THE ROOTS OF CIVILIZATION

THE ROOTS

Revised

**THE COGNITIVE BEGINNINGS
OF MAN'S FIRST ART,
SYMBOL AND NOTATION**

OF CIVILIZATION

and Expanded

Alexander
Marshack

MOYER BELL LIMITED

Mount Kisco, New York

THIS BOOK IS DEDICATED TO ELAINE
WHO LIVED THROUGH ITS DIFFICULT
MAKING AND HELPED BEYOND MEASURE.

Published by Moyer Bell Limited

Copyright © 1991 by Alexander Marshack

**LIBRARY OF CONGRESS
CATALOGING-IN-PUBLICATION DATA**

Marshack, Alexander.
    The roots of civilization / Alexander Marshack.—Rev. and expanded

p.   cm.

Includes bibliographic references and index.
    1. Paleolithic period. 2. Art, Prehistoric. 3. Thought and thinking.
    I. Title

GN772.M29   1991
930.1′2—dc20   91-16132
                 CIP

ISBN 1-55921-041-9 C1

Typesetting by Books International, Deatsville, Alabama; Printed in Singapore by The Palace Press; Distributed by Rizzoli International Publications, Inc.

CONTENTS

A BACKWARD-LOOKING FOREWORD

We enter the 21st century with the great question of who and what we are as "humans" and how we became "human," that species named *Homo sapiens* or the wise and thinking species, still largely unanswered, though it is being addressed from a thousand directions.

The question of who and what we are and how we became human became a question of scientific inquiry in the Western or European world during the 19th century. It was in that century that the political and economic expansion out of Europe, which had already entrenched itself in the Americas and was making these two great continents "European," conquered or invaded much of the remaining world. Part of that expansion involved the development of new technologies and inquiries. Early in the 19th century the young Charles Darwin, nearing 23, sailed from Devonport aboard the HMS Beagle, a ten-gun brig, as part of England's effort as an expanding empire to map the seas, coasts and resources of the world. To do this the Beagle carried on board a recently invented accurate ship's clock or chronometer. This allowed a ship to determine its longitude, or its position east or west on the earth's globe, by matching the time on the clock with an observation of the position of the sun, moon or stars in the sky. The accurate clock made it possible to match the precisely moving map of the sky to the time on the clock and to therefore indicate where the ship was at that moment both on the earth and under that shifting sky. The effort to place oneself functionally and practically in time-and-place is an exceedingly ancient human behavior. It was evident in an earlier cultural form, as this book documents, in the European Ice Age. It was evident also a century after Darwin, when the "space age" began in the latter half of the 20th century and satellites made it possible to map the earth with greater precision and to pinpoint the position of ships and any other point on the earth. And also recalling the earlier sailing vessels, these satellites now made it possible to picture and map the distribution of certain resources on the earth.

That, however, was only one of the time-and-space inquiries carried out on the Beagle. Darwin was on a different kind of time-and-space inquiry. As the naturalist on board he was assigned to study the different species on the lands they would touch. Some species might be of economic value, others of interest to the natural sciences. Cataloguing, comparing and describing the diversity of living species had become in the 18th and 19th century part of the Western process of inquiry and expansion. It had already led to comparative models and charts of the diversity of creatures in the plant and animal kingdoms with "man," of course, always at the top of the ladder or tree of being. The question of how this diversity had come about was being debated in the 19th century at the time Darwin sailed. But the solid earth itself had recently been discovered to be constantly in change and flux. The layers of the outer earth that had accumulated one above the other and were visible where the earth had ruptured or shifted indicated that the earth had gone through cycles and processes of change in an enormous depth of time. As Darwin sailed his distant seas to far shores there were, therefore, two types of 19th century "time" or "time-and-space" inquires or processes on board; the practical and functional navigational time that placed a ship and coasts on a chart or map of the earth, and the less precise time of the natural sciences which were attempting to place living things and even the earth itself into some sort of processual and functional time-and-space frame or model. In the "space age" it was the satellite that, like the earlier and slower sailing vessels, continued to visualize and map the distribution of certain resources on the earth.

One can somewhat inadequately describe these 19th century "time-factored" efforts as different types of visually mediated, observational inquiries, for that is what they were. They were based on what the 19th century eye and culture sought and could see and model. But there were other visual inquiries and discoveries being made in that century and they, too, began to shape the image of "man," or the human, and "his" place on earth. A few years after Darwin published his epochal *The Origins of Species* (1857), instigated by the things he saw on the voyage of the Beagle, the French neuroanatomist Paul Broca autopsied the brain of an adult who, when he lived, had lost the capacity to speak—though he had retained his other human capacities and could understand the speech of others. Broca discovered a major lesion in the frontal area of the left hemisphere and announced that the production of speech resided in that damaged brain area of the left hemisphere of the human brain. The study of "man" and human capacity had entered a new and still infant stage. In the century that followed the architecture of the brain and the functions or capacities that were lost or disrupted by injury to the different areas or structures of the brain was painstakingly mapped and diagrammed. As I now write, new imaging techniques have begun to map the split-second changes that occur in electrical activity and blood flow across both the whole brain and in different areas of the brain as a person performs different types of tasks. A spatial "time-factored," processual map of cognitive processes and the changes they produced in brain activity was being created. The processes of language it was found were, actually, dispersed in a network within the brain. Broca's early static image of a damaged local brain structure and the cataclysmic results that occurred when it was injured was being replaced by dynamic computer enhanced images and maps of the normal and abnormal brains as they functioned in different tasks. This not only represented an increase in technology and knowledge, but a change in the way of "seeing" or visualizing the extraordinary complexity of the brain that in Darwin's time was considered to be an unknowable "black box." It is this central and crucial aspect of the human that Darwin could not incorpo-

rate in his descriptions of the evolved human capacity. In the 19th century Darwin had stated that the processes that separated humanity from other species and even from other primates and the great apes was the capacity for language and the increased capacity to make and use tools. What he did not discuss, because he could not (and that Broca did not discuss because he could not), was that the manufacture and use of tools and the capacity for language are each ultimately dependent on the capacity of the brain to perceive, categorize, evaluate, abstract and model the processes and objects of the *visual,* perceptual world, and the capacity then to deal with these in diverse cultural ways. These are all, including language and tool use, cognitive processes. It is the visually perceived and evaluated world and visually-mediated or imagined concepts that humans talk about. It is the visually-mediated world that tools deal with. Darwin himself, though he did not realize it, had used this preeminent human capacity for visual evaluation, categorization, abstraction and modeling in accumulating his massive library of observations on living and extinct species and he had then used this capacity in formulating his theory. He had used the capacity for visual evaluation as much, and perhaps, more than he had used either hand-held tools or language. The 19th century, nevertheless, gave to the 20th century the strongly entrenched hypothesis that the human species is best described, not in terms of its overarching *cognitive* capacity, but in terms of its capacity for language and tools. This 19th century concept and definition of the human has in one form or another dominated or colored all inquiries into evolution of humans and the human capacity. The more difficult question, the one concerning the complex ways in which the human brain mediates its different, but ultimately visually-based and visually-referenced capacities, including language and tool-use, has only begun to be addressed.

There were other 19th century concepts that would influence our present ideas concerning "man" or the human. Systematic archaeology, for instance, began in that century. It provided the first evidence for early, "primitive" stone tools; it provided the first skeletal evidence for early ancient forms of "primitive" or archaic humans. These findings tended to validate Darwin's hypotheses concerning evolution and the nature of "man" and in the 20th century these inquiries became one of the major efforts of a mature archaeology. But in mid 19th century archaeologists also discovered examples of "art" from the "Reindeer Age" (now called the "Ice Age"), from that period before history when the extinct woolly mammoth, woolly rhinoceros, as well as herds of wild horse, bison and reindeer roamed Europe. The discovery of "art" in the European Ice Age, made by people with an anatomically modern skeleton and a new tool kit, led to the belief that human art and language began at that time and place, in the Ice Age of Europe, and with these humans who made both better tools and exquisite "art." This was the belief when I began my research in the 1960's, precisely one century after the discovery of Ice Age "art." It is still believed by many archaeologists that art and language began at this time and in this place. The archaeological record, however, can be deceiving. Ice Age skeletons, for instance, often wore beads and beads were also found in the homesites and so it was assumed as well that the capacity for "self-awareness" began at this time and in this place, with these humans and with these beads. These beliefs, however, were largely a product of 19th and 20th century European history, they were a product of its ethnocentrism, and of the fact that archaeology began in Europe. Ice Age archaeology had, in fact, become entrenched as a measure and standard for discussions concerning the evolutionary transition from earlier forms of humanity and human culture to fully modern human capacity and culture. But that Ice Age evidence, which is documented and discussed in this book, is skewed. Actually, it merely documents the human capacity as it was expressed in one time and place, in one context and in that one set of conditions. When the climate changed, that extraordinary Ice Age culture collapsed. Human capacity, however, did not collapse and it produced a new adaptation. Why and how art and language began is, therefore, still an open question. The answers will not be found in the soil or in any of the piecemeal and scattered discoveries of archaeology or paleontology, the study of early hominid skeletons. But some part of the answer may eventually be approached from a different direction, by those inquiries which are directed towards understanding the ways in which the human brain and the human capacity deals with and mediates the increasingly complex and changing worlds that it both creates and faces.

The 19th century gave us other paths to the human and these, too, relate to the book that follows. Comparative anthropology, the study of human behavior in different cultures, developed as part of the same European expansion that sent the Beagle and Darwin on their journey. Reports on the extraordinary diversity of human cultures and customs began to accumulate. Darwin himself, early in the 19th century, was astonished at the primitive state of "savagery" he saw among the native Terra del Fuegians at the southern tip of South America. Late 19th century anthropologists found, that despite these apparent differences among cultures, that human societies revealed fundamental similarities in their cultural patterns and modes of behavior. As a result of these studies and with the assumption of basic "similarity" numerous models of the typical, "primitive," hunting-gathering culture were proposed; these models changed every few years as more and better data were accumulated, documenting the unexpected variety and complexity of these supposedly "simple" cultures. Archaeologists, nevertheless, tried to use these constantly changing models to explain the past in terms of the present and, at the same time, to explain the present in terms of the past. But the Ice Age culture of Europe could not be explained by these comparisons. The hunting-gathering cultures that were still functioning in the 19th and 20th centuries were almost all at the peripheral margins of the earth's subsistence territories. The European Ice Age cultures were not, however, living at a periphery. The culture represented a long, slow, 25,000 year development in what was a unique and exceedingly rich and variable geography and ecology. This functional, conceptual time-and-space variety was depicted in their "art." No other hunting-gathering culture has ever had precisely this set of conditions or produced this range of referential art. The Ice Age "cultural explosion," actually an exceedingly slow development, can not therefore be explained by comparisons with those marginal hunting-gathering cultures that managed to survive into the historical present, often battered by, surrounded by, or in contact with other cultures. These were some of the concepts and problems I faced when I began my research. Like Darwin, I began a long voyage of inquiry that resulted in a huge collection of data. Like Darwin I had been prepared to "see" and to ask questions in a certain way by the concepts and questions of my time. Like Darwin, I was faced with the 19th century belief that language and tools were the essential marks of the human. But the inquiry was, nevertheless, different and it became increasingly different as the research grew.

This book, a report on some of that voyage, introduced the then new concept of "cognitive archaeology." As such the inquiry did not involve an attempt to find the origins or the "first" of anything. It was an analytical attempt to describe the way in which early modern humans, in one time and place, saw, abstracted, symbolized and imaged their world in time-and-space. This is therefore not a book about "art" but an inquiry into human imagery as a form of reference, and an inquiry into the human capacity to create models, metaphors and symbols of perceived or imagined objects, species and processes in cultural time-and-space. It has assumed, almost intuitively, that the potentially variable and changeable human capacity for "seeing" and imaging, and for dealing in diverse cultural modes with the variable, changing, visually-mediated world and reality is a crucial human capacity. The Ice Age represented one moment in which that capacity was able to function as it has seldom functioned before or since in a hunting-gathering culture. The products that were created, using bone, stone and paint, were never created in precisely this form or with such variability and richness by any other hunting-gathering culture. It was a moment in which the human capacity to think and image the world was able to create the first widespread and complex body of image and symbol so far found in the archaeological record. This book is a report on the inquiry that began to "see" that imagery differently.

Since the first edition was published, the materials in more than one hundred museums and collections in dozens of countries were studied at first hand and innovative analytical work was undertaken in more than a dozen of the more important French and Spanish caves. This second edition is in large part the result of these intense and broad studies. It is of significance that these studies have not contradicted any of the basic concepts in the first edition, but have greatly enriched and deepened them.

In some measure the research initiated by this book has become part of other larger and broader efforts. It has become part of that new subdiscipline of archae-ology called archaeoastronomy. It has become part of that subdiscipline that has now been formally termed "cognitive archeology." In 1974, after the first edition of this book was published, I was invited to present the annual lecture to the Boston Neurological Society. In 1984 I was invited to present the annual James Arthur Lecture of the American Museum of Natural History on evolution of the human brain. In 1987 I was invited to deliver the annual luncheon lecture before the American Association of Physical Anthropologists, specialists in the study of early hominid and human skeletons. In 1988 I presented the annual invited lecture before the Eastern Psychological Association. In 1989 I delivered the first annual McDonald Lecture at Cambridge University, .for the McDonald Institute of Archaeological Research, which had recently been constituted to pursue the subdiscipline of "cognitive archaeology." In 1989 I also delivered the keynote address at an international conference on Palaeolithic Art organized by the Prehistoric Society of Great Britain and Oxford University. It attempted to address the "cognitive" problem of the surprising complexity that I had found in use of female images during the Ice Age. In 1991 I was elected a Fellow of the American Association for the Advancement of Science, the leading interdisciplinary "For innovative research on Upper Paleolithic art and symbolic systems, and for (study of) the development of notational systems in nonliterate societies, both ancient and recent."

None of this means that all of the results of the research have been fully accepted. That is not the way science works. It does apparently mean, however, that the questions that were asked and many of the analytical methods that were devised were considered valid and that they and the results have become, two decades after the first edition of this book was published, a part of the ongoing and broadening inquiry into the nature of being human.

—Alexander Marshack

PART I
NOTATION: THE SEARCH

CHAPTER I

THE SEARCH BEGINS

The "space age" began—formally—with the launching of the Soviet satellite Sputnik I into orbit around the earth on October 4, 1957. On that day direct exploration of the solar system and eventual exploration of the moon and planets began as well. Man and his instruments had moved off the earth and away from the thin envelope of air that surrounds it.

Actually, of course, the "space age" had begun earlier, for it was the culmination of developments in technology and science that were neither national nor limited to that event or that decade. It had begun, as formally, with preparations for the International Geophysical Year (1957–1958), a worldwide research program in which scientists of almost one hundred nations had cooperated to study earth-sun relationships. Artificial earth satellites were among the devices and techniques that had been considered possible by the scientists planning the Geophysical Year. Satellites and rocket space probes had been discussed and scheduled, and satellites were eventually orbited by both the Soviet Union and the United States.

By chance I had written the first American book explaining the scientific programs of the International Geophysical Year.

Toward the end of the summer of 1962, with the expanding space programs of the U.S. and U.S.S.R.

already on the way toward the moon and planets, with plans for launching astronauts into outer space already programmed, and with the technologies of space changing the time and distance relations among parts of the world, I sat down to write a book with Dr. Robert Jastrow, then head of the Theoretical Science Division (Goddard Space Flight Center) for NASA, the United States space agency, and also chief of the space agency's Institute for Space Studies in New York (Columbia University). Dr. Jastrow was one of the young physicists drawn to space research in the administrative explosion of the IGY space effort and in 1959–1960 he had been chairman of NASA's first Lunar Exploration Committee.

The book we had contracted for was intended to explain "how" man reached that point in science and civilization to make it possible to plan a manned landing on the moon, and at the same time it was to explain the modern scientific and engineering problems involved.

As the writer, I had the task of supplying the historical and scientific background for the lunar program. Having outlined the book and begun the research, I found it was an almost impossible task—at least difficult within the scope of my original concept and outline.

I spent a good part of 1963 in travel through the United States for the space book. Somewhat earlier I had met with space scientists in the Soviet Union at their laboratories and institutes.

In the United States, I had begun with President John F. Kennedy's science adviser, Dr. Jerome Wiesner; gone on to the Administrator of NASA, the United States space agency, James Webb; then to the Executive Secretary of the National Aeronautics and Space Council, Edward G. Welsh; on to the National Academy of Sciences space board; to the generals, colonels, scientists, and engineers of the Air Force and its associated laboratories; to the planners and scientists of NASA, Rand, the System Development Corporation; the presidents, vice-presidents, managers, engineers, and technicians of the big aviation-space corporations; and finally to the university researchers and professors, including Nobel Prize winners who had entered space research from branches of science as different as molecular biology and brain research or astrophysics and higher mathematics.

I met hundreds in this early phase of the space effort and had long discussions on the administrative, economic, political, military, scientific, and engineering problems involved. I probed the personal backgrounds, plans, and hopes of the men participating in the programs. The preparations for that little book were as careful as I could make them.

What surprised me was that not one person I met knew clearly why we were going into space or how it had come about. Each man had one story and his opinion, each had the rationalization of his own speciality and background, whether in science, engineering, politics, war, or business.

Though all were in the massive effort and each had the proper skill and training, not one had the ability to explain the cross currents and processes—historical, intellectual, psychological, symbolic, social, political, international, to name a few, or even to explain the full range of the scientific and technical problems involved.

It was difficult, then, as the researcher, to get a clear picture of how or why the space age had developed, or what, except in a limited way, it meant. The most I could do after one year of travel, questioning, research, and reading and after five years of prior familiarity and preparation was to report the scene, capture a few of the personalities, explain the science, problems, and plans and give some of the fragmented historical record.

Perhaps the difficulty was that I was asking questions of interest to me, the answers to which could not be found on the surface. Clearly, the questions and their answers were not necessary for success of the space effort. Apparently it was not necessary for man to know fully "why" he succeeded. He needed only the skills and the stories to succeed.

I had another series of small difficulties in the writing. At one point I needed a few pages on the historical background of the space age, going back to the first civilizations and the apparent beginnings of mathematics, astronomy, and science. These few paragraphs turned out to be among the most difficult and frustrating I had ever tried to write. Even my explanations of the complexities of space physics and space engineering were easy in comparison. The reason, simply, was that there were not enough facts. Looking at the early history of science, mathematics, astronomy, and at the early history and prehistory of man, I was appalled at what seemed the inadequacy of the record.

Nothing as complex as the space program, or as complex as modern civilization or modern man, could have derived from the incomplete and primitive creature imagined and documented in the scientific journals.

Reading and leafing through the scientific texts in the quiet of the New York Public Library, searching for my few words on the origins of science and civilization, I had a profound sense of something missing from the valid human image. It was a feeling and an intuition, for I had no knowledge of other facts. There was a double frustration, then, in my attempt to understand the space age.

This feeling of "something missing" in the archaeological record was based in part on my life and sense of the world, on my own experience as to the way things were done, and on my travels around the earth. Over some twenty years I had been a journalist in Asia and Europe, a news writer, a book and drama reviewer, an art reporter, a photographer, a script writer, a producer-director of plays, and a science writer. I had dealt in the events man made and in his ways of telling them. Before sitting down to write, I had watched the first American astronauts in their training. Then from the control room, as science consultant for a television network, I had watched the complex preparations and the computerized launching into orbit of the first American Mercury capsule.

What I had, then, was a feeling about man, his efforts, and the space age based on impressions both old and fresh, gathered in every corner of the earth.

My interest in space and science had been kindled, in part, because these were human activities, culturally specialized products of the human brain, and to me, therefore, not much different from politics, religion, art, or war. I could not in my thoughts, while writing and searching for the meaning of man and the space program, separate Dr. Jerome Wiesner, Special Assistant to the President for Science and Technology, or Yuri Gagarin and John Glenn, the first Soviet and American astronauts, or Dr. Lloyd V. Berkner, the scientist and science administrator who had suggested the International Geophysical Year to the world's

scientists, from the extremely primitive natives I had met in New Guinea and Australia, or the starving farmers I had seen in India, or from the men who, thousands of years before, had hunted mammoth, reindeer, and bison and had painted the caves of Ice Age Europe, or from the later men who first farmed or built cities around the Mediterranean.

Some of these feelings were substantiated, as I read, by the archaeological evidence. There was no essential difference, for instance, between the first fully modern man of some 40,000 years ago and ourselves, either in brain size or general skeletal measurement. Going back still further in time, archaeologists and paleo-anthropologists were now beginning to imply a higher intelligence and more complex culture for proto-human and near-human "Stone Age" men than previous researchers had dared allow. The tool kits of pre-man and proto-man were turning out to be extraordinarily complex and varied. In fact, near-human toolmaking had recently been pushed back by archaeological finds in Africa to nearly two million years ago and, as I was writing, the evolutionary beginnings of the creature who would be man had been put back to some twenty million years, the period during which he seems to have stepped on to the path of his own development, as opposed to the path taken by monkey and ape.

The trend of these new findings heightened the sense I had of inadequacy in the traditional image of prehistoric man and his culture.

There was another, related problem. Searching through the historical record for the origins of the evolved civilizations, I was disturbed by the series of "suddenlies."

Science, that is, formal science, had begun "suddenly" with the Greeks; in a less philosophically coherent way, bits of near-science, mathematics and astronomy, had appeared "suddenly" among the Mesopotamians, the Egyptians, the early Chinese, and much later, in the Americas; civilization itself had apparently begun "suddenly" in the great arc of the Fertile Crescent in the Middle East; writing (history begins with writing) had apparently begun "suddenly" with the cuneiform of Mesopotamia and the hieroglyphs of Egypt; agriculture, the economic base of all the evolved civilizations, had apparently begun "suddenly" some ten thousand years ago with a relatively short period of incipience, or near-agriculture, leading into it; the calendar had begun "suddenly" with agriculture; art and decoration had begun "suddenly" some thirty or forty thousand years ago during the Ice Age, apparently at the point during which modern *Homo sapiens* man—as one theory had it—walked into Europe to displace Neanderthal man.

Coming fresh to the archaeological evidence and interpretations, and asking new questions, I now felt uneasy about the "suddenlies," though each "sudden" development apparently extended over generations and even over hundreds of years.

Art, agriculture, science, mathematics, astronomy, the calendar, writing, the growth of cities—these things that make up civilization—could not, it seemed to me, have happened "suddenly." They must have come at the end of many thousands of years of prior preparation. How many thousands was the question.

I sensed this preparatory process years before while trying to track the origins of the International Geophysical Year. Behind each discovery, each scientific law and question, there was always a vast, descending preparation, always more than the practicing scientist knew.

I could not, therefore, easily accept theories relating to man's "sudden" cultural innovations, particularly since these cultural manifestations appear in the rock and soil layers of the archaeological record with what seems to be an already complex and highly developed lore, mythology, symbolism, and method, a complexity that existed for all the languages, cultural groups, and peoples involved in the early civilizations.

Some acknowledgment of long incipience appeared in the scientific literature. Professor Richard A. Parker had written a monograph on the origins of the official Egyptian calendar, introduced about 3,000–4,000 B.C. This governmental, dynastic calendar was based on a solar day count and a stellar astronomy, the start of the solar year of 365 days being the morning on which the star Sirius, the brightest star in the sky, first appeared in the eastern dawn sky, around July 19. Near this day the Nile began to flood, marking the beginning of the agricultural season and the return of "life." Parker states that there seems to be a more ancient, predynastic lunar calendar in Egypt whose tradition is lost but whose remnants are implied in the

early dynastic symbolism, ritual, and religious calendar. So, too, the first calendars of the cities of Mesopotamia are lunar, with the addition of solar, stellar, and planetary observations. The evidence seemed to imply an ancient simple lunar tradition, with a month that began with observation of the lunar crescent. The earliest known Chaldean calendar, for instance, seems to have been lunar with alternate months of twenty-nine and thirty days, an already sophisticated arithmetic breakdown.

The early Hindu calendar was lunar, with observations of sun and stars helping to measure and determine the seasons and year. The early Chinese calendar contained observations of both the sun and moon but also seemed based on an ancient tradition that was probably primarily lunar. The lunar month in China began not with the crescent but with the dark, or invisible, "new" moon. The official, priestly calendar of the Central American Mayans was solar, but the Mayans had developed a late, historic culture and there are indications of a basic, earlier lunar calendar among the South and North American Indian traditions. The Peruvian Incas, for instance, had a solar calendar, but their division of the year into twelve months hinted at an earlier lunar tradition. In each of these developed agricultural civilizations, therefore, there is evidence of an early lunar observation and calendar. In view of these hints it did not seem to me that agriculture had led to the calendar, but rather that agriculture and the calendar were products of an exceedingly long development in human culture. But how old?

Again, more with feeling than knowledge, I could not easily accept the theories on the origins of agriculture. It was supposedly something that had evolved in limited areas as a kind of technological shift in a relatively short period, during the transition from hunting and gathering. The evidence, apparently, lay in the soil, for one could trace the evolution of settled villages, the evolution of agricultural tools, such as sickles and grinders, even the development of wheat, barley and corn from the wild to the domestic. One theory said that agriculture had begun with the accidental sprouting of seeds in the garbage heaps of hunting and gathering groups, probably noticed in the springtime by women, since they were the gatherers of shoots, roots, nuts, and the kernels of wild wheat and barley. However, even such simple discoveries and "accidents," in order to be culturally recognized and used, are long prepared for. Besides, how could the apparent indigenous beginnings and development of agriculture in the widely separated areas of Egypt, the Middle East, Asia, and the Americas be explained by such overly simple, random "accidents," all of which occurred at certain, comparable stages of cultural development?

These were not separate activities or discoveries. Agriculture, astronomy, the calendar, mathematics, science, writing, art, and even religion were products of the single, basic human brain. There was nothing, however, in the archaeological record or theory to indicate how this brain had functioned, in time, and with the accumulating, developing materials of culture and with the changing but near-constant realities of the world, to create at one stage these seemingly "sudden" cultural manifestations.

This was not the fault of the scientists or of the sciences but was in large part due to the inadequacy of the prehistoric, archaeological evidence.

The study of prehistory and the science of archaeology were roughly a century old, having begun in the second half of the nineteenth century. They were still new sciences devoted, essentially, to the finding, classifying, categorizing, and dating of the remnant products of the human hand and brain. These products are in large part the ruin, waste, garbage, discards, burials, and accumulations of human living, including bits and remnants of rite, symbol and myth, and record-keeping in later *Homo sapiens* times. Having dug up the remains, there follows the necessary first task of putting these products in their proper chronological order. After classifying them according to style and type, there then follows the attempt to interpret man's cultural evolution by the chronology and interrelation of these products. In the end, the archaeologist and prehistorian have the difficult task of trying to re-create the image and meaning of past human life from these accidental, remnant, discarded products which, for one reason or another, have managed to survive. This attempt at re-creation is not easy, and there can never be complete certainty, for the record is partial and can never be complete.

Many sciences have come to help the archaeologist and prehistorian. The most important aid in this century has come from nuclear physics and chemistry with their technique of dating the decay of the radioactive substances found in the archaeological and geological layers. The biological sciences have helped with analyses of the skeletal remains of animals and humans, pollen analysis of the soil samples, and even sea core analysis of the types of organisms accumulated on the sea floor. These chronological and biological sciences have helped the prehistorian re-create the general climatic and ecological conditions of the human past, period by·period. But, important as these results are, they remain only first steps in the developing science of man's origins. They set the stage for man, but they do not deal with man himself.

When we turn to man, the evidence is equally limited. In the area of prehistory, the most important materials for almost one hundred years have been the stone and bone tools that reveal an evolving tool skill with increasingly complex and specialized tool kits. Unfortunately, it is impossible to reconstruct the range of man's evolving culture from these tool industries. So, too, the remains of his meals indicate only some of his more basic efforts to stay alive.

With the appearance of evolved man, we begin to get the evidence of artistic and symbolic materials: burials, sanctuaries, decorations, and finally representations of animals and humanlike figures, signs, and symbols. What these "meant" to the makers in the period before history has been the subject of endless conjecture and theory. The archaeologist and prehistorian have had some help in attempting an interpretation from the anthropologists and ethnologists who have studied and compared living primitive societies. But it has been a limited help, since anthropology and ethnology deal with certain selected cultural products of the human brain: language, ritual, custom, lore, mythology, kinship and marriage, status, forms of exchange, symbol, art, religion, technology. These are aspects of culture that can be isolated, collected, compared, and classified. But these comparisons and classifications of cultural products, of man's relation to them and of their own interrelations, do not explain man and his brain. They merely clarify differences, changes, and developments in the product and of uses of the product, and it is therefore the *product* and not either man or his brain that lies at the core of these ethnological and anthropological studies of "man." Anthropology and ethnology offer merely a series of comparisons and analogies. They provide a certain sort of data and evidence, but they explain nothing.

Nevertheless, these studies are necessary for an understanding of man and his development. After enough evidence has been gathered from these archaeological and comparative studies, one has a chronology and an accumulation of evidence that make it possible to begin the attempt at an explanation of the human process. In the last century there have been many such attempts to explain man, each using the newly acquired, if limited, evidence of its time. These attempts were based on selected aspects of human behavior or on samplings of specific products of the human brain. They have ranged from broadly evolutionary theories based on the archaeological and paleontological evidence to chemical and biological explanations of man and have included psychoanalytic, psychological, anthropological, sociological, economic, technical, philosophical, religious, and even statistical and mathematical models. What I felt in recalling and returning to these theories and models of man was that they offered a part, a series of insights, but that the whole somehow escaped.

Sitting in the quiet rooms of the libraries, I was continually faced with the problem of the limitation of the evidence and theories. They were and felt partial and secondary.

There was one last important series of questions.

Some years before, while writing my book on the International Geophysical Year, I had been struck by the thought that each of the scientific programs, from study of the oceans, air, climate, earth, ionosphere, sun, cosmic rays to the rocketry and satellite programs, was "time-factored,"[1] and that the Geophysical Year itself was a "time-factored" call to the world's scientists to conduct simultaneous measurements and observations during a period of violent solar activity, the peak of the eleven-year sunspot cycle. Science, I surmised, was another of man's "time-factored" and "time-factoring" activities.

In the spring of 1962, therefore, while trying to get those few paragraphs of historical and prehistorical background for the book, I had a talk with Dr. Ralph Solecki, associate professor of anthropology at Columbia University in New York. Dr. Solecki, an archaeologist, was excavator of the cave site at Shanidar, in the Zagros Mountains of Iraq. At Shanidar, Neanderthal man had lived, and then thousands of years later early modern man had left evidence in the soil to indicate some of the steps he had taken as he slowly turned from full-time hunter and gatherer to part-time farmer and then to village builder.

I asked Dr. Solecki how it had happened. What skill had modern man brought with him to Shanidar that made this transition possible? Agriculture, I said, is an extraordinarily complex activity, requiring not only tools, but also the proper skills, stories, myths, and explanations. Besides, I continued, it is a "time-factored" activity, extending over the whole year, and therefore completely unlike the assumed primitive hunt which might begin and end in a day. What archaeological evidence was there for man's use of such "time-factored" skills? These would certainly have been necessary to make the transition from hunting and random gathering to agriculture possible. Solecki laughed, and said that I was asking questions that archaeologists had not yet dared ask. They were still trying, carefully and slowly, to establish the chronology and sequence of events for this period, and the soil held only the bones and tools of man, some evidence of his burial and building customs, and a few of the images of his religion. There was no evidence of his many other skills and stories.

Were they perhaps indicated, I asked, earlier, say ten, fifteen, or twenty thousand years before agriculture in the Ice Age? Solecki smiled and said that was again asking more than seemed possible. However, he continued, if there was an answer, the one man who might possibly know was André Leroi-Gourhan of the Musée de l'Homme in Paris, one of the outstanding authorities on the cave art and symbolism of Europe during the Ice Age.

[1] The concept of the time-factored process in the hard sciences is today almost tautological, since all processes, simple or complex, sequential or interrelated, finite or infinite, develop or continue and have measurable or estimable rates, velocities, durations, periodicities, and so on. However, the sciences which study these processes are themselves "time-factored," since the processes of cognition and recognition, of planning, research, analysis, comparison, and interpretation are also sequential, interrelated, developmental and cumulative.

On June 13, 1962, I sent a letter to Dr. Leroi-Gourhan:
"Dr. Solecki has suggested that I write . . . I have a single
difficult question and he stated that you were perhaps
the one person who could answer it . . .
"Is there any indication or evidence that the time of painting or drawing [in the cave art] was either seasonal or
periodic . . . ? "Much of the cave art is . . . ritual. Most
primitive ritual is, in one way or another, 'time-factored.'
It would not seem that the long journeys into the interiors
of the larger caves were haphazard in time. They should
have occurred at the change in a season or a phenomenon:
the mating or rutting time of the herds, the migration
times, the beginning of the rains, the end of hibernation
for the bear, the first killing in the spring or autumn, or
the time the hunter left winter shelter for the open campsite, or the time of ceremonial initiation.
"The literature indicates that the drawings and paintings
were used in hunting magic and perhaps in fertility and
initiation rites. These should be seasonal. Is there any evidence of a 'time-factored' root in Ice Age art?"

Within a week I had an answer.
"I was very much interested in your letter. And I found
your question of particular relevance. The fact is, I think
the use of the Upper Paleolithic cave sanctuary could very
well have had a seasonal character. But at the moment I
do not see how this can be demonstrated.
"As a matter of fact, it is now clear that the painted or engraved works were created as a single more or less monumental ensemble just as any sanctuary of classical times . . .
Certain sanctuaries were apparently visited only once . . .
others, such as Lascaux or the Combarelles which can be
reached easily, were visited often . . . traces of the visitors
remain visible in the countless scribblings next to the
principal works. It is reasonable to assume that these visits
occurred during definite seasons, but I would not be able
to indicate which.
". . . you allude to the magic of hunting and to fertility and
initiation rites . . . none of the prehistoric rites can be properly proved or reconstructed except with the help of the
imagination, and using as a starting point ideas borrowed
from present-day primitives. In this sphere everyone is free
to improvise his own interpretations.
". . . thus I am convinced, as you are, that prehistoric man
did not do things haphazardly at no matter what period,
but I am unable to tell you his patterns.
"There is, however, some evidence for the seasonal character of the cave visits: the paintings definitely seem to
repeat the same theme, and this persistence would indicate
that the subject was probably a mythical one. Seasonal
celebration of a myth is so widespread that I believe one
might see here proof in favor of your hypothesis."
I had my answer. But it was, of course, no answer.
And there did not seem to be any.

By April of 1963 I had almost finished the book on
space and so turned back to fill in those paragraphs on
the beginnings of science. I was still trying to explain
"how" it had begun in Egypt and Mesopotamia. I
went to my files and found an article I had clipped and
filed without reading, from the June 1962 SCIENTIFIC
AMERICAN. It concerned a small scratched bone that
had been found at Ishango, a Mesolithic site at the
headwaters of the Nile. The tiny bone had been
scratched by man about 6,500 B.C., some two or three
thousand years before the first dynasty appeared in
Egypt. The article had been written by a Belgian co-
worker of Dr. Solecki, Professor Jean de Heinzelin,
archaeologist and geologist, of the University of
Ghent and the Royal Institute in Brussels. De Heinzelin had gone to Africa in 1961 as a member of an expedition sponsored by Columbia University. Both the
article and the bone puzzled me. There seemed something wrong with de Heinzelin's interpretation, and
there seemed, also, something hauntingly significant
about the bone. It was, again, only a feeling, similar to
others I had had in reading the science journals. But it
now seemed as though this bone should, somehow,
contain the answer I had requested of Drs. Solecki
and Leroi-Gourhan, perhaps because I had raised just
these broad questions about the beginnings of science,
art, and civilization in the book on my desk.
I looked at the photos and drawings of the bone for
perhaps an hour, thinking. I got up for coffee, still
thinking, and came back. How does one "decode" or
translate or interpret scratch marks 8,500 years old,
created by a culture that was dead and by a man who
spoke a language that was lost? Scratch marks that
had been made 2,000 to 3,000 years before the first
hieroglyphic writing? And, besides, what proof could
there be of any interpretation? As Dr. Leroi-Gourhan
had suggested, we seemed to be forever stuck in the
realm of guesswork and imagination.
What went on inside me for that hour was odd. I was
churning with the broad, encompassing insights of an
unfinished book, and I was disagreeing with an interpretation that seemingly went against what I had
written. It was a dull, blackened bit of scratched bone,
about three and three-quarter inches long (9.6 cm),
and would one day end up in a museum under glass,
with a caption, probably, about the enigmatic, undecipherable activities of prehistoric man.

I decided to try a hunch, based on ideas suggested by the book I was writing. In fifteen minutes I had "cracked the code" of the Ishango bone. Or, at least, I felt I had come close to it. I was dizzied.

It seemed too easy, and I distrusted it. Yet an excitement burst in me like a fever. It had something exalting and frightening in it. I piled my nearly finished manuscript and the notes for the book on space in a corner of my desk, and for two days I tried to disprove my solution, making graphs, doing computations, going anxiously to the library and searching almost desperately to prove myself wrong.

For I had a contract and delivery date for the manuscript on the moon, and I was aware of the danger in pursuing the maverick idea.

Much as I tried, however, I could not disprove my too easy "solution." Reading all I could lay my hands on that dealt with the archaeological evidence, and doing computations into the night and morning, the most I could do was to retain the possibility that I might be right. And bit by bit, it seemed to me, undecipherable mysteries of the prehistoric past began to fall into line with the "solution."

I realized that if this solution was right or even approached some sort of validity, it would perhaps be necessary to rewrite much in the histories of science, art, religion, and civilization and to reinterpret some of the meaning of man and his intelligence. This I was neither equipped nor prepared to do. But, at that moment, neither was anyone else. I knew also that the ability to ask a question, or to have a hunch, or even to do research, was no proper preparation for the difficulties, discipline, and patience a scientific solution would require. Yet I could not stop.

For five weeks, as I dug into the spreading ramifications of that bit of bone, I could not sleep. I had a driving urge to bring the solution to Dr. Solecki or mail it to Professor Leroi-Gourhan in Paris, to get a quick confirmation or denial. But I did not dare. The insights that had led to the seeming solution were far too tentative still and in my mind I could see all the dangers of a too early presentation.

So I put the book that was almost ended aside and I took my seeming solution of the Ishango bone, and I went with it into the past, slowly, carefully, through all the records and scientific literature, to see what it could tell me about the beginnings of man and his culture. And I kept going back, fifteen, twenty, thirty, forty, and fifty thousand years.

At the end of one year I had a tentative manuscript. I carried this new book to my editor, more to explain the delay than to replace the lunar book. After one week I received a letter:

"I've just finished reading your manuscript—I mean really reading it. I must say I'm flabbergasted. It's an amazing work of imagination, carried out with a persistent exploration of detail that just seems unbelievable. Whether or not this thing revolutionizes anthropology and archaeology, no one can fail to be impressed . . .

"It's clear that no one person can evaluate it . . ."

The letter went on in detail. He was, he wrote, not convinced.

In one sense these were my feelings as well. I was in awe at what the findings seemed to indicate and had my own uncertainty as to whether they could be entirely true. I was called some weeks later to meet with the president of the publishing house. He said that I had evidently submitted an extraordinary manuscript. "If you were in my position, would you publish it?" "No," I answered. The book was not ready for publication. It required a long, careful checking and proving. I had worked only with the materials in libraries, and one could never be certain about the scientific renderings. I must go to Europe and examine the archaeological artifacts. Besides, the ideas in the book had not yet been shown to specialists in the field. Before publication I would need their evaluation and criticism. This would require time and funds, and, if I were a publisher, I said, I would hesitate. He agreed, and stated that he was, after all, a small publisher.

I brought the manuscript to McGraw-Hill, posing the problem of the necessity for proof and validation. After reading the manuscript, the editor and managing editor agreed to wait and to some extent to fund the cost of validation.

In the summer of 1964 I telephoned Professor Gerald S. Hawkins, astronomer at the Smithsonian Astrophysical Observatory, Harvard University. Professor Hawkins had published a paper in the English science journal NATURE on the alignments of Stonehenge, in England. The massive, open, circular stone structure had puzzled prehistorians for centuries, and Professor Hawkins had apparently been able to prove that at least some of the alignments were astronomical and calendric. I explained the problem to Professor Hawkins. He asked for the manuscript, did a Fourier analysis of my material, examined my arithmetic, my analytic and astronomic methods, and said yes, I seemed to be correct in methodology and in at least a portion of the findings.

The next step, he suggested, was to place the results and the problem of their feasibility before a leading prehistorian.

The American archaeologist most concerned with the Upper Paleolithic of Europe, the period of the Ice Age, was Professor Hallam L. Movius, Jr., of the Peabody Museum of Archaeology and Ethnology, Harvard.

When I returned to New York I telephoned Professor Movius at his archaeological dig at the Stone Age rock shelter or "abri" of Pataud in the village of Les Eyzies-de-Tayac in the Dordogne region of south central France.

"Professor Movius? This is a Mr. Marshack in New York. I am calling at the suggestion of Professor Hawkins. I think I have solved some of the notations of the Upper Paleolithic... some of the meaning of the art..." A pause, and then from France: "There are no 'notations' in the Upper Paleolithic!" We spoke for some twenty minutes and he finally said, "I'll see you at Les Eyzies next week and we'll see."

I arrived in Les Eyzies with two volumes of manuscript and presented my results for some eight hours over a period of two days in the workroom that had been constructed under the rock overhang. When I had finished and was exhausted, Professor Movius and I stepped out and looked down on the small valley. The narrow, swift Vézère twisted like a serpent below. The sun, setting behind the steep limestone hills, bathed the river red.

The valley had been occupied for more than a hundred thousand years. At the Abri Pataud, where we stood, the occupational levels went back to Neanderthal man. Fifteen minutes away by auto, along a bank of the Vézère, was the site of Le Moustier, after which the period of Neanderthal man is named the Mousterian. A few steps from where we stood was the site of Cro-Magnon, from which modern European man takes his name.

This valley had seen men, with subtle variations in Stone Age culture, come and go. The ice, some few hundred miles to the north and west, had come and gone in cycles. The climate in the valley had changed many times, the animals and plants had changed, and, when the last ice had finally receded from the mainland of Europe some 8,000 to 10,000 years ago, the complex Ice Age culture of man in this valley had shifted and evolved, as it had been doing also throughout Europe.

Today the valley is surrounded by vineyards east, west, north, and south. It is a gourmet center of agricultural France, renowned for sauces, pâtés, wines, and truffles. Farmers' houses are built against the cliffs, on soil containing the prehistory of man.

The valley is one of the most thoroughly excavated areas in the world, having been probed by four generations of prehistorians. The study of European prehistory had, in part, been born here. Archaeological diggings, some a hundred years old, were spotted along the cliffs and overhangs on each side of the narrow river. Professor Movius was himself coming to the end of about six or seven years of digging and had excavated more than 50,000 artifacts from one dig at the foot of the great gray and yellow rock overhang that shadows the village of Les Eyzies.

We looked across the valley. Professor Movius said that what I had done could be the "breakthrough" they had been waiting for.[2]

If I was right, not necessarily in all, but in one part, in one instance or one example, it was revolutionary. The results confirmed his own opinion of early Cro-Magnon's high intelligence.

Standing on the ledge in early evening, Movius explained the problems for acceptance of new ideas in

[2] Six years before, Professor Movius had published a monograph on the Stone Age shelter of La Colombière, along the Ain River, in the drainage of the Alpine ice sheet in eastern France. He had found a small pebble engraved with drawings of animals and strange linear marks. Writing of this art and symbol, he said:
"...it is patently obvious that the documents... whether paintings, engravings, or sculptures, must be deciphered. To allude to them as 'probably for ceremonial purposes'... begs the issue and contributes nothing material and germane to our understanding of the purpose behind the artistic accomplishment."
Hallam L. Movius, Jr., "Aspects of Upper Palaeolithic Art," in THREE REGIONS OF PRIMITIVE ART, Lecture Series Number Two, Museum of Primitive Art (New York, 1961), pp. 14–15.

the scientific community and the need for a proper series of steps. I must proceed both with haste and caution. I must leave France at once, talk to no one, and show no one the manuscript. I must publish as soon as possible to establish priority, but not too much, merely a short introductory paper. Above all, I must return to Europe, as I had suggested, to check the European materials firsthand, to see if the insights I had gleaned in the library held in the field. He agreed that one could not trust the traditional scientific renderings of the archaeological material.

I published a short, two-page introductory paper in SCIENCE, the journal of the American Association for the Advancement of Science, November 6, 1964, in which I explained briefly some of the findings. With the publication of that article, the concept of a notation in use 30,000 years ago, during the Ice Age, received tentative acknowledgment as a theory and hypothesis.

Following publication of the little paper, the Wenner-Gren Foundation for Anthropological Research of New York awarded me a grant to study the Upper Paleolithic materials in Europe, and the Bollingen Foundation awarded me a fellowship for preparation of the findings for publication.

In 1965, I returned to Europe, carrying the two volumes of manuscript, a camera, and a tiny Japanese binocular microscope, which had cost $15.

At the Musée des Antiquités, outside Paris, slowly, even painfully because of the difficulty in using a toy microscope, I worked out new analytic procedures. In the second week of work, the meaning of some of the ancient scratches "cleared," and the manuscript— at least that part that dealt with the notational thesis— seemed verified.

I reported to the Wenner-Gren Foundation that it was now necessary to check the bulk of Ice Age artifacts in all the collections of Europe. This time, however, I would need the finest possible micro and macro optical equipment, both for analysis and documentation of the findings.

I returned to Europe carrying a few hundred pounds of microscopic and photographic equipment and research apparatus, some on loan from Nikon Camera (Ehrenreich Industries). The accumulation of new findings at the end of a few months was so huge that my car could hold no more. It would take years to publish what I had found in a few months.

The Wenner-Gren Foundation scheduled a one-day conference in New York on February 4, 1966, for a presentation of these first results to a group of American archaeologists, anthropologists, and specialists in related fields. They had been called together for an evaluation and criticism of the method and findings. Professor Movius was chairman of the conference and those attending came from Yale, Princeton, Harvard, the University of Chicago, Cornell, the University of Pennsylvania, the University of California, the American Museum of Natural History, the Smithsonian Institution, Rockefeller University, and other institutions. It was agreed that the method and findings were new and perhaps represented a "breakthrough." But it was felt that the scientific community would have to await full publication before it could judge the significance of the results.

In 1966 I presented two short papers on the methodology and findings to the VII International Congress of Prehistory and Protohistory in Prague and delivered a monograph on the methods and results for publication by the Laboratoire de Géologie du Quaternaire et Préhistoire, the University of Bordeaux. I was put on staff as a researcher with the Peabody Museum of Archaeology and Ethnology at Harvard University, to work under Professor Movius with funding from the National Science Foundation. The first steps had been taken in setting up a new technology and in raising new questions and problems in the search for the "meaning" of early man.[3]

The ideas and findings that follow are new, and I have attempted to show how they were formed and grew. A series of monographs and papers have been prepared for archaeological and anthropological journals, in which the problems, methodology, and findings are presented within a more rigorous framework. What follows, then, is the tale of a deduction, the story of the making of a skill. It gives some indication of the generalizations, insights, hunches, and questions that were, in the beginning, not yet science, but which slowly evolved a new technology. It raises the

[3] See Appendix, Collections of Materials Examined and Photographed 1965–1970.

questions in the order I raised them, and it touches on those searches I made in a wide circle in and out of the field of archaeology and without which my work could not have proceeded.

The research is being refined, improved, and widened even as I write. What is important is that the track out of these early studies continues to lead in many new directions.

* * *

After the manuscript was completed but before this book was issued, I published a long analytical paper documenting the use of the microscope to study, not notations or "calendars," but the different ways in which animal images were used and reused during the Ice Age.* This mode of animal use was often different from that in any other known culture, yet for two decades no attention was paid to that seminal study. It was only as this second edition was being prepared that a few researchers in France, representing a new generation, began to validate the concept of variable image use and reuse.

In that early paper I indicated that a single animal image, whether in homesite "art" or in the cave sanctuaries, could be reused or renewed by the addition of some part of the animal and that it could also be "killed" by repeated overmarking with darts or spears. That paper, one of the important analytical papers in the study of Ice Age "art," is still not known

*Alexander Marshack, "Polesini, a reexamination of the engraved Upper Paleolithic mobiliary materials of Italy by a new methodology." *Revista di Scienze Preistoriche*, 1969, Vol. 24(2):219–281.

or mentioned by many Ice Age archaeologists. That study not only suggested that there were variable uses but probably variable meanings for a single species or animal image in the Ice Age, a suggestion that went against long standing and persistent attempts to find the single "proper" meaning for animal "art" or for a particular animal image or species.

In this introductory chapter I discussed my discomfort with the archaeological tendency to think in "suddenlies," to believe that the object or artifact in hand represents the "first" or the "beginning," or that the place at which an object was found represents the point of origin. During the decades since the publication of this book that tendency to think in "suddenlies" has continued as an article of faith. Cultural events may, of course, happen "suddenly" but the preparation for such events is often long and, for the archaeologist, usually hidden.

When in 1868 the Ice Age skeletons of modern humans, 30,000 years old, were found in a burial in the tiny cave of Cro-Magnon in the village of Les Eyzies in southwest France, a set of sea-shell beads

The head of a deer incised on a small non-utilitarian fragment of bone from the late Ice Age site of Polesini, Italy. The head is clumsily overengraved with a number of added muzzles that destroyed the original fine engraving of a realistic muzzle, while the head has additionally been "killed" by many darts

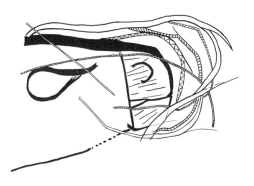

made at different times, in different styles and with different points. The analysis suggests an image that was apparently used ritually and symbolically at different times and in different ways. The same process occurs in the French and Spanish Ice Age caves (See Fig. 121a, p. 236).

was found in the burial. For more than a century it was assumed that these represented "the first" or earliest instance of human personal decoration or, as one colleague has claimed, "the beginning of self-awareness" and therefore also the beginnings of social, cultural complexity and even the beginnings of modern human language. The research described in this book and which has continued since then has indicated that items made of perishable materials, including twined cords and thongs, materials which do not last in the soil, probably existed thousands of years before the manufacture of beads. Twined thongs and cords are, in fact, regularly depicted on the images of supposedly naked Ice Age females, the popularly termed Ice Age "Venus" figurines (Chapter XIII and Marshack 1990a). Perishable items of personal decoration were probably made by the Neanderthals who inhabited Europe before the Cro-Magnons. The microscopic analysis of a bone working platform from the classic Mousterian site of La Quina, shortly after this book was published, found that the Neanderthals had been cutting skins, probably for making clothes and personal adornment, and perhaps for making thongs with which to bind and haft tools (Marshack 1989, 1990a, 1991a,* and Appendix).

The inquiry deepened as I began to investigate the deep roots of many modern human capacities, capacities that went back in earlier and less developed form to the primates. Slowly, over some three to five million years, these changed and evolved in mosaic fashion to finally function in the enlarged human brain as mediator of that complex set of capacities that seem to have exploded so "suddenly" and to have been put to complex and variable use in the European Ice Age. Each of the seeming cultural "firsts" of the Ice Age, I began to argue, apparently had antecedents that occurred earlier or elsewhere. This book is a record primarily of that so-called "explosion" of culture and symbol that occurred in one period and one region. Complex symboling traditions were surely occurring earlier and elsewhere though they have not yet all been found. This book is therefore an analytical description of the first widely dispersed and complex body of imagery so far to appear in the archaeological record. But it is not a description of the beginning of image and symbol. "Suddenlies" are seldom born out of themselves or out of the void. All "suddenlies," as I have noted, are in some manner prepared. There is evidence for a very early use of ocher for coloring by Homo erectus, c. 300,000–250,000 BP and perhaps earlier. There is evidence, being debated, that the later Neanderthals buried their dead and even made beads. A search for the reasons for that "explosion" of culture that took place at one time and place, in Europe during the Ice Age, is part of the ongoing inquiry.

*A. Marshack, "Evolution of the Human Capacity." YEARBOOK OF PHYSICAL ANTHROPOLOGY (1989), pp. 1–34.
A. Marshack, "The Female Image: A 'Time-Factored' Symbol. A study in style and modes of image use in the European Upper Paleolithic." PROCEEDINGS OF THE PREHISTORIC SOCIETY. (1990a), Vol. 57(1):17–31.
A. Marshack, "A reply to Davidson on Mania: Early Pre-Upper Paleolithic Problem-Solving." ROCK ART RESEARCH (1991a), Vol. 8(1):47–58.

CHAPTER II

A BIT OF BONE

High in the eastern mountains of central equatorial Africa, surrounded by steep hills, lies Lake Edward, one of the headwater sources of the Nile. It is a fair-sized lake, some 50 miles long and 30 wide.

As the plane flies, Lake Edward lies a thousand miles above, or south, of the "first" cataract at Khartoum, in the Sudan. This is the first cataract one meets coming down from the mountains toward Egypt, but it is the sixth cataract if one begins at the other end, in Egypt, at Aswan, and struggles southward up the long river.

If, however, you go downriver on foot, heading north as the shore winds, it is more than two thou-

sand miles from Lake Edward to the "first" cataract, and another thousand before you get to Aswan in Egypt.

If you go downhill from Lake Edward to the west, into the flatlands and another drainage of these mountains, you come to the new central African nation of Congo, touching on the Atlantic. If you go east, you pass Uganda, Kenya, and Ethiopia before coming to the Indian Ocean.

On the shore of this distant lake about 8,500 years ago—three thousand years before the first "towns" of farm life appeared in the valley of the Nile—there stood a tiny fishing village or community.

The man who lived at this site, now called Ishango by the archaeologist, stood at a sort of halfway point in the development of modern man and civilization. Jean de Heinzelin, the geologist-archaeologist who helped excavate Ishango, wrote of this man:

"... some of the molars we found were as large as those of *Australopithecus*, the prehuman 'man-ape.' Moreover, the skull bones were thick ... approximately the thickness of Neanderthal skulls ... On the other hand, Ishango man did not have the overhanging brow of Neanderthal and other earlier forms ... his chin was shaped like the chin of modern man ... the long bones of his body were quite slender ... this adds up to a unique picture. No other fossil man shows such a combination ... Primitive and even Neanderthaloid in part, Ishango man was nevertheless a true *Homo sapiens* ...[1]

"Ishango man was ... a true *Homo sapiens*, possibly Negroid [de Heinzelin conjectured] who represented the emergence in Africa of an indigenous Negro population from an older Paleolithic stock ... Most students now believe that modern man did not descend from any single stock but from a mingling of many stocks that arose independently in a number of Paleolithic [earlier 'stone-age'] communities."[2]

De Heinzelin is not referring to man's early primate origin millions of years before, but to the more recent evolved, migratory toolmaker and hunter who was already quite manlike and was already divided into what some prehistorians consider to have been "races."

The tools Ishango man used are "extremely crude and completely unlike any unearthed at other African sites" of this period, and "all of them resemble tools of the Paleolithic far more than those of the Mesolithic."[3]

The Mesolithic is the name given to the relatively late cultures, 10,000 to 4,000 B.C., which developed in different areas after the great ice had melted off most of Europe, ending the Upper Paleolithic and its hunting cultures. It was a revolutionary period in which new types and styles of tools began to be made and in which formal agriculture, that is planting for harvest, began to be practiced in primitive forms. De Heinzelin stated that besides primitive tools, Ishango man also left large numbers of "grinding and pounding stones ... to pound seeds and grain for

food ..." and these "argue for a relatively advanced stage of culture ... On the whole their cultural habits seem comparable to those of their contemporaries in Europe."[4]

At this time, about 8,500 B.C., in the Middle East agricultural developments had gone much further than either at Ishango or in Europe. Within the Zagros Mountains of Iraq, and extending down to Palestine, a true agriculture was already being practiced, and agricultural tools, such as the sickle, were being made. Ishango man was primarily a lakeside fisher far from these revolutionary centers, and the tool he developed furthest was the harpoon.

Ishango lasted a few hundred years, then one day was buried in volcanic ash. The sudden ash must have blacked out the sky, then settled on the area, closing the book on the tiny shore community.

It was a minor story, in a backwater. There was apparently nothing special about this man. He was a "Neanderthaloid" who, according to de Heinzelin, was also a cannibal, for he apparently occasionally ate his neighbors, but "cannibalism was not uncommon among Mesolithic peoples."[5] There was no reason he should have an important place in the story of man.

But, de Heinzelin continued:

"The most fascinating and most suggestive of all the artifacts at Ishango is not a harpoon point but a bone tool handle [Fig. 1 a, b, c] with a small fragment of quartz still fixed ... at its head ... it may have been used for engraving or tattooing, *or even for writing of some kind. Even more interesting, however, are its markings: groups of notches arranged in three distinct columns. The pattern of these notches leads me to suspect that they they represent more than pure decoration.*"[6] (My italics. A. M.) (See also Fig. 2 a, b.)

What de Heinzelin went on to suggest about this tiny scratched tool haunted me and kept me for an hour or so, perplexed, and in hard thought.

"In one of the columns [the notches] are arranged in four groups ... of 11, 13, 17 and 19 ... In the next they are arranged in eight groups [of] 3, 6, 4, 8, 10, 5, 5 and 7 ... In the third they are arranged in four groups of 11, 21, 19 and 9. I find it difficult to believe that these sequences are nothing more than a random selection of numbers ..."[7]

[1] Jean de Heinzelin, "Ishango," SCIENTIFIC AMERICAN, Vol. 206 (June, 1962), p. 113.
[2] Ibid., pp. 113–114.
[3] Ibid., p. 106.   [4] Loc. cit.   [5] Ibid., p. 113.
[6] Ibid., pp. 109–110.   [7] Ibid., p. 110.

Looking at the pictures and sums this seemed reasonable. But at a later sentence I balked.

"... Take the first column, for example: 11, 13, 17 and 19 are all prime numbers (divisible only by themselves and by one) in ascending order, and they are the only prime numbers between 10 and 20. Or consider the third: 11, 21, 19 and 9 represent the digits 10 plus one, 20 plus one, 20 minus one and 10 minus one."[8]

also close together. Then, again after a space, comes the 10, after which are the two fives, quite close. *This arrangement strongly suggests appreciation of the concept of duplication, or multiplying by two.*" It is of course possible that all the patterns are fortuitous. But it seems probable that they were deliberately planned. If so, they may represent *an arithmetical game of some sort, devised by a people who had a number system based on 10 as well as a knowledge of duplication and of prime numbers.*"[9] (My italics. A.M.)

Fig. 1 a, b, c
Bone tool with engraved sets of marks and a chipped quartz point from Ishango, the Congo. Mesolithic.

A Mesolithic "Neanderthaloid" man at this stage of arithmetical play? I wondered. De Heinzelin continued:
"The middle column shows a less cohesive set of relations. Nevertheless, it too follows a pattern of a sort. The groups of three and six notches are fairly close together. Then there is a space, after which ... four and eight appear—

The years of prior research, including my work on the book that now lay on my desk, hinted that somehow this was an error. It was part of a feeling for the way in which man thinks.

De Heinzelin ended:
"... this knowledge ... may have spread northward. The first example of a well-worked-out mathematical table dates from the dynastic period in Egypt. There are some clues, however, that suggest the existence of cruder systems in predynastic times. Because the Egyptian number system

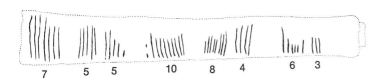

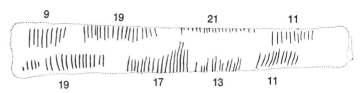

Fig. 2 a, b
The engraved marks on the bone tool from Ishango, according to de Heinzelin (© Scientific American 1962).

was a basis and a prerequisite for the scientific achievements of classical Greece, and thus for many of the developments in science that followed, it is even possible that

[8] Ibid., pp. 110–111.

[9] Ibid., p. 111.

the modern world owes one of its greatest debts to the people who lived at Ishango. Whether or not this is the case, it is remarkable that the oldest clue to the use of a number system by man dates back to the central Africa of the Mesolithic period. No excavations in Europe have turned up such a hint."[10]

It is not easy to say why I balked at de Heinzelin's explanation. But after sitting awhile, haunted by what *might* be a solution, I made a number of assumptions, none of which had been made before, yet all of which were implied in the book on space that lay almost completed on my desk.

I had returned from California six months before. I had watched war games being played for the United States Air Force on huge electronic computers, mathematical chess games in which armies of varying strengths were deployed, confronted, and wiped out in whole or part in the fraction of a second, and in which countermeasures were taken as swiftly. I had recently met with scientists who were planning the lunar and planetary shots for the space program and with the men who were training the astronauts; with bio-engineers and cyberneticists who were using computers to measure or interpret electrical patterns of the brain, the functioning of the DNA molecule, the developing fetus in the womb from conception to birth. In Washington I had spoken with mathematicians who had worked out by computer the ability of the American economy and industry to land a man on the moon before the Soviets. In Houston I had seen the lunar effort scheduled and computerized down to the last bolt, dollar, day, and week. I had watched the astronauts in training and had seen an orbital launch. I had met with men who were trying to release usable nuclear energy by fusion and men trying to create life from inert chemicals. I had met those doing research and using mathematics at the highest, most advanced levels. These were, as far as I was concerned, the most advanced examples of man "the toolmaker" and man the thinker. They were using mankind's most advanced tools and concepts. I had attempted to place this man, and the space program, at the end of a long historical development.
It was when I went, immediately after these inter-

views, to the archaeologists, the historians, and the prehistorians, that the evidence failed me. For I could find no thread that led reasonably from pre-man and early man, from the toolmaker, the chipper of stone and bone, the maker of hand axes and scrapers, to the complexities of civilization and science. A hand tool is not a process, and a stone ax is not a culture.
The bones and stones were meaningful only in their interpretation, as evidence of the growing skill, intelligence, and activity of the hominid creature who slowly became man. But how this evolving intelligence was used, and how the tools were used, had to be conjectured.
Even the skeletal fragments indicated only aspects of man's evolution, including evidence of a growing cranial capacity and a larger brain. But what "intelligence" was, and what the evolving brain did—besides direct the chipping of stones, the making of fire, and the occasional eating of neighbors, could not be adequately conjectured. Along the road language had evolved and with modern man art had burst forth, and still later agriculture had been born.
Relying on the hard archaeological evidence, one felt as though culture had simply "happened" when the brain grew larger. It was as though the hominid brain, evolving, had stumbled on skill after skill.

I tried thinking "from the evidence." Since the cranial capacity of *Homo sapiens* had not varied greatly since his first appearance in Europe, I made the assumption that the basic functioning of the brain was the same then and now, and that man before history and in the Ice Age was not much different from what he is now. What differed primarily were the facts, ideas, and relationships with which this brain was educated and with which it worked, not the manner of its functioning, its ability, or its capacity and intelligence.
This was not a stark assumption, and archaeologists and anthropologists had been tending towards it. But there had been no attempt as yet to apply this generalization and assumption to the archaeological evidence. If one did, one might get new results.
I had other, comparable thoughts. I had found that the scientists, mathematicians, and engineers of the space program, both in the United States and the

[10] Ibid., pp. 114, 116.

Soviet Union, and the psychoanalysts and psychologists I knew, were not any more "intelligent" than those I knew who were artists, writers, painters, film producers, dancers, sculptors, politicians, generals, businessmen, or thieves, nor were they different, for that matter, than the illiterate foragers, hunters and farmers I had met and lived with in primitive areas of the Pacific and Asia. Of course, there *was* a difference, but it was in culture and skills, in application and motivation, in the contemporary materials with which each brain was working, and not, it seemed to me, with the brain itself.

Having made these assumptions, I had to make others, until finally I was questioning, in one way or another, many of the accepted, basic theories concerning man's intelligence, instincts and activities —his magic, fertility rites, rites of initiation, rites of sacrifice, his art, symbols, and even the meaning of religion itself.

It was not that ancient man did not participate in these activities, but that science had given these activities labels at a distance that tended to be classificatory, clinical or even derogatory as though they were essentially early and, therefore, "primitive" manifestations. Yet, as activities of the same brain we have today, they could not have been much different from the activities that the brain conducts today.

Having gone this far, I had to make what seemed to me new assumptions about the activities of the brain. Some weeks before, in a chapter of my book about the moon, I had written that the brain was essentially a "time-factored" and a "time-factoring" organ. It was evolved over millions of years, it grows and develops anew in each individual, it matures *sequentially* with inputs from the organism and the environment, it remembers, it reacts, it plans, it participates in the dynamics of relations and processes outside of it. The concept of "time-factored" and "time-factoring" was neither simple nor easy.

Here, of course, I was treading on what was, perhaps, uncertain ground, and I had to be careful. In the lunar book I had worked with ideas that help explain why, as I sat at my desk, I approached the Ishango bone as I did. I had written that the tools (of stone and bone), the art, the stories, the ceremonies, the religion, and even language itself, all served, in a sense, the same general purpose. They made it possible for man to structure and organize an increasingly complex "time-factored life."

At its simplest, I was assuming that early man was *not essentially a toolmaker,* that is, a creature whose ability to stand and to grasp and use things in his hands had been the primary advance leading to culture and civilization.

I was assuming also that language, as a tool of communication, could not be understood merely as symbol-making and the exchange of meaning. The activities of early man, including his other evolving skills and culture, could be understood only in a "time-factored" and "time-factoring" context. This is stated simply but, as indicated above and explained later, it is an extraordinarily complex concept.

Looking at the Ishango bone I therefore asked: Why should an adult Mesolithic man—or woman—before history and agriculture, be playing arithmetical games? Certainly not as the child plays with water, mud, sticks, or stones, testing, enjoying, and developing his manipulative skills and knowledge of these things. Adult intellectual games, including arithmetical games, all have some kind of storied meaning. This holds whether the number games are used in magic or divination, in astrology or gambling, or whether the numbering is used as a storytelling and remembering device, say to recall an event, or to indicate a tattoo or a ritual pattern. This "storied" content for number thinking existed in the early arithmetic and geometric skills and games of the Egyptians, Babylonians, and Greek Pythagoreans, and it exists today for all branches of mathematics. Considered as an abstract skill, numbering may perhaps be thought of as "pure" and unrelated to storied meaning, but psychologically it is, nonetheless, a symbolizing and cognitive process. As such, it is always "time-factored" and "time-factoring." Number games, for instance, are "time-factored" as a *sequential* skill, in the process of setting up the problem, in the process of playing, in the symbolic acting out of the problem or drama, in the assumption of a solution to come, in the attainment of a solution, and in the assumption of a constancy in the rules of the game. It is also "time-factored" as tradition and lore, for the skill is taught, learned, and played repetitively. Numbering is also "time-factored" whether the story it tells is meant to be a one-time, chance reading *for now,* or whether it is intended to have a meaning that is to be repeated periodically or eternally. As a process of brain function, it is not an abstract system of rules nor a simple game. With these general thoughts I assumed it was far more than a mere game of numbers that was being played in the Mesolithic.

It seemed to me that the bone from Ishango, instead of representing a simple arithmetical game, was more significantly some sort of *notation*—arithmetic or not—and that it had been intentionally made for some purpose, whether playful or useful, and that it contained some storied meaning.

Note

Research since de Heinzelin's 1962 article and since the first edition of this book was published in 1972 has established that the inhabitants of Ishango were not "Neanderthaloid" but were, instead, an early, if somewhat archaic ancestor of modern native Africans. The debate over the place of human origins, first raised by Darwin in the 19th century when he suggested that Africa was the continent of origin, has resurfaced in a debate over the place, not merely of early hominid origins, but also of anatomically modern humans. A comparative study of the genetic material MTA/DNA found among all living humans has suggested a possible origin for modern humans in South Africa at perhaps 100-000–200,000 years ago. The debate over the relevance and meaning of this MTA/DNA data and the precision of the suggested date rages as this edition goes to the printer. Was there, in fact, one "point" and date of origin for all anatomically modern humans?

Lake Edward, on the border of Zaire, has been renamed Lake Rutanzige. Of greater importance for this book, Ishango has been redated and has been moved backward thousands of years to a period long before the "mesolithic" and longer even than before the beginnings of agriculture. (See page 32.)

CHAPTER III

THE ANCIENT BONE FROM AFRICA: ISHANGO

Martin P. Nilsson, the Danish historian, in his work PRIMITIVE TIME RECKONING (1920),[1] had indicated that most primitive peoples of whom there is record had some knowledge of time reckoning and made use of either the stars or moon or both. His "primitives," though, were almost all of our time, those studied by the anthropologist or those whose records were left us in writing.

My first assumption, then, was to ask if this series of odd and different "counts" on the prehistoric Ishango bone could be related somehow to a time count and perhaps to a lunar count. The lunar count would be the simplest possibility for an early system of time reckoning and might, for instance, include a recognition or count from full moon to full moon or from invisibility (new moon) to invisibility or from crescent to full moon.

There was nothing in the series to indicate it, for lunar phenomena are periodic and regular events, and there seemed to be no regularity in this series of "numbers," except for that arithmetical regularity that de Heinzelin had noted.

Well, then, let us try a different tack. Add the numbers

[1] Martin P. Nilsson, PRIMITIVE TIME RECKONING (Lund, Sweden: C.W.K. Gleerup, 1920), Eng. trans. F. J. Fieldan (Oxford Univ. Press, 1920).

in the right-hand column: $11+13+17+19=60$, and in the column to its left: $11+21+19+9=60$.

Could each line represent two months? Could the two lines together represent four months of lunar notation, one scratch representing one day? But how does one check such an assumption, particularly since the series is broken down so strangely? Besides 2 months do *not* give 60, and 4 months do *not* give 120. Two lunar months add up to 59 days ($29.5 \times 2 = 59$), and 4 months give 118 days, not 120. These counts of 60 might, therefore, represent some other sort of notation or numbering system.

Or, if this were lunar, perhaps our Ishango man did not keep a true calendar of set months, but used a system of observation and did not begin or end observations or make his notations at precisely the same day each month? This would not be unusual in a primitive system of lunar observation and notation. In that case his month or moon period might be longer than a strict astronomical count, at least for a period of two months. How could one tell? And what of the third line which contained only 47 or 48 marks? This would be the count for a month and a half. Why would anyone mark only a half month?

I puzzled this as I looked at the photographs and drawings of the bone. Could I perhaps assume that in an early possible notation Ishango man, consciously or unconsciously, indicated what he was doing, or what he meant? Not specifically, but generally? I had no right to make this assumption, except for the belief that his brain functioned as ours. With this assumption, though, I tried to see if I could "read" the scratches.

Look at the photographs and drawings. You will note that the groups are made at different angles and in varied sizes.

The sequence of 19 is broken down, for the eye, into 5 and 14. Could this separation have meaning? The next sequence of 17 has a swelling of some six scratches toward one end and, of these, some seem to be higher and visually separated from the rest. Following it is a sequence of 13, and this seems to contain the smallest scratches in that line of 60 marks.

Could these differences be a clue? Could they have a meaning? Or were they the "accidents" of a crude draftsman?

In the next series of 60 scratches there is a sequence of 21 very small scratches. Could these smaller marks be significant? Could they be similar in concept to the lesser sequence of 13 in the previous line?

Let us assume, I thought, that these differences do have a meaning, and that they represent, in some way, the phases or periods of the moon.

If you watch the sky each night and count the days of the waxing and waning moon, you will find that the number of days between one invisibility and the next is either 29 or 30 days. One cannot observe the astronomically precise $29\frac{1}{2}$ days. Instead there may be one, two, or three nights without a visible moon, with two as an average. The observer of this uneven visual month might mark it off as 28 or 31 days. But if he is off by one day here or there in his notation he will *always* be corrected by the next series of lunar phases. For the phases of the moon are accurate, though the observer and his notations may not be. The method is, therefore, self-correcting over a number of months.

Let us break the lunar month down further. From day of invisibility to the full moon is approximately 15 days. If you make a mark on the day of invisibility and proceed to the day of full moon you should have 16 marks, representing the 15 days. But again, for the observer, this is not a precise count and he may mark 14, 15 or 16 days from invisibility to full. Once more these variations in notation will *always* be corrected by the next phases of the moon.

There are other problems. The day of full moon and the day of invisibility are not always easy to pinpoint observationally. In fact, full moon, half-moon, invisibility, and the last and first crescents that come before and after the days of invisibility, might be observed correctly most times, but often within a day or two. Perhaps, then, it was not a single day but a *period* of a number of days that was important for the notator.

Returning to the Ishango bone, let us assume, therefore, that the five visually separated marks which begin the sequence of 19 represent a lunar *period*. We do not know which. The remaining 14 marks would then represent an earlier or a later lunar period. The 17, 13, and 11, on that line, would then also be lunar periods. With these assumptions one can take each of the three sides or faces of the bone and in a simple series of tests try to determine if the groups could be sequential lunar periods.

However, we have no idea where on the bone to begin, in which direction to proceed, or if the rendering by de Heinzelin is entirely accurate. Nor do we know, assuming this to be lunar, if we are to begin on the day of invisibility, the days of the crescents, the day of full moon, the days of half-moon, or with some period that includes, precedes, or follows these.

Nevertheless, despite these uncertainties, we can make rough tests of a lunar assumption.

We have a number of controls or checks on the tests: the invariant precision of the lunar phases themselves, the invariant sums of the different groups of marks, and the possibility of aid from the visual differences within each group and from one group to the next. We can also assume that the groups on each line were made in order, no matter from which direction.

My first tests indicated that there seemed to be a lunar phrasing along each side. The tests, however, could not be certain, for a lunar "phrasing" in a short series of 4 or 5 different counts might easily be accidental. The possibility would be made stronger if the lunar phrasing were found to be continuous from one line to the next. A consistent lunar phrasing in a long series of 15 or 16 different, apparently random numbers would be rare.

However, in trying to test for a continuous reading of the bone we are again faced with the problem of where to begin, and the direction and order of making.

Once more I had to make an assumption, based again on the feeling that the Ishango brain functioned as ours. I assumed that, if this were notation, there was probably a "logical" order to the making. One could not go helter-skelter to find an arrangement that fit. If a man begins at one end, he proceeds to the other, and finishes. He then either starts back going in the other direction, or else he returns to the side from which he started originally and proceeds again in the original direction:

However, if he marks one face going in one direction and then when he comes to the end, turns the bone 180°, perhaps because the bone was now awkward in hand, and then marks the second face in the same direction as the first, B would look to us like A. Whatever the system, however, it should be consistent for the maker. And *if* this is a lunar notation, then the lunar phrasing itself could give us clues as to the possible order of marking. We can, therefore, now make our tests among the possible alternatives.

For this test we can begin with the 19, broken down into 5 and 14. What do we do with the 5? Let us assume that, being a small *period,* it represents the days around either full moon or invisibility. Let us also assume that Ishango man did not necessarily notate the *day* of full moon, but a full moon period, nor the day of invisibility, but a period that either began or ended with one of the crescents. We have no right to make these assumptions, but they are being made in order to be tested.

The Bushman of South Africa celebrates the full moon with dances for *three* nights. These nights are the period of the full, strong, healthy moon. Then slowly, according to Bushman story, the moon begins to die as the meat of his body is cut from him by that great hunter, the Sun. From this period to the invisible moon there are some 13 days. The Bushman does not use numbers and so he retains an observational and story 13 and not a numerical 13. At invisibility, according to Bushman story, the moon is almost dead. He never quite dies. And then he grows again.

Let us assume that the 5 visually separate scratches represent some such lunar period.

Now we can make a graphic working model of the lunar month and measure the groups in the three series of lines against it. Such a model must be astronomically precise, but so made that it will allow us to judge whether the groups of marks could possibly be observational and notational lunar periods, allowing for the difficulties and uncertainties that we have discussed, and the controls we have established.

There can be no leeway in the tally, except for that small margin of variation offered by observation and notation of the moon. So, for instance, if our count is 16 days from invisibility to the day of full moon, it cannot be 16 days to the next invisibility. It must be less, either 13, 14 or 15. And if the count is 14 days from invisibility to the full moon, the next invisibility will come in either 15 or 16 days. These variations will be corrected or adjusted by the following phases.

For this test reading we hold the bone in the left hand, with the quartz point to the right, and make our marks beginning near the quartz head and moving to the left; we then turn the bone 180° and go again towards the left on the next line; once more we turn the bone 180° and go again towards the left. The same reading will be achieved by the "logic" of going to the end of the line in one direction and heading back in the other.

Now look at the chart (Fig. 3).

ing, either the full moon or the day of invisibility. If we end before either of these turning points, we must begin on the next line the same number of days before these points, or more precisely on the next day. The same process holds if we end after these turning points. In this way it is possible to make the model work for groups and sequences of any length.

A first look at the chart indicates that we *may* have a lunar phrasing here. It is not astronomically precise, but it is, nevertheless, *possible* as an observational notation.

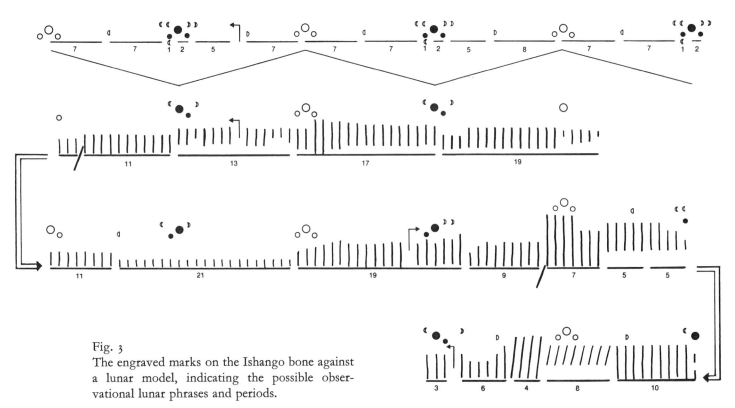

Fig. 3
The engraved marks on the Ishango bone against a lunar model, indicating the possible observational lunar phrases and periods.

To make the model work, we have worked out a simple technique of correction. Since the model is based on a two-month period of 60 days, and since there are only 59 days in each two months, we must move the notation forward one space in every 2 months in order to make the notations and observations match the model. We do not count this empty space, and count only the notational marks, but we indicate this space by an arrow in the direction of our count: ⤒ or ⤓. To simplify the reading of the linear scratches we will use the vertical lines of the graph paper as the notational points, instead of using the square. When we come to the end of a line we do not continue by merely extending and continuing on the line below, but must proceed from the relation of the last mark to either of the days of turn-

If we assume that a group of marks will either end or begin on a day of observation of a lunar phase, then some groups will, of course, end on the day before the new visible phase, while others will end on the *day of* the phase observation. The next group of marks, either beginning with the observation of a phase or not, will then go on to the day before, or the day of, a phase change and observation. In a non-arithmetical observational system both ways of ending and beginning could be equal to the maker.

With this thought you will notice that there is a close tally between the groups of marks and the astronomical lunar periods. The full moon periods do seem to contain a number of days, as we had originally assumed possible. The small marks that make up the sequences of 13 and 21 do contain periods of invisibility but no full moon, a visual differentiation that *seems* to make sense. The visual differentiations, in general, *seem* to be the results of a differentiation in thought at the time of marking, and while we have no certain proof, there are indications that they could be lunar.

This first crude test of the counts, worked out from the photographs and drawings of the Ishango bone, presents us with the *possibility,* then, that we may have a lunar phrasing and notation. It gives us no certainty, one way or the other, but also it does not eliminate the lunar possibility. In fact, a number of other readings in the long series of tests that were conducted gave even closer lunar approximations.

Having gone this far I had an almost desperate desire to hold the bone in hand so that I could see and feel it. Perhaps I would find clues to clarify these long counts of 17, 19, and 21 that included lunar points within them, or somehow clarify the other differences between the groups. Perhaps I could determine in which direction to read, or where to begin, and certainly whether de Heinzelin's rendition was correct.

Two years later I located the Ishango bone, packed in cotton and sealed in a glass vial, in the laboratories of the Musée d'Histoire Naturelle, the Royal Institute, Brussels. I found it to be a heavy piece of brownish-black stone, the bone having petrified or disappeared by action of water and chemistry in the soil, to be replaced by other minerals. By this time I had worked out and refined certain techniques of analysis for scratched or engraved artifacts. The result of that later analysis indicated an extremely close tally to the reading and breakdown presented here. It offered additional evidence of smaller periods within the long counts and these clarified the lunar phrasing.[2]

Without any certainty about the results, I had taken a number of new steps. I had shown that what had seemed to be a Mesolithic number game or decimal system to the excavator could instead be the result of a sequential notation, *perhaps* notating the lunar phases and periods. Whether my answers and results were entirely right or wrong was only partially important. The questions and techniques were new and might lead to new insights and findings regarding prehistoric thought. By my questions I had been forced to devise tests for this prehistoric material that had inherent controls, and similar tests could now be used on other examples with comparable markings. Perhaps, though I could not be sure, I had stumbled on a technique and result that could help "crack the code," not of a grammar or writing but nevertheless of some of man's earliest intellectual activities. "Intellectual" because it was not, apparently, art, but rather notation—though one can see implied tendencies toward decoration in such accumulations; "intellectual" because it was not toolmaking, though to the extent that notation may have been a useful procedure, it was an intellectual or cultural "tool."

I was faced with many questions, and I had to be cautious. I had only the evidence of a single bone, and by itself one bone could neither confirm nor disprove any assumption. Besides, the assumptions went against everything that had until then been written about prehistoric man.

Having gone this far, I had to ask the relevant question: *why* should Ishango man have been interested in making a notation, and particularly a lunar count? Without knowing a motive, I tried to assume possible reasons.

Let us assume that when the dry season had become perceptible and burdensome, some months after the rains had ceased, the Ishango hunter moved from the drying hills and valleys to the lakeside. At this time he became a fisher and perhaps a hunter of water birds, and was close to a source of water. Perhaps Ishango man lived at the lakeside permanently, and it was not he but the animals, herds, and water birds that came to the lakeside. Let us say that the arrival either of man or a species occurred in the dry season in this year, sometime around a full moon, the day of full moon falling some five days after the arrival. Perhaps it was not man or animal but a long-absent, well-known star that appeared at this time on the horizon in the dawn or dusk sky and this heralded the new season. In any of these cases, we might have something like our reading of the Ishango bone.

Perhaps five or five and a half months later the rains began and the lake started to rise. We have here a series of realistic, natural periods, points that could be recognized and marked notationally and ritually. Since Ishango man was also a gatherer of nuts and seeds, the times of gathering and pounding might

[2] See Chapter 14, Figs. 224 a, b, c and 225.

also be included in the sequence of seasonal recognitions. Since Ishango man was also an engraver or decorator—the bone is an engraving tool—the time of tattooing, decorating, gaming, of ceremony might also be indicated or implied in the notation. All this, of course, is conjecture, but it does seem to be within the realm of possibility for a hunter and fisher of the Mesolithic.

It is perhaps enough to have indicated the *possibility* that Ishango man used a system of notation, possibly lunar, and to have devised certain preliminary techniques of analysis.

The *possibility* is important, for if our hypothesis and conclusion are valid, civilization may have been built as much on such time-factoring or time-factored skills as on the handmade, hand-held tools that we find in the layers of the soil.

I had asked new questions and had devised the means to go out and test those assumptions with other examples.

Note

As I was preparing this edition, some papers were mailed to me by Professor Alison Brooks. Brooks had been one of Hallam Movius's students at the Abri Pataud in France when I had visited him in the 1960's. These papers, appearing more than two decades after I had puzzled over the Ishango bone, startled me—and they placed this volume, "suddenly," in a different perspective. Brooks and her colleagues, including de Heinzelin, had gone back to re-excavate Ishango in the 1980's in order to date any excavated organic materials by new and more precise methods.

The dates obtained suggest that the Ishango tool with its sets of marks, its inset point, and its association with bone harpoons, was 20,000 to 25,000 years old. Bone harpoons did not appear in Europe until 10 or 12,000 years later, around 10,000 BC; however notations appeared in Europe about 30,000 years ago. Significantly, around the time of Ishango, grinding and rubbing stones appear in other parts of Africa; these appeared in paleolithic Europe at a far earlier date, around 250,000 BC.

The anatomically modern humans at Ishango were different than those in Ice Age Europe, and the climate, ecology and culture were different as well.

But the human capacities were clearly comparable. I had assumed that the Ishango notation indicated changing seasonal behavior and movements of humans and animals. The new excavations at Ishango and at neighboring "Ishangian" sites document the presence of a complex, mixed ecology that included lakeside, savanna and forest, with prolific fishing in some seasons and a use of other seasonal resources such as crabs, snails, tortoises, ostrich eggs, small and large mammals, and a probable gathering of seasonal seeds, fruits and roots. Weighted digging sticks—that is, weighted by stones with central holes—appear further south in Africa at this time, in Zambia, and suggest a seasonal search for tubers and roots. Digging sticks, stones with holes, grinding stones and containers for holding plant materials, the hafting of stone tools, all document a variable use of the concept of the "hole" in Africa long before the beginnings of agriculture. But concepts of the "hole," including a hafting of tools, were also present in paleolithic Europe before the appearance of anatomically modern humans.

If interactions among dispersed human groups in tropical Africa during this early period were also seasonal, the Ishango notation may have helped to structure social life and group interchange in an environment totally different from that in mid-latitude Ice Age Europe.

We therefore need to discuss, not the points and places of supposed origins and beginnings for such cultural processes, but a use of the potentially variable human capacity within a diverse range of conditions and contexts. If notation did exist in tropical Central Africa before the beginnings of agriculture and animal domestication, what part did these time-factoring traditions and concepts play in the creation of the new economic strategies that would follow? Similarly, what part did the time-factoring concepts of the paleolithic hunter-gatherer of Europe play in the post-Ice Age "mesolithic" cultures of that region?

A. S. Brooks and C. C. Smith. Ishango revisited: new age determinations and cultural interpretations. The African Archaeological Review (1987) 5:65–78.

A. S. Brooks and P. Robertshaw. The Glacial Maximum in Tropical Africa: 22,000–12,000 BP. In The World at 18,000 BP. Vol. 2: Low Latitudes C. Gamble and O. Soffer (Eds). (Boston: Unwin, 1990) pp. 121–169.

CHAPTER IV

TRACKING THE HUNTER ON PAPER

Turn back and look again at the Ishango bone (Figs. 1 and 2). Assuming it to be notational, and possibly lunar, could such an extraordinarily complex cultural tool have been the development of one small group of "Neanderthaloid" fishermen living in relative isolation on the distant shores of a lake at the headwaters of the Nile? It did not seem reasonable. Skill of this kind would seem to have taken thousands of years to develop.

Once again, then, I made an assumption—with no precedent and no evidence to guide me, and with only a general hypothesis concerning the functioning of the human brain. I assumed that what Ishango man could do, other men could do, with varying degrees of skill. I assumed that the ability to make a notation of sorts was perhaps inherent in man. If this were true, then writing might be a late stage in the cultural development of this ability. There might also be the possibility of finding the notational skill exhibited in other examples of Mesolithic engraving and perhaps even in earlier periods. The chances, however, seemed small. There was no hint in the literature that this was possible. Archaeologists, prehistorians and anthropologists had never raised the question concerning the possibility of such a cultural beginning.

Nevertheless, I assumed the possibility and the probability of a long development for this apparent notational skill and at once took a huge leap backwards from Ishango man, ten, fifteen, twenty, even twenty-five thousand years, and in distance went thousands of miles from the high, equatorial headwaters of the Nile.

I went to western and middle Europe and to the time of the last Ice Age, to that time when a new breed of man had appeared, having either entered or evolved on the continent, displacing or eliminating or merely following the hunter who had roamed for almost a hundred thousand years the valleys, hills, and plains of Europe—Neanderthal man. There is still a blank in the record of events that must have occurred between the disappearance of Neanderthal man and the coming of the new man and his culture, though some hint that they are related groups with an ancient common ancestry is present.

This new man in Europe was modern *Homo sapiens,* the man of today, and his best-known representative was Cro-Magnon, big boned, high browed, powerful, tall, standing at times six feet four inches, and not much different from many Europeans of today. There were other representatives of modern *Homo sapiens* who entered or appeared in Europe around this time, including one who was smaller, of more delicate bone, almost frail in comparison, Combe Capelle man, apparently related to the Mediterranean peoples of today. There were other *Homo sapiens* types as well about this time in and around Europe and in the Middle East.

This modern man appeared in Europe "suddenly" about 37,000 years ago, carrying a number of new types of tools, though some are still related to those that had been made by Neanderthal man. More important, he appears, apparently for the first time, with a skill in art, a skill for making images and symbols, that soon blossomed in every form: painting, sculpture, decoration, drawing, and engraving. He appeared also with a skill in music, as excavated bone whistles and flutes from the early Upper Paleolithic indicate, hinting at ceremony, ritual, and perhaps dance. What is important for our search is the fact that these early modern men were already divided into subcultures that have been named for differences in their tool styles—the Perigordian, Aurigna-

cian, and Gravettian. As mentioned, there are also seeming skeletal differences among the carriers of some of these subcultures. One presumes also differences in language and in the details of myth and lore. The priority and origin of these subcultures have not yet been determined, and even the terminology and classification are still being debated. But as of today a Perigordian (Châtelperronian) level seems the earliest in Western Europe (*c.* 35,000 B.C.); a Gravettian level is early in Czechoslovakia (*c.* 27,000 B.C.) and may have evolved in south Russia; while the Aurignacian culture, brought by Cro-Magnon man (*c.* 32,000 B.C.) may have evolved outside of Europe in the Near East. Each of these tool cultures or industries shows traits that indicate it was evolved from tool traditions used by earlier forms of man. We are forced to conjecture a continuity, both for the tool industries and for broader cultural developments. In any case, the influences of these three subcultures of early modern man sometimes merge and run contemporaneously in Europe.

The great ice lay a mile and more thick in places during much of this time, and at its maximum it came as far south as mid-Germany, south Britain, and Czechoslovakia (see Fig. 28). Snow and ice were also piled in vast broken seas on the mountains and in the valleys of middle and southern Europe, clogging the Alps and spilling down into eastern France and filling the valleys of the Pyrenees between France and Spain. The climate, weather, and cloud cover of Europe were, therefore, probably different from what they are today. Between the vast northern ice sheet and the mountain ice of the Alps there was an ice-free corridor of gently rolling hills that ran east and west through Czechoslovakia to Russia. Here herds of cold-climate mammoth roamed and the mammoth hunters lived. Further south, in France, the cold-climate reindeer herds lived and still further south, in Spain and Italy, were animals of a more temperate climate. The climate of Europe through this second half of the last Ice Age warmed and chilled in small cycles, but it is still referred to climatically as the Ice Age. The archaeologist, however, talking *from the tools* of the new man who was in Europe at this time, calls it the Upper Paleolithic or Late Stone Age.

This early modern *Homo sapiens* has left evidence around Europe of graves, shelters, houses, fires, and

34

thousands of stone tools in various stages of making and use. He has also left *hundreds of scratched, notched, and "decorated" bones and stones.* These are found in all the soil layers of the Upper Paleolithic, beginning with the bottom layers of the Perigordian, Aurignacian, and Gravettian, and going up the layers to the time of the melting of the ice, the final phase of the Magdalenian. These strangely marked bones and stones continue to be found in soil layers overlying the Magdalenian, representing the Mesolithic period of the post-Ice Age cultures, and they are found even in the Neolithic, the period of transition to agriculture. They are also found in one form or another in Africa (the example from Ishango) and the Americas. In addition to these linear compositions, this early man in Europe left hundreds of engravings and paintings of animals, human figures, signs, forms, and symbols, both on the small portable artifacts and on the cave walls. Sometimes these are associated with the strange series of marks and sometimes not.

The question was obvious: could the marks, scratches, sequences, and signs of the Ice Age be, like the later Ishango marks, notational and, therefore, in one way or another, time-factored and time-factoring devices? If so, dare we assume that we could either "read" or interpret them?

A summation of what is known and generally accepted about ancient man has been prepared under the auspices of the United Nations Educational, Scientific and Cultural Organization (UNESCO) with the help of leading scholars around the world.[1] It includes a 215-page review of the prehistory of man by Jacquetta Hawkes. The bulk of this report deals with what has been learned from the hard evidence of man's tools, his sites and his occasional skeletons, with a small chapter on his art and some paragraphs concerning his religion. There is no mention or illustration of the early Perigordian, Aurignacian, or Gravettian markings, nor of the more complex Magdalenian compositions. There is no hint or recognition of a *cognitive skill* capable of notation. Nor is there any mention of the sky, the seasons, the year, the sun, or the moon.

No wonder. For how could the archaeologists make sense of these scratches, when no two examples are ever alike, and the marks are so irregular and apparently random?

When the prehistorians did attempt tentative interpretations of these markings, they at first assigned them to man's urge to "decorate," or to his "need to fill an empty space," or to doodling in rare moments of leisure. Somewhat later, these marks were assigned to hunting magic, the so-called *marques de chasse,* by analogy compared to rites occasionally practiced by hunting peoples alive today. These early interpretations were not based on a "reading" or analysis of the Ice Age marks but were generalities and assumptions based on their appearance which both classed and quickly dismissed the whole body of markings. As presumed magic they were felt to be indecipherable, as a possible "tally" of animals killed they were not felt to be culturally significant.

In recent years there have been new attempts to analyze these Upper Paleolithic marks, both on the engraved artifacts and in the caves. The most recent and the most important, because it is the most carefully prepared and the best documented, considers the body of marks, symbols, and animals, often associated together in the caves, as "sexual," indicating a philosophical duality (Leroi-Gourhan). In 1957 there had been a single attempt by Karel Absolon of Czechoslovakia to infer for the Upper Paleolithic, as de Heinzelin had for the Mesolithic Ishango bone, a decimal system of numbers, a counting by tens. The majority of prehistorians, however, remained unconvinced by such theories, uncommitted and perplexed. The Abbé Henri Breuil of France, the father of Upper Paleolithic art interpretation and rendition, never attempted either a systematic interpretation or analysis of these marks.

Paolo Graziosi, director of Italy's National Museum of Anthropology and Ethnology and editor of a leading European journal of prehistory, RIVISTA DI SCIENZE PREISTORICHE, published one of the first comprehensive anthologies of European prehistoric art, including both the cave paintings and the decorated and scratched bones and stones.[2] Graziosi, too,

---

[1] Jacquetta Hawkes and Sir Leonard Woolley, HISTORY OF MANKIND: PREHISTORY AND THE BEGINNINGS OF CIVILIZATION. (New York: Harper & Row, 1963.)

[2] Paolo Graziosi, PALAEOLITHIC ART, translated from the Italian (New York: McGraw-Hill, 1960).

attempted no interpretation. He stated that the scratchings and decorations seemed to be somehow related to the realistic art, may have stemmed from it or may have led to it, and he let it rest. He gave no examples of the simple, early Perigordian, Aurignacian, or Gravettian scratches. Of the signs and symbols on the cave walls he says either that "it is impossible to venture an interpretation" or that "It would be futile to attempt an explanation of this truly cabbalistic composition."

Leroi-Gourhan, who developed the theory that implies a sexual meaning for such marks when they appear in the cave compositions, in 1968 recognized that the small engraved bones and stones pose a special problem. At the early Upper Paleolithic (Châtelperronian) site of Arcy-sur-Cure, representing the culture that immediately follows the Mousterian of Neanderthal man, a site which he excavated, he found "bone fragments with regularly spaced parallel incisions on the edge . . . [Such] objects date from the later stages of the Upper Paleolithic and were long ago named 'marques de chasse,' 'hunting tallies'. . . the idea of the hunter conscientiously making a notch on his small stick every time he brought down a mammoth is more entertaining than plausible. Whatever the purpose of these objects, their occurrence throughout the Upper Paleolithic is a remarkable phenomenon—the earliest representation we have of a rhythmic arrangement with regular intervals, the beginning of the evolution that led to the ruler, the musical staff, the calendar, and the peristyle of the temple. The span of the Châtelperronian extends probably over several millennia, corresponding to the theoretical epoch of transition between the Mousterian culture of Neanderthal man and the cultures directly assigned to present-day man."[3]

But what these "bones with regular incisions" might have meant in their time he does not conjecture, though by inference they provide comparison to the so-called sexual symbols of the caves.

So much for the markings. There had also been a few scattered attempts by students of Ice Age art to compare the animals and symbols with the astronomical and calendric animals and symbols of the later civilizations in Mesopotamia, Egypt, Crete, Greece, Asia, and the Americas, and by these comparisons to impute an astronomical knowledge to prehistoric man (Breuil, Bourdier, König, Hentze). One researcher even claimed to recognize stellar constellations in the markings (Baudouin). But these were comparisons and analogies that could not be verified and they were, therefore, generally dismissed as unscientific.

Searching through the literature, then, for some clue to help me, I could find nothing. The situation remained as Professor Hallam L. Movius, Jr., of the Peabody Museum, Harvard, had summed it up: one waiting decipherment.

Using the questions, insights, and preliminary techniques derived from my analysis of the Ishango bone, I turned hesitantly to the markings and sequences of the European Ice Age. I proceeded with caution. A bone with few scratches or markings would tell me nothing. It could mean anything or nothing. At this stage of the search I needed examples with at least thirty markings, and preferably more, and I needed bones that were reasonably whole and unbroken. In fact, the longer and more complex a series of marks was, the easier it would be to determine if it was notational or lunar, the less possibility there would be for repeated chance correspondences with the phases of the moon.

For almost one year I studied the drawings and photographs of Ice Age artifacts in the scientific journals, making copies, comparing examples, doing computations, making charts. There was no certainty about the precision of any single illustration and so I had to do thousands of analyses and computations to arrive at what I felt to be an average, an understanding of the way in which these markings might have been made, and I had always to do my computations and judge my results within the possibility of a large or small error in the drawing. At times I felt like a man trying to structure a building with oozing sands of the sea. Slowly, however, the assumptions and computations, the comparisons and the eliminations of possibility began to give me feelings that at times approached certainty.

In mid-continent Europe, below the northern ice, in the corridor stretching from Czechoslovakia through Poland into the Ukraine and eastward to Siberia, was a vast forestless tundra of flat land, rolling hills and passes, and cold rivers and streams along which the herds of mammoth fed, migrated, and roamed.

[3] André Leroi-Gourhan, TREASURES OF PREHISTORIC ART, trans. Norbert Guterman (New York: Harry N. Abrams, Inc., 1967), p. 40.

Hunting these herds around 27,000 B.C. was an exceptionally skilled and intelligent *Homo sapiens*. In skeleton and brain capacity he was modern man, in culture he was an astonishingly sophisticated human. At this early date, the archaeological diggings show, he built huts and even large houses of skin, mammoth bone, reindeer antler, wood, clay, and stone, against the wind and cold (caves were rare in this heartland of Europe); he used coal and bone as fuel (wood was not as common as he might have wished in this cold time, and fresh bone, with the fat still present, burned well); he sculpted animals and human figures from ivory and from a clay that was mixed with bone ash and perhaps fat, and he then fired his clay figures hard in ovens or kilns; he buried his dead with ornament and ceremony; he used red and black color symbolically and decoratively; he wore leather and skin clothes, including what seems to have been a parka or arctic hood for the head, and he costumed himself with rings, bracelets, necklaces, and carved ivory headbands; he even ground and polished stone to make objects of unknown use (in the old chronology polished stone does not appear until some 20,000 years later, in the Mesolithic, after the ice had melted).

In UNESCO's PREHISTORY, Jacquetta Hawkes gives a description of an excavated living site:

"The earliest actual remains of man-made buildings date from Upper Palaeolithic times and come from Czechoslovakia, southern Russia and Siberia . . . three huts lying within a few hundred metres of one another [are] at Věstonice on the lower slopes of the Pavlov hills in Czechoslovakia . . . set near small springs and on a specially prepared floor hollowed from the slope of the hill . . . One of them was roughly oval . . . 15 by 9 metres [49 × 30 feet] and floored with limestone grit . . . Five hearths [fireplaces] in shallow depressions ringed with flat stones lay along the centre line, while small pits that may have been for storage had been dug just inside the house wall . . . This long house with its several hearths is judged to have been the communal dwelling of a family hunting-group or clan . . .

"The other hut was smaller, nearly circular . . . with a floor partly sunk into the hillside . . . The whole hut was enclosed in a circular wall of limestone and clay . . . This must be the most ancient true wall built by human hands

known to survive on earth. More remarkable still is the hearth in the middle . . . the base of a beehive-shaped oven or kiln . . . The layer of soot contained more than two thousand clay pellets . . . and . . . with them some fragments of the clay modeller's art—the heads of two bears and a fox, some unfinished statuettes . . . In short, it seems that this was a kiln, the oldest ever to have been discovered, and that it was used to harden clay figures . . . the excavators believe that this was . . . the quarters of a Palaeolithic medicine man, the sacred den where he shaped and hardened the images of beasts and of women to be used in his hunting and fertility rites."[4]

This sophisticated, mid-European, East Gravettian Ice Age mammoth hunter lived far—in terms of time, geography, and basic culture—from the fisher and gatherer of the equatorial hills of Ishango in Africa. This Gravettian culture spread with variations and additions as far west as France, England, and Spain, and as far east as Siberia, with some indication that it may have reached China. It was not an isolated, backwater culture, but one that was sufficiently dynamic and successful to have adapted itself to different regions, climates, and ecologies, and one from which later successful cultures evolved.

For our purposes at the moment, the important thing is that this early modern man made scratches and series of marks and sequences on bone and stone.

Sitting in the silent libraries and plodding through the scientific journals and studying the illustrations of this culture, I was fascinated by the complexity and richness of the markings. Some seemed purely decorative, others were certainly not. Preliminary tests with the illustrated examples indicated the possibility that there were dozens of pieces with both complex and simple notation in Czechoslovakia and Russia.

Fig. 4 a, b
Line drawing of the engraved marks on a bone fragment from Kulna, Czechoslovakia (after Breuil). Upper Paleolithic.

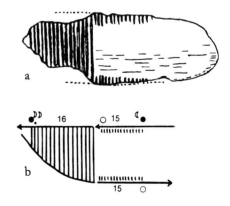

One of the simplest examples was a scratched reindeer bone (Fig. 4 a) from the Moravian mammoth-hunter

[4] Hawkes and Woolley, op. cit., pp. 134–135.

site at Kulna, Czechoslovakia, not far from the mammoth-hunter houses just described.

The markings are divided into groups, and each group is differentiated by size and place. It is an odd, unbalanced composition, and it does not seem to be decoration. For one thing, the fragment seems to have been neither a tool nor an ornament. After my analysis of the Ishango bone, it was my assumption that it might be notational, that the bone might be a "slate."

The markings are so simple that the possible ways of making and, therefore, the order of reading the sequences are few. One can either begin at the right or the left, with the large marks, or with one of the groups of small marks. The totals of each group are also simple: 15–16–15. Each of these is the count for an observational half month (Fig. 4 b).

We can illustrate one possible consecutive reading beginning at upper right and going sequentially to bottom right. If we assume a beginning on the day after the visible last crescent, on the day of invisibility, the sequence of fifteen small marks ends on the day before full moon. The day of full moon, then, begins the next large sequence of sixteen, and this ends on the day of invisibility. The next fifteen small marks would begin, observationally, with the day of first crescent, and take us exactly to full moon again:

We have, then, the *possibility* of an observational lunar notation, with the indication, once again, that such a notation does not necessarily imply a full month. The arithmetical regularity that seems at first to be present would then represent different observational periods, and could argue *against* a system of numbers. Each fifteen, for instance, begins and ends at a different but logical observational point. To the man making the two fifteens—if this is a lunar notation—the *periods,* and not the numbers, would have had an equivalence, representing the "period of the growing moon."

It must be stressed that the seeming regularity is not necessarily arithmetic, but may be due simply to the lunar periodicity. Karel Absolon of Czechoslovakia, excavator of many important East Gravettian sites including the one described at Věstonice, sensed, after years of handling such scratched bones, that they

were non-decorational, and he surmised that they might be arithmetic. But his assumption of a decimal system was not proved even in the examples that he gave.[5] The Kulna bone, and the many other examples I analyzed in the literature, hinted that the arithmetical patterns that Absolon thought he saw were the result of his modern arithmetical education and way of thinking and the result of suggestions he had received from anthropologists working with living primitives that do count. It was not based on analysis of the internal evidence, the markings themselves.

Let us now go eastward into Russia. At the mammoth hunting site of Gontzi in the Ukraine, a short ride west of Kiev and within what is today the rich agricultural farm belt of the Soviet Union, there was found deep in the soil a point or tip of mammoth ivory. It had never been used as a tool, nor had it been shaped or worked. But it had unusual markings, so delicately and precisely scratched they looked as though they had been made by a jeweler using a diamond stylus and a magnifying glass. It had, of course, been engraved by the point of a chipped flint and by the rough hand of a hunter or shaman. The Soviet scientific journals referred to it as a "decorated" tusk.

The tusk comes from the general area in which, it has been conjectured, the East Gravettian culture may have originated, but the example seems to be late and may date from the period that is comparable to the Magdalenian of western Europe, the time near the end of the Ice Age. The dating, apparently, is not certain. In any case, it is an evolved example of these markings.

We see it both unrolled and as it looks along one face (Fig. 5 a, b).

Could it be decoration? Hardly. We seem to have a number of sequences, or groups of marks, made along a horizontal line. These groups are separated by wide spaces, and each series is internally divided or differentiated by marks that are longer and shorter. Some marks are made over the horizontal and some below, a few cross over. There also seem to be "figures" or symbols at points in the sequence. Clearly the compo-

[5] Karel Absolon, "Dokumente und Beweise der Fähigkeiten des Fossilen Menschen zu Zählen im Mährischen Paläolithikum," ARTIBUS ASIAE, Vol. XX, 2/3 (1957), pp. 123–150.

sition is neither haphazard nor random. It is intentional, but not "decorative." It must then be, in one way or another, notational.

But of what? We cannot tell. If, however, we assume it to be notational, then it must be "time-factored," both in the making and in the meaning. The marks must have been made and conceived sequentially, one meaning and one stroke following the next. The man making the composition must have known the "story" or meaning that was being structured by the sequence. In such a system each mark is symbolic, representing one unit of something, and the whole represents something else as a "sum." It need not, however, be either writing or arithmetic.

Was this the record of the days or events in a hunt, a journey, a migration, a ritual, a myth, an initiation, a dance? Was it a record of the days of waiting from first snows to first thaw, or from the short winter nights to the spring calving? We cannot tell. But each of our conjectures, as you will notice, is a time-fac-

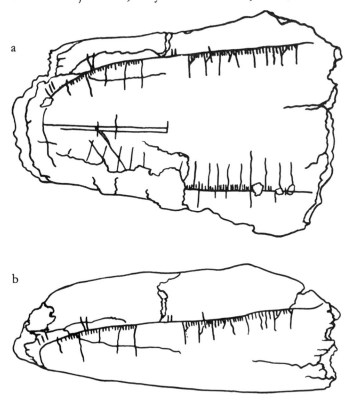

Fig. 5 a, b
Line drawing of the engraved marks on a mammoth tusk from Gontzi, the Ukraine (after Scerbakiwskyj). Late Upper Paleolithic.

tored sequence. At this stage of research it was impossible for me to test any concept but the lunar, since it alone offered the necessary controls.

Where do we begin? The question is crucial in the analysis of any sequence.

We have a horizontal line that arcs around the point of the tusk, and despite the one break it seems to be continuous. We can, therefore, assume a beginning at one of the ends. The horizontal line helps us in tying together the large groups, as it must have helped the maker. We "read," then, either right to left or left to right along the line. Because of the arc we would seem to begin at the thick end of the tusk and go around the point. With these tentative assumptions we can make our first tests.

Do we count the "signs" in the first group, top right, as one or as two or three marks ($\vee$ and $\curlyvee$)? This is the only group that has these particular multiple signs, and so we can run tests for each alternative possibility.

It is not necessary to give all the details of the tests, which, though simple, took many hours. It is important, however, to understand the process I was engaged in. I was trying not so much to solve the notation as to understand the ways-of-thinking involved. It was an attempt in which I assumed that I could understand and re-create those ways-of-thinking, despite a difference in language and culture, at a level that was more basic than either language or culture because the process was human, kinesthetic, and cognitive and because the brains of the maker and the interpreter were more or less equivalent. This is a process of interpretation similar to that indulged in by the archaeologist, for instance, when he tries to re-create the steps involved in toolmaking.

Rather than give all the details of the analysis, I shall indicate the types of questions I asked, since these are important aspects of any research.

Now, if the lunar hypothesis is correct, I thought, it may be possible to conjecture about the meaning of the "signs" and the large and small lines. Certain that I was wrong, but searching for some clue as to the *possible* meaning of the notation and marks, I asked *hundreds* of questions.

Could the "signs" represent points in the story or observation of the month? Could the angle containing the tiny mark represent the "hidden" or "swallowed" moon, the day on which the moon is missing from the sky, the day of invisibility? Could the open angle at the beginning of the first group be a sign for the beginning of a series? Or, if each sign was a multiple count, could the added angled stroke represent a day in which there was no observation of the moon? Or was it a day on which something special happened? In the same way, could the long lines represent evenings of clear observation of a phase of the moon? Could the marks above the horizontal line be a different kind of symbol than those below? Could they say something in sum about the month or period or sequence just completed? The first group, for instance, ends with two marks that are above the horizontal (   ). Could these be saying: "we have just had two invisibilities, and now we head for the third"? At the end of the next, second series we have three marks above the horizontal. Could these be saying: "we have just had the third invisibility"? Following the two upper series, and at the bend of the arc, we have a "sign" that *seems* to close out the previous sequence or period, as if to say: "we have just had two months (   )

containing three invisibilities (| | |)."

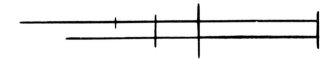

If the first group ended at invisibility, and the second series, therefore, began with the first crescent, could the long lines be read and would the two marks that fell above the horizontal, over marks 18 and 19, be days of rite and ceremony?

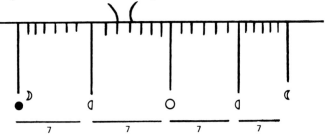

Or were these days when something happened? I went on in this way through the full notation.

After the long series of questions and tests in which I had used the lunar model, it was apparent, for instance, that if the "signs" of the first series were considered as one mark or unit each, the series would begin a few days before invisibility and last crescent (Fig. 6). But if each "sign" was considered as a mul-

tiple count, the series would begin some 4 or 5 days earlier, just after the full moon period.

In total, there seemed to be a four-month-plus period. This is one third of a year, beginning with one season and ending with another.

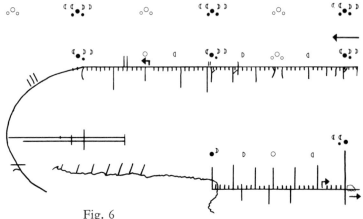

Fig. 6

The engraved marks on the Gontzi ivory against a lunar model, indicating the possible lunar phrasing and the placement of the notational symbols.

I doubted if I was entirely right. But it was not important, at this point, to be right in all the details.

Let me summarize. I was attempting to reconstruct a sequential notation, and I was assuming that each point in the notation represented a different point of meaning, or of observation, or a different point in the story or drama of the moon.

Each of the four "moons," or months, was different in specific breakdown and signs and, therefore, different, it seemed, in the stories it told or the details of observation. It could be that the odd breakdown indicated a non-lunar sequence.

I therefore had to ask, could there be a different story or series of events for each of the four months, realistically and observationally, as well as ritually and mythologically? The moon, of course, tells only one basic story: birth, growth, fullness, decay, and disappearance, with rebirth and growth again. But could it be that the frame of this structure could hold a different story or pattern for each of the months in a season or year?

Once again, knowing that I was wrong and merely to see how such stories might work against the odd divisions and signs of the Gontzi bone, I tried to create tentative stories, searching for a possible way-of-thinking rather than for precision. For any stories, if there were any, must remain forever lost.

Let us assume that the first month tells the story of the lunar hero who is swallowed by some beast spirit, real or fantastic. It is a story belonging to one season. The second month could then tell the story of the same hero in adventure with some other seasonal animal or spirit god. The notation could then have the storied or symbolic point, the ceremonial days, in the sign above days 18–19. Perhaps the story was strengthened or accompanied by a non-lunar phenomenon or observation, the first rains, the arrival of the first birds of spring, or something of the sort. The non-lunar phenomenon would then fall within the proper lunar month, or seasonal "moon." We are missing the third month in the break of the tusk, but it is clearly indicated. The fourth month with its many lines above and below the horizontal could then indicate a different ceremonial, ritual, or storied period, say of the hero's journey to the deep source of the waters and floods, or the plants of life.

It would be absolute presumption and stupidity to think that such stories are even close to the truth. The sequence, for instance, may have referred to the practical round of a hunt or migration. But as a way-of-thinking such a storied re-creation does *seem* to give some sense and meaning to the non-arithmetical order of marks, signs and groupings.

Was the re-creation valid? Or was it a work of my imagination, without relevance to the markings? If the analysis had even minimum validity did it mean that the Upper Paleolithic had notations that were purely observational, the stories held in mind, and that others might be largely storied, the lunar sequences kept in mind?

As you can see, there could be no certainty in the analysis of this one example, except perhaps for the certainty that it was a "time-factored" notation. For me, however, the *possibility* that it was lunar seemed strengthened by the hundreds of examples I had studied, many of which seemed best explained by a "time-factored" or lunar hypothesis.

I was doubly admonished to caution by Karel Absolon, who in trying to defend his theory of a decimal number system had written:

". . . it is not altogether easy to establish the number of strokes exactly because the outer surface of fossilized ivory and bone is often defiled or damaged by corrosion (chemical, the interweaving with plant roots, larval, worm-eaten, etc.) and the count of lines that are beginning to decay must always be done with a microscope or binocular magnifying glass."[6]

My paper in SCIENCE, "Lunar Notations on Upper Paleolithic Remains," November 6, 1964, gave the two tentative examples from Kulna and Gontzi, and two from the period after the ice had melted, the Mesolithic of Spain.

Having learned and questioned as much as I could from the journals, and having studied all the Upper Paleolithic examples I could find in the libraries, I now went, with a toy microscope, to Europe.

[6]Ibid., p. 138.

* * *

For a quarter of a century, after publishing the first edition of this book, I scoured Europe for the artifacts I had puzzled in the literature. When I flew to the Soviet Union to study the Gontzi tusk I learned that it had been lost in World War II, with other archaeological materials. The loss was tragic. The Gontzi tusk would have been crucial for if I were correct in my analysis, sequencing a linear notation in the Gontzi manner would have created a serpentine image if it were extended (Fig. 6 a). One would "read" it by starting at the right, reading to the left,

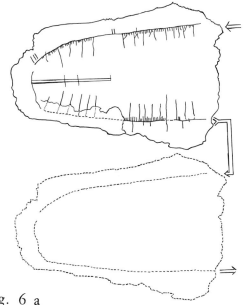

Fig. 6 a

descending to the next line and reading toward the right. At the end of the second line one would descend and begin again reading towards the left. This boustrophedon form of reading, "as the ox plows," had been used in early forms of writing among the later agricultural civilizations. The Gontzi tusk could have confirmed that boustrophedon mode. The serpentine, boustrophedon mode of notation showed up, however, in other Ice Age examples from Western Europe, many of which are described in this book (See Fig. 9). Besides, as I studied the materials from Russia and the Ukraine, I found an unexpected wealth of unpublished analytical evidence documenting a variety of symboling traditions, as rich as any in western Europe, including unexpected symboling modes. (See the Appendix.)

There was also, I found, more than one type of "notation." A shaped piece of mammoth ivory from the Russian plain had been a tool, perhaps a stake driven into the ground to anchor a tent, had cracked and so became a scrap available for marking. Microscopic analysis indicated that it had been marked with a tally or score perhaps made during an evening of gaming or gambling (Fig.6 b,c). Short sets of marks were incised at the top in different directions, usually upon short containing lines, and these containing lines were incised in different directions. The sets of marks on these lines were sometimes engraved down-

ward, sometimes upward, at times above the containing line, at other times below. The composition did not constitute a "design" but was apparently a "random" accumulation made by different engraving tools at different times. It was not a continuous, linear notation, nevertheless the mode of engraving small sets on containing lines suggested a tradition similar to that found on the Gontzi tusk. These data documented symboling modes that had never before been reported for the Ice Age (See Chapter VII). The analyses provided fascinating insights into early symbol. The use of visual cues such as containing lines and empty spaces, and the use of different angles of marking to separate sets, had already been suggested, for instance, in my study of the Ishango bone and the Gontzi tusk. On the Kostenki ivory these had apparently been used to accumulate a "tally." Because of the random, unorganized nature of the accumulation this was not a tally of animals killed, or of days or of months. The structure was, in fact, too irregular for any long-term record-keeping. The evidence that began accumulating both confirmed and altered the concepts in this book. A quarter of a century later these continuing studies would become part of the thinking that would aid in the solution of the most complex notation to come from the Ice Age (See Chapter VII).

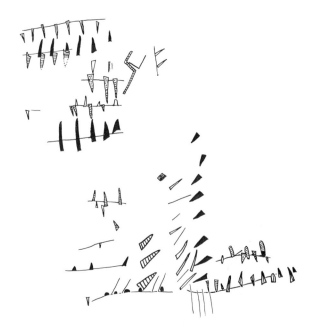

Fig.6 b,c

42

CHAPTER V

NOTATION: THE BONES

The Musée des Antiquités Nationales is about a half-hour's drive from Paris, at Saint-Germain-en-Laye, along the river Seine and off the track for the tourist. Once the summer palace of kings, it is today the ugly, heavy-stoned repository of France's pre-Christian past.

In its drab, poorly-lit side rooms, in badly displayed cabinets without electricity, lay the colorless, almost meaningless accumulations of Upper Paleolithic materials, crowded under glass with their aged yellowing labels. There were more than twenty cabinets of engraved, prehistoric, Upper Paleolithic materials on exhibit and more than twice as much locked away in private rooms and drawers of the palace.

When I walked into Mauss Hall, the main exhibit room of the prehistoric period, I had the sudden chill feeling of an intruder in an abandoned graveyard. There was a huge silence in the musty air of the high-ceilinged stone chamber.

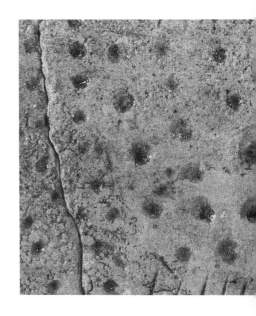

I walked with a sinking feeling past the cabinets. The large collection of browned, broken, and weathered bones, with their scratches and forms, seemed impossible to attack.

I spent a day handling pieces from all periods of the Upper Paleolithic, early Aurignacian to the end of the Magdalenian. The next day I still did not know where or how to begin. I put odd pieces for a few minutes under the microscope and examined the marks in close-up. It seemed an increasingly impossible task. My work with the drawings had not prepared me for the decay and complexity I held in hand. I was picking up piece after piece that seemed partial, broken, or non-notational.

I realized that if I began my search by seeking only those pieces that seemed to be notational or lunar I might find a piece, or a few such pieces, among the mass of materials here or elsewhere in Europe. But this would be a search by default, directed to prove a hypothetical point. If I were right, I would have to prove my point in a single cabinet, with the limited random sampling offered by a small collection of bones and stones. If I failed in this random sampling, there would be no point in performing the agonizing search through the other cabinets or through the rest of Europe for some chance piece that might give the proof. Either notation was common in the Upper Paleolithic or there was no notation.

In Mauss Hall, cabinet number one began in its upper left hand corner with engraved pieces from the earliest periods, the Aurignacian and Perigordian, and it ended at far right with engraved pieces from the Magdalenian. It was a fair sampling, then, of man's markings across nearly 20,000 years, and I would have to find the answer, one way or another, among these bones.

In the upper left corner of the first cabinet was a small, somewhat ovoid bit of bone (11 cm) that had been shaped and worked flat on both faces. Its main face was intentionally pockmarked in a small 1¾ inch area (5.2 cm) with a seemingly chaotic, haphazard pitting, obviously made by man. It was as far from the ordered, precise linear sequences I had studied in the libraries as possible.

It is presented here in enlargement (Fig. 7). The bone was just big enough to be held in the palm of one hand while it was being engraved by a tool held in the other.

It had been found at the site of the Abri Blanchard, in the Dordogne region of France, more than fifty years before, and it came from typical Aurignacian layers and had been made by early Cro-Magnon man. These same layers of the soil at the site of the Abri Blanchard held stone blocks containing paintings of two oxen that had fallen from the rock wall of the shelter. The shelter also contained engravings on stone of forms that resemble the female vulva, similar to other vulvar shapes found on bone and stone in this general period as far east as Czechoslovakia and the East Gravettian.

The tiny, pocked plaque, then, had come from a relatively complex, sophisticated culture, rich in symbolic art. This bit of shaped bone may or may not have been used as a tool, but it did not seem as though the marks were meant to be decorative.

Examining it superficially as I carried it to my work desk in the museum library, it seemed to be a perfect example of non-notational random marking. Using a small, single-lens hand magnifier, and a jeweler's eye-piece I had bought for a dollar and a half, I began the examination. I turned the bone slowly in the beam of a powerful lamp. It seemed hopeless. There were all sorts and styles of marks in the pocking.

Fig. 7
Engraved and shaped bone plaque from the rock shelter site of Blanchard (Dordogne). Aurignacian.

Then, as I worked it back and forth in the light, it became clear that there was something here that "made sense." There were groups of marks that were made by a hooked or arced stroke. Some of these were made by a fine, sharp point and others by a thicker point; some of these arced from right to left, others from left to right. Other marks had been punched without turning, while still others had been made with a limited half turn, to form a bit of arc.

It soon became clear that one style of stroke or one style of point had been used to make a limited number of marks, usually in a horizontal direction, and totalling one, two, three, four, five, six, seven, or eight.

I put the bone under the somewhat higher magnification of the microscope and carefully, over many hours, turning the bone and shifting the lamp, examined and plotted the "ballistic" print of each mark (Fig. 8). At one spot in the jumble of marks, in a corner at upper left, there were four arced or hooked strokes, made by the same flint point (ζ). These were not made in a horizontal order, but formed a rough square. Finding this square suddenly cleared the whole image.

Since the marks to the right of the square were arranged horizontally, these four marks must represent a "turn," two heading in one direction, two in the other:

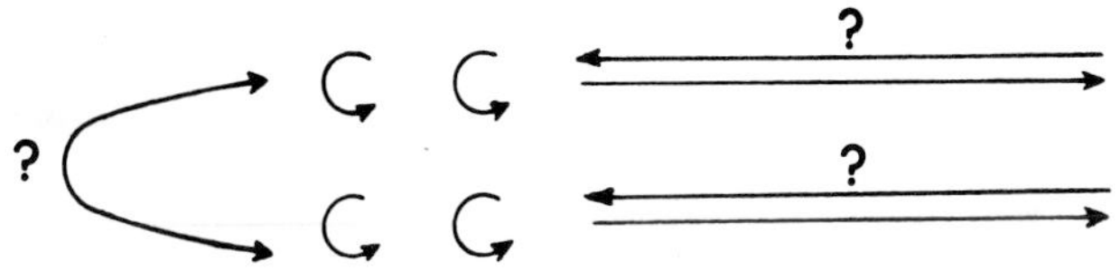

Fig. 7a

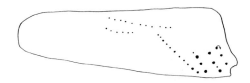

I did not know in which direction the "turn" pointed, but having found a point of turning the "chaotic" form took instantaneous shape. It was a

Fig. 8 (Next page)
Detail. The engraved marks on the main face of the Blanchard bone.

45

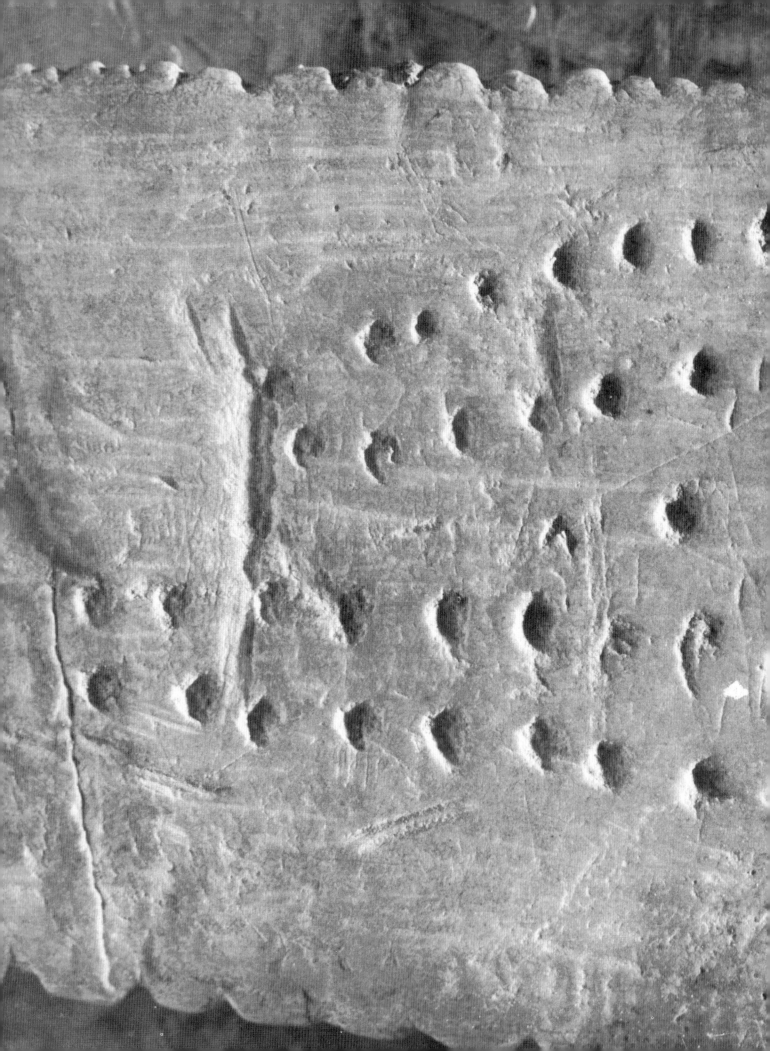

serpentine figure composed of 69 marks, containing some 24 changes of point or stroke (Fig. 9). The final image was:

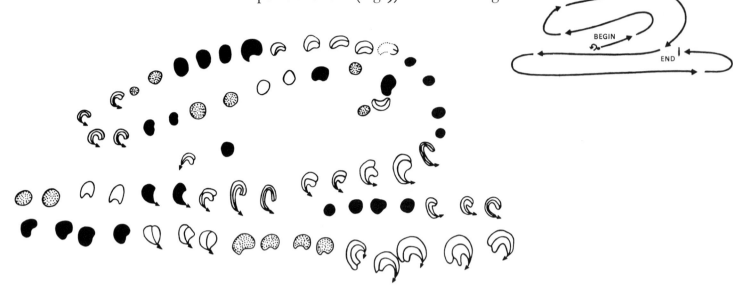

Fig. 9
Schematic rendition of the engraved marks on the bone from the Abri Blanchard as determined by microscopic analysis, indicating the differences in the engraving points and the strokes structuring the serpentine form.

Obviously the pattern was not random. It had been made on purpose. It had been made sequentially. Even now, after clarification, I knew it could not be ornament or decoration, for any man making an ornamental composition 1¾ inches in size would not have used 24 changes of point and stroke to make 69 close marks. It was inconceivable. Besides, it did not look or feel decorative. It must, therefore, be notational.

The man making this notation had possibly made it over a period of time, perhaps over a long period if the changes of stroke and point were a clue. And he had accumulated the notation, stroke by stroke, to structure an image. The image must, therefore, have been in his mind before he began, as he worked, and when he was done. The final image, then, must have had some meaning, and the meaning was somehow related to the notation. In fact, the meaning must have been known before the notation was started. But what meaning?

The long work in New York libraries now came to my aid. I would not have recognized this sequential pattern without that preparation. But, in addition, I had lived with the waxing and waning moon in thought so long, had been watching the phases in the sky, and had played with the technique of simple notational systems so often, that I now felt at home with this odd, serpentine figure. I had, on my own, begun to call the waxing and waning the "turning of the moon." It was a turning that was implied, for instance, and structured into the working and visualizations of my lunar model, a turning around the period of full moon and invisibility.

I had also learned from studying the drawings of the bones that any sequential notation inevitably structures an image, which is then recognized by the maker, non-arithmetically, as a "sum." Even a straight line series would do this.

Could this odd figure be lunar? Was this Aurignacian man thinking as I had?

I tested the figure against the lunar model. Assuming a beginning around invisibility, I conjectured that the arced, crescent-shaped mark in mid-figure was perhaps the last visible crescent, and the start of the notation. I then laid off the 69 marks sequentially against the model. The result was astonishing (Fig. 10 a, b).

If this were lunar, the days of invisibility fell at the right, at a point of turning, and the full moon periods fell at the left, at a point of turning, while the half-moons (our "quarter-moon") all fell in mid-figure. If lunar, we had a visual, kinesthetic, and symbolic representation of the waxing and waning which at any point indicated to the maker where in the lunar month he was, and it did this non-arithmetically. When the maker had finished his notation, the full serpentine figure represented two months or "moons." Because of my previous work I was even prepared for the fact that the notation ended at the half-moon.

Could this be chance? Was I seeing what I wished to see, what I had prepared myself to see?

There were also edge-marks on the bone, at the top, bottom, and along one side. Using the same technique of microscopic analysis and counting I found there were 63 marks, made by 40 points ($\pm$). This sum was three months, beginning on a day of last crescent and ending on a day of invisibility.

Fig. 10 a
The engraved marks forming the serpentine image on the Blanchard bone against a lunar model, indicating a possible two and a quarter month notation.

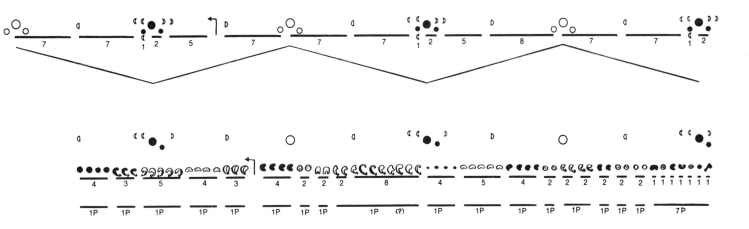

The reverse face of this bone had, on an uneven and unfinished surface, a number of groups of marks in linear order that totalled 40. The full sum for the bone was 172, plus or minus a few, and this came close to six months ($29.5 \times 6 = 177$). Could this bone contain the notation for six months, a half year or two seasons?

Was the use of two flat faces and three edges a form of kinesthetic and visual separation and division, to differentiate periods and "moons" for the maker? Did the serpentine figure on the main face represent some special period? If this were a lunar notation, how did it relate to the animals and symbolic figures made in the Aurignacian, including the female figures and vulvar images? What was its relation to the painted caves found in the area around the Abri Blanchard?

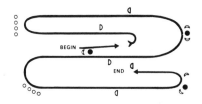

Fig. 10 b
Schematic rendition of the serpentine form on the Blanchard bone indicating the placement of the lunar phases according to the test conjunction with the lunar model.

Lying next to the bone from the Abri Blanchard, in the upper left corner of the cabinet, was a bone of roughly similar size, shape, and color. It too had been shaped and worked, but it was more purely ovoid. Whether or not it had been used as a tool, the marks were not ornamental. It was covered on both faces by a completely different style of marking.

It is shown in an enlargement of both faces (Fig. 11 a, b).

The bone came from the Abri Lartet in the Gorge d'Enfer. The shelter had been named after the pioneer excavator of the site, Edouard Lartet, the French magistrate who gave up law for paleontology and archaeology

Fig. 11 a, b
The two faces of the engraved and shaped bone plaque from the Abri Lartet in the Gorge d'Enfer (Dordogne). Aurignacian.

and who, in 1863, with a British businessman, Henry Christy, had begun excavating in the Vézère valley. It was Lartet who found the first accepted evidence of engraved prehistoric art—the figure of a mammoth. The Abri Lartet lies a few hundred yards downriver on the Vézère from Les Eyzies and the Abri Pataud that Professor Movius was excavating. The marked bone was found in a lower, early Aurignacian level at Gorge d'Enfer and dated from 30,000–32,000 B.C., a time that may have been a comparatively warm phase between Ice Age peaks, and it was, therefore, somewhat older than the bone from the Abri Blanchard, which came from a middle Aurignacian layer, somewhat higher in the soil, perhaps some hundreds or thousands of years later, and from a site that was a few miles to the north. Despite these differences, the two engraved bones come from the same general culture and area.

When I picked up the Gorge d'Enfer bone from the cabinet, I knew only that the yellowing label said that it had been found exactly one hundred years before, in 1865, and had been placed in the museum collection in 1870. I learned later that it had been well-known and had been one of the early important finds in the new study of prehistory. It had, in fact, been an example of the typical difficulty that surrounded early attempts at interpretation of such bones.

Edouard Lartet and Henry Christy had given a description of the bone: "... This specimen has been of necessity strongly impregnated with gelatine for its preservation; and it is difficult now to form a notion of its real structure ... so we hesitate to come to a decision as to whether it is antler, hard bone, or ivory. It may possibly consist of the last-named substance ... especially as a worked piece

Fig. 12 a, b
Schematic rendition of the engraved marks on the bone from the Abri Lartet as determined by microscopic analysis.

Fig. 12 a

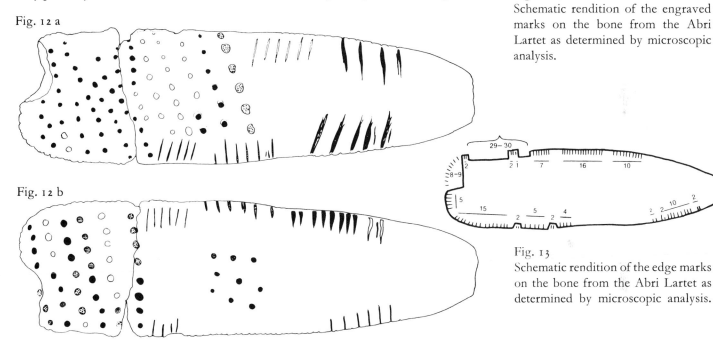

Fig. 12 b

Fig. 13
Schematic rendition of the edge marks on the bone from the Abri Lartet as determined by microscopic analysis.

of Elephant's tusk was found with these specimens in the Rock-shelter at ... Gorge d'Enfer, just as a fragment of tusk was found in the cave at Cro-Magnon."

They then gave a description of the markings:
"... [there is] a minute marginal notching, probably for ornament. The series of shallow cuts near the edges, and the somewhat systematically arranged pitting, on both faces, are very puzzling,—if indeed they were intended to mean anything at all. The reader will observe that the groups of cuts differ in direction, shape, and number; but in this some may see a character of value. It is difficult also to say if the combination of oblique transverse lines of pits was made on a premeditated plan. The several lines have not the same number of pits, nor is the arrangement of the latter vertically symmetrical. Though the isolated group of pits on the flat face gives *nine,* when counted either vertically or transversely, yet neither this nor the groups of notches constitute for certain any indication of a system of numeration,—nor indeed are we sure that they belong to any intelligible plan of marking."[1]

[1] Edouard Lartet and Henry Christy, RELIQUIAE AQUITANICAE, edited by Rupert Jones (London, 1875), II. Description of the Plates, pp. 98–99.

Nothing had been added to this cautious, hesitant analysis of the bone in a hundred years.

Having followed our long preparation and analyses, you can see at once that the *lines* on each face are made in groups, by different points, at different angles, and with different pressures. They were, therefore, *not* made at the same moment, with one rhythm, one thought, and one tool in hand. They are, therefore, "time-factored" and probably notational.

The lines on the first face total 30–31, the count for one month; on the second face the lines total 35, 4 or 5 marks over an observational lunar month. But, as we have seen, in a non-arithmetical notation system this does not contradict the possibility of a lunar phrasing.

Slowly, carefully, painfully, I worked for a number of days with this bone, examining each mark in a moving beam of light to cut through the gelatin that filled the engraving. I found that the rows of dots on each face were made by many different points and strokes, varying from punched strokes to partially twisted strokes, from shallow pits to deep, pointed holes. I then diagrammed the dots on each face by these differences. I added 2 seemingly lost dots in the breaks at the edges (Fig. 12 a, b).

Fig 12 a, b; Fig. 13. Preceding page.

I then moved to the edge-marks and by counting, measuring, and averaging for the breaks, I reconstructed the probable full count along the edges. Here too the microscope showed that there were groups differentiated by points with varying cross-sections (Fig. 13).

The total for the full bone (plus or minus perhaps 3 or 4) came to the nearly precise total for eleven months. Face one had 118 marks, precisely 4 months; face two had 90, precisely 3 months; and the edges had 121 plus or minus, close to 4 months.

These totals were based on the obvious division of two faces and the edges. But in what order were they made? Which groups of lines came first, which group of dots? Were the lines or dots made first, or the edges? Do we read from right to left, or vice versa? How then do we test the possibility that this is a lunar notation?

One way, of course, was to run a long series of tests, including every conceivable combination and order. The long examination gave the clues that speeded the operation and limited the number of tests required.

Notice that the lines on each face are made with a free use of space, while the dots are cramped at a side, or placed between the lines. On face number one, the dots at the left are made from edge to edge of the bone, but when they reach the lines they do not go to the edge, ending above them. It was obvious, then, that on this face at least the lines were made first, the dots later. The same free use of space was used for the lines on face two— the dots were cramped to a side, and the nine dots between the lines seemed to have been added last of all.[2] I now could begin my tests.

[2] Four years later I found another plaquette from this site and level in the basement of the British Museum, London, within the Christy Collection. It is similar in shape and size and, though broken and heavily encrusted with a soil accretion, it shows the same linear markings organized in groups with a free use of space on each face and similar markings along the edges. The dots, however, are missing. It seems to offer another indication that the dots were added later and the full composition accumulated slowly.

The first test went from lines to dots on face number one, then from lines to dots on face number two, and finally to the edge marks. The lines were read from right to left, beginning at top right, then the bone was turned 180° and the dots were read from right to left, going down.

The linear sequence that resulted was then put against the lunar model. On this model the lines were indicated as lines, the dots as dots (Fig. 14).

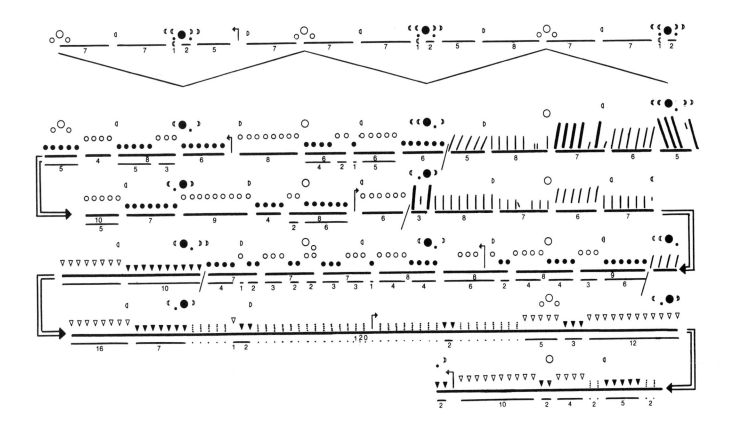

Each row of dots was grouped together, while the division of that row into tool differences as indicated by the microscope was put below it. The difficulty, of course, was that the gelatin made a complete and final reading of these tool differences uncertain.

The result, after the long days of analysis and work, was again startling. There was a near-perfect lunar phrasing and breakdown, perfect, that is, within the small errors allowable in a non-arithmetical, observational system of notation. This first test indicated that each sum of lines, on faces one and two, began or ended at a crescent moon, and that each smaller subgroup of lines, as far as could be determined through the clear gelatin, made a lunar phrase.

Among the dots, each row contained a lunar phase, and each row usually began or ended at a phase point. It also seemed from my first attempts at microscopic examination that the lunar breakdown and phrasing of the dots would be sharpened by the removal of the gelatin and a re-examination. One can see this on the chart, where the rows begin to be subdivided. The edge-marks, as a group, began at last crescent and ended at invisibility 4 months later.

Fig. 14
The engraved marks on both faces and the edges of the bone from Lartet against a lunar model, indicating a possible lunar phrasing in the sets and subsets.

It would, of course, be possible to find another order for these line-dot-edge groups, but the inherent phrasing of the groups would not change. It seems, then, that the same general way of thinking was being used here as on the bone from the Abri Blanchard. The man making this notation had begun by holding a blank slate in his left hand, slowly filling it up "period" by "period," using a series of flints in his right hand, perhaps turning the bone as each face filled. By doing so over a length of time, he was able to differentiate the phases of the moon and the months by the style of marking, the direction of reading, and their place on the bone, whether face or edge. When he was done he had a visual record and recall of the seasons and "moons" of the past year and he now, presumably, could begin a new slate with the two-or three-month season that followed and began the new year.

These few paragraphs oversimplify a difficult process of analysis and omit the profound implications of the findings. Let us therefore briefly consider what the analyses of these two bones imply.

I had taken in hand and analyzed two bones at random, yet the long work and preparation of the year before had allowed me quickly to stumble on a number of new findings and to begin the construction of a new technology. The technique of microscopic analysis had unexpectedly helped to verify the notational thesis; it had perhaps strengthened the more specialized lunar hypothesis and had apparently opened the way for its possible final verification. This, of course, could not be done with only two bones from one general period and region of France.

Significantly for the research, I now had a rapidly growing series of interlocking controls, each of which checked and helped the others. There were the numerical "counts," groups and sequences engraved permanently on the bones. There were the invariant phases of the moon. There was the visualization offered by the lunar model. There were the new facts being revealed, example by example, by the microscope. And slowly, as the work proceeded, there would be the possibility of accumulation, comparison, and grouping of results.

With the microscope one can often determine how many tools or points or grips or styles of stroke were used to make a composition or a sequence of marks. This will often help in deciding whether a composition is decorative and ornamental or notational. For if it was made at one or two sittings with one or two tools, with one concept and one rhythm, it could be decorative. If it was made by many points over a long time, it was probably not decorative.

In addition, since in many cases we can now subdivide the gross, visual, numerical counts by their microscopic and ballistic point differences, we have increased the effectiveness of both arithmetical analysis and the lunar model.

With the help of the microscope, therefore, we can attempt to reconstruct certain sequential processes of thought involved in the making of a composition.

Here is another minor example of microscopic analysis. The bone from the Gorge D'Enfer just analyzed was covered with ocher, a red paint made from ground hematite or other iron oxide. The color was added to the bone after the engraving and is found deep in the marks. Red ocher is common on engraved objects. Was red added to each notational subgroup as it was made, as a sort of printer's ink, to make the marks stand out against the white of the fresh bone? Or was red added at the end of long periods, or at the completion of the composition in a symbolic and ritual gesture, perhaps involving the concepts of death, blood, birth, and renewal? Were all engraved parts ochered or only key parts? Was an engraved bone ochered many times, as certain cave engravings were overpainted? Were tools ochered or only symbolic and notational objects? Were the uses of ocher many, so that on one bone it had one meaning but on another a second meaning? These are not easy questions, for Ice Age man used ocher to redden corpses, graves, shelter and cave walls, and female figurines. He might have used it to color parts of his body and as part of his ceremonies. As far as the marked bones and stones are concerned, we can now *begin* the attempt to find some of the answers.

In this problem, as with the marks, the microscope helps reconstruct certain processes of thought and action.

* * *

Much of the analytical data became relevant only as the research proceeded. It became clear, for instance, that the last images added to a symbolic composition that had been accumulated over time were often organized differently or placed outside of a composition and that they could for that reason be important as an indication of non-decorative intent. This process of later addition is suggested, for instance, by the nine marks in the center of face two of the Lartet bone (Fig. 12 b). The subsidiary marking on the rear of the Blanchard plaque (Fig. 7), where sets of dots with no apparent design or structure were carefully incised (Fig. 7a), also suggests a non-decorative, but symboling intent. It was only after a study of all the Upper Paleolithic marking traditions that it became clear that such subsidiary sets of marks had symbolic intent and meaning.

The idea that such compositions might have been made over time was strengthened when I studied, not the marking, but the nature of the artifacts themselves. The microscope, for instance, indicated that the front end of the Blanchard plaque had been broken back as though it had been used as a pressure flaker for sharpening or retouching stone tools, while the rear of the plaque showed the high polish it had received when it had pushed against the palm of the hand during this process. It was clear that the notations had been incised on a tool that could be carried in a pouch to be used for retouching when needed and could therefore also serve as an available surface for symbolic marking. Portable objects of multiple and variable, practical and symbolic, use are well-known ethnographically and are found among the highly mobile hunting-gathering aboriginals of Australia. The edge marks on the Blanchard plaque were rounded and polished, suggesting that it had been gripped firmly. But the polish was greatest towards the rear half where it was gripped, and less polished towards the front where it was not. This type of evidence, concerning the long term retention and use of a practical artifact that was also used for symbolic accumulations was noticed early in my studies but I did not at first consider it significant (see Fig. 19a–c; and note p. 196). However, the importance of the material on which notations and symbolic accumulations were incised continued to grow, and as it grew the nature of my interpretations changed.

The bone plaquette from Lartet in the Gorge d'Enfer, for instance, may also have been a pressure flaker, but the primary "edge" marks (Figs. 12 a,b) were not made as gripping marks; they were incised not on the edge itself but on the surface from the edge inwards, towards the interior. The straight edge merely served as a "containing" line for structuring these sets on the flat face. The lightly incised and unstructured marks along the true edge may therefore have been gripping marks. I had appended them at the end of the lunar model (Fig. 14) but they could be eliminated without affecting the near perfect tally of the highly structured and clearly differentiated sets and sequences on the bone's surface.

As the research progressed it became clear that the nature of the artifact and the nature of the incised material, as well as evidence for the long term handling and use of an artifact were as important as the analysis of a single mark or a set of marks. It became clear that the objects that were marked with "notation" were usually those carried about because they were practical in some other way or because they were small and light and easily incised. This developing insight began to change the nature of the inquiry and my understanding of the artifacts I had first published in this book. I found that some of the heavy and difficult to incise artifacts of stone, for instance, did not contain notations but were often, instead, surfaces that had been used within a homesite for ritual marking and the accumulation of different types of symbols, motifs and designs. (See comments to Fig. 15, page 82; Fig. 18, page 86; Fig. 86, page 195.)

PART II
BACKGROUND TO THE STORY

CHAPTER VI

THE HISTORY OF PREHISTORY

AN ASIDE

Apparently as far back as 30,000 B.C. the Ice Age hunter of western Europe was using a system of notation that was already evolved, complex, and sophisticated, a tradition that would seem to have been thousands of years old by this point. Apparently it was also in use by other types of modern man, such as Combe Capelle man of the East Gravettian culture in Czechoslovakia and Russia and by other peoples and subcultures in Italy and Spain, as we shall see. The tradition seems so widespread that the question arises as to whether its beginnings may not go back to the period of Neanderthal man.

What is significant, though I have presented but two examples, is that this notation was a cognitive, time-factored, and time-factoring technique.

These facts are so new and important they require the widest possible interpretation and evaluation. They raise profound questions concerning the evolved intelligence and cognitive abilities of the human species. We cannot, for instance, assume that Ice Age man was an "astronomer" or a "scientist" in the modern sense, or even that he used a modern system of arithmetic. It is clear, too, that the notations we have analyzed are not yet writing as we know it. Nevertheless, the roots of science and of writing seem to be here. Apparently we have archaeological evidence for use of the same basic *cognitive processes* that appear later in science and writing.

The results raise questions as to how much we can infer from the evidence on hand about the origin of man and his culture. But they raise equally important questions about the sciences that are involved in the study of man. They ask how the scientist, as a modern cognitive man no different genetically from the Ice Age toolmaker and notator, deals with the information and evidence he has. For at least part of the validity of the findings rests on the cognitive abilities and skills of early man as much as on the comparable cognitive abilities and skills of the modern researcher. For five years, as I worked with the archaeological materials of the Ice Age and post-Ice Age, gathering data and facts in collections across Europe, I read the new evidence concerning the evolution of man, his intelligence, behavior, and culture, the history of the study of prehistory, the psychology of intelligence and cognition, and the nature of both the scientific method and scientific insight. I wrote a full subsidiary volume in the attempt to explain and understand the growing body of my research results. Without the insights and facts gathered in this continual, peripheral research and writing, it would have been impossible to proceed stage by stage with the enlarging analysis. In telling the story, I retain portions of this free-ranging querying and research, partly to clarify the analytic problems as they arose, and partly to indicate why the research went where it did.

The search for the origins of man grew out of the changes wrought in the European concept of time and space, and of biological processes occurring in time and space, brought about by the technical, economic, political, and geographic expansion of the fourteenth-and fifteenth-century Renaissance and the subsequent period of European colonialism and industrialization. Digging in the soil of Europe to construct roads, buildings, railroads, sewers, canals, and tunnels and while mining ores and fuels, men slowly uncovered the geological history of the earth and the sequential record of evolutionary changes in life forms in the layers of the soil. Samples of plants and animals from every corner of the world were being brought to central collections in Europe, and the classification of life forms was initiated. The fossils found in the geo-logical layers made the changes occurring in these life forms through time apparent. The explorations of the sea voyagers brought back evidence of man in diverse stages of "savagery" and civilization, with hints that human culture was itself subject to degrees of development and evolution.

Charles Darwin (1809–1882) grew up in this adventurous period of exploration, collecting and classifying, with the search for origins and causes that always followed these accumulations, comparisons, and classifications. As a boy he was a collector of shells, insects, birds, minerals, and specimens of sea life. He had undoubtedly read of Captain Cook's three-year voyage by sail around the world (1772–1775), a voyage that was still fresh and had been made possible by England's development of an accurate ship's clock or chronometer, one of the essential basic instruments of modern navigation and exploration. Cook had aboard a botanist to collect plant specimens around the world. After college, and almost by accident, Darwin was appointed the "naturalist" aboard the *H. M. S. Beagle,* a ten gun brig headed for a five-year voyage of exploration for the purpose of doing chronometric measurements around the world and completing the work begun by Cook, that is, fixing time zones and longitudes and the distances and positions of shores and islands for England's navigators and geographers. The voyage was important not only because the young Darwin collected biological data that eventually led to his theory of evolution but also because it was in the line of those practical, technical space and time measurements that finally conquered sea, earth, and air and led to the space age of the twentieth century. The voyage itself was one part of the commercial and scientific expansion by which the nations of western Europe both conquered the earth and collected its resources and evidence.

Darwin, though, was on a different sort of "time search." He knew the recently published work of the former law student, Charles Lyell, which presented to English readers the combined geological and paleontological evidence that had been gathered from around the world.[1] Lyell stressed that geological changes within the earth were exceedingly ancient

---

[1] Charles Lyell, PRINCIPLES OF GEOLOGY, 4 vols. (London: John Murray, 1834).

and continuous. Species, he argued, shifted geographically and some had become extinct in the competition and struggle for existence. Lyell discussed the geological and evolutionary theories of the day (Lamarck, Hutton, Smith). Studying the range of climates and conditions around the world and noting that these changed, he surmised that changes in environment could cause extinction of species, yet he did not speculate on the *origin* of species. Darwin received Lyell's second volume, dealing with biological problems, during the voyage at Montevideo, Uruguay.

He mulled the worldwide problems posed by the book. He collected samples of living plants and creatures and as many geological specimens as possible. Before long the ship was an overcrowded museum. In a fascinating series of observations and comparisons made "in time and space" off the coast of South America, he reached those first temporary insights and made those first queries that would lead eventually to his theory on the mechanisms involved in evolution.

Among the small, gray, grim volcanic islands of the Galapagos on the equator, some five hundred miles west of Ecuador, he saw species of bird, lizard, and turtle that differed island to island in some of their anatomical structures, yet all lived near one another in the *same* environment. In his journal of September 1835, he wrote:

"... the different islands to a considerable extent are inhabited by a different set of beings. My attention was first called to this fact by the Vice-Governor, Mr. Lawson, declaring that the tortoises differed from the different islands, and that he could ... tell from which island any one was brought ... I never dreamed that islands, about fifty or sixty miles apart, and most of them in sight of each other, formed of precisely the same rocks, placed under a quite similar climate, rising to a nearly equal height, would have been differently tenanted."[2]

"... [a] most curious fact is the perfect gradation in the size of the beaks in the different species of Geospiza [finch], from one as large as that of a hawfinch to [as small as] that of a chaffinch ... there are no less than six species with insensibly graduated beaks ... Seeing this gradation and diversity of structure in one small, intimately related group of birds, one might really fancy that from an original paucity of birds in this archipelago, one species had been taken and modified for different ends."[3]

"... several of the islands possess their own species of the tortoise, mocking-thrush, finches, and numerous plants ... [and] I must repeat, that neither the nature of the soil, nor [the] height of the land, nor the climate, nor the general character of the associated beings, and therefore their action one on another, can differ much in the different islands."[4]

"... As the archipelago is free to a most remarkable degree from gales of wind, neither the birds, insects, nor lighter seeds, would be blown from island to island ... the profound depth of the ocean between the islands, and their apparently recent (in a geological sense) volcanic origin, render it highly unlikely that they were ever united; and this, probably, is a far more important consideration than any other ... Reviewing the facts here given, one is astonished at the amount of creative force, if such an expression may be used, displayed on these small, barren, and rocky islands ..."[5]

"... both in space and time, we seem to be brought somewhat near to that great fact—that mystery of mysteries—the first appearance of new beings on this earth."[6]

Trained as a "naturalist," a collector, and a comparer, Darwin had been able to distinguish slight differences of structure in a single species and a single environment—differences that were separated in space as in an island-scattered laboratory. He had seen and compared certain subtle differences in visible structures, and he therefore wondered about the processes that had created these changes across time and space.

When he returned to England he pondered the somewhat similar results obtained by the "scientific" farmers of Europe who were altering forms of life, creating changes in the structures and behavior of domesticated birds, plants, and animals through selective breeding. The farmers were choosing those individuals for breeding that had "by chance" the features they desired until slowly they evolved a new brand

[2] Charles Darwin, JOURNAL OF RESEARCHES INTO THE GEOLOGY AND NATURAL HISTORY OF THE VARIOUS COUNTRIES VISITED DURING THE VOYAGE OF H.M.S. BEAGLE ROUND THE WORLD, Ernest Rhys, Editor (New York: Everyman's Library, E. P. Dutton & Co., 1906), p. 379.

[3] Ibid., pp. 364–365.   [4] Ibid., p. 382.   [5] Ibid., p. 383.
[6] Ibid., p. 363.

or breed. It was not a different environment that was the determining or causative factor here either, and Darwin postulated a process in nature by which such changes occurred, not by use or by changes in environment, but almost by chance. These chance mutations were transmitted *selectively* to the next generation as a result of the struggle for existence and the survival of the fittest individuals. Environment, therefore, *did* play its part, not in forming the change but rather in *weeding out* the unfit, in selecting the fit for survival.

But what caused the mutation or change in the first place? In THE ORIGIN OF SPECIES, he wrote:

"I have . . . sometimes spoken as if . . . variations . . . were due to chance. This, of course, is a wholly incorrect expression, but it serves to acknowledge plainly our ignorance of the cause of each particular variation."[7]

It was more than a hundred years after THE ORIGIN was published before some of the basic molecular mechanisms and processes of heredity and evolutionary change were found in the cell, the gene, the chromosome, and the RNA and DNA molecules. There is still debate as to whether the molecular mechanisms and structures being uncovered explain all of the processes involved in evolution and in the formation of broad classes and genera. Nor is it yet clear how much of the evolutionary process is due to "chance."

The story is well known. Yet rereading it and THE ORIGIN as I worked with the Ice Age materials, I was struck by the nature of the research and the findings. The cognitive aspects of this discovery, one of the most important in the history of science, were those usual in science, though the discovery itself was unique.[8] But what seemed extraordinary to me was that similar or comparable cognitive capacities seemed to be indicated in the Upper Paleolithic culture and materials of the Ice Age hunter. Differences in results were of course huge, since the materials that the brains worked with were different, but the difference was not in the way that the human brain functioned.

Darwin was prepared for his research and queries in part by Lyell, but more broadly by his age. The journey of the Beagle itself, for the computation of practical time-space coordinates and the collection of biological and geological specimens, was one expression of that expanding age, in its way comparable to exploratory voyages in the first decades of the space age. But what seemed significant to me was the fact that Darwin had available a huge body or library of contemporary fact for analysis and comparison. The ordering, classifying, and comparison of the earth's living and prehistoric species had been begun by men like Cuvier and Lamarck. Geologists had shattered the dogmatic Christian concept of a limited time that had supposedly begun with six days of Creation, and had shown that the "solid" earth itself was dynamic and subject to change and growth. Explorations by foot, horse, and sea had shown the diversity of climates, species, and human cultures. Naturalists were collecting huge quantities of observations on differences in the characteristics and behavior of species in every corner of the globe.

Despite the conflicts of the emerging, expanding, or competing European nations, the earth was being "conquered" essentially by one culture, the Western. This culture spoke different languages and warred within itself, as well as against other peoples and cultures; but it was a culture that, nevertheless, kept a single "library and museum," a single body of knowledge. It was creating a new tapestry of time-space data and this, in large measure, was what made the new sciences possible. It was within this one great "library and museum" of Western culture that Darwin worked and within which the science of the origins of man was born and developed and within which my own research in the Upper Paleolithic, for instance, was done. The inputs of data, the chances for comparison, and the range of time-space information involved in modern science are different from the more limited range of inputs reaching the brain of the Upper Paleolithic hunter, but the cognitive processes involved in the recognition and use of structures, patterns, and processes in time and space and, therefore,

[7] Charles Darwin, THE ORIGIN OF SPECIES (New York: Collier Books, 1962), p. 138.

[8] Unique, but only to a degree, for in precisely the same series of cognitive steps, Alfred Russel Wallace, the teacher-turned-naturalist-and-collector, studying insects and plant samples from South America and Asia, came to a conclusion similar to that of Darwin.

in the "human" solutions reached, I sensed, were comparable.

The insight seemed strengthened the more I read of the history of the science of prehistory.

Darwin worked for twenty years on THE ORIGIN OF SPECIES, struggling through a huge documentation concerned with the varieties of species and their comparisons. Significantly, during that long time he avoided writing about man. But that he had been thinking about man in terms essentially modern is indicated in the youthful notes he wrote aboard the *Beagle* and by one lone statement in the closing paragraphs of THE ORIGIN:

"In the future I see open fields for far more important researches. Psychology will be securely based on the foundation well laid by . . . Herbert Spencer, that of the *necessary acquirement of each mental power and capacity by gradation* (my italics. A. M.). Much light will be thrown on the origin of man and his history."[9]

This statement was carefully limited, for Darwin had thought more deeply than he was saying. Twenty years before he had written in his journal:

"If we choose to let conjecture run wild, then animals, our fellow brethren in pain, disease, suffering and famine— our slaves in the most laborious works, our companions in our amusements—they may partake of our origin in one common ancestor—we may be all melted together."[10]

When Alfred Russel Wallace questioned Darwin as to whether he would discuss "man" in the forthcoming ORIGIN, Darwin replied:

"I think I shall avoid the whole subject, as . . . surrounded with prejudices, though I fully admit . . . it is the highest and most interesting problem for the naturalist."[11]

Nevertheless, despite his caution, Darwin was already at work on this "most interesting problem." He was collecting evidence on comparative anatomical differences and similarities between man and animals, as well as comparative evidence on their life processes and behavior patterns. He would publish these facts comparing man and animals a dozen years after THE ORIGIN in THE DESCENT OF MAN.

[9] Charles Darwin, THE ORIGIN OF SPECIES, p. 483.

[10] Francis Darwin, ed., LIFE AND LETTERS OF CHARLES DARWIN, 3 vols. (London: John Murray, 1888), Vol. 2, p. 6.

[11] Ibid., p. 109.

It is important to note that Darwin had worked out his theory of evolution through a comparative study of *living* creatures, though the geological and fossil evidence was always in mind. While writing THE DESCENT OF MAN, Darwin again relied on the living evidence, since there was no archaeological or geological evidence he could use concerning the anatomy or existence of early man. The evidence, however, was beginning to accumulate even as he was writing.

In 1838, two years after Darwin had returned from his voyages aboard the *Beagle,* the first example of Ice Age art was dug from the soil of Europe in the cave of Chaffaud (Vienne) by A. Brouillet, a notary and amateur digger. It was a Late Magdalenian engraving of two hinds accompanied by a strange handlike symbol on a piece of bone. Since the existence of a human culture older than the supposed Biblical dates of the Creation and Flood was not at that time held in Europe, the engraving was assigned to the near-historic Celts. Cave paintings from the Upper Paleolithic were also beginning to be found about this time but without great interest being taken. Dates and initials from this period are still scratched into the walls and over the paintings of certain caves in France.

In 1837, the year in which Darwin sat down to begin writing THE ORIGIN, a French customs official at Amiens, just across the English Channel, began picking up chipped flint tools and animal bones in the commercial gravel and sand pits of the region. Jacques Boucher de Perthes was a collector and hobbyist, a novelist, poet, playwright, occasional politician, and president of the local scientific and literary club. He had been touched by the same general winds of intellectual change and surmise as Darwin: the concepts of the new "natural sciences," including geological concepts concerning vast periods of time in formation of the earth, the bones of long-extinct animals in the layers of the soil, even the first theories of evolution by men like Lamarck, and by the archaeological discoveries of "antiquities" from the early civilizations around the Mediterranean.

In 1837, Boucher de Perthes recognized that the chipped stone objects he found in the soil of France were man-made and ancient. He presented his findings to French scientists but was coolly dismissed. His method of arguing process from observable visible structures was similar to Darwin's, but his preparation and the amount of data he had were more limited. He not only deduced that the tools he found were man-made, but he explained that, since they were taken from deep layers of the soil, they must be extremely old.

"If we attribute . . . the formation of the beds to successive deposits, we have . . . the history of the soil . . . [and] when the deposits of sediment . . . offer a growth so slow that centimeters represent centuries, who can believe that several thousand years could be sufficient to lift up eleven meters [37½ feet] and more of these layers . . . ?

"The formation of the peat is also a proof of the [length of] time . . . required for the deposits of sediments. In the [country] where one has used the peat bogs since time immemorial, nobody has seen the peat grow in any noticeable manner. One rightly concludes that it takes centuries to produce a thickness of several centimeters . . .

"Well, Sirs, in this bed of diluvium, covered by several meters of black compact peat, I found the traces of man. I collected several beautiful axes . . ."[12]

For twenty years, the period during which Darwin was gathering his documentation and writing THE ORIGIN, Boucher de Perthes was mocked. In 1859, the year in which THE ORIGIN was published, two English geologists, John Evans and Joseph Prestwich, crossed the channel to meet Boucher de Perthes at his site near Abbeville. They looked at the layers in the gravel pits, saw the bones and tools still imbedded in the soil, and were convinced. That year Prestwich read a paper to the Royal Society, "On the Occurrence of Flint Implements, Associated with the Remains of Animals of Extinct Species in Beds of a Late Geological Period . . ." With that paper, the study of the prehistory of man was formally and "officially" born, though as early as 1790 the Englishman John Frere had found and recognized chipped stone axes in a pit at Hoxne, Suffolk, with the bones of large extinct animals.

The publication of THE ORIGIN and vindication of Boucher de Perthes put "man before the flood," or ante-diluvian man, suddenly on stage and stage center. He became the subject of an intense debate and study, a developing inquiry that after more than a century is still progressing.

In 1863, Darwin wrote to Lyell concerning Boucher de Perthes' work:

"I knew something about his errors . . . I looked at his book many years ago, and am ashamed to think that I concluded the whole was rubbish. Yet he has done for man something like what Agassiz did for glaciers."[13]

Despite this statement by Darwin, however, it should be made clear that it was not man, but the *tools* of man, that Boucher de Perthes, like John Frere, had found and recognized. The fact is important because it is the stone tools that have remained a major part of the hard evidence and documentation for thinking about prehistoric man and his culture. In large part, the tools have both formed and limited the scientific thinking about early man.

The concept of "man the toolmaker" had been born. It came almost as though in proof of Darwin's implication of a "struggle for existence" and a "survival of the fittest." The evidence of the tools seemed to verify the concept that man had evolved *because* he was a toolmaker and because his evolving hand and thumb, his front-focusing eyes, his upright posture and his larger brain had, together, made him a toolmaker and therefore ultimate master on earth in the struggle of "tooth and claw."

This concept of "man the toolmaker," based on the evidence of the stone tools, was related to and strengthened by economic developments, the rapidly expanding Industrial Revolution with its successful materialism and technology. Political, social, and philosophical arguments were raging in these years around problems created by the new technology and economy, or the "means of production," problems concerned with a proper division and distribution of the products of the new machines and industries.

The idea that man had risen from a crude, primitive stone toolmaker to a sophisticated toolmaker using metal and steam, in an evolutionary sequence, seemed to offer both an explanation and a rationalization for the bitter problems of that day, involving the "struggle for existence" and the "survival of the fittest" for millions of persons. The debate included, by implication, not only the conflict of classes and groups involved in the Industrial Revolution at home, but also races and peoples involved in Europe's colonial ex-

[12] J. Boucher de Perthes, "On Antediluvian Man and His Works," trans. Stephen Heizer from "De l'Homme Antédiluvien et de ses Œuvres," IN MAN'S DISCOVERY OF HIS PAST: LITERARY LANDMARKS IN ARCHAEOLOGY, Robert F. Heizer, ed. (Englewood Cliffs, N.J.: Prentice-Hall, 1962), p. 91.

[13] Francis Darwin, op. cit., Vol. 3, pp. 15–16.

pansion and her political and economic conquest of the world. The best "toolmakers" seemed owners of the best culture and therefore most destined to succeed.

Darwin, however, working as a scientist with living species and with occasional fossils rather than with the politics of his time or with the still-sparse archaeological materials, did not overstress this toolmaking ability. He was more interested in what seemed to him the more important evolved intellectual and relational abilities of early man. Unfortunately, the evidence for these other attributes of early man was not, in Darwin's time, being found or recognized in the soil.

In these years, beginning in mid-nineteenth century, the accumulating tools of early man, found in descending levels of the soil, led step by step towards the recognition that there was a sequence and a chronology in the development of human culture. The tools provided one more blow to the rigid Christian dogma of a sudden human creation. For us it may be more important to realize that this formative stage in the study of prehistory was based on a series of cognitive steps common to all science. There was the recognition and accumulation of the evidence and then a comparison of the visible structures. The differences in tool styles were noted, and a classification of the types or forms was begun by their style of making and their place in the levels of the soil. The prehistorian had begun to work with a time-factored set of observations and comparisons. He was developing a sequence and chronology. When the research reached this stage, it became possible to deduce from the changes in structures and forms and from the sequences something of the processes involved. There was nothing mysterious or difficult, then, about the birth of this new field, and in less than a decade the study of these early stone tools had become a sophisticated specialty. The stone tools were being found increasingly all over Europe.

Before Boucher de Perthes, antiquarians in Scandinavia recognized that tools being dug out of their soil represented three stages of evolution, the oldest made of stone, the next of copper, the last of iron.

"We know that [they are] older than Christendom, but whether by a couple of years or a couple of centuries, or even by more than a millennium, we can do no more than guess."[14]

In 1843, while Darwin was writing THE ORIGIN and Boucher de Perthes was excavating his chipped tools, a twenty-two year old Danish lawyer-turned-archaeologist, Jacob Worsaae, formulated the concept of *comparative archaeology* by recognizing the "three ages," *Stone, Bronze* and *Iron,* "referable to three distinct periods." However, he had no dates. Next, from the evidence in the soil, there came a discussion of man's economic stages. In 1868, the Dane Sven Nilsson wrote:

"The earliest tribes, of which we find traces in every country . . . belonged to a race of beings standing on the very lowest point of civilization: . . . rough-hewn stone-flakes, their hunting and fishing implements; no domesticated animals except the dog; no cattle, no agriculture, no written language. Between this . . . and the most cultivated state of society . . . there are many intermediate degrees or stages of development."[15]

He surmised a series of stages from "savage" to herdsman to farmer to the final organized nation. But again, these were ideas without an adequate chronology and without dates.

In 1865 the English banker and politician John Lubbock wrote:

"Of late years . . . a new branch of knowledge has arisen; a new Science [geology] has . . . been born among us, which deals with times and events far more ancient than any which have yet fallen within the province of the archaeologist."

He continued:

"Archaeology forms . . . the link between geology and history . . . the men of past ages are to be studied principally by their works . . . From the careful study of the remains which have come down to us, it would appear that Prehistoric Archaeology may be divided into four great epochs.

I. . . . when man shared the possession of Europe with the Mammoth, the Cave Bear, the Woolly-haired rhinoceros, and other extinct animals . . . This I have proposed to call the 'Palaeolithic' Period.

II. The later or polished Stone Age; a period characterized by beautiful weapons and instruments made of flint and

[14] Glyn Daniel, THE ORIGINS AND GROWTH OF ARCHAEOLOGY (Harmondsworth, England: Penguin Books, 1967), p. 91.

[15] Ibid., p. 107.

other kinds of stone; . . . For this period I have suggested the term 'Neolithic.'[16]

Step by step the study of prehistory was beginning to structure the evidence of the tools *in time;* it was beginning to reconstruct an intelligible sequence for one aspect of man's early cultures.

In this period an example of early prehistoric man was excavated. The fossil skull and bones of an unusual "man" were dug up in 1856–1857 in a limestone cave in the Neanderthal gorge, between Düsseldorf and Elberfeld in Germany. Prussian zoologist and anatomist Herman Schaaffhausen described the find:

". . . the extraordinary form of the skull was due to a natural conformation hitherto not known to exist, even in the most barbarous races . . . [the] remarkable human remains belonged to a period [before] the time of the Celts and Germans . . . The cranium is of unusual size . . . extraordinary development of the frontal sinuses . . . The forehead is narrow and low . . . Both thighbones . . . like the skull . . . are characterized by . . . unusual thickness . . . There is no reason whatever for regarding the unusual development . . . in the skull . . . as an individual or pathological deformity: it is unquestionably a typical race character . . .

"Sufficient grounds exist for the assumption that man coexisted with the animals found in the diluvium; and many a barbarous race may, before all historical time, have disappeared, together with the animals of the ancient world . . ."[17]

In 1858, thirteen years before Darwin's DESCENT OF MAN, it was too early to accept the "humanity" of such a seemingly primitive form. Schaaffhausen's analysis was not accepted, for this creature could not be a "normal man." Though science was breaking the bind of Christian concepts in time by new ideas in astronomy, cosmology, geology, and archaeology, and though the evidence was strong for an ancient past and evolution for lower forms of life, European man's image of *himself* as the special creation of God, standing as a chosen being at the top of the scale of life, was deeply personal. The idea of a relatively re-cent primitive human form touched profoundly on his private prejudices and fears and threatened his religious beliefs and cultural myths.

Besides, the Neanderthal bones constituted a single find, and the layer in which the bones were found was not certain. Scientists of the day could not adequately, therefore, "think in time" with this evidence, either chronologically or comparatively, that is, in terms of other skulls of the same or of earlier periods. Even Lyell could write of the Neanderthal skull:

"When on my return to England I showed the cast of the cranium to Professor Huxley [an outstanding public defender of Darwin's theories], he remarked at once that it was the most ape-like skull he had ever beheld. Mr. Busk . . . added some valuable comments of his own on the characters in which this skull approached that of the gorilla and chimpanzee. . . ."[18]

We know today that Neanderthal man preceded modern man in Europe and, therefore, belonged to the Middle Paleolithic or Mousterian period. Below Neanderthal man in the layers of the soil there have been found skulls and bones of men who were apparently not as specialized as Neanderthal and were perhaps closer in form to modern *Homo sapiens.* Large-brained and big-boned Neanderthal man may have developed as an evolutionarily specialized branch of this ancestor of modern man. One theory states that it was from this earlier, near-modern *Homo sapiens* that one branch, developing in a widespread area of relative genetic isolation, apparently led to the aberrant Neanderthal form. The other line of development, perhaps in an area of greater mixing or different selective pressures, led to modern man. The archaeological evidence is still too scanty to make the full story certain.

Scientists in 1858, unable or afraid to call Neanderthal a European, called the creature an idiot, a diseased person, a wild savage, a near-ape, a pre-Christian Celt, a Russian Cossack, or a lower form of man such as Europeans believed existed in primitive tribes of Australia, America, and Africa.

Darwin himself did not know what to make of this uncertain find with its "well developed and capacious" skull. He was more interested in the possibility of a

[16] John Lubbock (Lord Avebury), PREHISTORIC TIMES AS ILLUSTRATED BY ANCIENT REMAINS AND THE MANNERS AND CUSTOMS OF MODERN SAVAGES (London: William & Norgate, 1865), pp. 1–3.

[17] D. [H.] Schaaffhausen, "Discovery of the Neanderthal Skull," In MAN'S DISCOVERY OF HIS PAST: LITERARY LANDMARKS IN ARCHAEOLOGY, pp. 117–122.

[18] Charles Lyell, THE GEOLOGICAL EVIDENCES OF THE ANTIQUITY OF MAN (London: John Murray, 1863), p. 79.

find that was clearly below man on the evolutionary scale, with a brain that was significantly smaller. He suggested that it was in the soil of Africa, where the large apes still lived, that one might possibly find the ancestor of man and ape. But he issued a warning:

"We must not fall into the error of supposing that the early progenitor of the whole Simian stock, including man, was identical with or even closely resembled, any existing ape or monkey."[19]

The evidence did not come in Darwin's lifetime. It was 1891, nine years after his death and near the close of the century, that the first of the so-called "missing links" implied in his theory of man's evolution was found.

Eugène Dubois was born in the Netherlands in 1858, in that crucial period around publication of THE ORIGIN, acceptance of Boucher de Perthes, and publication of the Neanderthal find. He grew up in the years of intense debate concerning evolution and man's origins. He studied medicine, became a lecturer in anatomy, but in his twenties decided to search for the "missing link."

The Netherlands controlled the East Indies archipelago (Indonesia), the group of volcanic islands that begin a few miles from the mainland of Southeast Asia and stretch almost three thousand miles into the Pacific. In a time of lower seas, they had once been joined to the mainland of Asia. The climate had apparently always been equatorial, and man's "ape-like" ancestors, Dubois reasoned, may once have walked over.

Dubois requested an appointment as surgeon in the colonial forces and in 1887, at twenty-nine, he sailed for the islands. After two years of searching in a deep level of an old stream bed of the Solo River in Java, within an area in which natives had long been collecting bones of "giants," Dubois found a fragment of lower jaw containing some humanlike teeth. He continued digging and found a brown, fossilized skull, with a brain smaller than man's and a receding apelike forehead. The brain was larger than an ape's, and it was difficult at that point to tell if the creature was closer to ape or to man. The next year Dubois found a thighbone in the same layer. As an anatomist, he

recognized at once that it belonged to someone who had walked upright on two feet, like man.

In 1894, Dubois published his facts on the creature he called *Pithecanthropus erectus,* the "erect man-ape." When the bones were shown in Europe the following year, they were disclaimed by some scientists as not being man, by others as not being ape. At least one scientist, D. J. Cunningham, however, wrote that it was

"in the direct human line although it occupies a place on this considerably lower than any human form at present known."[20]

This creature was *not* Darwin's early progenitor of both ape and man, for he was already far along the road to being modern man. Today's archaeologists have renamed him *Homo erectus,* placing him late on the hominid line, far from the ape.

The furor that had raged around Darwin's DESCENT now broke out again around *"erectus."* It must have seemed comparable to Dubois. Scientists and church leaders found it difficult to believe that this apelike creature was related to man. It was even harder to believe on the basis of a single find in a far land made by a young, amateur archaeologist. Dubois locked up the bones in a Netherlands vault where they remained unseen and unexamined until the twentieth century. Once again an important find could not be properly assessed because there were not enough data for comparison and not enough with which to think adequately in time and space.

It had been hard, at first, to accept early man's tools and as hard to accept his skeletal remains. It had been equally difficult in the beginning to accept clues as to the intelligence and culture of early man. Engraved bone materials from the European Upper Paleolithic had been excavated before Darwin's ORIGIN. They began to show up in increasing numbers in the second half of the nineteenth century. Bones with engravings of mammoth, bison, deer and other familiar animals were being unearthed at many sites. With these images there were also being found those odd, marked bones containing signs, symbols, geometric forms, and sequences and series of lines which remained inexplicable. Note was taken of paintings in the caves, but

---

[19] Charles Darwin, THE DESCENT OF MAN (London: J. Murray, 1891), p. 176.

[20] D. J. Cunningham, "Dr. Dubois' So-called Missing Link," NATURE, Vol. 51 (1895), p. 429.

these were less regarded than the engraved bones. In 1864, a Dr. Garrigou visited the cave of Niaux, in the Hautes-Pyrénées region of southern France. The cave contains superb paintings and engravings of bison, ibex, horse, and trout, as well as strange symbols. The doctor entered one line in his diary:

"There are some paintings on the wall: what on earth can they be?"

It was not until Lartet and Christy's RELIQUIAE AQUI-TANICAE was published posthumously in 1875 that the presence of a body of beautiful art and of strange, undecipherable markings on the mobiliary materials was adequately documented. Henry Christy was

"a hat-maker and banker who, among other things, introduced Turkish towels into western Europe. His Turkish Towels were exhibited at the Great Exhibition of 1851 and were allowed to be called Royal Turkish Towels after Queen Victoria had ordered six dozen for her own use. This Exhibition fired Christy with an interest in comparative ethnography and from 1851 until his death in 1865 his main interest was travelling and collecting."[21]

Christy supported Edouard Lartet financially. Lartet, a lawyer, amateur archaeologist, and paleontologist, dug in southern France, and in 1863 Christy took part in Dordogne excavations with Lartet which led to the "beginning of systematic Upper Palaeolithic archaeology."[22]

Yet as late as 1879, when a Spanish landowner, Marcelino de Sautuola, discovered paintings of bison, deer, and horse on the walls of the cave of Altamira, the paintings were condemned as fraudulent and received no mention at the International Congress of Prehistoric Archaeology and Anthropology held at Lisbon, 1880. In 1895—the year in which *Pithecanthropus erectus* was presented by Dubois and dismissed—a report on the discovery of prehistoric paintings and engravings in the cave of La Mouthe in the Les Eyzies region of France was met likewise with complete skepticism.

This sketch of a few early steps in the search for the origins and prehistory of man reveals that, by the beginning of the twentieth century, there was available a handful of significant but disparate facts, a number of important theories and insights, but equally as many questions and doubts. The available hard evidence was not completely understood, since it was still too sparse for adequate comparisons and evaluations.

Early in the twentieth century a pattern of research and findings began to emerge concerning the evolution of man and his culture, particularly as more evidence began to be accumulated in time and space. Stone tools and humanoid skeletons began to come from every part of Eurasia and Africa, and examples of Late Paleolithic art were also being found across wide areas in quantities sufficient for comparisons, for the beginnings of classification, for initiation of a workable chronology, and for attempts at interpretation.

The sciences involved were essentially the same as those used by Darwin and Boucher de Perthes: geology, paleontology, paleolithic archaeology, behavioral psychology, with the addition of a new branch of evolutionary science, genetics. New techniques and skills had been developed in these sciences. But, significantly, despite the new data and techniques, the cognitive processes involved in each of these sciences were still those used by Darwin and Boucher de Perthes. These were the basic, evolved, "time-factored" and "time-factoring" visual-kinesthetic capacities I had become aware of in my broadening studies of the Upper Paleolithic notations.

Since my analyses of the Upper Paleolithic markings continued to raise theoretical questions, at least for me, concerning this basic human cognitive capacity, it may be useful to look at some of the cognitive elements involved in the scientific effort to unravel the origins and development of man. I shall refer to these same potential cognitive capacities when I discuss early man, though he, of course, worked in a different cultural and reality context.

First, it should be noted that each of these sciences posed similar problems for cognition, raised the same sort of questions, and gave comparable answers. Each, therefore, represented a specialized case or a specialized skill. Each was an example of the more generalized evolved human capacity for time-factored and time-factoring thought. The differences between these sciences and the Upper Paleolithic notations, it seemed

[21] Glyn Daniel, ONE HUNDRED YEARS OF OLD WORLD PRE-HISTORY, Peabody Museum Centennial Lectures, October 7, 1967, pp. 12–13 (Unpublished Ms.)

[22] Ibid., p. 13.

to me as I studied both simultaneously, was that in the twentieth century contemporary culture and the way of life had presented scientists with a more complex, more specialized, and wider-ranging series of facts, problems, comparisons, classifications, and chances for cohering and theorizing.

Geology, for instance, begins with an analysis of *visible structures,* the diverse layers and formations of the earth, and then proceeds to search for the processes of their origin and change. Where structures are deep in the earth, they are reconstructed or "visualized" cognitively by measurements and computations. Paleontology deals with a comparison of the *visible structures* in the anatomy of living and fossil creatures, and then proceeds to an analysis of their possible functions and origins. Archaeology deals with *visible structures* that are the products of man; it then proceeds to a comparison of the styles and techniques found in these artifacts, attempts to establish their chronology, and finally moves to "process," to a search for the relation of these products to man's culture. Behavioral psychology studies and compares instinctual, behavioral, or learning patterns that are, in this sense, *visible* and *measurable* structures within the different species. After accumulation of enough comparable data, it becomes possible to seek an evolutionary order or hierarchy for these patterns of response and learning. The psychologists are aided in this work by comparative structural and functional studies of the brain and nervous system extending from lower creatures to man. These neurological structures and processes, like other biological structures and processes, can also then be placed in an evolutionary hierarchy. Genetics deals with *visible* or *measurable* structures, processes, and patterns that are involved in the hereditary process. These range from gross anatomical structures and visible behavior and instinctual patterns down to cellular, chromosomal, and molecular processes and structures. Genetics also deals with those statistical and numerical patterns and ratios that emerge in time and space within species populations as a result of the transmission of these structures and processes from generation to generation.

While the materials, the results, and the techniques differ in these sciences, *as far as the human brain is concerned, the processes of preparation, search and research, recognition, comparison, analysis, and deduction are the same in each.* The process always includes an adequate or proper cultural and individual preparation for thinking in time. It always involves a recognition and a comparison of patterns in structures and forms. It always involves the ability to recognize a *time-factored process* involving these forms, patterns, structures, and measurements.

It is this time-factored, time-factoring, and visual-kinesthetic cognitive ability that is the human basis of science—of the physical sciences and of sciences that deal with life and man. The nature of the problems and the questions varies as cultures develop and as the levels of reality in which man is interested become more specialized and as the quality and amount of the evidence change, but for the brain these are merely differences within a basic class of input.

This does not, of course, mean that there are not individual differences in ability and aptitude or that certain population groups are not culturally less prepared than others for "scientific" thinking. But it does mean that these differences vary around the genetic norm and mean, the basic species ability.

With this understanding of what I sensed in my reading of the sciences involved in the study of man, I can now turn to recent, twentieth-century research into the origins and prehistory of man, explaining more about the nature of the search and a bit about the nature of early man himself, the object of that research.

The Abbé Henri Breuil, the "father of prehistory," led it through the important early stage of its growth in the first half of the twentieth century.

Breuil, born in 1877 in France, grew up during the debate on evolution. A great-uncle had been an "antiquarian" collector and a friend of Boucher de Perthes. Amateur and increasingly professional digging had become a middle-class and aristocratic hobby in France, since history and prehistory lay everywhere underfoot. Breuil was probably handling antiquities and artifacts as a boy. At ten he wrote a school paper on the excavation of a Neolithic grave in the cave of Aurignac.

An aunt was married to the cousin of a geologist-archaeologist, d'Ault du Mesnil, and this distant relative introduced the boy formally to prehistory. He took Breuil at the age of fifteen to see the Somme valley gravel pits that Boucher de Perthes had "discovered" more than half a century before and in which d'Ault du Mesnil was now doing his own digging. These are the commercial gravel pits that Breuil would use later to help establish the chronology of European prehistory.

In 1895, at 18, Breuil entered a seminary. It was the year in which Dubois made his dramatic presentation of *Pithecanthropus erectus,* and it seems reasonable that the controversy over the "missing link" should sooner or later have been discussed at the seminary, for Breuil was being taught by the Abbé Guibert, a student of natural history and a believer in evolution. The Abbé gave the young Breuil French publications on anthropology and archaeology, with the advice: "There's a lot to be done in prehistory—you ought to tackle it."

That year, 1895, d'Ault du Mesnil announced that the Somme gravel layers revealed that primitive, crude "Chellean" tools were earlier than more sophisticated "Acheulian" tools and that the Acheulian tools were earlier than those of the still more advanced "Mousterian," the tools of Neanderthal man. D'Ault du Mesnil also found bones of warm-climate hippopotamus and rhinoceros in the Somme gravels, coming from an interglacial period some 400,000 years ago.

In 1896, d'Ault du Mesnil took the nineteen-year-old Breuil to a dig. Here he met the physician and archaeologist Joseph Louis Capitan, who introduced him to the new methods of classifying stone tools and to current methods of archaeological excavation. With Capitan, Breuil dug for the first time.

At twenty, Breuil began a serious study of the natural sciences: geology, geography, botany, physiology, and physics, that same cluster of sciences of the nineteenth century that had trained Darwin. That summer he visited Les Eyzies in the Vézère valley and met the schoolteacher-archaeologist Denis Peyrony excavating there. He traveled south to the foothills of the Pyrenees to see the cavern of Mas d'Azil and visited the cavern of Gargas, where he saw the mysterious Paleolithic prints of human hands on the cave walls. At the end of that memorable summer Edouard Piette showed Breuil his extraordinary collection of Late Magdalenian art, beautifully engraved and sculpted bone and ivory statuettes, bâtons and tools he had dug up and acquired. The Piette collection,

too, contained bones with the odd signs and sequences, many of which "looked" like writing or symbol-making. Breuil was stunned at the complexity and beauty of the works in the Piette collection and decided to specialize in the "Reindeer Age."

In 1899, Breuil began digging at Les Eyzies, at the site of Cro-Magnon—some few yards from the site of Abri Pataud that Professor Movius would later excavate—and at La Madeleine. He had entered manhood prepared by the theories and archaeologists of the late nineteenth century.

At twenty-three, in the late spring of 1900, Breuil was ordained, but, by choice and request, never became a cleric with religious duties. In 1901, at twenty-four, he was back in the Vézère valley during the excitement of the summer in which the art found in the local limestone caves was finally recognized as genuine (Les Combarelles and Font-de-Gaume).

As a boy, Breuil's hobby had been "nature," the observation, recognition, naming, and collecting of specimens, much as it had been for Darwin. In college he continued copying living forms. This drawing and classifying of insect varieties and plants developed his eye and skill for noting, classifying, and rendering comparative differences in shapes, forms, and details, a skill that was to serve him as it had served others from Leonardo da Vinci, Cuvier, and Lamarck to Darwin. That summer Breuil turned this sharpened and trained ability to copying and comparing the works of man. He wrote while at Les Eyzies: ". . . how we slaved yesterday! . . . I traced eighteen of the beasts . . . I spent ten hours in the grotto; I am half dead, I am aching all over . . ."[23]

The following year, 1902, Breuil and the nearly sixty-year-old prehistorian Emile Cartailhac, Professor of Prehistory at Toulouse and the dean of French archaeology, went to Spain to check the cave of Altamira. Twenty years before, when "there could be no such thing," Cartailhac had proclaimed that the paintings in Altamira were impossible and false. Now the two examined the paintings by candlelight, lying on their backs, and Breuil measured and copied them. On their return, Cartailhac published a recantation

[23] Alan H. Brodrick, THE ABBÉ BREUIL, PREHISTORIAN (London: Hutchinson & Co., 1963), p. 56.

and apology, "Mea culpa d'un sceptique," and the art of the prehistoric cave-sanctuaries was suddenly, and formally, an accepted scientific fact.

At a dramatic point in the recognition of Ice Age cave art, Breuil had become the prime copier and illustrator of that art. He was launched on a career that was to include the illustration, comparison, analysis, and classification of this art as well as of the tools of prehistoric man.

In the first half of the twentieth century it was too early for an evaluation or interpretation of Ice Age art that went beyond such generalities as "magic," "myth," "representation," "abstraction," "ritual," or "decoration." It would be a half century before the accumulation of hundreds of engraved examples and the discovery of more than a hundred painted caves would make the beginning of a scientific analysis and comparison possible. It would be a half century before Karel Absolon of Czechoslovakia would conjecture about a decimal system of counting in the engraved markings. It would be almost a half century before Annette Laming-Emperaire and André Leroi-Gourhan of France would be able to recognize and then compare patterns in the compositions of the cave art. The first comparisons of this art were non-analytic analogies between the animal pictures of the Ice Age and the religious animals of the early civilizations, animals whose rites and myths were known to be astronomic, seasonal, or calendric. Breuil himself made such a comparison in 1909, comparing the symbolic and ritual bulls of Mesopotamian and Egyptian art with the bison found in Ice Age art.[24] These were tentative comparisons without possibility of proof.

There was one thing that could be done with some degree of proof and certainty, and Breuil did it. With his insight into forms and shapes and on the basis of the tools and art already discovered, he began to set the house of prehistory in *chronological* order.

Early in the century he outlined a development of art styles in the Upper Paleolithic, covering a period of some 20,000 years. He theorized a development that began with simple animal outlines and evolved to the multicolored animals of the late cave paintings. He

[24] Henri Breuil, "Le bison et le taureau céleste chaldéen," REVUE ARCHÉOLOGIQUE, Vol. XIII, series IV (1909), pp. 250–254.

surmised that "realism" in the depiction of an animal developed slowly towards "abstraction," until an animal was finally represented by a few sparse, barely recognizable strokes.

He traced a seeming development of art styles from the basic naturalism of most Upper Paleolithic animal art to the seeming "degeneration of art" that appeared after the ice had melted in the Mesolithic. Later he spent years trying to sort out the styles and chronology of the post-Ice Age rock paintings found in Spain and Africa. As I write, Breuil's chronology of art styles is being revised by better comparative methods, and his theories concerning the art are being re-evaluated; nevertheless, his chronology remains the standard to which all later revisions must refer.

Breuil clarified the main sequence of Upper Paleolithic tool cultures by a comparison of their styles and techniques and by noting their place in the soil layers. He was the first to claim that the Aurignacian was a separate culture in Europe thousands of years before the complex later groups of Magdalenian cultures.

The general sequence in Breuil's chronology of tool styles is accepted, though the precise dating, evolution and relation of these tool cultures, including such questions as their origin and distribution, are still the subject of debate and research. Even the names of the so-called "cultures" are still debated.

Breuil also unravelled the sequence of the six diverse Magdalenian "cultures" which close out the Ice Age in Europe. But again, the six may be evolutionary stages of one culture or represent a mixing of groups, and the final determination has yet to be made.

With the general sequence of tools and art in the Upper Paleolithic apparently clarified, Breuil turned to the far older cultures of still-evolving man in the Lower Paleolithic. These deeper levels of the soil held no art, only bones and primitive tools.

In 1904, at the Somme gravel pits at Amiens, France, he had met an elementary-school teacher and amateur archaeologist, Victor Commont, who was digging there. Commont had found different styles of primitive tools in the Lower Paleolithic layers. There were roughly chipped pebble tools in the earliest levels (Chellean) but also somewhat better made tools (early Acheulian). The tools were associated with the bones of an ancient warm-climate elephant. In more recent layers, Commont found more evolved tools, the typical Acheulian hand ax. These later tools also lay with the bones of warm-climate animals. In these French gravels with which Breuil was now quite familiar, one had clear glimpses of exceedingly old tool cultures developing and varying in time and related somehow to changes of climate.

Breuil helped place these early European cultures in sequence. By a comparison of the tools, the animal bones, and the sequences of the soil, he pushed the Chellean pebble tools, primarily crude hand axes, which he renamed the Abbevillian, back to the warm period in Europe known as the First Interglacial, between the Günz and Mindel glaciations, a relatively warm period that occurred some 500,000–400,000 or more years ago. These were the tool cultures of the early, evolving men who preceded by hundreds of thousands of years the Mousterian culture of Neanderthal man. Breuil recognized that more than one tool culture or style existed in Europe during these early periods, an Abbevillian and a Clactonian in the First Interglacial mentioned above, and an Acheulian and a seeming Levalloisian in the second, Great Interglacial. Tools made by the Levallois technique were also found in the later Mousterian. Did this mean that different types of early man lived side by side? Did one stock evolve towards Neanderthal man, the other towards *Homo sapiens?* One could not tell. There were not yet enough tool sites and there were not enough human skeletal finds.

The Abbé Breuil had taken the necessary first steps in classification and "time-factoring." There were, however, great gaps in knowledge and many unanswered and even unasked questions. In 1932 and 1936 Breuil crossed the English Channel to dig in the Thames River valley. The stone tools found in the gravel layers of this part of England were similar to those found in the Somme valley. Louis Capitan had indicated the possibility of contact between the hunters of the two river valleys in a time of lower seas and with dry land between England and the continent. In the Swanscombe gravel pits, ten miles east of London, Breuil dug up early Abbevillian (Chellean) and later Acheulian tools, lying again with the fossils of warm-climate animals. Diggings over vast areas were uncovering the tools of early man in Europe, Asia, and Africa. Who were these extremely early men? How widely were they scattered? What did they look like? How intelligent were they?

Into what form did they finally evolve?

The fragments of a human skull without a jaw were found around this time in the Acheulian layers of the Swanscombe gravels by an English digger. The skull, apparently that of a young woman, was more than 100,000 years old.

Though the fragments were earlier than Neanderthal, they seemed almost modern, so close in brain size and appearance to modern man—with slight variations such as thicker bone—that it was theorized that Neanderthal man of Europe may have developed as an aberrant side branch of hominid evolution. But could one make such generalizations from one incomplete skull? If a jawbone were found, would it change the picture?

According to the theory, modern *Homo sapiens* would have begun to evolve on a line indicated by the Swanscombe skull, perhaps in the Middle East as skeletal finds there seem to indicate. According to this theory, European Neanderthal man would have evolved his specialized characteristics in relative separation or isolation, much as Darwin's finches and tortoises had in the Galapagos. The Swanscombe skull had a brain capacity of 1,325 cc., not far from the mean of 1,350 cc. for modern man, but less than the 1,600 cc. of the largest Neanderthal skull. But there is a problem. Despite the seeming genetic and cultural isolation of classical Neanderthal man in and around Europe, he continued to develop not only his skeleton and brain, but an increasingly human and sophisticated tool kit and general culture. The suggestion that humans originated in South Africa from a variant of *Homo erectus* while the Neanderthals evolved in Europe from a different variant raises questions concerning the level of "human" capacity that the dispersed groups of *erectus* had reached since the Neanderthals and modern humans had each evolved problem-solving capacities superior to those of *erectus*. This question of capacity is not addressed by physical anthropologists who are primarily interested in morphologies or skeletal structures and their implications. My research has attempted to describe the "different" but clearly "comparable" cognitive and problem-solving capacities of Neanderthals and modern humans as seen in the archaeological record.*

*See Appendix: Marshack 1984 a; 1985 a; 1988 a,b,d; 1989 a, b, d; 1990 a; 1991 d.

THE NEW PREHISTORY

This brief account of some of the efforts to track early man's origins and culture has indicated some of the data and some of the problems and questions. Perhaps of more importance for my research, it has shown us the nature of the cognitive efforts involved and, by doing so, revealed also the limitations and potentials in this phase of research. This should help in placing my own work in context and in assaying its limitations in terms of the data, the problems, and the questions.

By mid-twentieth century, when I turned to the science journals for help, it had become possible to think—not only backwards and forwards in time, as one went up and down the layers in a dig—but also *horizontally* in space. In the same way that Breuil could compare the Acheulian layers of the Somme valley in France with those of the Thames valley in England, prehistorians had begun to track and compare different Stone Age cultures across Africa, through Europe and the Middle East, and into Asia.

It had also become possible for archaeologists to study certain crucial sites horizontally by extremely careful excavations of ancient living floors or working areas. By analyses of the tools, bones, and refuse, one could attempt to reconstruct the processes and types of activity that were indicated, and one could then compare such living floors to other sites of the same or of earlier and later periods.

At the same time the archaeologists were plumbing down into still deeper, older layers, seeking that "progenitor of man" that Darwin had written of. These very old levels with their primitive tools offered important though indirect clues to an understanding of the later notations and art. It is interesting that the tools were so primitive that they went beyond the training and understanding of the Abbé Breuil, since he was most at home with the more evolved, sapient cultures, those closer to modern man. Since in my research I was searching for the origins of a certain evolved level of cognitive capacity as revealed in the Upper Paleolithic materials, it will be useful to describe these mid-century findings and their implications.

In 1925, certain "missing links" began to be found on the African continent, as Darwin had suggested they might be. The first was found accidentally in a commercial lime quarry near Taungs, South Africa. It was lower on the line of evolution than either Dubois' *Homo erectus* of Java or the maker of Europe's Abbevillian (Chellean) pebble tools. *Australopithecus,* or "southern ape man," was so named because the Taungs skull of a child was found in South Africa; however, he was not an ape, and he may have originated further north. The approximately four-foot-high adult creature would have looked "apelike" to us, though *Australopithecus* was an already evolved hominid whose ancestors had, millions of years before, separated from that branch of the primates that became apes. His line was so ancient that the australopithecines had had time to evolve into separate genetic subgroups, even as the apes had. Though *Australopithecus* was small, roughly the size of a chimpanzee, and had a small brain, that brain was already larger than a modern chimpanzee's and was comparable in size to that of a gorilla, whose body size is many times that of this early hominid.[25]

In general, the australopithecine brain was not only larger and presumably more evolved, but it was also functioning in a manner and with information completely different from an ape's. Raymond Dart has shown that *Australopithecus* could walk more or less upright, could use his hands freely, and perhaps made tools of bone and horn that could be used for clubbing, clawing, stabbing, and cutting. At least one group of the australopithecines were hunters and regular eaters of meat.

But if he made tools and stood erect, did that mean he was already "man"? The early definition of man as a "toolmaker" would seem to imply this. Was one group of these australopithecines on the line that led directly to modern man? The answers began to come in the next years, not, however, from South Africa. The evidence began to come from equatorial east central Africa, not far from the late Mesolithic site of Ishango on Lake Edward where the engraved bone tool with a quartz tip had been found, the tool that had set me on my path of research.

---

[25] Brain volume: chimpanzee, 394 cc.; gorilla, 498 cc.; *Australopithecus,* 435–600 cc.

Lake Victoria, like Lake Edward, lies in the upland Western Rift valley, that great north-south fault of earth uplift and valleys and of ancient tectonic and volcanic activity that, with the Eastern Rift, divides Africa in two. Victoria and Edward are headwater lakes that feed into the White Nile. Other rivers are also fed from these uplands, the Congo that flows westward towards the Atlantic, the Zambese that flows eastward toward the Indian Ocean. Early hominids must have followed these river valleys in all directions. The upland forests and hills still contain chimpanzee and gorilla. But it was the river and lake shores and the flat savannahs that, for millions of years, provided the ecology and way of life that supported and helped in the genetic selection of the evolving hominids.

Olduvai Gorge on the Serengeti Plain east of Lake Victoria was formed in relatively recent times by tectonic uplift and shearing. This created a cliff 300 feet high in places with exposed layers of accumulated soil and mud going downwards and backwards more than 2,000,000 years. At the lowest levels of these layers, paleontologist and archaeologist Louis B. Leakey, and his wife, Mary, found extremely crude chipped stones and pebbles that seemed to be "man"-made. The Abbé Breuil, in his day the foremost authority on early tool styles, refused to accept these Oldawan pebbles as evidence of toolmaking. They were too primitive, too crude, too early, and too uncertain. Besides, the skeleton of the supposed manlike creature that might have made them was, in Breuil's time, unknown.

In July 1959, while the first experimental satellites were in orbit around the earth, Mary Leakey found the skull of a short, wide-framed, low-browed, man-like creature, a youth about eighteen years old, with great jaws and large flat teeth that apparently indicated he had lived on nuts and tough plant fibers. Around the skull on the living floor of the ancient campsite were crude Oldawan tools of quartzite and lava, as well as bones of mice, lizards, snakes, and birds that had once been eaten. Leakey estimated the level to be 600,000 years old. The tools, apparently, were "man"-made and the "man" had been an eater of flesh. But was *Zinjanthropus,* or the "nutcracker man," as the Leakeys named him for his vegetarian

teeth, the maker of the tools? Had he, seemingly a vegetarian, been the eater of animals, or was he eaten? At first, Leakey claimed that *Zinjanthropus* was the first "true man," evolved from the somewhat more primitive *Australopithecus* in the south, that he was the "visualizer and fashioner of artifacts."[26]

A number of minor clues appeared in these exceedingly early levels which were perhaps as important as the evidence of the skull and tools. The site had been located near a lake abounding in fish and crocodiles. Some of the animals killed and eaten had been the young of larger species. One tool seemed to be a bit of animal bone that had been used as a leather or skin smoother or polisher. The stones used to make the tools seemed to have been brought from some distance. There were implications that the hunter knew, and to some extent certainly used, the seasons in a specialized way: the season of waterbird migration, the season of egg laying for bird, crocodile, lizard, and snake, the season of calving or the dropping of mammalian young, and probably the season of roots and nuts. There was an implication that he knew his range and territory in a specialized, time-factored way, that he had a primitive and roughly specialized tool "kit" for diverse activities and materials and perhaps for use in different areas; in other words, that he had begun to make himself at home in a time-factored, complex geometry that was far from apelike, a complexity that would deepen and widen as brain and body evolved.

The next year, 1960, the Leakeys found the battered skull of an eleven year old child who had apparently been murdered. Although it was lying two feet below *Zinjanthropus* and was therefore a far earlier creature, it was more advanced and had a larger brain. The two feet of soil represented almost a quarter of a million years.

In 1961 radioactive dating of the volcanic ash from the *Zinjanthropus* levels tripled the apparent age both of the Zinj youth and the pre-Zinj child, pushing them and toolmaking back in time to 2,000,000 and 1,750,000 years ago. Toolmaking had been pushed into the Pliocene age, which came before the drastic changes of climate that would begin the Pleistocene,

[26] "The 'First Unquestionable Man'," NEW YORK TIMES (October 11, 1959), Section E, p. 11.

the next age that would include the four slowly waxing and waning ice ages of the north, the first of which, the Günz glaciation of the Alps, may have begun about 1,500,000 years ago, and all of which were to affect evolving man's environment in Eurasia and Africa.

In the second half of the twentieth century, science was changing the nature of the questions being asked concerning life, evolution, and man. While the archaeologists and paleontologists were widening their search for the record of man's origins and development, psychologists were beginning to unravel the nature of higher cognition and intelligence; molecular biologists were seeking clues to basic processes in genetics, life processes, and thought; astronomers had begun to theorize on the possibility of other planets around other suns in other universes containing other forms of evolved intelligent life. The United States and the Soviet Union had arrived at advanced plans for lunar and planetary exploration, the most complex undertakings yet in the use of man's capacity for time-and-space activity.

In the next years, while I sat in libraries or traveled through Europe in search of Upper Paleolithic man, the Leakeys and a new generation of archaeologists were digging in the blazing sun of Africa. The Leakeys discovered the remains of a three-and-a-half to four-and-a-half foot high hominid of 1½ to 2 million years ago, apparently an omnivore with small teeth capable of eating animal flesh as well as plants and insects. It had a well opposed thumb that made it skilled in gripping and working objects and a curved arch in the foot that provided an erect, near human gait. It had a cranial capacity between 643 and 720 cc, more than the largest known australopithecines, but less than that of *Homo erectus* who appeared shortly after. This early hominid seemed to be on the generalized line leading to man, while the australopithecines seem to have taken a more specialized vegetarian road. It appeared that it was this more intelligent hominid who made the Oldawan tools. The Leakeys named this new creature *Homo habilis*, that is, the "handy, skillful, acute, vigorous."[27]

Above *Homo habilis*, the Leakeys found a still more evolved hominid, *Homo erectus*. He had a brain capacity of 1000 cc. Groups of vegetarian australopithecines continued to live in Africa with *Homo habilis*, but though they may have made tools (as even chimpanzees can), they had reached a dead end and had more or less stopped evolving. Their specialization for chewing plants may have put them in an ecological niche within which they were conservative, in contrast to the increasingly complex and variable way of life that was being made possible on the *habilis* line. Apparently, it was not toolmaking that was the essential skill in eventual success on the hominid line, but variability in thinking as well.

We surmise that this hominid was able to think and work *in time and space* far beyond the great apes. This increasingly generalized time-and-space capacity may have been one of the determining factors in the screening for those successful individuals and groups who led to the evolution of modern humans. If so, the anatomical changes and enlarging brain, including the better tools and an omnivorous diet, would merely represent aspects of this more general trend towards an increasing conceptual and productive capacity. We shall discuss this later. The development of an omnivorous diet in a two-handed, bipedal, far-ranging hominid had a profound influence on selection for variable cognitive, problem-solving capacities. A strict vegetarian is a specialized creature, suffering a sharper deprivation of range in dry seasons and years of drought and in longer periods of climatic change and drying. The omnivore can appropriate some of the river and lakeside range of the vegetarian in extremely dry seasons besides supplementing his diet with other foods and skills elsewhere. He can live off fish, birds, eggs, insects, and underground or hidden game. It may have been that in the long, slow screening process elicited by climatic changes, the omnivores able to function better in time and space, individually and in groups, simply replaced a less able, more specialized and therefore boxed-in hominid form.

After I had written the preceding pages there was a burst of discovery and a flood of new questions and theories. In 1975 the American archaeologist, Don

[27] It is now accepted that *Homo habilis* evolved from a bipedal form of early hominid, perhaps an australopithecine or the ancestor of the australopithcines who were his contemporaries.

Johanson found fragments of the most complete early hominid skeleton known till that time, at Afar in Ethiopia a thousand miles northeast of Olduvai Gorge. The skeleton, two and three-quarter million years old, was of a 65 pound female three feet eight inches tall. "Lucy," representing a pre-*Homo habilis* hominid, had a brain no larger than a chimpanzee's but she walked upright. Her fingers and hands suggested that she could climb a tree effectively if she needed to escape. Though small, the 375 to 500 cc. brain was probably already restructured for upright walking and for increasingly adaptive two-handed problem solving. Did she make tools? At the time "Lucy" was discovered, Jane Goodall was reporting that chimpanzees were making and using tools of perishable materials such as twigs and leaves and were even using natural hammers of stone and hard wood for pounding nuts. Had "Lucy" gone with her two-legged stride and more efficient hands to places where she could use new and developing skills and make a greater variety of simple ad hoc tools for diverse foods in different seasons? Was she already beginning to create a realm in time-and-space different from that of the great apes? Was it this capacity for variable problem-solving that would be selected for in evolution to create the larger brained maker of stone tools, *Homo habilis*? Could she exploit lake and riverside and then move out to the fringes of forest and savannah in different seasons? Whatever the answer, these early hominids were walking into a new set of opportunities in functional time-and-space.

Shortly after "Lucy" was discovered, Mary Leakey, in 1978, stumbled on an ancient layer of hardened volcanic ash at Laetoli not far from Olduvai, that had been crossed by three upright, bipedal hominids (a male, a female and a youngster). They had left their footprints in the ash perhaps a half million years before "Lucy." One can assume that the near human stride was carrying a still small brain, but one that was mediating a bipedal stride and a more efficient, developing, two-handed skill. These australopithecines, or ones like them, were walking across an unforested landscape towards eventual hominization. An intriguing approach entered the debate in 1987. It was concerned not with the variety among early hominids, but with the time and place of modern human origins. A study of the microscopic genetic material—mitochondrial DNA (MT/DNA)—which at birth is passed only from female to female, found that among the different human types dispersed across the earth, the measurable changes in MT/DNA suggested that modern humans had "originated" from one female or one set of females at one point of time in South Africa perhaps 200,000 years ago. A heated debate arose concerning the accuracy of the method, the precision of the date, and the suggestion that there was a single point in time and place for modern human origins. Of greater importance, this model did not explain why groups deriving from that supposed African "point" of origin, created the first major "explosion" of image and symbol to be seen in the archaeological record only 175,000 years later in the region of Europe (and Siberia) during the Ice Age. A comparable "explosion" of early art, symbol and image did not occur anywhere else. Other regions, of course, had symbol systems, but not of this quality and variety.

There was another problem. The MT/DNA model of African origins did not explain or describe the "human" capacities of the Neanderthals who had evolved in Eurasia at the moment modern humans were supposedly evolving in South Africa. The Neanderthals had adapted to a sequence of changing climates in northern latitudes, had used the same Mousterian tool kit and subsistence strategies as anatomically modern humans when these groups came in contact, and had engaged in a range of "human" productive and creative activities before they made contact with modern human groups and before they eventually disappeared. The place of the Neanderthals in the development of the human capacity for symboling is under intense debate. The disappearance of peoples and cultures under the impact of a different technology in historic times, suggests that there may have been a clash between hominids at two different developmental stages of their culture, between cultures with a different technological and social, historical development, rather than a major clash of "species." Were the carriers of the modern human skeleton more intelligent or had they merely acquired a more efficient set of conceptual adaptations as they spread northward through different climates and ecologies, while the Neanderthals were constrained to the adaptive strategies they had acquired in a more limited realm?

Neither traditional morphological studies or studies of MT/DNA address the question of what it means to be "human," or what it means to fail or succeed at some point in time as an aspect of human capacity. These questions, however, began to be asked in the research. I have written about the evolution of the human capacity, about the "comparable" but "different" capacity of the Neanderthals and the reason that the unique "explosion" of art and symbol occurred in Ice Age Europe. The success of the Ice Age cultures of Europe, from 35,000–10,000 B.C., is documented in the archeological record primarily by "imperishable" artifacts and materials that have, by chance, lasted. They provide a picture only of the way that the modern human capacity was used at that time and place, under those conditions, and with the materials that have been preserved. Change any one of the conditions or materials, without a change in the capacity of the humans involved, and the picture would be different. Besides, one must assume there was a long history of cultural behavior in preparation for the Ice Age "explosion," a history that is missing from the soil and that occurred in complex forms and with a wide and variable use of perishable materials. When the Ice Age ended and the climate changed, the cultures disintegrated (more rapidly in fact than the Neanderthals disappeared), and the art which had peaked in Europe toward the end of the Ice Age, disappeared. The population, of course, did not disappear. The archaeological record, therefore, provides us with the skewed impression of a sudden collapse in human creative, artistic capacity. It was, of course, the conditions that changed, not the capacity.

In the research that began with the preparation of this book a difficult and intriguing set of questions was, therefore, being addressed. What were the nature and range of the early evolving and evolved human capacity? How did it evolve? What role did these developing capacities play in adaptation and selection and the eventual creation of "modern humans"? How did the developing capacity to think in time-and-space and to categorize objects, processes and relations in a variable and changing time-and-space realm affect evolution, language as a mode of reference, and image and symbol as a referential mode of depiction?

It will be generations before the story of man's origins and development is adequately known. Great blanks exist between every important find: gaps in geography and time, gaps in the sequences of skeletal development, gaps in the tool sequence and the cultural materials, gaps in theory about the artifacts and the evolution and behavior of man.
Nevertheless, in the decade preceding Breuil's death in 1961, the study of man's origins and prehistory had reached a point where new comparisons, generalizations, and insights had become possible. One hundred years of groundwork and spadework had prepared the materials, the questions, and the researchers. It is clear that in the first stage the primary evidence and its analysis could do no more than hint at the complexities in the evolving hominid capacity or at the diverse factors involved in the uses of the tools and the later art.
The situation was comparable to that which prepared the way for Darwin. In the late eighteenth and early nineteenth centuries one could begin the classification of living forms in European collections and the development of a sequence for the soil layers and their fossils without knowing all the processes involved. So, too, from mid-nineteenth century to mid-twentieth, one could collect the archaeological and paleontological evidence, begin clarifying the chronology of hominid forms, track the sequence of evolution in such structures as tooth, hand, foot, hip, posture, and brain size, and lay out the chronology of tool forms and art without knowing all the processes involved. The fact we must recognize, then, is that the "hard evidence" does not present us with a process, but with the outline of certain aspects of the process. Nor do comparisons or statistical curves of changes in tool styles or percentages or graphs of changes in anatomy present us with a process. They are measurements of changes in the remnant products of culture or evolution. They

merely *hint* at the processes involved. Nevertheless, with the accumulation of this evidence and with a chronology, it was possible to begin asking the next, necessary questions. In a sense, I had been forced to ask some of these questions.

What cognitive and behavioral changes had evolved on the hominid line? Were the artifacts found by archaeology a reflection of these changes?

In the second half of the twentieth century, increasing possibilities for interpreting early man's way of life and cognitive problems were strengthened by new techniques. First, there was an accumulation of increasingly precise information about changes in climate and patterns of rainfall, advances and retreats of the northern ice, changes in plant and animal life, and even information about related changes in sea levels and coastlines, sea temperatures, and sea life. These facts set the stage; they described the environment of early man and the nature of his ecology; they gave us some insight into his daily and seasonal problems and how they varied and changed. Second, radioactive analyses of the biologic and geologic materials in the strata were providing an increasingly precise dating and chronology, not only for the changes in climate but also for evolutionary changes in skeleton and brain size, and for cultural changes one could read from the tools. Each of these "time series" checked the accuracy and increased the significance of the others.

In addition, as mentioned earlier, hundreds of archaeological sites in Europe, Asia, the Middle East, and Africa had made it increasingly possible to think *in time*—not only vertically, that is, up and down the layers—but horizontally as well, in terms of the distribution, migration, and dispersion of cultures and peoples in each period. The full chart or model of the combined time-space evidence had begun to look like a tapestry of interwoven threads. Even the many blank spaces in the model had by now become informative, since they indicated to some degree what evidence was still needed and where to look and why. It was at this point, in 1962, that I began my inquiries. The accumulating facts were supplying the *background* to man's development, but they told too little about the evolving hominid brain or about the way in which that brain was adjusting to and handling the dynamic,

expanding, increasingly complex, "humanized" world. As a result, the prehistorians of early man were beginning to express a frustration similar to one I myself had felt coming to their journals.

Glyn Daniel, editor of the English journal ANTIQUITY, wrote:

"Old World archaelogy is now in possession of a vast body of information before which the student quails and indeed before which the professional often boggles. The problem is how to organise and interpret this material meaningfully, a problem from which so many old-world archaeologists turn with a sigh of relief to their own cabbage-patch: it is so much easier to arrange your artifacts in pigeon-holed compartments than ask yourself why you are doing it and what it contributes to human history . . . without a sense of history, and of historical problem, archaeology can revert again to mere collection: and there is always the danger of a new antiquarianism."[30]

In mid-twentieth century, the classifications and comparisons of the chipped stone tools were nevertheless *beginning* to reveal something about evolving man's general intelligence and cognitive abilities. This information would begin to add meaning to my own studies of those other products of the human brain, the art and the notations.

Professor François Bordes of the Laboratoire de Géologie du Quaternaire et Préhistoire of the University of Bordeaux had brought the technique of archaeological excavation to such precision that it was possible for him to perform "micro" analysis of each square inch in a dig and to reconstruct the complete horizontal assemblage of tools and tool waste on the single floor of an ancient occupation site. With this care in excavation, so different from earlier searches for beautiful, whole, or "significant" examples, it was possible to type and classify the tool kit in each occupational level, to determine the techniques by which each type of tool was made, to count the number of each type at each level, and then to compare the assemblage at one level with that of higher and lower levels. In this way, one could begin to get a picture of evolving man's varying and developing tool kit, his developing skill in toolmaking, and, by inference, a clue to his varied, changing activities and culture.

[30] Glyn Daniel, ONE HUNDRED YEARS OF OLD WORLD PREHISTORY, pp. 46–47.

Bordes found that the Mousterian culture of Neanderthal man in Europe contained a kit composed of 63 different tool types, indicating a wide range of specialized skills, needs, and activities. The Mousterian kit and tools developed and evolved in time. Other studies revealed that the pre-Mousterian Acheulian culture had a tool kit with fewer tool types, but a kit that served, nevertheless, in almost the same general range of activities. The Acheulian hunter of more than 200,000 years ago used at least 26 tool types, including hand axes, cleavers, picks, borers, scrapers, knives, and points. The post-Mousterian, modern *Homo sapiens* cultures of the Upper Paleolithic periods showed a rapid expansion in their tool kit, 93 types of chipped stone tools being classified, apart from a large and diversified kit of bone tools. In each of these early periods, of course, the implied use of wood, plants, plant fibers, and skin or leather could not be determined, while the tool "types" Bordes found were not always clearly differentiated, and their uses could only be generally guessed at.

By comparison, classification, counting, averaging and charting, Bordes was able to show that even in one broad culture, such as the Mousterian, tool assemblages and kits varied from site to site and period to period. Sometimes a kit or assemblage would be absent in one layer, then reappear in a later level. The meaning of these findings was not at first clear, but they did indicate a diversity of skills and activities with possible changes in plant and animal usage at different sites and in different times, as well as possible changes in the specialized activities of different groups, part of which may have been adaptations to different conditions.

Slowly, using the basic human capacity for recognition, comparison, and classification and the ability to think in time from a series of structures and comparisons, the prehistorians found that the stone tools were hinting at changing cognitive and adaptive processes in the developing human cultures.

A similar precision in excavation by Professor Movius of Harvard, at the Abri Pataud in Les Eyzies, revealed fascinating facts about the settlement and living patterns of the Upper Paleolithic hunters. By a careful analysis of the fireplaces, or hearths, beginning with the early Aurignacian and going up to the end of the Ice Age, he found that in the early and later Aurignacian the groups living at the Abri were small, probably family groups. These Aurignacian family groups living along the valley would probably have been interrelated by "marriage," would perhaps have had certain communal hunting activities, particularly at certain seasons, and perhaps shared seasonal rituals and ceremonies. But the population density was seemingly small. Later, Upper Perigordian hearths were wider, hinting at some specialized group living in a "long house" built against the rock overhang and implying · larger, more complex social units. The fireplaces of these Upper Perigordians of about 20,000 years ago hinted at changes in population density, in social relations, and possibly in the interrelation of these larger groups among themselves and to the herds. These Perigordians had learned to cook food in vessels by dropping fire-heated stones into a liquid. They even had a drainage ditch through their site to run off excess water. Such findings and hints were fascinating, but limited and rare. It would be years before comparative evidence of this sort had accumulated in sufficient quantities to give a rounded picture of the evolving social complexities of early man.

Bordes and Movius represent the generation that followed Breuil. Their students and followers had begun pushing these new comparative, analytic, and statistical techniques towards even greater refinement, and were asking the tools and the sites for answers to even more subtle questions.

Lewis R. Binford of the University of New Mexico and his wife, Sally, are members of this generation of statistically and mathematically oriented prehistorians. By careful analysis of the tools and their distribution on the habitation floor, they have attempted to reconstruct some of the more subtle subdivisions of labor among the early Neanderthal hunters. For example, the distribution of one kind of Mousterian artifact, the "denticulate" or sawtooth type of stone tool, led the Binfords to theorize that this tool was used by females at certain kinds of tasks and at certain kinds of locations within a rather complex Neanderthal settlement system.[31]

[31] Lewis R. Binford, "Methodological Considerations of the Use of Ethnographic Data," Paper presented in Session VI, MAN THE HUNTER CONFERENCE, sponsored by the Wenner-Gren Foundation, University of Chicago (1966), p. 3.

The Binfords were attempting cognitive reconstructions far beyond those common to traditional archaeology:

"... if a group of people ... are engaged in a specific activity, such as hide-working, they would employ a number of different tools—knives, scrapers, and possibly pins for pinning down the hides or stretching them. The number of tools used in hide-processing will be directly related to the number of individuals engaged in the activity and the number of hides processed .. [yet] the proportions of the tools used would ... remain essentially constant. If after the ... hide-working, the group began to manufacture clothing, a different set of tools might be employed, along with some of the same tools used in hide-working ..."[32]

According to the Binfords, some of Bordes' Mousterian assemblages indicated that they had been used at butchering sites, others that they were used at the base-camp or home sites where meat, skin, and bone were prepared for use and consumption. The sawtooth or "denticulate" tool assemblage might have been used by Neanderthal women for "preparing plants and possibly scraping bones."[33]

The implication of a complex Neanderthal society with seasonal sites and tasks and with occupational and sexual specialization both at the home site and in the field implied a level of intelligence, cognition, culture, and interrelation not till then conjectured for Neanderthal man nor part of the central theorizing that had been going on about man's evolving intelligence. The Binfords ask the question that prepares for the next stages of research:

"Is there directional change through time evidenced in assemblages from a single location which suggests evolutionary or situational changes in human behavior?"[34]

Sally Binford, doing a comparison of Mousterian tools found at sites in the Middle East and of the number and kinds of animals killed, has asked what these Mousterian remains can tell us about Neanderthal man's adaptations, not to the European Ice Age but to the ecology and climate of what is today Israel-Jordan-Lebanon. The results and interpretations are speculative and still controversial.

Earlier theories held that during this period in the Middle East, Neanderthal man was undergoing anatomical changes in the direction of modern man. In Europe he seems to have been evolving on the classic Neanderthal line while adapting to the conditions of the growing ice. Sally Binford has adduced that Neanderthal man in the Levant seemed to be making increasingly heavy *seasonal* use of different ecological niches or regions of his area, as part of an increasing use of herd animals, wild cattle (Bos) and fallow deer over smaller prey. These wild ungulates have a feeding cycle which was apparently enhanced by the increasing aridity of the Early Würm: migrations between the wet season and dry season grazing grounds. The relatively damp coastal plain would have provided summer pasture; the inland, more elevated plains of the western slopes of the coastal mountains would have been the winter grazing ground. The far eastern slopes were dry and almost desert. Grasses along the western uplands would have offered the migration routes through which "large numbers of animals pass[ed] ... on a regular seasonal basis."[35]

This hypothesis of a slight drying and of changing patterns of adaptation in time and space occurring with forms of evolved man transitional between Neanderthal and modern man suggested to Sally Binford simultaneous changes in the size and interrelation of the human groups. Larger numbers of humans would have come together, particularly during migrations; "the large-scale systematic exploitation"[36] of these herds would have required new kinds of joint activity similar to those found later in the Upper Paleolithic of Europe. These new interrelations in time and space may have changed kinship and marriage relations, unifying wider bands. Arguing from the still sparse evidence of tool and animal types found in the Mousterian levels and the evidence of changing human skulls, she writes that the adaptive changes

[32] Lewis R. Binford and Sally R. Binford, "A Preliminary Analysis of Functional Variability in the Mousterian of Levallois Facies," AMERICAN ANTHROPOLOGIST, Vol. 68 (April 1966), p. 242.

[33] Ibid., p. 256.

[34] Ibid., p. 270.

[35] Sally R. Binford, "Early Upper Pleistocene Adaptations in the Levant," AMERICAN ANTHROPOLOGIST, Vol. 70, No. 4 (August 1968), p. 708.

[36] Ibid., p. 714.

"would have greatly increased the rates of gene flow, thus producing one of the conditions leading to evolutionary change."[37]

Using an entirely different set of archaeological materials but thinking in a similar cognitive mode, I was coming to related and comparable time-factored conclusions.

This chapter was intended to do a number of things. It has told some of the story of prehistory to help us understand the changing problems involved in the study of early man. It has placed my notational research in context with the archaeological research based on the tools and sites.

It has used the story of prehistory itself as an example of the evolved, time-factored, and time-factoring human capacity, the cognitive ability to think sequentially in terms of process within time and space. This book and chapter are themselves examples of this species ability.

It has implied that the early hunters, in a different culture and with a more limited range of available comparisons and facts, used this basic ability to structure their lives and lore.

It has shown how recent the study of prehistory is and how tentative the results are. The chapter has indicated the limitations inherent in the evidence and in methods of research at each stage. No one person in the story had all the evidence or the complete solution to the problem on which he has working. He could work only with the preparation, the evidence, and the questions of his time. The same would hold for my research. The limitations were no different for the Upper Paleolithic hunter.

We can now turn to the Upper Paleolithic markings to see what this body of evidence can tell us.

[37] Loc. cit.

PART III
NOTATION AND ART: THE RESEARCH AND THE IDEAS

CHAPTER VII
NOTATION: EARLY AND LATE

Some months before my first study of the Ice Age notations was published in 1970* I received a letter from François Bordes who was director for prehistoric archaeology in the Dordogne region of southwest France. The Abri Pataud in Les Eyzies, where Hallam Movius was excavating, was in Bordes' territory. Bordes was about to publish my memoir on Ice Age notations in the French language. He informed me with some excitement that a fragment of bone had just been excavated in the east of France and that it contained the most complex composition ever to come from the Ice Age, actually from the end of the Ice Age. It was more complex than any

*A. Marshack, NOTATION DANS LE PALÓLITHIC SUPERIÉUR. (1970a).

Fig. 15 a

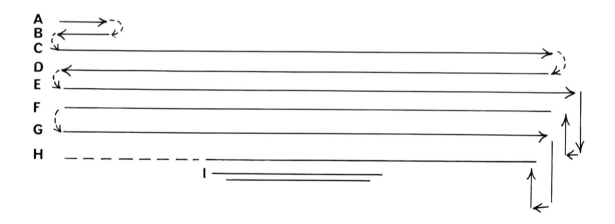

Fig. 15 c

Fig. 15 b

composition I was then in the process of publishing and Bordes suggested I might want to study it.

I flew to France carrying cameras and, by now, a modern binocular zoom-microscope and, on a shaky wooden table in a small bare room not far from the excavation, I began the slow, careful examination. The engraving was more complex than I could at that time fathom and it raised hundreds of questions. I took voluminous notes and made microphotographs at each point of puzzlement. A few years later (1973*) I published a tentative report stating that the engraving seemed to be a "lunar-solar" notation but that a full analysis would have to wait. It took

◀ Fig. 15 a, b, c
The two faces and one edge of engraved pebble from Barma Grande (Grimaldi). Breakage and deterioration of the surface on face (b) have removed some of the engraved marks. Probably Upper Perigordian.

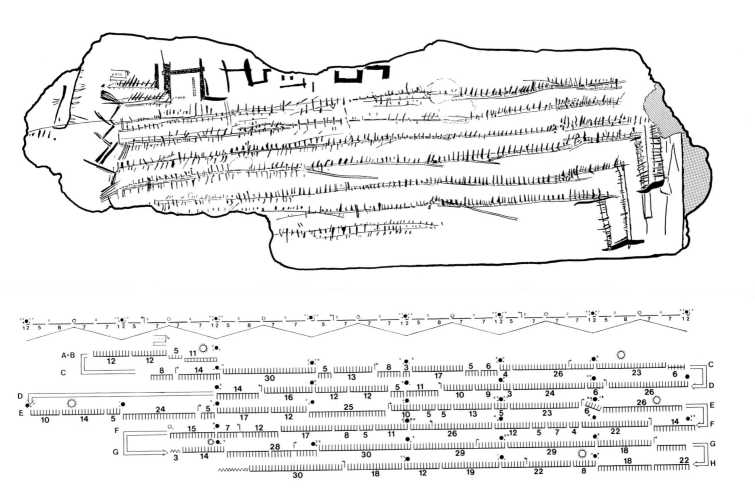

Fig. 16 a, b, c
Schematic rendition of the engraved marks on the Barma Grande pebble as determined by microscopic analysis.

twenty years to "break the code" of that composition and when this occurred, the unraveling occurred at precisely the moment that young archeologists in Europe and the United States had begun to publish arguments that notations could not possibly have existed in the Ice Age and that the microscopic method could not be used to ascertain notation. I summarize the "decoding" since it was not dependent on microscopic cross-sectional analysis of single marks but on a determination of the changing strategies involved in a complex sequence of visual, symbolic, problem-solving.

*A. Marshack, "Analyse preliminaire d'une gravure à système de notation de la grotte du Täi (St. Nazaire-en-Royans, Drôme)." (1973)

The fragment of a bovid rib, 3½ inches long (8.6 cm), was found at the Grotte du Taï (Drôme), a site on the Isère river, a tributary of the Rhône. It may never have been a tool when it was taken from a scrap heap near the habitation site (Fig. 15 a,b) since it was already deteriorating and flaking when it was picked up. It was then cut at the right and a section was snapped off. The reshaped fragment, now a plaque small enough to be held in one hand while it was marked with a tool in the other, was then used as an easily carried surface for the accumulation of the most complex composition to come from the Upper Paleolithic. Weathered bone, unlike fresh bone, is comparatively easy to incise. Many of the engraved lines and marks, in fact, cross over the areas of missing flakes that had earlier spalled from the weathered fragment.

At first glance the surface seemed to have been incised with nine or ten horizontal lines (A to I in Fig. 15) which were overmarked with tiny strokes. Microscopic analysis, however, revealed that these were not single horizontal lines, but were instead composed of very short sections, one appended to the other, with one subsection often overlapping or crossing the next. Each of these short subsections was then incised with its own set of marks. The scale of marking was roughly that of the marking on an inch ruler (with 32 marks to the inch) or on a millimeter rule. An analysis of the short subsets accumulated on each containing line indicated that they were made by different tools and with different rhythms of marking (Marshack 1973, 1991*).

Some sets were incised upward and some downward, suggesting that the bone had been turned 180° for the engraving of neighboring sets. This suggested that the marking had been made at different times since this was not the way that a rapidly made decorative composition would have been incised.

The twenty-year-long unraveling of the strategies involved in the accumulation proceeded by stages. At far right, near the snapped edge, for instance, the horizontal rows E–F and G–H terminate in two abrupt right-angle descents. These verticals appended to rows E–F and G–H are connected by a horizontal bar at the bottom, and each was engraved with its own set of tiny marks. It was clear that the engraver had not planned his accumulation properly, since more space was clearly needed at the end of row E to complete a "required" sequence of marks. The last mark on row E at right, in fact, actually crossed into the broken edge. It was at this point that the first vertical was added and marked with tiny strokes. The accumulation then ascended on the next vertical, which was appended to horizontal row F, and the marking continued towards the left.

Having added descending and ascending containing lines to rows E and F, the engraver was now forced to take account of the lack of space that had been created on the next two rows (G and H) and again added descending and ascending lines. The composition, therefore, consisted of

*A. Marshack, "An Observational Lunar, Probably Lunar/Solar Notation from the Terminal Upper Palaeolithic of France. CAMBRIDGE JOURNAL OF ARCHAEOLOGY. (1991)

a serpentine or boustrophedon sequence, a sequence that progressed "as the ox plows" (Fig. 15). Just as the four marks at upper left on the Blanchard plaquette (Figs. 8 and 9) revealed a "point of turning" within a continuous sequence, with the "turns" falling at a lunar phase, so the "points of turning" on the Taï plaque (at E/F and G/H) suggested a continuous sequence with the "turns" occurring at the end of far longer periods. It soon became apparent that the notation represented a non-arithmetic, observational solar year, divided into two halves, with each row or "half year" consisting of 5 to 7 lunar months. Since the lunar and solar years are not of equal length (354 days for the lunar year, and 365 + for the solar year), the second half of any year could not begin until there was an observation of the sun at the winter and summer solstice. As a result there was a period of waiting for the solstices at both the right and the left. This swing from solstice to solstice is what one observes on the eastern and western horizon as the sun moves back and forth during its six month swing from winter to summer. The analysis revealed, however, that these periods of waiting were handled differently at the left and the right. At the left the extra marks were added not on a descending or ascending vertical but, because of the descending zig-zag (at that position they were added), above or below the main horizontal containing line (Fig. 15 d).

If we begin with A + B as the opening period of 40 days, then A + B + C equal 7 lunar months of 208 days (29.5 x 7 = 206.5). The next row, D, has 148 marks, an accurate five lunar months (29.5 x 5 = 147.5). The sum of days in A + B + C + D equals 356, a quite accurate notation for one lunar year (12 x 29.5 = 354). However the division of that year is peculiar. A + B + C equal seven months, not six, and D is therefore only five months long. Seven plus five equals 12 months.

This odd breakdown occurs also within the next set, E + F. Line E has 180 marks, an almost precise lunar observation for six months (29.5 x 6 = 177), but the descent at far right contains a seventh month of 29 days (11 + 18 = 29). This was the awaited month required to close out that "half" year with an observation of the sun. The returning notation on line F was 161 days or 5½ months (161 ÷ 29.5 = 5.45 months). The sum of marks on E + F was 369 (180 + 29 + 161), a proper count for an observational solar year. A count of all the marks in G + H (G = 158, H = 136) gave a sum of 294, the sum for 10 lunar months (295 days). There were marks missing,

however, in the portion of bone absent at bottom left and these could have supplied a month or two. These initial sums, derived from a study of the microscopic data, while startling, presented a problem. How did the short subsections marked above and below the horizontals at left fit sequentially into these large sums. An analysis indicated that these added subsections almost always represented a non-arithmetical observational lunar period or month (Fig. 15 d and e). The full primary notation on this main face of the plaquette was for 3 ½ years.

Just as the marking on the reverse face of the Blanchard bone provided

Fig. 18 a, b, c ▶
The three sides of a bâton of antler, 13¾ inches long, from Le Placard (Charente), containing a hole, the sculpted head of a fox and sets of engraved marks. Lower Magdalenian.

Fig. 17

evidence of non-decorative notational marking, so the reverse face of the Täi plaquette supplies a subsidiary notation (Fig. 17). Discrete sets of marks were again incised on horizontal containing lines. This notation on the reverse face apparently helped to complete the fourth ritual or economic year.

It should be noted that the primary analytical evidence for notation has been "cognitive." The analysis was concerned with the strategies involved in forming a sequential continuous accumulation; while counting was used toward the end of the analysis, the determination of notation was not dependent on counting. While the microscope was used in the analysis, the determination of notation was not dependent on cross-sectional determinations by use of the microscope. The counting represented analytical sums by the researcher; these sums need not have been of concern to the original engraver. During the analysis the microscope was used primarily to determine the length of a horizontal containing line, the differences within and among sets, the number of marks in each subset, the marking above and below a line, and the differences in the direction, rhythm, pressure and type of marking in the sets and subsets, etc. (Fig 16 a–d).

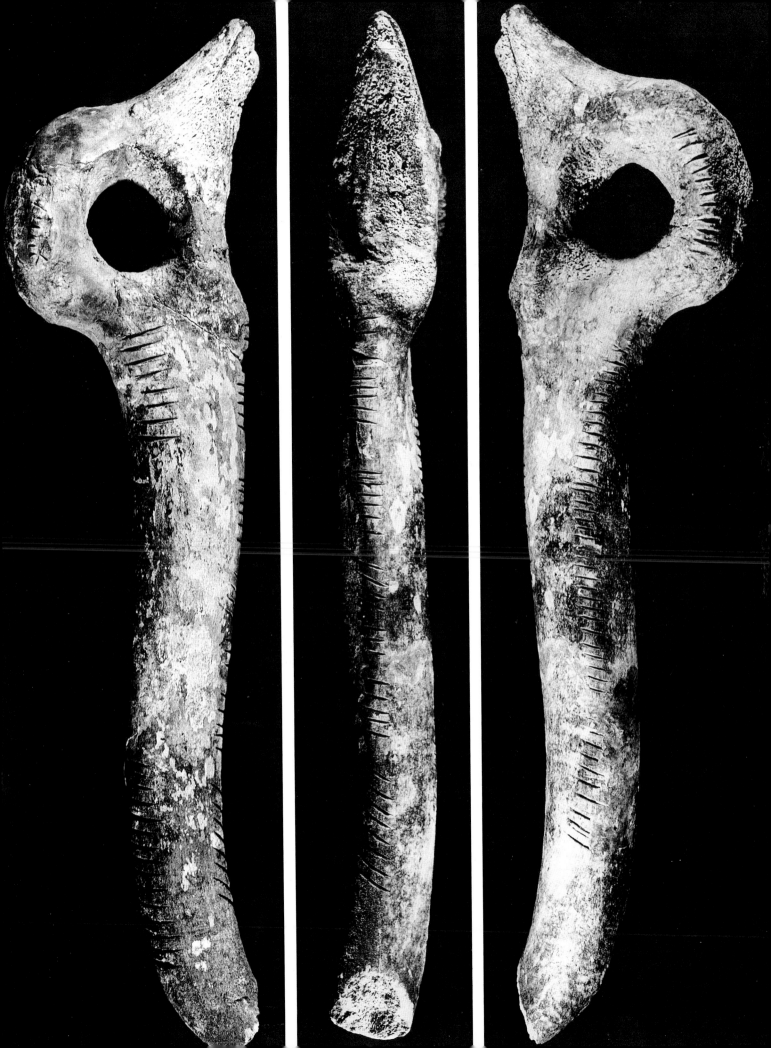

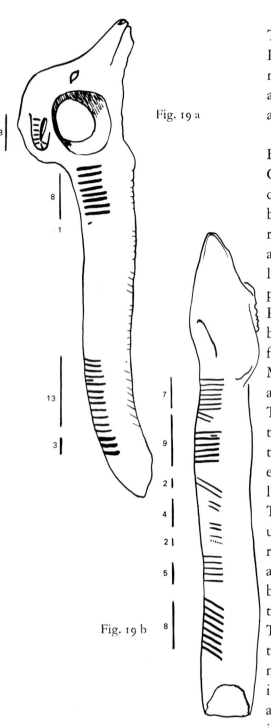

Fig. 19 a

Fig. 19 b

Fig. 19 a, b, c
Schematic rendition of the sets of engraved marks on the Placard bâton as determined by microscopic analysis.

The Taï plaque was an easily carried fragment of a scrap bone. By the time I completed analysis of the Taï composition I had found other examples of notation on scraps of waste bone (1970b)* besides accumulations on artifacts such as batons, flutes and pressure flakers which were carried about and used for long periods.

From Magdalenian III, the site of Le Placard in the department of Charente, just north of the Vézère valley in the Dordogne, there comes a classic example of one of those mysterious worked bone objects that have been have named *bâtons de commandment*, a name that indicates a presumed ritual purpose (Fig 18a, b, c). These bâtons begin in the Aurignacian and are found with increasing frequency as one goes up the Magdalenian levels. They usually, but not always, have a large hole in them and in later periods may have many such large holes. Paolo Graziosi, in his book PALAEOLITHIC ART, states: ". . . often the fragility, delicacy and beauty of the decorations seem hardly compatible with practical and frequent use."[2] This delicacy becomes more pronounced later in the Magdalenian; the early bâton from Le Placard is rather large and feels like a club when in hand.[3]

The bâton has the head of a smiling fox sculpted at one end. On one side there is a sculpted ear, on the other side the ridge of the large hole *seems* to serve as the ear. The bâton is marked by groups of series of marks on each side and along the bottom, or belly. The meaning of these marks, like the purpose or purposes of the bâtons, has remained unknown.

The Abbé Breuil illustrated the marks as simple series of linear scratches, undifferentiated except by size and placement. The microscope, however, reveals an unexpected complexity. The marks seem to have been made by at least 25 different points. At two places, where the bâton had been broken and glued, the microscope revealed the presence of marks beneath the glue. These are presented as dotted lines (Fig. 19 a, b, c).

The reconstruction, based on microscopic analysis, seems to prove that this bâton, whatever its original or primary purpose, was marked with a notation. Is it lunar? Since the sculpted head is "realistic," are the marks in the ear intended to represent hair? On the other face, do the marks along the ridge represent hair? The engraved art of the Upper Paleolithic is often quiet realistic, with hair and fur clearly indicated. Is this a crude attempt at realism?

*A. Marshack, "Upper Palaeolithic engraved pieces in the British Museum. BRITISH MUSEUM QUARTERLY. 35 (1–4):137–145.

[2] Graziosi, op. cit., p. 40.

[3] Microscopic analysis by the author over a period of five years has documented the fact that some bâtons were put to frequent heavy use, that others show none, that some were heavily decorated or marked notationally or symbolically, that others had no markings. The documentation and significance of these findings will be presented later. At this stage I had only the two marked bâtons described in this chapter.

We have seen that the Upper Paleolithic engraver uses visual kinesthetic aids for separating his notational groups. Let us, therefore, test the possibility that the marks were placed where they were, in this case, for notational purposes and lay the groups sequentially against a lunar model. We begin with side number one, holding the bâton in the left hand with the hole to the left and reading from right to left, including the marks around the hole. Still holding the bâton in the left hand, we give it a quarter turn and continue reading along the belly, again right to left. After finishing the bottom, the bâton is turned so that the head is not upside down but faces to the right, and we continue reading again right to left (Fig. 20).

The result is an extremely close lunar tally. Each change of point, stroke, or grouping, and each change to a new side, occurs at a visible lunar phase. The apparent exceptions occur where there are so many changes of point that a long lunar phase is impossible.

There is a high probability, then, that here is one more example of a visual and kinesthetic system of lunar notation and differentiation. The full notation covers a bit more than four months and therefore includes the beginnings of at least two major "seasons."

Two early theories assumed that these bâtons were used either for softening leather thongs which were run back and forth through the hole, or for bending and straightening shafts. Some bâton holes do show friction wear, yet others are too fragile for rough use and some with many holes seem too complex. Let us pause, then, for some observations and questions.

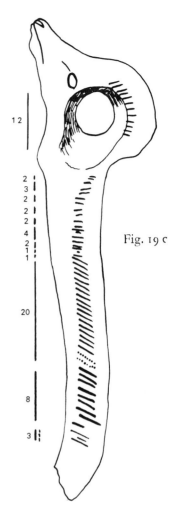

Fig. 19 c

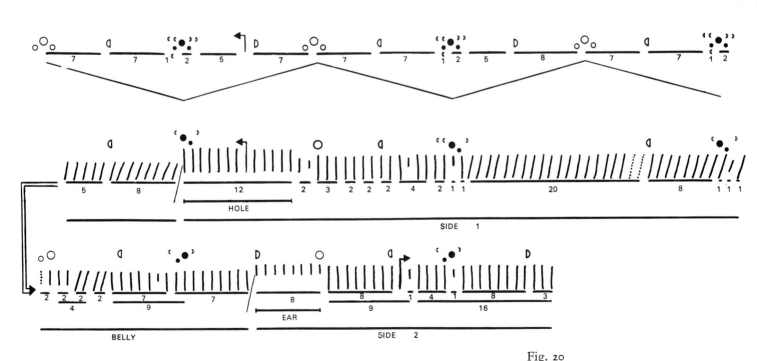

Fig. 20
The engraved marks on the three sides of the Placard bâton laid sequentially against a lunar model, indicating the possible lunar phrasing.

The plaques from Blanchard and Lartet may, as a result of our analysis, seem to be non-utilitarian slates intended primarily for notation. However, microscopic analysis of the hand polish and the pressure wear on

Fig. 22 b
Detail. Enlargement of the middle portion of the first "form" at extreme right of the Le Placard bâton, Fig. 22 a, indicating the intentional structuring of two almost parallel lines met by a third at an angle. At right are three faint parallel lines and an angle engraved at a still sharper angle. All marks in this figure are made by the same sharp point. See full form on page 93.

these objects indicates that they were also used for some practical purpose. The bone from Blanchard shows considerable hand polish along the back edge and the edges of the rear wider half. The edge notches in these areas are all rounded by hand wear. Yet the narrower front half of the bone shows no polish along the edges, indicating that the plaque was held firmly but was not used as a knife or polisher. The point is broken back by pressure as though the bone had been used as a fine retouch pressure flaker for chipped stone tools. This plaque had been used as a tool over a considerable period, indicating the possibility of slow accumulation for the notations. In contrast, I have found that other utilitarian plaques were intentionally broken when their use was ended to turn them into notational slates. Scraps of bone such as the Taï fragment had also been picked up or shaped for notational purposes. We find, then, a complex tradition in which tools and slates reveal a practical and a symbolic sense of coming of time, as well as varied techniques either for utilizing or making notational slates and marking off units of time.

This cognitive aspect of notation may not seem different from the practical intelligence involved in the understanding that the coming cold of winter required warm furs and that these must be ready before the first frost and snows. Nevertheless, it is different, since time is here *symbolized,* abstractly and cumulatively.

Why were tools used as slates and bones fashioned for that purpose? Could not the marks have been more easily scratched on a wooden stick? It is possible that wooden tally sticks were used, but, if so, they are lost. Fortunately, the Upper Paleolithic cultures made extensive use of stone and bone, and these last. Later, when the ice melts and the herds grow scarce, when the climate changes and the forests take over, wood begins to be used more and more. Engraved bones become scarce, and the evidence for tallying also becomes sparse except in areas where bone or amber were worked. Upper Paleolithic records may also have been kept on painted skins, with knotted thongs, or by an accumulation of pebbles or seeds, and again the evidence would be gone.

The fact is that bone has certain advantages. A bone slate is small and long-lasting, it can take an exceedingly fine scratching better than wood. Being relatively small, a bone slate can be carried in pocket or pouch more easily than one carries a large wooden stick, and in a culture of high mobility, where a man could not carry too many belongings, the small slate would be the more practical. Besides, wood may not have been widely or readily available, while bones were accumulated in great heaps at most sites and acted as a permanent source of scrap material.

Since the problem of portability exists in a hunting culture, the man who was carrying a bâton either poked through a belt or hung on a thong through the hole, whether as a ritual or working object, might find it convenient and practical to make his notations on this slate that was with him daily. Or, if the bâton broke or its primary purpose was ended, he now had a clean bone surface at hand that could serve as a slate. Such notations on a bâton would then be either related or unrelated to the primary purpose of the bâton. We cannot as yet tell which. Or were there ceremonial and practical bâtons, as there are in later periods ceremonial and non-ceremonial knives, axes, daggers, vases, and wagons? Earlier we saw the Mesolithic tool from Ishango, with a quartz engraving tip, that had been used for notation. Was there a connection between the uses of that tool and the notation?

If, apart from any practical uses, a bâton was also a ritual object, it may have been used by the shaman (priest) or chief, or by the head of a family group. In that case, the notations may have had ceremonial or administrative uses. But in a culture that counted "moons" there may also have been other persons keeping a notation for other purposes: perhaps for a voyage, visit, or march, or for a menstrual or pregnancy record, or for a private period of initiation. There might be differences, then, in the sort of notations kept.

Fig. 21
The main face of a broken bâton, 7 ¼ inches long, from Le Placard (Charente), containing sets of engraved marks. The head of the bâton is broken off. Middle Magdalenian.

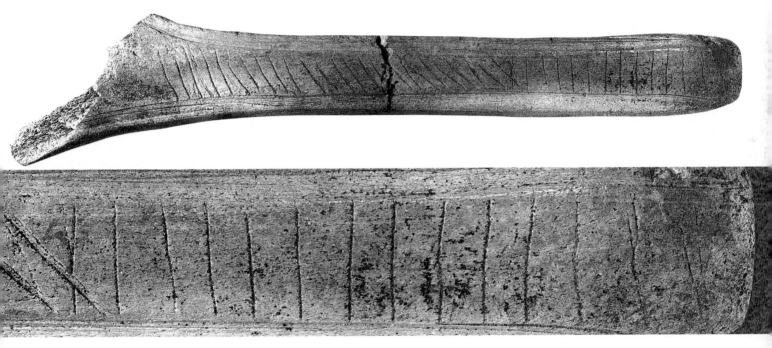

Fig. 22 a
Detail, bottom portion of the Le Placard bâton indicating the series of parallel marks that are preceded at right by "forms" engraved by other points. A series at left is engraved at an angle. (See Fig. 22 b opposite.)

In cabinet number one at the Musée des Antiquités Nationales, not far from the large bâton, lies a smaller, fragile, better-worked bit of bone, discolored a dead gray with time. It is the handle of a bâton, with the head and hole broken off, but with the arc of the hole visible at the break. It too comes from Le Placard, apparently from Magdalenian IV, and may be a few years, a few hundred years, or a thousand years later than the bâton with the head of a fox. Since it is a fragment, it has not been considered an important find. It is marked in what has been traditionally called decoration in a "geometric" style (Fig. 21).

The bâton has been worked to create four flattened sides, and on one of these there is a raised platform on which the markings were made. The handle itself is unbroken and the markings on it are complete. It is possible, then, that we have all the markings originally made.

Microscopic analysis of the main face (Fig. 22 a, b) revealed sets of parallel

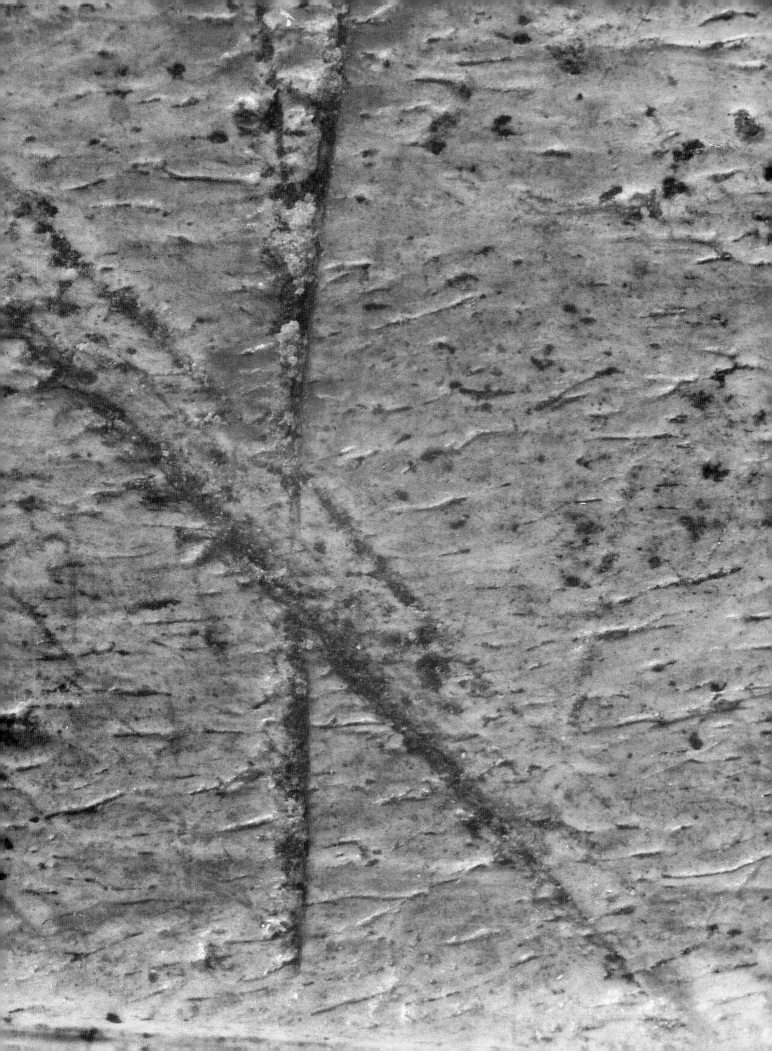

lines made by 10 different points, with groups that seem to contain "symbols" and "signs."

At one place a mark at the end of a series of 14 lines, all made by a sharp, thin point, is crossed over by another point that scratched a flat floor with two small points at each side ($\vee\!\!-\!\!\vee$) (Fig. 23). This broad stroke begins the next series. Since the broad stroke crosses over the fine stroke, it must have been made later, and the full sequence on this face begins at the right and reads to the left, toward the hole.

The sequence begins with an odd, delicately scratched sign, visible under the microscope (see Fig. 22 b):_____

It is composed of 9 strokes. This is followed by a somewhat curved "Y" of 2 strokes, made by another point:_____

This is followed by a series of 14 strokes, made by still another point; the last ends with 2 small appended strokes:_____

The next series, made by another point, has 1 appended stroke at the end. The full sequence on this face, with the counts by changes and differences of point, is shown in Figure 24. At the end of the series there are 10 strokes made by two points, in a 5 and 5 breakdown. Then, as though this fills out all the available notational space on this side of the bâton, *over* this, and between the last 5 long strokes, there are added 10 light strokes.

◄ Fig. 23
Detail, the main face of broken Placard bâton. The last mark of the series of 14 crossed over by the first mark of the series of 8, showing the differences in the points engraving each group. Also visible at the top is the fine mark appended at an angle.

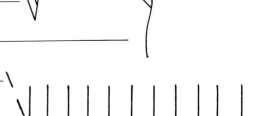

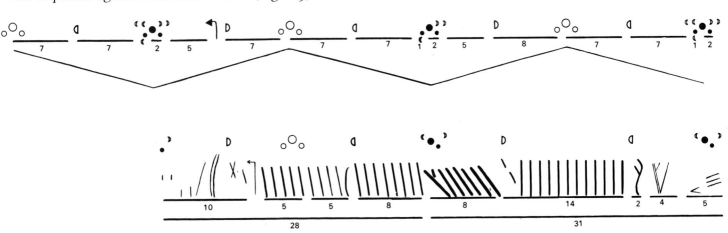

All the marks on this face are intentional. It is obvious that this odd sequence of figures, counts, and groups is not ornamental or decorative, and that it is notational. Is it lunar? Assuming one stroke per day, we lay the sequence against our lunar model (Fig. 25).

Fig. 24
Schematic rendition of the engraved marks on the main face of the Placard bâton fragment indicating the differences in the engraving points and the grouping, as determined by microscopic analysis.

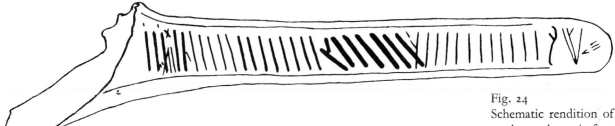

There is an absolutely perfect tally for 2 months, beginning at last crescent and ending on the first day of invisibility 58 days later.

We seem to have in this series a development of notational technique—

Fig. 25
The engraved marks on the main face of the Placard bâton against a lunar model, indicating the lunar phrasing of the sets.

recalling the accumulation of cueing marks of the Taï Plaque—in which seeming "signs" or multiple marks, made by appended strokes of arms and groups of angles, are used to indicate points of change in lunar phase. How are they used? The lunar model reveals that on the day of an expected lunar observation around a phase point a small stroke is used, as though an observation of the moon was impossible on that day and the stroke represented a day of waiting. On the next clear day of observation the new series begins with a different stroking. Interesting also is the indication of a notational significance for the "quarter" moon, the visible half-moon. None of this is difficult to understand. It is once more a visual notational technique. It is non-arithmetical and it is cumulative. Remember also that this bâton was engraved some 5,000 years before agriculture formally "began" in the Fertile Crescent of the Middle East and some 10,000 years before the formal "beginning" of writing.

On the reverse face of this bâton, scratched so faintly that even when held in hand most of the markings are invisible, yet clear under the microscope, is another unusual composition (Fig. 26). Once more there is certainty of notation, apparently for two lunar months. The lines, however, are so faintly scratched that a ballistic determination of point differences is difficult, and some exceedingly faint lines are difficult to prove.

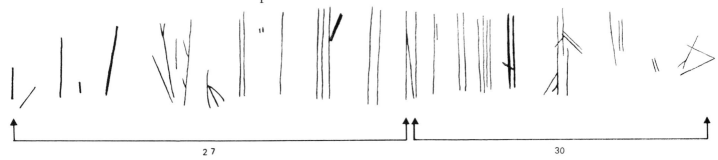

27   30

Fig. 26
Schematic rendition of the faintly engraved lines on the reverse face of the Placard bâton fragment indicating the intentional grouping of marks, as nearly as could be determined by microscopic analysis.

This Magdalenian IV bâton reveals a further stage in the development of the notational technique and a possible development in the care and precision of lunar observation and use.

A third style of marking, a development of that style of parallel stroking overengraved to make a crosshatching, occurs along one side of this bâton. It, too, gives a sum for two months.

These Le Placard bâtons prepare us for the complex "geometric" compositions of Magdalenian V and VI that end the Ice Age. Before proceeding to these, however, we should turn back to the period that comes between the Aurignacian-Perigordian cultures and the Magdalenian—the strange, instrusive Solutrean.

The Aurignacian and Perigordian, though roughly contemporaneous, are called different cultures on the basis of their tool kits and projectile points. Some Perigordian tools hint at a connection with the earlier Mousterian cultures of Europe or North Africa, while the Aurignacian styles may have come from the east. Eventually they mixed, while still other later styles seem to have come in from the east (Gravettian).

About 21,000 years ago, during a period of great cold, the layers of soil in the Dordogne region of France reveal what seems to be a sudden "disappearance" of these Aurignacian and Perigordian cultures. There then appears, in the levels above, a "new culture." It was discovered first in the Vézère valley near Les Eyzies, at the site of Laugerie Haute, by Lartet and Christy, but it is called the Solutrean for a dig at Solutré, further east in France, toward the Rhône and Alpine foothills. The culture itself extended down to Spain. At that time an ice sheet covered the Alps not far from Solutré, and much of England, Ireland, and northern Europe was under the great continental ice sheet.

Who were the people of this "new" culture? Were they invaders? Or did they represent a *technical* revolution created by the older cultures under influence of the new conditions? Or had a new set of ideas entered Europe? Suddenly in the layers there are exquisitely chipped flints, particularly projectile points. The rest of the tool kit remains the basic one of the earlier period. At Laugerie Haute, for instance, the Aurignacian ends; there is a blank layer of soil indicating a period of extreme cold when the valley was perhaps unoccupied and then a thin layer with early or proto-Solutrean tools. It is as though a people carrying the beginning of a new culture had entered briefly and passed through the valley.

Some 2,000 years later, about 18,700 B.C. (Carbon 14 dating), the true Solutrean is already in the Vézère valley. Layer by layer one can follow the development of the tool styles. The exquisitely retouched flints become more abundant, the flint work becomes at times experimental and virtuoso. Philip Smith, a student of the Solutrean, has written:

"Some [flints] have such thin cross sections . . . it is difficult to imagine how they could have served any utilitarian purpose. Indeed, they may have been show-pieces and luxury items."[4]

In late levels such decorative "tools" make up almost fifty percent of the flints.

The slow development of these tool styles hints at a local growth for the culture, though an impetus may have come from as far east as Hungary. Toward the end of this period the first bone needles with eyes or holes for thread appear in the layers. The simple, tiny needle may seem a minor tool, but it may have had large cultural significance as a "time-factoring" tool, perhaps indicating a more skilled, varied industry for preparing skins and furs for the *future*—possibly fitted clothes, tents, vessels, and infant cradles—to be used during the bitter winter snows, or during the spring and summer migrations and movements. Leathers and furs, in order to be sewn and worn, must be dried, treated, and worked into soft-ness, and the whole, from killing to stretching to softening to making of needles and sewing, may indicate a complex activity over many months,

[4] Philip E. L. Smith, "The Solutrean Culture," SCIENTIFIC AMERICAN, Vol. 211 (August 1964), p. 90.

Fig. 27
(Pages following.) A chart of the sequence and approximate chronology of the Upper Paleolithic "cultures" of Europe. The names are based on regional tool styles or on the archaeological site or region in which these tools were first found. They do not refer to "culture" in the sense of clearly defined social or symbolic variation.

Of necessity the names and the chronology are based on the current stage of research. It is probable that these cultures had a range of mobility and dispersal which allowed for the diffusion and infusion of technical as well as symbolic influences.

Presented at the bottom are selected examples of Upper Paleolithic and later Mesolithic notation or marking in various styles. These examples, covering a range of some 25,000 years, are more fully illustrated and discussed in the book.

The climatic graph depicts the approximate temperature variations within the Dordogne region of France, one of the centers of European tool and symbol development during the Ice Age. It is based on soil analyses conducted by Henri Laville of the Laboratory of Pleistocene Geology and Prehistory, the University of Bordeaux.

Fig. 28
(Pages 98–99.) Map of Europe indicating the maximum extension of the ice during the Upper Paleolithic. Also shown are the approximate extensions of the coast lines due to the lowered seas. Archaeological sites and painted caves are clustered in certain coastal or river valley regions. See appendix for site names.

CHRONOLOGY:

APPROXIMATE
TEMPERATURE
VARIATIONS
(DORDOGNE,
FRANCE)

DATE B.P.

COLD

WARM

EUROPEAN
"CULTURES"
BY REGIONAL
TOOL STYLES

EAST	SOVIET UNION
CENTRAL	CZECHOSLOVAKIA
	GERMANY
FRANCO-CANTABRIAN	FRANCE (DORDOGNE)
	NORTHWEST SPAIN
MEDI-TERRANEAN	EASTERN SPAIN
	ITALY

FRANCO-CANTABRIAN

MOUSTERIAN COMPLEXES

EARLY UPPER PALEOLITHIC (SJELETIAN...ETC
AURIGNACOID-OLSCHEWIAN TRADITIONS

AURIGNACOID TRADITIONS

MOUSTEROID   AURIGNACIAN

AURIGNACIAN
BASAL   INTER-
EARLY   MEDIATE   EVOLVED

(CHATELPERRONIAN)
PERIGORDIAN   I   II

AURIGNACIAN

AURIGNACIAN

LA FERRASSIE

BLANCHARD

LARTE

NOTATIONS:

OTHER

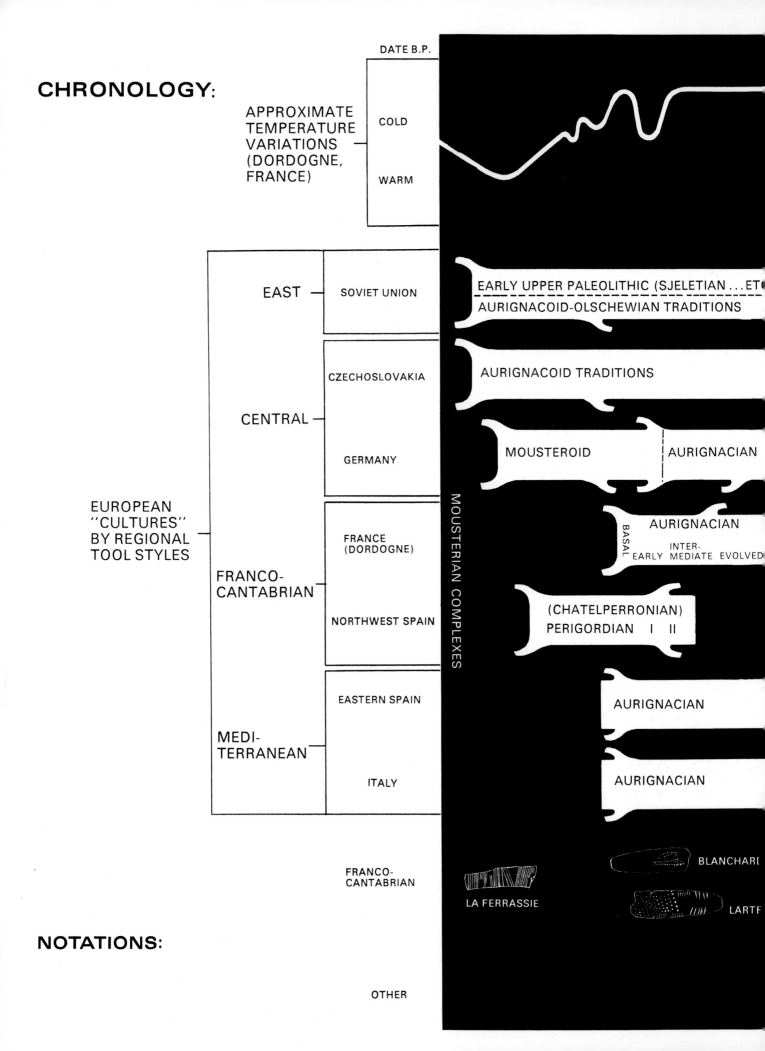

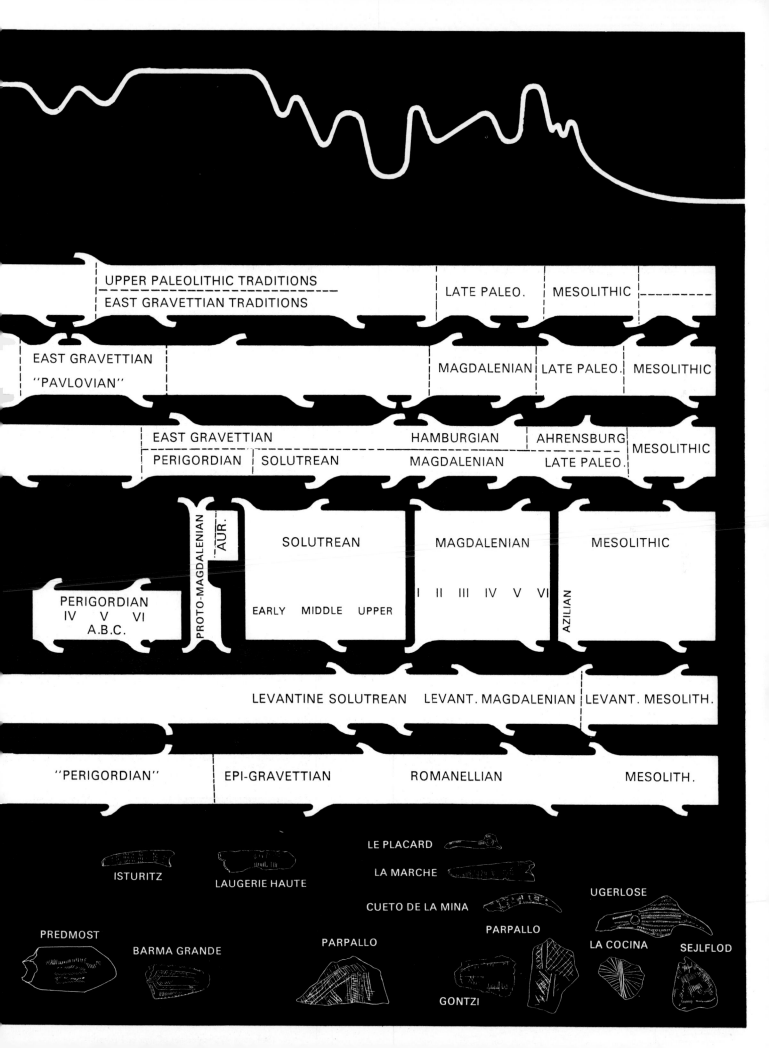

UPPER PALEOLITHIC TRADITIONS

EAST GRAVETTIAN TRADITIONS

LATE PALEO. MESOLITHIC

EAST GRAVETTIAN

"PAVLOVIAN"

MAGDALENIAN LATE PALEO. MESOLITHIC

EAST GRAVETTIAN HAMBURGIAN AHRENSBURG

MESOLITHIC

PERIGORDIAN SOLUTREAN MAGDALENIAN LATE PALEO.

PROTO-MAGDALENIAN

AUR.

SOLUTREAN

MAGDALENIAN

MESOLITHIC

PERIGORDIAN
IV   V   VI
A.B.C.

EARLY   MIDDLE   UPPER

I II III IV V VI

AZILIAN

LEVANTINE SOLUTREAN   LEVANT. MAGDALENIAN LEVANT. MESOLITH.

"PERIGORDIAN"   EPI-GRAVETTIAN   ROMANELLIAN   MESOLITH.

LE PLACARD

LA MARCHE

ISTURITZ

LAUGERIE HAUTE

CUETO DE LA MINA

UGERLOSE

PARPALLO

PREDMOST

BARMA GRANDE

PARPALLO

PARPALLO

LA COCINA   SEJLFLOD

GONTZI

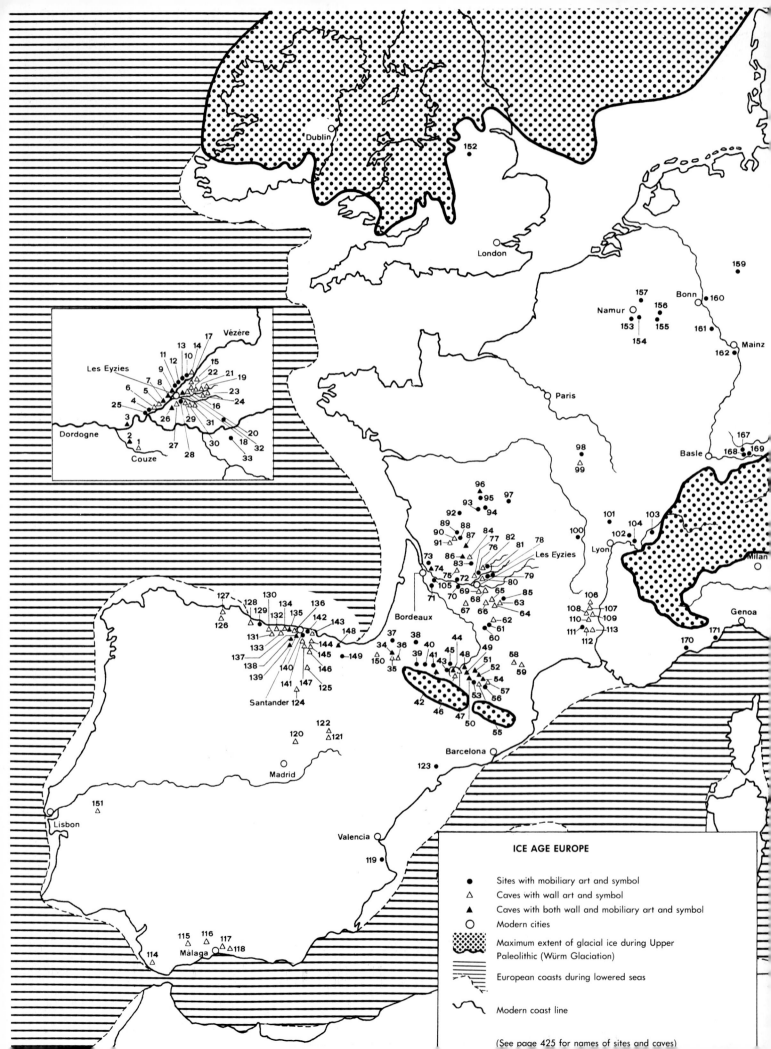

ICE AGE EUROPE

- ● Sites with mobiliary art and symbol
- △ Caves with wall art and symbol
- ▲ Caves with both wall and mobiliary art and symbol
- ○ Modern cities
- ▨ Maximum extent of glacial ice during Upper Paleolithic (Würm Glaciation)
- ▤ European coasts during lowered seas
- ⌣ Modern coast line

(See page 425 for names of sites and caves)

Berlin

Warsaw

197

196

Desna

198

Seym

199 Lipeck

200 Siberia

Voronezh

201

Don

195

Kiev

194

Prague

192

193

187 188

186

Brno 185

189

163

Munich

183

184

Vienna

191

Odessa

Budapest

190

174 Venice

Belgrade

173

175

176

Rome

177

178

180

179

202

182

203

181

Palermo

with a knowledge of how many pieces must be sewn, with what furs from what animals, and by what season or "moon." The needle was an advance in technique, but the process may have begun long before with the borer, piercer, and awl, and with a cruder tying by thongs instead of thread.

Toward the end of the Solutrean the climate grew mild and the herds of cold-weather animals of the tundra, the source of food and skins, probably lessened or moved north, forcing a change in the culture and density of the Solutrean hunters. The late Solutrean sites are now smaller and contain fewer tools. Then suddenly the climate changed again and grew bitterly cold, and the Solutrean culture this time "disappeared." At some digs there is a blank layer of soil lying over the Solutrean before the next cultural phase appears. When it does, this "new culture," the early Magdalenian, is using the eyed bone needle developed earlier.

Fig. 29
Non-utilitarian fragment of bone from Laugerie Haute (Dordogne) with four sets of engraved marks. Solutrean.

Fig. 30 a, b
Detail and schematic rendition of the engraved marks on the Laugerie Haute fragment indicating the differences in the points doing the engraving and in the spacing, rhythm and grouping of the sets, as determined by microscopic analysis.

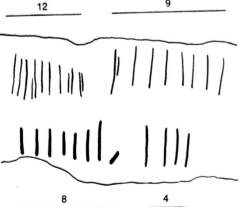

The full Solutrean covers some 4,000 years (Fig. 27). While it lasted. the hunters of the Solutrean culture were in motion, either following the herbivore herds seasonally or by long-range colonization and immigration. They spilled over the Pyrenees into Spain and down to the southern coasts of the Mediterranean facing Africa, and went north into central France (Fig. 28). They lived in rock shelters and caves when these were available, but in open campsites when they were not.

This is the limited, unsatisfactory story presented by the evidence of the sites, the tools, and the refuse. What about markings on bone and stone from this period? Do they reveal a cultural continuity with earlier, and perhaps later, Upper Paleolithic peoples?

A small bone fragment from the Solutrean comes from Lartet and Christy's dig at Laugerie Haute and looks like a bit of scrap bone that was picked up from the rubble heap to be used as a slate. It is marked with a complete, unbroken notation: four simple groups of marks, each made by a different point, and each group separated visually by spacing and rhythm of marking (Figs. 29, 30 a, b).

The breakdown and count are simple. A test conjunction with the lunar model gives us a sequence that, in our reading. begins with the last crescent and ends a month later on a day of invisibility:

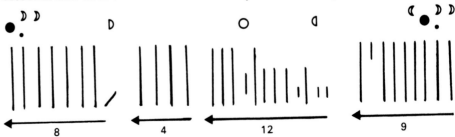

This is the basic Upper Paleolithic style, and it occurs on a non-utilitarian fragment. From a Solutrean site some two or three days' walk north from Laugerie Haute, at the dig of Fourneau du Diable ("The Devil's Furnace") comes another non-utilitarian slate, a bit of bone from a bird or small animal that contains two unbroken sequences (Fig. 31 a, b). The breakdown by point differences and the count give us two hunter "moons" or months (Fig. 32 a, b) and the conjunction with the lunar model reveals another accurate observational lunar phrasing (chart, Fig. 32 c).

Fig. 31 a, b
Non-utilitarian bone (engraved on two sides) from the site of Fourneau du Diable. Solutrean.

Fig. 32 a, b
Schematic rendition of the engraved marks on the bone from Fourneau du Diable indicating the sets, as determined by microscopic analysis.

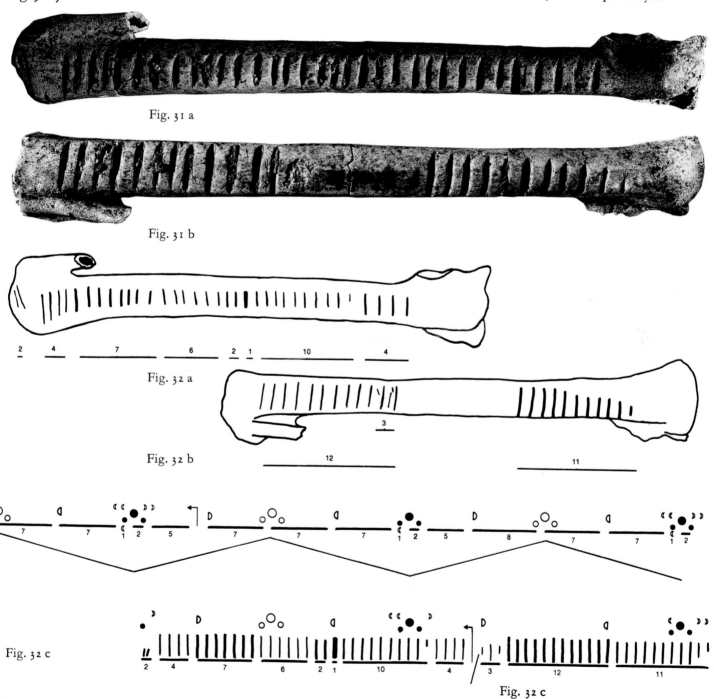

Fig. 31 a

Fig. 31 b

Fig. 32 a

Fig. 32 b

Fig. 32 c

Fig. 32 c
The engraved marks on the bone from Fourneau du Diable against the lunar model, indicating the possible lunar phrasing.

These are simple linear notations. There are many examples of more complex techniques. A fragment from the foothills of the Basses Pyrénées in southwest France, perhaps a week's walk from Laugerie Haute

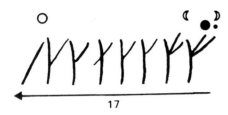

17

Fig. 33 a, b ▶
The two faces of an engraved and marked limestone from the site of Parpallo, eastern Spain. Face (a) is engraved by a sharp chipped point, face (b) is marked by a rounded pebble. Solutrean.

and the Vézère, contains a number of simple linear sequences, as well as this separate grouping. This sequence from the site of Isturitz recalls the earlier Perigordian and the later Magdalenian notations.

Crossing over the Pyrenees from France and going south along the Mediterranean coast of eastern Spain, one finds Ice Age art as far as the southern coast, within sight of Africa across the sea. One of the major sites for a study of the variability in Ice Age imagery occurs midway down the eastern coast of Spain at the cave of Parpallo, the district of Valencia, in the hills about five miles inland from the Mediterranean.[5] More than 1,000 engraved and painted limestone slates, made over thousands of years, were found in the cave, ranging from tiny flat plaques the size of a large coin to large, heavy slabs of rock. Some were so lightly engraved that one can see the lines only in a certain angle of light. The plaques go from the Aurignacian through the Solutrean and early and Middle Magdalenian. There is a symbolic continuity not only in the use of limestone in preference to bone (there were no huge herds of reindeer, bison, mammoth in this region), but in the making of "geometric compositions" no two of which are alike. The compositions represent a tradition that continued in this region past the Ice Age, into the Mesolithic and Neolithic. There are occasional animal images: deer, wild cattle, horses, lions. But the most common images are accumulations of band motifs and interconnected serpentine forms. These marked fragments of limestone were neither useful, beautiful nor decorative, yet the tradition continued for thousands of years. Collections of incised stones occur at other sites, in France at La Marche, Limeuil, Enlène, and in Germany at Gönnersdorf, but these usually contain human or animal images, whereas at Parpallo and other Mediterranean sites "geometric" compositions predominate.

This east Spanish culture had contact with the northern Franco-Cantabrian cultures; however, the major influence seems to have involved ideas coming along the Mediterranean coast from Italy to southern Spain and even crossing the narrow span of the Mediterranean to North Africa. Aspects of a geometric style occur in other parts of Ice Age Europe, and are also found in the decorated caves, but it is most common along the Mediterranean coast. The "geometric" tradition does not change greatly but develops local styles that continued in Spain and Italy into the Mesolithic and Neolithic (see Chapter XIV, "The Step Toward History"). The accumulation of these geometric images posed one of the crucial challenges to the notational hypothesis.

At first, the evidence for cumulative or periodic marking on these stones seemed to suggest that they were "notational," but a ten year study of the Ice Age and Mesolithic symboling traditions across Europe, from Spain

[5]Luis Pericot García, LA CUEVA DEL PARPALLO (Gandía). Excavaciones del servicio de Investigación Prehistórica de la Excma. Diputación Provincial de Valencia (Madrid: Consejo Superior de Investigaciones Científicas Instituto Diego Velázquez, 1942).

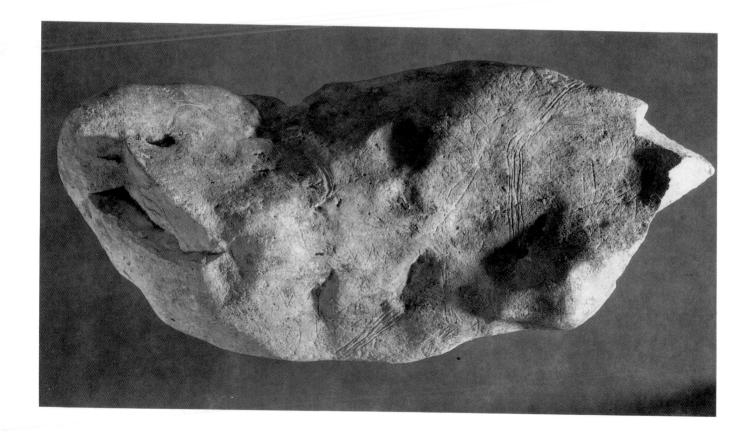

Fig. 34 a, b
Schematic rendition of all the intentional marks on the two faces of the limestone from Parpallo indicating the sets, the overengraving and the division of each surface into sequential areas of marking, as determined by microscopic analysis.

and Italy to Germany, Scandinavia and the Russian plain, revealed dozens of symbolic marking and accumulation systems. These traditions involved the periodic, ritual marking and accumulation of motifs, rather than notations. It seemed as though the act of marking a motif, or of

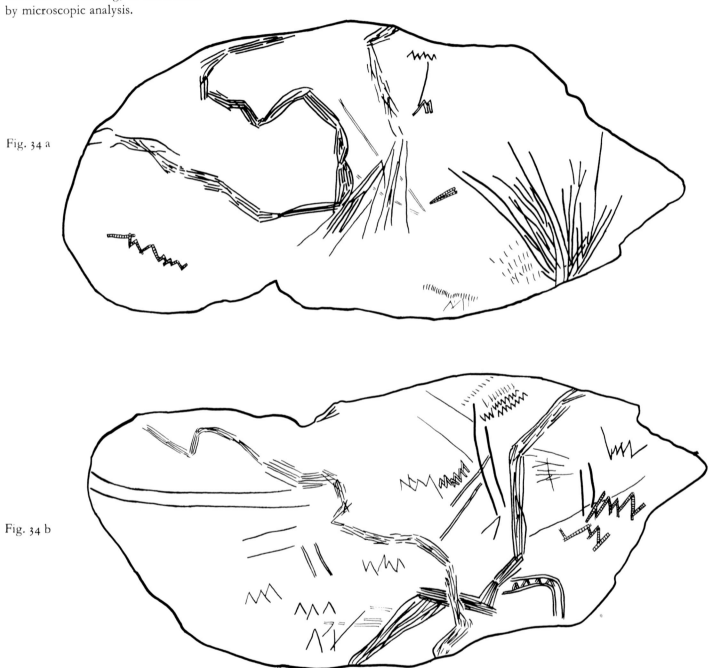

Fig. 34 a

Fig. 34 b

accumulating motifs over time, was itself a symbolic behavior as they were apparently made at the proper place and time and for the proper purpose. This unexpected "time-factored" and locational symbolic behavior provided a new, significant insight to the concepts first presented in this book. The process of periodic symbolic marking itself had, of course, been documented in my early paper (1969) and my papers on the use of animal images (1970 a,b) (see p. 19). But the accumulation of abstract, non-figurative motifs at certain sites and times added a complexity to the use of image and symbol in the Ice Age that had never been noted.

clear that the slate had been used to record or notate "something," for the compositions on each face had been structured sequentially, group by group. Microscopic analysis revealed that the groups were often composed of series of short lines that either crossed over and were contained by longer lines or were crossed over by these longer lines to conclude that group. (Fig. 34 a, b). Each such group formed a "set." There was no I found that accumulations of the zig-zag or serpentine "macaroni" motif occurred across all of Ice Age Europe in regional styles, usually on non-utilitarian and not easily portable fragments of stone, antler or ivory. This contrasted with the easily portable or curated objects of bone that were used for notation. These geometric motifs, often accumulated in

Fig. 35
The engraved and marked lines on the two faces of the Parpallo lime-stone against the lunar model, indicating the possible lunar phrasing.

Fig. 36 a, b ▶
The two faces of a broken, engraved bâton made of antler from the site of Isturitz (Basses-Pyrénées). Upper Perigordian.

Fig. 35. Preceding page.

Fig. 37 ▶
Schematic rendition of the engraved marks on the first face of the bâton from Isturitz indicating the sets and subsets and the probable differences in engraving points, as determined by microscopic analysis. The sequence of engraving is from right to left.

Fig. 39 ▶
Schematic rendition of the engraved marks on the second face of the broken bâton from Isturitz indicating the sets, subsets and forms and the probable differences in the engraving points, as determined by microscopic analysis. The direction of engraving is varied, the composition totally different from the first face, and the sequence, therefore, is undetermined.

large numbers at a site, may have represented a *seasonal* form of ritual marking at these sites. They may, therefore, have been indirectly related to the notations, which represented a different and more specialized type of "time-factored" symboling behavior.

Microscopic analysis of a heavy oval limestone block (10 ⅜ inches long; 26.5 cm) from the Upper Paleolithic site of Romanelli, Italy, documents one mode of accumulating the serpentine/zigzag "macaroni" motif (Fig. 33 a,b and 34a,b).* Two serpentine bands were begun at different times, one on the upper and one on the lower edge, by incising a "comet" from which there then flowed a twisting riverine ribbon constructed of short appended sections that wrapped itself around the stone. Each ribbon began on the first face, but wrapped itself around the stone to return to that face. After they were made, the zigzag/band motifs were repeated a number of times in extremely abstracted form as simple zigzags and empty double lines. I have suggested that these motifs represent a water-related symbolism and a form of seasonal ritual marking found primarily at particular riverside, waterside sites. Within the concept of a "time-factored" economic and symbolic culture, this mode of periodic motif marking, like the periodic marking of notations and the periodic use of animal images, suggests a culture which often was producing not "art" but symbols related to different aspects of the processual, temporal and spatial complexity found in Upper Paleolithic of Europe.

I close this chapter with an example from the Perigordian.

From the Basses-Pyrénées site of Isturitz in southern France, whose sequence we saw above, there comes an engraved bone, perhaps deer antler. It resembles those Magdalenian bâtons of later periods which have a hole or holes and which, as was discussed, are often too fragile to have been subjected to hard use. The practical and possible symbolic uses of these bâtons have been the subject of much theorizing, as have the decorated "daggers" of the Solutrean mentioned above. The remnant arc of the typical bâton hole is present at the thick end of this Perigordian example (Fig. 36 a, b).

The microscope revealed that the bâton has two clearly differentiated faces, each of which is engraved with a composition in a different pattern, as though each was intended to serve as a separate slate.

*Marshack, A. "Exploring the mind of Ice Age Man." (1975)
Marshack, A. "Aspects of style versus usage in the analysis and interpretation of Upper Paleolithic images." (1976)

Marshack, A. "The meander as a system: The analysis and recognition of iconographic units in Upper Palaeolithic compositions." (1977)

The bone is round and the marks on face number one are made not horizontally along the length of the bone but vertically in bands that recall the earlier vertical dot series on the plaque from the Gorge d'Enfer. On this face there are eight groups of marks made by nine different points (Fig. 37). The notations on this face go slightly around the bone at top and bottom, as illustrated. Only one sequence goes around the bone in a circle, the last group near the tip, as though being at the narrow end it

Fig. 36 a

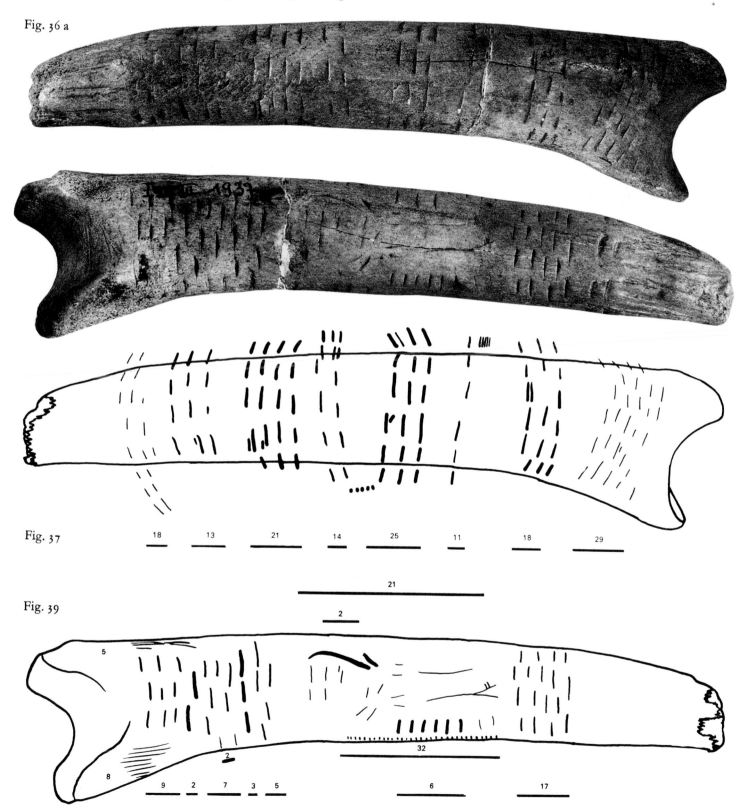

Fig. 37

| 18 | 13 | 21 | 14 | 25 | 11 | 18 | 29 |

Fig. 39

needed more space. The count for this face is precisely five months. Against the lunar model, reading from right to left, the sequence gives a relatively close lunar tally (Fig. 38). What we seem to have is a non-arithmetic, visual-kinesthetic accumulation composed of subgroups whose counts never go beyond eight, organized into larger groups which

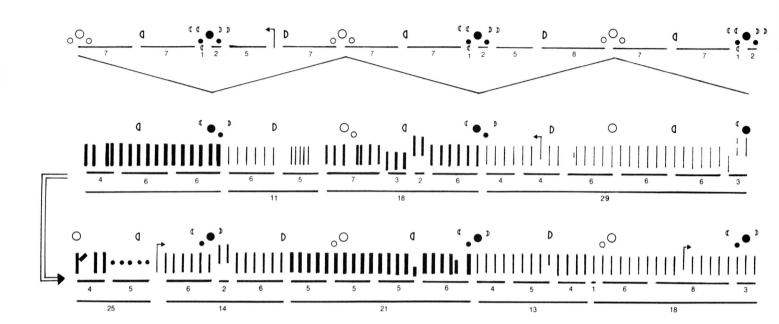

Fig. 38
The engraved marks on the first face of the Isturitz bâton against the lunar model indicating the possible lunar phrasing.

Fig. 39. Preceding page.

may have offered the intended "sums," since they give the more consistent evidence of an observational lunar phrasing. There is therefore the hint that it was the long period rather than the shorter subgroup that was the culturally significant element. Such accumulations could have been used in a hunting, migratory, ritual, or pregnancy context.

The reverse face of the round bone contains a complex notation, made by some eleven to twelve different points in a number of different styles of marking (Fig. 39). It includes one extremely faint horizontal linear series of small marks and a number of vertical series. It also includes what looks like a number of random markings, but two, by comparison with other forms found in the Upper Paleolithic of France, are probably intentional and may represent the horn and ear of an ibex. The total on this face is four months, though the sequence in which the groups were made is uncertain, and a conjunction with the lunar model therefore equally uncertain.

The archaeological materials excavated from Perigordian layers include a great variety of notational styles, all similar to styles we have already seen.

If these analyses and interpretations are correct, then there was a common, basic tradition of notation in all the European Upper Paleolithic cultures, and this notation was cumulative, "time-factored," and possibly lunar.

CHAPTER VIII

TIME-FACTORED THOUGHT

From the Russian steppe and tundra westward to the Atlantic and south to the foothills of the Pyrenees, over the mountains and along the warm seacoasts of Spain and Italy, the hunting cultures of the Ice Age have left evidence of notation. These scratched and engraved bits of bone and stone, dug from the soil layers of all periods of the Upper Paleolithic, roughly 35,000 to 10,000 years old and contemporary with the "birth of art," raise profound questions about the nature of evolved human cognition and intelligence and human culture and society. The questions are as important and difficult as those that were asked in mid-nineteenth century in the time of Darwin. The an-

swers, as we have seen, are only partly implied in the archaeological materials, and it is the evidence of notation that gives us clues of a new depth.

If, as was done often in the second half of the nineteenth century, we consider man during his evolution or hominization as basically a toolmaker, then it is relatively easy to trace a line of development in this toolmaking ability through the biological fossil evidence: the evolution of the grasping hand, the mobile thumb, the front-facing stereoscopic eyes, the small non-carnivorous teeth and the weakening jaw, the upright posture, the arched foot, and finally the enlarging skull holding an expanding convoluted brain, which supervised the increasingly complex muscular coordination of eye, hand, and foot.

The amount of information one can obtain from the excavated anatomical evidence—like the information deducible from the tools—while basic, is limited. Even within these limitations, there is sufficient new evidence to indicate that early concepts concerning toolmaking and hominization were wrong. The origin of humanoid toolmaking has been pushed back to a creature who was not yet human within any acceptable scale of brain size, and there is evidence that early hominids not on the line that led directly to modern man were also making tools. Other species and creatures have also evolved limited, specialized forms of toolmaking and use. In an earlier chapter we saw that the tool kits and habitation floors hint at a hominoid social and cultural complexity far back in the evolution towards man. It is probable, therefore, that the tool was only one aspect of a wider, cognitive, cultural evolution.

By the Mousterian period, Neanderthal man, for instance, was not only engaged in complex adaptations to his environment, but was also engaged in complex ceremony and rite. By the Upper Paleolithic, modern *Homo sapiens* was capable of representational art and notation. This combined late evidence would seem to indicate that quite early the evolving hominid must have had some means of communication or "language," a capacity and skill that evolved as part of the increasingly complex way of life and culture he was structuring. But how much language, and to say what at each stage, has not yet begun to be investigated. It was certainly more complex than can be deduced by analogy and from studies of the primates. In our efforts to understand the notations we must make the effort.

It was the first thought of prehistorians involved in the late nineteenth-century debate of science against the church that the newly discovered evidence of prehistoric art and ceremony revealed an evolution of man's "spiritual" and "religious" side, as opposed to his developing "practical" or "aggressive" side as indicated by the tools. This philosophic division of man into two or three parts was an attempt to save his unique "spiritual" place at the top of the ladder of creation. Man, the argument went, may have ascended biologically during his evolution, but once near the top he had been given, or he had achieved, a "soul." The debate took many forms and was argued within the church as well as within science.

Jacquetta Hawkes, in her summary of prehistory, states:

"The . . . weakness of archaeology as a proper basis for history is its helpless dependence on material remains and the resulting tendency to over-emphasize the first of these two great ways of human endeavor [the technical as opposed to the spiritual] . . ."[1]

Dissatisfaction with the limitations of the hard evidence was repeatedly expressed in the first half of the twentieth century, even while important evidence was being excavated. The most elaborate statement of man's "spiritual evolution" was developed by a co-worker of the Abbé Breuil, Father Teilhard de Chardin (1881–1955). Teilhard de Chardin, like the Abbé Breuil, was a scientist and a churchman, a Jesuit without a pulpit. An excellent geologist and archaeologist, he dug for early man in Europe, Africa, and Asia. He was part of the team that excavated at Choukoutien in China in 1932–1933 and made the important discovery of a fossil hominine midway on the road to modern man, the popularly known Peking Man or *Sinanthropus Pekinensis*, "Chinese Man of Peking." This early man was related in time and in his stage of evolution to Dubois' Java Man of South Asia and to the early Abbevillian (Chellean) man of Europe that Breuil was familiar with. Teilhard excavated some of his early tools.

But though Teilhard helped find some of the "hard evidence" related to man's evolution, his thinking and feeling went beyond the artifacts and fossils. As a Christian philosopher and a Western scientist, he tried to bridge the gap between evolutionary science and Catholicism. To do this, he conceived of all life and physical matter, and of time and evolution, as a spiritual drama which proceeded toward a predestined peak that was human and Christlike. He sought to bring cosmology, geology, archaeology, paleontology, and evolution, with their vast panoramas of time and process, in tune with the Catholic concept of man's "creation." This "creation" could no longer be considered sudden, as stated in the Bible, but now

[1] Hawkes and Woolley, op. cit., p. 106.

proceeded slowly and aspired towards the evolution of a spiritual creature with a "soul." Evolution, Teilhard wrote, had begun with physical matter and had gone beyond physical matter to thought and consciousness. Teilhard's ideas were fought by the Catholic Church during his lifetime, but since his death he has become an important figure in and out of the Church in the continuing debate over the "meaning of man."

We do not need such concepts in discussing man. If we think of man's cultural activities and thoughts as specialized products of the evolved brain and its processes, then we can, if we wish, label some of these products and processes as "practical," others "spiritual," or some as "intellectual," "cognitive," or "rational," and others as "emotional," "irrational," "instinctive," or "symbolic." But we must be clear that we are doing so primarily as an aid in the attempt to understand man's mind and as part of a continuing and expanding analysis. These words are generalizations representing abstract universals and classes. They are not descriptions of process, nor explanations of them. They are at most comparisons between certain forms of behavior, between products, patterns, or processes of brain function. While such comparisons are helpful, they are neither adequate descriptions of behavior nor adequate explanations of the processes involved in behavior. They are labels for patterns we can recognize, and they represent categories we have devised, none of which are yet adequately understood. In much the way that we can compare aspects of behavior, evolving tools and tool styles, developing art and art styles, changing styles of pots, baskets, temples, and graves, and man's symbols, myths, and kin relations, so we can compare any of the specialized products of the evolving human way of life. But in every case, we are dealing with a *comparison of products,* products of the brain and of the culture that brain is able to maintain in time. Yet these products are not man, nor do they define or describe him.

The specialist in the styles or forms of man's work is therefore a student of by-products of the human process. He is a student of the way in which these by-products compare, interrelate and change. Only by inference can they be referred to the brain and its processes, to thought and cognition. It should be clear, then, that when the archaeologist or anthropologist

excavates or accumulates material, classifies, categorizes, labels, cross-indexes, dates, compares, averages, and charts such products and draws inferences from the data, he is dealing—as he must—with selected, limited, remnant, and measurable products of the brain, with *aspects* of the human process.

Of course, this is all that the researcher into the origins of "man" often has to work with. The result is a tendency to take these products to be the meaning of the human process and to judge the quality or stage of a culture, or the intelligence of the man involved, by comparing and judging these cultural by-products. In archaeology there is also that limitation due to the stage of research and theory. We noted some of this in the history of prehistory. A new find raises new questions, and new questions almost always uncover a body of new, if limited, facts. But not only the hard data and the theories they engender are limited and specialized. Scientific terminology, which often seems to imply information, often as not indicates a lack of information. Words such as "art," "decoration," "tool industries" and "assemblages," "magic," "ritual," "mythological," or "symbolic" are used in anthropology and archaeology to classify or describe—but do not adequately define or explain—certain products or forms of behavior. Recognizing these inadequacies and limitations, we can now return to the archaeological evidence asking new questions about the making of man, trying to avoid old labels and classifications. I ask these new questions in terms of the evolving cognitive, time-factored and time-factoring capacities and potentialities of the human brain.

In the winter of 1930, Teilhard de Chardin visited the Abbé Breuil at his office in the Institut de Paléontologie Humaine in Paris. He handed Breuil a piece of blackened bone.
"What do you make of that?"
The Abbé examined it...
"It is a portion of a stag's antler."
Then, according to a reconstruction of the scene in the first published biography of Breuil,[2] the Abbé continued,
"It was, when still fresh, exposed to fire and it was worked with a crude stone implement, probably not of flint, some sort of primitive chopping tool."

[2] Brodrick, op. cit., p. 11.

"But that's impossible. It comes from Choukoutien," Teilhard said.

"I don't care where it comes from, it was fashioned by a man, and by a man who knew the use of fire."

The bit of antler had come from a site 35 miles southwest of Peking, China. Portions of an early "man's" skulls and bones had also been found at the site. In the early 1930's this man had not yet been adequately classified. From his skull, though, it was clear that he was earlier than either modern man or Neanderthal man. It was some years before it was realized that *Sinanthropus Pekinensis* lived more than 500,000 years ago, and that in the general stage of his biologic evolution he was related to Dubois' somewhat earlier Java Man of about 700,000 years ago and to the maker of the Abbevillian (Chellean) stone tools found in France and England, and that he was related also to the maker of the Chellean tools that the Leakeys found in Bed II at Olduvai Gorge, Tanganyika.

Peking Man was, therefore, an intermediary stage of early man, evolved beyond *Homo habilis* and spread across Eurasia and Africa. He had been dispersed long enough to have become "racially" diversified, that is, to show skeletal differences, though he may not have been divided into separate "species." Peking Man had a brain capacity of about 1,100 cc. (a range of 900 to 1,200 cc.) compared to the 745 cc. of the largest *Homo habilis* skull yet found in Africa and compared to the 1,400 cc. average modern human brain capacity (with a range of 1,010 to 2,000 cc.). Dubois' Java Man of 200,000 years before had a brain capacity of perhaps less than 900 cc., and an earlier example from Java was even more primitive. Discoveries in lower, earlier Chinese levels have uncovered the remains of a man with a brain smaller than that of Peking Man. A skull of Chellean man found by the Leakeys in Bed II of Olduvai Gorge and roughly of the same age as Peking Man had a capacity of about 1,000 cc., roughly that of Peking Man. This evolved man of the intermediary stage, who was approaching modern man, has been named, as a group, *Homo erectus*. Peking Man of Choukoutien is the example that has so far given us the richest site with the most revealing finds about his culture.

Not long after the Abbé Breuil looked at the burned stag horn, charcoal from a hearth or fireplace was found at Choukoutien in Peking Man's levels. This charcoal remains one of the earliest evidences for the use of fire.

Eventually chipped and flaked stone tools and bones apparently splintered to make points were found at Choukoutien. Also found were the skulls and occasional limb bones of some forty individuals, human bones, including those of fifteen children, evidently showing indications of cannibalism. Signs of heavy impact as of blows were on many skulls, and arm and leg bones were broken as though to get at the marrow. These few human bones lay with large numbers of animal bones, the remnants of far more regular meals.

On the basis of this evidence, we might make some assumptions.

We do not know when or where fire was discovered. By 500,000 B.C., however, it was part of Peking Man's culture. Since the climate in northeast China at the beginning of this period in the Middle Pleistocene was cool, fire may have been as important or as integral a part of that culture as the stone tools.

The demands of a fire culture are strict. While the lore of firemaking and of fire use might vary from one early culture to another and in different geographic areas, it can vary only within limits imposed by the necessities of making and maintaining a fire. We must assume, then, that the brain capable of maintaining a fire culture would be capable of learning that wet wood would not burn as well as dry, that most spring or summer wood with the sap flowing thick would probably not burn as quickly or as well as dead or winter wood, that scraping or cutting a branch in the spring could foul or gum the hand, that green grass or reeds do not burn as well as yellow or brown, that summer leafing wood smoulders, that the wood you wish to use that day must be kept out of the rain, that one does not stand close and downwind of heavy smoke, that the wood that cracks sharp in breaking burns best, that in the cold of winter fire serves most, that in the night it offers light and warmth and safety since most wild animals fear fire. Assuming a practical knowledge such as this as a minimum, we see that Peking Man—with or without a large use of language—had created a skill and lore that was time-factored and time-factoring, and that this lore and culture was almost entirely "artificial," that is, self-created and self-perpetuated, though it was based on processes in nature. It was bound by the necessities of fire maintenance and by the possibilities and limitations involved in human life in the mobile, shifting, periodic, seasonal, and daily reality.

Far more symbolically[3]—and, again, with or without a large use of language—fire is "alive." It must be tended; it needs a home and place out of the great winds, the heavy rains, the deep snows; it must be constantly fed; it sleeps in embers and can die, yet it can also be blown back to life by the breath; it can burn a hand; it sputters angrily and brightly with animal fat; it dies entirely in water; it whispers, hisses, or crackles, and therefore has a variable "voice"; it uses itself up, transforming a large weight of wood to gray ash, while climbing by smoke and savor to the sky, at last disappearing in the wind; one can carry its spirit or "life" on a burning branch or ember to make a second fire. To a man with fire, then, there is a continuous involvement in a complex, dynamic process which creates its varying, yet "artificial," demands, relations, comparisons, recognitions, and images.

More important, perhaps, fire ties one down in time and thought because of the constant requirements in maintaining it. These demands may have been greater at the beginnings of fire culture, particularly if early man used fire without an adequate skill in sparking or making it. In the old anthropological and archaeological concept, fire "freed" man to live in new climates and lands. But clearly, it also *bound* him strictly, culturally and functionally. Even if it freed the hunter temporarily, while the women and children were rooted safe around a fire, the group was bound in time and place.

Five hundred thousand years ago, then, by evidence of the charcoal in the hearths at Choukoutien, we can assume within limits of some certainty that the life of Peking Man was already structured in time, artificially and culturally, across long seasonal periods and within shorter diurnal periods.

Now, not all men on the Eurasian and African land mass may have been using fire. The evidence is still too sparse to tell. One way or another, for an understanding of evolving man, this would make no great difference since the use of fire is a question of cultural

specialization. For us the significant fact is that *Homo erectus* could *think in time* and *think of process* in ways and with a depth that were far beyond the capability of other creatures, and already beyond that of *Homo habilis*.

It was a clear foreshadowing of the more complex time-factoring and time-factored skills and relations to be found in the later Middle and Upper Paleolithic cultures, structured by Neanderthal man and *Homo sapiens* with larger brains. It foreshadowed the time-factored complexities of agriculture that would follow after the last ice had melted.

What we have, *comparatively,* is a huge leap from *Homo habilis, Kenyapithecus,* and the animal world. But it was not a *sudden* leap of the "spirit" or mind. The ability and the skill had evolved from that available to a smaller brain with less advanced skills and time-factoring potentials.

We do not know the extent of language involved in the fire culture of Choukoutien, nor specifically what portions of the brain had evolved to develop the language facility, but we *must* assume that there was communication at least adequate to maintain the lore and skill of fire.

In Peking Man, the fossil jaws show some of the skeletal parts, including the fossa, that seem to indicate the presence of muscles which are used in speech. But even without such evidence, whose significance is still being debated, we can assume a minimum communication. Peking Man may have had a sound, word, or gesture (or some combination of these) for "fire," and probably for "good-wood-burning" or "bad wood," and perhaps for the "approaching rain" or "snow," and perhaps even a general word indicating the death or absence of fire.

We must also assume that a child, during the Middle Pleistocene, growing up in the protection of a cave, shelter, or camp where fire was used, saw and learned what no other creature had ever seen or learned. The "imprint" of fire and of the fire relation was maintained through his lifetime. In this sense man was domesticating himself to his own self-created and artificial culture. This ability of the individual to adapt, within limits, to a new life situation, even an artificial one, belongs to most animals. In varying degrees it is one of the potentials of all life. One sees it later when

[3] Symbolic in the sense that the use of fire involved a cognitive, visual recognition and comparison of processes and relations.

man domesticates and trains animals, animals that could adapt to, but could not create or maintain, artificial cultures. The specific ability to create and maintain a continuous, dynamic, changing, and increasingly complex, time-factored, artificial culture is human. It belongs to the evolution of the brain.

For the *Homo erectus* child, fire became automatically part of his reality: part of his sense of time, his use of time, his sense of place and distance, his sense of direction around the center, his kinesthetic awareness of the differences between summer and winter, day and night, rain and no-rain. In some sense, too, fire must have become part of his subconscious imagery, an image in dream, an image below consciousness that meant warmth when he was away in the cold, an image of home and place. It was, then, a kinesthetic reference, a time reference, a geometric reference, and it could be all these without a large use of words.

In addition, the infant, and then the child, growing up in a camp where there was fire, would learn that the same adults that fed and tended him also fed and tended the fire, and he would probably sense that the fire was there before he was. If, when the men were at the hunt, it was the women who maintained the fire, it would have been easy to symbolize woman as the "mother who feeds" in terms that included the hearth and home fire. These are relational equations and recognitions; they are not grammatical or logical in terms either of explanation or language.

All this is assumption and, despite the implications of complexity, it is probably too simple. For *if* language was present, then fire would also be woven with story. If the hunting family was seasonally nomadic, the hearth at the winter cave shelter to which the group always returned may have had a different value or name or story than the temporary campfire, and there may have been a relighting ritual, or simply some effusion of laughter at return to the winter hearth. At this primitive level of possible "story," the details of cultural behavior or telling would probably vary from family to family and area to area far more than would the hard and necessary fire lore. But the details of such "stories" or behavior patterns are not important. What is important is the attempt we are making to deduce a level of potential and inherent capability at the *Homo erectus* stage of human evolution. For it would be out of this developing and widening capa-

bility—rather than out of a more basic animal inheritance of instinct and signal-response reaction, or out of manipulative skills for toolmaking—that modern man came.

Assuming this to be part of the developing, evolving process, we can conjecture that in the Middle Pleistocene, though not all groups may have been using fire, not all may have been living in caves, and not all may have had the same level of culture, they would all have been able to structure more or less equivalent kinesthetic and cognitive complexities in time and space.

The evidence is still sparse. Nevertheless, we can stay with the evidence. Take the stone tools, for example. At Choukoutien they are relatively crude. But the crudity is comparative, and the tools are far in advance of the earliest pebble tools at Olduvai Gorge, a million and a half years before. Archaeologists have excavated a few roughly broken pieces of quartz and a few crudely flaked pebbles. Yet what was excavated was a tool *kit,* with tools that could be used for different purposes, upon different materials, and therefore at different times. There were chopper-like cores, and flakes trimmed to points or scraper-like edges, and bones that had been fragmented to get points. The kit could be used variously on flesh, fur, skin, bone, and wood.

Most of the pebbles had come from the bed of a stream nearby, but faceted crystals of quartz found with the tools had come from granite hills some miles away, to the north and south.

We can make the assumption, therefore, that the pebbles from the stream bed, the quartz from the distant hills, and the wood for the fire (or the wood to make pokers, diggers, spears, all long since decayed), did not come from the same spots in the hunter's territory. They could not be gathered at the same time, or at the same time by the same individuals. The gathering of each would be specialized in time and place, and perhaps also by age and by a person's role in the family. There is the possibility at this early stage, then, of cultural and occupational specialization.

The lore and skill of making and using a tool is different from the lore and skill of fire. It requires a different kinesthetic knowledge and learning, a different sense of the potentiality of materials, a different sort of manipulative skill, and a knowledge, for instance, that the stone tool can be used in certain ways against bone, wood, or flesh.

Once again, these skills require an evolved level or capacity for kinesthetic and relational understanding, learning, and teaching, *with or without* a large use of words. This is the minimum that we must assume. But the cultural and cognitive complexity revealed by our analysis would seem to indicate also that by the time of Peking Man there must have been a range of communication adequate to maintain that cultural complexity.

It is necessary, then, to look a moment at this matter of language and communication. If, on the basis of the hard archaeological evidence, we are permitted our prior assumptions, we must now make others. Peking Man was not, as the popular image would have him, a mere hunter, crouched dumb around a fire, with an appetite for meat and sex and a propensity for cruelty and anger. He was a man with a working knowledge of time, place, and the direction and bounds of his effective territory, with a working knowledge of materials, and with some cultural specialization. He was, therefore, "sophisticated" in a near-human, or near-modern way.

Now, assume that into his valley a carnivore came, some feline, now old or wounded, a maverick, not belonging to the district or to any of the prides or family units whose habit and range were known in that valley. The lion or tiger may have killed an infant, or a woman gathering berries, or a youth gathering pebbles for tools at the stream, or even a hunter stalking a deer. Among the apes, such as the baboon, the presence of a carnivore is communicated by particular sounds and a specific and communicable anxiety, and the males assume a role of protecting the band. With Peking Man and his near-modern human brain we assume a greater skill in communication. If, for the moment, we assume that this communication was done at a minimum level of spoken language, we would get the gesture and perhaps the sound for "lion," some gesture or pantomime indicating that he was old or wounded and dangerous, that he had already killed "one of us," perhaps even indication that the victim had been a woman or child. Then the direction of the killing, or the track of the feline, or the lair would be pointed out. With these assumptions—and with a minimum of language—we already have

the beginning of story, related within what was a common lore, symbolism, and understanding, not only of lions, but of certain gestures and sounds, distances and directions.

Assume that within this communication it was also indicated that the lion had already fed and was not therefore at that moment dangerous. Not only have we been told about the past, but we are now being told about the immediate future. Assume also that it is gestured among the males, simply by pointing to the horizon or sky in the east, that tomorrow ("at dawn") they would hunt that particular lion.

None of this would seem beyond the scope of the maker of tools and fire. Somewhere along the line of evolution towards language and speech, and hominine culture, such communication became possible and necessary. A large portion of it, as we can see, could have been accomplished within a realm of understanding and communication that was basically mimetic and kinesthetic, based on non-verbal recognitions—even though elements of early speech may also have been used.

Assume now that the lion was killed, and the kill was carried home. There might be some indication or acknowledgment to the old and the women that it was a young male who had made the kill, his first. This might be indicated either in the young male's attitude and behavior, or in his having cut up and brought back some prime section of the lion, or by some other sort of miming. In this communication we would not only have the report of a past hunt, but also the report of a character development, a "growing-up." A new relationship to the young hunter would have been established by the telling.

So in this one assumed series of events and communications there is a time-factored and time-factoring use of *story* that is already distinctly human. It has all been done by communication at some distance from the two killings, and by performing, playing out, or communicating meanings related to the past, present, and future.

In the old archaeology and anthropology, based entirely on a strict interpretation of the bones and tools, such "storied" assumptions would have seemed gratuitous and unscientific. But given the possibility of an evolved and "storied" notation in the Upper Paleolithic, ceremony and ritual in the Mousterian period of Neanderthal man, and the clues to cultural complexity of Acheulian man and earlier *Homo erectus,* such assumptions begin to be necessary.

In this same, tentative manner we can query the significance of the bit of stag antler shown by Teilhard de Chardin to the Abbé Breuil. The broken animal bones of ancient meals found at Choukoutien indicate that deer made up a large part of Peking Man's diet. He was a persistent hunter of the creature. Assuming a time-factoring ability at a near-modern human level, is it possible that a hunter who was a relatively advanced maker of tools and user of fire, with a knowledge of the properties of wood, stone, skin, and flesh, would have failed to note the diurnal and the seasonal behavior of his prime source of food? There is the dawn and dusk feeding habit of the deer, the rutting time of the stag in the autumn, the periodic shedding of the hard stag antlers in late winter or early spring and then the slow beginning growth of new, soft, velveting antlers that continue to grow, branch, and harden. Could he have failed to notice the spring dropping of the fawns, or the enlarging of the pregnant does? Could he have failed to hear and recognize the braying and battling of the stags in rutting season, the period of the dramatic clash of antlers? These not only represented a regularity and periodicity of animal behavior but, for the hunter, they also represented a periodicity and difference in his main food source and in the materials of bone, antler, and skin available at different times. These facts probably also represented differences and periodicities in the skills and types of "stories" involved.

Assuming the possibility of such recognitions by the hunter of the Middle Pleistocene, is it possible that the children of Peking Man—who saw the killed stag, fawn, or doe brought to the camp, and who watched the stag's antlers being freed or broken for use, and who at long range saw the animals grazing or drinking, and who heard the distant braying and clash of the stag's rutting ritual—did not act or play either at "hunter-and-deer" or at "battle-of-the-stags," especially in the dramatic season of the rut? Of course we cannot know. But at one point in the developing hominid culture this sort of play-at-the-hunt or play-at-the-animal must have become part of the self-education and training of the boy. If the length of his childhood or maturation was somewhat shorter than

for modern man, he would be accumulating the skills and lore of his region and the hunt for some eight to thirteen years before he went on his first grown-up hunt for large game.

If the play-hunt evolved in this way, we would have here the development of a specialized, child's "storied" and time-factored relation to the large animal, learned as a seasonal game before the child could go to kill in company of the adult males. The behavior of large animals, both herbivore and carnivore, would in this way, and through the miming stories told by the adult hunter, have been culturally adapted into the lore of the group. Again, this was a process that was possible without a large use of language—given the near-human brain and a use of mime, symbol, and dance-like gestures.

In addition, if, as the evidence implies, Peking Man was a regular hunter in a large range, with a regular hunter's skills, and not a random and accidental hunter as are some apes, then he would not have failed to note and use the seasons of animal migration, whether of herds of camel, horse, buffalo, or elephant, or of flocks of birds. There was a hint of such recognition and use a million years before, in *Homo habilis,* with a lesser brain.

With the animal bones at Choukoutien there were also found quantities of a cool-climate wild cherry seed. Could Peking Man have failed to note the yearly round of flower, fruit, berry, cone, and nut, or have failed to note from which bush, tree, or hill the yearly and seasonal bounty came?

These recognitions would all seem to be within the limits of possibility for Peking Man. For one thing, *Homo erectus* was omnivorous and had been evolving in that line for millions of years, and to be successfully omnivorous requires a knowledge of the range and potential of the differing sources and resources of each season. The omnivore requires a minimum larder for the worst season and can indulge in a maximum during the best season. Effective use of the minimum season would have become increasingly necessary as he moved into northern latitudes, with their sharper seasonal differences. One does not, for instance, go seeking fruit in early spring, hunt for the soft delicacy of the new fawn in mid-winter, or climb for birds' eggs in the fall.

The point is that man, the omnivore and hunter, had

moved into the problems and realities of a widening, increasingly complex and dynamic time-factored geometry. In part this was based on the periodicities of nature, in part on his own self-created, self-domesticating, artificial culture, and in part on his evolving anatomy and brain. It was the interrelation of these factors that must have played a selective part in evolution, choosing those who could best think and function "in time."

From our point of view in this book, the increasing capacity for creating and maintaining this new hominid level and way of life lay in the time-factoring and time-factored processes and potentialities of the evolving and expanding brain.

I have implied "stories" without evidence, just as I have implied "communication." We must look again at this problem, for it leads directly to the notations and the art of early *Homo sapiens*.

Paleontologists have written much about the development of language in early man, primarily in terms of the evolving capability of jaw, teeth, tongue, muscles, and the enlargement of those areas of the brain which supervise their motor action. Language in this limited physiological sense is the ability to vocalize sounds that are recognized as symbols with meaning. In my assumed instances, however, I implied a vast amount of communication—expressed, recognized, and understood—which was not entirely vocal or semantic, but which would nevertheless have required a near-human brain for the expression, recognition, and understanding.

In part, as we saw, this communication involved concepts and processes in time and space, and the symbolic communication of these time-factored meanings was, I have suggested, one measure of the evolving human capacity. Such near-human communication would have been of a special sort.

In the assumed examples, meanings were expressed in terms of the *local* geography in that valley or territory, and in terms of the specialized knowledge, culture, and skills of that hunting group, the knowledge available and possible at that moment in prehistory and in that valley. This was not, then, a generalized knowledge of animals and seasons, but a specific knowledge concerned with the animals on hand at that time, in that place. Nevertheless, the capacity, both for under-

standing and communication, was general, that is, it was at a stage in evolutionary development already higher than that possible for *Homo habilis* and different in kind from that possible for apes and other animals. To the extent that "story" was involved, communication and knowledge were *beginning* to be abstracted and therefore to be generalized as "cultural coin," capable of being inherited. The beginnings of an accumulation of knowledge and of a cultural comparison of facts would have been evident in these "stories."

There is an important element in human and, apparently, near-human communication, then, that goes profoundly beyond the physiological ability to manipulate the tongue and articulate words. It is not merely a matter of "understanding" or "meaning" but concerns the nature of what is meant and understood. It includes memory and the capacity for comparison,[4] for learning, for mimetic and kinesthetic understanding, for synthesizing and abstracting relational concepts and concepts in a time-factored geometry. This evolved hominid communication would include the capacity for expression and recognition of feelings and "states." Because of this complexity, speech would have been only one aspect, perhaps simultaneous, of that broad, evolving, non-verbal process involved in communication and symbol-making.

Once voice and brain had evolved to the point where the hominid could utter syllabic words, these words would not, in the early stage, have been used as *defined* symbols, abstracted in meaning, as we define words today in a dictionary or in a course in a foreign language where one word refers to, or is compared with, another word. Nor would words have been used merely to "name" things. On the contrary, it would seem that the words would, in large measure, have been used *as part* of a communication of meaning that could be understood only within a process or relation, or if they referred to a process or relation. Only then could words be symbolic and be understood in reference to the non-verbal process or relation. A cry or a specialized word of warning at the presence of a carnivore is perhaps the simplest example. But the non-verbal content of such a pro-

---

[4] Among other things, comparisons of forms, rates, processes, directions, distances, materials and substances.

cess or relation would *always* have had a meaning more important and inclusive than could ever be contained in the word or words. To understand the evolution of language one must therefore understand the scope of the visual-kinesthetic, non-verbal, cognitive aspects in hominid communication.

The adult male hunter ar Choukoutien, 500,000 years ago in northern China, standing at the cave mouth and looking down his valley, must have had a series of functional references in his head—not always semantic or transferable into words. These references would have run to points in every direction the eye could see, and they would have been "time-factored." They would include memories of place and events, the lore of animal behavior, a knowledge of the potential changes of season and animal activity, a knowledge of the specialized hunting and gathering skills involved for each part of the day, each season, and each animal. As he looked out across the valley he probably also had a sense of time implied by the angle of the sun in the sky and the shadows across the valley and by the inferred or remembered walking or hunting distances to some point, or across and beyond the valley territory. If a word was used as a reference within this context, it would refer possibly to some communicable, common experience among the adult hunters.

The word, then, like the stone tool and fire, was an adjunct and a product of the increasingly complex, widening, time-factored, time-factoring capacity and potential of the hominine brain and its culture.

As I have indicated, though a word and the knowledge it referred to would often have been specific to a valley and a hunting group, the ability and the potential were innate and were becoming *increasingly generalized*. A woman in a local hunting group could probably, therefore, look down the valley from a cave mouth and have a different series of specialized time and space references than those of the hunter, involving skills and words that related perhaps to the range of her child's wanderings or to the plant and water resources of each season. For male and female, child and adult, therefore, there would be in any group specializations of skill, knowledge, and communication. These were becoming increasingly possible because of the generalized character of the brain's evolving capacity. The hominid brain could increasingly function with references and meanings in time and space across a widening diversity of natural and artificial or cultural conditions.

If now we assume, as we must, an evolutionary process for the development of this hominine ability to communicate time-factored meanings, then we have one measure of insight, without any direct evidence, of the way in which evolving hominid words and vocalizations would probably have been used with increasing complexity at various stages of development. This would have entailed not only a development of manipulative "language" skill but simultaneous and equal developments of the generalized cognitive skill, the hunting skill, the stages in a child's education and maturation, the possibility for diversification and specialization in adult social life and interrelations, and so on.

It would also follow that fear, threat, pain, anger, frustration, hunger, illness, dependence, desire, puberty, menstruation, old age—that is, expressable or recognizable emotional or physical states—would, at different stages, also find component words or gestures. Such communication concerning hominoid states would also entail a common awareness that was essentially time-factored and non-verbal, referring to processes and relations with a large measure of emotional, kinesthetic, or mimetic understanding.

Without assumptions such as I have made, it would be difficult to begin an interpretation of the early hominine cultures or the later Upper Paleolithic, *Homo sapiens* cultures. I have attempted here to shift the emphasis from the skills of toolmaking and language as the primary expressions of hominine culture and culture transmission to a broader, more inclusive, and more generalized human capacity. Toolmaking and language are aspects and products of this evolving capacity. But it is the evolution of the broader, time-factored and time-factoring capacity, including the skills of toolmaking and language, that leads eventually to the notations and art.

These concepts are important, for they were part of the intuitive insights that allowed me to proceed with the research, and they hinted at the reasons that such research was possible. Since notations and art were products of man's evolved kinesthetic and cognitive capacity, and since this capacity was broader than that involved in a specific toolmaking skill or in the physiological skills required for the articulation of one language, I could, with a comparable cognitive capacity, try to re-create some of the specific uses.

If tools and words are specialized products of this evolving generalized capacity, can we follow even one hypothetical thread in the long development that leads from these to art and notation?

We can probably assume that a word used by an adult *Homo erectus* such as Peking Man would quite often imply, or tell, a "story."

The spring flower that we today call by some Latin classifying name, early man might have named, "he, yellow after the snows." The complex of meanings in this simple statement would have included for that hunter in that culture a recognition of the round of years, the dearth of winter, and the spring thaw and flood. Within the local knowledge it might also have had reference to the spring coming of the great herds or flocks of water birds in the time of "he yellow." The name, then, implied reference to a "story," to a *relation or process* which was understood, teachable, and communicable. It was a recognition with meaning in time and space.

I am not here discussing the origins of specific words or any language but rather the origins of "story" and the uses and meaning of story. "Story" refers to the nature of the communication of meaning and, even more, to a certain sort of meaning which is time-factored, relational, and concerns process. In specialized and limited ways, animals communicate primitive elements of "story," that is, of process and relation, and I shall look at this problem in another place. At the human level there is a wide, changing, developing, and diverse interplay of meaning, understanding, and recognition between a mother and infant *before words* are used intelligently between them, and this pre-verbal interplay includes the communication of relatively complex "storied" meanings.

What then is "story"? The simplest definition is that it is the communication of an event or process—that *is* happening, *has* happened, or *will* happen. There is a beginning, something happens, and there is a change or result, an understood solution: act one, act two, act three. It is in the nature of the "story equation" that it must always be told in terms of someone or something. There is, in fact, no other way to tell a

story. This holds whether one uses words, mime, dance, ritual, or refers to the symbolism of dream and trance. It holds in the more primitive "storied" communications of lower forms of life, and it holds in the evolved and specialized human "story" categories: magic, religion, ceremony, rite, lore, reportage, history, science. In the hominid on the way to becoming man, the time-factored and time-factoring content and complexity contained in story would have evolved as the brain itself and human culture evolved.

In this sense a "name," when names would begin to be used by early man (perhaps as I surmised for the yellow flower), would always imply or tell a story, whether the name was that of a person, a non-person, an object, or a process. This is not the same as saying that the name is a "symbol," for a symbol implies that the relation of the symbol to the object or idea is somewhat static and constant. The "story," by definition, is not. This is not as odd or as difficult as it sounds, for even today, if you think about it, you will find that every name you can think of is part of a storied reference. Even the simplest names, the nouns or words such as "man," "woman," "old man," "infant," "boy-with-changing-voice," "girl-first-menstruating," "mountain wearing green" or "mountain wearing white," all imply stories. Such stories would, of course, differ somewhat in each culture, with each person, and with the age of the person, but as a reader you nevertheless sense at once the "stories" implied and contained in such words.

It is by such storied references, as much as by repetition and rote, that a child learns language, whether it is a name or the word for a relation or process. The first expressions and vocalizations are parts of elementary "story," from the primitive cry of hunger or discomfort to the first words. These words could be "want," "mamma," "eat," or "don't"; the word is simple but the meaning is a relation or process told in terms of someone or something. As the child grows the circle of references, meanings, and stories widens, increases, and matures, and the meanings of these first words change. Hardly any important word maintains a constancy of meaning for an individual in his life. Now, at some point in hominine evolution this time-factoring, time-factored use of words began to be possible and began to evolve.

When at last formal names would come to be used for

a person or thing, they too would be largely storied and comparative. The name might be a generalized one such as "mamma," or more specific such as "old one," "broken foot," "fast foot," "deer catcher," "lion killer," or "long eye." Such names would be recognitions of some storied aspect, specialization, or process, or they would refer to a description that was part of a known story or a common understanding. At a later stage in the development of culture one might give the child a name at birth, referring to an ancestor, totem, spirit, or to some prior owner of a name and story. One could then change it or add a new name or subname at adolescence and growing up, or after the child had participated in the story of initiation; still another name might be added or taken when the man had performed some storied act of courage and skill. It should be clear that in modern times we do exactly the same. We change a person's name or status continually, at time of birth and at times of baptism, confirmation, graduation, by the acquisition of a degree, title, office, or rank, and even when one acquires the adult status of being called simply "Mister" or "Missus," "citizen" or "comrade." Each of these names implies a story, a process, and a development. For the brain using these names as references, they have meaning only in terms of processes in time, mutually understood and recognized. Names, then, are time-factored and time-factoring tools, and we might assume that, like the stone tools, they evolved in complexity and use as the brain did.

This short discussion of a few possible uses of early language is an oversimplification. But it does indicate the evolving uses of language and story as part of the increasingly complex cultural continuity that was being created and maintained.

To sum up, *Homo erectus* was a near-modern human who, with or without a large use of spoken language, was capable of maintaining and communicating evolved cultural complexities, and it was this generalized ability to understand and communicate the time-factored meaning of a "story" or process that was perhaps the basic, humanizing, intellectual skill. Our only evidences for these assumptions are the charcoal, the stone tools, the animal bones, the skulls, and the cherry pits.

There was other evidence found at Choukoutien, and

it leads us one step deeper into the human problem. The excavated skulls and limb bones of Peking Man show evidence of what seems to be "cannibalism." The base, or *foramen magnum,* of at least one skull seems to have been broken to get at the brain, and a few limb bones have apparently been split to get at the marrow. Other bones of the near-human skeletons—except for the jaw or chin—are missing, as though they had been left outside the cave or at the spot of killing or dismemberment. Only the head, then, and an occasional limb seems to have been brought back for apparent eating.

Like the charcoal and the stone tools, this evidence raises questions that are, in essence, time-factored.

Before we can discuss the evidence, it will be necessary to touch on the problem of "cannibalism" and "aggression" for, like the debates over toolmaking, intelligence, and spirit, there is a continuing debate over man's "animal instincts" and "innate aggression," and the evidence of killing and storied death appears with the art and notation of the Upper Paleolithic.

Early man was a killer of game, and like certain primitive peoples of historic times (in Europe, the Pacific, Asia, Africa, and South America) he was apparently also a part-time cannibal. The meaning of this apparent cannibalism differs vastly among prehistorians and anthropologists. Carleton S. Coon, in his THE ORIGIN OF RACES, a study of the development of human types, wrote:

"With . . . few exceptions . . . nearly all the available skeletal material from the Middle Pleistocene, and some from the Late Pleistocene also, commemorates the ancient practice of man eat man. This does not mean that for hundreds of thousands of years every human being ended up in someone else's stomach; but if you are eaten, your bones have a better chance of being preserved for posterity than if your body is simply abandoned. Being tossed into a garbage dump is better from the archaeological point of view than being left for wolves and hyenas on the lone prairie.

"Moreover, the great cannibals of the world are farmers whose tiresome starch diets make them crave meat, as for example the Caribs, Papuans, and Azande. Hunters eat one another only when starving, not just for protein, but for calories. As the Sinanthropi were hunters, we may assume that the scraps of well-picked human bone which they threw into the cleft at Choukoutien represented moments of extreme hunger. Had the entire population been eaten over the thousands of years that this site was occupied, the excavators would have found the remains of thousands of Sinanthropi instead of a scant forty."[5]

This is a common-sense, time-factored theory, based on the evidence and related to belly hunger. Completely different is the interpretation of Alberto C. Blanc, of Italy who wrote:

"The evidence for the ideologies of the pithecanthropian races is almost nil . . . except the most valuable evidence furnished by the *Sinanthropus* site Choukoutien . . . selection has doubtless been performed so that essentially almost only the skulls of *Sinanthropus* have been brought into the cave, a circumstance that strongly points to the practice of head-hunting . . .

"F. Weidenreich was able to reconstruct an almost complete skull . . . Only one area is completely missing . . . the area . . . around the *foramen magnum*. The reconstructed skull . . . offers, therefore, an astonishing resemblance to the mutilated skulls of the 'early' and 'late' Neanderthals and to the skulls mutilated for the purpose of practicing ritual cannibalism in the Bronze Age of Germany and by . . . present head-hunters from Borneo and New Guinea . . .

"It may be pointed out that the mental functions and psychical *Einstellung* that form the background of ritual cannibalism may also be traced in the classic Mediterranean world, where the ideological crises undergone, possibly in the late stages of prehistory, may have produced a transition from an archaic effective cannibalism to a symbolic cannibalism . . . The urgent need (a typically human psychological feature) of establishing a relation with the unknown and mystic link between life and death . . ."[6]

"Now, this intentional [Neanderthal] mutilation is *identical* to the one presently produced by head-hunters of Borneo and Melanesia with the object of extracting the brain and eating it for ritual and social purposes, one of which is the necessity for assigning a name to the newborn. In certain tribes of New Guinea a newborn child receives a name only after the killing and beheading of a man whose name is known . . . The mutilated skull is kept as a sacred object in the home until the death of the new bearer of the name . . . This gruesome custom is practised by tribes that are not particularly bloodthirsty or aggressive and have rather high morals . . ."[7]

"... the evidence proves a constant complexity in human beliefs that is ever present, both in the so-called 'primitive' societies and in 'civilized' cultures."[8]

The theory here deals with psychological need rather than belly hunger. But it primarily describes and compares styles of cannibalism, rather than explaining or deriving it. For the concept of a "psychological hunger" to establish a mystic link with death and life is a generalization which, like the concept of "instinct," may help us in our research, but it is not for that reason a scientific explanation of the process.

The problem is among the most difficult in the attempt to understand early and modern man. The vast and complex evidence from the Upper Paleolithic related to killing, "aggression," and the notations and art will be examined later. Now I touch on the problem to ask new questions.

In the nineteenth century scientists believed that man had taken a huge step beyond the animal with his toolmaking ability. Implied was the idea that the hand-ax was an extension of the carnivore tooth and claw, and therefore a factor in the life-and-death struggle for individual and species survival. We have seen that the use of a hand tool involves far more, culturally, than a substitute canine tooth or claw.

In the twentieth century research into animal and human behavior has begun to change our understanding of "aggression." Centers for release of aggressive behavior have been found in the brain and have been artificially triggered and inhibited, and many of the hormonal components of aggressive action have been determined. Nevertheless, aggressive behavior was found to be extraordinarily complex, not easily explained by either neurological or hormonal processes. Aggressive behavior has been found to be interrelated with other processes of species behavior, development, maturation, interaction, experience and cognition. Old concepts concerning innate, constant, and separate "instincts" to kill or to defend had to be changed, even for the carnivore. Nevertheless, the idea of a single "killer instinct" is still current, based on a too-easy application of Darwin's ideas and the findings of behavioral psychology. It is based on the idea that man is basically "animal" and *therefore* "aggressive"; that he has developed his tools *for killing* but

[5] Carleton Coon, THE ORIGIN OF RACES (New York: Alfred A. Knopf, 1962), p. 432.

[6] Alberto C. Blanc, "Some Evidence for the Ideologies of Early Man," in SOCIAL LIFE OF EARLY MAN, ed. Sherwood L. Washburn (Chicago: Aldine Publishing Co., 1961), pp. 133–134.

[7] Ibid., p. 126.

[8] Ibid., p. 120.

has not evolved those instinctive inhibitions that would keep him from killing his own kind. This over-simple, storied description of man is quite similar to earlier religious theories that held man to be innately "good" and "evil," because the evidence, as anyone could see, was there. Similarly, the archaeological evidence of battered skulls and broken limb bones, from *Homo habilis* and *Australopithecus* to *Homo erectus*, *Homo neanderthalensis*, and *Homo sapiens*, is there, and there is, in the later art, the evidence of symbolized killing. As much as anything in the record of early man, the evidence requires an answer but more than is supplied by the concept of belly hunger, mystic union with death, or innate animal aggression. What is needed is an understanding of "aggression" and of "instinct" as *components of evolved behavior* in all species and then for man, as a more highly evolved species, an understanding of the evolved and evolving roles of "aggression" and "instinct," their relation both to the evolving brain and to its product, human culture. It is a different sort of question that is needed to get a different sort of answer.

Konrad Lorenz, director of the Max-Planck-Institut for Behavioral Physiology in Bavaria, West Germany, is a founder of "ethology," a branch of psychology that deals with the biology and genetics of animal behavior. He and his school have found that even "aggressive" vertebrates, such as the mammalian carnivore, and "aggressive" creatures lower on the scale of evolution, such as the lizard, snake, and fish, do not under normal, average conditions kill and eat their own species. He postulated that it was the "innate aggression" of animals that had made it possible for them to develop the cooperative behavior patterns which structure an animal society based on family, rank and status, dependence and love—forms of behavior that, according to Lorenz, have their origin in redirected, masked, or sublimated aggression. The problem, he has suggested, is that the instinctive, ritualized controls over aggression that were evolved by animals over millions of years have not had time to evolve in man. He has, therefore, theorized an uncontrolled animal aggression in the psyche of man, with man's culture as the basic restraint. Lorenz has tried to understand aggression in man but not sequentially or analytically in terms of the way in which it *evolved* in man towards new levels of com-

plexity as brain and way of life changed, but *comparatively* as though it had not evolved but had retained an uncontrolled animal immediacy.

Working not with animals but with man, Sigmund Freud, the founder of psychoanalysis, theorized that man is essentially "aggressive" and "sexual" in relations within his own species. Man, Freud suggested, foreshadowing Lorenz's insight into animals, has the capacity to sublimate, to shift, and to redirect this aggression symbolically and culturally.

According to Freud, this basic human aggression led a group of sons, some time in prehistory, to kill the father who ruled over the women. A late extension of this theory suggested that this early murder led to an eating of the father, implanting guilt in the sons and fear for themselves in a repetition of this primal crime and, therefore, a need to prevent such future murders by the establishment of taboos, cultural admonitions against both incestual sexual desires and all murders too close to home. From his study of emotional, neurotic disease in modern man, Freud has tried to understand what he considered to be the prehistoric development of cultural taboos and restrictions. He postulated a clinical drama as though it had been an actual definitive stage in man's cultural evolution. He did not realize that such stages proceed through levels of biologic and cultural capacity and complexity.

Freud also theorized that man's abhorrence and fear of death were the results of a "projection" by those living; a symbolic shift of aggressive feelings onto the dead; an unconscious equation whereby it was felt that the dead could think, behave, and be as demanding, threatening, and hostile as the living. This was a valuable insight into one form of modern, human, non-verbal storymaking: the ability to project into an abstract nonexistent domain a possible future "action" to which one reacts in the present. In this way, too, the past, the person long dead or killed, becomes present and affects the future. What is important here is not the clinical or cultural aspect of the equation but the *evolved* time-factored and time-factoring capacity.

Anthropologists in the field have found that there is no rule concerning either taboos or aggression. There are diverse cultural norms; cultures that are aggressive and others that are non-aggressive, and cultures that are sometimes one and sometimes the other; there are cultures that express a fear of the dead, and those that do not. The subject, then, is neither simple nor covered by any single theory. The most one could say regarding human "aggression" was that a range of potential aggressive behavior was present, a range more complex than in lower animals. The problem is crucial, and the research, theories, and insights on "aggression," killing, and cannibalism continue to grow. At Choukoutien, in the early *Homo erectus* levels of Peking Man, the skeletal remains contain the parts of fifteen children (infants and juveniles) as well as the bones of men and women. The complexity of this early evidence, which continues into the Middle and Upper Paleolithic and into the Mesolithic and Neolithic, is not answered by the theories of Freud or Lorenz, that is, by theories of aggressive rivalry between males, of aggressive feeling against the father, or by theories of aggressive defense of the territory against threat. Human bones at Choukoutien are too few in comparison to the number of animals killed to indicate a persistent hunting and killing of men. In addition, if the bones are evidence of cannibalism, we cannot be dealing with a cannibalism for food, since the bulk of the body meat was not brought home.

What we might have is evidence of an eating primarily of the brain and perhaps of the marrow—and this would, again, not be an example of simple feeding to fill the belly. There is also a possibility that the heads were buried until the flesh and brain were decayed and that the skulls were then used for vessels and cups. We do not know. But within the range of these possibilities, in each case, we are far beyond simple animal aggression, carnivorous feeding, innate animal ritual, or the neurotic clinical equation. It would seem that we have, as Blanc suggested, evidence of a *storied,* occasional, or selective killing or use of man's body and bones; it need not have been, as Blanc suggested, a mystic union with life and death.

Since there is no theory at present adequate to help us, it becomes necessary once again to redefine our terms, particularly such terms as "aggression," "cannibalism," "killing," and "murder," and to seek meaning for these words in terms of species content and evolving man.

This redefinition will be needed as we proceed in our study of Upper Paleolithic behavior, art, and notation, but the full discussion must be held for another place. Now we return to the notations and art, one aspect of man's time-factored thought.

CHAPTER IX

VAULT OF THE SKY

As the hominid who was to become man evolved and spread across Africa and the central land mass of Eurasia, he changed his body, his intelligence, the animals he hunted, the plants he gathered, his tool kit, the range and complexity of his domain, and probably his group relations and his "stories." The climates, ecologies, and diversity of the seasons also changed.

One set of things did not change: the round of day and night, the rise and set of the sun in the east and west, and the phases of the moon. These, in fact, for almost two million years were the only constants he had, except for birth and death. The angle of the ris-

ing and setting moon and sun on the horizon and the angle that the paths of the sun and moon made in the sky might vary in Africa, Europe, the Middle East, and China, and in different seasons, but the periodicities and the sequences did not substantially change.

Now, at some point—perhaps not in the *Homo habilis* stage of 2,000,000 to 1,500,000 years ago—but certainly in the *Homo erectus* stage of 700,000 to 400,000 years ago, man had evolved sufficiently to create and maintain a complex time-factored culture. The root of this capacity was the enlarged brain with its evolved, specialized structures and processes for visual and kinesthetic coordination, conceptualization, memory, and cross-referencing. This brain had not been evolved for viewing the sky but for coping with the time-space realities encountered in daily and seasonal living on the ground. At one point, however, this brain, standing on an upright spine and with the windows of the front-focusing eyes able to swing 180° and from ground to horizon to zenith, must have been able to discern a pattern related to bodies in the sky and directions in the territory. The beginnings of the process may have been no more complex, millions of years before *Homo erectus,* than a standing primate's curiosity in the open field at the rising and setting ball of the crimson sun, or at a full, copper moon hovering on the eastern horizon. Perhaps at this early date it was only a recognition, perhaps a curiosity at some particularly dramatic sunset as the disc of the sun slipped in and out of purple or reddened clouds. Perhaps the full moon brought a foot stamping, a hand clapping, or a "hoo-hooing!"

Whatever the details, slowly the evolving conceptualizing brain must have been capable of distinguishing a pattern: to differentiate between sun and moon, to recognize phases in the moon. I am discussing an increasing capability and potential, evolved for other purposes, and not necessarily a developed cultural fact. At one point, *if* a father pointed out a full moon to a child, the child would have achieved a "cultural awareness" for a shared periodic phenomenon. The next month, perhaps, the child could have pointed it back to the father.

Clearly the capacity *must* have been evolving because at one point it was evolved, and at one point, too, the recognition and the "communication" would have been possible. No matter where this early man who was capable of recognizing a pattern in the sky migrated, some aspect of this recognition would go with him. Climate, animals, and landscape might change as he wandered, but the sky went with him, and to that extent he was psychologically and culturally "at home" anywhere on earth.

By the time of *Homo erectus* and cave-dwelling Peking Man, we have a hominid with a brain capable of maintaining a fire culture and able to utilize both seasonal and geometric references.

A cave or rock shelter is a fixed point, facing a fixed horizon. If it faces east, a man in the entrance will catch the ball of sun rising each morning. Once a month he will catch the sliver of the crescent or dying moon hovering in the eastern dawn like a flint chip, the back of its arc pointed at the sun still under the hills.

If the shelter faces west, a man will see the newborn crescent moon some two days after it has disappeared in the east, but now it is on the evening, western horizon as the sun sinks, the back of its arc once again pointing at the sun. This crescent will return each 29 to 30 days to some spot over this western horizon.

If the shelter faces south, our man can see a more complex pattern. If a lip extends out from the cave to serve as a floor for fire or observation, he might catch a large part of the two dramas mentioned above, occurring in the east and west. But he will also catch other lunar patterns.

The full moon appears in the eastern sky opposite the sinking sun in the west. It keeps its face towards the sun as it rises and the sun sinks and, as the full moon rises and journeys across the sky heading to the west, the sun, behind the earth, has begun its journey to the east. When, at night's end, the full moon is now in the west, the sun is already in the east awaiting the dawn. This full moon is high in the night sky about midnight, lighting the valleys and the hills of the earth. Facing the hidden sun, it is lit by the same light that is pouring daylight on the other side of the earth. In certain seasons, it is possible for a man in a cave or shelter facing southerly to watch the complete full moon sequence.

The half-moon, or "first quarter" as we call it, comes some seven or eight days before the full moon. It is already high in the sky at sunset and is moving towards the west, and it goes down about midnight. The second half-moon, which we call the "third quarter," comes seven or eight days after the full. It does not rise in the east till about midnight. It then reaches its highest point in the sky about sunrise. It is visible high in the sky in the morning light, the arc of its back facing towards the eastern sun. These are rough estimates of the general lunar pattern occurring at different places in the sky and at different times. The precise angle of the moon in the sky varies slightly by season and over longer periods, and the sun also varies its place on the horizon, season to season.

A man in a cave facing east, in the middle latitudes of

Eurasia, would see the sun rise and set toward the north on the summer horizon, and toward the south on the winter horizon. Because the angle of the earth's axis shifts season by season in relation to the sun, the cave facing south would catch the winter sunrise and sunset but would begin to lose it as winter ebbed and the spring approached. Since this shifting pattern of the rising and setting sun on the horizon with each season is more obvious in European and mid-Asian latitudes than it is in equatorial Africa, it would have been visible to Peking Man at Choukoutien and to later Paleolithic man in Europe. We cannot know at what level of cognition it was observed by Peking Man. We can only state that this shifting solar pattern is a periodic process, repeating in twelve months. On the other hand, the shorter, more dramatic lunar pattern is recognizable in a matter of days. We do know that by the time of *Homo sapiens* in the Upper Paleolithic the capacity and potential for recognition of long-term patterns was present. To what extent it was culturally recognized and structured is now the question.

To continue with the patterns of the sky: in general, the last crescent, sunrise, and the rise of the full moon were primary events towards the east; the first crescent and the sunset were primary events towards the west and here the full moon also sank; when half-moons were highest in the sky, they marked the time of sunset and sunrise. For observation and recognition of these patterns, a rock shelter or cave was the best possible place for a man, since it was a fixed point within a time-factored, periodic geometry.

There are variations in these movements. The path of the orbiting moon is at an angle to the equator of the earth, and the earth orbits the sun with its own changing angle. The precise place of the rising and setting lunar crescents and the full moon therefore shifts along the horizon. The full moon rises towards the northeast in winter and towards the southeast in summer, the reverse of the solar movement. There are other, more subtle patterns, but these for primitive man must have seemed erratic since the periodicities are extremely long and require record-keeping and mathematics for their clarification. The primary observational dramas are the lunar phases, their general direction of origin and disappearance, and the general westward motion of the moon in the sky.

These phenomena belong to the sky and are invariant, and we can assume that hominids, perhaps at the stage of *Homo erectus* but certainly at the stage of *Homo sapiens* when men had used a permanent rock shelter for a number of generations (facing either east, south, or west), saw these patterns and recognized them. What we do *not* know is the level of the *cultural* recognition, the myth-making, and the utilization.

There were other time and geometry clues for the cave dweller. In the cold climate and latitude of Peking Man and later in the cold climate and latitude of *Homo sapiens* in Ice Age Europe, even during the somewhat warmer interglacial periods, a family that made its winter living quarters in a rock shelter or cave mouth knew that a shelter that faced north was "bad." It caught the icy blasts from the arctic, blowing wind and snow and the fire smoke, and it did not catch the warming sun through the day.
If the cave or shelter faced southerly at a good angle, it caught the winter sun through much of the day. In the winter, when the warmth of the pale sun was most wanted, it hung low in the sky and gave less heat, but it did shine deep into the shelter or cave mouth where it was needed, warming the skin and even the ground and rocks.
When the first snows lay thick in the valley, and when the rivers were frozen, the sun reached its low point on the horizon. It rose late, and it set early at a point far to the south among the hills. It crossed the sky in so low an arc that it almost looked you in the face: Then slowly as the winter deepened, and the cold grew worse, the sun began to climb higher in the sky each day; the sun's rays did not reach as deeply into the cave or shelter. But at this point the spring thaw could be only two or three full or crescent moons away.
The rise and fall of the path or arc of the sun through the sky with each season is, then, like the phases of the moon and the sun's seasonal position on the horizon —invariant. If a family used a shelter for a number of years, even if only a winter quarters, then without any story, myth, or ritual these were changes that child and family saw, sensed, and therefore "learned." The correlation of sun angle with the times of bitter cold, short days, absent herds, and returning warmth and thaw could not easily be missed.

I have discussed an environmental constant (the patterns in the sky) and the evolution of a cognitive conceptual capacity. Not all early men, however, lived in caves.

Turn to the description of the East Gravettian mammoth-hunter who engraved the bone from Kulna (Fig. 4 a). Here was a hunter who lived among gently rolling hills that lacked the caves found in the valleys of southern France, Spain, the Middle East, and China. The herds were vast and sufficient to support a hunting culture, but even in interglacial times the winters were bitter, winds blowing unhindered from the north. The hunters, therefore, built huts, tents, or houses. Sometimes these were dug slightly into the earth to protect against the icy winds and snows.

At Pavlov, near Dolní Věstonice, Czechoslovakia, the camp stood on the slope of a low hill, facing north into the wind. Below the camp, at the foot of the hill, was a small river or stream. On the softly rolling plain one could see the horizon north, east, and west. Herds of mammoth, like fleets of ships, could be followed on this vast tundra.

Behind the camp, to the south, the hill continued to rise. On the horizon, like a huge tower, there stood an upthrust cliff face, shaped like a giant or a towering church. This rock of Magdenburg was a fixed point, an obelisk standing in the rear. The open site, under the sky, was also a fixed point, with a view of the patterns of sun and moon. The rock, therefore, served as a sun marker to the south, by which one could measure the height or angle of the sun, winter and summer. In the winter the sun came low to the head of the rock and cast a long, cold shadow.

These hunters had a different skeleton and a somewhat different culture than the cave dwellers of France and Spain. They presumably had a different language. But they were *Homo sapiens,* and at the same point in evolution and with the same cognitive capacity, and they had structured an equal or comparable complexity in their time-factored culture. They had different environmental conditions, but nevertheless had two fixed points and a fixed horizon and could observe the periodic sequences of the sky while they watched the land colors go from green to brown to white, saw the coming thaw, the roaming herds, the flights of migrating birds, and felt the changing directions of the winds in each season. None of this, of course, lies in the layers of the soil.

In my tentative first analysis of the engraved ivory from Gontzi in the Ukraine (Fig. 5 a), I assumed that a notation of this apparent complexity in a culture at this stage of development *required* "story," whether the notation was lunar or mnemonic, for remembering either events or a tale.

I also assumed that *Homo sapiens* living permanently or seasonally at a fixed point such as a shelter or camp, through a number of generations, is capable of noticing and recognizing patterns in the sky *without* story.

The questions these two viewpoints raise are many.

To what extent is the capacity to recognize and use a time-factored pattern or sequence—in the sky or in a notation—innate to *Homo sapiens?* To what extent is this an evolved capacity for *potentially variable cognitive behavior?* If potentially variable, how will it express itself in different individuals and cultures? What is the range and limitation of this variability? What part does culture, including language and story, play in making possible these recognitions and their uses? If notation is present in the archaeological materials, does it have to be—as I at first assumed—lunar? Would not man at a certain level of evolved capacity be capable also of other forms of notation, so that one culture, or different cultures, could use many forms, including allied, non-notational, or non-sequential forms of symbol-making? If the notations were lunar, what were the minimum concepts and techniques required in their making, an analysis of which might allow us 20,000 to 30,000 years later to test and either prove or disprove such possible use?

The Swiss psychologist Jean Piaget has studied the steps and processes by which a child develops its ability to understand and operate with objects and concepts. He has found that the child begins to think spatially, arithmetically, sequentially, and in time *before* it has an adequate use of language, that is, before verbal culture has played a large part in the formation of these concepts. The general level of this potential capacity is innate for each age, though it changes and develops as the child matures and deals with the increasingly difficult problems of reality and culture, and as the child extends its range, territory, and activities at each age.

The cognitive capacity that Piaget has studied is, then, time-factored, as a process of potential variability that has evolved in a particular, specialized way. It has evolved to allow a longer childhood during which more advanced, complex stages of cognition can develop, *sequentially,* as the body matures and as the child reacts to the signals, stimuli, and processes of reality, both kinesthetic and cultural, building memory, developing skills, absorbing culture, increasing the range of data feedback. And it is time-factored also because the processes the child deals with are themselves increasingly complex, time-factored processes. Piaget studied the innate potential variability at each age, but in terms of modern, Western culture—using rulers, bottles, colored chips, triangles, cubes, squares, and clocks, as well as comparative concepts such as measurement, rate, size, angle, number. It is the potential, however, that we are interested in, since Upper Paleolithic man with a hunting culture in a different time would have had a different set of objects, forms, skills, processes, questions, and words to deal with. What Piaget finds is significant then for understanding the *range* of innate potential intelligence in man and, therefore, the cognitive possibility for an early notation.

In a paper dealing with the way in which children form mathematical concepts, he wrote that a child does not acquire its notions of "number and other mathematical concepts" from teaching, but that these largely develop spontaneously.[1] The attempt to instill mathematical understanding too early results in rote learning, whereas true understanding comes with time and cognitive maturation.

Piaget found that a child of five or six can learn the *names* of numbers and, if ten pebbles are laid in a row, he can call off these names, but if this linear arrangement is broken, the child's certainty as to the total is lost. He has learned the names but does not understand the "essential idea of number," that the quantity of units remains the same when objects are scrambled.[2]

But a half year or more later, at six and a half or seven, the child will have formed the idea of number even if he has not been taught to count. Given an equal number of red and blue chips and asked which group has "more," he will discover that each has an equal number by matching reds against blues. At this age he will discover that no matter how they are arranged, the number remains the same. He has learned the principle of conservation of quantity, a logical concept that spontaneously prepares the child for understanding the idea of number. Earlier, at five, the child believed that, if the pebbles or chips are close together they are "less," if stretched apart they are "more."

Piaget's experiments clarify certain stages of cognitive development. It must be noted, though, that the way in which these experiments were formulated constituted a form of teaching, since asking a question or setting up a problem with a question creates a cultural ideogram and determines the nature of the possible answer.

Piaget has found that a child learns spontaneously to understand cardinal numbers (one, two, three, etc.) and ordinal numbers (first, second, third, etc.) as he grows and learns to distinguish that one object is before or after another "in time or space, that is, in the order of enumeration."[3] He spontaneously discovers these spatial relationships and has a working geometry of space and time before he has acquired the verbalization for these concepts. The ideas come, not by teaching, but by stages of maturation.

At about three the child can distinguish certain figures, such as a circle or cross, and determine if they are open or closed. However, he cannot yet draw a rectangle or triangle or express their "Euclidean characteristics."[4] In the next stage, he begins to understand spatial concepts.

If a child of about four is asked to place upright sticks in a straight line between two other sticks about fifteen inches apart, he merely places one near the next and ends with a wavy line. He cannot project the idea of a straight line. After four, he may form a straight line with the sticks by aligning them to a table edge. But at about seven, he can build a straight line fence

[1] Jean Piaget, "How Children Form Mathematical Concepts," Reprint from SCIENTIFIC AMERICAN, Vol. 189 (November 1953), p. 2.

[2] Loc. cit.

[3] Ibid., p. 3.

[4] Loc. cit.

in any direction by shutting one eye and sighting along it. He has grasped the idea of the angle of vision. At about seven, too, he senses the angle of vision of another person looking at the same object. This is the necessary cognitive beginning for interpersonal cooperation in time and space, whether for hunting, for games of throwing and hurling, or for modern technology. He can finally coordinate different perspectives at about nine or ten. He can visualize the difference between his point of view in looking at a "range of mountains," and that of the experimenter, behind the mountains. The child is at the stage of cooperative hunting. At this stage, culture and story have already intruded.

At this stage, too, he begins to understand the stability of directions. He will not only sight with one eye, but may raise his hands parallel to structure the direction. In a similar way he begins to understand the idea of constant length.

Place two toy trees on a table, then place a cardboard wall between them. The youngest child thinks the distance has changed; he cannot add up the two parts to make a total distance. At five or six a child believes the distance has been reduced, the wall having used up some of the space. Near seven, he begins to realize that intervening objects do not change distance. He is beginning to function in time and space at an adult level.

By stages he learns to judge and measure the comparative heights of objects, spontaneously learning how to establish a comparison by use of a stick or rod. He finally learns that the whole is composed of parts and that one can substitute units and still retain the whole. Slowly the child has approached the idea of number, distance, measure, and serial order apart from the use of an arithmetical system of numbers. He also learns to make three-dimensional measurements, constructing coordinate axes by references to natural objects: a wall, a tree, a floor, a rock, a table. Assuming this capability to be innate in man, one can perhaps assume that the early hunter could recognize the passage of three or six full moons, representing seasons, before he could divide these months into twenty-nine or thirty numerically precise day units. With the acquisition of a system of notation in the Paleolithic, this ability would have begun to be culturally formalized. The Upper Paleolithic evidence indicates that the full development was, cognitively and culturally, rather complex, as we shall see later. To some extent, Piaget recognizes the complexity for he has also studied the stages in a child's use of language and the development of his spontaneous conceptions of time, motion, velocity, sequence, series, causality, and the processes of nature. Of special interest is Piaget's study of a city child's conception of sun and moon and of his developing ideas concerning their visible processes.[5]

Piaget has been a pioneer of research into certain aspects of the maturation of human cognition, as Freud pioneered a time-factored approach to the genesis and dynamics of emotional and symbolic equations in human neurosis and behavior. He has not asked questions relating to the evolution of these cognitive processes nor has he studied the difference between a generalized, potential capacity and the specific cultural expressions of that potential. Still, the research begun by Piaget has relevance for education within the increasing and extraordinary complexity of modern life. We should note the nature of this research Piaget began in describing and classifying the stages and modes of cognition in a child. His analyses deal largely with measurable, observable, and comparable products at each age. It is far from being a scientific explanation of cognition or intelligence, but merging its data and insights with those being obtained from biological sciences and with the insights such as those in this book, we may slowly approach an adequate understanding of human intelligence and cognition.

For my research with the Upper Paleolithic notations it is perhaps sufficient to have indicated that human intelligence is beginning to be approached in a scientific way, not as an "absolute," but as a process that is time-factored, evolved, developmental, specialized, diversely structured, limited, and potential. The possible stages in the evolution of this human cognition have hardly begun to be discussed. Nevertheless, for our research it is important to recognize the presence of an increasing body of experimental evidence that

[5] Jean Piaget, THE CHILD'S CONCEPTION OF THE WORLD, trans. Joan and Andrew Tomlinson (New York: Humanities Press, 1960).

has relevance to the archaeological materials, to the size of the skulls, and to the evidence that a time-factored, arithmetic-geometric cognitive capacity evolved in man.

The hunter of the Upper Paleolithic, standing in his shelter or camp in the half-light of dusk or dawn and looking at his sky and horizon, judging the weather and feel of a day, had non-verbal recognitions of the season and, if the sky were clear, of the phase of the moon and perhaps the angle of the sun.

I assume in addition that he had stories for clear or overcast sky, when the moon was visible, or if the sun was rising or sinking. There would have been, then, a range of recognitions and stories. The evening or morning sky, based on experience and group knowledge, would have been involved in the hunter's thoughts with the tasks of the coming day, a kind of "storytelling" which had more or less known alternative possible endings, hazards and efforts. The sky of mid-latitude Europe was more variable, seasonally and daily, than the sky of Africa or the Middle East, and in some sense each day's sky had to be "judged," the tasks of each day made variable.

I have stated that the capacity to understand and communicate a "story" was perhaps the basic, humanizing intellectual and social skill, the primary tool and technique of developing human culture, but I touched on it sparsely and briefly. Let us look at it a bit more carefully in terms of the patterns of the sky and of those cognitive elements, verbal and non-verbal, that would be involved in observation and a use of notation.

The Upper Paleolithic hunter had a vast store of skills and knowledge, in amount and quality far beyond that available to *Homo erectus*. This included not only knowledge of sky, season, and animals, but of materials and processes. He knew the quality and uses of hide, bone, antler, fat, coal, charcoal, wood, fire, stone, and he had an extremely varied and useful tool kit. He knew the specific qualities of mud, frozen ground, snows, ice, the varieties of stone, the various plants, the colors of charcoal, oxides, and clays, and the technical processes of decoration on body, bone, stone, and shelter or cave wall. He knew how to make structures, whether tents, huts, corrals, pits, nets, fireplaces or drainage ditches. He knew the varied uses of story and notation and the symbolic uses of magic, ceremony, and music. He probably knew the lore of drafts relating to fire and smoke, and he had a range of uses for fire from diverse forms of cooking to the hardening of wooden shafts or clay figures to the use of oil lamps for lighting shelters and caves. Not all of this knowledge could be put directly into words, any more than the simple crafts and skills of today can be put entirely into words.

In an earlier book I had noted the non-verbal ability of the hunter to understand and utilize certain natural laws and phenomena:

"Consider a few of the phenomena the modern geophysicist studies and uses scientifically. Early man used these phenomena intuitively and with skill. The cave dweller had no concept of *gravity,* yet he could 'use' gravity.

"He could dig a pit and trap a falling animal. He could scare herds of horses and send them tumbling from a cliff. He learned the craft and skill of the spear, and then invented a 'pendulum' spear-thrower to increase its range and force. He developed the bow and arrow and learned to aim the arrow high, over its mark, since gravity brought it down in an arc, and he learned to shoot to one side since the wind carried the arrow.

"He learned to 'use' centrifugal force. He learned the trick of the boomerang and, while he did not know the laws of things hurled into the air, he developed the skill to allow for the curve a bent, whirling stick makes when it is thrown. He invented the bola, three separate stones on strings, that whirls about a center when thrown, and wraps itself around the legs of the hunted animal to deliver it tied and helpless. He used the slingshot which made use of a whirling, centrifugal force, this time upon a small stone. He learned . . . the art of the blowgun which uses a burst of breath from the lungs to fire a dart.

"The ballistics engineer . . . may not know how to shoot an arrow or hurl a boomerang, but he uses the same facts of gravity, air resistance and expenditure of energy to hurl a missile into space . . .

"Modern scientists did not discover gravity, but they learned how to measure and compute its effects mathematically . . . The phenomena of the world have not changed. What has changed is the state of our knowledge . . ."[6]

In these instances, the process included both a sequence of recognitions and a series of efforts to obtain a desired effect. The hunter was thinking in space and time, non-verbally, kinesthetically, and sequentially,

[6] Alexander Marshack, THE WORLD IN SPACE (New York: Thomas Nelson & Sons, 1958), pp. 14-15.

but nevertheless with the "equation of story," the sense of sequence and change as part of a process.

Now the child in an Upper Paleolithic family could, to an extent, learn some of these skills "spontaneously" at the right age, in Piaget's sense of a developing capacity, as well as by imitation and kinesthetic participation in group activity. There is however, a more specialized form of human knowledge about process, and it utilizes language and symbolic story in the teaching and the learning.

The capacity of a child to understand a story is different than that of a teenager, the teenager different than that of an adult, the adult different than that of a senile oldster. Each has a different core of knowledge and capacity, either for understanding a story or for participating in a relation. Yet the adult explaining a phenomenon to a child usually tells it instinctively *at the child's level*. He knows that it is a story for the child and that the comparatively "true," or adult, story will come later—perhaps, as many cultures have devised it, in the initiation rites of the teenager or, as with modern man, sequentially in the stages of schooling, books, and professional experience.

Automatically, then, because of the developing capacity and needs of each child, there is a separation into levels of reality and story, and these are usually understood by the adult to be just that. This does not necessarily mean that the child's story is considered "false," and that the initiation rite is considered "true." For such comparative judgments are possible only when there are alternative possible stories available for the child, the teenager and the adult, one of which is considered "truer" for each age group, or true at a different level. In a more or less uniform early culture without cross-cultural comparison, this modern problem of the comparison of story validities probably did not occur, at least not in contemporary terms. Nevertheless, the *capacity* for comparative judgments of "validity" among stories would have been present in the Upper Paleolithic. It would have taken cultural forms different from those with which we are familiar.

I have been theorizing about aspects of *Homo sapiens* intelligence and culture and particularly about "story." These hypotheses do not have the same possibility of proof that the more structured analyses of the notational materials have. Nevertheless they indicate the explanations I sought and made, almost of necessity, as the evidence grew in complexity and quantity. It became apparent as I worked that a documentation of the notations, though adequate for a scientific paper, could not explain or encompass the range of the associated symbolic evidence that began to unfold. Nor would it have explained the notations. I was forced to my inquiries into "story."

When the adult *Homo sapiens* hunter saw the phases of the moon, he could presumably explain them to a child, to a teenager, or to himself, in each case differently and in each case in terms of the knowledge and mythology he had. These explanations would probably have included the lore of killing and eating, the lore of the weapon, the tool, the net and the trap; they would probably have included emotional and relational components such as fear, courage, skill, the relations of child to parent, man to woman, tribe to tribe, man to animal; part of the explanation might have included a story of escape, deceit, incompetence, fumbling; it might have included less certain concepts such as references to the canyon of the dark, the world of the deep, the domain of the waters, the land of the sky, the realm of the mountain; it might also have included concepts of process such as change of form, size, or sex. The possibilities are large, but the limitations are sure, because there is nothing else that can be included in story or explanation but what is known or considered possible in a culture, and it must be told in terms of someone and of something happening. I earlier described the tale told by the African Bushman about the lunar phases in terms of the cutting of meat from a full animal with a subsequent healing and recovery. This does not mean that the hunter did not see the phases of the moon accurately, or recognize other complex patterns in the sky or nature. For the recognition of a pattern is one thing, and its explanation is another. The ability to recognize a complex pattern, we have seen, belongs to the species. This is the reason that we can today recognize an Ice Age notation, test whether it is lunar, and still not know the stories that were told with it and, in fact, possibly be wrong in interpreting or reconstructing the stories. For the patterns we recognize and our explanations of them are also separate.

In just this way the factual knowledge the early hunter

had can be separated from his stories. Nevertheless, we cannot assume that the Ice Age hunter himself would have been able, consciously and in words, to separate his stories from his hard, factual knowledge. For he probably used one to understand and teach the other, and the words and names he used would have had a storied content. The story might, in fact, seem to him to be the definition of the phenomenon, since it would be his only way of explaining or describing it, even while its practical cues and uses were unstoried. Now, a good story not only helped the hunter learn, but the human ability to recognize or see a story helped him to recognize and see a pattern *in terms of story*. If, for instance, he "knew" that the gods (or animals or plants) could change their form or residence, it was no surprise for him to see the flower bloom in season, the butterfly emerge from a cocoon, the snake from its sheath, the child come from the womb, or the moon wax and wane. Nor would he be surprised at the sudden, unpatterned, aberrational event, the earthquake, the shower of meteors, the eclipse, or the epidemic. It would be cohered, explained, and put in context by story. If he knew that thunder came in the summer, for instance, it would not have been difficult to explain either the anger of the storm or the hammering of the heavenly toolmaker and to expect it to come each summer in terms of a repetition of the story.

The storytelling skill, then, helped him to see and recognize process and change, to widen his references and comparisons, to "understand" and to participate in them in storied terms, and it enabled him to tell and foretell them. One assumes, then, that the kind of stories a man tells—in this case a hunter's—helps him to unify the extraordinarily diverse phenomena and processes of his life; and since a story is an *equation,* a cognitive form for abstractly structuring and dealing with process and relation, the uses and complexities of the story form would change as the culture became more complex. For us the important thing is to recognize that the innate, evolved *Homo sapiens* capacity for storied thinking has probably not changed significantly in the last 40,000 years.

What I call, perhaps too simply, the "story equation" has been the subject of study by diverse branches of the science of man. The anthropologist has collected the myths, religious lore, and rites of cultures, running to hundreds of volumes. The anthropologist Claude Lévi-Strauss of France has taken the forms and the structures of these myths as the human reality, the storied equations as the validity of men's thoughts and relations, and he has analyzed and compared the mythological structures that various primitive cultures have built. The American psychologist Jerome Bruner of Harvard University, a follower of Piaget, has studied the cognitive strategies or equations used by a child in solving a problem. Sigmund Freud initiated the study of the origins and uses of the neurotic, behavioral equation, which is a form of symbolic "story." His followers have widened the effort by extending Freud's dream and symbol analysis to include a study of group behavior, myths and symbols, and their retention or change through time. In each of these areas the scientist is studying a storied process, some specialized time-factored product of the brain, the same brain that made the notations and art of the Ice Age.

Piaget has studied a modern child's changing concepts of sun and moon and their visible processes. He used abstract words such as "sun" and "moon"; nevertheless, he found that the child considered them alive. A different story would have been told by each child if the names of these two sky bodies were, in his culture, Sky Bull and Sky Cow, or Big Hunter and White Fleeing Deer, or Great Father and Great Mother. There would have been a difference in story also if there existed no scientific explanations in the adult world with which to frame questions but if only storied explanations and storied names were available. The potential cognitive capacity of a modern and Ice Age child would be equal, and they would develop through comparable stages; the sun and moon are also the same, and the human ability to recognize their patterns would not have changed. But the precise "cognitive strategies," to use Bruner's phrase, and the details of the relational and neurotic equations, to use Freud's concept, would vary according to the diverse cultural and reality problems faced in the two periods.

We have, then, both a potentiality and a limitation in the development of the story skill.

How would an early notation relate to these problems of cognition and story? Let us begin in the period before notation appears in the archaeological levels and look at the evidence of the stone tools. The tools offer a record of more than 2,000,000 years of development; notations appear as a cultural fact only with modern man.

I have indicated that the first pebble tools, such as those found at Olduvai Gorge by the Leakeys, implied a developing ability to think and perform in time, sequentially, with a complex series of time-factored recognitions. Before seeking the pebble, one had to know what the pebble could and would do; after finding the pebble, one had to know that striking one stone upon another would chip it. Even at this simple level, one had to know the proper sequence of coordinated movements. After the tool was made the hunter or digger had in mind, though not in words, a variable range of activities and skills related to that pebble tool, and these included a lore of animals and materials, such as the potentialities of the sharpened stone on skin, bone, and flesh, or on soil and tuber. Early forms of sequential tool-seeking, tool-using, and toolmaking are found in other creatures of many species, but the increasing complexity, potential duration, and range is one of the important behavioral hominoid differences.

We have, then, early evidence for an evolutionary step in cognition, though we are perhaps not yet far beyond the kinesthetic intelligence that simply grasps a stick, a bone, or a stone to strike an animal. Earlier than *Homo habilis,* the evolving hominoids must have recognized that an *unworked* stone or club could break a skull or the back of a small animal, or else split a bone or nut. The fact that one stone could break another stone is, therefore, not a great leap forward. But it is a step, since the breaking of a stone was not intended for immediate eating of the stone. Some apes are at this stage of crude toolmaking. The hominoid may at first have learned that a stone can be broken by hurling, or be chipped by dropping. A kinesthetic "knowledge" or capacity for the breaking of things was there at this primate level. What evolved was the coordination of this capacity as sequential thinking, with increased memory, feedback, and visual-kinesthetic inputs, extending from hunger to the search to the breaking of the stone, to the use of it to break a skull or back or to split a bone or to crack a nut.

Now if we go to the next stage, to the evolving hominid on the way to being *Homo erectus,* when slightly larger animals were hunted and killed, certainly over a larger, more varied territory, then we have a creature with new kinesthetic problems. For one thing, the larger animals have a tougher skin, a thicker skull, a heavier bone, a greater speed, a wider range of foraging territory, and more meat to be cut and separated from the skin and bones. Your evolved kinesthetic logic now tells you that you want a more efficient cutting edge, and your evolved manipulative-cognitive capacity allows you now to chip the stone more carefully, a number of times on each side to increase the sharpness of the cutting edge.

The brain capable of this increase in kinesthetic and time-factored thinking was using that capacity not only to shape tools but more generally to conceptualize "in the round" not only in terms of the tool in hand but in time and space, in the skills of the search and hunt, and in the skills of protection and shelter.

By the next stage, the *Homo erectus* stage of Peking Man and the use of fire, tools were being chipped roughly around the full pebble, except perhaps for the hand grip on top, to form a generally useful chopper or scraper. It is a larger brain that is capable of this increased kinesthetic thinking, a larger brain in a more evolved body, probably capable of a wider walking, running, hunting, and foraging range. This near-man could not only conceptualize and work his stone more carefully "in the round" but could also structure all his activities across a wider range, for longer periods, with greater care and complexity. This *Homo erectus* level of toolmaking requires an interrelated series of sequential, controlled blows to create one or another intentional design. These specific skills are the product of the more generalized evolved capacity. This is evident in the other finds. *Homo erectus* was not only chipping a diversity of stone tools; he was using bone, and it must be assumed in this context that to some extent he was creating different types of tools at the right time, in the right season, at the proper place, for the specific animal or task. In the making of his stone tools each stroke now depended on what the blow before had done. The elements in such complex skills would have been taught and learned sequentially. For one tool in the kit there may have been hundreds of cognitive-kinesthetic steps involved, all cohered and "understood" without a use of words.

By the time of the near-modern man who made the tools in the Abbevillian levels of the Somme gravel pits that Boucher de Perthes excavated and that the Abbé Breuil put in chronological order, biface tools were being chipped by a careful sequence of sharp blows on one face; the stone was then turned over and another sequence of blows was made so that the fractures met, until at last a full, pear-shaped core had been sculpted. Techniques for chipping varied in different parts of the world during this stage, but in general the cultures continued to develop better cutting or working edges and more complex tool kits. An analysis of the cognitive concepts and skills involved at each stage in the development of toolmaking would indicate the extraordinary evolutionary development of the combined kinesthetic, cognitive, and sequential skills increasingly involved.

By the time of Neanderthal man, the stone tools are exquisitely conceived and wrought, and the range of specialized tools, points, and edges comparatively large. The same mind is already involved in complex territorial specialization, in ritual, and in ceremonial burial. When we reach *Homo sapiens,* there is a still more evolved tool kit and the evidence of art and notation, indicating a further development in time-factored culture.

It is interesting that the toolmaking skill had evolved as a sequential activity that increasingly approached the abstract, time-factored thinking required for sculpture, the shaping of slates, ceremonial objects, artistic compositions, and sequential notation. The Upper Paleolithic hunter who shaped a slate and then made a series of notational marks with tools chipped for the purpose of engraving was the inheritor of an evolved capacity.

At one stage and before the appearance of notation, this evolving brain could probably increasingly recognize and conceptualize the "shapes" and phases of the moon. This may have been done in many ways. We can conjecture one with relevance to the toolmaking skill. It is possible that in some group the first sound or name that was given to the moon, or to one of its phases, was a kinesthetic recognition, much like that of the African Bushman's meat-cutting recognition. But in this particular case, perhaps, the crescent moon may have been named for the first flake chipped off a pebble; the full moon may have been named for the waterworn, rounded untouched pebble, the half-moon for the tool. It may not have happened, but it is within the realm of possibility, in terms of the potential capacity and the culture. Before a name had been given to each phase of the moon, the phases would have seemed "understandable" to a brain capable of shaping a form, of chipping a pebble, and of obtaining crescent flakes and a "half-moon" tool. The name, then, when it came, could have represented a recognition, a comparison, a process, a story meaningful in that culture.

Turn back and look at the engraved sequences presented in Chapters V and VII. You will find that the sequences will have assumed a meaning at this point of our analysis they did not have at first. Like any member of *Homo sapiens* we have been helped to see a pattern and a process *by story,* and while doing so we have been using our basic visual-kinesthetic, time-factored, and cognitive ability.

Now turn back to the early explanation of the lunar model in Chapter III (p. 30). As an introduction, it was purposefully simple. We now need an explanation a bit more advanced.

We must forget everything we know about the week, the month and the year. We must forget the seven-day week, the 29-, 30-, and 31-day month, and the 365¼-day year, for these are a result of relatively late cultural divisions and subdivisions developed by the first agricultural civilizations of the Middle East and Nile some 5,000 years ago. Though the root of this late development, apparently, goes back to the Ice Age, we can assume no such numerical, calendric division in the Aurignacian of 32,000 years ago.

We must assume that the marks and scratches, in their early stages, did not represent numbers; they were not numerals as we know them, or part of a system of numbers. They could not, in the Aurignacian, be manipulated as numbers, as we do in our decimal system, in multiples of 5, 10, 20, 60, or 100.

This may be difficult since we are trained to think in numbers. If we see 3 scratches, or 9 scratches, or 30 scratches, we think of them as "3," "9," and "30" and they seem related as numbers in a decimal system. Instead, we must think of these scratches as forms of notation; we can then try to reconstruct how they might have been used *if* they were lunar. At first, perhaps, a hunter on a long hunt may have made a scratch, and then the next day another. If he began with the new moon, or the day of invisibility, and ended with the full moon, he had 14, 15, or 16 scratches. If he ended with the new moon, he had 28, 29, or 30 scratches.

Considering the difficulties of observation and the problems of weather, this rough figure is not hard to understand.

But we must be careful. We are *assuming* that our Upper Paleolithic man could not count, and we are assuming that he began his notation at some logical point such as the new moon or the full moon. We are also assuming that he was making scratches to record the "phases" of the moon. None of these things need be true.

It is doubtful, for instance, that the Ice Age hunter was much interested either in an abstracted number system or in "keeping records" in a modern sense for modern purposes, or that he had any understanding of the modern astronomical concept of the "phases of the moon."

Why, then, should he have kept a lunar notation? Here we return to our prior assumptions.

Against the phases of the moon he told a story, or he told many stories. And against the phases of the moon he held at least some of his rites and ceremonies, which is another way of telling a story. And against the phases of the moon he structured his practical, social, cultural, and biological life.

If this is true, then the notations might have been "remembering marks" in a well-known story, a story perhaps as old as language itself, or as old as language when it had developed to the point that it could carry a complex story. The skill in notation would in such a case have developed *after* the astronomical, observational lore and stories were known, perhaps for remembering and perhaps for teaching.

I have been informed by Professor Ward H. Goodenough, University of Pennsylvania, editor of *American Anthropologist*, that in the Caroline Islands of the Pacific, natives keep "count" of the days in a lunar month by having a different name for each day and major phase. One remembers thirty names the way we remember the seven days of the week or the names of the twelve months. This is a way of counting, but it is *not* numerical. And for us, too, each name is storied.

One of the primitive hunting peoples still living is the Stone Age Australian aborigine. He may at one time, thousands of years before, in a different land and a better environment, have had a different specialized culture and lore, but the general level of his cognitions and skills might not have been far different than it is now. He is today an isolated, undeveloped, and perhaps even a regressed hunter-gatherer. Yet the Australian aborigine in some areas still uses notation on "message-sticks." These superficially and at first glance look like the notations made by the Ice Age hunter. We must be careful of such analogies. The archaeological evidence we have from Europe of 32,000 years ago indicates that the Ice Age hunter, on a different line of economic and racial development, in a richer, more complex environment, had taken cultural steps beyond those available to the present aborigine. Nevertheless, the Australian message-sticks are significant, not because they are "comparable" products but because they operate at similar levels of cognition. They have been studied as a minor aspect of the complex Australian aborigine culture.

G. Horne and G. Aiston give a summary of the uses of these sticks in a few tribes:

"Message-sticks are frequently in use amongst the Wonkonguru, but seem to be employed chiefly for two purposes. In the first place as a token of good faith, and secondly as memory help for numbers. The blacks' command of numerals is very limited, so this latter use was quite necessary.

"An example of the first is to be found in the message-sticks sent with the men of the red ochre and the *pitcheri* expeditions. These were carried to the owner of the commodity in question from the old men of the tribe that sent the messengers. Apparently they conveyed no actual message, but were simply the same as when in old days a king sent his signet ring for a token showing the messenger's genuineness and also from whom the request was made. The real message was always in these cases given by word of mouth through the messengers.

"In the second case it was sought to convey also the number of sleeps or moons before a thing would occur, or the number of men or women or old men who were expected at, say, a corroboree [a ritual, ceremonial dance]. The meaning of the sender was to be conveyed by various signals. Thus I was shown a stick with three notches on one end. This, I was told, meant that in three sleeps the receiver was to be ready to serve in a pinya (a revenge party) . . .

". . . I have a message-stick which was sent round by one of the Anula tribe in the far north and was accompanied by a plume of white cockatoo feathers fastened on the end of a stick. This was a call to a corroboree. It was apparently a conventional design, of crosses and v's, the cuts being rubbed in with red ochre . . .

"There seem to be three classes of message-stick amongst the Wonkonguru. First the mnemonic, where nicks are cut in the stick which mean so many moons, or men, or bags of ochre, or some meaning that the bearer supplies *viva voce* or by his appearance. The second is the conventional, where the chief idea of the native is to 'make 'em pretty fella.' But certain regular designs are followed and different patterns may mean exactly the same thing. The message is given by certain ways the man is painted or things that he carries, if he does not actually speak. But generally the message-stick is simply a guarantee of good faith.

"Quite often the appearance of the marks themselves seems to have a significance, so the burnt-in knife-cuts on one seem to accentuate that it is a message to fight. The sticks may be coated with yellow or with red ochre . . . Sometimes they are dotted with minute spots, which are often enclosed without pattern in spaces, sometimes arranged in bands, either single, double, or treble; or they may be like the leaves of trees.

"These bands are said to take the place of the nicks cut in the stick and to have different meanings according to the number of conjoined bands. Thus single bands might mean women, double bands young men, and treble bands old men. The message then would run: Send so many women, so many young men, and so many old men. The appearance of the messenger would convey that it was a corroboree or whatever it was.

"The third sort of message-stick is the rarest, and it definitely shows places and things. This is apparently either to point out a direction to a given locality, or is the description of the place . . . The message-sticks can therefore be classified as the mnemonic, the conventional, and the pictorial."[7]

These message-sticks are then an extremely primitive

form of notation, still far from writing and arithmetic. We cannot assume that their specific cultural uses in Australia were the same as in Ice Age Europe.

Nevertheless, there are similarities. The message-sticks are one indication that the Australian aborigine has evolved culturally to the point where he lives in economic and cultural contact with neighboring groups of the same basic culture, and that these interrelations are structured both in time and space and are maintained by a common understanding and story. These interrelations are dependent on both verbal and non-verbal referents and symbols. A comparable evidence for complex interrelations in time and space is apparent in the kin and intermarriage structures that the aborigines have developed. The message-sticks are an indication of the cognitive, visual-kinesthetic, time-factored, and story levels reached by all *Homo sapiens*. A dot, or a scratch, was a unit with a meaning and story.

A painted or engraved composition, even when not realistic or figurative, often had a complex, storied meaning. Though concepts of number, quantity, geometry, and constancy were involved and could be notated and indicated, transmitted and read, these were not *arithmetical* in the sense that we use a system of numbers or coordinates. Finally, we find in the aborigine a *sense* of unit time and of time in sums that is capable of being notated, and that at times was notated, but which has other verbal and non-verbal means of expression and communication. There was the indication of a "day count" in terms of "moons" or "sleeps," a concept of sequential time which makes up a unit or duration. C. P. Mountford, a leading ethnologist, adds that "sometimes there were notches, the length of [a] journey in days."[8]

At other times message-sticks indicated the length and distance of a journey in terms of a sequence of water holes. There has even been uncorroborated mention by an author with the government native health service of the use of a notched stick by women to record their months of pregnancy.[9] The true mea-

[7] G. Horne and G. Aiston, SAVAGE LIFE IN CENTRAL AUSTRALIA (London: Macmillan, 1924), pp. 22–24.

[8] Charles P. Mountford, ART, MYTH AND SYMBOLISM, Records of the American-Australian Expedition to Arnhem Land, Vol. 1 (Melbourne: Melbourne University Press, 1956), p. 466.

[9] Xavier Herbert, CAPRICORNIA (London: Rich & Cowan, 1939).

sure of the depth, scope, and complexity of aboriginal time-factored thought, however, is found in the round of seasonal economic and ritual or storytelling activities.

Donald F. Thomson, an Australian anthropologist, has studied the aborigine's economic activities in a way that has meaning for our study of the Upper Paleolithic cultures, since aboriginal time-factored thought, utilizing both seasonal activities and time-factored stories, while completely different in detail from that in Ice Age Europe, is at the same level of human cognition. Our comparison, then, should not be of the product, but of the process:

"In the interpretation of the evidence provided by archaeological investigation it is important to realise its limitations, and to appreciate the complexity of the factors involved . . . an onlooker, seeing these ['stone age'] people at different seasons of the year, would find them engaged in occupations so diverse, and with weapons and utensils differing so much in character, that if he were unaware of the seasonal influence on food supply, and consequently upon occupation, he would . . . conclude that they were different groups . . . little would remain to suggest to an archaeologist of the future, forced to depend upon the examination of old camp sites and such artefacts as resisted decay, the extent and complexity of the culture.

"Within the bounds . . . of a single . . . territory a people may spend several months of the year as nomadic hunters, in pursuit of bush game, wild honey and small mammals, and exploiting the resources of vegetable foods . . . A few months later the same people may be found established on the sea coast in camps that have all the appearance of permanence or at least . . . semi-permanence, having apparently abandoned their nomadic habits. They will remain in these camps for months on end, engaged now in fishing and in the harpooning of dugong and turtle from canoes; leading, in fact, the life of a typical fishing and seafaring culture. In each case the camps and the house types, the weapons and the utensils, are of a specialised type and related to the seasonal life . . . (the) relatively rich material culture . . . would . . . leave only the slenderest evidence for later archaeological investigation.

"The seasonal factor is recognised by the aborigines themselves, and stressed by the fact that they have classified the types of country, as accurately and as scientifically as any ecologist, giving to each a name, and associating it with specific resources, with its animal and vegetable foods, and its technological products . . . in spite of this com-

plexity, this sophistication, which is not generally credited to people of a 'stone age' culture, little enough would remain on account of the ephemeral nature of the greater part of the material used, to provide a key to the true state of affairs or even to correlate as part of a seasonal cycle the occupational sites which are visited regularly at the appropriate season. Too often the nomadic movements of such people have been regarded as merely aimless or random wanderings; studied at first hand they assume a very different character. It cannot be emphasised too strongly that these movements, each circumscribed and conducted within well-defined limits and definitely related to a season and a food supply, take on a very different aspect; seen in true perspective, they form a regular and *orderly* annual cycle carried out systematically, and with a rhythm parallel to, and in step with, the seasonal changes themselves."[10]

Of one aborigine group, the Wik Monkan, Thomson writes about the

"orderliness of their lives . . . the systematic way in which every activity is planned and carried out . . . manifest in the methods of collecting and preparing food, and in every technological process which is carried out, and [which] is well illustrated in the systematic method employed for the classification of plants, animals, and material objects connected with domestic or social life . . ."[11]

The Wik Monkan divide the year into five named seasons, each with distinctive climate, food supply, and activities, and specialized forms of huts or shelters. Thomson gives a detailed account of the skills and activities of each season.

What the archaeological record would not show, however, and what this economic analysis of the group also does not show, is the nature of the cognitions involved and the nature of the stories that make of these activities, and of the other human interrelations and activities, a cultural whole.

The literature on the Australian mythology is vast, for though still a "stone age" hunter, he has developed and specialized his storytelling and symbol-making skill to an extraordinary degree. It is this that has helped him coalesce the complexities of his culture with its interrelations in time and space. What is significant and has not been particularly noted or stressed is the amount of hard knowledge and observational

[10] Donald F. Thomson, "The Seasonal Factor in Human Culture," PROCEEDINGS OF THE PREHISTORIC SOCIETY, New Series, Vol. V, Part 2 (1939), pp. 209, 211.

[11] Ibid., p. 212.

lore contained in this mythology. One of the most beautiful poems ever composed is an aboriginal song sung seasonally, which relates the adventures of the Moon and Evening Star (Venus) in an early time.[12] The qualities of the precise seasonal detail in the observation of nature that it contains are awesome and, when these portions are separated out from the tribal referants and names, even paraphrased, the song is breathtaking. The myth concerns the death and rebirth of the moon as repeated in the phases. Outside of such richly mythological structures, the aborigine more simply recognizes and names the four phases of the moon: new moon, half-moon, three-quarter-moon and full moon. Moon and sun are both anthropomorphized, the moon being masculine, the sun feminine. In addition, some tribes describe the phases in terms of other forms or of animals, the half-moon, for instance, in one case being said to look like a seated opossum.

The American Indian of historic times, at a higher level of cultural and economic development than the Australian aborigine and of different racial stocks than the aborigine or the Ice Age hunter of Europe, showed a similar capacity and skill. He also used message-sticks and tally-sticks, and kept records of events, historic, mythological, or ceremonial.

At the time of contact with the European navigators and colonists of the western expansion in the sixteenth century, the American Indian represented a conglomerate of peoples, languages, and cultures at various levels of development and regression, from the high Inca (Peru) and Aztec (Mexico) to groups living in marginal subsistence from the Alaskan north to shellfish and fishing cultures of the near-Antarctic Cape Horn. The Indians were neither homogeneous in their levels of culture when found nor in their levels of development when diverse groups first arrived in the Americas. They came, apparently, in "waves" from Asia and the Pacific over a period of perhaps 20,000 or more years and represented various stages or levels of Upper Paleolithic and post-Ice Age culture.

The specialized, evolved, and remnant uses of notation, art, symbol, rite, and story found in the Americas varied widely, and the uses and skills of tallying, counting, and arithmetic also varied. One cannot, then, speak of the American Indian as one speaks of the Australian aborigine, as a people more or less homogenous in stock and culture. Nevertheless, for our purpose, the American Indian as a group will serve since, being *Homo sapiens* and at the furthest extreme of human dispersal from Africa and Europe, he used the same basic processes of cognition, time-space orientation, notation, and story and developed the same techniques and cultural products. The notations of the American Indian, though extremely varied and more evolved than those of the aborigines, served cultural purposes not much different than they did in Australia.

A small notched message-stick of the Seneca, with a hole at one end for a knotted string, looks exactly like certain Upper Paleolithic notched bones and some Australian message-sticks. It contains a marking of days, calling chiefs to a particular ceremony at a certain time. A small tally-stick of the Onandaga with twenty-seven notches was a "condolence" record, listing twenty-seven chiefs who had died. A tribe of the Sioux at the end of the eighteenth and beginning of the nineteenth centuries had a "slender pole about six feet in length, the surface of which was covered with small notches, and the old Indian who had it assured him [Clark] that it had been handed down from father to son for many generations and that those notches represented the history of his tribe for more than a thousand years back to the time when they lived near the ocean."[13]

At the Museum of the American Indian, Heye Foundation, New York, there is a long, four-faced "calendar stick" of the Pima Indians, Arizona, that represents forty-five years of notation, with one unpainted notch for each year and with other painted notches and dots representing important events to be remem-

[12] Ronald M. Berndt, "A Wonguri-Mandzikai Song Cycle of the Moon-Bone," OCEANIA, Vol. XIX (September 1948), pp. 16 to 50.

[13] James Mooney, "Calendar History of the Kiowa Indians," SEVENTEENTH ANNUAL REPORT OF THE BUREAU OF AMERICAN ETHNOLOGY 1895–1896, Part I (Washington: Government Printing Office, 1898), pp. 142–143.

bered in each year, such as the "raid" of one year, the meteoric shower of another, the earthquake of another, the flood of still another, or the great snowstorm of another. Each year had its unit mark, and each year also had its specialized mark and story, either as an edge-mark, a series of dots, a colored mark, an angle-mark, a spiral, and so on. This was essentially a nonnumerical "counting" and remembering system and one could go back "twenty-five" years by twenty-five marks and by twenty-five stories. Superficially, this record stick looks like those found on bones and stones of the Upper Paleolithic.

Another technique of notation involved painting. There is a painted Sioux buffalo skin in which the sequence of time, in unit years, is not linear but spiral, recalling the way time was structured on the tiny Aurignacian slate from the Abri Blanchard (Figs. 9, 10). It includes seventy years of notation, starting from the center and working out from right to left. Among the Plains tribes past years were usually counted by winters, each winter being known and named for some event taking place at the time, instead of being numbered as is our custom. To keep track of the sequence of winters, painted charts were prepared in which the successive year was remembered by a symbol bringing to mind the event the recorder thought most important or characteristic.

Running together with these storied tribal year counts were other time-factored counts, sometimes notated and sometimes oral. There were day counts indicating distances on a journey or hunt. There were non-numerical lunar month "counts" for economic and ceremonial purposes. The month list, for instance, might include mid-winter names like "Snow Moon," or "Hunger Moon"; spring names like "Awakening Moon," "Salmon Moon," "Grass Moon"; autumn names like "Leaf-falling Moon," "Bison-fighting Moon," and beginning winter names like "Long Night Moon." Tribes differed in the names they used, but they were of this sort.

At a later time I shall discuss the complexities of these widely dispersed historic systems of time-factored notation and geometry and their relations to the European Upper Paleolithic traditions. Here I point out only that the *cognitive skills* involved were essentially the same as those used by the hunter of Ice Age Europe and by the Mesolithic fisher of Ishango at the

headwaters of the Nile, though the peoples, languages, cultures, stories, and the specialized uses and techniques of the notations differed. The American Indian notations on wood, skin, bark, and knotted cord or leather would long since have decayed except that an occasional example obtained from an Indian chief or priest was put into a museum collection or was buried in the dry sands of a culture like the Inca of Peru.[14]

Another peripheral people, racially related to some of the Mongoloid "Indian" peoples who came from Asia and Siberia over the Bering Straits along the Arctic Circle, today lives on a small group of equatorial islands in the Indian Ocean, off the coast of Malaysia and Sumatra.

Isolated from the full impact of historic influences from the Chinese, Arab, Hindu, or European proselytizing cultures except for a small trade in such items as coconuts and knives, the relatively primitive farming and fishing natives of the Nicobar Islands use a highly evolved system of notation that includes marking off of the days of a sea journey, as well as a more specialized lunar calendar. The people are Mongoloid or "Indo-Chinese":

"The Nicobarese are a Mongolian people who in prehistoric days passed over to the islands from the opposite shores of Burma ... or Malaya ... their language has affinities with the Indo-Chinese languages as represented nowadays by the Mon language of Pegu and Annam, and the Khmer language of Cambodia, amongst civilized peoples, and by the languages of a number of uncivilized tribes in the Malay Peninsula and Indo-China."[15]

The Nicobarese lunar calendar sticks are engraved on soft, white tropical wood cut to look like a dagger or knife. They look similar to the bone "spatulas" or "knives" of unknown use found in the Upper Paleo-

---

[14] The most significant of the North American Indian calendar sticks is a rare, early nineteenth century wooden year-stick that notated the days and phases of the lunar month. Exceedingly close to Upper Paleolithic lunar notations in appearance and concept, it will be discussed in detail in a later publication. Robert H. Merrill, "The Calendar Stick of Tshi-zun-hau-kau", CRANBROOK INSTITUTE OF SCIENCE, Bull. 24 (October 1945).

[15] George Whitehead, IN THE NICOBAR ISLANDS (London: Seeley, Service, & Co., 1924), p. 226.

lithic of Europe, from the Solutrean to the Magdalenian, objects which often contain notations. The style of these Nicobarese notations recalls that of the Upper Paleolithic, for the periods are differentiated both by count and by the angle of making. One month is placed opposite another to create a chevron effect in which one month gives the measure for the other, and, when space runs out, one month may be engraved over another to create a hatch effect. An example from the literature, apparently indicative, is presented in Figure 40, a Nicobarese calendar stick for at least eight months.[16]

Kenrata, which I have been able to analyze, seems to have evolved from this and gives a rough 10+10+10 = 30 count, a system in which the lunar sub-phases are apparently not observed or indicated, but it is the whole month that counts (Figs. 41, 42).[18] This system is interested in the *sums of months* that make up the Nicobarese six- or seven-month "year." During one year the monsoon wind blows from the northeast, in the other from the southwest. This Kenrata is often used to measure the years in the growth of a child.

The general kinesthetic-visual-cognitive thinking involved in this style of notation is so similar to that

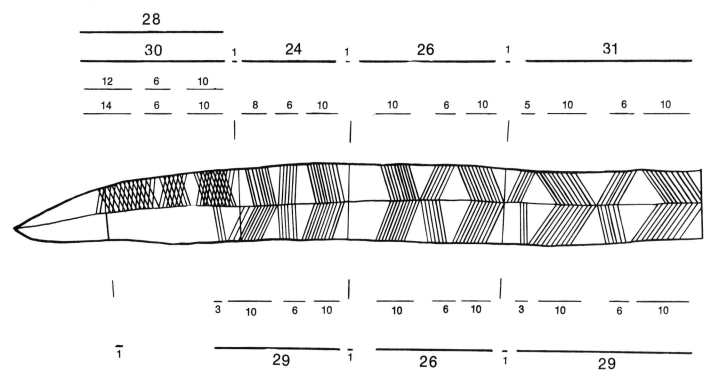

The author writes that

"the notches are meant to go 10–6, 10–4 = 30. When the notches fill one side of the *Kenrata* they commence on the other, and thus keep tally for quite a while."[17]

The lunar phrasing by this system is:

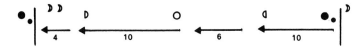

It is not always precise, and requires an occasional 11, 3, or 5 count. A second sort of tally system on the

found in the Upper Paleolithic of Europe that it is uncertain whether we are dealing with the evolved remnant of an ancient notational tradition or merely a similar expression of the cognitive capacity.

Significantly, the Nicobarese used a *naming* system for every day in the lunar month, with a name for each

[16] E. H. Man, THE NICOBAR ISLANDS (London: Royal Anthropological Institute, 1933), p. 95.

[17] Loc. cit.

[18] Collection, Museum of Archaeology and Ethnology, Cambridge University.

change of phase, and they broke this down even further with a name for each phase *period* consisting of a number of days, such as the period of the "waxing moon," the "disappearing moon," the "full moon." This was a subsidiary oral system whose presence lay behind the notations and could not be determined from an analysis of the *Kenrata*.

processes, however, are similar to those of the peripheral peoples I have discussed.

The first thing one notices when one looks at the hundreds of Ice Age bones and stones with scratched sequences, and at the signs and notations on the cave walls, is that no two are ever exactly alike.

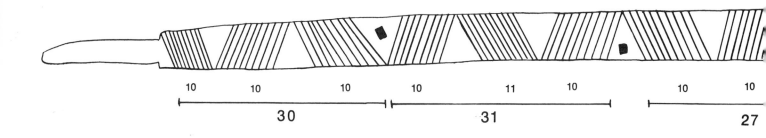

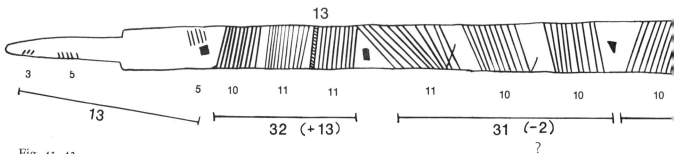

Fig. 41, 42
Schematic renditions of one engraved face on two contemporary lunar calendar sticks from the Nicobar Islands. Indicated are grouping of sets by alternating angles, use of periodic marks of division, apparent marks of subtraction and terminal subsidiary sets within and outside of the primary notation. Reverse faces are in same style.

These are aspects of a highly evolved space-time culture, in which the day is subdivided and in which sun and stars are observed and distances, directions, ceremonies and activities are "measured."

Other islanders of Southeast Asia and the Pacific, representing other races, have used other calendric systems. Moving to the central land mass of Eurasia, to the Siberian and northern territories and to peoples along the northern Pacific coast, areas and cultures from which the American Indian groups came, one finds an extensive tradition of seasonal and lunar observation, notation, and myth. The complexity of these Asian traditions, which point backward to the Upper Paleolithic and eastward to America, requires discussion and analysis at a later time. The cognitive

For the scientist who may be trying to make sense of these marks—and many have tried—the difficulty, on the face of it, is huge. In fact, if one approaches them as "writing" or as arithmetical counting, it is impossible. For there is often not much internal patterning among the sequences nor material available for precise stylistic comparison between examples. Some sequences, particularly in the later stages, may contain fifty or more marks without any apparent differentiation. There are occasional signs or symbols among the notations, but even these vary. One cannot, therefore, "crack the code," as scientists have cracked the codes of the ancient structured writings of the early civilizations from Egypt, Mesopotamia, Phoenicia, and Crete, or as they cracked the codes of the number and astronomical systems of many of these early civilizations. If one approaches the marks as mnemonic, that is, as a storied notation, it is also impossible to perform analysis, because the reference would be not to a periodic, constant pattern but to a random patterning. Fortunately, the engraved bones do indicate a consistent grouping by "periods" made sequentially and therefore lunar tests can be made of their patterns. How do we reconstruct or re-create a lunar notation at a level so early that we assume the man making it could not count, read, or write?

In the analysis that follows I will use numbers and simple arithmetic, but merely as analytic tools.

Begin at the right:

Since we are using numbers in our analysis, we can easily have a numerical uncertainty in the count of

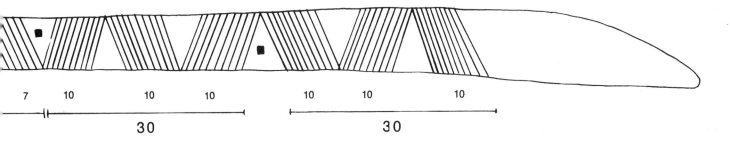

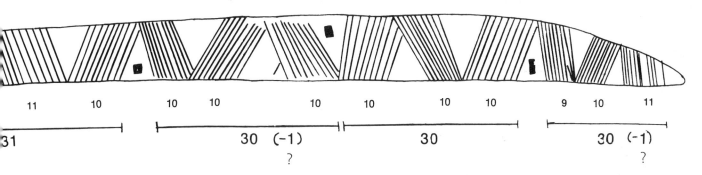

The month as the astronomer measures it is approximately 29½ days long. But if you make a mark for each day you cannot count the half-day, and the month would be either 29 or 30 days. If you made marks only on days in which the moon was visible, it would be 27 or 28 days, because the moon is in the earth's shadow and invisible one, two, or three days each month. The astronomer calls this the "new moon" and signifies it as one day, but for the observer it may be more. A person notating a month and beginning on the day he saw the first crescent over the western sunset and making one mark a day until he saw the last crescent on the eastern horizon would have only 27 or 28 marks. The next notated period would then contain 29 or 30 marks if it included the two days of no moon and went to the next observable crescent, the last of the month. If he notated past the last crescent to the first crescent some days later, he would have 33 marks. To the maker of such a notation, the 27 and the 33 could easily represent "two moons."

any one lunar month, but this would be corrected or clarified by the length of the next month, a correction by the moon itself that will persist as one goes on through a long series of months.

Now, let us assume that the observer is interested not only in the month or "moon" but also in the full moon, the half-moon, or the crescents, perhaps because the story of the lunar month makes one of these a day of recognition or ceremony. There is another difficulty. A phase is not easy to determine to the precise day. Even in the twentieth century the modern Muhammadan using a lunar calendar in a region of clear skies, and using a month that begins on the day of the first crescent, and using an arithmetic that allows him to know when the month should approximately end and begin, has difficulty and local disputes over the precise day on which the first crescent may have been seen by this or that observer.

If you take the full moon as a *period of days,* you have a division of the month into two notational periods of unequal length. Let us say the full moon period is thought of as three days—the days of power, maturity, or fullness. This means that your month will be divided observationally and notationally and by story into a complex series of periods:

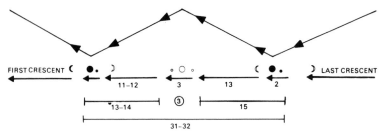

The problem is that the month, though it is divided into periods, is not divided into four equal periods. There are also one or two days in which no moon is visible, and there is the extra half-day that sometimes gives a long observational month, with the next time being short. But these problems would bother only a person trying to use numbers to divide the month. It would not bother a person telling the story of the phases, for the story is always the same, nor would it bother a person using names, since he can merely use one name for one month, no matter what its length, and another name for the next.

The problem, then, is not in the whole month but in the phases. There is, in fact, a simple non-arithmetic way of solving the problem of the whole month which begins to approach arithmetic. Say you dig a hole and each day from the day of first crescent you drop in a pebble. By the time you reach the last crescent you have 28 pebbles in the hole. There are then two days of invisibility and you drop in 2 black pebbles. You now have thirty pebbles in the hole and one month is gone. These 30 pebbles are your measure. If you now make a notch on a stick or a bone, or paint a mark on a wall, you have that one month indicated. If on the next day, the day of first crescent, you begin taking out one pebble a day, you will find that when the hole is empty you are back to the day of the first crescent. Your last pebble on that day would be a black one, which means that the crescent has moved forward one day. You now start over that same day, dropping in a plain pebble in place of the black. In this way your thirty pebbles can be used for a 59-day, two-month period, with one black pebble being an extra at the end of each two months. This is no more difficult than the games children play.

There is no similar, simple way of solving the problem of the phases and quarters. If you are interested in the half-moon, full moon, and crescents, you will have to wait for these points from one phase to the next. They are not an equal number of marks apart. If you are not interested in numbers, this makes no difference. If, however, in a simple way you begin to be interested in numbers, then it is not hard to work out a system using your fingers. You would quickly

realize that, if you begin on the day after the last crescent and count 10 fingers, you arrive at the half-moon:

One hand, or 5 days later, you arrive at the day before the full moon *period*:

One hand after the full moon period, or 5 days later, you arrive at the day before the second half-moon, within a day or two.

You wait your day or so for the half-moon and then on the next day count one more hand of 5 days and you arrive at the last crescent. This is a rough, simple kind of arithmetic that would work more or less like a notation system. Your hands and experience and stories would tell you on what day, approximately, to expect a phase, though because of weather and the variations in the moon itself, you may not see it on the day you expect.

There is, of course, no evidence for the use of such a system in the Upper Paleolithic, and I worked it out merely as a possible system that might have used the simplest possible sort of counting, by fingers, to fore-

ment of a tradition, so let us see what the problem would look like to a man making scratches. Observationally, the days from first crescent to first half-moon are eight:

This eight can disappear notationally if the observational periods are made so, dropping the crescent

tell the phases, but not yet a number system where large sums were required.

There is a danger here. I am assuming a level of cognitive ability that is modern, with a possible use of such constants as the periods of the moon and the hands. The system, then, is possible, but such a system would not have been used unless there was a *cultural* reason or need, practical, ceremonial, or economic. A man leaving on a hunt or a journey for a five-day period may be told to be back in "one hand" *before* the next quarter, or a number of family groups might be asked to assemble for a ceremony at the "full moon," three hands from the first crescent. This is conjecture, but it does indicate a possibility for development when the time-factored geometry and the interrelations of a culture had become sufficiently complex and precise. The lunar system would then be "at hand" as a common measure for all peoples at this level.

These, then, are conjectures, and the fact is that we have only the marked bones. These engraved sequences imply a somewhat late stage in the develop-

from the eight:

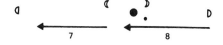

Or the eight can appear as an entirely different lunar period, beginning, say, with the last quarter:

If you look at a marked bone with short sequences, it will be difficult, then, to determine if a lunar phrasing is present, or which periods may have been notated. The uncertainties lessen as the number of marked periods made in sequence increases. Each group of marks will then maintain and clarify the general lunar phrasing. Sequences running to many months will often begin to give indications—both by their counts and by other notational means (spacing, angle of marks, signs, etc.)—of the important points around invisibility. A typical lunar month as it might be observed and notated is presented in the full lunar model designed for the purposes of the research:

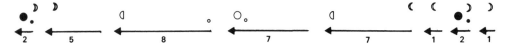

But within this basic lunar phrasing there are many other observational and notational possibilities. Because of normal observational difficulties that can occur, representing a day in either direction, the observational phrases or points may vary so:

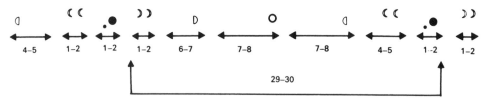

These possibilities can be increased, since in times of bad weather groups may be merged. In addition, one can either end or begin a period on the day of an observation, or the day before or after. Because the small groups can be made up in so many combinations, ordinary counting and totalling at this late date in the twentieth century is an inadequate analytic tool, except to give rough sums as a guide.

The lunar model was devised for these reasons and to make it possible to visualize patterns through the uncertainties. It presents *two* forms of visual breakdown, one indicating the astronomical observational points, the other indicating the possible endings or beginnings of periods around these points. By putting a sequence of many periods against this model, one can visually determine if there is a possible lunar phrasing involved. With this as a first step in a sequence of analysis, we can then make more complex tests.

In using the model, however, we must remember that the man making his marks probably had other sorts of aids: stories, names, kinesthetic-visual cues, and perhaps even an early form of finger counting that would not be indicated in the observational phrasing. In addition, he may have been primarily interested in months, that is, in longer periods to mark off his seasons, and not at all in the smaller periods, except perhaps now and then for an important one. Somehow, if a lunar notation were used, there would have to be a number of subsidiary cultural systems involved. By reference to current primitive peoples, we have seen how these are utilized.

Now let us turn to the evidence.

CHAPTER X

THE BONE OF THE EAGLE

In cabinet number one at the Musée des Antiquités Nationales in 1965, there lay a tiny gray, broken bit of hollow eagle bone. It was some 4½ inches long (11 cm), had been cut by a flint knife at one end, and was broken at the other. It came from a level approximately 13,000 to 15,000 years old, was dated as late middle Magdalenian and came from the same site of Le Placard that gave us the two earlier Magdalenian bâtons.

Worked or decorated bird bones are not uncommon in the Upper Paleolithic. Some have blow holes cut into them, indicating their use as whistles or flutes, and they can be blown to give a high, piping, flute sound.

At first glance the bone seemed to have been scratched lightly with an exceedingly fine engraving on three sides. The main face had a series of large multiple angles; along the flat sides were long rows of tiny angles that looked like inverted " λ 's." At first glance the markings

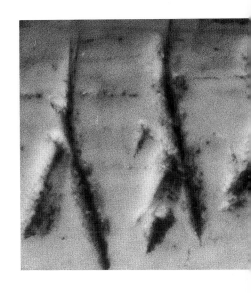

looked like decoration, a balanced geometric patterning. The bone was too fragile to have been put to any practical use, and this particular example did not seem to have been cut as a whistle. It may therefore originally have been intended for some "magical" ceremonial, sacred, or even notational use (Fig. 43 a, b, c).

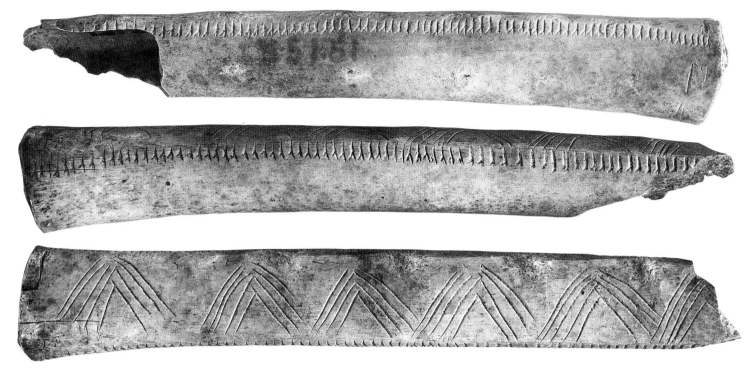

Fig. 43 a, b, c
The three faces of an engraved fragment of eagle bone from the site of Le Placard (Charente). Middle Magdalenian.

The tiny, careful " λ 's" were a puzzle. The Abbé Breuil had called such marks the abstract, degenerate, simplified images of horned animals. The large and small angles were also similar to markings that André Leroi-Gourhan, Europe's leading authority on Upper Paleolithic art following Breuil's death, had called "sexual signs" when found on the cave walls. They did not, however, seem to be animal or sexual signs here. In any case, the markings were late in the Upper Paleolithic tradition of engraving.

Under the microscope the gray bird bone became a "library"—which I sat "reading" and pondering for many days. The hard, tight composition of the bone and its burial in dry soil had retained an absolutely clean, unweathered surface that still maintained its original shine. Except for graying with age and drying, it felt and looked like new bone. It was the tight bird-bone composition that had made possible the original sharp, clean engraving. These marks were easier to "read" than the crumbled engraved edges of the pebble from Barma Grande and better than marks often found on somewhat softer, more easily decayed animal bone. In fact, this was the best bone I had yet put under the microscope, in terms of the uniformly high quality of the preserved engraved line. Under the microscope the fine " λ 's" seemed, once again, to have been made by a jeweler using a lens, though they had been made by a hunter using a chipped tool of stone or flint. The spacing and size of the small marks were comparable to the printed marks along the edge of a centimeter ruler. When they had been cut into the bone, they must have been as easy to read as my modern ruler with its black, painted marks.

What was astonishing was the complexity of these tiny marks. One can "read" a modern inch or centimeter ruler, though there is no language involved, because one has learned the *system* and because there are periodic, recognizable marks to indicate a half, a quarter, or one unit of measure. Looking at this ancient series of engraved marks, I was haunted by the feeling that a similar visual "system" was involved.

The first thing that became clear, as I focussed on each mark under the microscope, was that these were not " λ 's," but that each mark was rather composed of a long vertical with an appended "foot," the foot at an angle: _____

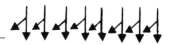

What was even more surprising, looking at one mark at a time, was that the vertical was always made by a different point than the foot. The marks were all so small that it did not seem that a man would change his tools first to make the verticals and then the feet. Nor did it look as though it was the same tool cutting first a vertical stroke, then making what appeared to be a different foot by holding the tool at an angle. The composition, in fact, was too complex.

Slowly, going carefully from one mark to the next and making notes and drawings for each stroke, turning and studying each mark in a varied light, the notes began to accumulate. At the end of the first week I had so many notes I was overwhelmed. It was only then that I could begin summing and grouping the results. Finally, I began a sequential reconstruction of the marks and, after that was done, a statistical analysis. Piecing the microscopic analysis together in the silent, chill library, almost 15,000 years after the eagle had flown and man had cleaned the bone to make his scratches, induced a strange excitement. Slowly the pattern emerged

At one end the bone was broken, at the other end cut. I could not tell what was missing in the break, but I did know that the series began or ended near the cut and that from the point of view of analyzing the structure of a series, I could consider the cut end as the "beginning." I there-

Fig. 44
Detail. The opening sequence of marks on the first face of the Placard eagle bone showing the differences between the points engraving the first 7 verticals and the next series of verticals as well as the feet.

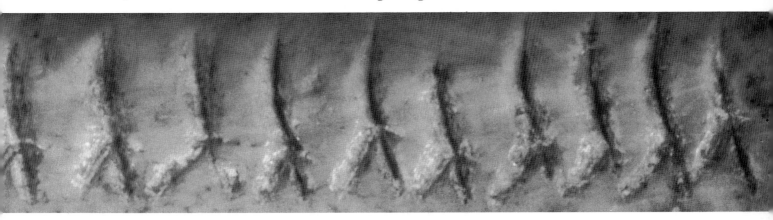

fore began with the series of marks at the top, above the points of the large multiple angles, with the broken end of the bone held toward the left and the cut end towards the right (Fig. 44).

The analysis is simple, though given in detail. When it is ended you should be able to "read" at least some of the bone.

The microscope showed that the first 14 marks were made by *two* different tools or points, the verticals by a point that made a sharp, deep track ($\vee$), the feet by a tool that made a somewhat wider, almost rounded mark ($\diagdown\!\diagup$). These differences are clear in the photo enlargement of the beginning of this series (Fig. 44). The "count" of the opening sequence, therefore, is:

After these 14 marks the microscope revealed that the next series of verticals was made by still a different, or *third* point. It created a double track and had either an entrance or an exit that flared apart.

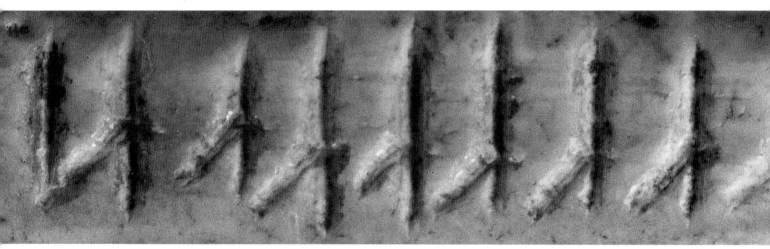

Fig. 45
Detail. First face of the Placard eagle bone. At right are the last three verticals of the series of 15, followed by the first six of the series of 29. The sixth mark in the 29 lacks a foot.

The walls of this series of strokes had a wider angle than the first 7 verticals, but narrower than the first 7 feet. This series of verticals, all made by this new point, had a count of 15:

The feet on this series of 15 were made by still another tool, the *fourth*. It is clear in the photo enlargement. This is a wide, shallow mark with a floor that has a double track: ($\diagdown\!\diagup$). Startlingly, the microscope revealed that this tool was used to make all the remaining feet in this series of upper marks. The verticals, however, continued to be made by a change in points.

After the 15 verticals, the next verticals were made by a point that cut a cleaner, sharper floor groove and that also had a different entrance and exit. This is clear when you compare the photo enlargement of this series (Fig. 45) with marks from the earlier series at the same enlargement. These verticals totaled 29:

These 29 are followed by a group of 4 vertical strokes made by an unusual point that drags two extremely far apart parallel grooves with a slightly higher, flat floor between them. At first the impression is of a double line, but the microscope shows that they are made by a single point ($\bigvee\!\!\frown\!\!\bigvee$). These 4 strokes are clear in Fig. 46, which also shows the end of the prior series and the beginning of the next, following series. The photo shows three different tools in the verticals, but the same tool being used for all the feet.

The series after the 4 runs to the break in the bone. The track is narrow, but it drags a wide angle at the right ($\diagup$). The top of the stroke, whether as entrance or exit, is pointed and extremely sharp.

There is something extraordinary about this particular arrangement of points. They could have been made in only one of two possible sequential orders. The logic of the series is immutable, that of a closed system. In

Fig. 46
Detail. Middle marks on the first face of the Placard eagle bone. At right the last two verticals of the series of 29, then 4 verticals by a different point, followed by the first two verticals of the series of 25. All feet are engraved by the same point. Four engraving points are documented in the photo.

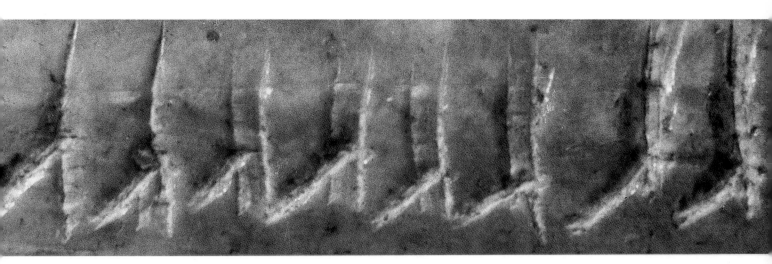

this sense it is similar to the serpentine figure from the Aurignacian of the Abri Blanchard we analyzed earlier.

For the analysis to determine whether this odd grouping could be notational and, if notational, whether it could be lunar, I continue to assume a "beginning" at the right, near the cut of the bone. The structure of the sequence will not be affected if we call it beginning or end.

The first seven verticals had to be the opening marks. There is no alternative. These are then followed *either* by the next 15 verticals, or by the 7 attached feet. There is no other choice. Since both the count of 7 and the count of 15 are lunar "phrases" we are not sure which may have come next:

Choice A) _____

Choice B) _

If we assume choice A there is only one possible solution for the series. Since the same foot, made by the same point, is attached to all the remaining verticals, which are themselves made by four *different* points, the verticals *must* have been made before the feet were applied. There is no alternative. The order for the periods under choice A would then be:

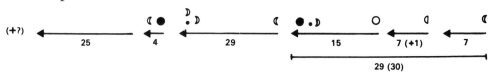

The lunar phrasing is clear. After the 25 plus verticals, which continue past the break in the bone, the final 50 plus feet would have been added. This is one possible reading; there now remains the other possible order.

If we take choice B, then *all* the verticals must have been made first, in sequence. All the feet would then have been made later, in sequence. Again there is no alternative. The reading of the verticals in this possible order is:

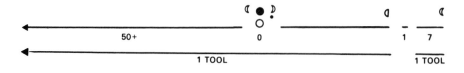

The phrasing is almost precisely the same, but it now includes the loss of the 7 feet. Since 7 is a lunar phrase, the loss does not change the general lunar phrasing, and this is clear. In the supposed reading above, the opening month is short a count of 7, 8, or 9 to the new moon period.

If we now add the feet to this reading of the verticals, we get an unusual count. In the middle of the third series of verticals, the 29, there is one vertical that has no foot (see Fig. 45). The empty vertical occurs as the sixth mark of this series. Now, assuming the sequential order of all the

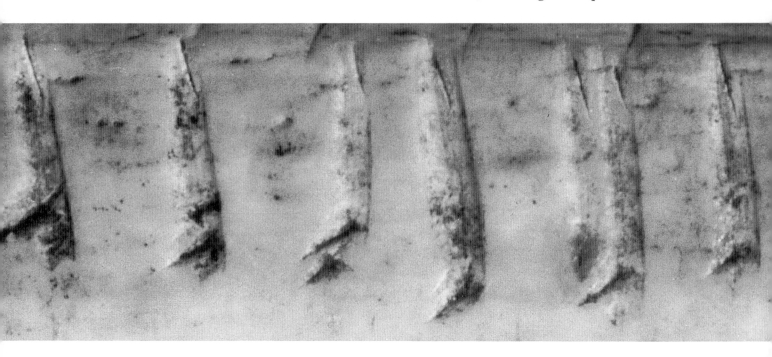

Fig. 47
Detail. Middle of the opening sequence on the second face of the Placard eagle bone showing the difference between the points engraving the verticals and feet. One vertical lacks a foot, another has a doubled foot. Compare the prints of these marks to those on the first face.

feet in our reading, this is mark number 28 of the verticals that lacks the foot. If the foot series began with the first crescent, this would mean that the empty vertical was the place of the expected last crescent, or first day of invisibility. The foot sequence then looks like this:

The evidence of a lunar phrasing, therefore, appears also in this second reading. We cannot as yet tell whether the first or the second reading is better, but we may find the answer before the analysis is through.

We now go to the second series of small marks, the lower series, below the large, multiple angles (Fig. 43 b).

Analytically, this series begins in the break of the bone, at right. We cannot tell how many marks are missing. We do, however, know that this series *ends* precisely and accurately near the cutting of the bone.

When we put this series under the microscope, beginning at the right near the break, we find at once that the verticals are made by a point different from any we have yet seen. It roughly resembles the point that made the 4 broad verticals on the upper series, but it is narrower and it tracks a sharp point through the floor (⌣).

The feet attached to these opening verticals are again made by a different tool (Fig. 47). A count of the verticals made by the first point is 25, including the remnants of marks visible along the line of the break. This is the same number as was counted in the break of the upper series, and both seem to have a similar number broken off. Perhaps later this will help us to determine how many are missing and how large the piece of missing bone is.

Fig. 48
Detail. Central marks on the second face of the Placard eagle bone. At right is the last mark of the series of 25, then 7 verticals by a different point. These 7 contain 17 feet. Not shown is the next series of 43 verticals by still another point. The feet and verticals of all series are made by different points.

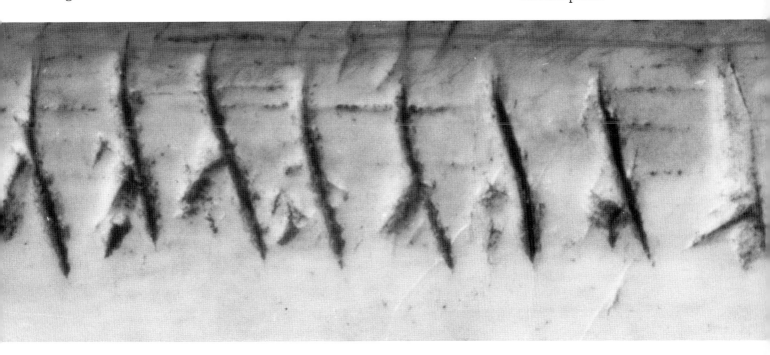

The feet attached to this opening series of verticals are made by a different point, but these feet end with the verticals. This reminds us of the small series of 7 and 7 that opened the upper series.

Just as there was a blank vertical in the upper series, we notice something unusual in this series. One of the verticals has a second vertical close to it, and this has no attached foot. This makes us pause and ponder. In the upper series we noticed a sequence of normal verticals, and then a blank space among the series of attached feet. It was the feet that indicated a notational "point." Here, however, it is the *vertical* that seems to indicate

a notational point in *its* sequence. Then in the foot sequence that is attached there *also* seems to be an indication of a notational point, because no foot is attached to this vertical. However, two vertical marks further, there are *two* feet on *one vertical*. It is almost as though three separate notational points are indicated in a single area, one for the verticals and two for the feet. This is the sort of complexity that can help us in our analysis.

The doubled verticals are marks number 16 and 17 in the 25. The odd breakdown of this series is:

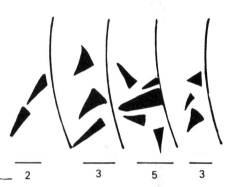

◀ Fig. 49
Detail. The last vertical and foot of the series of 25 and the first vertical and foot of the series of 7 and 17 indicating that four different points did the engraving.

When we turn our microscope to the series of marks that follows these verticals and feet, we notice something even more unusual. The vertical strokes are angled differently and the feet are not single but in most cases are multiple. It is almost as though at this place in the notation there was a "scatter" of feet, as though the man making them had marked time, or waited (Fig. 48).

This is the most interesting "period" we have come upon and we shall approach it carefully.

Figure 49 is an extreme enlargement of the last vertical and foot of the prior series of 25 and the first stroke and two feet of this new series. The photo clearly shows that at least 4 different points were used.

The microscope reveals that there are 7 verticals in this series and *17* feet. Microscopic examination of verticals 4 through 7 of this series shows the plurality of feet. These four verticals, the last of the 7, are seen to have this accumulation of feet under the microscope: _____

The reconstruction of verticals and feet in this sequence gives us: _____

Fig. 48. Page 153.

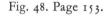

The series that follows again uses different points both in the verticals and the feet. This is clear in Figure 48. This series continues with one tool for the verticals and another for the feet to the end of the bone. The count is 43 verticals, 43 feet.

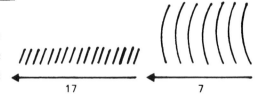

In our analysis of these two series of marks the upper series was complete at the beginning, broken at the end. This series is broken at the beginning, complete at the end. We can therefore attempt a reconstruction and lunar test by backtracking. If we are dealing with the consistency and regularity of a lunar phrasing, this should cause us no difficulty. The only thing we must be aware of is that the schematic diagrams that follow point forward in the direction of the notation and go right to left. We are analyzing the marks, however, from left to right.

As in the upper series, we do not at this point know if the verticals were made first as a group, with all the feet following, or if there was some more mixed procedure. Once again, we can try the alternatives.

Assuming first that the feet of each period were made after the verticals, we begin with the *ending* of 43 verticals followed by 43 feet. The total is

86, for 3 lunar months, lacking the days of invisibility at each end:

Continuing to work backwards, we come next to the intriguing small central sequence. Laying it out from the prior first crescent we get:

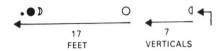

Finally, backtracking *to the feet* of the beginning series we get:

We cannot continue sequentially into the verticals, for we run into the break and are missing both verticals and feet. To continue we would have to estimate the number of missing feet and verticals. It is clear, nevertheless, that we have a rather close lunar phrasing here. We can now test the alternative possibility, that of all the verticals made first, followed by all the feet next.
We backtrack, beginning with the feet:

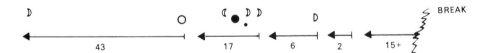

The general lunar phrasing of the periods is still indicated. In this case as in the previous reading, the doubled foot could represent a day of no observation, waiting the next visible phase. We next try the verticals:

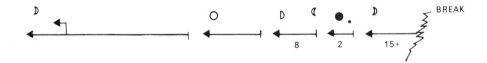

Again we have a lunar phrasing, and the doubled vertical could be, in the surmised manner, a day or days of no observation. There can be no doubt then that what we have in these periods is a lunar phrasing. It would not be possible to achieve this unique ordering of periods and this changing of points (there are 13 to 14 changes of point on this single fragment of eagle bone), except for notational purposes made over an extended period. It is not necessary to go into all the details of analysis made in the reconstruction and in my estimate of the amount of bone and the number of marks that were missing. I here present the drawings of the two side sequences as determined by microscopic analysis (Fig. 50 a, b).

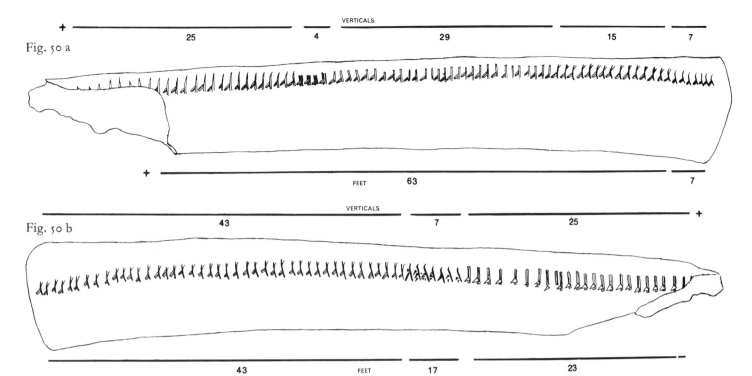

Fig. 50 a

Fig. 50 b

Fig. 50 a, b
Schematic renditions of the engraved marks on faces one and two of the Placard eagle bone indicating the sets among the verticals and feet, as determined by microscopic analysis.

I also present my final test of these two engraved series against the lunar model (Fig. 51 a, b). The tests include an equal amount of estimated bone added to each side, with an almost equal number of marks added to each series (9–10). The differences in the number of added marks required the measurement of slight differences in the amount of bone missing along each side, and the amount of bone added depended on enough to complete the angles on the main face and some space to the end.

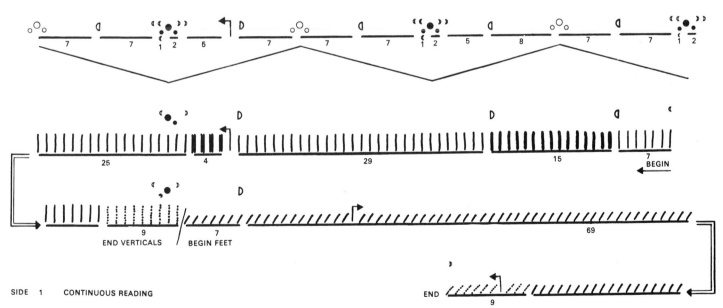

SIDE 1   CONTINUOUS READING

Fig. 51 a
The engraved marks on the first face of the Placard eagle bone against the lunar model indicating the lunar phrasing.

Fig. 51 b. Next page.

Now if your look at these tests you will find that where the marks form a sequence not interrupted by the break in the bone, the lunar phrasing is precise. Every indication of notation and variation that we found by microscope is at an observational point. The 4 wide marks on side one come after the half-moon and are days of waiting for the last crescent. Even the "zero" point of the feet on side two seems to come at the time of the *expected* last crescent, and the doubled foot that comes soon after falls on the day of the expected first crescent; the doubled vertical comes on a day of the expected half-moon. It may be, then, that what we have found is evidence of an extremely simple notational technique for "waiting," and that in each case the *observation,* because of bad weather or invisibility, was made on the day after the expected phase.

As you can see, side one can continue sequentially into side two. The total for the two sides is six months plus six months, precisely one lunar year.

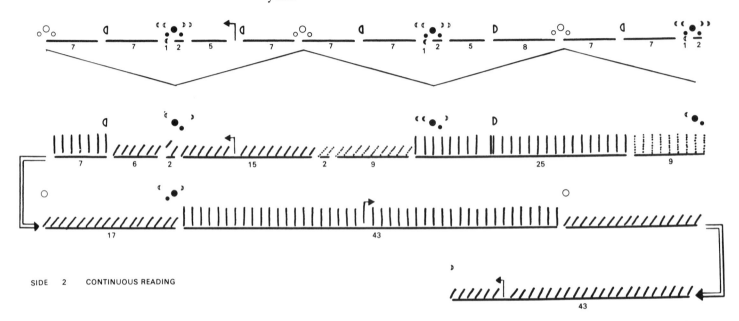

SIDE 2 CONTINUOUS READING

Fig. 51 b
The engraved marks on the second face of the Placard eagle bone against the lunar model indicating the lunar phrasing.

Also interesting is the indication that *usually* all the verticals are made first, all the feet after. But this is not a rule. The exception on this bone comes before and within the complex central series of 7 and 17 on face two. This may indicate that here, somehow, was a place or month of "turning" in the year.

Analysis of the angles, symbolically related to the lunar series, will have to wait.

Now, if this analysis of the engraved eagle bone is even partly correct, there are a number of assumptions that must be made. First, that this system of putting "feet" on a series of vertical lines probably developed from the earlier, simpler system of parallel lines that were crossed over by a second series to give a hatch effect and by the system of making a series of sequential angles that contained extra marks at important points. We saw examples and variations of this early tradition on the Perigordian pebble from Barma Grande, the Solutrean example from Parpallo, and the Magdalenian bâton from Le Placard. This notational technique, therefore, had some 10,000 to 15,000 years to develop.

When we looked at the early notations of the Aurignacian, I suggested that there may have been a knowledge of "counting" by some system or other, but that this was neither apparent nor provable in the notations. The Aurignacian "counts" indicated that the periods were in general short, and probably observational. At this point, however, we *must* assume—*if* these Magdalenian series are notational—that the man making the long counts of 43 plus 43 for a sum of three months or a count of 86, and the man using the system of the one-to-one double-tracking, one foot usually made on one vertical, *knew how to use numbers of a sort and sums,* though he probably used a system of counting that was not ours. He apparently also knew that lunar periods were of a certain length and were repeated regularly, as well as that phases were roughly predictable within a day or two.

Perhaps more intriguing, it seems, at least by implication, that the notation on this eagle bone was not the primary observational system. There was apparently another technique being used in the tribe or group, and our bone seems to represent a *subsidiary* notation made by some specialized person using an evolved, local technique for some purpose, perhaps ritual or ceremonial. The maker would seem to have had knowledge of, contact with, or use of a different, separate, *more basic* day-to-day lunar notational system.

I therefore assume a long, slow development of observational and notational knowledge over a period that covers some 20,000 years from early Upper Paleolithic to Late Magdalenian.

These are conjectures based on the careful analysis of one bit of broken, engraved bird bone. The fact, of course, is that when I finished my analysis, I had nothing but the tantalizing *possibility* that what I had stumbled on might be correct. One bone and one example, especially of such assumed complexity, could prove nothing. It *seemed* valid to me only because it apparently stood in the tradition and at the end of what looked like a logical development. But I could have been too anxious to see it so. One example does not prove a cultural tradition, nor prove the presence of anything as complex as a system of counting, notation, and observation that apparently also included a knowledge of the "year."

There now began a separate story of search.

In 1907 Edouard Piette, one of the founders of nineteenth-century European prehistory and archaeology and the major collector in his day of Upper Paleolithic artifacts, published the first and still classic anthology of Ice Age art, his own collection of mobiliary or portable objects sculpted and engraved on bone, L'ART PENDANT L'AGE DU RENNE ("Art during the Age of the Reindeer"). It was this collection that had stunned the young Breuil and influenced him to specialize in prehistory. It is still the most important single collection of Ice Age art.

The first plate in Piette's large, oversized volume of colored illustrations contains two small drawings of an engraved eagle bone from Le Placard with exactly the same kind of markings as on the eagle bone from Le Placard I had just analyzed.

It looks like the same bone, but a careful comparison indicated that it was not. It is a "sister bone," with similar multiple angles on the main face and with the same series of verticals plus foot marks above and below. But the shape of the bone is somewhat different. The break at one end is not as ragged, and at the other end, which has been cut by a flint knife, there was also cut a blow hole indicating that this bone had been used as a whistle. The multiple angles, also, were more numerous and more complex.

The possibility was breathtaking. From the same site, the same period, and the same level, there existed a bone of the same bird, engraved in exactly the same style. It may have been made by the same hand, certainly it was made in the same tradition by the same culture. Two matching finds such as this must be extremely rare and I know of no other like them in the Upper Paleolithic. If my analysis of the first bone was correct, and if the first bone was notational in an evolved technique, then this could be verified or disproved by the "sister" bone.

There began one of those intriguing stories that is possible perhaps only in France. The Piette collection at the Musée des Antiquités Nationales is in another wing and on a higher floor, but closed to everyone, public and researchers. By will of Edouard Piette, implemented by the Countess de Cugnac, Piette's granddaughter, no one could approach the materials. In preparing a photographic index of the huge collection a short while before, certain pieces had been damaged and a rigid prohibition had been imposed.

There was an agonizing attempt to get permission to walk into the room to see if the piece was there, and it was refused. It took a year and a half to gain permission to enter the Piette room, merely to look through the glass of the cabinets. The piece was missing.

I was informed by the Countess de Cugnac that the Le Placard eagle bone had disappeared some thirty years before. It might have been swallowed up in World War II, and that was it.

For one year I searched in all the back-room drawers of museums in France and asked every specialist I met if he knew of this fragment of eagle bone. It seemed permanently lost. Then I found it, accidently, in the tiny archaeological collection of the University of Poitiers, Faculty of Science. It had been used by Professor Etienne Patte, now retired, to write a paper, "Remarks on Some Prehistoric Patterns," in the *Revue Anthropologique,* 1934. In that paper Patte had written that the sign ' λ ' had "a value more than ornamental, the small mark is never omitted, though it is extremely small."[1] Patte suggested it probably had some sacred or magical intent (Fig. 52 a, b, c).

Under the microscope the little bone exploded into a complexity greater than the sister bone. The same technique of verticals made by one point and feet by another was used here. In addition, there were verticals *with-out* feet ($\lambda\lambda\lambda$ $||$ λ $\lambda\lambda$), verticals with double feet ($\not\lambda$) and verticals that had been formed into angles (V) as though verticals that had once been made close together and without feet had here been

---

[1] Etienne Patte, "Remarques sur quelques figurations préhistoriques," REVUE ANTHRO-POLOGIQUE, Nos. 1–3 (January–March 1934), p. 55, trans. A. Marshack.

merged (Figs. 53 a, b; 54 a, b). There was also an unusual "figure" light-ly engraved at the end of the second series: | (|)'

I present the results of my analysis and a final rendering of the two notated sides in line (Fig. 55 a, b).

Clearly, what we have is notation, in the same style and technique as on the first bone. Using the technique of measurement and estimation I had used on the first bone, I deduced a possible length of missing bone and a minimum loss of 7 and 11 marks in the break for each side. I then placed the reconstructed sequences against a lunar model (Fig. 56 a, b).[2]

Figs. 53 a, b; 54 a, b. Pages following.

Figs. 55 a, b; 56 a, b. Pages 164–165.

The tally is precise within the bounds of lunar observation and those techniques we saw before. One side notates six, and the other seven and a half months. This is a "long year."

The Nicobarese and some groups of North American Indians utilized the same sort of lunar calendar and faced similar problems in adjusting the lunar to the tropical, or solar, year of the seasons. The techniques and uses of lunar notation and observation were not precisely the same as in Ice Age Europe, but the cognitive *problems* were similar.

Richard I. Dodge wrote:

"The Indians measure time solely by days, by sleeps, by moons, and by winters[3]... There is no Indian word synonymous with our word year. 'From

Fig. 52 a, b, c
Three faces of a broken eagle bone whistle from Le Placard engraved in the same style as the prior eagle bone fragment. Middle Magdalenian.

[2] A full analysis of the Placard eagle bones, including the angles of the central faces, appears in: Alexander Marshack, NOTATION DANS LES GRAVURES DU PALÉOLITHIQUE SUPÉRIEUR, Mémoire 8, ed. François Bordes (L'Institut de Préhistoire, Université de Bordeaux, 1970).

[3] Richard I. Dodge, OUR WILD INDIANS (Hartford: A. D. Worthington & Co., 1882), p. 396.

Fig. 53 a
Detail. The central marks on the second face of the Le Placard whistle indicating the two vertical marks without feet that divide the sequences to the right and left. There may be an extra mark, not engraved as an attached foot, placed between the two central dividing marks.

Fig. 53 b
Enlarged detail. The mid marks in the

winter to winter' is the nearest approach to it. The year commences at the first fall of snow.[4] [thus] Some years [may] have more moons than others. One year may have only ten moons, but the next . . . may have fifteen[5] . . . A moon commences when the first streak of its crescent can be discovered in the west, and lasts until the next one appears, but the days of the moon are neither numbered nor named[6] . . . an Indian of the middle Plains will to-day designate a spring moon as 'the moon when the corn is planted;' tomorrow, speaking of the same moon, he may call it 'the moon when the buffalo comes.' Moreover though there are 13 moons in our year, no observer has ever given an Indian name to the thirteenth."[7]

figure above indicating the differences in the points engraving the three series and the feet at the right and the left. Note spacing and rhythm differences between the central two marks and the sequences on either side.

Indian calendars were more varied and complex than Dodge indicates, but the problems and ways of thinking are what concern us.

[4] Ibid., p. 398.   [5] Ibid., p. 399.   [6] Ibid., p. 397.   [7] Ibid., p. 398.

Now, *if* these two sister bones from Le Placard represent an evolved tradition of lunar notation—apparently more advanced in the Upper Paleolithic than in many later Indian traditions—we should find other examples from this period in Europe, since the Ice Age culture of the Magdalenian had spread from south central France and Spain as far as Czechoslovakia and Poland.

The most complex, mysterious, and "cabalistic" of the Ice Age compositions are those found on certain engraved bones from Magdalenian IV,

Fig. 54 a
Detail. The central marks on the first face of the Le Placard whistle of eagle bone indicating the pause in the middle for extra engraved marks and seeming "signs." Note the difference in the engraving points, the rhythm and the spacing of the marks to the right and the left of the mid marks.

Fig. 54 b
Enlarged detail. The mid marks in the

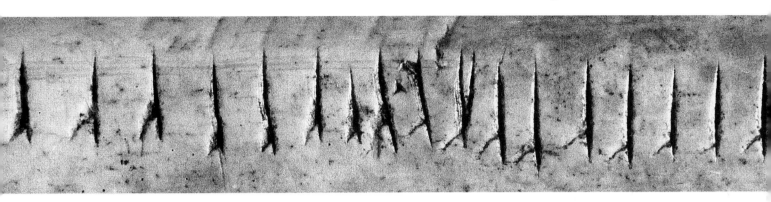

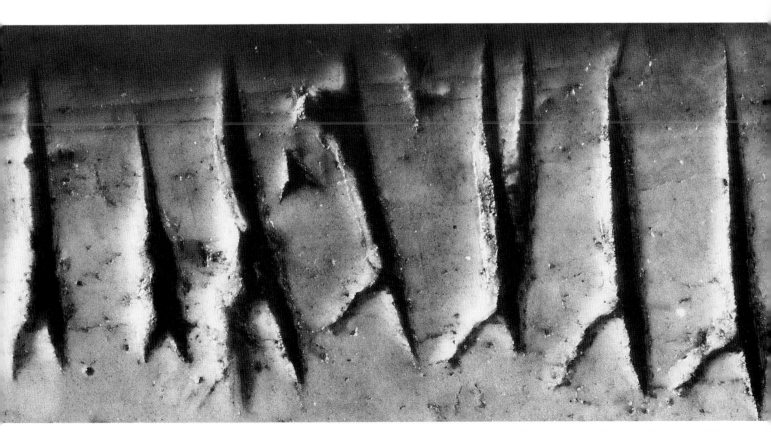

V, and VI, the cultures that terminated the Ice Age, cultures which changed when the climate and way of life changed.
I present the line renditions of compositions on nine of these bones, in most cases as they were presented in the early literature by the Abbé Breuil and others (Fig. 57 a, b, c, d, e, f, g, h, i). Laugerie Basse is a short

figure above indicating the angle with an attached foot, added marks not attached to any verticals and the differences in the points engraving the feet, the verticals and the added marks.

Fig. 57 a–i. Page 166.

walk from Les Eyzies on the Vézère, which runs southwest to the Dordogne. The Abri Mège at Teyjat is a few miles from Le Placard, somewhat north of Les Eyzies. Bruniquel is further south, and Gourdan, Mas d'Azil, and La Vache are more than a hundred miles to the south, in the

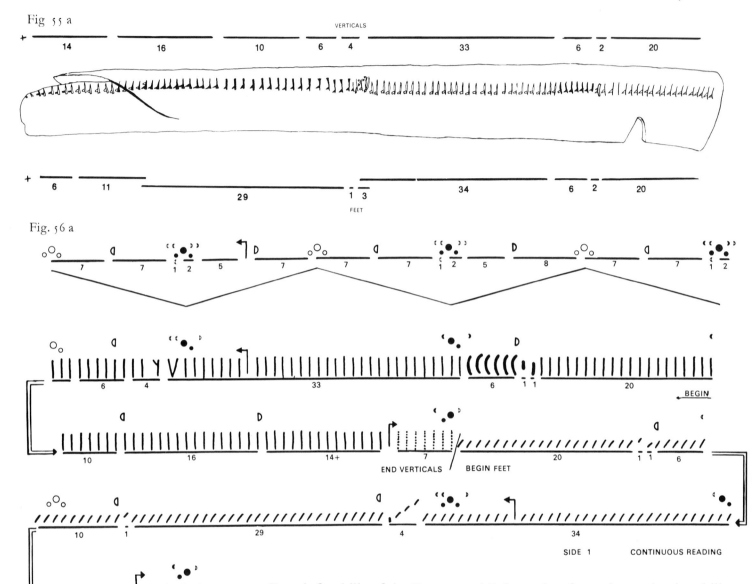

Fig 55 a

VERTICALS

FEET

Fig. 56 a

BEGIN

END VERTICALS   BEGIN FEET

SIDE 1   CONTINUOUS READING

END

Fig. 55 a, b
Upper drawings. Schematic rendition of the engraved marks on faces one and two of the Placard eagle bone whistle indicating the sets among the verticals and feet, as determined by microscopic analysis.

French foothills of the Pyrenees. All these sites formed one riverine, hill and valley culture in southwest France, the drainage of their rivers going toward Bordeaux.

As you can see from the line drawings, these engraved bones contain representational art and symbols. But in each case, also, there is a block or area of notation separated from the art. The art in these nine examples represents fish, seal, horse, deer, the hind legs of a frog or "anthropomorph," an ant or other insect, and a plant or vegetable form or motif. One piece contains an unusual image that looks like a fish head but which may be a geometricized image of the female form (Fig. 57c). I will analyze some of the art in a later chapter. At this point I am interested only in the conjunctive blocks or rows of notation, for this material is obviously non-representational, and it can be subjected to the analytic techniques we have devised.

Of the art and symbol it is perhaps not necessary at this point to do more than indicate that each figure could reasonably represent the image of a "time-factored," seasonal process, phenomenon, or myth.

Examination of these pieces—except for the fragment with horse

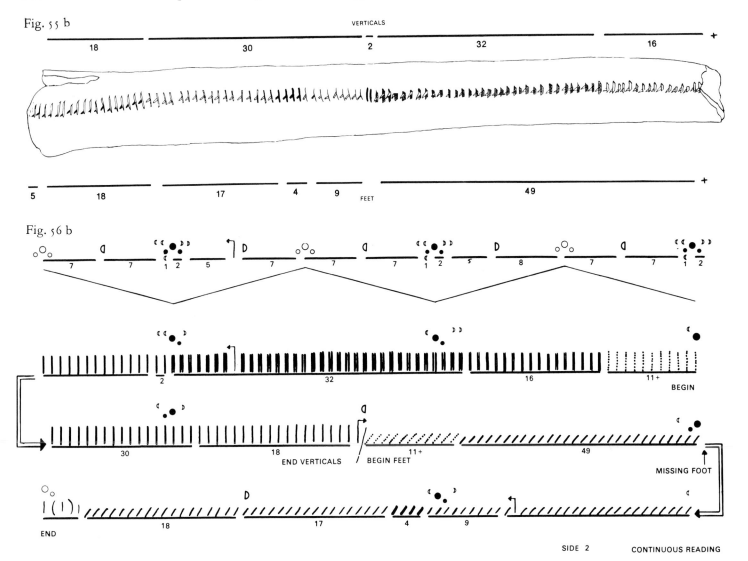

Fig. 55 b

Fig. 56 b

SIDE 2   CONTINUOUS READING

heads —at first suggested that the blocks of tiny marks were made in the "vertical-foot" tradition documented on the Le Placard eagle bones. A subsequent study of the marking traditions from sites in France, Spain and the rest of Europe—including the Taï notation (Fig. 15 a,b)—demonstrated an unexpected variability in these marking traditions. The same visual effect could be created in different ways. Marks that appear to be "feet" can result from incising a stroke downward over the rounded edge of a rod, with an abrupt change in the direction of the stroke as it drops around the curve; the effect can be achieved by incising across an engraved horizontal containing line, with an abrupt change in the direction of the stroke when it crosses the groove; it can be created by

Fig. 56 a, b
Charts. The engraved marks on both faces of the Placard eagle bone whistle against the lunar model indicating the possible lunar phrasing and placement of the engraved points of differentiation.

Fig. 57 a–i

Notational Sequences with Figurative and Symbolic Art. Upper Magdalenian.

a. Mas d'Azil (Ariège); b, c, d, e. Abri Mège, Teyjat (Dordogne); f. Laugerie Basse (Dordogne); g. La Vache (Ariège); h. Gourdan (Haute-Garonne); i. Bruniquel (Tarn-et-Garonne).

a, h. after E. Piette, *L'Art pendant l'Age du Renne,* Paris, Masson et Cie. (1907), Fig. 92 and Plate LXIII; b, c, e. after Capitan, Breuil, Bourrinet and Peyrony, "L'Abri Mège,"

Fig. 57 a

Fig. 57 b

Fig. 57 c

Fig. 57 d

Fig. 57 e

Fig. 57 f

Revue de l'Ecole d'Anthropologie, Vol. XVI (1906), p. 209, Fig. 71: 1, 2, 5 b; d, f. after Breuil, "Les subdivisions du Paléolithique Supérieur et leur signification," *Compte Rendu du Congrès International d'Anthropologie et d'Archéologie Préhistorique,* 14e sess., 1913 (2e edn., 1957), p. 208, Fig. 29: 5, 13; g. Collection Romain Robert; i. Collection de Lastic Saint-Jal, The British Museum.

(g, h, i are schematic renditions by the author.)

Fig. 57 g

Fig. 57 h

Fig. 57 i

adding feet to verticals, a notational mode I have since been able to document in other examples.

Lying in a display cabinet at the Musée des Antiquités Nationales at Saint Germaine-en-Laye was the lower end of a bone rod or point which had on its upper fragment the heads of four stags with antlers in different early stages of growth. In Magdalenian "art" stags are usually depicted carrying the fully developed late summer or autumn growth of branched antlers, near the time of rutting. The set of marks may therefore represent a period

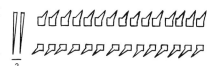

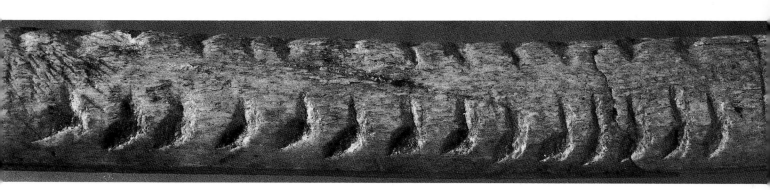

of antler growth before the autumn rut. There are 2 + 15 + 14 + 2 strokes, suggesting the days of invisibility and a crescent, followed by 29 days of the month followed again by 2 days of invisibility and a crescent. Did this set therefore symbolically represent the period or "moon" depicted by the heads? If so, we may have an ability to count with no indication of the method or system used in the counting. Analysis of the

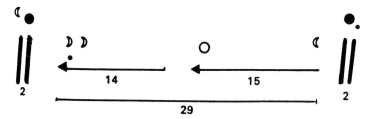

Taï notation also suggested an ability to count small sets at a time. Of particular interest are the 13 tiny marks added at a later date. Such later additions do not occur in decorative compositions but are common in notations and the ritual accumulation of symbolic motifs. These fragile, breakable points, perhaps used in hunting, may have been made and engraved in the seasons that are depicted in their imagery. This mode of seasonal depiction, associated with a block of notation, is seen in Figs. 60, 84 and 102. It may also be of interest that the horse heads, Fig. 57 a, represent a typical Magdalenian, Pyrenean style of schematically rendering the head of the *summer* horse. The morphological indication of the area

Fig. 58 a
Engraved portion of a larger bone from the Abri Mège (Fig. 57 b) containing the block of notation.

Fig. 58 b
Detail. A single row of the notational marks on the Abri Mège bone indicating the sharp, angled strokes. The opening two linear marks and the lightly engraved subsidiary series are at opposite ends.

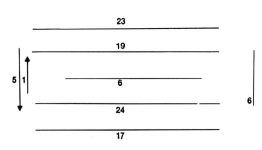

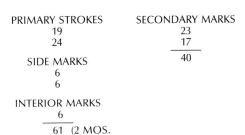

PRIMARY STROKES	SECONDARY MARKS
19	23
24	17
	40
SIDE MARKS	
6	
6	
INTERIOR MARKS	
6	
61 (2 MOS.	

Fig. 59
Schematic rendition of the notational marks on the bone from the Abri Mège, Teyjat, indicating all the subsidiary marks, as determined by microscopic analysis. The intentional secondary and subsidiary marks are one clue to a notational accumulation. The counts are based on a tentative assumption that on this bone the angled marks are single strokes.

of the teeth (the zigzags) and the jaw muscle leading to the ear make these abstractions look like a bridle and halter. This species-specific morphology, which is visible in summer, disappears with the growth of heavy winter hair.

The second bone with a relatively complete "notational" sequence has the head of a fish, the tail of a seal and an image I have interpreted as a water-related female figure (See Fig. 186 b). There are 3 + 19 + 2 marks in the upper row and 3 + 24 in the lower, with 6 marks between the rows providing a sum of 61, perhaps representing the important period after the spring thaw when salmon begin their first migratory run up river and seals follow them far inland. Significantly, there is a subsidiary marking, 40 tiny strokes added within the primary notation, suggesting a repeat or an extension of that two month period. Since each of the creatures associated with these blocks of marks represent a seasonal presence we may have another example of the way seasonally relevant periods or phenomena were symbolized in the Magdalenian of the Franco-Cantabrian area and in those areas to which the Magdalenian culture dispersed (Germany,

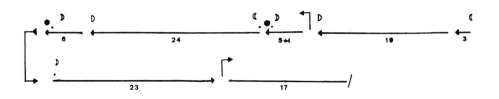

Czechoslovakia, Poland). (See Figs. 83, 135.) No other Ice Age culture depicts animals with their seasonal and sexual characteristics. Depictions in the rest of Ice Age Europe tend to be of the generalized mammoth, lion, horse, bear, etc. (See Fig. 131, 132.) The ecological, geographical and climatological reasons for this regional development of naturalistic animal depiction are now being researched.

CHAPTER XI

IMAGE OF THE WORLD: TIME-FACTORED ART

The caves and bones have, as their major illustrations, the representations of animals, and these animals, particularly in the caves, are limited to a basic repertoire of certain species, though the repertoire of animals varies in different periods and regions. In general, the cave art is more limited and "specialized," that is, it contains fewer minor creatures than the mobiliary materials, a lesser number of snakes, fewer birds, no insects. In addition to the animals, there are other images in the caves and on the smaller stones and bones: signs, symbols, notations, anthropomorphs, sorcerers, magicians or dancers, and feminine figures, sometimes a full feminine figure and sometimes an abstracted feminine form.

The meaning of these images was, at first, guessed at vaguely as "religious magic." The animals were thought to be primarily involved in cults of hunting magic for food and of fertility magic for increase of the species.

Fig. 61
Fig. 61
One face of the bâton of Montgaudier showing two engraved seals, part of a fish and other forms. Upper Magdalenian.

We have already looked at two kinds of Ice Age marking, and neither fell into these traditional categories: the notational bones and bones with notations and associated images. Let us look at a third class of composition.

6. Creatures and flower engraved between faces of bâton. Direction of gravity for creatures: ↑, for flower: ←

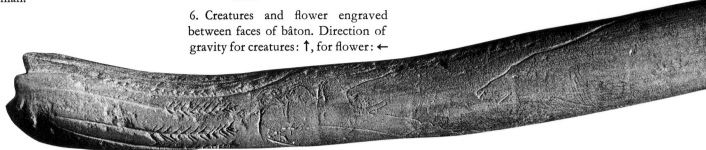

3. Three plants, perhaps drawn third, with bâton turned 90°. Direction of gravity for image: ←

Fig. 60
Early drawing of bâton of Montgaudier (Charente), unrolled to show both faces (after Breuil and St. Périer). Only major creatures identifiable. Microscopic analysis indicates errors in this drawing for each form.

Fig. 65 a
Detail. The three plants at the bottom of the Montgaudier bâton. Such forms had often been called barbed weapons.

5. Ibex, sprout and form, last images engraved on face with bâton in original position. Direction of gravity: ↓

4. Male salmon perhaps drawn fourth with bâton hole at left. Direction of gravity for image: ↑

2. Bull seal engraved after and behind female, in perspective, and more simply drawn.

One of the early discoveries of complex Magdalenian engraving was made in the 1880's at the site of Montgaudier, a short walk from Le Placard. Figure 60 is a line rendition as presented by the Abbé Breuil.[1] It

Fig. 60

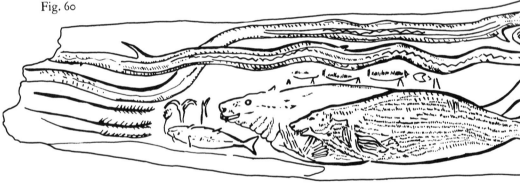

shows the two faces of the round bone unrolled to present a single composition.

It is a long bâton (14.5 inches, 37.2 cm) of reindeer antler, unbroken and with a single large hole at one end (Fig. 61). It is engraved with realistic, delicate, detailed drawings of two seals, male and female by their form and size, and on the other face are two serpentine forms, both apparently male. The beauty of these Upper Paleolithic drawings surprised the early prehistorians. But they were also perplexed. The site of Montgaudier is today more than a hundred miles from the sea, and during the last phases of the cold Magdalenian, when large quantities of water were locked up in the ice sheets that sat on Europe, Asia, and North America, the sea was much lower and the coast was still farther west. The men at Montgaudier

[1] H. Breuil & R. de Saint-Périer, LES POISSONS, LES BATRACIENS ET LES REPTILES DANS L'ART QUATERNAIRE, Archives de l'Institut de Paléontologie Humaine, Mémoire 2 (Paris: Masson et Cie., July 1927), p. 147.

1. Female seal, perhaps first image on face. Direction of gravity for seal, indicating position baton was held: ↓

Fig. 63 a
Detail. The schematized ibex head on the Montgaudier bâton with an "X" on its brow. To the left is a sprout with leaves and roots (see page 172).

were seemingly inland, hill-dwelling reindeer hunters and not coastal fishermen. How, then, could they draw such realistic seals? The puzzle has remained. Breuil's rendition of the bâton appears occasionally in anthologies of Ice Age art, without explanation of this problem of the inland seals.

The bâton is a random piece at the Musée d'Histoire Naturelle in Paris, which has only four or five examples of engraved Upper Paleolithic materials. The small collection is not often seen, even by specialists. The

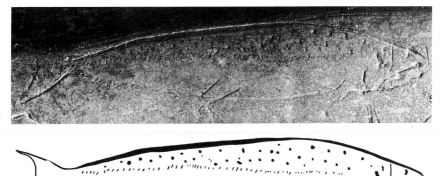

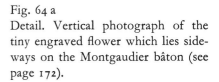

Fig. 62 a
Detail. Photograph of the salmon on the Montgaudier bâton indicating the open mouth, the salmonid markings and the hook on the lower jaw which appears on the male salmon in season of spawning.

Fig. 62 b
Line rendition of the salmon as determined by microscopic analysis.

bâton, when I picked it up, was covered with a protective film of wax put on perhaps half a century before. It was through this film of wax that prehistorians, when they came, saw the engraving. After I cleaned it carefully for a full day, the details became clear, and these gave a sudden new meaning to the composition and to Ice Age art.

In front of the two seals is a fish, upside down in relation to the seals. The Abbé Breuil had written that in this

"beautiful engraving of a fish ... determination of the species is somewhat uncertain. It has been termed a salmonide by G. de Mortillet, who has given the engraving an incorrect rendition, since the fish in the original engraving has the mouth closed, a fact that we have ourselves ascertained. It is true that the dorsal region is decorated like a trout or salmon, but the dorsal fins are not drawn..."[2]

Because of the shape of the slim rear and the tail, the Abbé Breuil decided that the fish was "without doubt a common mackerel."

[2] Ibid., pp. 44–45, trans A. Marshack.

Fig. 64 a
Detail. Vertical photograph of the tiny engraved flower which lies sideways on the Montgaudier bâton (see page 172).

Fig. 63 b
Line rendition of the Montgaudier ibex and sprout, as determined by microscopic analysis.

Fig. 64 b
Line rendition of the Montgaudier flower indicating the pedicel, sepal, leaves and petals, as determined by microscopic analysis.

Figs. 62 a, b; 63 a; 64 a; 65 a.
Preceding pages.

Microscopic examination *after* cleaning showed that the mouth of the fish was, in fact, open. More important, it showed that the lower jaw had that hook or "kype" that the adult male salmon develops in the season of the return to the rivers and the time of spawning (Fig. 62 a, b). The shape of the tail and the lack of a dorsal fin would seem to have been the artist's simplification due to the shape of the bâton, since the dorsal line runs along the edge of the flat face of the bâton and an upper fin would have had to be drawn over the edge, at right angles to the main surface, and would not have been seen when the fish was viewed straight on. Besides, mackerel also have dorsal fins, if of a different size and shape. The Abbé Breuil, then, was wrong. Salmon appear in inland Ice Age art even further upstream than Montgaudier.

These seemingly minor details are important, because the behavior of seal and salmon in relation to each other is seasonal and precise. Salmon, migrating to their spawning grounds upriver, begin to leave the warmer salt seas soon after the first thaw of early spring has begun to carry the cool, sweet meltwater downriver to the sea. They begin to enter the estuary or river mouth with the first big sea tide of the spring (often at full moon), a tide which carries the salt water some distance upstream, near the end of March or the beginning of April. At this time, there is the spring run, the dramatic "first fish" of the year. There is also a later, larger, end-of-spring or early-summer run in June and a still later autumn run. It is the earliest run that sends up the bigger salmon. Often the seals, which prey on the salmon gathering near the coasts and in the estuaries, follow the salmon upriver, particularly after their own early spring molt and mating is over.

J. G. D. Clark, an authority on the economic culture of prehistoric Europe, has observed that occasional seal bones have been found at Upper Paleolithic sites in the Dordogne valley. They appear in an Aurignacian level in the Vézère valley and in the Magdalenian on another tributary of the Dordogne river, the Isle. He states that probably "the seals were slaughtered in the immediate neighborhood of the sites ..."[3] even though the kills were made some 114–120 miles [190–200 km] from the present coast and, by presumption, even further from the Ice Age sea. Modern seals have been found on the Oder, flowing into the Baltic, and on the Rhine and Loire, flowing into the Atlantic, as far as 240 miles [400 km] from the sea in their pursuit of salmon. Says Clark: "they were seen at least occasionally by the cave artist."[4]

It may be, then, that seal and salmon together were dramatic "signs" of the coming of spring, "first fruits" in a sense, *after* the thaw. When we turn to the twisted serpentine figures on the reverse face of the bâton, we

[3] J. G. D. Clark, "Seal-hunting in the Stone Age of Northwestern Europe: A Study in Economic Prehistory," PROCEEDINGS OF THE PREHISTORIC SOCIETY, New Series, Vol. XII (1946), p. 17.

[4] Loc. cit.

have the Abbé Breuil's statement that, though they have been called eels, the presence of the male penis in the drawings, the long slender shape, and the markings make him sure the figures are a common non-poisonous grass snake. Common European snakes of the family *Colubridae,* as Breuil terms them, emerge from hibernation in the early spring to mate and form breeding pairs. These serpents are amphibious and can be seen snaking across streams in the same season as the first salmon and the occasional seal. Whether the serpentine forms are snake or eel, they are linked to seal and fish as "signs" of the returning spring.

The microscope now revealed a number of astonishing minor forms. Just in front of the fish is an indeterminate series of marks, meaningless in Breuil's rendition. The microscope showed this to be a carefully drawn, exquisitely rendered sprout, including roots and first leaves or branches (Fig. 63 a, b). Here was another sign of spring. Above and to the right of the shoot was the schematized, simplified head of an ibex with "crescent" horns and large ears. The muzzle was made by a few triangulating lines, and the brow seemed to be crossed out. This mammal, too, has strong seasonal habits and calves in the spring. The ibex appears as a subsidiary animal in much of Ice Age art, and we shall look at more examples later.

Between the seals and snakes an odd series of forms was revealed by the microscope to be three creatures of the damp soil or water bottom. What look like the pointed ears of these creatures are a series of symbolic angles. In front of these creatures was an image, carefully drawn by a series of sure, clear, careful strokes. It turned out to be a budding flower (Fig. 64 a, b). As one followed the strokes through the microscope, re-creating the sequence in which they were made, the flower became certain.

At the bottom or far end of the bâton was a series of forms that looked like barbed harpoons of the type considered to be drawn for "hunting magic" by some authorities, forms that have recently been called barbed "masculine" or sexual signs. Under the microscope it was evident that these are impossible harpoons; the barbs were turned the wrong way and the points of the long shafts were at the wrong end. However, they were *perfect* plants or branches, growing at the proper angle and in the proper way at the top of a long stem (Fig. 65 a, b).

Every image, then, including the three creatures of the damp soil or water, was seasonal and representative of early spring, perhaps mid-April to May in Ice Age Europe. Though seal, salmon, and ibex were eaten, the images in this cumulative composition were not intended as "hunting magic" in the traditional sense. They were time-factored and storied images of creatures whose comings and goings and seasonal habits were known, and they *represented* the birth of the "new year," if not calendrically and arithmetically at least observationally and probably in story. Even where the images were overtly "sexual," they were sexual only in the context of a seasonal manifestation.

This bâton represents a class of European, Upper Paleolithic engraved composition, common in the Late Magdalenian. It contains no notations

Fig. 65 b
Line rendetion of the three Montgaudier plants, as determined by microscopic analysis.

Plant image in the hall of engravings, the "apse," Lascaux.

and no symbolic "signs" more abstract than the crossed-out ibex, the plants, and the small angles, perhaps the last marks to be engraved. Until recent years, such compositions were considered magical, related to the hunt and the increase of animals, tokens in one sense of desperation and dependence and therefore of supplication and invocation. Now "magic" of many sorts, including rite and story, was certainly involved in the Upper Paleolithic culture, and it was probably involved with these images *at the season of appearance* of the species or forms. But there is clearly something more here, something different, something that goes beyond belly hunger or psychological need. It is in line with the cognitive developments we have been following. We shall look at the meanings of these time-factored images, stories, and myths and of the "magic" that may have been involved in the representations later after we have examined other examples of these Late Magdalenian compositions.

From the last stages of the Upper Paleolithic Ice Age culture, Magdalenian VI, there comes a dagger, polisher, or spatula with engravings on two faces. It was found at the site of La Vache in the Pyrenean foothills of southern France and was excavated by Romain Robert, an insurance agent and one of the more energetic and competent "amateurs" in France, president and founder of the Société Préhistorique de l'Ariège, and one of the discoverers of the important Ice Age cave of Rouffignac in the Dordogne.

The dagger (Fig. 66 a, b) has the fine head of a doe on one side; with it are a number of "minor" subsidiary images. Near the ears are three serpentine wavy lines that look like snakes or water. Below the doe is the schematized head of an ibex in exactly the same tradition, but more finely drawn, than the ibex on the Montgaudier bâton. One horn is symbolically "crossed out" by a double stroke. Below and to the right of the ibex are two flowers and the quickly sketched indication of a third. The flowers are in full leaf and many-headed. The composition on this face and the "symbols" seem to represent spring and early summer.

On the reverse face is the head of a bison with mouth open and tongue out as though bellowing. It is, therefore, probably a male in the time of

Fig. 66 a, b
The two faces of an engraved bone "knife" or "polisher" from the site of La Vache (Ariège). Final Magdalenian.

Fig. 67 a, b
Line rendition of all the engraved marks on the La Vache knife as determined by microscopic analysis.

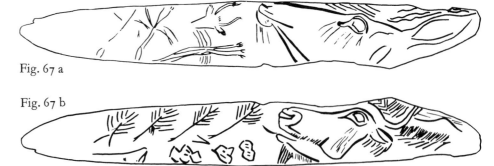

Fig. 67 a

Fig. 67 b

rutting, roughly around September, when the bulls bellow at night and butt and battle in the day. Below the bison are plant forms, but these are without flowers and seem to be either bare autumn branches or conifer leaves. One plant form looks like a bent, drooping flower, the last of the season. With these are three unusual forms that, under the microscope, look like nuts, seeds, or pine cones (Fig. 67 a, b).

In the same tradition, but somewhat more schematic and ornamental, is the fragment of a dagger or polisher from Fontarnaud à Lugasson with the antlered head of a stag and four flowers (Fig. 68 a, b). Above and in the horns is a broken-off image that looks like a feather or branch, an

Fig. 68 a

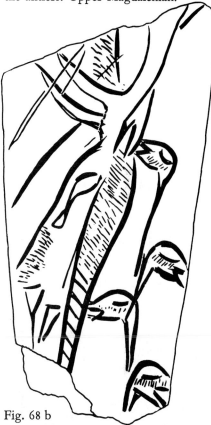

Fig. 68 a
Bone fragment from Fontarnaud à Lugasson (Gironde) with the schematized head of a stag and flowers. A feather or branch is engraved above the antlers. Upper Magdalenian.

Fig. 68 b
Line rendition of all intentional marks on the Fontarnaud à Lugasson fragment showing the feathered form in the antlers and the long lines crossing the antlers, as determined by microscopic analysis.

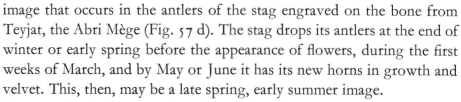

image that occurs in the antlers of the stag engraved on the bone from Teyjat, the Abri Mège (Fig. 57 d). The stag drops its antlers at the end of winter or early spring before the appearance of flowers, during the first weeks of March, and by May or June it has its new horns in growth and velvet. This, then, may be a late spring, early summer image.

An exceedingly fine example of an animal, apparently a chamois, and a schematic flower in full bloom comes from Laugerie Basse, near Les Eyzies (Fig. 69).

Fig. 69
Line rendition of a chamois with a tiny horn associated with a schematized flower on a fragment of bone from Laugerie Basse (Dordogne), as determined by microscopic analysis. Upper Magdalenian.

Fig. 70 a
Engraved and deteriorated bone fragment from La Vache (Ariège) with two facing capridae and a schematized bird in flight between them. Final Magdalenian.

These examples of compositions containing animals without notations, but associated with plants, are common in the Late Magdalenian. Stylistically, they tend to be realistic, though they may also occasionally be abstracted and schematized. There are also examples of animals alone, of plants alone, of animals with fish, and of fish with plants. Unless we

recognize that these compositions contain "related" images and that they are related *at least by season,* we are left only to admire the art or to talk vaguely of general "magical" or decorative purposes, or else to seek "sexual" meanings in the associations, relationships and combinations.

From the hill site of La Vache that gave us the doe, bison and plants, and again from the end of the Magdalenian, there comes an engraved bone with a goat and perhaps a saiga antelope facing each other and with a schematized bird between them (Fig. 70 a, b). The composition recalls the art of the late symbolic and calendric religions of the agricultural city cultures which often had two facing, horned animals with a bird between.

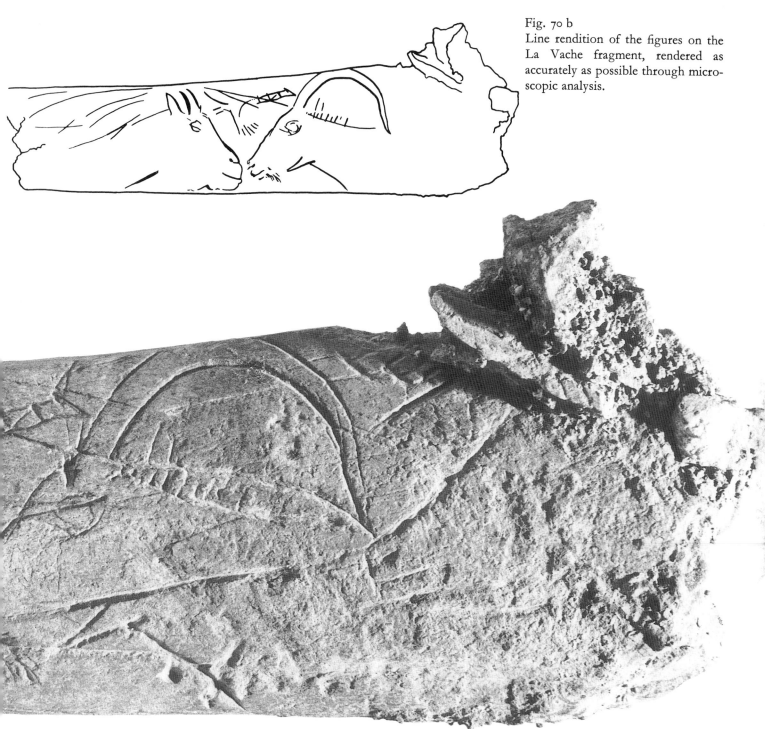

Fig. 70 b
Line rendition of the figures on the La Vache fragment, rendered as accurately as possible through microscopic analysis.

Another engraved bone from La Vache presents us with two animals, one clearly a doe, with two fish behind (Fig. 71 a, b).

From Raymonden, near Périgueux in the Dordogne, there comes a broken fragment that has two animals, apparently two ibexes or goats, one of

Fig. 71 a. Next page.

Fig. 71 b
Line rendition of the engraved composition on the La Vache fragment, as determined by microscopic analysis.

Fig. 71 a
Engraved bone fragment from La Vache (Ariège) with the head of a doe and two fishes. The remnant of a second animal is at left. Final Magdalenian.

which is apparently lying on its side. When the bone is turned around, we see the heads of three kids and two flying, small birds between the major animals. Each of the two large animals has a "sign" of two marks on its body. The image, with the birds and kids, is of April and spring (Fig. 72 a, b). The "double sign" of two marks in the prone adult

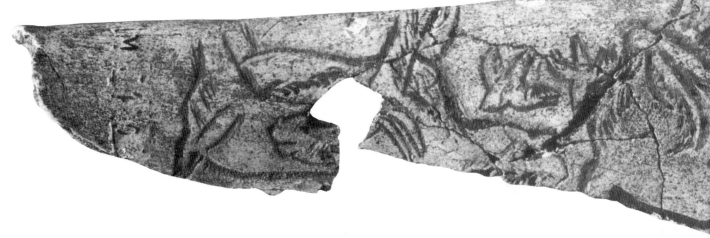

animals, like the crossed-out ibex horns, may be "sacrificial" or ceremonial related to rites of the season, and we shall look at such signs later.
A small plaquette or disc from the late Middle Magdalenian of Laugerie Basse shows a cow on one face, her calf on the other (Fig. 73 a, b).
A second disc from the same site shows a long-legged fawn as though

Fig. 72 a
Engraved bone fragment from Raymonden (Dordogne) with a complex composition that was engraved in two stages. Two adult animals were engraved, the bone was then turned 180° and overengraved to complete the composition. Upper Magdalenian.

Fig. 72 a

Fig. 72 b
Line rendition of all engraved marks on the Raymonden fragment as determined by microscope, revealing two adult capridae with a double mark in each and in reverse the heads of three kids. Two birds are between the animals. The whole is an image of spring and perhaps of rites of that season.

Fig. 73 a, b. Pages following.

Fig. 74 a, b. Pages following.

Fig. 73 a, b
The two faces of a bone disc from Laugerie Basse (Dordogne) with a cow on one face and a calf on the other. The two faces form a combined image of spring. Late Middle Magdalenian.

newborn and unable to stand, and on the other face the fawn is standing in an awkward, long-legged stance (Fig. 74 a, b). From the last stages of the Upper Paleolithic, Magdalenian VI, and the site of Le Morin there comes a group of piglike bison, oddly drawn, but with the bison horns visible. The bison calf is marked with a spear or "sign" (Fig. 75).

From a different area of Ice Age Europe, from southern Italy, where a

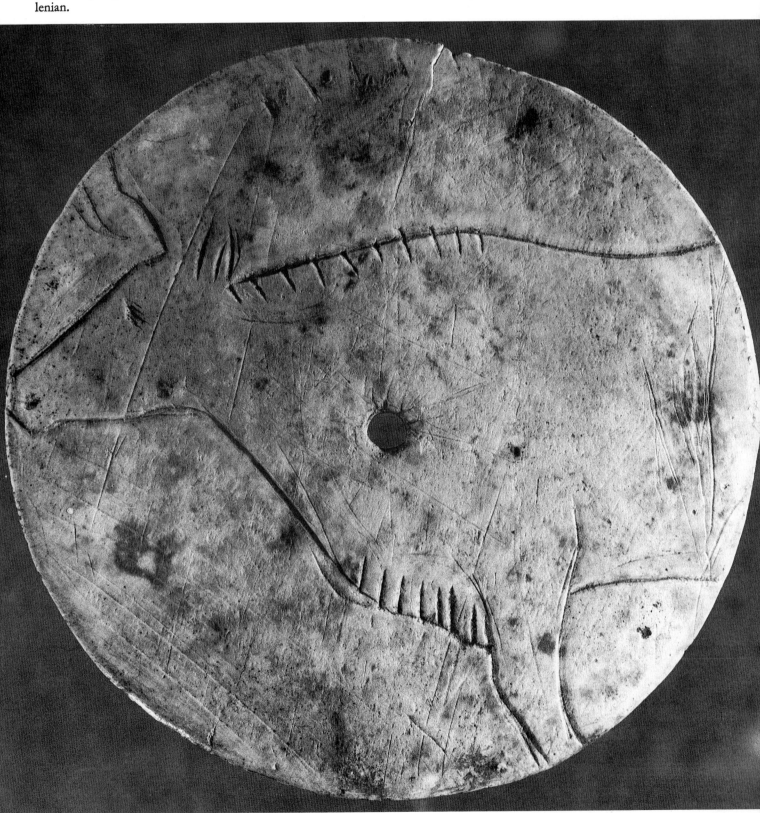

warmer, more temperate climate and ecology supported a somewhat different adaptive hunting culture, there come a number of engraved pieces from the late Upper Paleolithic relevant to the problem of the seasonal image.

The cave site of Paglicci, in the Apulia region of southeastern Italy facing the Adriatic Sea, contains the red paintings of two seemingly pregnant

Fig. 75. Page 184.

Fig. 74 a, b
The two faces of a second bone disc from Laugerie Basse (Dordogne) depicting a fawn resting on the ground on one face and standing stiff-legged and awkward on the other. The two faces are images of spring. Late Middle Magdalenian.

horses and the prints of human hands. In the archaeological levels engraved bones were found.[5] The first is a fragment of bone that has the engraving of a wide-eyed bird with long beak and crested head (Fig. 76), a Spoonbill *(Platalea Leucorodia)*, a migratory water bird still common in Italy, that arrives in the springtime for nesting but winters in Africa. The young bird has a shorter bill than the adult, and, as here engraved,

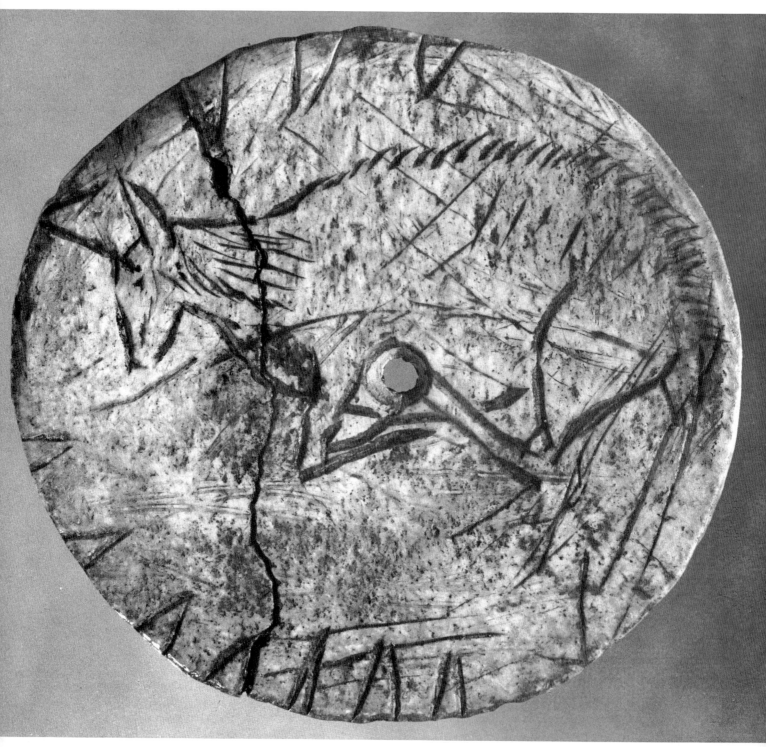

[5] Francesco Zorzi, "Pitture Parietali Paleolitiche Scoperte nella Grotta Paglicci presso Rignano Garganico," MEMORIE DEL MUSEO CIVICO DI STORIA NATURALE—VERONA, Vol. X (1962), pp. 265–282.

it is not yet fully arced, implying an image of late spring. The second example, larger and more complex, presents a scene or composition unique in Upper Paleolithic art. It shows a duck apparently superimposed or seated on an oval nest which is full of eggs (Fig. 77). A serpent has encroached on the nest, its head among the eggs as though to steal. To the right is a small bird of a different species with elongated beak, perhaps

Fig. 76

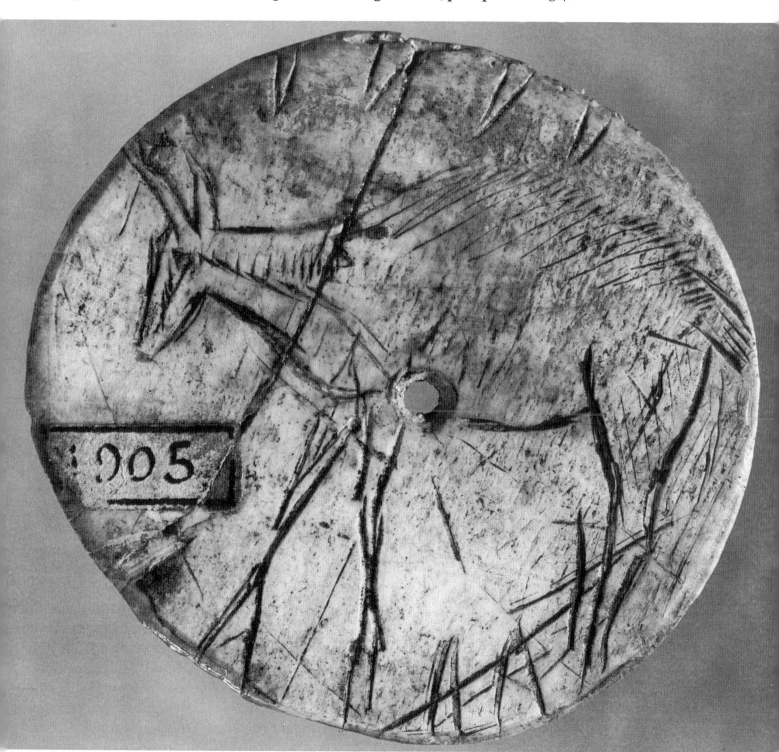

a hummingbird. The primary image seems to be the reportorial scene of a snake intruding on an occupied nest, a clearly seasonal image. The en-

Fig. 76
Bone from Paglicci (Apulia) with crested head of young spoonbill. Late Upper Paleolithic.

Fig. 75
Engraved bone fragment from Le Morin (Dordogne) depicting two adult bison and a spring calf. The calf carries the double wound mark and has the line of the weapon engraved on its body. Final Magdalenian.

Fig. 77
Schematic rendition of composition on bone from Paglicci (Apulia) apparently depicting scene of a snake stealing eggs from a nest containing a seated duck. Microscopic analysis reveals duck was engraved first, nest

graving had been inked over for easier viewing in the museum display. Cleaning off the ink, however, microscopic analysis of the image revealed that the nest was engraved *over* the duck and the snake over the nest. The reconstruction implied a sequential composition in time, apparently representing a series of seasonal events: the arrival of the flocks of ducks, after this the building of nests and the laying of eggs, and finally the theft of eggs by the snake. The time span was certainly many weeks and the composition was not conceived, engraved, or understood as a single image. Nevertheless, it is seasonal and observational and it was probably "storied" as well.

The list of such "seasonal" Ice Age compositions with fawns, calves, snakes, fish, birds, and plants is relatively large, and it is surprising that

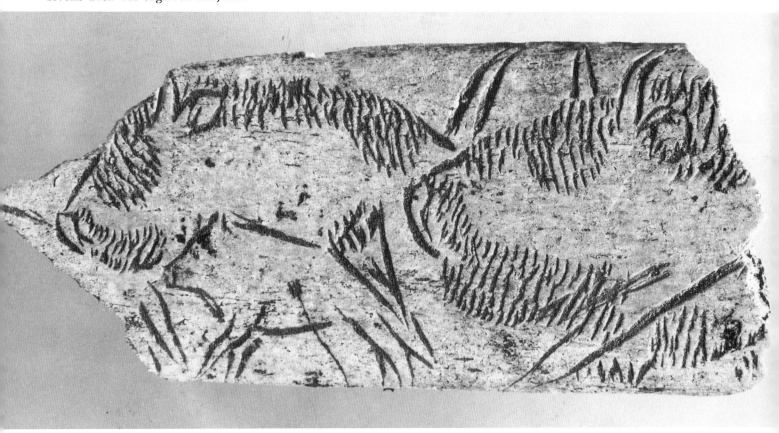

Fig. 75

was engraved over the duck and snake over the nest, perhaps indicative of a sequence of events in the spring. At right a smaller species of bird, perhaps of the summer. Late Upper Paleolithic.

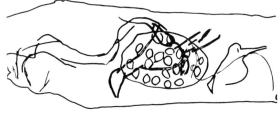

an earlier effort was not made to compare, evaluate, and interpret them. An appealing seasonal image is of an Ice Age grasshopper in a composition of birds and what look like pupae or insect eggs. It comes from the site of Les Trois Frères in the Ariège region of southern France (Fig. 78 a, b), and it is clearly an image of summer and warm weather.

The most dramatic of these seasonal, realistic representations are, perhaps, those depicting stags and bison bulls and even ibex in the late summer and autumn rut. The art is often so strong, and the examples so numerous, that one practically hears the ancient clashing of horns and tusks and the belling and bellowing of the males, year after year. These species do not rut in the same moon or month. The ibex may rut a month or so after the late summer rut of the bison, at about the time of the reindeer rut and perhaps a month before the rutting of the stags of red deer.

A long-antlered, head-high stag in its full-throated autumn rutting bellow is depicted on a bâton from the site of Les Hoteaux, on the river Ain in eastern France near Switzerland (Fig. 79 a, b). The image occurs often. On a pebble from Limeuil, near Les Eyzies in south central France, there is the head-high, tongue out, open-mouthed image of a stag (Fig. 80). On a bit of slate from Labastide, further south in the Pyrenean foothills, another is crudely but forcibly drawn (Fig. 81 a, b). On the cave wall at Lascaux there is a magnificent stag bellowing (Fig. 82). There are other examples of the bellowing stag, engraved and painted.

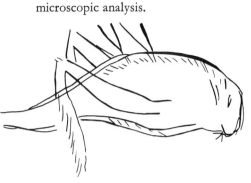

Fig. 78 b
Detail. Line rendition of the grasshopper on the bone fragment from Les Trois Frères, as determined by microscopic analysis.

Fig. 78 a
Bone fragment from Les Trois Frères (Ariège) depicting bird legs, grasshopper, grass and perhaps insect pupae. Upper Magdalenian.

Fig. 79 a
Bâton from Les Hoteaux (Aïn) with baying autumn stag. Upper Magdalenian.

Related to this image of the autumn stag is the engraving of two bull bison butting, from the Magdalenian site of Pekarna in Czechoslovakia (Fig. 83), a seasonal activity of the summer, July to September, with a peak in a cool climate around August. At Laugerie Haute, between Solutrean and Magdalenian levels, there was found a *bâton de commandement*

Fig. 79 b. Preceding pages.
Detail. Baying stag.

Fig. 80
Engraved stone from Limeuil (Dordogne) with the head of a baying stag.
Upper Magdalenian.

with two mammoth butting. This is one of the earliest known examples of a realistic, seasonal, "sexual" composition, though the exact rutting season of the mammoth is not known.

These images are instantly recognizable. There is another class of composition, however, in which animals are associated with notations or with abstract symbols and even with "darts," "spears," or wounds that were once considered evidences of hunting magic. The butting bison from Pekarna is one example, the two ibexes from Raymonden another.

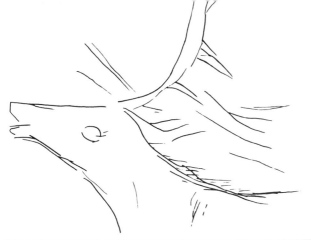

Fig. 81 b

Fig. 81 a
Engraved stone from Labastide (Haute-Pyrénées) with the head of a baying stag. Upper Magdalenian.

Fig. 81 b
Line rendition of the baying stag on the Labastide stone, as determined by microscopic analysis.

Fig. 82
Painting of a baying stag in cave of Lascaux (Dordogne). The autumn

Fig. 81 a

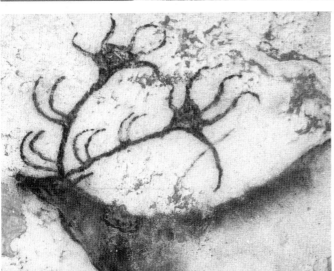

Fig. 82

stag is associated on wall with geometric forms, cows, pregnant mares, notational sequences and possible weapons and plant motifs related to the other animals. Images together present a composition that is perhaps comparable in symbolic complexity, if not in precise meaning, to the two faces of the La Vache knife (Fig. 67 a, b) and the La Marche bâton (Fig. 88) combined.

Fig. 83
Line rendition of an engraved bone from Pekarna (Moravia) depicting three bison bulls, two of which are butting (after Absolon). There may be marks of wounding or killing. Upper Magdalenian.

Now, if some of the associated markings are notational and lunar, and if some of the animal images are representative of seasonal behavior and interrelations, the compositions containing animals, notations, and symbols may tell us something, if only a little, about the meanings they contain.

Fig. 84
Broken ivory plaque from La Vache (Ariège) with the outline of a molting bull bison. Ear and horn are clearly engraved, the eye is exceedingly faint, the nostril may be a fault in the plaque. Above, below and to the rear of the bison are three groups of notation in different styles. Final Magdalenian.

From La Vache, which has given us a number of seasonal compositions, there comes a beautifully shaped piece of ivory, broken at one end, that has the schematic image of a bison bull engraved on it. The eye is faintly engraved, the horn is quickly and imprecisely drawn, and the mouth

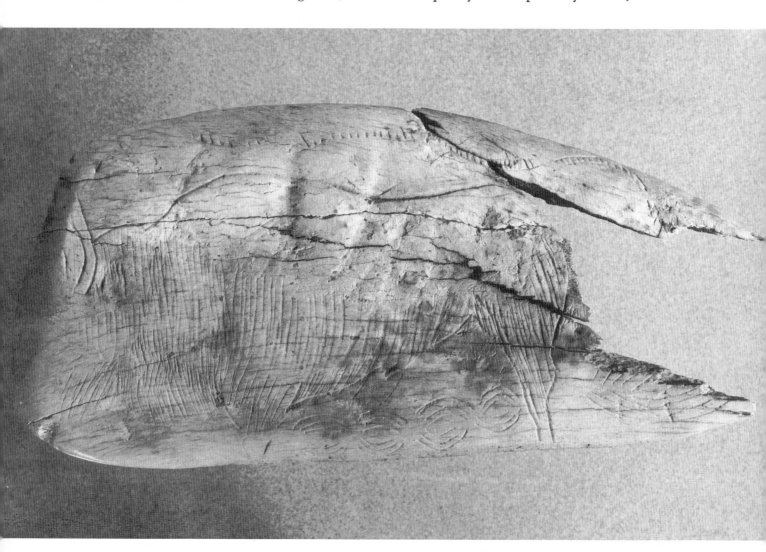

seems to be more a fault in the bone than an intentional mark. But the bison body is clear and detailed, as though the meaning was in the body. The bison fur is patchy, the top almost naked. The molting season of the bison begins in the spring, so that if the hunter wants a buffalo robe for wearing or for covering the floor of his shelter, he must plan to get the full, healthy autumn or winter hide. In any case, the hunter would know his seasons of changing fur. The bison may be more or less bare some two or three months, from spring to summer, and by the time the buzzing mosquitoes have begun to swarm, he is uncomfortable and irritable. The bulls are particularly hairless at this time and love to wallow in the cooling, protective mud of a stream (Fig. 84).

Seasonal images of molting, like images of rutting, are common. There is a molting bison painted at Lascaux (France) and one at Altamira (Spain). There is a brilliantly detailed molting musk ox, whose molting period is the same as the bison's, engraved on a pebble from the Upper Perigordian site of La Colombière on the river Ain (Fig. 85). On this pebble there is a similar generalization of the eye and an indeterminate face, as though to stress the nakedness of the molting animal.

If you turn back to the La Vache bison, you will notice that above and below the spring and early summer image of the bull, there is a marking

◀ *Note*, Fig. 83
The butting bison bulls represent the Magdalenian IV Franco-Cantabrian style and tradition of seasonal and sexually descriptive animal art that reached as far as Germany, Czechoslovakia and even Poland, c. 13,500 B.C. The earlier Gravettian animal art of Czechoslovakia, c. 26,000 B.C., produced only generalized images of a few species.

Fig. 85
Engraved, broken pebble from La Colombière (Aïn) with a molting musk ox. Lance or dart lines cross over and into the animal. Upper Perigordian.

Fig. 86 ▶
One face of an engraved, broken
bâton from La Marche (Vienne) with
rows of tiny marks grouped as blocks.
Middle Magdalenian.

that looks like notation. It seems to have been made after the drawing. By microscope the notational intent becomes clear, for the markings are divided into series made by different points. Each group is contained by a curved horizontal line that sometimes runs above the marks and sometimes below. The full composition, indicating the changes of point and the sums of the periods, is:

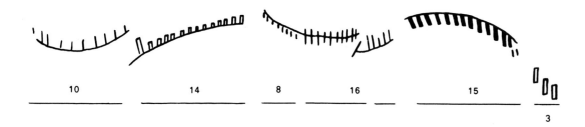

The sum of marks is 66, the rough count for a two-month period. If this were a lunar notation, it would break down so:

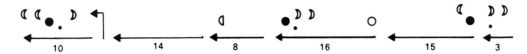

The phrasing is precise and goes a day or two beyond the first crescent. Below the bison is an odd set of arced figures that at first looks like four eyes and seems to have some specialized meaning. The microscope reveals that the full figure was made by a single point and therefore probably at one time. I hesitate to interpret this non-linear series, but the complete image is composed of 30 strokes and is made by a basic triple arc, with added marks in some sets:

To the right and rear of the bison is a broken series of marks that again looks symbolic or notational. It is made by 3 points and looks so:

Whatever the meaning of the marks, they seem clearly related to the spring-early summer bison, and perhaps they count the moons or days from the start of molt to the time of rut.

The bison and notation from La Vache occur on a flat slate seen as a single image. Let us look at a more complex engraving of an animal associated with markings. The site of La Marche, north of Les Eyzies on the drainage of the Vienne and Loire rivers, has given us, engraved on stone, some of the most complex pictorial compositions in the Upper Paleolithic.[6]

From this site comes a bâton whose top portion, if it had a hole, is broken off. The engraving on one face is complete, on the other partial (Fig. 86).

Fig. 88 ▶
Schematic rendition of all the intentional marks on the La Marche bâton, as determined by microscopic analysis. The pregnant mare, below, has five "sets" of darts associated with it, each engraved by a different point, in a different style and at a different time. The body of the second horse is missing in a break of the bone. The notations on the main face were accumulated from the top downward.

[6] These are being prepared for publication by Dr. Léon Pales, Musée de l'Homme, Paris.

Face one is engraved with rows of horizontal marks made as the bâton was held vertically.

The microscope reveals that these marks are made in groups, each engraved by a different point, and each block of marks is also subdivided into rows. Some blocks of marks are engraved in a downward direction,

Fig. 88

Fig. 86

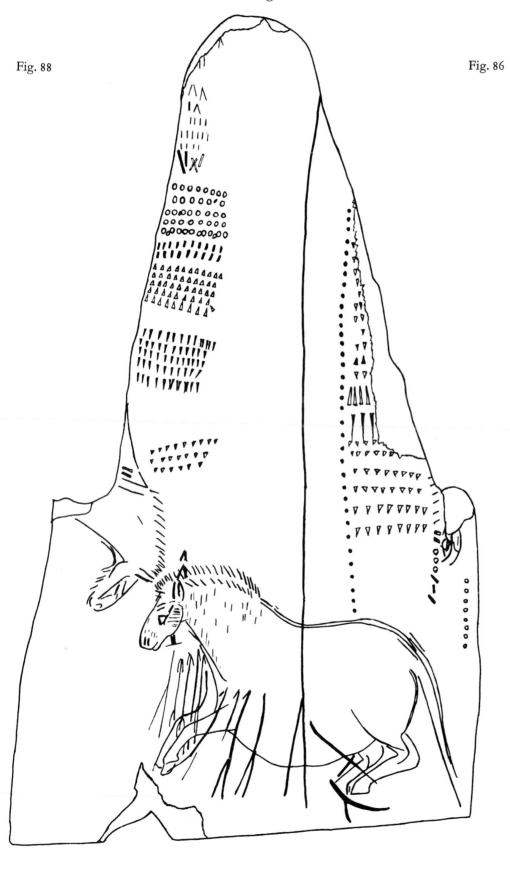

others upward, as though the bâton had been turned 180° for the engraving of some sets.

Figure 87 is an enlargement of two blocks of notation documenting the differences in tool and stroke for each block. The upper block is composed of strokes that impact at the top and tail out below. The lower set is composed of slightly twisted strokes made by a different point.

Analysis reveals that the composition is notational and begins at the narrow end and accumulates its rows and sets in a downward direction. On the second face is a subsidiary notation, some of which is lost in a broken portion. These marks also show differences in engraving points and changes in the direction of engraving.

At the bottom of the bâton is the engraving of a pregnant mare. The head of another horse is at left, representing the animal on face two. Its front hooves are visible at the break at right. The mare has five sets of marks associated with it, each set made by a different point: two sets of vertical darts, a single long dart with an angled back, and two wide angles (Fig. 88).

Testing the notational groups on face one for possible lunar phrasing gives a near perfect tally for $7\frac{1}{2}$ months. At least three months are notated on the second face (Fig. 89).

◀ Fig. 87
Detail. Enlargement of two blocks of marks in mid-bâton indicating that different points and styles of stroke were used for each block. The lower group was made by a slightly arced or turned stroke.

Note, Figs. 86, 88
In the Magdalenian period, bone tools would often become surfaces for different types of symbolic marking. Microscopic analysis indicates that the La Marche antler fragment had probably been a bâton that was originally marked on one face with notation and a horse. It had broken and the handle was then scraped and reshaped to become a pressure flaker for sharpening stone tools. It was then engraved on the second face with another notation and another horse which was periodically renewed, "killed" and marked with symbols.

Fig. 88. Page 193.

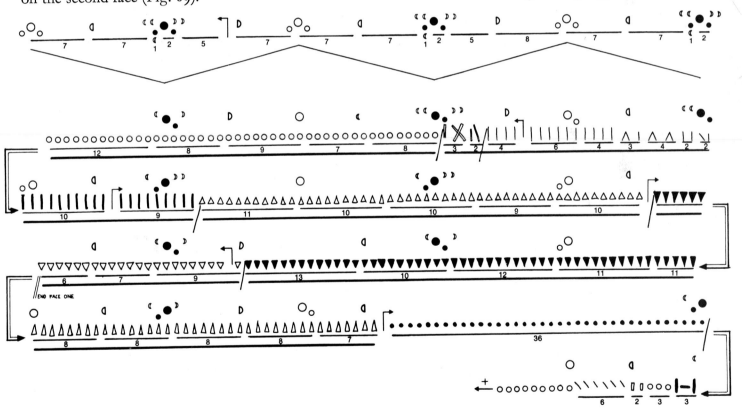

The mare drops its foal in the spring after an eleven month gestation and so the mare may be a seasonal image. The associated darts and signs may then represent rites, sacrifices or acts of participation related to the time of foaling. The combination of naturalistic "art," sequences of darts and signs, and a lunar notation hints at a complex time-factored symbolism and mythology.

Fig. 89
The engraved notational marks on the main face of the La Marche bâton against the lunar model, with some sets from the second face, indicating a possible observational lunar phrasing both in the sets and the subsets.

Plant engravings in Lascaux.

196

We can now move from compositions with animals, plants, fish, and snakes to compositions containing more complex, multiple "signs" and "symbols" and to images that have been interpreted as belonging to hunting and fertility magic or to ritual and sexual symbolism.

The most comprehensive analysis and comparison of the signs and symbols of the Ice Age has been made by André Leroi-Gourhan of the Musée de l'Homme and the Collège de France.[7] Like the work of the Abbé Breuil, Leroi-Gourhan's work marks a significant stage in the comparative analysis of Ice Age art and symbol. He has worked primarily with the caves, but his monumental classification and comparison of Ice Age animals and "signs" apply, in large measure, to the engraved materials. In a brilliant insight, shared by Annette Laming-Emperaire of the Musée de l'Homme, Leroi-Gourhan perceived that key animals in the cave art, such as bison and horse, were often associated with each other and that these "central" animals were of different species than the subsidiary animals, such as ibex, stag, and lion, often found in other areas of a cave. He also perceived that animals were not only associated with each other in what seemed a meaningful way in different parts of a cave, but that they were also associated with signs and symbols. In a tentative hypothesis concerning these associations, he theorized that these relationships found by statistical and comparative analysis, were "sexual," that is, they represented a general "male/female" pairing, a philosophical and religious view of the world as divided into two opposed "principles." As a result, all the signs and symbols, as well as the animals, were either "male" or "female."

My analysis of the art on the mobiliary materials, undertaken before I had knowledge of Leroi-Gourhan's results, indicated the validity of the first part of his insight, the meaningful association and relation of animals, signs, and symbols. But, as we have seen, the relationships were not necessarily "sexual," that is, concerned with a pairing of male and female opposites, but were rather more broadly cognitive in their meaning. When such associations did have a "sexual" content, it was often seasonal and behavioral, observational, or mythological. This does not mean that major processes, such as rutting, calving, molting, dropping of the antlers, battling of the males, and migration of species, did not—in story and symbol—have a sexual content or recognition, but that such content was not their central meaning. A goddess related to the spring calving or thaw, or a god related to the autumn rut, could, in Leroi-Gourhan's scheme, be representative of "female" or "male" polarity, if I may

[7] André Leroi-Gourhan, "La fonction des signes dans les sanctuaires paléolithiques," BULLETIN SOCIÉTÉ PRÉHISTORIQUE FRANÇAISE (LV, 1958), pp. 307–321;
"Le symbolisme des grands signes dans l'art pariétal paléolithique," BULL. SOC. PRÉHIST. FRANÇAISE (LV, 1958), pp. 384–398;
"Répartition et groupement des animaux dans l'art pariétal paléolithique," BULL. SOC. PRÉHIST. FRANÇAISE (LV, 1958), pp. 515–528;
"Réflexions de méthode sur l'art paléolithique," BULL. SOC. PRÉHIST. FRANÇAISE (LXIII, 1966), pp. 35–49;
TREASURES OF PREHISTORIC ART, trans. Norbert Guterman (New York: Abrams, 1967).

project from his theory. But the core of such a theoretical mythology would be a series of recognitions far broader and more complex than a mere division of the sexes. It would require a complex series of *time-factored* recognitions that could be simplified and explained only by story and with symbol via the use of male, female and non-sexual or bisexual characters. I shall return to the complexities of this problem later when we look at the "sexual" evidence more closely.

If you look at Leroi-Gourhan's list of Ice Age signs (Fig. 90), many of which are often associated with each other or with animals, you will recognize that our analysis has shown that some are *notations*. When found on the mobiliary artifacts, such notations are often, apparently, lunar. Our analysis has also shown that other signs on the list are more broadly symbolic and represent plant forms or even weapons and are thus neither notational in a unit sense nor sexual in the sense that they are either male or female.

I stress the difference between the notations on the mobiliary artifacts, which were apparently often lunar, and those found in the deep caves. Some of the painted and engraved chambers in the caves were extremely difficult to reach. It took hours to climb or crawl to these walls and hours to return. It would not seem that the notations on these walls would necessarily serve the same purposes as those on the easily portable bones and stones or on slates resting in a habitation site.

Nevertheless, a culture that had evolved a notational tradition as complex as the one we have been following on the mobiliary materials could easily have used notational and symbolic sequences of a different sort on the cave walls. We are dealing with a level of cognition and cultural skill. There is no reason, then, that a sequence of marks, dots, or punctuations found in the caves might not have served other notational purposes, might not have represented units of other reference. This would mean that the notations on the mobiliary materials and the notations on the cave walls would be related *as notations* in that culture but not that they necessarily had equal meanings, mark by mark. Having indicated a possible difference in the uses and meanings of these notations, we can also recognize that they were probably more closely related than these differences of meaning would suggest, since to some extent the same *stories* and *basic images* would be involved and these would be associated with the notations in the caves and those on the mobiliary artifacts. If one body of notation was lunar and referred to the seasons and species of ceremony and ritual, the other might have had reference to units involved in the ritual itself, perhaps ceremonial objects, weapons, dances, days, sacrifices, or participants.

As I pointed out, a number of "signs" in Leroi-Gourhan's classification look like the plant forms we have already seen in association with animals, fish, snakes and seals. Let us, therefore, see whether our continuing analysis will help us explain, a bit more precisely, the range of meanings, not necessarily sexual, in Leroi-Gourhan's comprehensive classification of signs and their juxtapositions. In this way it may be possible to incor-

Fig. 90. Pages following. The styles and patterns of Ice Age "signs" according to the classification of Leroi-Gourhan.

Numbers 1–36 are theorized as evolved "female" signs.
  1–10: Shield-like forms or "scuti-forms"
  11–13: Shield-like forms with appendices
  14–19: Bird-like forms or "avi-forms"
  20–29: House-like forms or "tecti-forms"
  30–36: Key-like forms or "clavi-forms"

Numbers 37–84 are theorized as "masculine" signs according to Leroi-Gourhan.
  37–50: Feather-like forms or "penni-forms"
  51–52: Incomplete outlines
  53–55: Bundles of lines
  56–67: Dots
  68–84: Lines

Numbers 85–126 are simplified "male" or "female" signs according to the theory of Leroi-Gourhan.
  85–104: "Female" signs
  105–122: "Male" signs
  123–126: Coupled or doubled signs of "male" plus "female" elements

The following comparison of certain types of Upper Paleolithic marking is useful and basic since it indicates some of the range and variation in Ice Age symbol usage. Such comparisons, however, can be used for other theoretical and analytic considerations than those tentatively proposed by Leroi-Gourhan. The present volume presents new techniques for the intensive internal analysis of many of these forms and has clarified their general usage or meaning in other terms.

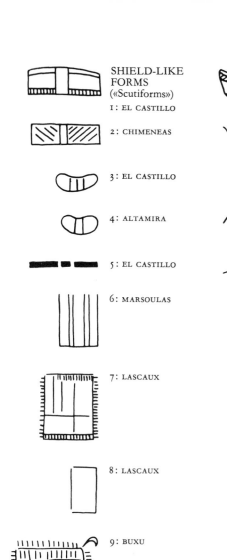

SHIELD-LIKE
FORMS
(«Scutiforms»)
1: EL CASTILLO

2: CHIMENEAS

3: EL CASTILLO

4: ALTAMIRA

5: EL CASTILLO

6: MARSOULAS

7: LASCAUX

8: LASCAUX

9: BUXU

10: ARCY

SHIELD-LIKE
FORMS
with appendices
11: USSAT

12: USSAT

13: LA PILETA

BIRD-LIKE
FORMS
(«Aviforms»)
14: LA PASIEGA

15: LA PASIEGA

16: ALTAMIRA

17: LA PASIEGA

18: EL CASTILLO

19: COUGNAC

HOUSE-LIKE
FORMS
(«Tectiforms»)
20: FONT-DE-GAUME

21: FONT-DE-GAUME

22: FONT-DE-GAUME

23: BERNIFAL

24: BERNIFAL

25: FONT-DE-GAUME

26: FONT-DE-GAUME

27: FONT-DE-GAUME

28: FONT-DE-GAUME

29: LASCAUX

KEY-LIKE
FORMS
(«Claviforms»)
30: NIAUX
31: TROIS-FRÈRES
32: LA PASIEGA

33: ALTAMIRA
34: PINDAL

35: BAYOL
36: BAYOL

FEATHER-LIKE
FORMS
(«Penniforms»)
37: LASCAUX

38: MARSOULAS

39: LASCAUX

40: LASCAUX

41: NIAUX

42: MONEDAS
43: MONEDAS
44: MARSOULAS

45: EL CASTILLO
46: LABASTIDE

47: LASCAUX
48: COUGNAC

49: LA PASIEGA
50: LA PASIEGA

INCOMPLETE
OUTLINES
51: BEDEILHAC

52: ARCY

BUNDLES
OF LINES
53: ARCY

54: LASCAUX

55: ROUFFIGNAC

DOTS

56: LASCAUX

57: LASCAUX

58: BEDEILHAC

59: EL CASTILLO

60: BERNIFAL

61: NIAUX

62: MARSOULAS

63: PORTEL

64: NIAUX
65: NIAUX

66: GARGAS

67: PECH-MERLE

68: LASCAUX

69: PORTEL

LINES
70: NIAUX

71: CULLALVERA

72: PECH-MERLE

73: USSAT

74: LA CROZE À GONTRAN

75: LES COMBARELLES

76: LASCAUX

77: ALTAMIRA

78: BEDEILHAC

79: ALTAMIRA

80: LASCAUX

81: ARCY

82: NIAUX

83: NIAUX

84: PINDAL

«Female» signs
85

86

87

88

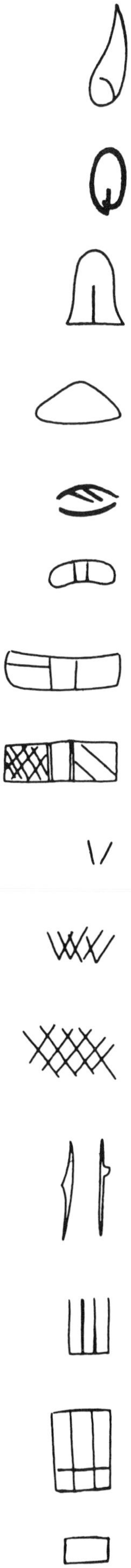

89

90

91

92

93

94

95

96

97

98

99

100
101

102

103

104

«Male» signs
105

106

107
108

109
110

111
112
113

114
115
116

117
118

119

120

121

122

Coupled «male/female» signs
123

124

125

126

Fig. 91 a, b
The two faces of a broken, engraved bone from Roc de Courbet, Bruniquel (Tarn-et-Garonne) depicting fish on one face and uncertain images on the other. Upper Magdalenian.

Fig. 91 c
Line rendition of one face of the bone from Roc de Courbet showing the two fish heads and the remnant of a fish tail at the left, as determined by microscopic analysis.

porate the factual elements in Leroi-Gourhan's statistical and comparative work into our own. Leroi-Gourhan's admittedly tentative hypotheses are among the most controversial in the field of the Upper Paleolithic, and it is necessary, therefore, to proceed slowly and by steps.

The plant form seems to be a crucial "sign" or "symbol" so let us examine its relations to the figurative art and the notations.

A fragment of hollow bone from the Grotte du Roc de Courbet at Bruniquel, midway between Les Eyzies and the Pyrenean foothills and on the drainage of the Garonne which meets the Dordogne below Bordeaux, has fish heads engraved on one face. The other face has four figures that the Abbé Breuil has called schematized fish tails, "isolated fins already evolved towards stylization"[8] (Fig. 91 a, b, c).

Fig. 91 a

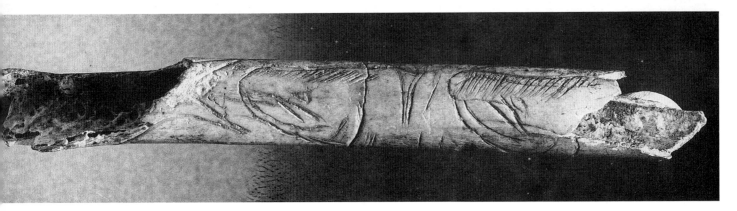

Fig. 91 c

Note
The hooked jaw and bulbous snout depict the male salmon at the time of the salmon run. Bruniquel is halfway into France from the estuary at Bordeaux. A comparable image of a male salmon was found at La Vache in the Pyrenean foothills. See page 274.

The microscope reveals that in front of the first fish on face one there is a simplified, schematized fish tail of an entirely different sort, made by sure, single strokes:

[8] H. Breuil and R. de Saint-Périer, LES POISSONS, LES BATRACIENS ET LES REPTILES DANS L'ART QUATERNAIRE, p. 84.

The man making this obvious fish tail would not, it seems, have made the unstructured, unbalanced images on the other face as tails (Fig. 92 a, b). Ice Age fish tails are usually made to capture the balance rather than the disorganization of the tail image, whether made in single strokes as above or in multiple strokes that indicate the rays. On the page on which the Abbé Breuil presents his drawing of the bone from Bruniquel, he presents the drawing of a bone with fish and plant or feather images from Laugerie Basse, near Les Eyzies (Fig. 93 a, b).

Fig. 92 b
Line rendition of two of the upright figures on the second face of the bone from Roc de Courbet, as determined by microscopic analysis.

Perhaps, then, the forms on face two of the Bruniquel bone represent plant images, but plants of a certain kind: not a single branch or twig, but an *irregular* form, a form that branches up and out. Perhaps, therefore, they are trees.

Fig. 92 a
Detail. The upright images on the second face of the bone from Roc de Courbet.

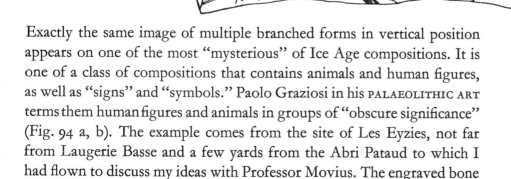

Exactly the same image of multiple branched forms in vertical position appears on one of the most "mysterious" of Ice Age compositions. It is one of a class of compositions that contains animals and human figures, as well as "signs" and "symbols." Paolo Graziosi in his PALAEOLITHIC ART terms them human figures and animals in groups of "obscure significance" (Fig. 94 a, b). The example comes from the site of Les Eyzies, not far from Laugerie Basse and a few yards from the Abri Pataud to which I had flown to discuss my ideas with Professor Movius. The engraved bone

Fig. 93 b
Schematic rendition of the basic composition on the bone fragment from Laugerie Basse indicating the fish with surrounding feathers or plants, as determined by microscopic analysis.

Figs. 93 a; 94 a, b. Pages following.

Fig. 93 a
Engraved fragment of bone from Laugerie Basse (Dordogne) depicting two schematic fishes seen from above and other images. Upper Magdalenian.

Fig. 94 a
Engraved bone fragment from Les Eyzies (Dordogne) with a scene containing humanoid figures facing an oversize bison and four trees. Upper Magdalenian.

Fig. 94 b
Line rendition of the engraving on the bone from Les Eyzies, as determined by microscopic analysis.

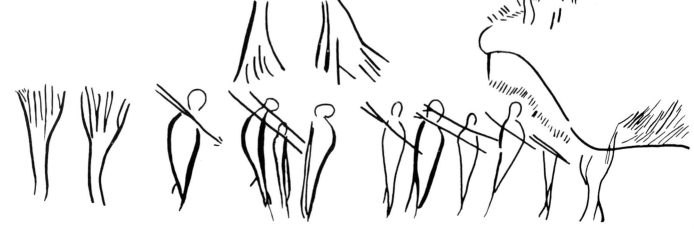

is housed in the local museum built into the limestone cliff that faces the Vézère and once served as a shelter for the Ice Age hunter.

Even without the microscope, it is clear that the forms are trees, that they have long narrow trunks and a random branching. In one form the branches flare out at the top in a way that could not be considered "fishlike" (Fig. 95 a, b, c, d).

The system of "reading" or notating around the edges of a flat slate is one that we have seen. Here the style makes two of the trees seem to stand upside down. Leroi-Gourhan, writing of this composition, states that it contains

"the forequarters of a bison and four forms that resemble alder trees bordering a kind of central path along which file nine small silhouettes carrying sticks on their shoulders … [a] peaceful procession of little men who seem to be walking toward a bison—they are so short they barely come up to the level of its fetlock."[9]

To Leroi-Gourhan, the significance of the scene lies not in the trees but in the relation of the little men to the bison, a "female" image.

Fig. 95 a, b, c. Pages following. Details. Photo enlargements of the four engraved trees on the Les Eyzies bone indicating that the upper and lower trees were made by different points and perhaps at different times. Compare the print of the point engraving the trees with that engraving the nearby humanoid figure.

Fig. 95 d
Line rendition of the four trees as determined by microscopic analysis.

The valley of Les Eyzies is small, yet clumps of trees and stands of wood may have run up the steep hills in the Magdalenian, and other species may have hugged the damp shores of the winding Vézère, much as they do today. If we assume that these bare, leafless trees, apparently not conifers, or evergreens, are time-factored and seasonal images, then the branches may have begun to bud and perhaps to flower from the end of April to the middle of May and to have dropped their leaves and seeds

[9] Leroi-Gourhan, TREASURES OF PREHISTORIC ART, p. 134.

in the fall. If we consider the oversize bison as a time-factored and seasonal image—whether as part of a rite, myth, ceremony, dance, or even sacrifice—then we have a composition or scene whose visual elements are neither directly sexual nor particularly involved in "hunting magic," at least not as far as the belly and next meal are concerned. If the bare trees are a sign either of early spring or of autumn-winter, the bison instead of being a "sex" sign might represent the season, or bison behavior in that season, and the image might be of the bison sacrificed or worshipped at the "proper time."

Not shown in any of the anthologies where this piece is popular, nor noticeable in the museum where one face only is displayed as "art," is an engraved image on the reverse side that looks like part of a schematized fish. It is cut off at the break of the bone:

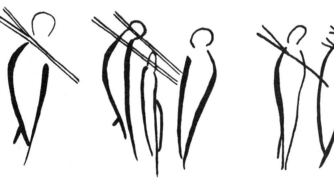

The microscope also reveals that the human figures or anthropomorphs, carrying "spears" or "sticks" according to Leroi-Gourhan, or struck through by spears or darts, are overengraved by four separate sets of lines. Each set is engraved by a different point, as though made at four different times. In addition, the two anthropomorphs directly under the bison were made by two different points. The tool prints making the other human figures are not as easy to distinguish and compare, owing to wear, but seem to have been made by one point:

DARTS BY 1 POINT   DARTS BY 1 POINT   1 PT.   1 PT.

If we are correct in assuming that the associated images of the trees and bison are storied or mythical, time-factored and seasonal, then we can place the whole dramatic composition within the context of the evolving culture and tradition we have been tracing. The composition, though it has no notations, is related to the notations and to compositions with notations, as well as to animals without notations but associated only with each other. Of course, we must be careful. We cannot assume that all the images and notations found in the Upper Paleolithic are part of the same, single "story." We can only assume, at this stage, that all are part of the one basic time-factored culture, and that within this culture there were many stories and rites.

We can also assume that the composition on this bone is related to the art of the caves. These decorated caves are scattered through the Franco-

Cantabrian area and have on their walls bison, darts, humanoid figures, and plant images.

If this composition represents a seasonal, mythological rite, the humanoid figures would represent elements either in the story, in the dance or ritual, or in the possible "sacrifice." But though the figures are either carrying "spears" or "sticks," or are themselves struck through, we cannot assume that they necessarily represent an image of direct "killing." Weapons can be ceremonial and can represent the power or the ability to kill, or the story of some mythical killing, just as ceremonial axes or swords have done in historic times. Even a "sacrifice" can be storied and can be danced, mimed, or sung, rather than real. In fact, the real sacrifice and true sacrificial weapons are also storied. There is a potential complexity in such storied compositions, then, that cannot be determined from the analysis of a single bone. We can, however, begin the process of analysis by proceeding as we did with the notations, by microscopy and by sequential reconstruction of a composition, by comparisons, by the clarification of related themes, and so on. Later we shall look more closely at the time-factored and time-factoring uses of myth and "sacrifice."

Fig. 96 a
Engraved bone fragment from Raymonden (Dordogne) depicting a bison head and spine, two detached front legs, humanoid figures and various signs. Upper Magdalenian.

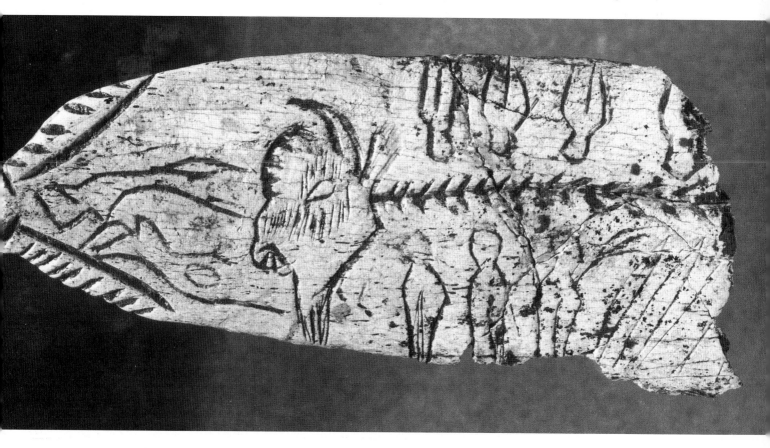

A bone slate with a composition containing a bison and humanoid figures comes from Raymonden, not far from Les Eyzies (Fig. 96 a, b), the site that gave us the spring image of the two birds and the kids. The bison head is intact, but the body is represented only by the spinal column. Even in the "x-ray" art of modern primitives, the body is drawn, so that

Fig. 96 b. Next page.

it may be that in this scene the parts of a newly killed bison are presented. In front of the bison are two unattached, well-drawn feet, facing each other awkwardly. The drawing of the bison head and feet is extremely good, and the man making it was a craftsman who did not waste strokes or distort, so the bison parts may have had some intentional meaning. Around the carefully drawn bison head march or stand faceless, poorly drawn "anonymous" humanlike figures.

Of this composition, Leroi-Gourhan states,
"we see seven little fellows disposed in two rows along the central path, which is occupied by a barbed sign [the spine, here interpreted as a weapon or a masculine symbol]; at one end of the path a bison's head and two legs seem to be lying on the ground, as though they had been cut off. One of the men carries over his shoulder not a stick or a spear but a kind of broom. Lacking more evidence, it is rash to interpret these objects, but apparently a 'bison and hunter' theme exists, recurring in caves and on objects in various forms."[10]

The "bison and hunter" image need not represent a hunt for food but, as seems more likely, a myth and rite in which the bison, or bison parts, and the manlike figures are related. In such a storied ceremony, any "killing" would be also storied and probably "sacrificial."

The artist drawing this bison is illustrating a different aspect of bison meaning and story than the artist of La Vache, who drew a bison without legs, with an indeterminate head, and with a body in seasonal molt related to notations. Nevertheless, both bison images and meanings may have been subsumed or coalesced in an encompassing myth, story, and ritual.

Each humanoid figure in the composition is "struck through" by a stroke or strokes, and it is difficult to know if these represent arms or legs, spears or darts. One figure has coming out of his chest the odd image that Leroi-Gourhan calls "a kind of broom" but that looks more like a three-pronged symbolic branch, and behind him the microscope reveals an image that looks like a two-pronged "Y." In front of the man with the branch is a series of lightly drawn images that look like schematic, incomplete forms, huge leaves, darts, knives, or spatulas. Similar images representing schematized weapons in a non-killing position or relation to the depicted animal appear in a number of Upper Paleolithic compositions.

Another complex composition of "obscure significance," containing animals, humanoid figures, and signs or symbols comes from La Madeleine, the site that gave its name to the Magdalenian period. The site is a short walk downriver on the Vézère from Les Eyzies, and it shared both the culture and seasons of the Dordogne region with the hunters of Raymonden and Les Eyzies. I present the line drawing of the unrolled, round bâton published by the Abbé Breuil (Fig. 97).

The drawing shows us two horse heads, an anthropomorph carrying a

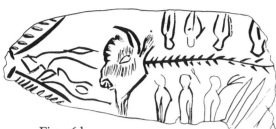

Fig. 96 b
Line rendition of all intentional lines within the Raymonden composition depicting in addition a branched and a forked sign, blade-like shapes and two sets of enclosed notches, as determined by microscopic analysis.

Fig. 99 ▶
Schematic rendition of the full engraved composition on the bone from La Madeleine as determined by microscopic analysis. The precise rendition indicates the notational character of the marks around the serpentine figure.

[10] Ibid., pp. 134–135.

long stick, and a snake or eel with an oddly branched tail and double neck marks.

The microscope reveals that Breuil's rendition is not completely accurate and that the anthropomorph is carrying a branch with two leaves or twigs arcing in a direction opposite to the one he presents. The mouth and eye drawn by Breuil are not really there but only seem to be there because of breaks and marks in the bone (Fig. 98 a, b).

Fig. 97

Fig. 99

Above the anthropomorph is a series of marks that were too worn to be examined for their prints, but which looked like "rain" only because the carefully structured linear sequences around the eel seem clearly notational. That this was a mythical or a ritual, ceremonial scene was apparent when the microscope revealed that the bâton had been heavily covered with red ocher, the symbolic color of life (Fig. 99).

Note a)

The eel, which I had originally thought might be an eel or a serpent has the rear caudal fin joined as a unit to the upper dorsal and lower anal fins, as well as the pectoral fins below the head, that are typical of the genus Anguilla. Eels, like salmon, are a migratory fish and their seasonal appearance in the rivers of the Franco-Cantabrian region was apparently noted by the Magdalenians who had increased both their use and their depictions of fish in this period.

If the figure is an eel, then the suggested seasonal relation of the "spring/summer" horse and the "spring/summer" fish within engraved compositions on bone during this period is strengthened. One must then address the referential and probably mythological aspects of such associations in the Magdalenian. Actually, serpents and eels are each seasonal referents, but from different realms or domains.

Note b)

The symbolic branch carried by the human figure may be reflected in the symbolic branch or plant described by Breuil as a "broom" over the shoulder of the human figure in Fig. 96 b. The symbolic use of plants in rituals and imagery has not to this day been adequately addressed in the study of Ice Age "art."

Now, the Upper Paleolithic cultures have left little evidence of a use of wood, except for the charcoal of the fires and the large and varied tool kit of bone and stone that must have been used at times on items of wood. Here, in the engraved double leaves or branches, is the first proof of a symbolic use of the branch carried in hand. The stick is too long for it to have been made of antler or bone.

Extremely interesting is the microscopic analysis of the linear "structure." The details hint at a notational system of some sort, of a sequence of lines and marks that are divided into groups or "periods." The full figure, differing significantly from Breuil's rendition, is:

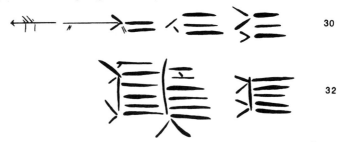

The style of marking is not one that we have seen before and so I hesitate, on the basis of this one example, to declare it lunar. However, it does seem notational, and a mere test of the sequences and marks gives us two months:

Interesting is the fact that the man carrying the symbolic branch is directly related to the two "floating" bodyless horse heads and the "rain," while the symbolic eel is directly related to the marking around it, and all are related by being on one bone. The nature of the relation must, in part at least, have been storied. The analysis we have been developing would indicate that the images are involved in time-factored, seasonal myths or rites, and that horse heads, like bison heads, had symbolic meaning.

The stories we cannot know, but the same visual elements appear in other "obscure compositions." Turn back and look at the Magdalenian bone slate with the three horse heads from Mas d'Azil in the Pyrenean foothills (Fig. 57a). The horse heads in single file look as though they were tethered by thongs, or as though they were intended to "follow each other" in linear sequence. The Mas d'Azil heads are not realistic, but are slightly abstracted and geometricized. Around these horses, above and below, there is a notation in the vertical-foot tradition. On the other face there is a subsidiary notation, of verticals, to which feet have not yet been added. If one estimates and visualizes a full slate and finishes the one broken horse head and then approximates the amount of notation that might be required to finish the bone at the spacing already indicated, one gets about five months, with one subsidiary month on the reverse face. There would be a minimum notation then, if the notation is lunar, of a half year. Does a horse head, then, indicate a "month," or does a series of horses indicate a "period," some season of the sun, or are these horse heads the image of a tribal story or rite related to a seasonal passage of time? Are these heads images in a story and myth that included a real horse in sacrifice? At this point we cannot tell. We know only that horse heads, isolated as pendants as at Isturitz where geometric horse heads similar to these of Mas d'Azil are cut out of bone, and those in the engravings seem to serve some symbolic, time-factored use. The meaning of the horse seems to extend in time.

Whether these are ritual horses, storied horses, signs for horses, sacrificed horses, or masks of horses, it is certain that they are not images in "hunting magic," as was thought earlier. The Mas d'Azil horses are related to the floating horse heads of the La Madeleine composition; both sets of horses are related to their associated notations, while the horses of La Madeleine are also related to the man with the branch and to the snake or eel; and all these horse heads are related to the horse head pendants and beads that are found in great numbers in these regions and may have been worn by a chief or "sorcerer" or a person wishing to be part of the continuing myth.

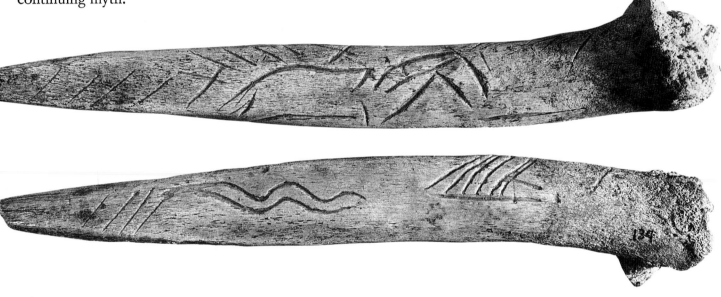

Fig. 100 a, b
The two faces of an engraved bone from El Pendo, northwest Spain, depicting a horse and a serpentine image, perhaps an eel, associated with sets of linear marks. Upper Magdalenian.

Step by step, then, it seems that we are increasingly able to make the necessary comparisons of images and compositions and ask the important new questions. One reason this is possible is that the use of combined images and a limited repertoire of images approaches a system of symbolic notation. It is cognitively similar to the unit notation of the lunar sequences in that it is based on the brain's capacity: on learning, observation, story, recognition, and the ability to synthesize and compose a "sum" of images.

To show how this cognitive ability works with more abstracted, less realistic images, I present another example from the Late Magdalenian, from the site of El Pendo on the northern Cantabrian coast of Spain. The culture and animals were the same as those in France (Fig. 100 a, b).

The bone shows on one face a quickly drawn schematic horse and on the other a schematic snake. The combined meaning is probably similar to that of the horse and snake combination from La Madeleine. The precise storied meaning remains obscure, or only hinted at in a possible ritual and seasonal context.

With the horse and snake on each face is a marking that seems to be notational. The markings are not in linear sequence so that analysis is difficult, but they do seem to be related to the horse/snake story. A simple count gives us 34 marks, roughly one month from new moon period to new moon period, perhaps representing two "moons."

I turn to another composition that uses images, symbols, and notations in sequence and contains other animals or forms we have been studying, the fish, the plant, and the ibex.

Fig. 101 a
The main face of an engraved bâton from Raymonden (Dordogne) depicting the head of a deer and other symbolic forms. Middle Magdalenian.

From Raymonden a mid-Magdalenian bâton presents an extremely complex composition. The engraving is worn, but the microscope reveals that all the intentional marks of the original are present (Fig. 101 a, b). The bâton is round but, holding it so that the side opposite the hole is the main face, one has in sequence the head of a deer, the tail of a fish, the schematic head of an ibex, and a form not quite recognizable. On the lower side are a branch and a seedling, followed by a block of notation. Above are a fish tail, an ibex, another odd image, and a block of notation. These were made sequentially, but we cannot be sure whether each face was made at one time or it was composed in the round. If it was composed in the round, the two fish tails may have been made one after the other and the two ibexes, one seemingly male, the other female, may have been made together. The notations, then, may have been made last.

In addition to these engravings, there are markings on each side of the bâton hole that seem decorative, but which break down so:

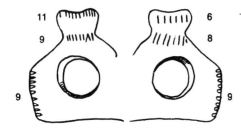

We cannot "read" these images and marks. Nevertheless, an extraordinarily complex composition has begun to seem organized, purposeful, notational, and part of a tradition that composed storied sequences or sums with a repertoire of images. The way of thinking is one we understand.

In the winter of 1968, after this book was almost completed, I visited a small, little-known collection of Upper Paleolithic materials at the Museo de Ciencias Naturales, Madrid. Under glass in a cabinet there lay a broken bâton engraved in an extremely complex manner. The complexity was of the kind that has been called "random," "undecipherable," or "geometric patterning."

Within this complexity, however, there were clearly recognizable forms, including notational sequences and symbolic images. Some of the images were instantly familiar. I examined the engraving by microscope, made notes, photomacrographs, and drawings, and left the museum without having worked out a cohesive analysis and reconstruction of the two faces (Fig. 102 a, b).

Fig. 102 a, b. Page 215.

After the manuscript was completed, I took my notes and drawings, enlarged my photos, and began the study again. I realized I had stumbled

on a unique example, the one composition in all Europe that validated the many hypotheses, theories, conjectures, and findings I had pieced together so laboriously in an analysis of hundreds of other examples.

The bone came from the cave of Cueto de la Mina near Oviedo in the Asturias region of northwest Cantabrian Spain. It was Late Magdalenian and had been found more than fifty years before.[11] The bâton is shaped like the one from Raymonden that I just described, but is broken off at the hole whose edge is still apparent.

On the first face there are two abstracted ibex heads, in the tradition of the "ibex sign" we have already examined (Montgaudier, La Vache, Raymonden). On this same face there seem to be two plantlike or barbed forms. On the other face there are at least three plant forms, each so different as to seem indicative of either species or seasonal variation.

One of the ibex heads is struck through or crossed out, a technique of marking an animal or its horns we have seen before on the Montgaudier and La Vache examples and which occurs on other Magdalenian examples with other animals. Each of the images, plant and animal, seems to be associated with its own group or sequence of marks, each of which is made in a different style, pattern, or rhythm. Some groups run horizontally, some vertically, some arc toward the right, others toward the left,

Fig. 101 b
Line rendition of all intentionally engraved marks on the body of the bâton from Raymonden, as determined by microscopic analysis. The composition is unrolled and includes animal, fish and plant images in varying degrees of realism and schematization together with notational counts. The composition was apparently engraved sequentially to tell a "story."

[11] Ricardo Vega del Sella, "El Paleolítico de la Cueto de la Mina," COMISIÓN DE INVESTIGACIONES PALEONTOLÓGICAS Y PREHISTÓRICAS, Memoire 13 (Madrid, 1916), Plate XXXIX: 2 a, b and Plate XL.

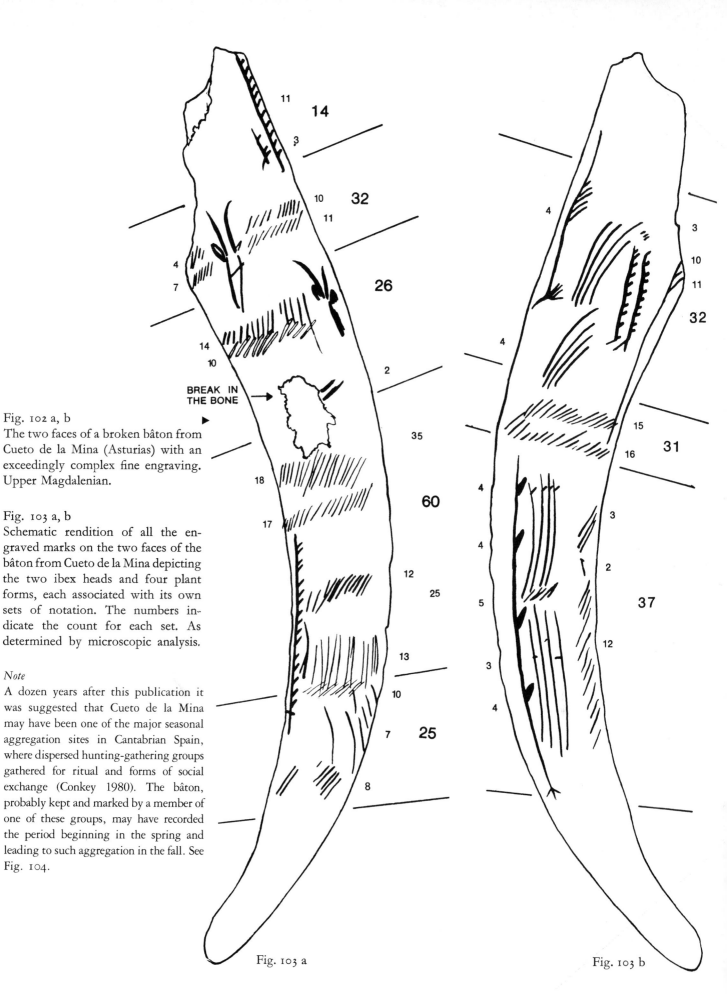

Fig. 102 a, b
The two faces of a broken bâton from Cueto de la Mina (Asturias) with an exceedingly complex fine engraving. Upper Magdalenian.

Fig. 103 a, b
Schematic rendition of all the engraved marks on the two faces of the bâton from Cueto de la Mina depicting the two ibex heads and four plant forms, each associated with its own sets of notation. The numbers indicate the count for each set. As determined by microscopic analysis.

Note
A dozen years after this publication it was suggested that Cueto de la Mina may have been one of the major seasonal aggregation sites in Cantabrian Spain, where dispersed hunting-gathering groups gathered for ritual and forms of social exchange (Conkey 1980). The bâton, probably kept and marked by a member of one of these groups, may have recorded the period beginning in the spring and leading to such aggregation in the fall. See Fig. 104.

BREAK IN THE BONE

Fig. 103 a

Fig. 103 b

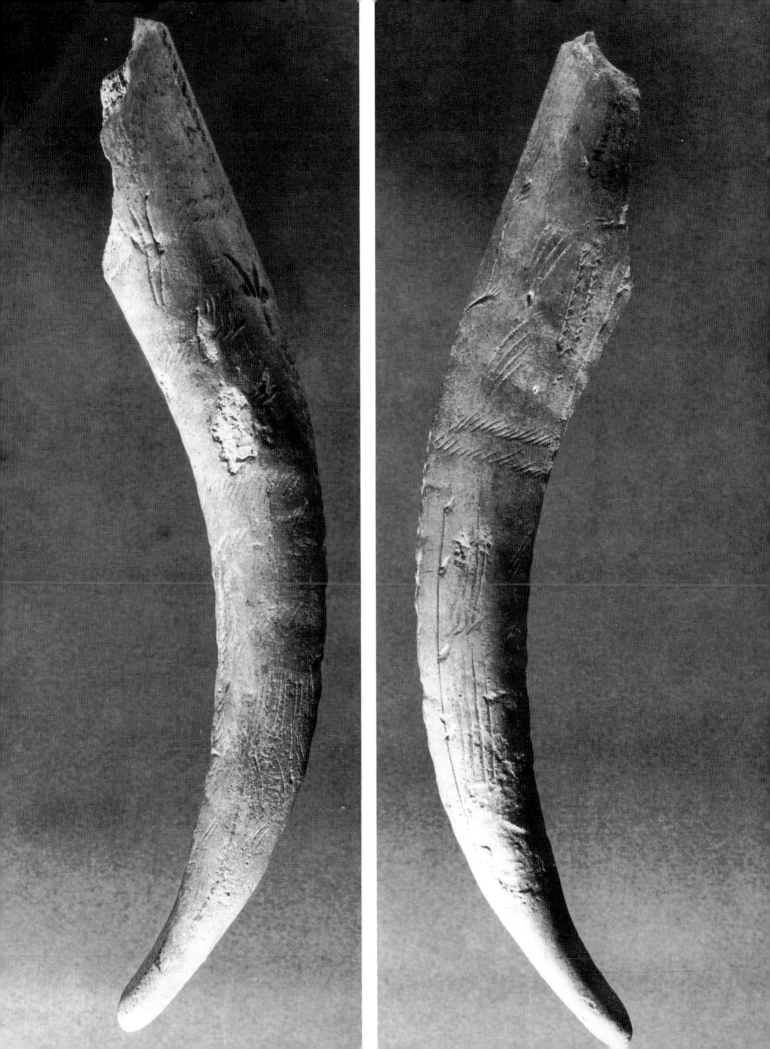

some are made at one angle, a closely related group is angled more steeply, some late sequences cross over earlier sequences, some groups are made by small strokes, others by long strokes, some sequences run as edge-marks on a face, others seem to include that long containing line that serves as an "edge" and makes a sequence look like a plant. Each of these techniques has been seen before. They comprise a range of notational styles that I have called a visual-kinesthetic form of differentiation. Unfortunately, because of wear and deterioration and the delicacy of some sequences, it is difficult at this stage of microscopic technology to determine the tool differences (Fig. 103 a, b).

This bâton is so important for an understanding of one of the uses of the bâtons, and of notation and the meaning of the art and symbol, that I present the symbols separately (Fig. 103 c).

The composition again unites ibex heads conceptually with plant forms. The Abbé Breuil has presented one of these forms (4) as the underbelly of a fish, with rayed pelvic and anal fins.[12] The microscope reveals the form to be more plantlike than fishlike, but whether one or the other, the nature of our analysis holds.

The forms or images having been separated from the notational groups, it becomes clear that they were intended to serve as symbols in relation to the sums of marks near each. This is a somewhat different technique of juxtaposition and relation than we saw in the French Magdalenian compositions of Figures 57 a–i, in which blocks of notation were separated spatially and visually from the symbolic art and in which the notational technique itself was more highly evolved. We have on this bone, therefore, the first sure validation of the symbolic use of art and sign in relation to notation.

The possible exceptions to my interpretation are those groups which look plantlike but which I have called sequences. These seem, by their placement and their complexity, to be examples of that style of notation which "contains" a sequence along a horizontal. We have seen this visual technique in a number of examples, including the Gontzi composition early in the research, the Perigordian example from Barma Grande, the preceding Raymonden example, and we can see it on an example from the same region and period as the bâton from Cueto de la Mina, a bâton from El Pendo (Fig. 140 b). One image that looks like these forms of linear notation but which I have called a plant is Figure 103 c–3. This form has both a cross line and an inverted angle associated with it, as well as groups of ordinary notations, indicating its probable symbolic intent. It is placed in a position like the plantlike form with notations on the other face. Despite these small uncertainties, the bone from Cueto de la Mina apparently serves as a "Rosetta Stone," explaining the general intent, breaking the code, and serving as a verification for the notational-symbolic complexity of Upper Paleolithic marking.

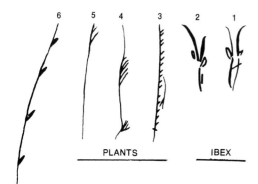

Fig. 103 c, 1–6
Line rendition of the images on the bâton from Cueto de la Mina, including 1) one ibex head, crossed out, 2) a smaller ibex head, 3) one plant with an associated angle sign and 4, 5, 6) three plants of different species or stages of growth.

[12] H. Breuil and R. de Saint-Périer, LES POISSONS, LES BATRACIENS ET LES REPTILES DANS L'ART QUATERNAIRE, p. 85, Fig. 36-6.

The counts in the notational groups as determined by microscope and the structures and placements of the images are seen in the line renditions (Fig. 103 a, b).

Fig. 103 a, b. Page 214.

If, as my earlier analysis has indicated, the ibex head is a symbol or sign of early spring—or of a myth, rite, or sacrifice related to that season—and if the plants (and the possible fish) are taken to be seasonal and storied signs, then it is possible to perform a simple juxtaposition in a test with our lunar model.

We begin at the thick end, then proceed downward sequentially on face one; having finished, we revert to the top of face two and again proceed downward (Fig. 104).

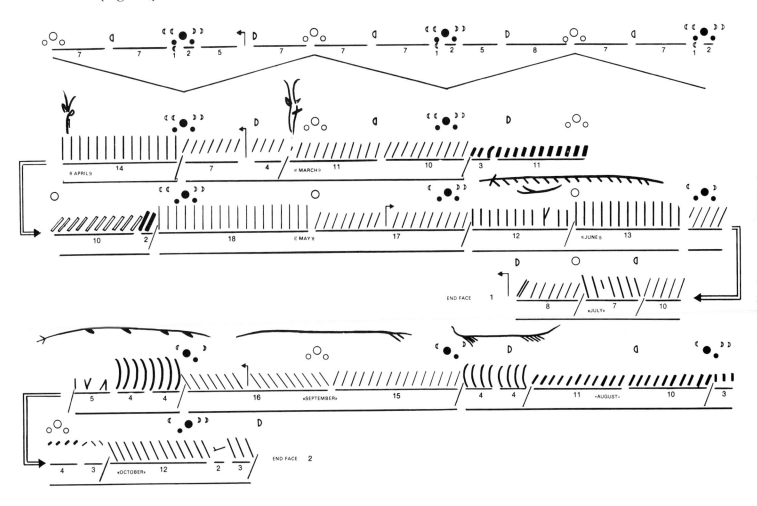

The conjunction reveals a precise observational lunar phrasing, spanning a period of almost nine months. A portion of bone is missing around the hole, and there may be some marks missing, particularly on face one. Each of the large groups comprises a lunar "month" and either goes from a crescent to a crescent or, as in the case of the 35 and 25 counts, forms a two-month period in which one month spans observations of the crescents and the other falls between crescents.

In this first reading the symbols are placed above the notations with which they are associated. The long plant form (5) stands next to a group of marks at its left, but it also rises from and crosses into the lower group.

Fig. 104
The engraved marks on the bâton from Cueto de la Mina against the lunar model indicating the possible lunar phrasing. The images appear as signs above their associated sets of marks. Hypothetically the notation in this test begins with the full moon of mid-February.

It may therefore be related to one or the other. Our conjunction reveals that the symbols are periodically, though not regularly, associated with certain months and seasons. If the ibex head that is struck through is indicative of an early spring rite or sacrifice, as implied in the Montgaudier and La Vache examples, then it may here represent a first spring sacrifice in the time of the thaw, roughly in the time of our month of March, the time or month also of the vernal equinox. With this tentative clue the notations on face one would begin in the winter, within our month of February, and would continue downward to the second quarter or half-moon of July, in mid-summer.

The microscope reveals that the markings on face two are complete, except perhaps for some faint marks that may have been eroded near the faint beginning 3 marks, where there is bone wear and deterioration. Face two in this reading runs from August through October with a different plant image for each month. The August image looks like a plant in full summer growth (or like the possible belly of a fish in spawning time if Breuil's interpretation is accepted), while September seems to be a reed and October seems to represent the nut-cone-fruit-seed image of a particular species.

Whether the reading of each symbol is correct or not, what we have here is clearly a calendric system combining signs and notations in a highly evolved Magdalenian style.

The technique of running a series of day-units (or month- or year-units) horizontally along an edge, with symbols juxtaposed above the days (or months or years) to indicate moments of significant rite, myth, observation, or seasonal change, appears in the historic Greco-Roman calendars, the Scandinavian calendar rune stick, the English Clogg almanac, the Siberian Yakut calendar, and on certain American Indian record sticks. Our early analysis of the engraved mammoth tusk from Gontzi, with a calendric notation along a line and with symbols above and at the end of sequences, seems to be an early example of this cognitive style. The difference between the style on this bone and that from Gontzi is that the groups here are not "contained" or structured linearly but fill up a face area by area, one of the typical Upper Paleolithic styles of notating, particularly in Spain and Italy.

On this bone from the site of Cueto de la Mina we seem to have an example indicating the integrated beginnings of arithmetic, astronomy, writing, abstracted symbolism, and notation. There is also the implication that these cultural skills were related to the economic and ritual-religious life of the hunting groups.

Since at this point we are seeking the general meaning of the plant image, with some hint as to its relation to the notations and symbolic signs and animals, let us turn briefly to the caves where plant images appear, associated with animals and other abstracted signs. These associations of barbed plantlike images with animals and signs have been recognized in the caves for a long time, but interpretation of these forms as plants was not established.

A recent summary of current theories concerning rock or cave art states that "... Palaeolithic parietal [rock] art contains no example which convincingly represents any kind of vegetation."[13]

We have seen that vegetation is clearly represented on the small mobiliary objects and that many of the so-called "barbed signs" and "masculine signs" in the caves probably represent plant forms.

Of these supposed barbed signs Ucko and Rosenfeld state:

"... signs shaped like feathers which are found engraved or painted on the bodies of some ... animals ... have often been considered to represent arrows but real Palaeolithic bone projectile points were either not barbed or were mounted to produce only a single barb, and fully biserial barbed harpoons only appeared in the final Magdalenian. These feather-shaped signs as well as many others such as dots and ovals, which have frequently been given a representational interpretation ... are here all classed as non-representational."[14]

There seems to be confusion, then, as to whether they are weapons or symbolic signs. Let us examine the forms.

The cave of Lascaux was discovered in 1940 by two boys and was closed in 1966 because algae contamination was destroying the paintings. It is the most famous of the French Ice Age caves and remains the supreme sanctuary of the Upper Paleolithic culture north of the Pyrenees. It lies upriver along the Vézère one or two days' walk from Les Eyzies and is part of the Dordogne culture that lasted from Aurignacian times to the end of the Magdalenian. As a main sanctuary, it may have been used in season and for the proper ceremonies by peoples from many sites over long periods. Most of the art, according to the Abbé Breuil, is Aurignacian-Perigordian, with some from the Magdalenian. Leroi-Gourhan, however, has placed the art of the cave at the end of the Solutrean to Magdalenian III and IV. Whatever the chronology, the cave and its art represent a relatively late development in the use of art and symbol.

The first volume illustrating the cave paintings in color, LASCAUX OR THE BIRTH OF ART, by art historian Georges Bataille, presents a horse painted in the Middle Magdalenian style (Fig. 105). There are three horses in this style, and the Abbé Breuil wrote:

Fig. 105. Next page.

"... Their legs are very short and their bodies very thick which give[s] ... the look of an old Chinese painting."[15]

According to Bataille, the horse is
"one of the most engaging figures in the entire Cave. Its light, sharp silhouette is so to speak anchored by the darker ochre color of some insignia ["sign" or "form"] which one may interpret as fletched arrows released in flight. ... [we]

[13] Peter J. Ucko and Andrée Rosenfeld, PALAEOLITHIC CAVE ART (London: World University Library, 1967), p. 187.

[14] Ibid., p. 100.

[15] Abbé H. Breuil, FOUR HUNDRED CENTURIES OF CAVE ART, trans. Mary E. Boyle from QUATRE CENT SIÈCLES D'ART PARIÉTAL, (Montignac, France: Centre d'Etudes et de Documentations Préhistoriques, 1952), p. 118.

may safely conclude that these … express the hunter's desire to bring down his quarry…"[16]

This hunting magic interpretation is the old one, and it was the Abbé Breuil who first called these objects "flying arrows." On the other hand, Leroi-Gourhan has called them barbed signs, sexual and masculine, and his interpretation is based on the fact that in the caves these signs are often associated with pregnant animals or with feminine symbols such as the vulva.

The analysis we have been following indicates the possibility of a different meaning. If we consider this horse to be female and pregnant—or female and potentially pregnant—then the image might be considered a branch and, therefore, a sign of late spring and the time of calving or, if the form is intended to represent a bare, sparse branch, it may be a sign

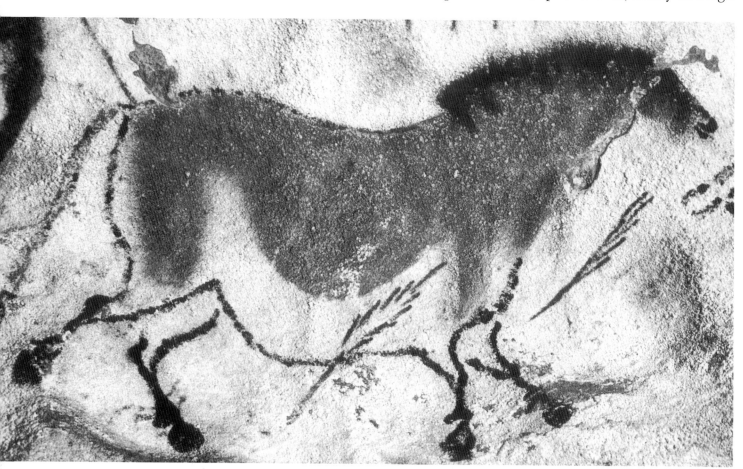

Fig. 105
A painted horse with a small muzzle from the cave of Lascaux (Dordogne) associated with plant images and a geometric form.

of autumn-winter. The branch in this composition may then be related either to the period of dropping of the colt or the period of the first apparent fetal enlargement, the first visible sign of the mare's pregnancy. Given the possibility of this sort of interpretation, a whole class of compositions or associations in the caves is given new potential meaning, with some hint as to the possible seasons of the rites or myths that may be involved.

But we must be careful. As spears or darts, or as phallic forms, these

[16] Georges Bataille, LASCAUX OR THE BIRTH OF ART, trans. Austryn Wainhouse (New York: Skira, Inc., 1955), pp. 82–83.

plantlike signs are badly and inaccurately drawn, whereas the animal art is comparatively superb. There is, however, another class of signs which clearly represents weapons. We shall look at these later. Here we must note that, as plant forms, the class under discussion can be "sexual" in the sense that it is related to fertility and the seasons of pregnancy, calving, or mating and the processes of birth, re-creation, and growth. But this is not biologic or symbolic "sexuality" in our modern understanding of the term, as something that is either masculine or feminine. On the contrary, a plant sign might be, at the same time, "feminine" and related to the pregnancy of the female, "neuter" in the sense that as "magic" of the seasons it helps bring on the pregnancy, and "male" in the sense that, like the stag's antlers, the branch grows and has its own power. Also, it might be a "male" object simply because it was used by a male shaman.

As you can see, the story can vary, and in fact all these stories could conceivably run together since they are not mutually exclusive as are facts in science or concepts in Western philosophy. What is important, then, is that we understand the nature of the human cognitive processes and recognitions involved, not only in these compositions but generally in mythological storied equations. With this understanding, we can begin that analysis and comparison that allows us to interpret *some* of the meanings in the "signs" from their relations to the animals and the notations.

At Lascaux, next to the "Chinese" horse, is a huge red cow with a number of simplified branches attached to and associated with it (Fig. 106). The

Fig. 106
A painted cow and a horse with a small muzzle from the cave of Lascaux (Dordogne) with associated plant images.

Fig. 107 a
Painted panel from the cave of Marsoulas (Haute-Garonne) with plant forms and notations (after Breuil):

Fig. 107 b
Painted panel from the cave of Marsoulas depicting a bison with signs in its body and associated with a plant image (after Breuil).

cow may be of roughly the same cultural period as the horse, but it is in a different style. Once again the branch has been called either a weapon or a sexual sign. Here I need only point out that mare and cow may be related to a plant form for reasons that are not necessarily "sexual" or phallic.

In the cave of Marsoulas, not many miles from the site of La Vache whose Magdalenian seasonal engravings we have seen, there is an unusual series of compositions. These, too, have been considered as hunting magic or as sexual. Many of the paintings are by now extremely faint, but

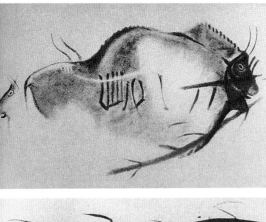

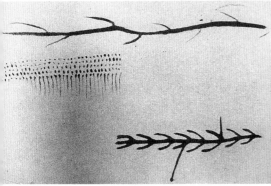

Fig. 107 c
Painted panel from the cave of Marsoulas depicting two plant images and notations (after Breuil).

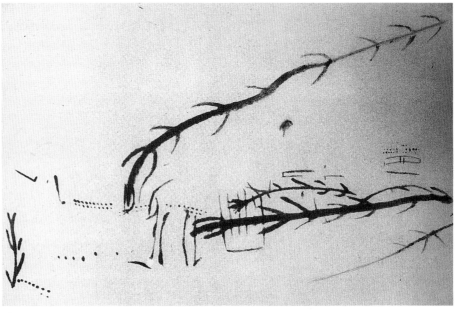

Fig. 107 a

the Abbé Breuil has done tracings and renderings that indicate the nature of the compositions and associations (Fig. 107 a, b, c)[17], and Leroi-Gourhan has done a schematic, simplified rendering of the main "tableau" (Fig. 108).[18]

Fig. 108
Schematic rendition of tne painted tableau or composition in the cave of Marsoulas depicting bison, horse, plants and notation (after Leroi-Gourhan).

[17] H. Breuil, FOUR HUNDRED CENTURIES OF CAVE ART, pp. 241–243.

[18] After A. Leroi-Gourhan, TREASURES OF PREHISTORIC ART, p. 447.

It is obvious that we have notation of some sort, related to the sign of the plant or branch, which is in turn related to the animals, in this case the bison and horse. One bison has a series of evolved Magdalenian signs within it, one of which looks like an abstracted hand. The stenciled copy of a real hand appears in many caves, and the hand is also engraved on mobiliary pieces. I will touch on the symbolism of the hand in a later chapter. The plant, however, as a spring, summer, or fall-winter image, more or less speaks for itself.

We find, then, that the art, symbols, and notations of the caves are related to the work on the bones. But similarity is not equivalence, for each represents a specialized aspect of a complex culture and mythology. The differences are indicated on a bit of bone from the Grotte de Lorthet in the Pyrenean foothills. A fork-tongued viper is surrounded by a rather indefinite decoration according to the illustration by the Abbé Breuil[19] (Fig. 109, a, b).

Fig. 109 a
Engraved and shaped non-utilitarian object of antler, probably ritual, from Lorthet (Hautes-Pyrénées), evidencing the polish of hand wear along all its edges and deterioration of the more faintly engraved lines. Middle Magdalenian.

Fig. 109 b
Line rendition of all the engraved lines on the object from Lorthet revealing a serpent, two rows of schematized young birds, two plant forms and possible signs, as determined by microscopic analysis. The serpent seems intentionally full and may be carrying eggs or young or may have recently fed.

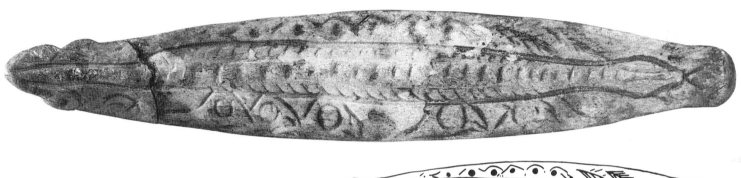

The microscope reveals that the snake has above it two plant forms and below it a schematic series of birds with huge eyes, while above there is another schematic series of birds of a seemingly different species. The composition seems to present us with newly hatched chicks and plants related to the snake. These are, in a sense, air and earth aspects of the spring. What the story was that related them or what the use was of this bone we do not know. The sculpted snakelike bone is common in the Upper Paleolithic; it here shows signs of long hand wear and polish but no marks of use as a tool, and it may, therefore, have served as a ritual, ceremonial object, belonging perhaps to a shaman or sorcerer. A similar bone from Gourdan, near Lorthet, and from the same period (Magdalenian IV), has a more schematic central snake with sequences of notation instead of drawings around it. One from La Vache has a horse, deer, and plant forms.

Neither snakes nor groups of birds are common in cave art, though snakes do appear. The branch or plant, however, seems to have been a

Fig. 110
Painted bull and sign in the cave of Lascaux (Dordogne).

[19] H. Breuil and R. de Saint-Périer, LES POISSONS, LES BATRACIENS ET LES REPTILES DANS L'ART QUATERNAIRE, p. 153, Fig. 71.

Fig. 111
Painted horse and associated sign in cave of Lascaux (Dordogne).

specialized, meaningful motif throughout the culture and mythology, and the snake evidently played a part in a range of ceremonies or myths. It may be that animals were sacrificed, that the snake was ritualized or symbolized, and that the branch or plant was used in ceremony. The complexity of a symbolic system, as we can see, cannot be explained by any single, unitary interpretation.

There is one sign at Lascaux that Leroi-Gourhan has called "feminine" because it is associated with a bull and because it looks as though it was derived from the female vulva, which in a more realistic image looks so: ▽ (Fig. 110). Others have called the image a weapon.

Fig. 112 a

Fig. 112 b

Fig. 112 a, b
The two faces of an engraved rib fragment from La Vache (Ariège) showing two horses following each other on one face and two facing saiga antelopes on the other. Final Magdalenian.

Fig. 110. Preceding page.

Turn back and look at the similar sign in the chest of the man on the bone from Raymonden, where it seems to be a symbolic simplified branch. Look at the branched stick carried by the man on the bone from Les Eyzies. Look at the sign associated with a running horse at Lascaux (Fig. 111). It is difficult to tell whether these are all the same image. It is clear, however, that they are not weapons. If they are images of objects that were carried, say a branch, to call them "feminine" may be an over-simplification.

If the new leafing branch was associated with the pregnant mare, cow, and doe of the spring, then the bare, stripped, triple branch of autumn might have been associated with the stag, stallion, and bull, and it could, perhaps, in this sense be called a "masculine" sign. We would then have images of objects carried or used in a ceremony related to the rite of the season and the season of the animal. If the three-pronged sign was a physical object carried in the hand, then the drawing or engraving is not the sign for a branch but the sign for a ritual object, stripped down and simplified, and it was the object that was the sign for a branch.

As the analysis continues, we are faced increasingly with the complexity of a symbolic culture, a complexity with so many variations that, despite

Fig. 113 a, b
Line rendition of the engraving on both faces of La Vache rib, as determined by microscopic analysis. On face one, a stallion is followed by a mare, a symbolic branch between them. On face two the facing male saigas are associated with a fish tail. All images on rib may be seasonal with storied interrelations.

Fig. 113 a

Fig. 113 b

the generalizations we are approaching, it is necessary to perform a careful, separate analysis of each object and composition.

From La Vache, which has given us other seasonal images, there comes a bone engraved on two faces (Fig. 112 a, b). Romain Robert, who excavated the bone, and L. Nougier, have given a description of the compositions:

"Main Face: Horses Following Each Other. The two heads look left, each similarly animated. The first head is stockier than the one that follows. Its mane is relatively short, and is made by short fine strokes. The details are particularly elaborate. The eye has a mobile lid, the mouth is clearly open and has a double line to mark the lips, the nose is large with a strong nostril also heightened by a double line. In front of the muzzle there are diverse lines which are too delicate to interpret. This first horse is undoubtedly male. [Fig. 113 a.]

"The second head is finer than the first, the muzzle is delicately thrust forward, the nose not as high, the nostril smaller but well outlined with a double line, the chin is smaller. The mane, more voluminous, is made with fine regular lines and descends at a 45° angle. In front of the muzzle there is an engraved branch, separated at the top and difficult to interpret ... This second head is perhaps that of a mare following her stallion.

"Reverse Face: The Facing Saïga Antelopes. The two figures constitute a true scene, that of two males facing, since it is only the males that have horns and indulge in furious combats. The antelope at left has a short head and a typically hooked, large muzzle, an essential characteristic of the saïga species. [Fig. 113 b.] "Slightly lower than the other, the first head is also engraved more lightly and with a more summary rendition. The eye is a single circle, and is surmounted by a single horn, curved and tilted to the rear. The ear is clear but small.

Fig. 114 a, b
The two faces of an engraved fragment of bone from Bruniquel (Tarn-et-Garonne) depicting horses differing in age and sex. Upper Magdalenian.

Fig. 114 a

"The antelope at right is better made, more deeply engraved, with greater realism and easily attains the perfection of the most beautiful engravings of the mobiliary art [of the period]. Its profile presents a perfect image of the saïga: muzzle lifted, the beautiful horns curved, head slightly raised, nostrils dilated to savor the air. It is in the position of an animal sniffing an adversary.

"The eye, slightly elongated, is outlined by the art of the eyebrow. The ear is partly hidden behind the long conical horn, very delicately tapered, the concentric spires indicating the sequential development. The theme—the combat of the males— is frequently found in the iconography of hunting peoples. It asserts itself as a persistent leitmotif in the gallery at Rouffignac, so rich in mammoths, the chief bulls of the herds in confrontation. It is found equally in the more recent rock art of North Africa, and is referrable to the same conditions of the hunting life...

"The theme supplies a background of strife and sexuality, related to the mysteries of animal fecundity, the chthonic gods [those of the earth] and the mystery cults of the earth mother.

"At the right of the combat theme, there is the end of the caudal fin of a fish, unequally divided, deeply engraved. The double curve finishing the piece allows us to suppose that the figure was never completed. A certain 'schematicism' is apparent, or a certain 'abstractionism,' as opposed to the realism of the saïgas. For a definitive interpretation of this engraving one should compare it with other, more explicit documents."[20]

The branch reminds us of the one carried by the human figure walking between two horse heads on the bone from La Madeleine and of one of the signs on the bone from Cueto de la Mina.

A representation of mare and stallion is found in material collected by Lastic Saint-Jal in the 1860's and now in the cellar reserves of the British Museum. It is a fragment from Bruniquel engraved on two faces with three animal heads on each face (Fig. 114 a, b, c, d). Face one shows what seems to be a large stallion at left, followed by a more delicately muzzled, smaller-headed mare. Behind the mare is the remnant of a smaller head, perhaps that of a colt. Face two begins with a colt at left, followed by what seems to be a young stallion, followed by what seems to be a mare with head held high. The microscope reveals that the composition on each face was made by the same point, and the differences are, therefore, intentional and comparative. The scenes are seasonal. Such

examples raise a question as to whether the small-headed Lascaux horse of Figure 105 is feminine and whether the horse at right on the engraved bone from La Madeleine (Fig. 98 b) is a mare and the second a stallion. Horses with exaggeratedly small, delicate heads or muzzles appear on cave paintings at a time when the engraved art indicates the ability to differentiate the large male muzzle.

If the analysis of male and female horse heads and the colt in a single composition is accurate, it is difficult to see how the horse, as a species, can be considered "male" as it is in the tentative theory of Leroi-Gourhan. That sexuality is involved is obvious, but the nature of that sexuality was apparently often realistic. This does not preclude the horse, as a species, from being involved *in myth* with femininity or masculinity, that is, with a male god or hero or with a female goddess, or with the ceremonies of a male group or a female group, or from being related to a season whose

Fig. 114 b

Fig. 114 c

Fig. 114 d

Fig. 114 c, d
Line rendition of the engraved horses on the Bruniquel fragment indicating the intentional differentiation among the heads according to age, size and sex. As determined by microscopic analysis. The total composition seems to represent a herd in the spring.

[20] Louis-René Nougier and Romain Robert, "Le 'Lissoir aux Saïgas' de la grotte de la Vache," BULL. DE LA SOC. PRÉHIST. DE L'ARIÈGE, XIII (1958), trans. A. Marshack, pp. 1–4.

Schematic rendition in line of a portion of a painted and engraved composition in the cave of Lascaux (Dordogne) depicting horses, bison, signs and geometric forms and accumulations of engraved weapons (after Laming-Emperaire).

symbolic astronomical representation or masked figure in a dance might be considered male or female. A stallion or a mare might be intentionally sacrificed in these myths. But the "masculinity" or "femininity" of the species cannot be inferred from the art. The difficulty in Leroi-Gourhan's thesis is compounded when we find that the horse is associated with the bison, with notations, with the lion, the snake, the fish, the bird, the hand, and with signs that seemingly represent water or rain.

At this stage in our analysis the attempt to interpret the plant as a clearly seasonal image seems simpler than the attempt to interpret the horse. The

Fig. 116 b
Line rendition of all the intentional marks on the Le Soucy fragment indicating the stylized dotted mane of each horse and the fact that each is struck through the chest by a non-decorative angled form. The large horse at left also has an angle sign below the head and a line thrust into its neck. As determined by microscopic analysis.

plant or branch, whether an object in ceremony or a symbol in story or an image of seasonal manifestation or relation, is almost certainly time-factored. Alone or with an animal, fish, or snake, the meaning was traditional and widespread, and it was apparently used at the proper time and place, and perhaps by the proper person. "Sexuality" of a sort might be inferred in its "power" for growth, but this power was not necessarily "masculine." Instead, this "power" would seem to have been one aspect of the seasonal behavior of all the wild life of the subarctic and temperate-zone ecology of Ice Age Europe.

Leroi-Gourhan's insight, then, in perceiving a relation between the sign and the animal is valid. The nature of that relation, however, cannot be simply categorized as "sexual." The meaning of each sign and symbol must be determined within the context of a complex tradition and in terms of each composition.

There is one sign at Lascaux that Leroi-Gourhan has at times termed "masculine" but which looks like an arrow or dart (Fig. 115).

Fig. 116 a

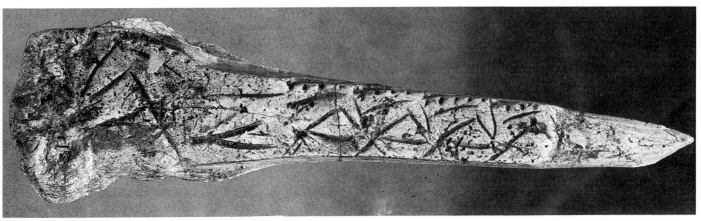

Annette Laming-Emperaire of the Musée de l'Homme in Paris has described the composition:

"a figure, which may represent a pregnant mare, is followed by a galloping horse about 3 ft 8 in. long, painted chestnut-red and black ... A black line may indicate the phallus. The figure is pierced by seven parallel darts pointing upwards, and an eighth and shorter dart is shown embedded in the region of its chest ... [a] bison, which is about 4 ft 5 in. in length, is painted brown with black legs. Its body is pierced by seven deeply engraved darts and overlaid with a few incised lines difficult to decipher. ... The central subject of this vast frieze is an enormous black cow (about 5 ft long) ... It was painted ... and then

engraved ... Both its hindlegs are placed on a latticed sign similar to those in other parts of the cave ... A third sign is painted slightly behind it ... The long frieze of horses was executed at an earlier date than the black cow, for several of the horses are covered by the cow ... they belong to the same artistic period." [21]

We have seen that some animals at Lascaux are associated with seasonal signs and perhaps these darts, which are clearly weapons and not plants, are related to a seasonal context. I approached the plant or branch in the caves via an examination of similar signs on the engraved bones. Let us do the same here.

A piece of bone from the Late Magdalenian, Magdalenian VI, comes from Le Soucy in the Dordogne. The point is broken, but the engraved por-

Fig. 117
Detail. Photograph of the lower right quadrant of an engraved stone from Labastide (Hautes-Pyrénées) indicating darts passing upward into a fish and over a symbolic serpent. Middle Magdalenian.

◀ Fig. 116 a
Engraved bone point or awl from Le Soucy (Dordogne) containing schematized horse heads. Final Magdalenian.

[21] A. Laming, LASCAUX, PAINTINGS AND ENGRAVINGS (Harmondsworth and Baltimore: Penguin Books Ltd., 1959), trans. E. F. Armstrong, pp. 87–88.

Fig. 116 a, b. Page 228.
Fig. 117. Preceding page.

tion is complete. It has five schematized horse heads with dotted manes (Fig. 116 a, b). The seemingly decorative composition, under microscopic examination, indicates that each horse is "struck through" by a sign or barb in the throat or chest. The marks are not random nor is each shaped like a dart or harpoon. This lack of realism occurs often in symbolic overmarking, and we shall see another example shortly. In any case, the marks seem symbolic, either of killing or of some other storied relation. Deterioration of the bone makes it hard to determine the tool differences to see whether the chest marks were made at one time or over a period. Other examples will help us understand the nature of such symbolic "killing" or ritual marks.

From the earlier Magdalenian IV site of Labastide, which gave us an autumn stag bellowing, there comes an engraved stone that has the simple outline of a fish, a salmon or trout, engraved by a sharp point. Through it are a number of "darts" pointing upwards, though they do not all look precisely like darts. The stone has not yet been published by Georges Simonnet, the excavator, so I give only a line rendering and portions of the photo documentation and explain the microscopic analysis (Figs. 117, 118, and 119).

Fig. 118
Schematic rendition of the engraved lines on the stone from Labastide indicating the fish with a renewed belly made by a different point and in a different style, the accumulated sets of darts and the symbolic snake.

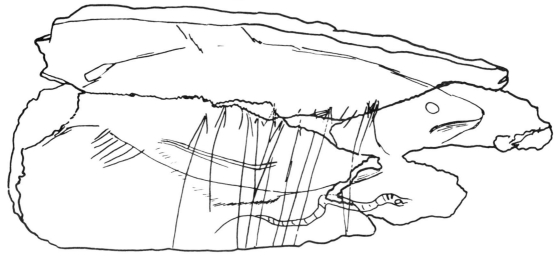

Fig. 119
Schematic rendition of the sets of darts engraved into the fish from Labastide, indicating the seven points engraving the sets.

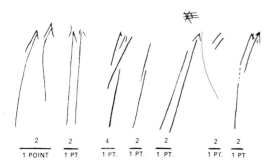

The composition looks like hunting or killing magic. But on the same face as the fish, below it and to the right, is the engraving of a snake. We have seen fish and snake associated before. Added to the fish, perhaps at a later date, is a second "belly" composed of numerous fine strokes, in a style different from the original outline, as though to indicate a pregnant female ready to spawn. Along the thick parallel edge of the flat shale stone there are a series of six arcs: ∩∩∩ ∩∩∩
Three are made by a wide point, three by an extremely sharp point.
There seem to be seven sets of darts made by at least seven points. Above them is engraved a geometric "figure."
The odd composition seems to imply "hunting magic" or scorekeeping. But it also indicates a seasonal context. The small snake has no darts in it and seems to be symbolic. Snakes are almost never "killed" with darts in Upper Paleolithic art. The arcs along the side seem also to be symbolic. We can hazard a guess that they may be 6 sky-arcs and therefore 6 days, or

6 sky-arcs and therefore 6 months, or perhaps they are an image of water. Whatever the snake and the arcs represent, they are *not* part of simple "hunting magic." Whatever the darts are, by their form of making and by their accumulation, they are not "sexual" signs. It may be, then, that what we have is a time-factored composition, made over a period and renewed or revised, whose meaning was related to the seasons of spring migration and spawning in autumn. The "killings" represented by the darts are, therefore, storied.

The questions raised by this composition are many. Were the darts on cave animals also made over a period of time, by different points, perhaps as the animals were overpainted and overengraved? Were the animals renewed to be "rekilled" in a series of rites or ceremonies? We note, again, a practical difference between the small engraved artifacts and the caves. The man *seemingly* "hunting" the fish could carry the stone with him for a long period, or have it near at hand, and he did one or the other as the accumulation of darts indicates. The man apparently "hunting" the painted horse of Lascaux could not carry the cave. He had to climb and enter to make his mark. Some caves with animal art are so difficult to get into and their painted and engraved chambers are so deep that hours were spent climbing inside, time was spent in engraving, painting, and ceremony, and more time was spent coming out. This would be a tiring and uneconomic activity for a hunter performing "hunting magic." In true hunting magic, one can draw the animal in the sand or scratch it on an open rock surface and perform the rite of magic killing quickly. Once again, then, it seems that in the caves these images of darts were not intended as hunting magic in the old sense, nor were they apparently sexual.

The most important document concerned with "killing" and symbolic weapons is an engraved bone from Paglicci, on the eastern coast of southern Italy, which comes from the late Upper Paleolithic. We have seen two seasonal images from this site, while the cave contains two seemingly pregnant mares drawn in red paint as well as the red paintings of human hands.

On the flat pelvic bone of a horse there are two compositions, one on each face.[22] The rear face contains the engraved head of a large adult bovine and the smaller, more delicate head of what seems to be a calf. The main face (Fig. 120 a, b) has the engraved figure of a running horse, depicting the realistic squat body of the wild Upper Paleolithic species. The muzzle is thick and heavy and the belly, though somewhat rounded as a species characteristic, is not exaggerated, so that this may be a stallion. Above the horse, the engraved head of a deer and another antlered animal were made later.

Microscopic analysis reveals an astonishing complexity. There are eighteen to twenty feathered darts in and around the horse, each made by a

Fig. 120 a, b. Pages following.

[22] Francesco Zorzi, "Pitture parietali e oggetti d'arte mobiliare del Paleolitico scoperti, nella grotta Paglicci presso Rignano Garganico," RIVISTA DI SCIENZE PREISTORICHE, XVII, Fasc. 1–4 (1962), pp. 123–137.

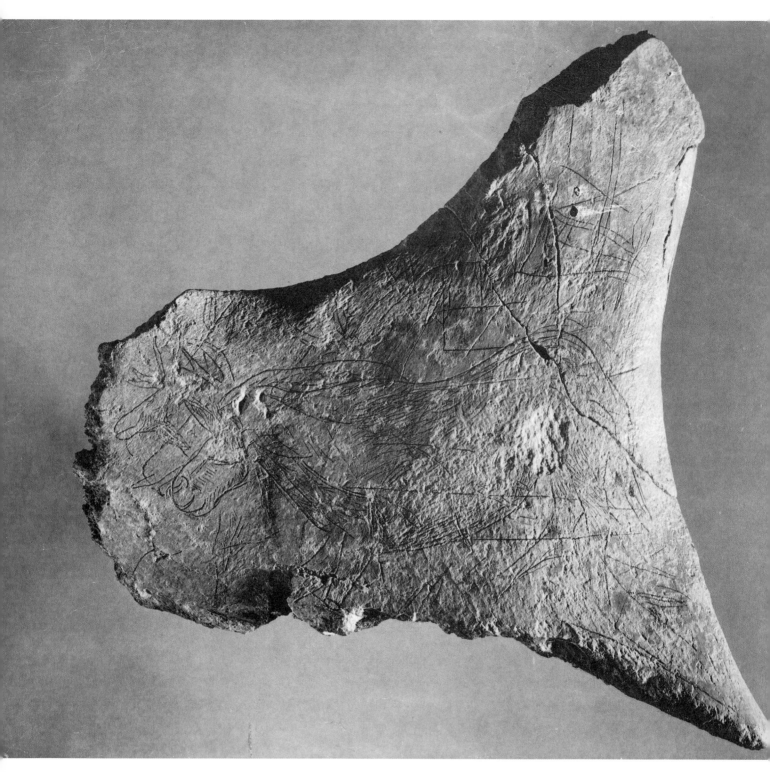

Fig. 120 a
Main face of engraved pelvic bone of a horse from Paglicci (Apulia) depicting a running horse apparently "killed" by flying darts. Late Upper Paleolithic.

different point and at a different time, as well as 6 or 7 horizontal darts without feathers that may have been made by one point and form part of a "set." The microscopic documentation of these and other Italian darts will be presented in separate papers.[23]

The composition is significant for what it tells us about Upper Paleolithic art. The horse did not represent a particular horse intended to be a victim

[23] A. Marshack, "Polesini: A Reexamination of the Engraved Mobilary Materials of Italy by a New Methodology," RIVISTA DI SCIENZE PREISTORICHE, Vol. 14 (1969).

on some day of hunting but was intended as a generalized image whose meaning was continuous. He represented a class and, to that extent, perhaps also a myth. The darts are short-term images representing a periodic use of the horse (as they did of the fish). The length of time represented by the sequence of darts we cannot as yet determine, but it would seem to

have been considerable. If they represent a participatory act of "hunting magic," we have at least eighteen to twenty such acts; if they represent some more generalized act of participation in a rite related to the horse myth, the period involved might have extended over months or years. In either case, the horse was an image whose storied meaning, existence, or "spirit" was continuous, not terminated by any one "killing."

We seem to have clarification for a number of theoretical problems. Weapons are weapons and not sexual signs, weapons can be differentiated from plant signs, and weapons or plants can be added cumulatively to an animal image. Microscopic analysis of the material from the Italian site of

Fig. 120 b
Schematic rendition of all the engraved marks on Paglicci bone indicating twenty-seven darts, nineteen feathered. The darts are made by twenty different points and in different styles and degrees of schematization, as determined by microscopic analysis. Two antlered heads were engraved above the horse at a later date. The total composition indicates an accumulation over a long time.

Polesini has also revealed that the feathered dart can be symbolized alone, as an image with storied meaning and relevance apart from an animal.

Now, if the art-and-story of the caves and mobiliary materials was either infrequent, periodic, or seasonal, then the apparent "killings" may have been symbolic, mythological, ritual, related to the season of the image or the occasional ceremony of the image. The story of the animal or the "killing" was repeated by overpainting or overengraving, by adding a sign or symbol, or by ceremony in front of the image.

This would indicate that in the caves where darts, spears, or harpoons are illustrated we have *substitute* mythological killings via art and rite. There may have been a true killing of the live animal as one aspect of the rite or story, but this killing would then also have been symbolic and not for food. Such symbolic killings are common, and the anthropologists and ethnologists have compiled a huge body of documentation that describes ceremonial or sacrificial killings among historic groups.

This evidence of symbolic "killing" and of the storied weapon requires that we be exceedingly cautious. It brings us to a number of crucial problems relating to human behavior and culture. What is the nature of evolved symbolic killing and aggression in man, either substitute killing in art and rite, or true killing of a living creature, animal or man? Is such symbolic killing by Upper Paleolithic man comparable to the earlier seemingly ritual killings of Neanderthal or Peking Man? How are such killings related to the more basic, instinctive, signal-response killings of animals, such as the sequence of killing evolved in the carnivore on the feeding chain? How are such symbolic killings by man related to the rare killings by an animal in territorial defense or killings that come about as a result of an artificial or unusual situation?

In a volume in preparation on the evolution of hominid behavior, I examine the fact that killing and "aggression," like most behavior, are sequential and time-factored. The idea of time-factored process is heuristic, an aid to conception. It is like saying that a physical object has size, shape, weight, and duration without knowing what the prime measurements and details are. Such statements are generally true, but they are too simple to be of use; they are only a beginning and guide to the necessary search for facts. I therefore now turn to Upper Paleolithic art and notation to seek some of the specialized meanings in the time-factored, symbolic killings. The problem is crucial, not only for understanding prehistoric man, but also for a general understanding of modern man and his art, rite, and war.

CHAPTER XII

TIME-FACTORED DEATH

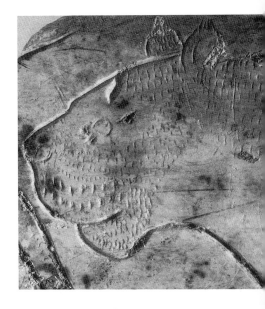

The cave of Les Trois Frères in the Pyrenean foothills of Ariège near Mas d'Azil is called "The Three Brothers" because it was discovered in 1912 on the family property by the sons of the Count H. Bégouën. Within the cave there is the engraving of a bear that has often been cited as a primary example of "hunting magic."

The walls of Les Trois Frères are overlain with thousands of engravings. I present a simplified version of one panel based on a Breuil rendition (Fig. 121 a, b). Says Breuil:

"... At ... top right [is] an archaic Bison [Aurignacian]; below, a Bear [Magdalenian IV] or rather the statue [engraving] of a Bear with many wounds represented by small circles, and with [what seems like] hay ... in its mouth ... it [is] covered with arrows and is superimposed on an archaic Bison ... it is pierced by arrows, seeming to spit blood and spotted like a Panther..."[1]

[1] H. Breuil, FOUR HUNDRED CENTURIES OF CAVE ART, pp. 169, 177.

Hay or blood, spots or wounds, it is a dramatic image.

The bison above has both a serpentine figure and angular marks upon it, the bear below has more circles, the horse at left is seemingly pregnant and has been renewed by the addition of a second face and perhaps a second belly.

The cave of Les Trois Frères is extraordinary for the number and variety of its engraved and overengraved images. The Abbé Breuil, tracing and copying the drawings, wrote:

"in certain years, in a month of work, I hardly deciphered more than one or two metres [about one or two yards]."[2]

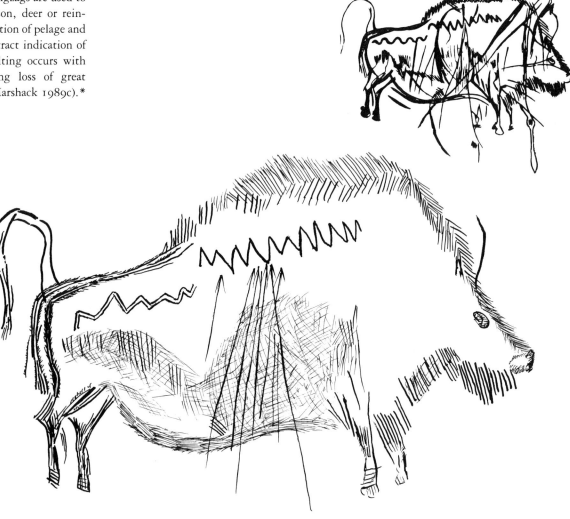

Fig. 121a
The drawing of a bison in the cave of Trois Frères (Ariège) from the first edition of this book. The bison is part of a complex engraved panel of many overmarked animals and a few human "shamanic" figures or "sorcerers." See Fig. 150 a-c. (After Breuil.)

* A. Marshack. "Theory and methodology in the study of the Upper Paleolithic signs." ROCK ART RESEARCH. Vol. 6, pp. 17–53. (1989c)

At first glance and early in my search for meaning, images like the bear seemed to represent a killing for "hunting magic." But the cave has a mass of images that are not directly related to hunting. There is one wall with a long linear sequence of red painted dots that, one way or another,

[2] Ibid., p. 167.

is notational. There are engraved bears that, according to Breuil, have been
"intentionally changed zoologically: one of these has the legs and body of a Bear and the head of a Wolf, and the second, a long arched tail like a Bison."[3]
There is a "Reindeer cow, normal, except for its front legs which have been changed into the legs of a web-footed creature;"[4] there is a second reindeer cow with the head of a bison. Such transformed or multiple animals occur in the caves as well as on the engraved small pieces, and they always imply "story" far more than do the simpler realistic images.[5]
At Les Trois Frères there are images of the lion, including one dramatic image in a chamber that Breuil has named "The Chapel of the Lioness":
"... On a rock shaped like an altar [a sort of table of rock], a Lioness with her cub is painted in black and engraved [on the front face of the rock table]; the cub is only engraved ... There are two versions of the Lioness's tail and three of her head ... [She] is the ... guardian of the Sanctuary, reserved for initiates."[6]
Breuil renders the "guardian of the sanctuary" with a number of arrows in her side (Fig. 122). There are also in the cave a number of engraved and painted "sorcerers," human figures dressed in animal masks and robes who are somehow related to these realistic, transformed, and "killed" animals.

Now, for an understanding of the art and the uses of the cave, it must be stated that, while bear and lion might have been eaten occasionally, they did not represent the major or usual diet. Large Ice Age herbivores were present in great herds, and the bear and lion were a rare, difficult, and dangerous prey. The intentional killing of any such animal must have been special; it required other techniques of hunting and a special allotment of time; it must have had some other intent and story than was used for either the tundra or forest herbivore. At Les Trois Frères bear and lion represent a small minority of the renditions. It is quite probable that the occasional killing of these animals was both seasonal and storied. The female European brown bear hibernates in the winter, entering her hiding-place among rocks, a rock shelter, or the hollow of a tree around October or November. She bears her young in hiding in a state of stupor or lethargy between December and February, during the coldest months, and the

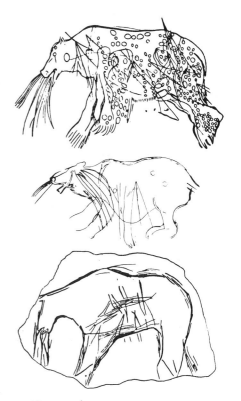

[3] Ibid., p. 177.

[4] Ibid., p. 176.

[5] A bone from Laugerie Basse has a horse associated with a fish; the horse has the feet and tail of a seal. An engraved horse from Lespugue in the Pyrenean foothills has a rear of fire or wind. At Lascaux a painted animal has two long, straight horns coming from its head, with large ovals and arcs on its body. At Le Roc de Sers there is the sculpted bas-relief of an aurochs with the head of a pig, leading a pregnant mare. These are not accidents of bad drawing and the artist's skill is always fine. I shall discuss such transformed "story" animals in another place. The South African ethnologist, Lewis-Williams, has suggested that such images were seen in shamanistic trance. But the extraordinary and variable transformations of animals in myths do not require trance for their creation. The literature on mythologically transformed animals is enormous. They often derive from equations of mythic transformation, not trance.

[6] H. Breuil, FOUR HUNDRED CENTURIES OF CAVE ART, pp. 156-157.

Fig. 121 b
Detail. Line rendition of the two "killed" bears in the Trois Frères composition indicating the darts, wound marks and the bleeding mouth and nose (after Breuil). Similar depiction on a piece of limestone from the neighboring cave of Le Portel again indicating a "killed" bear with wounds on the body and blood flowing from nose and mouth (after Marshack 1989 c).

Fig. 122
A painted and engraved lioness as rendered by Breuil showing a renewed head and tail, with darts in her side. The archaeologist Clottes has restudied the image and found that many of Breuil's suggestions of added imagery have faded or were not present. The restudy of Ice Age imagery begun by this book has created a huge body of such corrections and new interpretations.

cubs suck at the prone, lethargic mother through the winter. In the spring mother and cubs come out of hiding. It is possible that in the dead winter bear meat was sought, but it is also possible that a spring awakening was "celebrated" for non-eating purposes. Lions follow the herds; they are peripheral beasts, much like man himself. It is possible that they followed the herds of horse and bison rather than the far-ranging, fast-moving migratory reindeer, except perhaps when reindeer were locally present through much of the year or returned to a range in certain seasons. Horse and lion are often associated in the art. Did this mean lions were primarily foragers off the horse herds? Once again, then, the images of bear and lion bring us to questions concerning the seasonal behavior and movements of the animals.

The killing of bears in late fall would have provided excellent meat and fat. The ritual killing of bears in the spring, after their winter hibernation, was practiced in these Pyrenean mountains into the 19th century. It is possible that the Pyrenean Ice Age images of killed bears represented either early spring or late fall rituals in these same foothills. (See also Fig. 153 a,b)

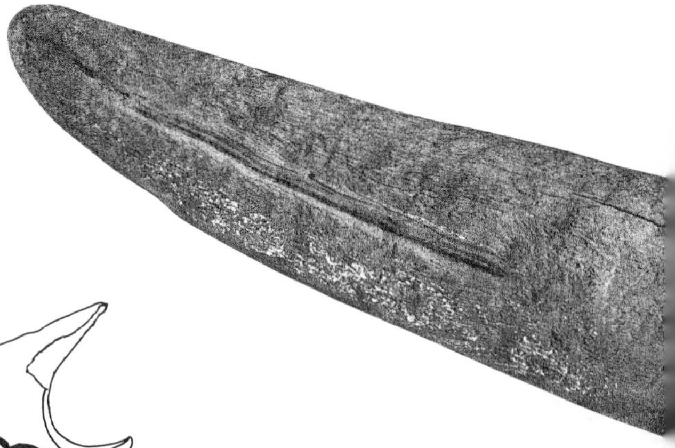

Fig. 123 a, b ▶
The two faces of a broken, engraved bâton from Massat (Ariège) with a bear head on one face.

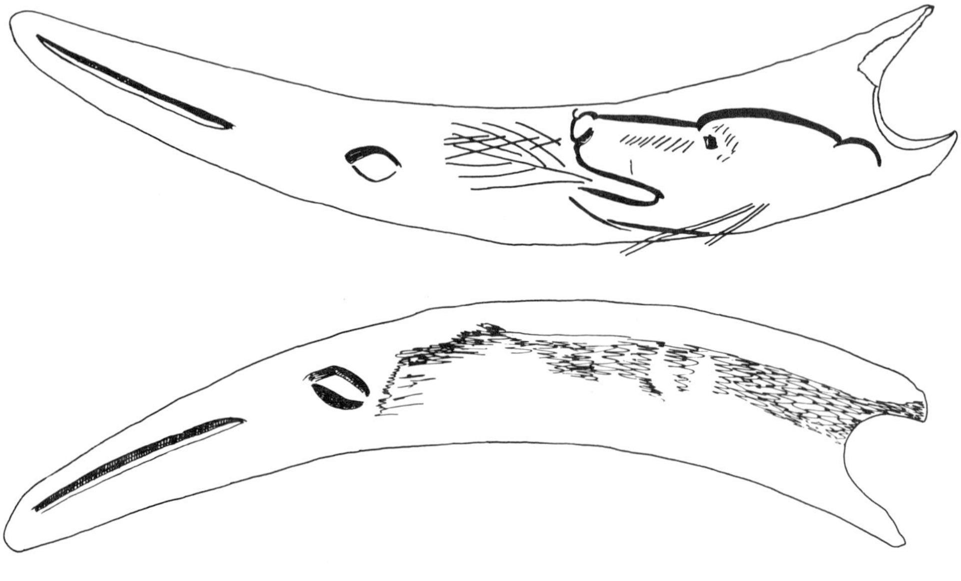

Fig. 123 c, d
Schematic rendition of the engraved marks on the two faces of the Massat bâton indicating the eyes and the curved beak of a water bird on both faces and the fact that the bear has a dart in its throat and is bleeding from mouth and nose, as determined by microscopic analysis.

There is an engraved bâton of deer antler found in the early 1860's by Edouard Lartet at the site of Massat, a short walking distance from the cave of Les Trois Frères (Fig. 123 a, b, c, d). It shows the engraved head of a bear with the same "hay" or blood spouting from the mouth that we find on the bear from the neighboring cave. Leroi-Gourhan has called the branchlike image issuing from the mouth and the small oval near it "sexual symbols." The example is so crucial to the argument of sexuality

238

as hypothesized by Leroi-Gourhan that I quote him in detail. After completing his analysis of the cave animals and signs and their juxtapositions and relations, he writes,

"it leaped to the eye that the ovals, triangles, and quadrangular signs were all more or less abstract variations on the vulvas which appear among the earliest works of prehistoric art. As for the dots and strokes, it was obvious that they are male signs, although their degree of abstraction is beyond any simple similarity of form. I suddenly recalled two decorated objects which had been published separately many times, and these furnished the final proof. The first is the half-rounded rod from La Madeleine [see Fig. 201, Chapter XIII] ..., the second a pierced staff from the Massat cave."[7] The Massat bone "shows ... a barbed sign ['male'] and an oval ['female']."

Though this engraved bear is one of Leroi-Gourhan's "final proofs" and has often been reproduced in modern anthologies of prehistoric art, it seems to be known through illustrations, for no mention is made of the fact that the bear is engraved on the sculpted representation of a schematized water-bird, a crane or heron. In fact, one of Leroi-Gourhan's sup-

[7] A. Leroi-Gourhan, TREASURES OF PREHISTORIC ART, p. 137.

posed "sexual symbols," the oval, forms the eyes of this bird. These appear on both faces accompanied by the slit that establishes the beak. These large fishing and wading birds arrive from the south of Europe and Africa in the late spring or early summer to nest and feed, and they come at about the same time as the first early runs of salmon and the first spring appearance of the amphibians and reptiles. Both the bears and the long-legged fishing birds are found at this time feeding in the streams during the fish runs, the bears pawing the migratory fish in shallow water. This apparent image of the bear-of-the-spring, or the bear-of-autumn-fish-run, associated with a seasonal water bird, has an engraved arrow or dart in its throat, a fact not mentioned or illustrated by Leroi-Gourhan. In addition, microscopic examination (Fig. 123 c) of the lines issuing from the mouth indicates that there is a set of overcrossing lines issuing also from the nose, much as they do in the cave engraving. The details of the composition seem to indicate blood, and the bear seems sacrificial and seasonal, rather than sexual or culinary.

Not far from Les Trois Frères is the Magdalenian cave of Montespan. A stream issues from its low-roofed entrance. There are a variety of engraved animals on its walls: horse and bison, an engraved bovine, an ibex, a bird, a hyena, and perhaps a hind. On the floor there are sculpted clay horses one of which has long undulating lines engraved at its chest and other marks on its neck. Another sculpted horse represents a pregnant mare. Against the wall is the remnant of a clay statue that looks like a lion. Breuil describes the main statue in this chamber:

"the headless statue of a Bear rises from the floor ... The animal is crouching, lying on its stomach; the forepaws are stretched out in front, the claws [on the right paw are] clearly indicated. The hindlegs are gathered under the body ... The surface of this 'dummy,' which is rather roughly made, is smooth as if worn by rubbing with a supple skin drawn over the clay surface. This wear is more marked near the neck; the head is not there, and was never modelled ... In the centre of the neck is a deep hole driving inwards, and signs that a wooden stump once supported a young Bear's head attached to the skin which clothed the 'dummy.'" The fragments of a bear's skull were found nearby, between the bear's paws. "The body of this Bear was stabbed by more than 30 javelin thrusts of various sizes, entering very deeply."[8]

Many interpretations of this bear have been published. In 1950, Paolo Graziosi of Italy and Romain Robert of Tarascon-sur-Ariège visited the cave. Graziosi reports he

"could see no trace of some of the details described ... The section of the neck did not appear to be polished at all ... The hole that is presumed to have contained a peg to support the head does not exist—at least, it is not large enough for its alleged purpose. There are several little holes here and there on the neck and chest, many of which, however, appear to be due to natural causes—the sort of small cavities in the clay that can be seen all over the cave. The largest hole, which appears to be artificial, is on a level with the chest ..."[9]

but could not have supported a peg.

[8] H. Breuil, FOUR HUNDRED CENTURIES OF CAVE ART, p. 238.

[9] P. Graziosi, PALAEOLITHIC ART, p. 152.

Apart from this insight into the uncertainties of visual observation, the bear is significant. The fact is that neither a bear skull nor a bear robe requires a peg, a robe placed upon wet clay would not polish it, and stabs by a spear into a draped bear robe resting on a wet clay statue would not necessarily be penetrating. The head of a bear recently slain could lie at the feet of the statue and still serve in a rite. We have seen an engraved bison head without a body and only a spine on the bone from Raymonden in the representation of a "bison ceremony." There is also the example of an engraved bear head without body and a naked spine from La Madeleine that Leroi-Gourhan mentions and that we shall discuss later. Whatever the details of the bear ceremony, peg or no peg, robe or no robe, stabs or no stabs, bear and lion images in this cave were symbols or characters in ceremonials, rituals, and mythic tales. Though "killings" may have been involved, ritual or real, it would seem these were not necessarily related to simple hunting magic or fertility rites seeking to increase the species.

A last example of cave art from these hills will show the complexity of these ceremonies.

Within the hill that contains the cave of Les Trois Frères, but on the other side of the hill, there is another cave, Tuc d'Audoubert, also discovered in 1912 by the sons of the Count Bégouën. It is not now connected to Les Trois Frères, but at one time may have been. In any case, both caves were local sanctuaries during the Magdalenian.

Breuil wrote of the cave:

"The river Volp … exit[s] at Tuc d'Audoubert, where it rush[es] out of the limestone hill. … The caves of Trois-Frères and the Tuc d'Audoubert, divided nowadays into two vast separate caverns, was once the ancient upper watercourse of the Volp and, really, a single cavern … The river flows out [of the cave] under a wide but rather low arch … the boat must be rowed for 80 metres upstream [into the cave] to reach the landing place, a bed of small gravel, which the Volp covers completely when in flood."[10]

The description is necessary to understand the art on these cave walls, since the Magdalenian hunter had a time-factored relation to the valley, the animals in the valley, the river, and the cave itself. Turn back to the bone fragment with the engraved grasshopper and birds found at Les Trois Frères. Here is a picture of summer, but was it summer in these foothills around the cave? Or was the engraving carried here from some other site that had been the summer camp? Was the rock shelter used all year or only through the autumn, winter, and early spring? Whatever the details, the flood waters of the spring thaw must have burst from the hill in an icy rush and have made entry into Tuc d'Audoubert impossible. When the thaw had ebbed and the water had fallen and had warmed somewhat, when the ground inside was firm and relatively dry, when the first salmon were coming upstream, perhaps in early or late May, when the mare was rounded and full and ready in a month or so to foal,

[10] H. Breuil, FOUR HUNDRED CENTURIES OF CAVE ART, pp. 153, 156, 230.

when the reindeer were getting restless because of the first insect pests, it may then have *begun to be possible* to enter the cave. But was it entered then, or in the summer, or in the autumn when the water was lower still? Or was the cave entered through Les Trois Frères? Perhaps the art of the cave can help us in determining the answer.

Herbert Kühn, of Gutenberg University in Mainz, Germany, gives us a romantic description of his first entry into Tuc d'Audoubert:
"Before us stretched the long range of the Pyrenees. Below, meadows and woods, then, rising above them, the high mountains already decked with snow... we set off ... After about half an hour's walk we got to a brook called the Volp, swift-flowing, gurgling, its bed strewn with boulders ... we had got to the cave's entrance, but ... could see no path, no aperture, nothing but a stream which disappeared into a hillside. [Count Bégouën said:] 'lie quite flat on the bottom, for the water almost touches the ceiling ... in winter and ... spring, the brook's so swollen that the cave gets water-logged and then there's no question of exploring ... [it] is quite often inaccessible even in the summer. The best time of year is now—autumn.'

"We got in and lay down on the planking ... it was soon completely dark. The rock-vaulting bore down upon us and in places scraped the tops of the boat's sides ... None of us said a word. It was sinister and ... terrifying ... eventually, the channel widened out and we could discern a strip of beach ... A few yards farther on the Volp pours down through a dark pit ... Suddenly, there they were. Pictures. Beasts engraved in the stones: bisons, reindeer, horses ... a bison's head ... shamans ... too, men wearing beast-masks, uncanny figures and weird. Another bison is struck by many arrows; ... From the head of a horse project P-shaped signs. ...

"... we entered a spacious chamber ... a fairy palace ... From the ceiling hung stalactites while stalagmites rose up. ... From time to time we could hear a drop fall onto the water's surface and in the uncanny stillness this ghostly drip, drip was most eerie.

"Then we got to the 'cat's hole' ... the way got narrower [and] we had to slither forward flat upon our faces ... More long passages, and then halls, further galleries and corridors and then something indescribably beautiful like some enchanted festival-hall ... fashioned ... of alabaster—a forest of stalagmites ... shimmering all white and pale yellows.

"... in a corner, behind a mass of stalagmites, are traces of human footsteps impressed in the clay. The footprints of naked feet ... of Ice Age Man ... stalagmitic matter overlies the marks .. If one examines the imprints closely one can recognize the marks of the wrinkles in the skin ... We moved forward again. Still more passages, more footprints ... another lake ... black, solid ... absolute[ly] immobil[e]. ... A lake full of dread—and unreal. More traces of Ice Age Man. One can make out the imprints of the heels, the balls of the feet, the toes.

"... we had been almost two hours in the innermost recesses of a mountain ... Then, without any warning, we were in the last chamber ... We could not suppress a cry. The Bison Sculptures. Each beast is about two feet long as we see it by the flickering light of our lamps. These sculptures are no primitive carvings, they are works of surprising plastic beauty ... The nearer of the two animals is a cow and behind her stands the bull just about to mount. Obviously a piece of fertility magic. Bisons ... had come to be rather rare beasts in Magdalenian times, so there was every inducement to enchant them that they might multiply.

"All around the sculptures, traces of men. We lift up one of the footprint-casts from the ground. They consist of nothing but heel-marks, only heels; and heels, moreover, of young men, of lads, say about thirteen or fourteen years old ... Why only heels? Why only the heels of children? Since there are no other imprints than those of heels, it is obvious that this must have been a dance-floor, used for some sort of cult-dance ... [perhaps] a bison-dance.

"... among [nearly] all so-called 'primitive' peoples ... there occur, at a certain stage in life, great festivals ... At these ... children are received into the society of the tribe. They are admitted as full-grown adults, men and women. In the case of hunting peoples, the neophytes are then allowed to hunt with their fathers, while with all such peoples the young are initiated into the mysteries of adult life. The boys and girls behold the marvels of fertility and fecundity, of the beginning of life ...

"We followed the traces, the footprints. These lead to the rock walls and they lead to five different spots. Everywhere we found phallic engravings, symbols of life, birth, beginning ... We had spent a whole day, nearly twelve hours, in the shrines of prehistoric men."[11]

There are questions. Among the phallic forms in the chamber were a few crudely modelled or rolled clay forms that have uncertainly been termed "penises," and on the wall were the so-called P-shaped forms that have been termed *feminine* signs by Leroi-Gourhan and others, images of pregnancy. On the floor there are some 50 juvenile heel prints, hardly enough for a "dance" of more than a couple of minutes for one youth at a time or a walk by a few youths when the floor was soft. Was the ceremony, then, limited to a few persons? Was it limited to a certain period? How were the bison sculpted of wet clay if not by adults who walked normally on their soles and not on their heels, and who knelt to work? Where were their prints? Was the floor smoothed for the ceremony? We may not ever know, so let us turn to the behavior of the species of animals depicted.

The mating of the bison occurs in late summer (August-September) when the cave certainly would have been relatively easy to enter. The wild horse in the renditions on many cave walls seems to be related to the nearly extinct wild horse of today, the Przewalski horse which is found now only in the Siberian Gobi desert. The Przewalski mare drops its foal between mid-June and the end of July in early summer, and it mates in late summer, around August-September. The pregnant mare is, therefore, a peak summer sign, when the sun is at its highest. The reindeer, on the other hand, calves earlier in the spring in May and mates later, in the fall.

Now, to assume that this combination of diverse images—phallus, mating bison, horse, "P" signs of possible pregnancy, and a ceremonial or ritual

[11] Herbert Kühn, ON THE TRACK OF PREHISTORIC MAN (New York: Random House, 1955), pp. 90–98.

dance—is clear evidence of fecundity rites for the increase of these species, one must also assume that there was some knowledge of the relation of mating to procreation, of the phallus to pregnancy, a knowledge that would have been present in the Magdalenian, thousands of years before agriculture and the first true domestication of food animals. It would also imply a knowledge of the fact that the late summer or autumn mating brought forth the late spring and early summer colts and calves. If this knowledge existed, it would have had an important bearing on the lore and ritual surrounding these animals. It would also have been another of the cognitions that would have been available to serve man in the subsequent domestication or half domestication of species when the climate finally changed. There is no reason, of course, why such knowledge should not have existed, at least in some "storied" form. The herd animals were easily observed and followed in their spring, summer, and autumn movements, and their patterns of mating and calving were open and clearly periodic and seasonal.

But, even assuming such knowledge, need the ceremonies have been for "fertility" purposes? Could not the same knowledge have been involved, not in "rites of increase" but in "initiation" rites? An initiation rite which introduces the juvenile to manhood, and at the same time tells him the story and teaches him the skills of sex, need not be a fecundity rite for increase of the species. There is an opposite side to this problem. It is important to realize that a rite that sought the increase of a species need not have been "sexual," unless one assumes a knowledge of insemination and impregnation. *From a story point of view,* one can seek increase by imitating the birth story and by offering a sacrifice to the spirit of the species, or to the god who created the species or supervises all life. We shall look at this problem in the next chapter.

We are, therefore, faced with many alternatives, and we do not have the answers. We know only that none of the theories put forth till now are satisfactory. We do know that the images are all seasonal and that the ceremonies and "killings" depicted were probably also seasonal

Tuc d'Audoubert contains a few mythological animals as well as the key-like, P-shaped signs. At Les Trois Frères, there is one red painted P sign on a horse near the highly placed, difficult to reach sorcerer who is the central figure of the cave. At Altamira in Spain, similar "pregnancy" signs appear with a doe. The symbolic and storied complexity is perhaps more revealing than any single interpretation. Renewed images, images of species, of killing, of pregnancy, of mating and sexuality, and evidence of ceremony and mythology seem linked together in a time-conscious, time-factored culture.

The lesser animals in the cave art pose the most intriguing problems and, like the plant, offer unique possibilities for interpretation. The mythological animals, for instance, were not species hunted or eaten, nor was their increase sought. The bear and lion were not main items of diet. The hyena, who is depicted rarely, was a peripheral scavenger of the herds and,

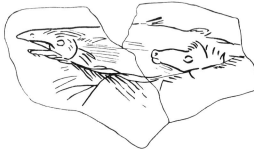

Fig. 124
Line rendition of a stone from Les Trois Frères (Ariège) engraved with a fish and the head of a small horse (after Bouyssonie).

as a carnivore, would hardly do more than attack the newborn, helpless calves of the herbivores. Like the lion, he would probably not be hunted as a regular item of diet, nor would his increase be specifically sought. His spring and summer attack on the newly dropped calves and on the weakened or injured in winter would, however, be noted, and he would have had his own story.

The lesser animals, both real and mythic, seem to offer us, then, certain key insights. This was true also, as we have seen, of the seal, the snake, and the salmon. A small engraved stone found at Les Trois Frères shows an engraved salmon, and within the body of the fish there is the engraved head of a horse, because of its delicacy perhaps a colt or a female (Fig.124). The whole is quickly drawn, a crude engraving on unworked stone. It looks as though it was done in one moment or for one period and then discarded. The first run of salmon at Les Trois Frères, if early, would have come at the time of rounded pregnancy in the mare, if later, in the time of dropping of the colts and, if still later, in the time of mating. The delicate horse head in association with the fish seems to indicate a spring or summer composition. The combination of horse and fish appears on many Magdalenian pieces from La Madeleine and Laugerie Basse in the Dordogne region down to the Santander region of northwestern Spain along the Atlantic. Often the combination of horse and fish is so decorative and stylized that it seems to indicate the presence of a traditional relation and story, one that could be simplified and abstracted and still be understood and recognized. Occasionally the horse is associated with a series of abstracted, symbolic fish. Occasionally the horse is with a bird, snake, lion, or branch, and on the cave walls he is often associated with the bison (see Figs. 108, 121 a). I present an example from the Magdalenian of Laugerie Basse, the fragment of a bâton that shows two horse heads on one face and two lion heads on the other, though because of the break, we see only the mane and ears of the second (Fig.125 a, b). That such compositions are related primarily neither to hunting magic nor to a sexual symbolism is shown not only by the range of such juxtapositions but also by the fact that in some instances within such compositions it is the horse that is "killed," in others it may be the "lion," but in most cases there is no indication of killing but only of a storied or mythological juxtaposition. In addition, the common practice of engraving a group of horses, lions, or fish seems to speak generically of a species concept. Such groups make it difficult to maintain the concept of an animal engraved as a symbol or sign for hunting magic or as an image to be used as an abstracted "male" or "female" symbol.

A subsidiary question raised by such compositions on utilitarian and non-utilitarian objects is whether objects had specialized seasonal uses, whether there was a tool kit and series of objects for spring-summer and perhaps autumn use and ritual.

Let us continue with the lesser animals. From the Pyrenean hills comes one of the truly superb examples of Magdalenian engraving, a pride of

Fig. 125 a, b
The two faces of a broken bâton from Laugerie Basse (Dordogne) engraved with the heads of horses on one face and lion heads on the other. Upper Magdalenian.

Fig. 126
The fragment of a rib from La Vache (Ariège) engraved with a pride of lions running under a series of schematic angles, perhaps representing rain or storm clouds. Final Magdalenian.

lions drawn with exquisite delicacy and realism, with legs and ears in perspective, with the front animals blocking those in the rear. It comes from the terminal, Magdalenian VI level at La Vache and is, therefore, an example that, in a sense, closes out the art and culture of the Upper Paleolithic (Fig. 126). Above these superbly realistic lions, there is a schematic series of angles and marks that looks like lightning-clouds containing

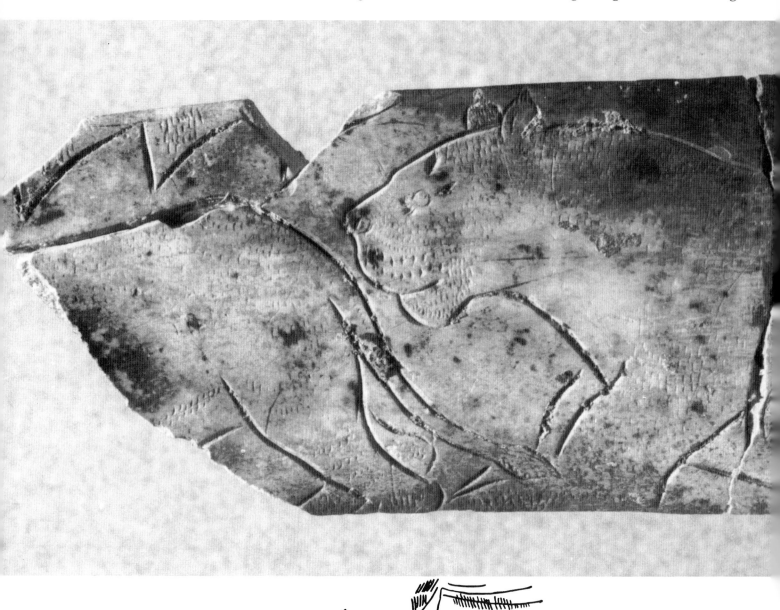

Fig. 127
Schematic rendition of engraved lions in the cave of Lascaux (Dordogne) associated with darts and geometric forms and signs. One of the lions is apparently bleeding from the nose and mouth (after Laming-Emperaire).

rain, or represents some other symbolism or even a notation. These are not lions, then, for art's sake, and not lions for eating or sexual symbolism. The angles might be interpreted as vulvar or "feminine"; but, as I will show later, such angles appear in a range of meanings. Whatever the meaning of the composition, it is clearly "storied," though the lions in their realism seem reportorial.

We have seen in these hills a lioness and cub on an altar, renewed, ceremonial, and apparently killed or sacrificed, and now we have an engraved bone with a lion "story." In the cave of Lascaux to the north, there is an early group of engraved lions in a narrow passage that is difficult to reach. Annette Laming-Emperaire writes: "... this tunnel had a special significance. The outstanding figures ... are a series of engraved latticed signs similar to those beneath the feet of the large black cow, an engraved horse and a group of felines, one of them pierced by seven darts, which is extremely difficult to interpret."[12] (Fig. 127.)

made to show how subjectivity can influence interpretation. It was my memory that originally suggested that the zigzags might be storm clouds. But this type of subjectivity could also have led to the Ice Age metaphor and image of storm clouds.

Note
In 1988 a fragment missing at the right was found.* It depicts the lion missing at right in a bounding gait, like the lion

[12] A. Laming, LASCAUX, p. 91.

*Buisson and Delporte. 1988.

at left. The authors also state that the double mark of a wound (a double-line "sign") is incised in the side of the central lion, to the right of the crack. This tends again to confirm the persistent argument I have made that images of "killing" represent one among the various uses to which animal images were put. The authors also suggest that the engraving, made on an animal rib, was intentionally broken or snapped near the wound. If so then we may be able to add another form of symbolic use to the composition, the "killing" this time of a composition, a symbolic act that goes beyond mere depiction. See Fig. 127.

There are other markings in the composition. One of the lions is spouting blood from mouth and nose. The lion, as a species and as a character in myth and rite, was apparently storied, and we are here faced with what would seem to be a specialized "storied" killing of a lion, which is at the same time associated with the horse and certain signs.

The images of bear and lion and their "killing" in art would seem, therefore, to be specialized examples of myth and rite, aspects of a broader, more encompassing, time-factored mythology and ceremonial.

Far to the east in France, among the foothills of the Alps in the lower valley of the river Ain, is the late Perigordian site of La Colombière, first excavated in 1913 by Mayet and Pissot of France and then again in 1948 by Hallam L. Movius, Jr., of the Peabody Museum at Harvard. The rock shelter of La Colombière was a temporary summer campsite used by Perigordian reindeer hunters during the height of the last glacial maximum, about 22,000 years ago, when the Alps not far from this valley were covered with thick ice.

Nine hand-sized pebbles engraved with animals and two engraved mammoth bones were found at the site. The style and quality of the engraved animals foreshadow the high Magdalenian art that would appear later in southwest France. The drawings are occasionally exquisite and, when well done, the craftmanship is as sure and as careful as on the Perigordian pebble from Barma Grande that we analyzed earlier (Figs. 15, 16, 17), engraved with notations, however, instead of animals. It would seem that a tradition using animal art, notations, and symbols, as we shall see, was present. Some of the engravings on the La Colombière pebbles are quickly sketched outlines, others are beautifully drawn, some stand alone, others offer a melange of figures, one over the other.

It is not the quality or style that is important for our analysis but the species represented and the details with which these species are presented, and what these species and details can tell us about the time-factored culture of these Perigordian hunters and the meaning of art and "killing" in that culture.

These Perigordian hunters, to a large extent, lived off the migrating reindeer herds and during the late spring followed them to their summer range in these cool hill valleys. How many miles the reindeer had trekked on their migration is not known, since different herds in different regions ranged from the nearly sedentary to those making journeys of hundreds of miles. In any case, this herd would have had its spring calves along. We might assume that lions preyed on these young animals, both here and at the spring calving grounds. The hunters themselves ate mostly reindeer. Movius writes of the food remains: "Reindeer is the form most frequently represented by [the] bones ... [The] remains of Horse were very rare. However, amongst the drawings there are no less than 12 figures of Horses ..."[13]

[13] Hallam L. Movius, Jr. and Sheldon Judson, "The Rock-shelter of La Colombière," AMERICAN SCHOOL OF PREHISTORIC RESEARCH, PEABODY MUS., HARV. UNIV., Bull. 19, 1956, p. 139.

Of 47 engraved figures, only 6 were reindeer.[14] In addition, there were 2 engraved bears, 4 felines (no feline bones were found), 4 rhinoceros (rhino bones were rare), 2 musk oxen (no musk ox bones were found), and other animals such as mammoth, red deer, chamois, and ibex. Movius does not think that chamois or musk ox were common in the valley at that time.

The finely engraved musk ox with a shedding coat we saw on a La Colombière pebble (Fig. 85) is an image of late spring and early summer. The musk ox molts copiously in great patches in May and June, and the new coat does not come until late summer in August and September. If there were no musk ox at La Colombière in the summer, are we to assume that the pebble represents the observation and possible mythologizing of early summer at another locale? If so, why was the seemingly realistic image carried to the summer camp? Or was the musk ox, though rare, ritually "killed" at La Colombière but not eaten?

Significantly, many of the reindeer engravings represent animals in their fall, winter, or spring state, but not in their summer state as they would have been at La Colombière, since quite a few of the reindeer are without antlers. The mature reindeer male drops his antlers in the fall after mating; one of the engravings is clearly of a male without antlers. The younger males drop them in late winter, about February. The females drop theirs soon after the spring calving, and by mid-summer they are growing again. The La Colombière pebbles even provide one engraving of antlers without a reindeer. These would have been found at another locale. From the evidence of the reindeer images, the pebbles were carried here with images of another place and time.

One of the engraved reindeer, carrying antlers, has a feathered dart in its throat and another in its stomach and it, therefore, represents a "killing"; but is this a summer scene or a fall one? Another, engraved on a mammoth bone, has a large, full set of antlers and is clearly an image of late summer or fall. These images, therefore, raise questions as to whether they are all equally and generically reindeer or belong to observations and representations of a number of places and times.

The horses raise similar questions. On one of the La Colombière pebbles there is a seemingly wild, windblown horse with odd serpentine arcs engraved within the body (Fig. 128). They recall the serpentine and arced forms found associated with engraved horses on mobiliary materials at other sites and in certain French caves. On the pebble that Movius found, one of the horses shows a laddered serpentine figure added over the mane Other animals on the pebbles have overengraved ovals with interior vertical marks. Whatever the precise meaning of such additions, they seem "symbolic," intended either to "renew" the use of the animal or to add meaning to it. But if horses were rare at the site, why were these recurrent horse images carried to the summer camp? Clearly, they were not intended for "hunting magic" at the site. Nor apparently were they

[14] "In addition, 4 of the figures shown may be either Reindeer or Red Deer." Loc. cit.

Fig. 128. See page 252.

Fig. 129. Pages following.
Broken horse of mammoth ivory from the site of Vogelherd (Baden-Württemberg) in south Germany. One of the earliest examples of sculpture known, it shows evidence of long handling, perhaps in ritual or ceremonial usage. An angle is engraved in its side. Aurignacian, c. 30,000 B.C.

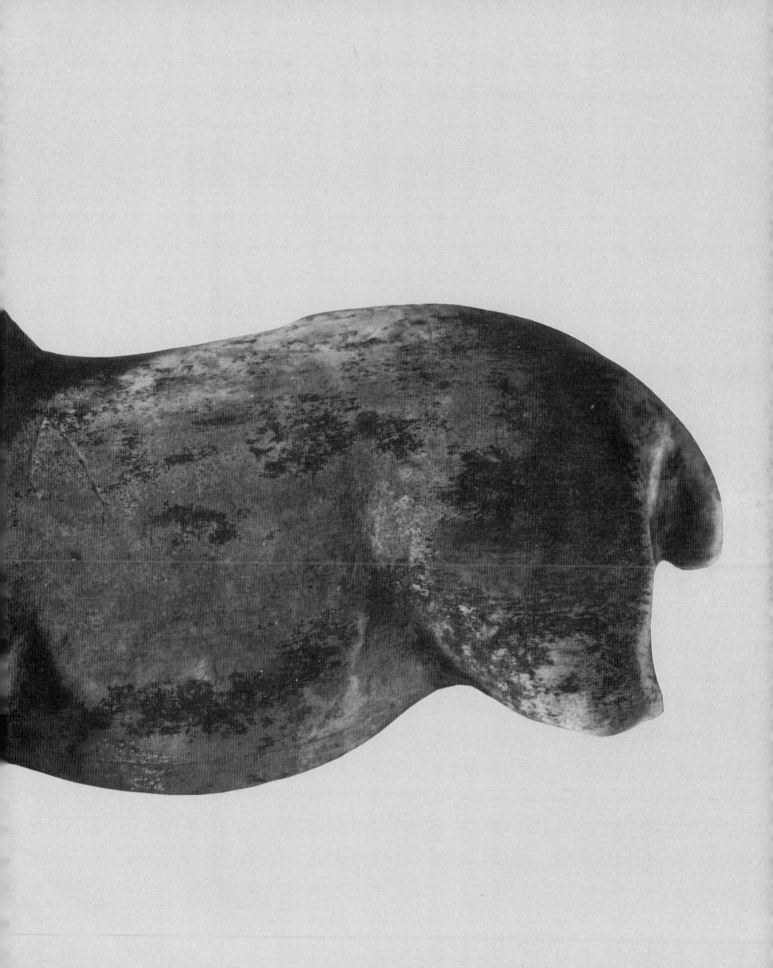

intended for sexual symbolism or fecundity magic related to the horse as a species, at least not for ceremonies performed at this site in the summer, in this area of few horses, and by a reindeer hunter.

There are other alternatives. As with the musk ox, we can ask whether the horse, though rare at this summer camp and, therefore, not regularly

◄ Fig. 128
An engraved pebble from La Colombière (Aïn) depicting a wide-eyed horse with a disarrayed mane and two series of connected serpentine arcs.

hunted or eaten, might not have been ritually hunted or killed as a sacrifice or offering rather than as food? Or perhaps the image was ritually or ceremonially used without a killing. The reasons suggesting such use of the horse are many. The horse engravings on the La Colombière pebbles indicate a symbolism of the horse and a renewal or reuse of the horse image, as well as a juxtaposition with other symbols. There is strong

The pebble shows both the wear of handling and use in hammering. Upper Perigordian.

Caption 130 a. See page 254.

Fig. 130 a. Preceding page. Pebble from La Colombière (Aïn) depicting a rhinoceros whose horns were renewed by different engraving points. Four darts, apparently also made by various points at varied times, are aimed at its underbelly. The accumulations indicate a repeated use of the pebble and rhinoceros image. The rhinoceros is engraved over two earlier animals. Upper Perigordian.

implication in these renditions that the horse—as symbol and image—had relevance and meaning beyond a single meal and beyond the moment surrounding the engraving. The horse myth or story, whatever its details, would seem to have had a continuity, a significance through time, as is suggested both by carriage of the engraved pebbles over a long period to various camps and the reuse of the horse image. The collection of pebbles, as Movius recognized, seems to have been the "religious" property of the group and, by evidence of the excavation, it was apparently lost in an accidental flood that swept it away. Professor Movius has stated that "it is considered very improbable that the drawings were actually executed at the shelter."[15]

The meaning of the horse image, though it cannot be precisely known, can, nevertheless, be roughly and generally understood as culturally time-factored, involving a story that, with the image, was carried through time and space. We have examined one Upper Perigordian pebble from Barma Grande with evidence of time-factored notation, apparently lunar (Figs. 15, 16, 17), so we can hypothesize that in the Upper Perigordian art and notation, though engraved on separate objects, were the products of a single culture, thoroughly modern in its use of symbol. The La Colombière pebbles date from *c.* 20,000 B.C. Earlier we examined a mid-Magdalenian bâton with a pregnant horse associated with notations (Figs. 86 to 89). This example, from La Marche, *c.* 13,000 B.C., represents a late development when notations and art had begun to appear in conjunction on a single piece. Before going on with our analysis of the La Colombière material, let us go back 5,000 to 10,000 years to the Middle Aurignacian, to the culture and tradition of the first modern *Homo sapiens* to enter western Europe, the Cro-Magnon hunter, to see what we can learn about the earliest animal art.

At the reindeer-hunting site of Vogelherd in southeast Germany, of roughly 30,000 B.C., there was found a number of exquisite sculptures carved in ivory, including figures of the horse, lion, bear, and mammoth. Figure 129 is the photograph of a small horse able to lie in the palm of a hand, sculpted in mammoth ivory. The little horse, carved with a stone knife, is one of the great masterpieces of human art. The aesthetic quality is as fine as in the best art of the later Upper Paleolithic, including even the high art of the caves. Each sculpted figure captures not only the form, but also the kinesthetic spirit, the distinctive quality of movement in each species. Since at this point we are not interested in comparative aesthetics but rather in levels of cognition, I point out that the culture making this animal art is the same that made the notations excavated at the Abri Blanchard in France (chapter V, Figs. 7–10).

The microscope revealed that the ivory horse had been beautifully carved in all details, including ears, nose, eyes, mouth, and a hatched mane, but that these sculptural details had been worn and polished by a handling of

[15] Ibid., p. 140.

many months, perhaps of years. In the shoulder of the horse there was engraved a relatively new "point" or angle ($\bigvee$). Whatever the meaning of the horse, it had been carefully made, kept, and handled or used for a long time and then it had apparently had a "killing." Again, all we can say from the one piece is that the image and the accompanying story, myth, or rite were, somehow, time-factored. The microscopic findings imply that the horse was not made for a quick use in hunting magic.

I assume the horse to be one aspect of a culture with a complex, integrated, time-factored use of symbol, a tradition that would culminate in the Late Magdalenian.

Returning to La Colombière, we note that the most intriguing of the pebbles, for our purpose in this chapter, shows a beautifully drawn woolly rhinoceros with four feathered darts in its belly (Fig. 130 a, b). This rhinoceros is engraved upon an earlier reindeer without a head, and the reindeer is engraved over a still lighter earlier figure. The microscope reveals that the rhinoceros has had its horns renewed four or five times, each renewal by a different point. The bones of rhinoceros were rare in the occupation level to which the pebbles belong. Since the engraved rhinoceros was renewed and also apparently "rekilled" a number of times—as far as the microscope could determine, the darts, though made by one hand, may have been made at different times—the image was used over a period of time, and its use may have been at a different locale.

From other sites and other periods there comes more evidence of this technique of renewing the image by the addition of a back, a stomach, a face, a mane, a tail, a tusk, a horn, or a trunk. In the caves the possibility that such renewals were made within a single period or culture is hard to prove. (See horse of Les Trois Frères, Fig. 121 a.)

An example of Upper Paleolithic art found by Edouard Lartet at the site of La Madeleine in the Dordogne in 1864 has the engraving of a mammoth on mammoth ivory. The microscope reveals that head, back, and tusks were renewed at different times and by different points. A similar, crudely engraved mammoth on ivory from the earlier Solutrean was found at Ober Klause, Bavaria, Germany. It has four sets of tusks, each set made by a different point at a different time. This evidence raises questions concerning the time-factored nature of the image, its continuity and the moments of its precise use. We cannot know the details of story or thought that accompanied its making, retention, and subsequent reuse. But we can understand the general cognitive processes and storymaking skills involved.

The La Colombière pebbles raise similar but more specific questions. Why were these images, not related to summer activities, carried to the site? Why twelve horses with storied additions when the remains of killed horses were rare, why images of musk ox when their bones were not found, why non-summer images of reindeer, why images of cave lion and cave bear when these were not major items of diet? Analysis of the pebbles shows that the engravings were made in diverse styles and with varying skills, as though they had been made over a number of years and by seem-

Fig. 130 a. See page 253.

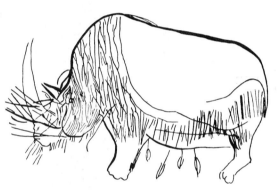

Fig. 130 b
Line rendition of the engraved rhinoceros on the La Colombière pebble indicating the original drawing of the head and the subsequent overengraving, as determined by microscopic analysis.

Fig. 132
The broken, semi-sculptural image of a running lion carved of mammoth ivory from Pavlov (Moravia), apparently an image of long-term use. East Gravettian or Pavlovian.

Fig. 131 a, b
Two views of a small lion head of fired clay from Dolní Věstonice (Moravia). Two stab holes were made into the wet clay before it was fired indicating a single use of the image. East Gravettian or Pavlovian.

Fig. 133
Detail. A non-utilitarian portion of mammoth tusk from Predmost (Moravia) engraved with irregular sets of marks made by different points and showing differential wear among the sets. East Gravettian or Pavlovian.

ingly different hands. This would tend to strengthen the implication of a "library" with meanings maintained by story. There are also indications that some of the pebbles were used. The pebble that Movius found, for instance, shows signs both of hand polish and of hammering as though it had been used for some practical purpose.[16] In addition, there are spring images, summer images, and autumn and winter images. From whatever point of view we approach them, we get time-factored questions and findings.

Since these were migratory reindeer hunters who moved in time and space on known paths, we might ask whether the images of renewals and killings are indications of sacrifice or of "first killing" to mark either the start of a season or the hunter's return to a new site or territory? The seasonal sacrifice or offering of a large animal resident in a range or territory might serve a variety of symbolic purposes. The sacrifice of a female or a calf in the springtime might serve other symbolic purposes. The killing of a non-food or a food animal at a time of non-periodic calamity or stress might serve still other traditional and symbolic purposes. In every case the equation would be the same, a killing not for food but, one way or another, a time-factored and storied killing.

If my earlier findings concerning the use of a time-factored notation are correct, the possibilities of a corollary use of a time-factored art, and of rites or ceremonies involving storied "killings," are strong.

North of La Colombière, about 27,000 B.C., the mammoth hunters roamed Czechoslovakia. The remains of their meals indicate that they ate primarily mammoth, horse, pig, and an occasional wolf. They sculpted or engraved an occasional mammoth, but the bulk of their animal art was concerned with the lion, bear, rhinoceros, and other minor animals such as owl and glutton. These are represented by tiny heads or full animals sculpted of an artificial clay made of powered bone, animal fat, and earth, and afterward fired and hardened. A lion head from the site of Dolní Věstonice had two holes jabbed into the skull and eye while the clay was wet (Fig. 131 a, b). It was seemingly crudely and quickly sculpted for a single use, perhaps as part of a ritual "killing," but it was not apparently intended as hunting magic to secure food. If this was so, the ritual killing could have been related to an actual killing, but this real killing of a lion would also have been storied, the act of making and killing the head having served as one part in a broader, culturally understood drama.

There is a sculpted ivory lion from Pavlov of this period that has a different intent (Fig. 132). This lion was not made quickly to be used once. Instead, it is the schematic rendering of a storied "decorative" beast comparable to the Aurignacian horse of Vogelherd, to the engraved Perigordian horses of La Colombière, and to later horse head pendants from Magdalenian France. It took time to make and was apparently intended

[16] The microscope has revealed that bone and stone objects were often used both symbolically and practically, with engraved symbols and art over work marks, and work marks and friction wear over art.

to last and serve as a durable image within this culture which had a lore of the lion.

These East Gravettian lions represent different forms or uses of art, but

each represents one aspect of a tradition in which lions and the killing of lions had a continuous meaning and significance and a specialized meaning at precise moments of rite.

The evidence of notation lends final weight to our interpretation of this East Gravettian art. The style of notation differs slightly from that in Western Europe, but the common origin is apparent. I present an extremely simple example from the site of Predmost, a large chunk of unworked mammoth ivory used as a slate (Fig. 133). Traditionally, such markings were called decorations in a geometric or chevron pattern. There are, in fact, examples of decorative patterns on bracelets, headbands, and ritual objects, and the microscope reveals that such decorations were engraved

Fig. 134
Schematic rendition of the engraved marks within the detail of Fig. 133 on the ivory tusk from Predmost indicating the angle, size and placement of the accumulated sets. As determined by microscopic analysis.

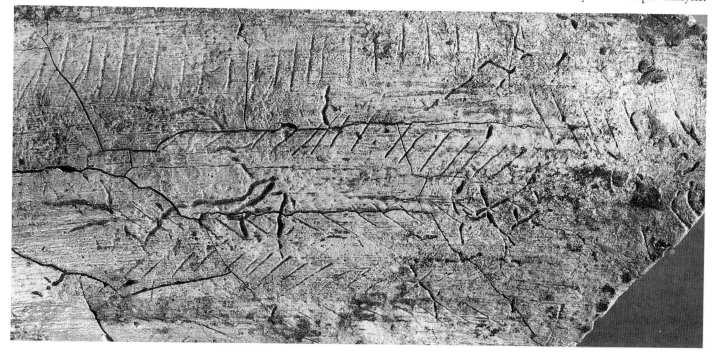

Fig. 135 a, b
The two faces of a ceremonial or symbolic bone knife from Pekarna (Moravia) containing three horse heads on one face, including that of a colt, and a bison and antelope on the other. The bison contains a serpentine image. The tip of the knife is missing, the muzzle of one horse reconstructed. Upper Magdalenian.

by one point. On this chunk of ivory, however, too heavy to be easily handled and never used as a tool, the markings were made in small sequential groups, each at a different time and by different points, angles, and pressures. Some groups show wear and deterioration; others are relatively new and fresh. A schematic breakdown as determined by microscopic analysis shows that there is no "chevron pattern," that what we have is notation (Fig. 134). The style of marking is in the Eastern tradition, one that made its marks at alternate angles, a regional style of accumulation that was used both in decoration and notation.

The range of symbolic usage in this culture, including female images, ceremonial burials, amulets, and costume pieces, implies a rich, inter-

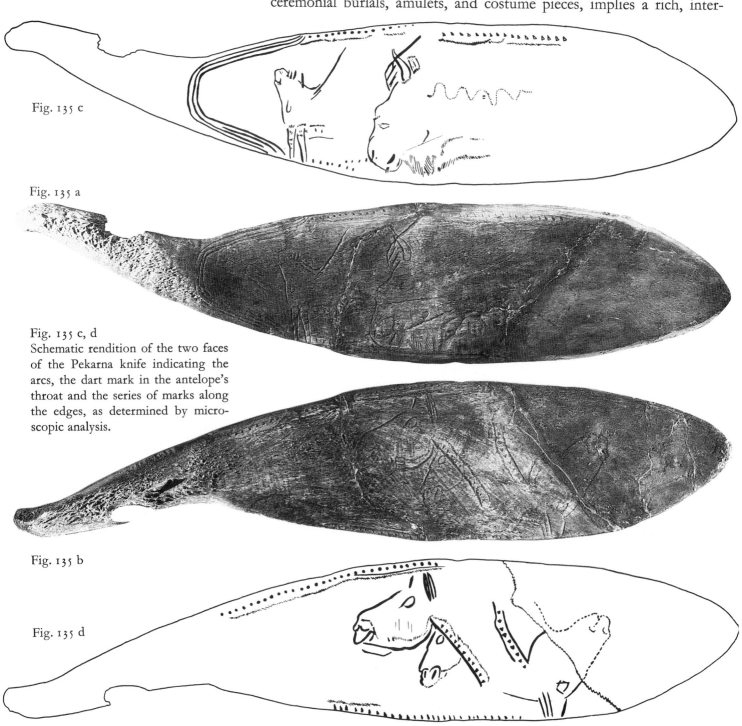

Fig. 135 c

Fig. 135 a

Fig. 135 c, d
Schematic rendition of the two faces of the Pekarna knife indicating the arcs, the dart mark in the antelope's throat and the series of marks along the edges, as determined by microscopic analysis.

Fig. 135 b

Fig. 135 d

related ceremonial and mythological lore. I shall discuss some of these in the next chapter.

After thousands of years the climate changed, the mammoth became rare, and a new way of life came to Czechoslovakia. The Magdalenian hunters who entered these rolling plains were hunters of reindeer and horse with ties to the culture of France. They did almost no reindeer art and, instead, engraved and drew bison, horse, fish, and other "lesser" creatures, almost always with symbolic, ceremonial, or seasonal reference. The art, symbols, and notations appeared in compositions of the evolved Magdalenian style.

The shelter of Pekarna, northeast of the Alps, lies near the industrial city

Fig. 136 a, b
The two faces of a second ceremonial or symbolic bone knife from Pekarna (Moravia) containing a horse on one face with a triple arc in its body plus signs and with a number of forms and signs on the second face. Upper Magdalenian.

Fig. 136 c, d
Schematic rendition of the two faces of the second Pekarna knife indicating the horse, the schematized fish and other forms and markings, as determined by microscopic analysis.

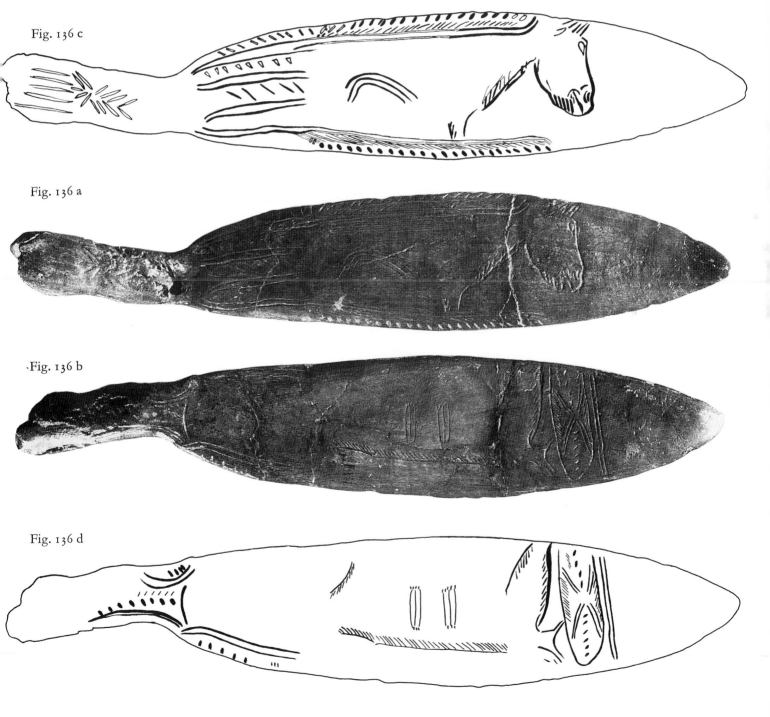

Fig. 136 c

Fig. 136 a

·Fig. 136 b

Fig. 136 d

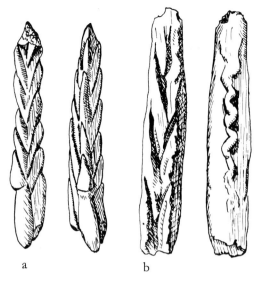

a   b

Fig. 137 a, b
a) Fragment of an ivory rod from Espélugues (Hautes-Pyrénées) in southern France in the shape of a plant with kernels and b) a fragment of ivory from Pekarna (Moravia) with a similar plant image on one face and a serpentine image on the other. Upper Magdalenian (after Absolon).

Fig. 138
Line rendition of the unrolled, engraved composition on a bâton from the Abri Mège, Teyjat (Dordogne), indicating a sequence in the engraving of groups of images (after Breuil). On the first face is a doe and three serpentine images. Behind are a stallion which has apparently been

of Brno, on the plain that was once the migratory route for animals and hunters to and from Poland and Russia. From this site there comes a shaped horse rib, perhaps a ceremonial dagger, engraved with three male bison, two of which are in a late summer or early autumn rutting battle. One of the bison has dart marks in its side and seeming blood trickling from its mouth. (See Fig. 83.) Once again, it would seem that it is not an animal being killed for food, but a beast "killed" in a special time.

A related series of decorated, apparently ceremonial knives from Pekarna, made from the lower jaw of the wild horse, contains images of horse, fish, bison, and antelope with associated notations and signs (Fig. 135 a, b, c, d). Significantly there are no reindeer. The microscope reveals that the daggers had been overpainted with red ocher, stressing their ceremonial nature. The microscope also reveals that there is a dart in the throat of the antelope which, as a horned ungulate, is perhaps equivalent to the ibex of France and Spain. It is engraved next to a bison that contains a schematic serpentine figure.

On one face of the broken dagger, there is the drawing of a mare and colt with what may be part of a stallion's head. On the other dagger there is a horse with three arcs in its body (Fig. 136 a, b, c, d). On the reverse face there is a simplified fish associated with a strange "X" form, almost a shield. The knives contain notation, seeming plant forms, other arcs, and possible insect pupae. A third knife has as its decoration the form of a schematized fish. A number of schematic fish made of pebbles were also found at Pekarna, engraved with symbols and signs such as are common later in the Mesolithic. Perhaps the most interesting of the images made by these reindeer hunters is a fragment of carved ivory which on one side has the deeply engraved image of a branch and on the other a carved snake (Fig. 137 b). Karel Absolon, who found the fragment, stated that

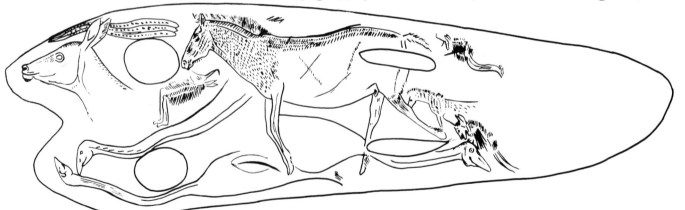

"killed" and a small horse, perhaps a colt. On the other face are three swans, the first two facing and the third turned away. One shamanistic barefoot dancer wearing a chamois robe and mask is engraved for each group of images; each is successively more schematized probably indicating their sequence of making. Upper Magdalenian.

the plant looks like a carved ivory that "suggests ears of corn" (or maize) found in the Magdalenian cave of Espélugues at Lourdes in the Pyrenees (Fig. 137 a).

The repertoire of images found across the Upper Paleolithic of Europe, therefore, suggests a storied, mythological, time-factored, seasonal, ceremonial and ritual use of animal, fish, bird, plant, and serpent images, and it apparently also includes at times what seem to have been selective and seasonal killing and sacrifice, either of the image, in rite, or of the real animal. The complexity and interrelation of these storied meanings cannot easily be explained by any generalizing theories propounding concepts of hunting magic, fertility ritual, or sexual symbolism. Instead, the art and symbol suggest a broad range of cognitions, cultural and practical, and a profound understanding of processes in nature and of the varieties of living creatures. They imply an understanding of diverse animal and plant ranges, directions, and seasons, all of which were unified by story, rite, and art. While the stories were, of necessity, "false," they were based on a careful observation. While the art was sometimes "realistic," it was always storied and, while it was sometimes abstract and symbolic, it had even then reference to a core of observation and cognition.

I now return to France and Spain, to a careful selection of a few little-known examples and some well-known for their beauty or their drama.

From the Abri Mège at Teyjat, the Dordogne, which gave us examples of

Fig. 139 a
A model of the unrolled, engraved composition on a broken bâton from Lorthet (Hautes-Pyrénées) depicting two stags crossing a stream with four leaping salmon among them. The sequence and manner of engraving indicates that the images represent a single scene or composition. Above the main stag are two schematic lozenge images in a different style. The total composition is clearly seasonal. Upper Magdalenian.

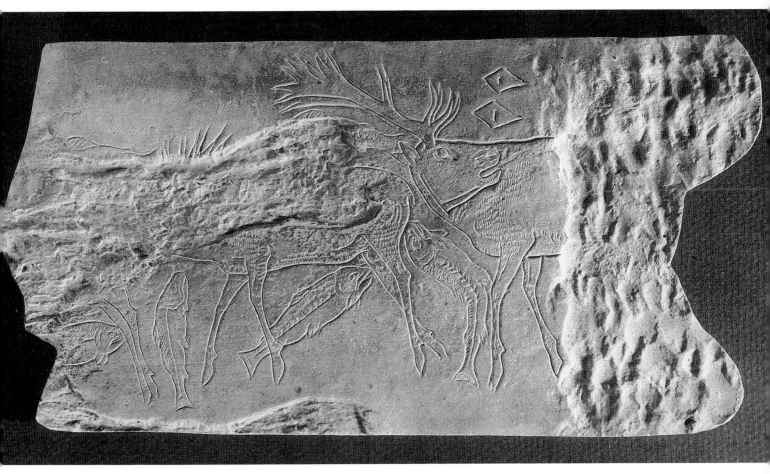

evolved notations in the vertical-foot tradition, there comes a Late Magdalenian bâton made of antler (Fig. 138).[17] It is a bâton with two holes, one round, the other oval and narrow. On one face before the round hole is a beautifully rendered, realistic doe or hind associated with three schema-

[17] H. Breuil and D. Peyrony, "Observations sur un bâton de commandement orné de figures animales et de personnages semi-humains," REVUE DE L'ÉCOLE D'ANTHROPOLOGIE, XIX (1909), pp. 62-76.

tized snakes that were drawn in after the deer. Together they seem to form an image of spring. Behind the hole is the figure of a shaman or sorcerer in chamois mask and robe. Behind the sorcerer there is a large stallion, running.[18] He is marked with "spears" and perhaps notated, the only animal so marked, perhaps representing a "sacrifice." Behind the stallion

Fig. 139 b
Detail. The turned stag head and the two schematic lozenge forms above it indicating the superb realism of the animal and the abstraction of the "signs" apparently engraved later and in relation to the seasonal composition.

is a small, unfinished horse, made later, apparently a colt. Together the horses seem to be an image of summer. Behind the two horses, there is a second shaman or sorcerer in chamois mask.

On the other face of the bâton are related or associated images. Around the large hole are the necks and heads of two swans, meeting as though in a mating dance. Behind the two swans is a third swan facing in the opposite direction, and near this swan is a third sorcerer in chamois mask, more quickly and crudely made than the other two. The nature of the composition on the main face and the arrangement of the figures in space indicate that the doe and snakes were made first, the horse and colt

[18] Though it has also been called a "mare" in the archaeological literature.

second. The sorcerers seem to have been squeezed in after the primary images, as though relating them to the symbolic creatures. The third swan and its sorcerer seem to have been made last. If the images are, as they seem, seasonal, it may be that the third sorcerer and the departing swan indicate an autumn image, as the first two swans may have indicated a late spring image. Does the combined imagery, then, relate to stories or ceremonies involved in a single cultural complex of seasonal recognition and rites? Was it a single shaman, the owner of the bâton, who performed a *sequence* of seasonal rites? Was the chamois his spiritual animal, in much the way that other masks of other shamans represent other horned animals? Is the chamois, in this case, comparable to the horned ibex image that we have seen in other seasonal contexts within this region of southwest France and northwest Spain? Could the ibex and chamois of myth be at one time seasonal signs, generalized characters in myth, and specialized spirits aiding a shaman? Within the possibilities of story and art, all are possible. More important, the analysis shows the difficulty of simple explanations.

From the site of Lorthet in the foothills of the Pyrenees, which gave us birds and plants around a snake, comes a Magdalenian VI composition on a broken bâton that depicts three deer, two of which are stags, one with a full head of antlers, crossing a river in which salmon are leaping (Fig.139a, b). Above the head of the stag who is turning as though being followed are two signs that look like eyes but have also been called schematized fish or vulva signs. The creatures are uniform in style and excellence and, by the manner in which the fish are drawn, deer, fish, and signs seem intended to form a whole. The image is seasonal and may represent the summer or autumn salmon run. In terms of numbers, the autumn salmon run is often the largest. This is the season when antlers have lost their velvet and when the dominant stag collects his harem. Since we see two stags, however, the image may depict the summer run of salmon, the season during which stags often depart from the hinds. In either case, the seeming schematic eyes may represent some seasonal relation to realistic images, perhaps the two "eyes" of the sky, the moon and the solstitial summer or equinoctial autumn sun, or perhaps some stellar-solar combination. That the signs are not schematized fish is indicated by the realism of the salmon; that they may not be vulvas is implied by the fact that there are *two,* offered almost as a single image rather than as images renewed, reused or added to. But whether they are eyes, vulvas, or signs and symbols of another sort, it would seem that in sum the composition is seasonal.

From the site of El Pendo in the Cantabrique region of northwest Spain comes a bâton whose appearance some specialists have declared to be in the likeness of a horse, but which Leroi-Gourhan has termed phallic (Fig. 140 a, b). On one face of the bâton, superbly and delicately drawn, is the head of a horse and two heads of does, and on the other face there is the head of a doe and a stag with growing antlers, apparently in the late spring or early summer velvet stage. On the throat of the horse are two

Fig. 139 a. Page 261.

Fig. 140 a, b. Next page.

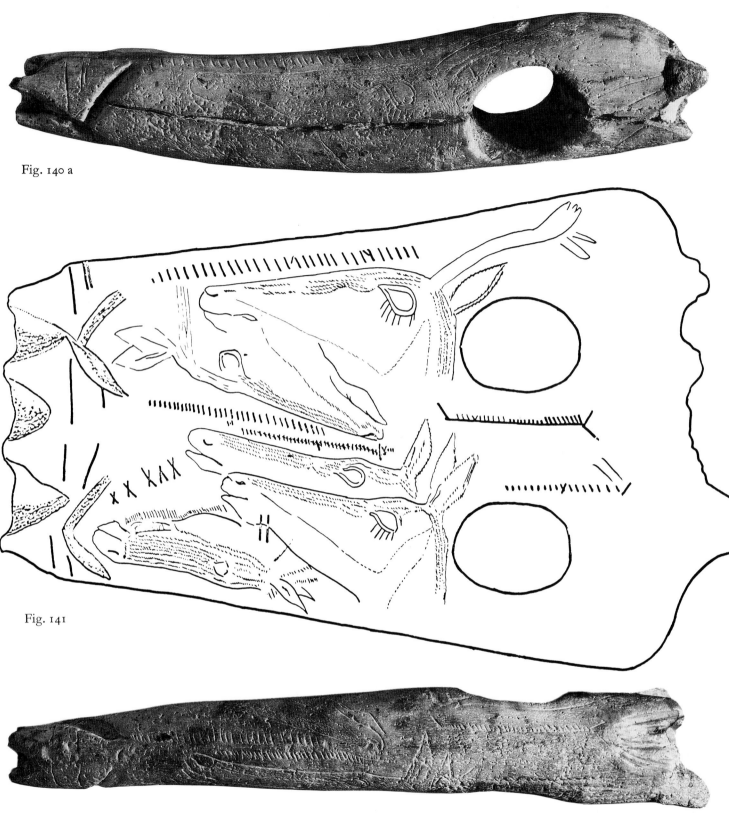

Fig. 140 a

Fig. 141

Fig. 140 b

marks that may be indicative of killing or "sacrifice." There are five animals; around the animals—above, below, and to the side—is a complex series of marks, all intentional and carefully grouped, most of them apparently notational. I present all the marks in their accurate microscopic count (Fig. 141). If they are all notational and if they are all lunar, they give us 6 or 7 months. There seem to be containing lines, lines of separation, and a few differentiating marks, and the group of 10 may be symbols of a different meaning. The breakdown is:

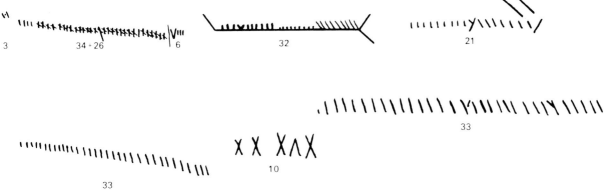

Examples of such interrelated compositions are numerous: horse, bison, deer, ibex, aurochs (wild ox), fish, plant, snake, seal, and bird—associated, storied, and seasonal; bison, bear, lion, horse, bull, rhinoceros, ibex, fish—occasionally "killed" in art and perhaps "sacrificed" in art and reality, but certainly storied, ceremonial and mythological.

It is important to note that it is in the Magdalenian that this repertoire of combined, composed images on mobiliary objects begins to become common and complex. The Magdalenian, north of the Pyrenees, was primarily a cold-climate, reindeer-hunting culture and, while the reindeer does appear in the art, it plays a relatively minor role. Reindeer representations are more common in some periods than others, but even when most common, the reindeer is a minor creature in the art. This has created a number of problems for specialists seeking to interpret the reindeer hunters' Magdalenian art and culture either in terms of hunting or fertility magic or in terms of a sexual symbolism. Obviously the meaning of the reindeer image is crucial for our attempt to understand the general meaning and development of this first art.

Leroi-Gourhan has made a comparative study of the frequency of appearance of the various animal species in cave art and on the decorated objects. He states:

"The statement has become almost standard that the reindeer occurs very rarely in cave art, while it abounds in the art of Late Magdalenian decorated objects. Actually, the reindeer appears on decorated objects in two separate periods—at the beginning, between the Gravettian and the Early Magdalenian, and at the end, in Magdalenian V–VI. During the intermediate period, although reindeer bones keep turning up in the kitchen refuse of the dwellings, the animal appears only very rarely among the strictly limited cast of animal characters most frequently represented on walls and objects: its place was taken by the stag. In the Late Magdalenian the reindeer again appears on objects, but nothing of this recurrence is discernible on the cave walls, except among the latest decorations at a few sites …"[19]

A reindeer-hunting culture with a somewhat different tool kit and a less developed use of art inhabited the rolling flatlands of north Germany about 12,000 B.C. during the Late Magdalenian period. This unforested

◀ Fig. 140 a, b
The two faces of an engraved bâton from El Pendo near Santander, Spain, containing the extremely fine engraving of a stag and hinds, one horse and six sets of notation. Upper Magdalenian.

◀ Fig. 141.
Schematic rendition of all the engraved lines on the El Pendo bâton indicating that the stag's antlers are apparently in their early velvet stage, that the horse has two wound marks in its throat and that one of the notational sets has been overengraved, as determined by microscopic analysis.

[19] A. Leroi-Gourhan, TREASURES OF PREHISTORIC ART, p. 107.

tundra had not long before been covered with ice and was still covered with ice in northeast Germany and Denmark. The reindeer herds were probably forced to longer seasonal migrations here than in the protected, warmer limestone hills of the Dordogne, or the foothills of the Pyrenees and the Massif Central.

To what extent these hunters of the Schleswig-Holstein area had roots in the earlier East Gravettian culture, with some lore perhaps learned from the French Magdalenian, it is too early to say, but they seemed to have something of both, including the bow and arrow of the east. In any case, they represent a peripheral branch of the late, evolved Upper Paleolithic cultures.

In 1932, Alfred Rust, an electrical engineer-turned-archaeologist, found hundreds of stone tools in a newly plowed field between Meiendorf and Ahrensburg in North Germany, not many miles from the city of Hamburg. In 1933 and 1934, he found the campsite, some 25 yards from what had once been an Ice Age lake. Almost ninety percent of the animal bones found at the site were reindeer, with an occasional wild horse or summer water bird, such as crane, swan, goose, and gull. An examination of the vertebrae and antlers indicated that all the reindeer had been killed in the summer, between July and September, the majority being young animals. The open-air camp, therefore, had been located at the northern summer grazing grounds of the herd, the summer nesting area also for water birds. The hunters had followed the herd, living off it. Each autumn, apparently, they left with the herd for some hillier, more forested terrain, perhaps in central Germany. Where the winter site was, or what the spring and autumn migratory routes were, could not be determined.

The only evidences of art were a few small, crudely engraved pebbles and bits of amber, and a few decorated tools. Significantly, no reindeer "art" was found; the engraved animals included two or three horse heads, what might be a feline head, and perhaps a bird. Fortunately, the accident of geography and climate has also preserved the rare and unique evidence of what seems to have been a reindeer ceremony.

On the ancient lake floor was the skeleton of a reindeer doe, its antlers intact, its bones showing no marks of cutting or breaking, but with an eighteen-pound stone in its rib cage. The cuticular stage of the female antlers indicated that it was killed in May or June, the period during which the reindeer hunters arrived at this summer campsite after perhaps weeks of spring migration by the herd. Rust believes that the animal was hurled into the lake whole with skin and antlers, as a sacrifice related to the end of the trek and arrival at the site. To what the sacrifice or offering was made, one cannot tell, since it could have been to any aspect of the time-and-space-structured myth: the "spirit of the lake," the area, the time, the herd, the safe arrival, or the "god" who supervised the round. The details are unimportant. It is the mythologizing of the sequence, the recognition of the process, the use of the symbol, with killing as a symbolic act, that are significant. In all, Rust excavated some thirty reindeer, each with a rock inside, in three lakes.

The ice continued to retreat to the north. The climate in north Germany warmed, birch and pine took root in the tundra, and forest animals began to move in. Four to five thousand years after the Hamburgian reindeer hunters had camped at their summer lakeside, and during the dying stages of the Magdalenian reindeer-hunting culture, a new group of northern hunters camped during the summer at lakeside sites near Ahrensburg. This was about 8,000 B.C., a period during which the post-Ice Age economic revolutions had already taken place further south and in which agriculture was already being practiced around the eastern Mediterranean. In north Germany Rust found, again, a number of reindeer apparently thrown into the water in the dried lake-bottom layer of this culture. More important, however, was the discovery of a wooden stake about five inches thick and seven feet long that had once stood in the water and had been crowned with the skull of a sixteen year old reindeer doe, the oldest reindeer skeleton found at the site. No art was found. The stick and skull were not "art," as we define art, any more than the sacrifice of an animal was art. But the pole-and-skull was related to art by being a symbol that served at a particular time and perhaps through an extended period as an image in a traditional and repeated story. In this sense art is just one specialized aspect of this complex, traditional use of story, image, and symbol.

We cannot know the details of the stories accompanying these reindeer rites and symbols, nor would conjecture solve the problem of details. We know only that the stories, rites, and symbols were time-factored and seasonal and that, in these two reindeer-hunting cultures at these lakeside sites, they were related to summer and to water and to the symbol of the animal. Whether there were also autumn or spring rites related to the periods of the rut or calving, or to the long night of winter, or the beginning lengthening of the days, or the start of the migration, we do not know. But some storied recognition of these processes would perhaps have existed.

For our purpose the most important find at Ahrensburg was a reindeer-antler ax, with a beveled, polished head, of a type that would be found later throughout north Germany and Scandinavia in the post-Ice Age Mesolithic cultures that have been broadly called the Maglemose. This Ahrensburg ax was engraved with what seem to have been both sequential notation and a form of symbolism, styles of marking that stem from the earlier Upper Paleolithic and appear also throughout the later European Mesolithic (Fig. 142).

Alfred Rust describes his find so:
"The shank back of the Lyngby ax has two groups of rows of notches lying next to each other ... the right is composed of groups which have [starting on the right] 5, 5, 4, 4, 5 (?) notches. The second row is less clear. It begins [on the right] with groups of 5 and 4, then 7(?). From the arrangement of the 6 last strokes, one might perceive groups of 2, 2, 2(?). [Fig. 143.]
"Our ax once carried 4 or more further rows of figures which have been removed by scraping so that only traces can now be seen ... For proof of the purpose of

Fig. 142
A reindeer antler ax from Ahrensburg near Hamburg, Germany, capable of being used for digging or in cutting soft wood. Ahrensburgian culture, c. 8,000 B.C.

Fig. 143. Next page.

these figures, better examples must be sought ... on which the figures can be more clearly pointed out." [20]

A microscopic analysis of the ax showed that all the marks of the main sequence could be determined and that both the counts and the markings were more complex than Rust had surmised. Two secondary sequences could only be approximated because they were originally extremely faint. A close-up of the primary linear series, with a linear rendition of the marks as determined by microscope, is presented in Figures 143 and 144. The

Fig. 143
Detail. Sets of engraved linear marks on the Ahrensburg ax. The two large series are subdivided into smaller groups. A faint third group is at top right.

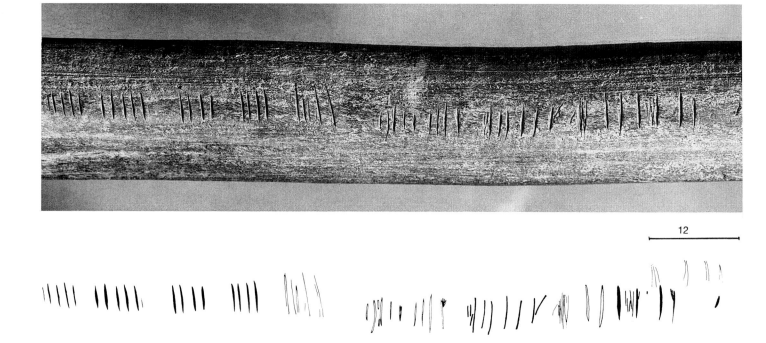

Fig. 144
Schematic rendition of the sets of marks engraved along one side of the Ahrensburg ax, as determined by microscopic analysis.

surface wear and deterioration make it difficult to determine "ballistic" prints or tool differences. Nevertheless, the broad visual groupings and their inner subdivisions could be determined. The total of the marks in this major series is ninety, or a possible three months. However, the only way such a breakdown could be considered a valid lunar series was if the separated groups were also to contain subgroups and points of visual differentiation within them, as revealed in the diagram. We saw this sort of sequencing in the French Magdalenian on a bâton from Le Placard (Fig. 26). Whether lunar or not, the markings seemed intentional, carefully varied and grouped, and notational. To show how the breakdown might work as a lunar notation, I present a schematic rendition showing where the lunar phase points would fall if one began with the day of invisibility (Fig. 145).

The faint marks on the ax that Rust had assumed were scraped off were revealed by the microscope to have been lightly scratched and apparently

[20] Alfred Rust, DIE ALT- UND MITTELSSTEINZEITLICHEN FUNDE VON STELLMOOR. ARCHÄO-LOGISCHES INSTITUT DES DEUTSCHEN REICHES (Neumünster in Holstein: Karl Wachholtz Verlag, 1943), trans. A. Marshack.

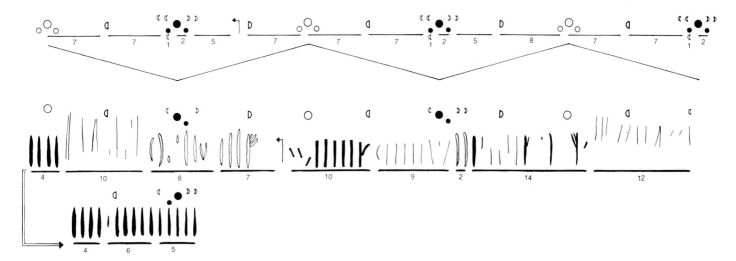

worn or polished off by handling. For this reason one may assume that they were probably made first and represent a form with a unit meaning which somehow precedes the linear sequences. The full form as revealed by the microscope gives us a triple hatching:

Such forms appear on later Mesolithic antler axes and on objects of amber and stone. We shall see some in the last chapter. The number of strokes vary irregularly and we cannot, therefore, assume it to be notational or lunar; however, it may represent irregular periods or sequences. Whatever its meaning, this type of form seems to have had a generalized meaning extending over thousands of years. It was, as we shall see, symbolic, periodic, repetitive, traditional, and storied.

The reindeer as an animal, in the flesh or in the bone, was periodically symbolic or ritual in this reindeer-hunting culture of the far northern peripheral region during the terminal stages of the Ice Age. This reindeer-hunting culture also seems to have made use of a tradition of notation whose roots go back to the early Upper Paleolithic. Since we are seeking the cognitive, symbolic roots of a tradition that seems to have been widespread throughout Europe, let us now return to the art of the central Magdalenian culture of France to see if we can find evidence of a ritual or sacrificial killing of reindeer or a symbolic use of its image.

From La Madeleine there comes a fragment of bone that shows two reindeer, one a male with the genitals indicated and with the ends of a large spread of antlers engraved above the back (Fig. 146). He is followed by a seemingly younger reindeer, male or female, without a full spread of antlers but apparently with a new beginning growth. Just over the right leg, in the shoulder, is the double mark of a spear wound. The spear itself seemingly passes upwards into the chest and through the body. There is precision in the depiction of the weapon and wound along a straight line. The first point of impact in the engraved line doing the "killing" is at bottom right; it then passes upwards. Significantly, the microscope reveals that this spear is engraved over the body lines of the chest and back, a clear indication of the sequential intent of this portion of the composition. That the "killing" may be symbolic and ritual is indi-

Fig. 145
The engraved marks along one side of the Ahrensburg ax against the lunar model in a test for lunar phrasing.

Note
This type of marking provided the greatest difficulty for the notational hypothesis since there is no strong internal structure except for the separation of small sets and the general breakdown suggested above. That there was intention, however, is apparent in Fig. 145. Irregularly structured marking of this type, found on tools and non-utilitarian objects in the Ice Age, instigated a 20 year long study of the variability in early modes of marking. It led to an investigation of the problem of determining intentional symbolic marking from other forms: cutting and work marks, tool testing, grip marks, decoration, ritual marking (Marshack 1977; 1979 a,d; 1983 a; 1985 c; 1990 b; 1991 c,d). The small sets in Figs. 144 and 145 probably could not be counted after they were made. But while they were being made they might have been able to indicate their position within a month or season (see Figs. 19 and 20). As an analytical and theoretical problem this concerns the nature of the human capac-

ity for abstraction, symboling and visual problem-solving. I am not quite sure how one verifies that such marking is notational, but I keep referring back to the valid Taï notation, Fig. 15.

cated by the microscope, which shows the bone to have been ochered red after the engraving, as though offering an added storied content to the composition of "killing." The sequence of composing the animals reveals that the reindeer buck to the right was made after the young reindeer at the left and that it, too, may have a spear shaft through it. Of particular interest is the double mark of the wound in the body of the animal as opposed to the single shaft of the spear. This double wound often appears as a sign of killing or sacrifice in the Upper Paleolithic, and it is here clarified as a "non-sexual" sign or image by its relation to the shaft. (See La Pileta horse, Fig. 197.)

Fig. 146
A fragment of engraved bone from La Madeleine (Dordogne) depicting a young reindeer "killed" by a dart as it follows an older bull. Upper Magdalenian.

Comparable to this image is one that appears on a Late Magdalenian bâton from the site of Kesslerloch bei Thayngen, an outpost of the French Magdalenian in the German-Swiss border region, which shows an exquisitely engraved reindeer buck with the genitals indicated (Fig. 147). There are no extraneous lines on the bâton face except for a wound in the shoulder over the right leg and an extended line into the back, creating a wound image similar to that from La Madeleine (Fig. 148). The inside of the bâton hole exhibits a high polish along the sides as though a thong had been habitually used in the hole for gripping the bâton. On the reverse face, opposite this exquisitely engraved, realistic reindeer, there is an unusual random scratching, clearly not notational, giving the appearance of grass or rain. The skill and care used in making the image on one face and the seeming random disorder on the second face are startling, and one may possibly assume a symbolic meaning for the "image" or sum of the marks.

Associated with the animal images as though in ceremony, there are occasional human or humanoid figures, sometimes in animal dress or mask, sometimes crudely generalized. These compositions have till now been considered as examples either of hunting or fecundity magic. In the engraved compositions with human figures that we examined from Raymonden, Les Eyzies, the Abri Mège of Teyjat, and La Madeleine, neither the act of killing nor sexual symbolism was apparent or stressed. At most, in the example from Les Eyzies the humanoid figures may be involved in some story related to sacrifice if, as our reading of the humanoid figures might suggest, it is the human figures and not the bison which are struck through. On the bâton from the Abri Mège the horse may have been "killed" but not the other creatures. Such possibilities raise questions as to the nature and variety of the ceremonies and rites in which man, animals, and symbols are related at specific times by story. It is evident that calling such compositions "magic" or "ritual" serves neither as a definition nor an explanation but merely says that they were used symbolically. Let us, therefore, with the help of the microscope, look at those few available compositions in which human figures are clearly related to animals.

From the Upper Perigordian site of Péchialet in the Dordogne comes a small engraved stone or schist that shows two men baiting, teasing, or

Fig. 147
A broken, engraved bâton from Kesslerloch near Thayngen, Switzerland, depicting a reindeer bull in its foraging or battling position with a wound mark in its shoulder. Upper Magdalenian.

Fig. 148
Detail. Photograph of the rounded double mark representing the shoulder wound on the Kesslerloch bâton with the line of the engraved dart pointing down towards the wound.

Fig. 149
Line rendition of the engraved composition on a piece of stone from the site of Péchialet (Dordogne) depicting two dance-like human figures around a standing bear, as determined by microscopic analysis. Upper Perigordian.

Fig. 150 a

Fig. 150 b

Fig. 150 a, b, c
Three engraved and painted sorcerers from Les Trois Frères (Ariège) wearing animal masks and skins (after Breuil). Each is partly nude and in a dance-like attitude. Traditional interpretation of last sorcerer as playing a pipe seems doubtful since it would have to be held by both hands.

hunting a standing bear (Fig. 149). The corrected rendition, based on microscopic analysis, changes the illustration that has till now appeared in the literature, a change just enough to be significant, since it removes what seemed a "phallus" from one of the men. That it is not a hunt in the ordinary sense is indicated by the fact that no weapon is illustrated, no wound appears on the bear. In "hunting magic" intended to secure success in a coming hunt, juxtaposition of the animal and the weapon or an indication of the wound are usually the significant productive elements. The hunter, psychologically, is often the dispensable element. Now, the killing of a bear at close quarters would require long, sharpened poles for stabbing and wounding or darts for hurling. They are the easiest of all representations, but they are not shown. Is this the image, then, of a ceremonial dance or of the ceremonial baiting of a bear? The presence of bear myths, ceremonies, and rites, almost always seasonal or periodic, from Scandinavia through Asia and into America in historic times, is enlightening.

It is interesting that of the many human figures found with animals in Upper Paleolithic art none have weapons in hand, whereas many do have ceremonial and symbolic dress or objects. It is only later, after the Upper Paleolithic is ended, when the ice is gone and the culture changes, that we get images of hunters at the chase with weapon in hand, and even here we cannot be sure that the hunt is not ceremonial and that the animals hunted and represented are not symbolic of seasonal rites. The Upper Paleolithic image is usually of a man naked, or robed in animal skins, often with body and hand attitudes that seem to stress the ritual, ceremonial nature of the relation.

In Les Trois Frères one sorcerer wears antlers, is barefooted, and has his genitals exposed; another wears a bison mask, carries bison hooves before him, seems also barefoot, and has his genitals exposed; a third also wears a bison mask and has his genitals exposed. The attitude of all three is dancelike, much like the attitude of the masked sorcerers on the bâton from the Abri Mège. These do not seem to be winter dances but, if they are winter dances, they were apparently not performed in the open and may have been limited to closed warm sanctuaries. The relation of the sorcerers to the engraved and painted animals around them on the cave walls seems to be mimed, danced, storied, and ceremonial (Fig. 150 a,b,c). The Les Trois Frères sorcerers seem to be involved in rite that is "sexual" only because they are naked and their sexual organs are exposed; occasionally, an image in such a composition is ithyphallic, that is, rendered with penis erect. Ethnology and anthropology abound in examples of ceremonies performed in semi-nudity without any overt sexual symbolism. We cannot, therefore, assume a "fertility rite," since a ceremony and story can be "masculine" without fertility connotation, and since a ceremony can generally be sufficiently excitable to cause erection; when this occurred it might be interpreted as a visible sign of masculine power and virility without fertility connotation. We must be careful, then, in judging such images of nudity, for we see in them what we consider to be sexual in terms of our repertoire of images and habits, our ethical and moral values concerning nakedness, and our knowledge concerning insemination and conception. The fact to be noted, however, is that the images do not show man either as a killer or a procreator. This does not mean that he was not a hunter and killer, for he was, or that he did not kill ceremonially, or that he did not have some storied explanation of the masculine role in procreation. It means only that simple explanations of the images and the ceremonies are inadequate, that questions must now be asked at a new level.

Though there are no human figures with weapons in hand shown hunting the animals, there are images that seem to illustrate hunting or killing. There is one crudely drawn Magdalenian image from Laugerie Basse in the Dordogne of a man reaching for a fish (Fig. 151). The original illustration in the scientific literature depicts a man with a round head seemingly reaching for a large fish with what seem to be a number of simple darts in

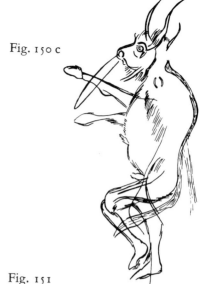

Fig. 150 c

Fig. 151
Engraved fragment of bone from Laugerie Basse (Dordogne) with the images of a huge fish, two humanoids

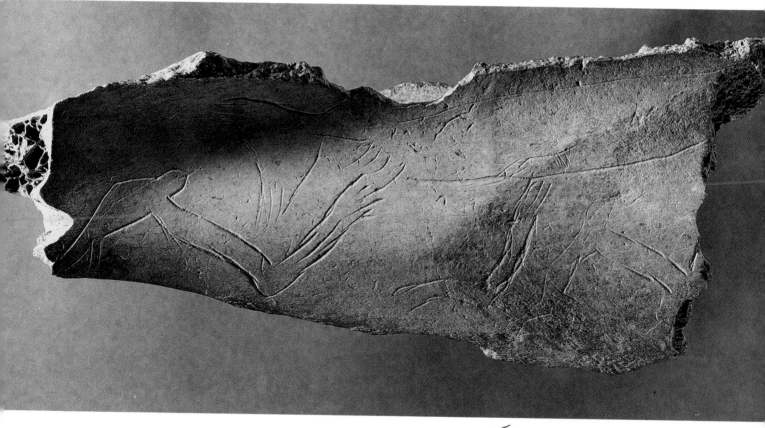

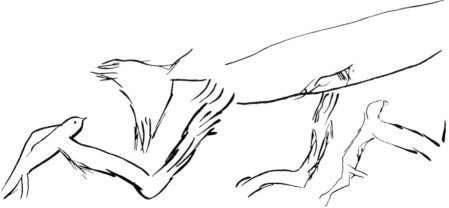

with upraised arms and one lone arm raised toward the fish. Upper Magdalenian.

Fig. 152
Line rendition of all engraved lines on the bone from Laugerie Basse indicating the bird-like heads on the humanoid figures, the absence of any weapons and the engraving of the pectoral fin, as determined by microscopic analysis.

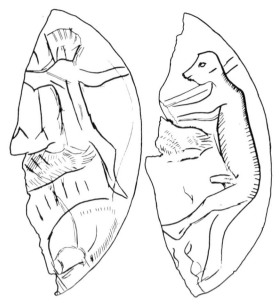

Fig. 153 a, b
Line rendition of both faces of broken, engraved bone disc or plaque from Mas d'Azil (Ariège) depicting on one face a masked dancer before the paw of a bear and on the other a naked dancer with a pole on his shoulder apparently baiting a bear. On face one, the subsidiary, associated figure is the head of a horse in reverse at right below. On face two, there is a plant-like figure, perhaps a flower.

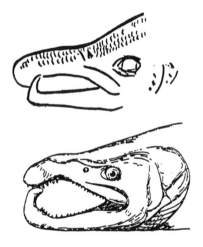

its side. The microscope, however, reveals that the "wound" is more complex than was illustrated. Instead of being an image of dart heads (a) ⋏⋏⋏ it is actually a complex figure (b). It may, therefore, represent the pectoral or dorsal fin of the salmon, which would fall at this point to the right of the anal fin in the lower quadrant and somewhat above the lower body line. The full image of the man and fish as reconstructed recalls a gesture of adoration more than the gesture of killing in a hunt, particularly since there are *two* additional arms added to the composition, each perhaps made at a later date and by a different point, but no added weapon. The fish is above the man, as would be proper for an object in adoration but awkward for a fish in water. Heightening this ceremonial possibility, the microscope also reveals that *both* men have beaked bird heads, a mask or sign we shall find again in mythologized compositions, but that would be meaningless in ordinary fishing. The corrected rendition in line is presented in Figure 152.

A broken roundelle or plaque from Mas d'Azil is engraved on two faces with human figures in dancelike stances before the paws of a standing bear. The microscope indicates changes in the traditional rendition which are of significance. One of the men is naked and the other is robed and masked (Fig. 153 a, b). On the side containing the masked dancer, below the bear's paw, upside down and in reverse, there is the finely engraved head of a horse (the image looks fishlike when not turned around). On the other face the naked "dog-faced" dancer carries what seems to be a pole on his shoulder held in two outstretched arms. The attitude of the man and the manner of carrying the pole in two hands indicates its use in dance ceremony or baiting rather than as a spear in the hunt, an interpretation strengthened by the attitude of the masked dancer on the reverse face. Before the naked man is a small, clearly engraved, curved "Y" sign and at his feet a serpentine figure that looks like a blossom.

The plaque comes from the near Pyrenean region that has given us seasonal compositions and evidence of a bear ceremony in a cave. We seem to have here two aspects of the bear rite, ceremony, or myth, with associated symbols and signs, including the horse, related to the bear story.

We are, therefore, faced with a dilemma. We have evidence of "killings" depicted in the art, of darts and spears within the animals, but these killings are not always, apparently, for food. When we do have food animals such as reindeer, horse, bison, aurochs, or fish illustrated, they are often depicted with a symbol or are themselves used as symbols; only occasionally are they killed or wounded. We have evidence of non-food animals such as the lion and the bear (perhaps a seasonal food) "killed" ceremonially or ritually and perhaps in fact. We have evidence of ceremonies with food animals, such as bison, horse, and reindeer, but these are not always depicted in terms of killing even though "killed parts" of the animals are involved. We have seasonal compositions without indication of rite or killing, but which imply a storied relation between the animals, birds, and plants. We have finally the evidence of a time-factored notation related to the animals and symbols and, by our analysis, also to the moon and perhaps to other phenomena of the sky.

The dilemma is neither unexpected nor insoluble. It is due to the complexity inherent and always present in *Homo sapiens'* use of art, symbol, rite, and story. It is the same complexity we find today in human culture, primitive or advanced, and it was already at a modern level in the Ice Age. Art and symbol are products that visualize and objectify aspects of a culture, and no one image in human art is ever entirely explicable in terms of that representation and the limited meaning of that one image. Nevertheless, out of the complexity of Upper Paleolithic art and notation certain tendencies do seem to emerge, the culture does seem to be becoming increasingly whole and understandable.

Let us look at a Late Magdalenian composition that combines these insights and findings. From the Late Magdalenian site of La Vache, which has given us a body of crucial seasonal images, there comes a long, thin, fragile bone that was apparently a ceremonial or ritual object, since it shows no marks of use. It is engraved around the circle of the bone, for it is too narrow to supply separate faces. I present a schematic rendition of the full, unrolled composition (Fig. 154).

Note

La Vache (Ariège), the foothills of the Pyrenees. The head of a seal and part of the upside down head of a lion engraved on a fragment of bone. Seals may have followed salmon halfway into France during their spawning run and have been hunted by lions on the river shores. The association of seal and lion may therefore be seasonal as well as mythological. The reversed positions of the heads may indicate that they were species from different realms.

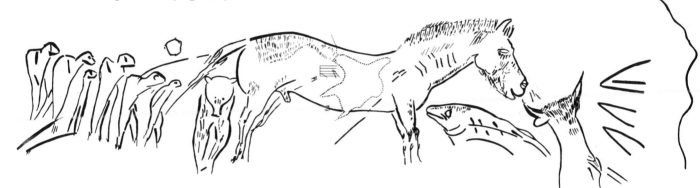

The engraving shows six generalized human figures following a magnificently drawn stallion, the central and major figure. The stallion has a thick muzzle, a phallus, and a normally arced stomach. There is a spear line entering from below and two exit marks from the nose, possibly of blood. The six humans, with heads bent forward and in quiet stride, seem reverential rather than aggressive, similar to the previous engravings of human groups (Raymonden, Les Eyzies). One or two of the figures are so small as to be possible youths. The second figure to the left of the horse has a phallus line that indicates the group may be naked.

An engraved line over their heads separates the first two humans from a circle that stands like a sun or full moon above the group.

It would seem that these form the primary composition, for the other images are smaller and are squeezed at odd angles into the remaining space around the horse. Under the tail of the horse is a bear standing front face. Since the bone is exceedingly narrow, though he appears under the horse's tail in the flat rendition, he may have been intended as the image on the reverse side in the round, or as the image above the horse, in which case

Fig. 154

Line rendition of the complete composition, unrolled, on an eagle bone from La Vache (Ariège), as finally determined by microscopic analysis. The primary, perhaps first engraving depicts 6 nude males, including two possible youths, following a stallion that has the wound marks of "killing" on his body, a spear shaft aimed at the wound, and blood lines coming from his nose. The horse contains an extremely faint geometric figure, comparable to those painted in Lascaux. Above the horse is the full moon or sun. A bear, a fish and a sacrificed or wounded bovine are later additions. Three angles may represent water. The men walk in tiny angles that may be grass. The dotted area is a missing piece of bone. Final Magdalenian.

275

he would stand with the disc on the line of separation. Before the horse is a fish, and the head of a wounded bovine seen from the rear. At the far right are three angles that at first look decorative but in other contexts have been found to imply "water."

The composition seems to contain an Upper Paleolithic pantheon, relating a primary animal, perhaps sacrificial, to a sky body and to three subsidiary animals from different realms, a horned and hooved creature, a fish, and a clawed omnivore, the bear. A number of "signs" seem to indicate spear, wound, blood, and symbolic water. The relation of the human group to these images does not seem to be aggressive, despite the possible killing of the horse and the bleeding bovine.

The bone was unavailable for microscopic analysis and had only just been published by Roman Robert when I was writing the chapter so it was not possible to determine if the images were accumulated or made at one time.[21] Despite this, the composition does seem to present the image of a seasonal, time-factored ceremony and myth involving man with a pantheon of creatures and symbols and involving him also in a number of ritual activities, from killing and ceremonial gathering to engraving the representation of diverse classes of symbol.

The art, symbols, and notations, therefore, imply a structure, continuity, and periodicity in the economic and cultural life of the Upper Paleolithic hunter. But the evidence, less directly, also implies specializations in the use of art and symbol: in terms of a child's stories and play; an adult's stories and rituals; a shaman's performance and role; the seasonal rites of a sex group, age group, tribal or kin group, with rites perhaps for the unexpected event. The evidence also indicates a variability and range in artistic expression: the animals vary, the combinations and juxtapositions vary, the seasonal behavior and significance of the animals involved vary, the contents of the caves vary, the masks vary, the bâtons and their stories vary. The quality of the art also varies: from superb, schooled, almost "professional" renderings, to quick, local and crude efforts, from objects intended to last to those intended for single use. Styles and techniques of notation also vary: locally, temporally, and in terms of individual skill. The notation in any period ranges from the comparatively sophisticated and evolved to the simplest, though an overall development can be traced and followed.

Art, symbol, rite, and notation operated within a culture that for some 25,000 years had a certain basic homogeneity, a hunting way of life with a lore and mythology based on that way of life. For us the important thing is the combined evidence for an evolved, modern, cognitive and symbolic capacity found in the earliest levels to the last. Though traditional categories such as magic and myth, aggression, symbolism, and sexuality are elements in the stories, the whole might more aptly, if awk-

---

[21] Louis-René Nougier and Romain Robert, "Scène d'Initiation de la Grotte de la Vache à Alliat (Ariège)," BULLETIN DE LA SOCIÉTÉ DE L'ARIÈGE, Tome XXIII (1968), pp. 13–98.

wardly, be called a "cognitive-and-time-factored use of art, myth, rite, and symbol."

The most famous and perhaps the most dramatic of the compositions containing the image of man and animal in juxtaposition occurs at Lascaux. It dates somewhere between the end of the Aurignacian-Perigordian, some 20,000 years ago, to the early Magdalenian of about 15,000 B.C. (Fig. 155).

In her book, *Lascaux*, Annette Laming-Emperaire writes: "... at the ... end of the Main Gallery ... the most amazing scene in the entire cave is painted ... At first sight [the] Chamber seems to be one of the least impressive parts of the cave ... the walls are marked and scored in all directions [and] difficult to decipher ... the ... walls have a patina; worn and smoothed by time and friction, they bear witness to the constant use and frequentation of this part of the cave. At the far end of [this] Chamber, ... a stone, highly polished, worn, and much blackened by the constant passage of countless human bodies, forms a kind of lip over a yawning pit ... [the] vault above is engraved with various animal figures, latticed signs ... in several colours, long bands of short parallel strokes, and clusters of diverging lines ...

"At the bottom of this shaft, which is about 16 ft deep, and must once have had to be negotiated by means of a rope, there is a small irregular chamber ... There is very little decoration on the walls. On the right-hand there is a painting of a small black horse's head ... [but] all attention is focused on the painted panel about 6 ft 6 in. in length ... at the base of the Shaft. The central figure is a bird-

Fig. 155
The painted composition in the "Well" of the cave of Lascaux (Dordogne). It depicts a naked bird-headed man with an erect phallus lying or falling before a wounded bison with its entrails spilling. There is a spear in the bison, a bird on a stick and an oddly branched form. The rhinoceros at left has six black dots near it. The composition contains diverse classes of image and symbol, each of which carries a different aspect of the meaning. Middle Upper Paleolithic.

The bird-headed man and the disembow-eled bison are among the most debated images of the Ice Age. The South African ethnographer, D. Lewis-Williams, has suggested that the composition not only depicts a shamanic trance but that a large portion of Ice Age imagery, including the notations (Fig. 15) and geometric patterns (Fig. 34), and even the other images in Lascaux, were either seen in, or were derived from, trance.

I have suggested that it is possible that the composition represents a shaman in trance, but that there is no proof. The disemboweled bison, like other images of "killed" animals in the Ice Age, suggests a ritual, symbolic "killing" as much as a killing seen in trance. The evidence for ritual, symbolic killing, often in a seasonal context, is abundant (Figs. 153, 154). The scene may as easily illustrate the killing of a mytho-logical bison by a mythological ancestor. The killing of certain animals in rituals of initiation, curing, crisis, renewal, and seasonal aggregation, are well known. The image may, therefore, be commem-orative or reportorial.

The bird poses an intriguing problem. It is often the spirit helper of a shaman. But it is as often a creature involved in myths of the seasonal return of life in the spring, or a seminal character in story and myth. Myths, of course, contain their own powerful images of transfor-mation and killing. Such myths and their narrative killings and transforma-tions are not derived from trance, but from the nature of the mythic process itself. Once a myth has been created it can appear as part of a trance and be incorporated into a shaman's repertoire of image and story.

I have therefore left the interpretation or origin of the scene open, as an aspect of the inherent variability and potentiality found in human culture. The effort to see Ice Age imagery in terms of trance, or in terms of any other single explana-tion, does not take account of the ex-traordinary complexity of the reference that one can find in an image or the variety that one finds in the composi-tions.

There is another problem. The tendency to use ethnographic analogy or suppos-

headed man drawn in black outline and very stiff in contrast with the supple lines of the other figures in the cave. The body is a mere rectangle with a black stroke indicating the phallus. Each arm is represented by a single stroke ending in a four-fingered hand, and the legs and feet, which are merely bent extensions of the legs, are not rendered in any detail. At the man's side lies a hooked stick; in front of him the schematized figure of a bird, likewise outlined in black, with a head precisely similar to his own, is perched on a pole which ends in a few short black vertical strokes.

"The man appears to be falling backwards. In front of him a bison ... in a some-what unusual style ... turns its head, probably the better to threaten him with its horns. [Or perhaps to see its own wound?] It is painted in black outline ... The interior of the body is brown, but it has not been painted—the artist has cunningly placed his bison where the clay is of a darker colour ... The animal is shown thrashing the air with its tail, which is stiffly and clumsily rendered. It is badly wounded, and its entrails are hanging from its body in large black loops. A long spear, probably the Bird-Headed Man's, is shown lying across its body over the wound.

"To the left of the Man a rhinoceros with two horns—the only rhinoceros in the cave—is shown moving away from the scene. This figure is lightly modelled in black, and in style is therefore closer to the paintings in the Great Hall of the Bulls and the Painted Gallery than to the Bird-Headed Man or the wounded bison. If in fact it is part of the scene, it does not seem to have been painted by the same hand; nor is the technique similar ... The painting is clearly incomplete, for the outlines of the belly, chest, and foreleg have been merely sketched in black line and never filled in. Under the upraised tail there are six black dots of doubtful significance, and slightly below them some black marks which may be traces of the imprint of a hand."[22]

Mme Laming-Emperaire interprets this composition:

"the bird-headed man appears to be dead or wounded ... The Palaeolithic human figures bear little resemblance to masked hunters. At [the caves of] Cougnac and Pech-Merle they are little creatures with heads vaguely reminiscent of a bird's, and their bodies are pierced with darts ... It is difficult to understand how the bird-headed man and the bird perched on a stake at his feet ... could further success of the hunt ... it seems more likely that [they] represent mythical beings who were perhaps connected in some way with the history of the ancestors of the group."[23]

She also writes that

"it is generally agreed that the hooked stick painted at the feet of the bird-headed man is a spear-thrower, the two short transverse lines at the opposite end to the hook being the butt."[24]

Leroi-Gourhan, on the other hand, declares that the bird on the stick, the hooked stick, the barbed spear, and the six dots near the rhinoceros are "masculine" and that the ovals under the bison are "feminine" and com-plementary to the spear, while the bison and the horse head opposite are somehow "sexually" related.

[22] A. Laming, LASCAUX, pp. 93–96.

[23] Ibid., pp. 191–192.

[24] Ibid., pp. 193–194.

The fact is that the hooked stick does not look like the spear throwers of the Upper Paleolithic that have actually been excavated. These have a small notch to catch hold of the spear at one end but contain no encumbrances along the face that would hold the spear, even at the other end, for this would make its use difficult or impossible. The "masculinity" of the objects depicted can be assumed only if one assumes that the ovals of the disemboweled bison are feminine and that the relation of the spear to the ovals is that of male and female. There is nothing, of course, to indicate such a "sexual" interpretation. Perhaps the "stick" was a plant image.

I begin the analysis in a different way. The polish on the sides and walls of the stones of the upper chamber indicates a frequent use of the passage. The complexity and number of the signs and engravings in the vault above the shaft indicate that this use was symbolic and storied. The presence of the rhinoceros at the bottom of the shaft, the one clear rhinoceros in the cave, indicates that it was neither used in hunting nor fertility magic, for in these cases the use of the rhinoceros as an art animal would probably have been more frequent and accessible. It would seem then that it was storied, specialized, and a character in myth or ceremony, whether it was made at the same time as the bird-headed man and the bison or not. In some way also it lent some aspect of story and myth to the shaft.

The bird-headed man poses another problem. We have already seen the use of a bird-headed man in what may be a fish ceremony. We have also seen birds depicted as signs of the season in association with animals. The bird image, like the ibex image, then, is not simple. The bird was apparently variously symbolized and storied, with different stories for water birds, tree birds, night birds, and birds of prey, winter birds and summer birds, and ritual or symbol birds. The fact that birds flew in the sky, came and went with the seasons or at different times of the day, flew to and from unknown realms, would have been part of the recognition and story. These are broad assumptions based on the cognitive ability of the hunter who was also the artist and on the observations available to him. These observations and stories would not be cognitively or generally different from those concerning the run of salmon, the presence of the seal, the dropping and regrowth of antlers, the fighting of horned animals in mating season, the pregnancy of females and the birth of the young, the leafing and dying of the plants, and even death itself. The *precise* meanings and uses, however, of bird bone, bird feathers, and bird symbolism and story would have been different.

One need not turn to primitive groups living today for knowledge of such specialized stories. For the Upper Paleolithic was early, and stories change, evolve, combine and abstract, particularly as ways of life change and as cultures meet and mix. Instead we must argue from the evidence and the ancient living reality, from the limits and possibilities available, and from the cognitions possible. Clearly the bird had a value and story of its own. It was specialized in habitat and habit, and these elements of the bird story or process were its "character," its explanation, and its "power." Its comings and goings could only be storied at this stage, and the bird was,

edly scientific explanations of some aspect of human behavior to explain the behavior of another period and culture is seductive and often false. The San bushman of South Africa, who practice trance and once made rock art related to their trance performances, never developed a culture as varied or as complex as that of the European Ice Age. They did not have as rich an iconography of the female (see Chap. XIII), they did not develop elaborate burials or manufacture as elaborate and complex forms of personal decoration. They did not develop comparable networks for the exchange and trade of symbolic resources and artifacts. They did not, therefore, reach a stage or level of cultural complexity, with the necessary symbolization of that complexity, that occurred in Europe during the Ice Age.

If we are to discuss the human capacity for cultural variability we cannot explain the symbolic products of one culture by the symbolic products of another culture separated by history, geography, level of development, and time. Precisely the same images and products can be used for different and contrary purposes. "Killing" can be used with the rationale of renewing or preserving life, but it can also be used with the rationale of destroying or ending evil and threat. Essentially the same image can be read differently in different cultures, and sometimes can be read into the same image in the same culture. We, as interpretors at a distance must therefore face the product as an expression of that potential variability, and seek the range of that variability, not the proof of a small hypothesis.

therefore, probably a sign and symbol not only of the season but more generally of an equation that recognized flight, disappearance, and return. The equation is simple, but hundreds of variations on this theme have been collected from the mythology and folklore of historic peoples. Since every story has a number of characters, the bird story in the Upper Paleolithic must have been told *in terms of other characters,* whether animals, spirits, gods of sky, plant, season, place, or in terms of the shaman who performed in a storied and ceremonial relation to all. In such assumed story, the bird would almost always play a subsidiary or specialized role.

If we now turn to the images in the shaft at Lascaux, we can ask a number of questions. Since every shamanistic performance or trance is, in a sense, also a story—the story of an event, a search, a journey, a hunt, a trickery, an escape, a fight, a miracle—the bird as a subsidiary or specialized character able to fly and return and associated with the shaman would have a certain storied validity. Was this bird on a stick, then, the image of the shamanistic spirit, or did the bird carry or lead the spirit of the shaman on a journey? Was it a messenger of the four-fingered "bird-god" in some seasonal myth related to the bison? Or did the bird-headed man wear a mask to indicate his bird aspect in this part of the story? Was this the image of a journey to a far land—say to the land of spirits or the land of death—which required a journey or return in bird shape or with bird help? Or was it a story in which the mythological bison was killed by the shaman with the help of the bird or in his trance shape as a bird? Is this the image of a seasonal sacrifice or periodic rite? The possibilities, as you can see, are vast, and it is probable that none of those I have mentioned is the truth. But as with the notations, the details of the story are unimportant. It is the generalized use of the symbol and of the storied equation, in tradition and in time, that is significant.

It is also important that we recognize in the culture—and in the one composition—the presence of combined realistic, symbolic, and mythological elements. The same Ice Age culture used the living, the symbolic, and the mythological bison and bird. In this example, the realistic images of the bison, the spear, and the disgorged intestines are probably mythical and storied just as much as the symbolic bird, the symbolic bird-man, and the hooked stick. As examples of story equation and symbol use, these are not much different from the storied use of animal antlers, masks, and robes before painted or engraved animal images or live animals.

Within this context we do not have to rely on such categories of story as "magic," "animism," or "totemism" to begin to understand the cognitive processes involved. Instead we can begin with an analysis of those basic psychological equations and strategies which use symbols and symbolic relations to indicate story and process and which always make the participant, artist, dancer, viewer, or dreamer a part of the story.

Though in the Upper Paleolithic explanations were by story and via image and symbol, there was a high intelligence, cognition, rationality, knowledge, and technical skill involved. Only the combination could cohere the early *Homo sapiens* complexity of economic, psychological, and social life.

CHAPTER XIII

SEX AND THE GODDESS

For some 25,000 years, from the earliest levels of the Aurignacian to the end of the Magdalenian and from France, Spain, and Italy through Germany, Austria, Czechoslovakia, the Ukraine, and as far east as Lake Baikal in Siberia, images of the human female have been found in the same Upper Paleolithic layers as the tools and with the engraved bones and stones containing sequences of marks, animal figures, signs, and symbols. These female images, like the notations and tools, were the products of different races or subraces and of people with different languages, stories, and specialized economies.

Since their discovery in the nineteenth century, these female images have been universally lumped together as "fertility symbols" associated with "increase magic" of man or beast, or more generally as images of the "goddess," the so-called Upper Paleolithic "Venus." In most cases, the

Fig. 155 a, b
Crude stone pendant of steatite with a pregnant female on one face and a flat, non-pregnant female on the other. Grimaldi, Italy, c. 26,000 B.C. (Marshack 1986, 1991).

Note
After writing these pages, I found the pendant on page 282 at the Peabody Museum, Harvard University. It seemed to validate many of the suggestions and questions found in this book. Depiction of the states of pregnancy and non-pregnancy indicates that these were differentiated and probably separately explained, mythologized and ritualized aspects of the feminine.

If the pendant was worn by a woman it may have been to ensure fertility and to reduce the hazards of pregnancy and birth. It is interesting that the bulging stomach is polished from handling. Differentiation of these states is significant since I have argued that female imagery in the Ice Age represented different aspects or categories of "the feminine" and that there were different classes of female imagery, each of which had its own range of meanings and uses.

images are naked or represent naked portions of the female anatomy. Occasionally they are associated in a single composition with sequences of marks, or with animals, symbols, or decorations.

The traditional interpretations have been based, first, on what the eye can see, for the female figures are often pregnant. They are also based on what is known from the history of religion and from a study of historic primitive peoples who often have a goddess who is mother of the creatures, or mother of the earth, sky, or waters, or mother of the tribe or gods, an ancient mother who may also be an intervening spirit in pregnancy and birth.

Except for such comparisons with goddesses or images of historic times, there has been no profound or careful analysis of the figures themselves, except in terms of their style, shape, or anatomy. There was no technique for any other form of analysis and no way to interpret the figures in terms of new data or concepts related to the complex Upper Paleolithic cultures. We now have a number of techniques, insights, and clues to make the beginnings of such an analysis possible.

We have seen that, though the Upper Paleolithic hunter killed for food, the act of killing and the animal itself were often storied. We know that this hunter made sharp and careful observations of the periodic and characteristic behavior of the animals and that he had a sense of the interrelation of phenomena. Aspects of his stories and knowledge appear in his art. We therefore assume that this brain, operating in this developed culture, would exhibit the same levels of cognition and comparison, the same storied equations, and the same efforts at coherence and unification by story and of participation in story in relation to the primary processes and functions of woman—including maturation, menstruation, copulation, pregnancy, birth, and lactation. Apart from these specialized processes, we might assume that the more generalized aspect of woman as "mother" would be involved.

If this is so, then the traditional theories concerning "fertility magic" would seem to be an oversimplification, much as theories of "hunting magic" were. But there are other theories as well, based on the anthropological and ethnographical studies of primitive peoples, theories that deal with sexuality in terms of the initiation ordeal that girls and boys often go through at puberty to enter adulthood, the taboos of menstruation or birth, the uses of sympathetic magic and idols for success in pregnancy, or of sacrifice and prayer in relation to these processes.

It is not necessary to begin our analysis of the Ice Age female figurines with these theories or findings, for each of these cultural expressions is merely a specialized, storied aspect of a human recognition of sequence and process—one in which a girl matures, develops breasts, develops pubic hairs, menstruates for the first time, and then sequentially or periodically changes her "personality" or "character," becomes accessible for mating, becomes pregnant but does not always deliver successfully, lactates or gives milk, cares for the infant, and eventually grows old.

If we accept the validity of that level of cognition, culture, and use of symbol apparent in the notations and art, we can assume that the equally meaningful time-factored processes and sequences related to women would also be storied and symbolized and that females would be prepared for these processes and would be given explanations at each stage. We would also assume a specialization in which there would be one set of stories for the child, one for the developing and one for the mature female, and a completely different set for the male, whose personality, role, sexual development, and processes are different. We would assume that unification or coherence of these separate sexual sequences would be attempted by story and storied interrelations among the age groups and sexes. The evidence from history and living primitive peoples presents us with an immense range of possibilities for such storied relations and equations. But they always exist, and they always serve to structure the cultural repetitions and sequences of the human biological and psychological context.

When we look at the female images, therefore, we are faced with a host of questions. Which *aspect* of the female process or myth is being depicted, symbolized, or given story? Is it the menstrual, the pubertal, the copulative, the pregnant, or the milk-giving? Is it a specialized or a general aspect of the myth and story? Is it the general image of the mother "goddess," the ancestress of the tribe? Or is it the female aspect which is related to birth and rebirth in all life and nature and, therefore, to a "female property"? Is it related to biological or seasonal cycles? Is the image related to the lunar cycle via the story of birth, death, and rebirth and by comparisons between the lunar and menstrual cycles? Was the image made to be used once for a specialized purpose and as one aspect of the wider myth, or was it a long-range image? The possibilities are large.

Now, processes, sequences, and periodicities of female, sky, and season were surely recognized. As we have seen, they could be explained and unified, compared and related *only by story* and, in story, only by the use of images, symbols, rites, ceremonies, and words, and by the use of anthropomorphized or humanized "characters," who had names and attributes and who are the necessary parts of any story. This is one conceptual key for an understanding of the Ice Age female image. It is based on our findings with the notations and art. The other will be an analysis of the female images themselves.

Let me repeat, for the concepts are crucial: every process recognized and used in human culture becomes a story, and every story is an event which includes characters (whether spirit, god, hero, person, "mana," or, in modern terms, element, particle, force, or law) who change or do things in time. Without knowing the story, we can assume that the reality of sexual maturation, function, and interrelation, male and female, was storied. Since every story can potentially end in a number of ways, efforts would be made to participate in the story, and, therefore, to change or influence the story or process or to become meaningfully a part of it. When such acts become traditional, we can sometimes call them "magic" or "religious." The specific content of these storied efforts would vary

Fig. 156. Page 284.
Sculpted, highly polished coal pendant from Petersfels, south Germany, depicting a stylized, abstracted female form whose primary features are the large buttocks and slightly bent knees. Upper Magdalenian.

Fig. 157 a, b. Page 285.
Side and front view of a crudely, quickly carved female figurine of coal from Petersfels, Germany, with the protruding stomach of pregnancy, an arced back and the absence of buttocks. The head, breasts and two legs are carved. The figurine lacks the polish of handling and may have had a short-term use. Upper Magdalenian.

culture to culture. But the cognitive, symbolizing processes would not change, and the basic nature of the storied equation would remain. Let us now look at the examples.

From a Magdalenian reindeer-hunter site at Petersfels in southwest Germany near Switzerland, not many miles from the Alpine glacial ice, there come a dozen tiny feminine figures sculpted in black coal. Petersfels is a tiny, family-sized cave and overhang that fronted a few feet from the icy stream which once flowed in a narrow valley from the glacial ice. There were probably other caves and shelters along the stream. Petersfels itself seems to have been big enough only for a "nuclear family." The tiny figurines each have a hole and may have been part of a necklace, or they may have been worn individually as pendants or amulets. They are prototype images of similar female images in bone and stone found to the north in Czechoslovakia, to the east in Russia, and to the south in Italy, France, and Spain. The basic form of this image is found from the Aurignacian into the Neolithic.

The most famous of these coal figurines is the largest, 1¾ inches high, a pendant with a hole through the top (Fig. 156). Others in the set are a third the size, and it seems incredible that they were carved by a stone knife while the bit of coal was held at finger tip. The figurine has been presented in the archaeological literature most often by a line drawing, perhaps because of the difficulties in adequately photographing so tiny a black object. It has not often been examined, even by those writing about it, because it lies in a small local collection. The early photographs and line renditions tell us nothing about the figurine but its shape.

The microscope reveals that the figurine is highly polished, not by carving or scraping but from handling or wear, while the hole indicates the signs of long use. The figurine, then, was intended to be a long-term image worn on a string, its general meaning extending across seasons and across diverse activities.

The image is as abstract as any in modern or primitive art. Though clearly feminine, it has eliminated vulva, breasts, stomach, head, hands, and feet. It stresses primarily the rear and a somewhat squatting, bent-knee posture, an attitude some archaeologists have termed the "buttocks silhouette."

This image has been much theorized. From the same site and level there was excavated another, equally tiny female figure made of black coal (Fig. 157 a, b). It represents an entirely different concept and image. It is a crude, upright, full figure with a slight arc to the back, an angular head, two breasts, a pregnant stomach, and an engraved line to differentiate the two legs. It has no hands and no feet. The microscope reveals that it was quickly, if surely, shaped. The cutting and scraping marks of the flint knife are still visible. There is no evidence of hand polish or wear, and it has been preserved almost exactly as it was made. There is no hole, nor any place for a hole, indicating that it was not intended as a bead or pendant. It is so tiny that standing it on its point in the earth as an "idol" makes no sense, and it is too tiny to have been carried safely for any length of time; besides, the lack of hand polish or wear eliminates this possibility. It is too small, and would have been too easily swallowed, to have been a child's doll. What we seem to have, then, is a female image made quickly and crudely for *one* limited time and use, probably related to pregnancy, but whether as part of a rite hoping for pregnancy or during pregnancy hoping for safe delivery or after birth as a thanks offering, we cannot tell. Because of the small size of these objects, and because they come from the same site and level, the technique of microscopic examination enables us to make a number of time-factored assumptions. There was, in this reindeer-hunting culture, a long-range myth related to "woman" and the female processes. Within the context of this myth, certain symbolic images were made for long-term use. In addition, crudely made images representing pregnancy and intended for a specific, probably ritual use were also made as one aspect of the broader, more encompassing myth and recognition.

The concept is new and is based on a new technique of analysis, so it requires additional examples for confirmation.

From Petersfels comes an unusual "bâton" of reindeer antler, a crude female silhouette indicating the head, buttocks, and the jutting belly of pregnancy. The figure is slightly arced as in the previous pregnancy figure (Fig. 158). On one side two engraved circles indicate the breasts, front face. On the other side there is a pit dug out by strong strokes with a stone knife. A light linear engraving may be symbolic. Around the edge of the bâton a single line was engraved as though to "contain" or "circumscribe" the image. The "bâton" is 6½ inches high (16½ cm), and the handle is about 3 inches high. It was not meant to be stuck in a hole or to be stood on end. It was intended to be held, but the grip is so small it seems to have been used by a woman. The microscope reveals that the scraping and cutting marks are still "fresh," showing no wear, polish, or deterioration. We have another female image, like the pregnant coal image, made quickly and crudely for some specific, limited ritual or ceremonial use related to pregnancy. The meaning of the encircling line, the pit, the engraved symbolic lines, and the details of the rite or ceremony in which the bâton was used cannot be known. But that this was a time-factored object, different in intent and use from the long-term pendant or bead, is clear.

These three Magdalenian figurines from one site raise questions similar to those that were raised in connection with the images of animals, the large bâtons, the pendants, and the discs.

One of the earliest figurines comes from an Aurignacian level at La Ferrassie in the Dordogne, near Les Eyzies (Fig. 159 a, b). It is approximately 32,000 years old, roughly contemporaneous with the animal art of Vogelherd and the notations of the Abri Blanchard. Below this level lay the artifacts of Neanderthal man, with evidence of ceremonial burials that contained symbolic and "storied" objects.

◀ Fig. 158. Page opposite.
One face of a bâton of reindeer antler from Petersfels, Germany, in the shape of a pregnant female in profile. The bâton has an arced body. The breasts are seen front face. The handle lacks the polish of usage and the bâton may have been made for a single ritual use. An engraved line seems to cut down the size of the buttocks. Upper Magdalenian.

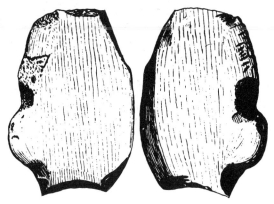

Fig. 159 a, b
Line rendition of a crude female figurine carved of reindeer antler from La Ferrassie (Dordogne) with series of engraved marks (after Peyrony). Aurignacian.

Fig. 160 a, b
Drawing of a broken mammoth ivory female figurine from Brassempouy (Landes), southwest France, with an engraved series of marks on its body (after Piette). Aurignacian.

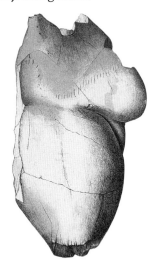

Fig. 161 a–d.   ▶
Four sides of a mammoth ivory figurine or bâton from Dolní Věstonice (Moravia) consisting of a pair of breasts and a somewhat arced back. Each side contains marks that are engraved in groups or sets. East Gravettian or Pavlovian.

The figurine, carved from reindeer antler, represents a small, perhaps pregnant, torso. It is without breasts, head, feet, or hands, but is marked by a series of small notches.[1] We cannot tell what the marks signify; they are, however, neither so placed and organized as to be decorative, nor sufficiently structured to be tattoo marks. We assume, therefore, that they are "storied" and somehow notational or symbolic, and represent one of the forms of intentional marking used by man before writing. They may be counting-marks of months or menstrual periods, or marks of "magic" or "ritual" made as prayer or offering in a storied participation in the desire for a successful pregnancy. The precise interpretation is unimportant. What is important is that the image—which might seem simply "female" or "goddess"—was *used* in some time-factored, storied way.

Apparently from a later Aurignacian level there comes a broken but beautifully sculpted ivory figurine. It was found by Edouard Piette at Brassempouy in the foothills of the Pyrenees in the late nineteenth century (Fig. 160 a, b).[2] The figurine is not obviously pregnant, but it depicts full mature breasts. Along the side of one breast and around the nipple are marks that do not seem to represent beads or costuming. Perhaps they are decorative or represent tattoo marks; if so, they are a form of symbolic marking. Since they are intentional, I assume they are somehow storied. Since the figure does not seem to be pregnant, perhaps they are related to lactation or to some more general story related to the female form.

There is no certainty as to the meaning of such figurines or markings, but we have begun to ask a certain sort of question, and we can begin the accumulation of data.

From the Aurignacian of Austria there comes the famous soft stone image of the "Venus" of Willendorf, a fat, abundant, faceless female in a crown of matronly waves or curls, with two stick arms and hands resting on enormous bosoms. Uniformly fat, but apparently not pregnant, she seems a generalized mother image. The statue was not marked, but it had been painted with red ocher, a symbolic and storied gesture comparable perhaps to marking. The red apparently signified, somewhat broadly, the blood color of life and vitality and, while it is conceptually different from linear marking, it represents but another aspect of storied participation in the broader myth.

These isolated female images from scattered sites must be compared cross-culturally, unlike the Petersfels examples that came from one level and site. Let us, therefore, look again at examples that come from a uniform cultural context.

From the East Gravettian (Pavlovian) culture of Czechoslovakia there come extremely varied female images which, because of their diversity, may help us in interpreting their possible meanings.

[1] Denis Peyrony, "La Ferrassie," PRÉHISTOIRE, III (1934), pp. 1–92, Fig. 50, p. 51.

[2] E. Piette, "La Station de Brassempouy et les statuettes humaines de la période glyptique," L'ANTHROPOLOGIE, VI (1895), pp. 129–151.

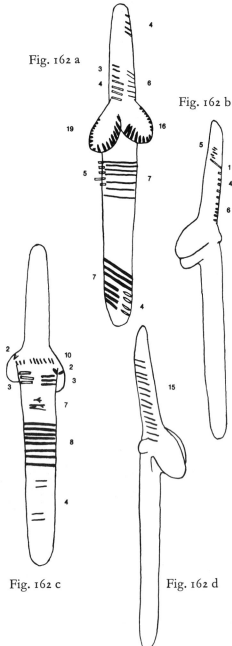

Fig. 162 a

Fig. 162 b

Fig. 162 c

Fig. 162 d

Fig. 162 a, b, c, d
Schematic rendition of all the engraved marks on the four sides of the Dolní Věstonice figurine indicating the division into sets or groups of marks engraved by different points, as determined by microscopic analysis.

A beautiful small ivory rod from Dolní Věstonice has two sculpted breasts (Fig. 161 a, b, c, d). The head is a long, empty, faceless neck and the body is an extension of the rod, slightly arced and curved backwards as in the Petersfels examples. The breasts have been notched along their edges and the rod is marked by series of lines. Karel Absolon, who found the piece in 1937, wrote in the manner of the time:

"Sex and hunger were the two motives which influenced the entire mental life of the mammoth hunters and their productive art[3] ... This statuette shows us that the artist has neglected all that did not interest him, stressing his sexual libido only where the breasts are concerned—a diluvial [Ice Age or pre-flood] plastic pornography. ... The whole body is decorated geometrically with horizontal and slanting lines of a significance unknown to us ..."[4]

Absolon assumed that this was an "erotic image" intended for male gratification.

The microscope reveals that both breasts were marked uniformly with a single point and that they were probably, therefore, "decorated" at one time. Whether decorative or notational, the marks apparently had some storied intent concerning the breasts, the dominant feature depicted. The other marks are more clearly notational. The microscope reveals that 17 or 18 different points were used to structure a number of separate groups or counts. A breakdown of these marks schematically indicating the tool differences and counts is presented in Figure 162 a–d. The markings are part of the East Gravettian tradition of notation, an example of which we saw earlier. Whether these refer to biologic periods, have ritual reference, are part of a storied tradition of decoration, or are related to the lunar tradition of notation, one cannot tell from a single example. It is not difficult, however, to make a test of the markings against a lunar model, reading in sequential order from one face to the other and going from top to bottom. Additional evidence establishing the presence of symbolic notation related to the human figure comes from a crudely sculpted piece of ivory, similar to images found in Russia and France, with only the head roughly indicated. This "human" figure was found at Pavlov, not far from Dolní Věstonice (Fig. 163). There are two rows of markings made by three points, enclosed and separated by long verticals along the side. The breakdown gives us a perfect "one month," going from day of invisibility to first crescent to full moon and again to first crescent:

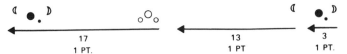

It is not only the possibility of a notation that is important in these examples but the fact that in one, all elements of the female figure and process

[3] K. Absolon, "'Modernist' Moravian Art 30,000 Years Ago," ILLUSTRATED LONDON NEWS (March 25, 1939), p. 469.

[4] K. Absolon, "The Diluvial Anthropomorphic Statuettes and Drawings, Especially the So-called Venus Statuettes, Discovered in Moravia," ARTIBUS ASIAE, XII, 3 (1949), p. 208.

have been eliminated except the breasts, a starkly abstracted image, carefully made, presenting the breast aspect of the "mother"—without the vulval or pregnancy aspect. The other is abstracted even further, so generalized and crude that the human shape is barely implied, yet it was carefully and precisely marked. Though both may be notated, there is no evidence that it was for the same aspect of the myth.

From Dolní Věstonice the breast aspect of the female is again represented by a series of eight beads in ascending sizes, the smallest less than a half inch across. Each is a pendant with a hole bored into a horizontal ridge carved on the back. Each is the image of two breasts with a headless, faceless neck, recalling the two breasts on a rod. I present an enlargement of the center piece, which is decorated on the front and has marks on the back (Fig. 164).

Necklaces or pendants with the double-breast image, worn singly or in series, come not only from the Upper Paleolithic but from periods after the ice had melted, when the economy and culture had changed; they have been found in the Mesolithic (Natufian) culture of Palestine at Mount

Fig. 163
Schematic rendition of crude anthropomorphic figure of ivory from Pavlov (Moravia) with two sets of marks engraved by three different points. East Gravettian or Pavlovian.

Fig. 164 a, b
Set of carved ivory beads from Dolní Věstonice in the form of the double breasts. East Gravettian or Pavlovian culture. The well-known central bead, when published alone has led to its description as a "phallus." However, when seen as part of the set of beads, within which the smaller beads lack the high central peak, it is clear that the beads represent the double breast image (see also Fig. 223).

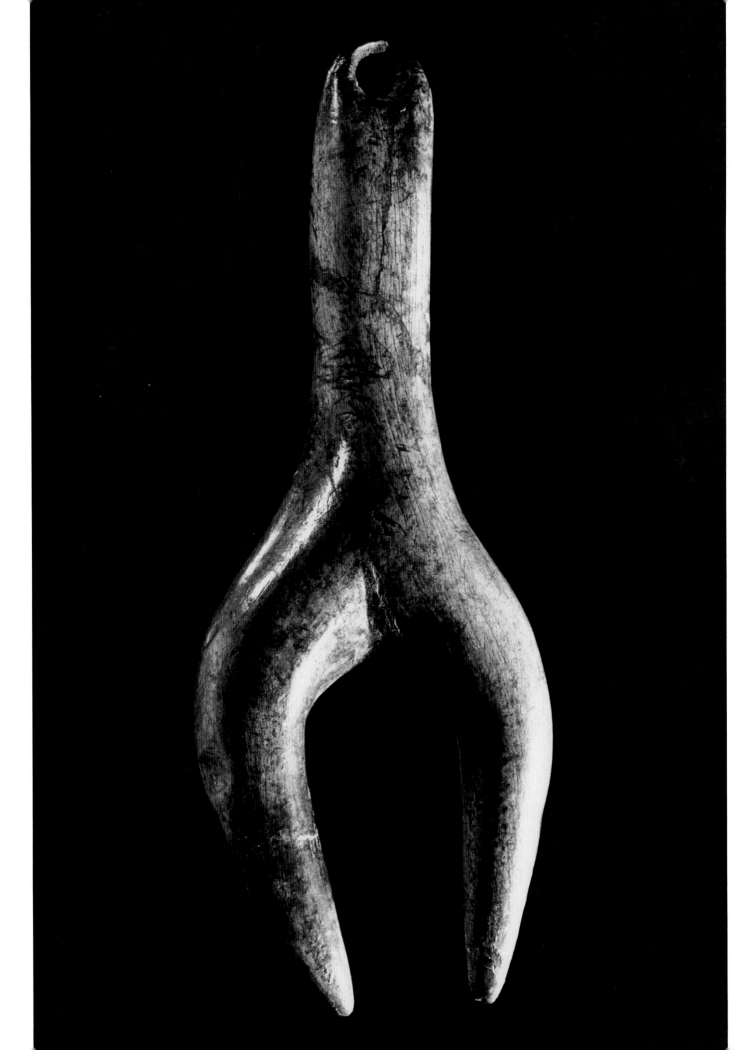

Carmel, in the cultures of the megalith builders of France and Italy, in the Eneolithic of Switzerland, and the Eneolithic tombs of the early Cycladic culture of the Aegean Islands, which predates classical Greece.[5]

It would seem that these breast images were both used and worn, not by the male hunter for erotic purposes, but by women, or else by a shaman or ritual person performing for women, helping them to participate in the story whose symbol was the flowing breast, a process whose power and effect came with maturity and fullness, a fullness that is clearly depicted in the ivory images. This is not the large-bellied pregnancy image, nor a menstrual or copulative image and, while we can assume that all these processes were storied within the unified myth and lore relating to women, the breast aspect could be separated from the whole as a distinct image with a separate story. We might conjecture that it was not worn by men, or by girls before menstruation, or by women before pregnancy, but we cannot be sure. Whatever its meaning, it was specialized.

From Dolní Věstonice there comes another female form (Fig. 165). It seems to be a fork, but has a hole indicating its use as a pendant. The image is without breasts, without stomach, and is not pregnant. All elements relating to these processes are missing. But in the highly polished figure there is one area around the vulva that has been differentiated and marked by a single stroke. Without full breasts, hips, or layers of fat, it seems almost the image of a girl or young woman or an aspect of young womanhood. The image and the intent seem to be entirely different from those in the breast figures, yet both belong to the one culture and time.

Reminiscent of this forked image is a later, Magdalenian image also with a hole, whose fork contains a quite realistic sculpted vulva, the truncated legs apart. In this case, the headless, elongated neck is the bâton handle (Fig. 166 a, b, c). The image is as stark and abstracted, despite its realism, as the images of breasts from Czechoslovakia. The microscope reveals that this bâton is marked by an extremely fine series of sequential marks made by different points and rhythms, marks which may be notational or otherwise storied (Fig. 167 a, b). The piece comes from Le Placard, which has given us Magdalenian notations, some of which were related to a lunar count. Could these, then, be notations related to menstruation or pregnancy, or to a rite related to one or the other?

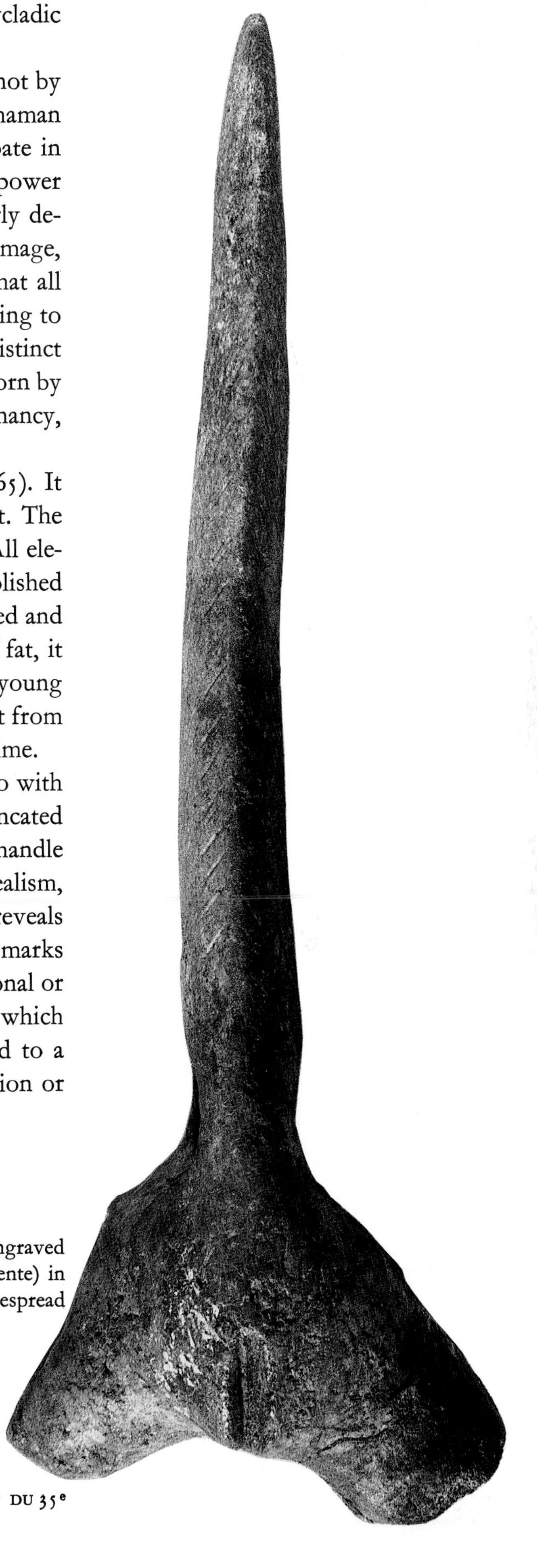

◀ Fig. 165.
A mammoth ivory pendant from Dolní Věstonice in the shape of a highly abstracted female form. All physical details have been eliminated except for the widespread abstracted legs and a vulva line. East Gravettian or Pavlovian.

Fig. 166 a
Front view of a carved and engraved bâton from Le Placard (Charente) in the form of a vulva with widespread legs. Middle Magdalenian.

Figs. 166 b, c ; 167 a, b.
Pages following.

[5] Marc R. Sauter, "Essai sur l'histoire de la perle à ailette," TIRAGE À PART DU 35ᵉ ANNUAIRE DE LA SOCIÉTÉ SUISSE DE PRÉHISTOIRE (1944), pp. 118–124.

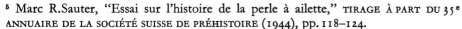

Fig. 166 b

Whatever the interpretation, the forked image, like the double-breast image, served as a sign or symbol of some specialized aspect of the female process and story.

Turning back to Czechoslovakia, we find even more abstract images of the vulva, small coin-like discs of stone and bone that have a single radial

Fig. 166 c

line from the center to the edge. I present one of these discs, 1³/₈ inches in diameter (35 mm), carved from a mammoth's tooth. It is somewhat worn, but the enlargement reveals the remnants of a carefully made, fine decorative notching or marking around the edge (Fig. 168 a, b). The disc and marks are too small for these to be notation. It is, therefore, a decorated piece, and one assumes that the "unbalanced" radial mark is intended to be part of the image and design.

How the image was used and to what aspect of the story it belonged, we do not know, but it seems to be a specialized image. The tiny discs were found in the grave of a man that also contained the statue of a nude male and a large stone disc with a great hole at its center that has been inter-

Fig. 167 a

Fig. 167 b

Fig. 166 b. Page opposite.
Side view of vulva bâton from Le Placard indicating the engraved marks.

Fig. 166 c. Page opposite.
Detail. The abstracted vulval form on the Le Placard bâton, conceptually formed by an angle and a line.

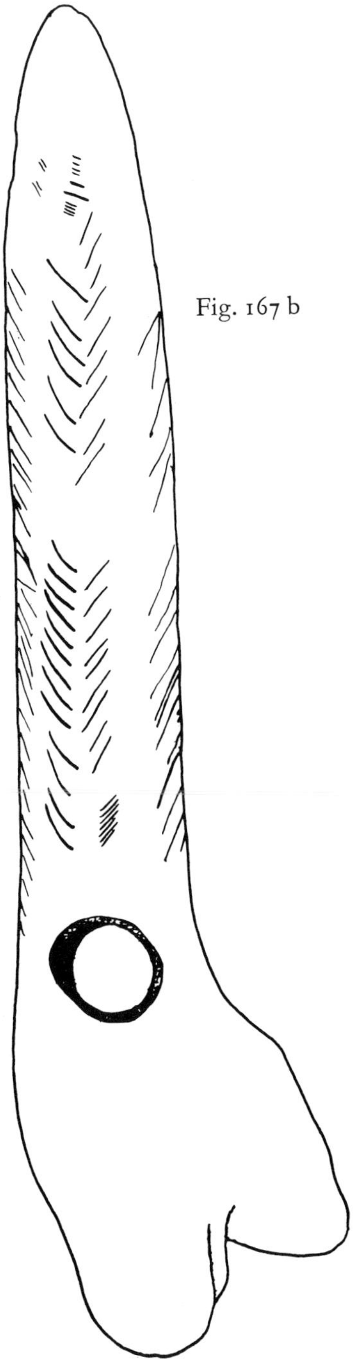

Fig. 167 a, b
Schematic rendition of all the lines on the Le Placard bâton indicating the engraving of series at diverse angles, and with strokes of different lengths and rhythms, as determined by microscopic analysis.

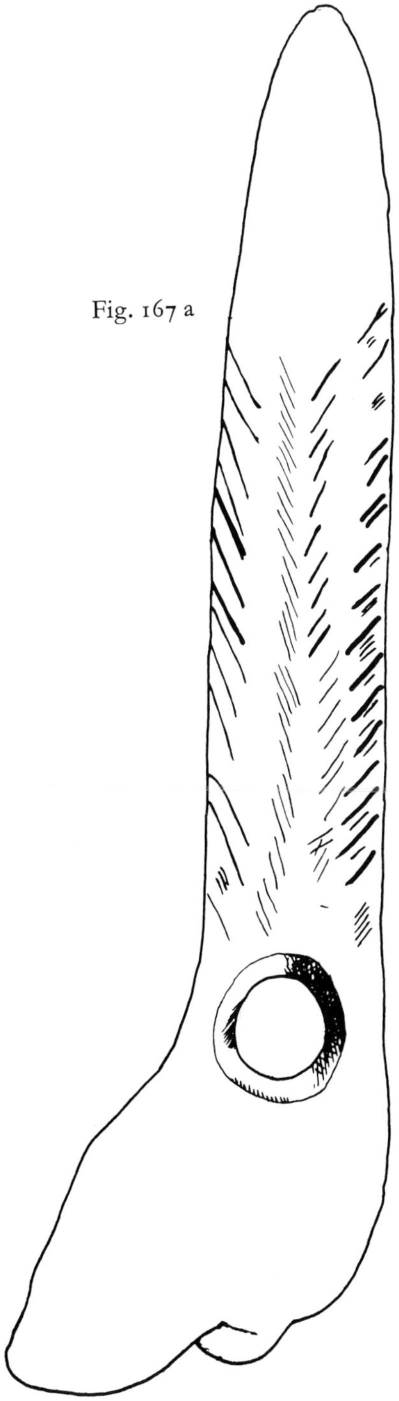

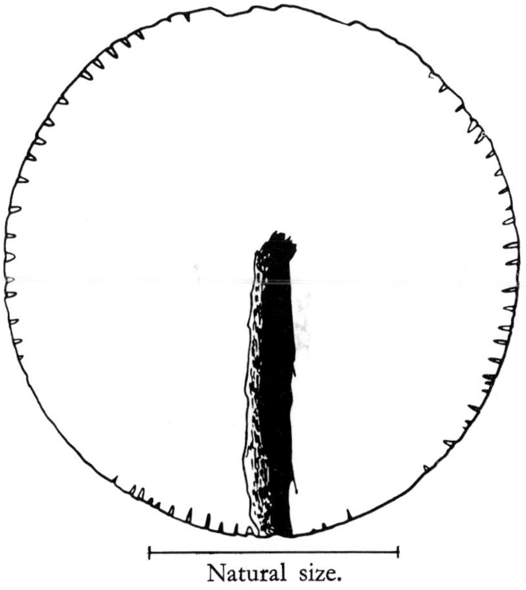

Natural size.

Fig. 168 b
Schematic rendition of the vulva disc from Brno indicating the two classes of marking, a representational line and edge decoration.

preted by some archaeologists as a "solar" or "sky" symbol. The microscope reveals that the small discs have spots of red ocher and may have been painted, or else they picked it up from the soil or by association with ocher in the burial. The presence of these discs in a male grave

Fig. 168 a. Next page.

indicates that at least part of the story or myth with which the vulva was involved extended to a relation with the male and into death, and that it, therefore, had a significance broader than mere femininity or "sexual" symbolism.[6]

The decorative edge on the disc is important for an understanding of the evolution of these symbols. As in the case of the double-breast image, the

[6]Female images of a different kind were found in the grave of an approximately eighteen year old male at Arene Candide, north Italy, and will be discussed later.

Note

Validation of the original suggestion that the vulva was a generalized symbol for renewal, periodicity, birth and rebirth came unexpectedly after this manuscript was completed. A headstone of sandstone found in the burial of a male at the German Magdalenian site of Oelknitz, c. 14,000 B.C., is incised with a single vulva, probably made for the burial. The same site produced a carved ivory figurine in the buttock/torso style of the beads from Peterfels made of coal, and the style of the hundreds of buttocks images incised on stone from the German Magdalenian site of Gönnersdorf (see comparable images in Figs. 179, 181). The beads were worn, the incised figures were ritually overmarked and accumulated at the homesite, and the vulva was placed in a burial. Gönnersdorf also provides us with the incised image of a phallus inside a vulva as well as the incised image of a buttocks image giving birth.

The variable use of female images across such a large span in time and space requires a major rethinking of our understanding of Ice Age symbol and image and of Ice Age knowledge concerning periodicity and process.

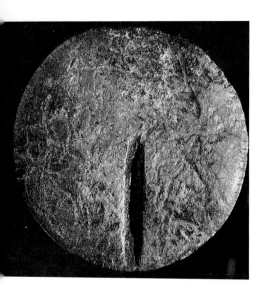

Fig. 168 a
Enlargement of a disc made from a mammoth tooth found in a grave at Brno (Moravia) representing an abstracted vulva composed of a circle and a line. There are engraved decorations around the edge. East Gravettian or Pavlovian. c. 26,000 B.C.

Fig. 168 b, c
Headstone, approx. 18 ¾ inches long (48 cm), found in male burial at Oelknitz, Germany. Magdalenian, c. 14,000 B.C. (Photos by Feustel.)

vulva had in time become isolated, abstracted, and symbolic to the point where it could be recognized in a simple circle with a single mark. One assumes, then, that the image and story were so well-known they were "understood" by every adult in the culture, that it was a traditional image

Fig. 169 a–h
Carved and engraved vulval images from the Upper Paleolithic.
a) Bodrogkeresztur, Hungary, East Gravettian; b) Laussel; c) Lalinde;

       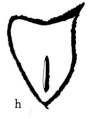

Fig. 169 a   b   c   d   e   f   g   h

d) La Ferrassie; e) La Ferrassie; f) Les Combarelles; g) Pergouset; h) La Ferrassie.

with a traditional story. This argues for use of this symbol over many generations, a use so ancient it could be decorated or embellished without loss of recognition or meaning. This is the process we indulge in today when we abstract, elaborate, and decorate the storied symbols and images of our modern religious, political, and national life. We, too, recognize the original and its story behind the abstraction, the elaboration, and the decoration. Such decoration of a traditional image is a time-factored aspect of symbol use. In the East Gravettian, from Czechoslovakia through Russia, the decoration of traditional images had itself become a tradition.

The abstracted vulva was, therefore, early, storied, and widespread. It appears in France and Spain without decoration from the Aurignacian to the Magdalenian, and with decoration further east (Fig. 169 a–h). There is also a pebble in the shape of a vulva from Polesini, Italy.

There are variations in the shapes and styles of these Upper Paleolithic vulvas: sometimes oval, sometimes triangular, sometimes realistic, sometimes decorated, sometimes alone, sometimes associated with the mother goddess or presented as a symbol and aspect of her story, sometimes in graves, sometimes associated with other symbols. These uses and variations increase our understanding of the complex, interrelated nature of the story and take it out of the realm of mere sexuality. It is not the anatomic "sexual" organ that is being symbolized, but the stories, characters, and processes with which the symbol had become associated. We shall look at other examples shortly.

To show how time and cultural change transform such basic images, I present a small double-breast pendant from the Magdalenian of Czechoslovakia (Fig. 170 a, b). It is crudely made, so abstracted and elongated that it has almost lost its resemblance to the female and her breasts. It is 12,000 years later than the double breasts of the East Gravettian mammoth hunter and was made by a reindeer-hunting culture and another people. Its general meaning, however, seems to have been similar to the earlier breasts, and is neither erotic nor pornographic. It would seem, therefore, to have been worn by someone seeking participation in the ancient story of the flowing breast, one aspect of the larger story involving the "mother."

From the East Gravettian of Czechoslovakia there come other feminine images representing other specialized aspects of the female myth and

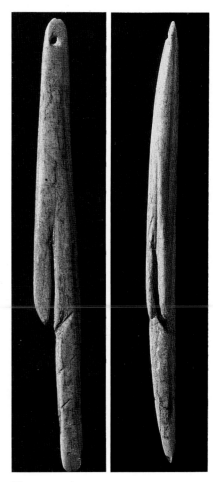

Fig. 170 a, b
Two sides of a bone pendant from Rytírská (Moravia) in the form of the double breast image. Upper Magdalenian.

Fig. 171 a, b. Pages following.
Front and rear of buxom female image of fired-clay from Dolní Věstonice (Moravia) which depicts neither pregnancy nor vulva. Hips are wide but buttocks are not protruding. East Gravettian or Pavlovian.

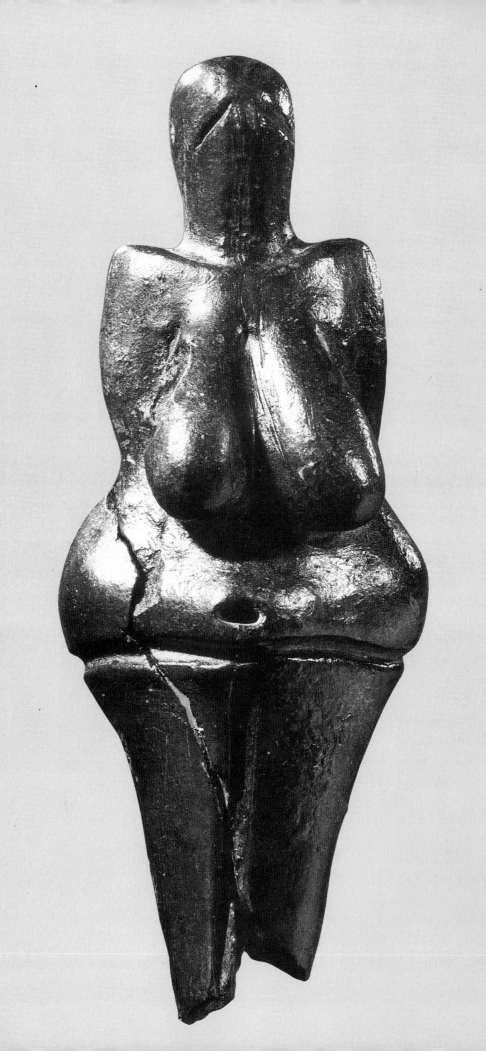

Fig. 171 c
Detail. The head of the "goddess" from Dolní Věstonice depicting an unreal schematized face with slit, mask-like eyes, a nose represented by a line drawn in the wet clay and the absence of a mouth.

Fig. 173 a, b
Torso of hematite stone from Petřkovice (Moravia) depicting the realistic body of a slightly pregnant young woman with an arced back, small breasts, narrow hips, defined vulva and the absence of protruding buttocks. The image apparently represents a different aspect of feminine myth than the clay "goddess" Fig. 171. East Gravettian or Pavlovian.

Fig. 174. Page opposite.
Small, two inch (50 mm), mammoth ivory head of a young woman from Dolní Věstonice (Moravia) with a coiffure and carved eyes, nose and mouth. East Gravettian or Pavlovian.

Fig. 172
Detail. Four holes in the top of the head of the female figurine from Dolní Věstonice, perhaps intended to hold a symbolic image of hair or growth.

story. The most dramatic are full-figure images of the so-called "mother goddess."

A small black figurine sculpted from clay and burnt bone and fired rock-hard comes from Dolní Věstonice (Fig. 171 a, b, c). It is an odd, haunting image, a "faceless" head with slit eyes, a stroke for the nose, pendulous

realistic breasts, truncated arms, upward-tilted angular shoulders and, despite the realism of the torso, a missing vulva. The combination of realism, abstraction, elimination, near-surrealism, and overemphasis indicates that we have a *traditional* image and form. The legs are broken, but other figurines in this tradition from Czechoslovakia show that the legs ended without feet in a rounded point. The image could not stand on its own and had either to lie down, be carried, or be placed upright in a hole as an idol. Most interesting is the top of the head, where four holes were made into the wet clay. It may have been that flowers, leaves, or feathers were put in the holes to serve as "hair," as Absolon suggests, which would then be symbols of the seasonal growth adhering to the goddess. The image, then, seems to represent one more aspect of the female story, not necessarily related to human pregnancy but including it perhaps in some general comprehensive aspect (Fig. 172).

Completely different from this formal, traditional, and somewhat unreal image of the "mother goddess" is an East Gravettian statuette from the site of Petřkovice, Czechoslovakia, carved from a piece of black hematite

Figs. 173 a, b; 174. Preceding pages.

Fig. 175 a, b
Front and rear of a fragmented female torso from Dolní Věstonice (Moravia) in which a slightly protruding stomach and the vulva are subtly carved and the buttocks are completely flattened. East Gravettian or Pavlovian.
Note
This crude early carving, c.26,000 B.C., has turned out to be one of the important Ice Age figurines. Not only was it ritually marked and covered with red ocher, but it was carved without head, arms or breasts. Schematization of the female torso are found in many styles throughout the Ice Age.

iron ore. It is an exquisitely fluid, if roughly carved, female image of a different sort, the realistic form of a young, pregnant woman, stomach bulging, with small, almost youthful breasts (one of which has broken off) and with the vulva region clearly carved. The same culture that made the symbols of the double breasts, the isolated vulva, and the comprehensive non-pregnant "mother goddess" made this image of a real woman in pregnancy. It is the same culture that made the quick, realistic clay images of bear and lion for the apparent ritual purposes of "killing" and the long-term image of the decorative lion. This young woman seems to be in the tradition of the quick image made for some immediate storied purpose, perhaps participation in approaching delivery or birth (Fig. 173 a, b). In this tradition of realism there comes from Dolní Věstonice a tiny ivory head, much worn with time, that gives us a delicate face with realistic eyes, mouth, and a hair-do (Fig. 174). The image is neither formal nor

Fig. 175 c
The rounded top indicates intentional carving rather than breakage. Ice Age figurines frequently have the deep cut across the belly, thighs and rear that represents a belt of twined perishable material, a mode of adornment that often marked the mature female (see Figs. 171). Perishable decorations made of hide may have been more common than beads and go back further in human culture (Marshack 1991). (Absolon photo.)

Fig. 175 a

Fig. 175 b

Fig. 176. Page opposite. ▶
Broken mammoth tusk from Předmost (Moravia) with an engraved, unrealistic, geometricized female form. East Gravettian or Pavlovian.

Fig. 177 a. Page opposite. ▶
Detail. The oval womb of the geometricized female from Předmost. The circle of the navel and part of the stomach are at top right. The chevron marks and the break in the oval around the vulval region are indicated, as are the vertical lines below that begin the legs.

traditional, and it may, therefore, have been made for some use involving a real person, living or dead. If this is so, it may have had a specific use different from the image of the pregnant young woman.

All this is conjecture, based on an analysis and comparison of the evidence, but it is conjecture within the realm of possibility for a *Homo sapiens* culture with a rich repertoire of interrelated images, symbols, and stories. In a culture using a varied system of images and symbols, it would be possible to mark, notate, and color the female figures, or handle them, or say words with them as an act of participation in the story. The meaning of such markings could vary from counts and calendric sequences to mnemonic notations, to storied and traditional decorations and patterns. The fragment of a figurine from Dolní Věstonice has on its back two groups or series of marks, each made by a different point (Fig. 175 a, b, c).

The microscope reveals it was also ochered red. Red ocher and symbolic marks both served as aspects of participation in the myth.

The most unusual female image from the East Gravettian of Czechoslovakia comes from the site of Predmost and is different from all the rest. Instead of being a simplified or abstracted image that was then decorated, it is itself a complex and geometricized decoration (Fig. 176).
Engraved on a mammoth tusk is a "human" figure, larger than any other from Czechoslovakia, with egg-shaped breasts that reach as high as the head, a circular stomach with a central navel, a horizontal oval womb, arced linear arms, and a triangular, horned head from which all realism is gone. The whole squat body looks like a face. Any element in the composition, if alone, would seem meaningless or decorative (Fig. 177 a, b).
Again, this is no erotic or pornographic image, nor does it seem to be an

Fig. 176

Fig. 177 a

image like those of the realistic young pregnant woman or the realistic coiffured head, nor is it an abstract symbol of some single aspect of the female process as was represented by the breast or vulva, nor is it, stylistically, the traditional female image of that culture, the small, hand-

sized, bountiful, realistically bosomed "mother." We might assume then that it is a representation of still another aspect of the story. The image, for instance, may have been made for use in a *group* ceremony. Perhaps it was used in a shamanistic performance and was, therefore, individualized and personalized by the shaman within the East Gravettian tradition of decoration. Perhaps it was an image of the mythical "female" beyond time and of no one place (and so without true body or face) who was either ancestress or mother of the land of death, or mother of horned animals, and who could thus be storied without any realistic attributes or form. We do not know. We know only that the range of female images and the many forms of presentation and use preclude any simple interpretations.

The sum of such images implies a time-factored, storied way of thinking. The complexity is heightened when we realize that this analysis of the East Gravettian female has not deeply or in detail related them to other symbolic and storied facets of that culture, to the animals, the sacrifices, the burial symbolism, the lunar notations, or the seasons and sky.

Whatever the spectrum of meanings in these female images of the Upper Paleolithic, the tradition of the image was carried into the Mesolithic and Neolithic cultures that followed. It was part of the intellectual, time-factored and time-factoring heritage that prepared the way for agriculture.

From the Magdalenian reindeer-hunting site of Pekarna, Czechoslovakia, there comes a small, white, ivory figurine in the tradition of the figurine in coal made by the reindeer hunters of Petersfels (Fig. 156). It is the buttocks image, beautifully abstracted. To a large extent this is the crucial image for an understanding of Upper Paleolithic feminine symbolism. It appears in so many diverse cultural contexts and in so wide a range of materials and styles that a beginning can be made in a study and comparison of its generalized and specialized meanings and uses. It can be traced in its development from early Aurignacian through the Magdalenian and into the Neolithic, where it appears in sites as widely dispersed as Rumania, Greece, and Spain (Fig. 178).

These buttocks images are sculpted and engraved, plain and decorated, sometimes symbolically marked, sometimes worn as pendants, sometimes held in the hand. They are sometimes alone, sometimes in series, sometimes associated with other symbols or with animals. Despite this diversity, they have been interpreted largely as belonging to a cult of "fertility magic" and have been compared to one another primarily because of their similarity in shape. The form is obviously significant, but terms such as "fertility magic," as we have seen, are inadequate. "Fertility magic" is one form of participation in the story and myth surrounding pregnancy and birth. But such "magic" varies in every culture, first, because fertility concepts and myths vary and develop. Pregnancy and birth, for instance, need not be "sexual" in a modern meaning of the term, that is, related biologically to impregnation and conception. But as knowledge increased, as the way of life changed, as the animals one hunted changed, the meaning of the female image would also change.

Fig. 177b. Page opposite.
Detail. The horned head of the geometricized female from Předmost. The ovaloid breasts are at each side below.

Note
Schematic drawing of the head of the female "spirit" from Předmost with the lined areas blackened to indicate the eyes, nose, mouth and horns. The intent of creating an unrealistic female "spirit" with a clearly differentiated stomach and womb may suggest that it is a mythologized and generalized metaphor of birth and renewal rather than merely a masked "human" image.

Fig. 178. Next page.
Abstracted, stylized female figurine of mammoth ivory from Pekarna (Moravia) which reproduces the large buttocks, bent knees and empty stomach of the coal pendant from Petersfels (Fig. 156). Upper Magdalenian.

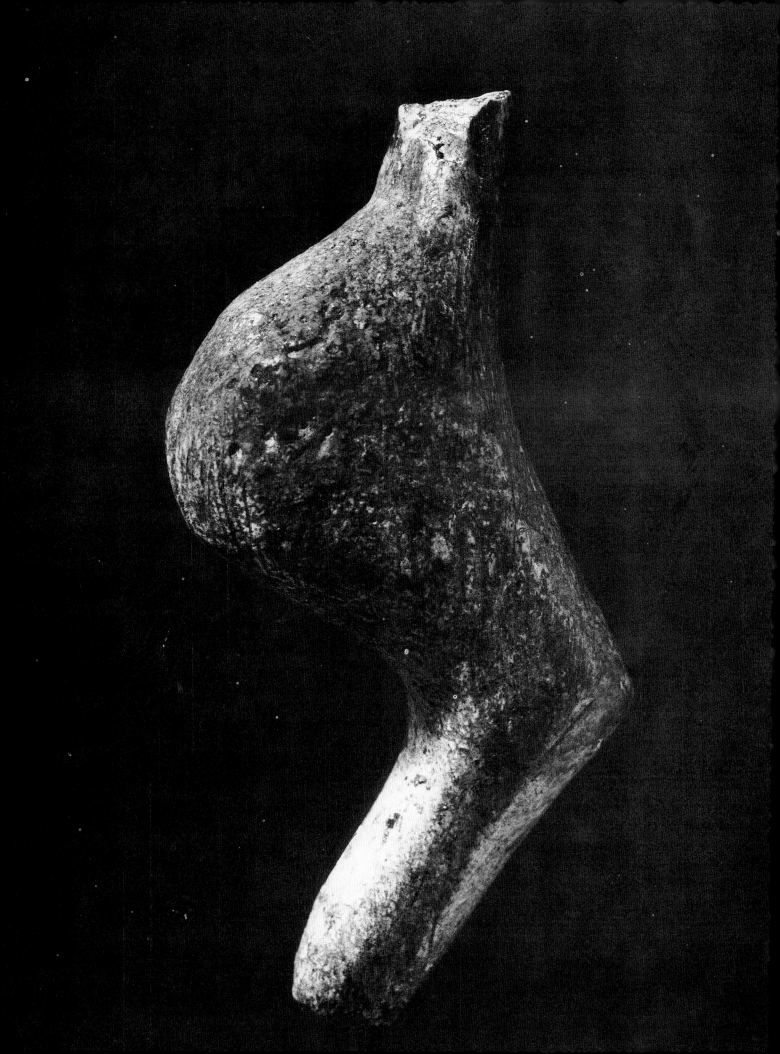

Besides, a generalized symbol such as the abstract female may entail repetitive, often periodic telling and participation. Such stories would probably have been originally based on a valid recognition of certain processes and their comparison with other processes. But in time the details of the myth would change, the processes included in the myth would change or widen, though the image might remain and though use of the image in time-factored stories might remain. Some possible uses of the female image have been discussed; still others are apparent in the Upper Paleolithic.

On the wet clay walls of the cave of Pech-Merle (Lot), south of the Dordogne, Aurignacian finger drawings of the female are found associated with mammoth and other animals of the period (Fig. 179 a, b). According to the Abbé Breuil, "The hanging position of the breasts . . . seems to be due to their crawling attitude,"[7] which apparently creates the buttocks attitude. These female figures are associated in the cave also with symbols, signs, hand prints, series of colored dots, horseshoe arcs, and serpentine meanders. The story of the female image seems to be related to the stories of these other images, and the animals, symbols, signs, and notations were, as we saw, time-factored.

Essentially the same female image, in a more evolved, abstracted form, appears on a limestone slab from the Late Magdalenian site of Fontalès, on the Aveyron, in the foothills of the Massif Central, south of Les Eyzies (Fig. 180). Twelve inches long and heavy, it was a slate that could not easily be carried about. The drawing presented here from the archaeological literature is too simple, for the actual markings are somewhat more numerous.[8] The engraving shows two female images, one with a circle within it, the head of a cervid, probably a deer, and the head of a bird, probably a goose. Each of these figures is associated with its own group of nearby markings or notations, and the impression is of a composition that contains four symbolic, accumulated, or time-factored images, and six or seven groups of associated markings.

The composition seems to relate the image and story of the female to the seasonal stories of the animals and to the tradition of symbolic marking and notation. In this sense, though thousands of years later, it is similar to the female figures at Pech-Merle and their association with animals, signs, and markings.

Other engraved, non-portable stone slabs make this time-factored aspect clearer. They come from Late Magdalenian sites in the Dordogne region of France and as far north as Hohlenstein in Germany, north of the Alps and not far from the Danube (Figs. 181, 182, 183). Each of these slabs has a number of engraved female figures of the "buttocks" form.

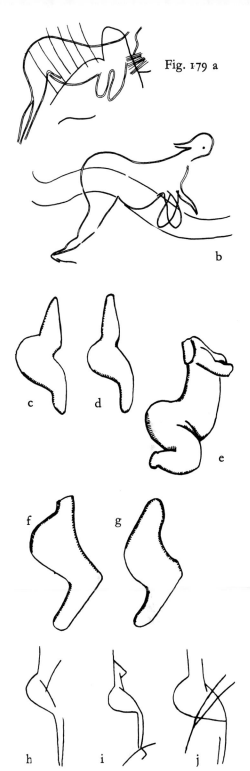

Fig. 179 a

b

c   d

e

f   g

h   i   j

Fig. 179 a–s. Above and pages following.
Line renditions of engraved and sculpted female images with the buttocks silhouette.
a, b) Pech-Merle; c, d) Petersfels; e) Sireuil; f) Pekarna; h, i, j) Hohlenstein; k, l, m, n) Lalinde; o, p) Fontalès; q) La Gare de Couze; g, r) Cucetini (Neolithic); s) Rond du Barry.

Figs. 181, 182. Pages following.
Fig. 183. Page 310.

[7] Breuil, FOUR HUNDRED CENTURIES OF CAVE ART, p. 267.

[8] Paul Darasse and Simone Guffroy, "Le Magdalénien Supérieur de l'Abri de Fontalès près Saint-Antonin," L'ANTHROPOLOGIE, Vol. 64, No. 1–2 (1960), Fig. 19, p. 31.

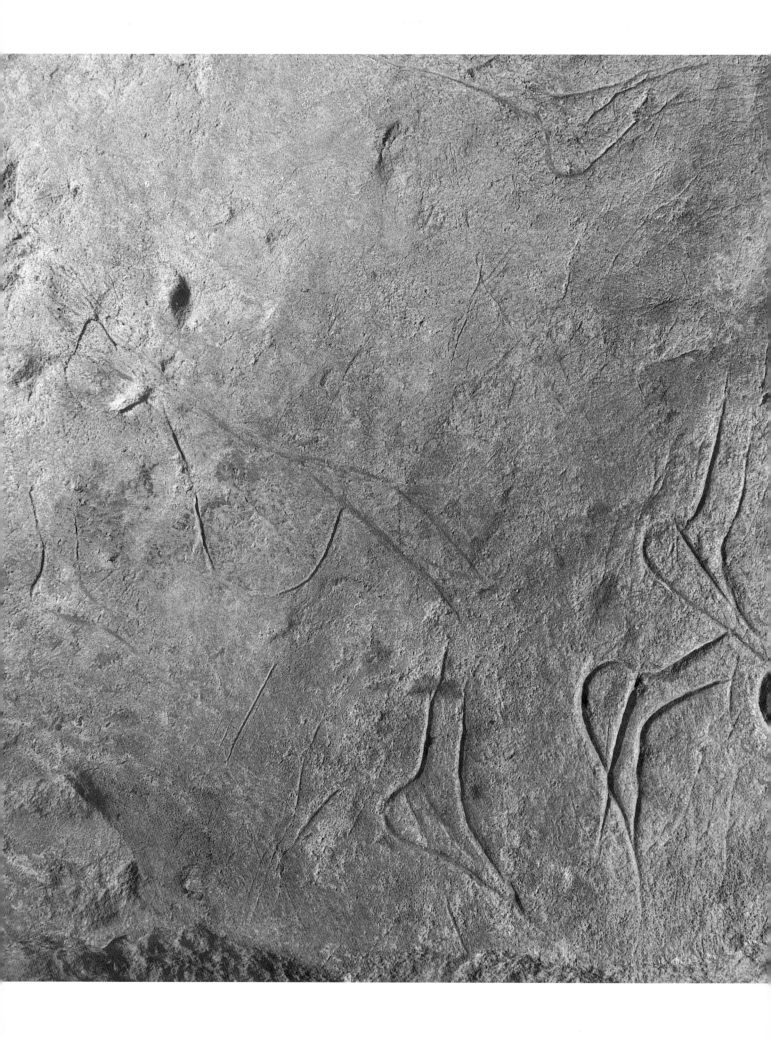

Fig. 179 k l m

n o p

q r

◄ Fig. 181
Engraved stone slab from Lalinde (Dordogne) containing an accumulation of female images with the buttocks form, each made by a different point and struck through by an engraved mark. Final Magdalenian. (Photo Alain Roussot, Musée d'Aquitaine.)

Fig. 182
Second engraved stone slab from Lalinde containing an accumulation of female images with the buttocks form, each made by a different point and struck through by an engraved mark. Final Magdalenian. (Photo Field Museum.)

s

From the comparatively realistic females of Pech-Merle, through the female abstractions of Fig. 179 to these schematic, almost calligraphic females there runs the thread of a generalized form or shape and a similar meaning. The images were both accumulated and put to persistent, continuous use.

309

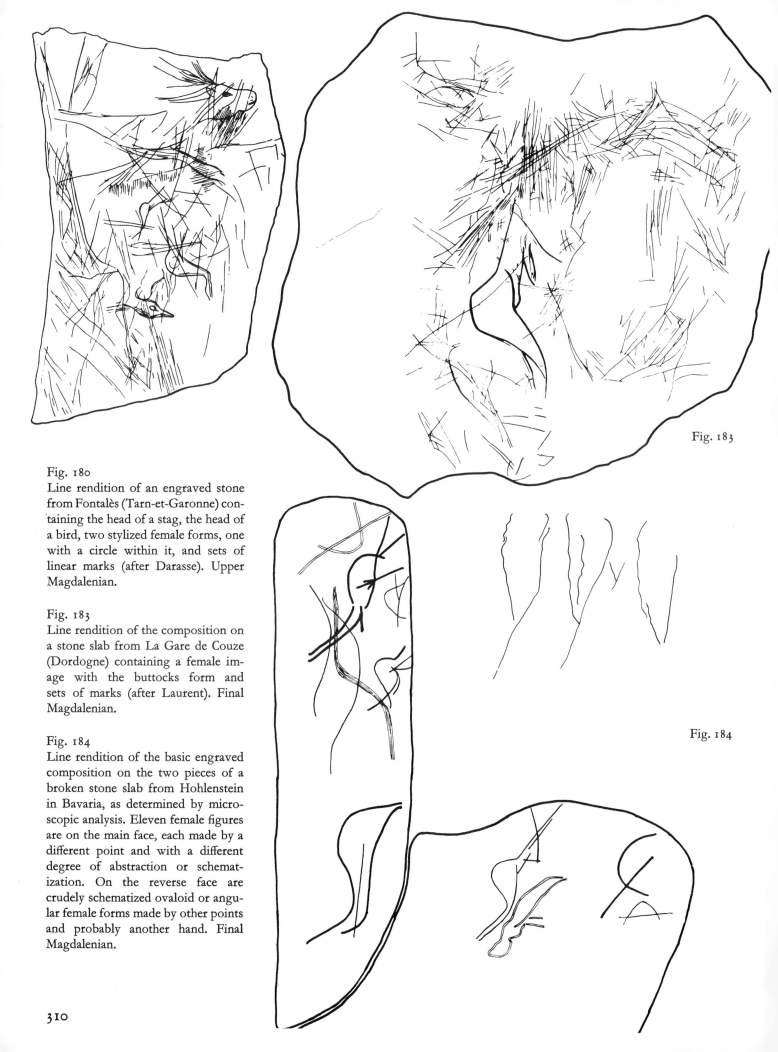

Fig. 180
Line rendition of an engraved stone from Fontalès (Tarn-et-Garonne) containing the head of a stag, the head of a bird, two stylized female forms, one with a circle within it, and sets of linear marks (after Darasse). Upper Magdalenian.

Fig. 183
Line rendition of the composition on a stone slab from La Gare de Couze (Dordogne) containing a female image with the buttocks form and sets of marks (after Laurent). Final Magdalenian.

Fig. 184
Line rendition of the basic engraved composition on the two pieces of a broken stone slab from Hohlenstein in Bavaria, as determined by microscopic analysis. Eleven female figures are on the main face, each made by a different point and with a different degree of abstraction or schematization. On the reverse face are crudely schematized ovaloid or angular female forms made by other points and probably another hand. Final Magdalenian.

Fig. 183

Fig. 184

I discuss one of these stones in detail to show the new information a microscope can give us. The Magdalenian stone from Hohlenstein, Germany, is broken, heavy, and was probably stationary in the habitation area except while being engraved. The engravings are in the style of those from France, though Hohlenstein was only a few days' walk from sites in Czechoslovakia to the north. The archaeological literature has presented the stone in line illustrations that indicate only three engraved feminine figures.[9]

The microscope, however, reveals that the main face of the slab is covered with incredibly complex overengravings as though the stone had been used over a long time, recalling the overengraving of the stones from Fontalès and the Gare de Couze. The microscope shows that, instead of three, there are at least eleven figures distinguishable on the main face, each made by a different point, each in a different style, each a different size, and each in a different stage or style of abstraction or simplification (Fig. 184).

Some of the engravings form the typical buttocks image; one has the breasts engraved (as on the stone from Gare de Couze), others are so simplified they are made by an arc and straight line, structuring an image like the so-called "P" sign. Still others form a more or less serpentine figure made by double arcs. There is also one human figure with head and arm faintly engraved. When I turned the stone over, I found three or four engraved figures on the reverse face, heavily encrusted with sand and mud. Washing the stone clarified the figures, images apparently made by another hand in a different style, but indicative again of the simplified female figure. These female images seem to include individual styles of representation as well as specialized aspects of the image. It does not seem that the person making the beautifully simple buttocks image with the breasts would have clumsily engraved the figures on the reverse face, unless they represented a different aspect of the story. Could these fourteen or fifteen figures represent months in the menstrual cycle, perhaps including pregnancy? Or are they more generalized images, representing some periodic rite or ceremony within the feminine myth?

If you turn to the forms on the other Magdalenian slabs, you will find that the figures are occasionally crossed over, or "crossed out," by added marks as though to end, change, or add to their meaning. One figure has an added circle, others are surrounded by associated groups of marks and sequences. Whatever the precise meaning of the feminine figure, some things are certain: it was made periodically and repetitively, it was a symbol that had a traditional story and use, it was engraved on stones that were not carried about and which, therefore, served as records of a sort in the habitation site. The engraved images on the Hohlenstein slab were not long-term symbols but imply a specialized, repeated short-term use.

[9] Karl J. Narr, "Die Altsteinzeitfunde aus dem Hohlenstein bei Nordlingen," BAYERISCHE VORGESCHICHTSBLÄTTER (München: 1965), p. 2.
Paul Darasse, "Dessins paléolithiques de la vallée de l'Aveyron, identiques à ceux de l'Hohlenstein en Bavière," QUARTÄR (1956), Fig. 2.

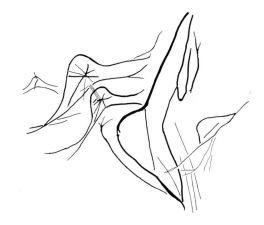

Fig. 182 a
Female images in different degrees of abstraction or schematization on the slab of limestone from Lalinde. Each is ritually struck through by lines. Two of the females have an indication of breasts, one has the line of an arm. As determined by microscopic analysis.

Fig. 185 a-j
Analysis of these ivory figurines from the late Ice Age site of Mezin (Ukraine) reveal that they were complex symbols. A schematic, armless, headless torso is engraved on the front; below is a huge vulva that was often ritually over-marked, a tradition noted on vulvas from the early Ice Age in France and

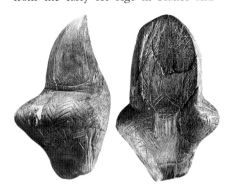

carved stone vulvas from the Russian plain. The carved shapes themselves, as abstractions of the female torso, are related to the late Ice Age "buttocks" images of West Europe. The designs on the rear, the multiple zigzag and the multiple geometric spiral or meander, according to the research of this author, may be generic abstractions of "time" and "process," derived from the seasonal water symbol and the serpentine, boustrophedon image of notation (see the late Ice Age Gontzi notation). (Marshack 1977, 1979 a, 1991 b.)

Since the short-term use was storied, implying participation in some aspect of myth, it would have been what we inadequately call a "ritual," "ceremonial," "religious," "magic," or "superstitious" act. The buttocks image appears on the cave walls associated with animals and signs, and this may imply a related, though slightly different, time-factored use.

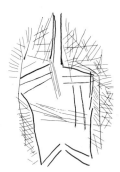

Fig. 185 k-p
Late Ice Age ivory female figurine from Mezherich (Ukraine) representing an extreme schematization of the Mezin style. The flat front has a deeply incised vulva which was renewed or reused three times by engraving triangular vulvas made by different points and pressures, above it. In the torso region is a two-armed cross which probably represents a schematization of the Mezin torso. The details presented here have not before been noted.

Once again, though we do not know the stories involved, the process is understandable. One can conjecture possible meanings in terms of the evidence available and perhaps approach a general meaning which will then be clarified as the evidence accumulates.

It is possible that the image was related to menstruation or to the cessation of menstruation and initiation of the months of pregnancy. But, though this may have been one aspect of its meaning, these images were also related in story to other processes, to the seasons, the animals, the seasonal habits of the animals, and to rites and ceremonies surrounding them. If such meanings did exist as aspects of the buttocks image, then the long-range, overall, sculpted female image, the "mother goddess" or "Venus," may have contained or cohered these and many more meanings across the year.

The problem of symbol usage is always, in this sense, time-factored. The name, the story, and the image of a god, goddess, or spirit lasts through time. But the use, renewal, and reference to the god or goddess is never constant; it is always specialized and limited. It is often partial, performed by a word, a saying, a gesture, or through a subsidiary image, a time-factored rite, or by reference to still another character in the story.

Whatever the full meaning of these female images, we know that they formed one aspect of a culture that used images, symbols, and notations for interrelated time-factored purposes.

Some of the answers may come with a better analysis of the engraved and sculpted images. Unfortunately, the granular composition of many of the stones makes microscopic analysis with present techniques difficult. It would seem that with better techniques a proper sequencing of the figures and their associated marks will be achieved.

Though this image is female and "sexual," it was neither erotic nor merely a form of "fertility magic." By story and usage it seems to be related to female processes, animals, birds, cave ceremonial and ritual, the seasons, homesite record-keeping, and the tradition of notation. There are within this tradition long-range images, short-range images, and compositions with interrelated images.

Slowly, as we proceed, the circle widens, but the meaning narrows.

The East Gravettian mammoth-hunting culture of Russia provides a different sort of evidence to help us in understanding these feminine images. The site of Mezin, on the Ukraine flatlands near a river feeding into the Dnepr that runs to the Black Sea and towards east Mediterranean Europe and the Middle East, has given us a series of small figurines that were first recognized as feminine by the Abbé Breuil (Fig. 185: 1a–9c).[10] They are unlike most western European figurines in being highly decorated. This decoration consists of chevron, angle, and meander patterns and certain

[10] After Z. A. Abramova, "Palaeolithic Art in the U.S.S.R.," ARCTIC ANTHROPOLOGY, IV–2 (1967), trans. from ARKHEOLOGIIA SSSR. SVOD ARKHEOLOGICHESKIKH ISTOCHNIKOV. Vyp. A4–3 (Moscow-Leningrad: Akademiia Nauk SSSR, 1962) by Catherine Page, ed. C.S. Chard, pp. 148–149.

Fig. 186 b

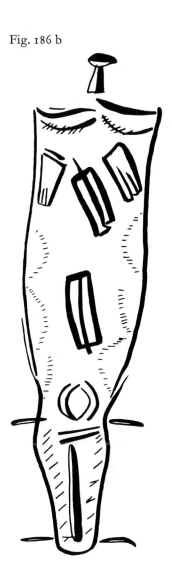

Compare this engraved image from the late French Magdalenian with the engraved schematic headless images with triangular vulvas below that appear on certain pieces from Mezin at left.

Note the body markings and the associated motifs: serpentine images on the Magdalenian piece and angle meander patterns on the eastern pieces. Note the doubled lines of the vulval triangles at left and the doubled lines of the oval on the Magdalenian figure. In one case the heads are missing, in the other there is a button head on a linear neck.

Note

The suggestions first made here were in large measure validated and expanded by microscopic analyses of these artifacts and traditions a decade later in the city of Kiev, the Ukraine.

Note

The suggestions made here have, since this book was first published, been discussed in subsequent studies and arguments concerning the place of the "goddess" in prehistory (see for example Gimbutas 1974, 1989). It has also been referred to in books attempting to argue a contemporary political and social position related to current and ancient feminine rights. The present research, however, has merely indicated that the female image in these early hunting-gathering cultures was a multivalent symbol with a wide range of uses and meanings.

standard symbols. These angular patterns had a traditional, evolved meaning in the East Gravettian culture, and they apparently remain as a motif in later Neolithic cultures, often again associated with feminine images. They were used as motifs in the ornamentation of East Gravettian bracelets and headbands and formed part of the structural style occasionally used in forming sequential notations.

These carved figurines apparently evolved from the image of the headless, long-necked female with extended rear or buttocks and flattened belly. On these images there is often engraved, in addition to the decorative patterns, the headless body of the "goddess" and a schematized vulva. Each of these three symbolic aspects of the feminine myth is drawn separately and is stylized differently. The engraved "goddess" has angular, seemingly multiple shoulders and multiple lines in the body as though to hint at the ribs, breasts, and the vulval region. Below the "goddess," on the flattened front of the figurine, there is usually a schematic, somewhat rounded, engraved triangle for the vulva. At times, the engraved "goddess" is missing and only the vulva and the linear patterns appear.

It would seem from the silhouette and form that this feminine figurine represents neither the specialized breast nor the specialized pregnancy aspect of the female story, but is somewhat more broadly mythologized. She is, in fact, quadruply stylized, not only by the inclusion of three separate feminine images (buttocks, goddess, vulva), but also by the formal decoration of the chevrons and the meanders. She, therefore, seems storied in a traditional, complex way, with specific and separate attributes, each of which belongs to the story. The total image is completely different from the more or less realistic, full-bosomed, fat, and sometimes pregnant figurines that are found in the East Gravettian and other European Upper Paleolithic cultures.

Since the tradition of the buttocks image seems to go back to the early Aurignacian and forward to the Magdalenian where it is associated with animals, notation, and evidence of a periodic telling and ceremonial, we ask whether these eastern figurines with their abstracted attributes and patterns are not also time-factored. The long-necked, long-bodied, often fiddle-shaped figurine with schematized vulva, at times surrounded or marked by chevrons, angles, meanders, or serpentine and spiral images, is found in the Neolithic and the still later agricultural cultures. These chevron, meander, and serpentine designs have been interpreted as water, sky, time, earth, and serpent images. This later agricultural goddess is also often associated with horned animals, fish, plants, and birds, and she is usually part of a lunar mythology with celebrations that are calendric and seasonal. The scholars of early agricultural lore have called her an overall earth and water goddess and "mistress of the animals." Could it be that the origins of the time-factored, multi-storied agricultural "mother goddess" appear in the Upper Paleolithic, thousands of years before agriculture? Could the time-factored lore and rites of the "goddess" be one of the cognitive, intellectual threads leading to and preparing the way for agriculture? Could these decorated images from Mezin represent this broad general aspect of the female myth? We need more examples. We know only that the "signs" on the figurines are related to each other.

Go back to the engraved Magdalenian bone from the Abri Mège, at Teyjat in the Dordogne (Fig. 57 c, p. 166), which depicts the realistic head of a fish, the tail section of a seal, and a block of notation containing three lunar months. The composition also includes a central, odd image that at first looks like the head of a pike or a moulting dogfish. Realistic images of pike and dogfish appear occasionally in Upper Paleolithic art. The microscope, however, reveals that the engraved, fishlike image is composed and decorated in an unusual, schematic, and oddly balanced way (Fig. 186 a, b).

Fig. 186 a
Detail. Photo of one of the engraved images on the bone point from the Abri Mège at Teyjat (Dordogne), Fig. 57 c, which also contains a fish, a seal's tail and a block of notation.

Fig. 186 b
Line rendition of the engraved image on the Abri Mège bone indicating that it is probably the abstracted "goddess" with a tiny head, doubled angular shoulders, doubled ovaloid vulva, a serpentine decoration perhaps representing water and symbolic geometric forms in the body. As determined by microscopic analysis.

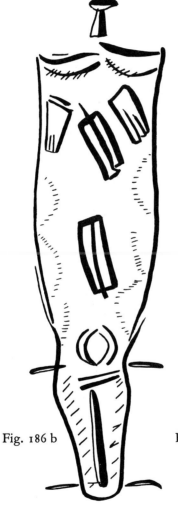

Fig. 186 b   Fig. 186 a

If you stand the image lengthwise—Upper Paleolithic artists often engraved compositions on a single face with images that were to be read sideways and lengthwise in sequence—then it looks like an evolved rendition of the earlier engraved goddess of Mezin, the Ukraine, with fiddle-shaped figure, double-lined shoulders, a circular, double-lined vulva, tapering legs without feet that look like those of the sculpted figurines, and a tiny subsidiary neck and head. Along each side there are three arcs in series made of small marks that form what seem to be serpentine or water images, similar to images we have seen associated with animals.

Within the body there are odd structures or forms. The two upper forms, placed like breasts, seem like three-fingered hands with outward-facing palms. The two larger, rectangular, central forms seem like paddles, notation boards or simplified "tectiforms," a geometric figure often found engraved or painted in the caves or on stones. The full composition has nothing fishlike in its details except for the one seeming "eye" and the seeming "mouth." The mouth, however, does not end as a mouth should but rather as do the legs of the sculpted figurines, while the circular and oval vulva is itself a motif of Magdalenian art.

I have already indicated that the creatures and plants associated with the notations on the bones, of which this is one, were seasonal and that fish and seal were images of late spring and summer and perhaps of early fall. If, as seems possible, this bone from the Abri Mège presents us with a combined image of notations, spring water creatures, and the schematized goddess, it may be that in this highly abstracted form we have another proof that she is a seasonal image related to the "rebirth" of life and to the period following the thaw and flood, the period of warmth and the return of fish, bird, and plant.

If this is so, then we must pause to ask some questions about this "goddess." Could it be that the periodic and regular female processes and their stories served as the basis for storied equations, explanations, and verifications for comparable periodic processes in nature? One does not need a philosophy of religion to see that, within the bounds of *Homo sapiens* levels of cognition and use of symbols and storied equations, there were few alternatives available for a hunting culture attempting to cohere its observations of reality. The structure of any regular, periodic phenomenon could be used to explain or incorporate any other. The story equation, by its nature, is infinitely open-ended at every point. In this way, just as the female goddess could be used in explaining and cohering stories about nature, so animals could be used as characters in stories explaining processes that were human, whether female processes of birth and pregnancy or more general processes of disease, death, dreams or trance, or even the origins of man himself.

This does not mean that observations of processes in nature were false, or that the goddess was thought of as "real," but rather that she was conceived of as an equation in story, representing and explaining what was observable and functioned. To the extent that she was a character in a story, she was "understood" in human terms; to the extent that she was a female character, her story was related to birth and to the male as a subsidiary and related character; to the extent that she was a character in a repetitive, periodic, continuing story, the group could participate regularly in her story and, through her, in a continuing "understanding" and retelling of the meaning of nature and process; to the extent that the group became part of the story in which she was a "mother," they themselves entered into the family of nature and animals; to the extent that they were part of her story and her family, they acted in terms of obedience, offering, sacrifice, prayer, and taboo—that is, in terms of relational and storied communication and participation. To the extent that she was a symbol, the symbol could be used at many points in the continuing myth. We do not need the mythological details to see that the story equation, using observations available to a hunting group, could structure such a symbolic use for the female image.

From the late Tardi-Gravettian site of Arene Candide in the Maritime Alps region of northern Italy, the grave of an approximately eighteen year old youth puts the problem in another context.[11] The youth, of the Mediterranean Combe Capelle type, was ceremonially buried with an extraordinary range of interrelated symbols, carrying the tapestry of Upper Paleolithic mythology into death and the future. The skeleton and grave, and probably the body, were heavily ochered red; under his chin there was yellow ocher. These colors may have had meaning related to life and light. On his skull was a beautiful cap of seashell beads from which hung pendants of the canine teeth of deer, whose shape is that of the buttocks image with the flattened, even concave, belly. The cap may have united sea, animal, and female myth. In one hand the skeleton grasped a long, curved stone knife, giving him a practical tool for future life. Near his upper arms were four *bâtons de commandement,* each with a hole, made from the tines of elk antler. Three of the bâtons were heavily engraved with groups of marks that, the microscope showed, were made by different points and were accumulated over a long period. The bâton holes showed the pressure wear and polish of use, probably as shaft straighteners. Here were practical and symbolic items probably used by the youth. The fourth bâton had no markings and may have been freshly made for the burial. Near the upper part of the body there lay a decorated bone pendant in the shape of the buttocks image, with a hole at the top. The microscope showed it was highly polished and was worn inside the hole from long use. The female buttocks image had been used in life, by the youth or someone else, and it was being used now in burial to extend its meaning into the afterlife. Near each knee there lay a quickly made, crudely carved bone figure shaped like an abstract "goddess" image, with a head and ovaloid body. The figures had no holes and the microscope revealed that, though deteriorated, they showed no polish of use in any area. Apparently the figurines had been made for the burial as part of the participation of the living in the myth and to strengthen the corpse's own participation. There were other symbolic items in the grave as well. Obviously the meaning of the female image in life and in death could not be explained except in terms of an encompassing story.

Much in this analysis of the Upper Paleolithic female image is conjecture, but it is conjecture that allows us to dispense with such undefinable, unmeasurable categories as "magic" and "religion," which neither adequately describe nor explain but simply classify types of behavior patterns and cultural products.

---

[11] Luigi Cardini, "Nuovi Documenti sull'Antichita dell'Uomo en Italia. Reperto Umano del Paleolitico Superiore nella i Grotta delle Arene Candide," RAZZA E CIVILITA A ANNO III, Vol. 23, No 1–4 (March–June 1942).

This goddess image, then, is not "sexual" in a modern usage of the term, since it is neither primarily copulative, pornographic, or erotic, nor surely cognizant of insemination and impregnation, though these aspects of the process may have been a growing, developing part of the story and the participation.

In this sense, the vulva, too, is to some extent a "non-sexual," that is, a non-copulative, non-erotic symbol, representing stories of processes that include birth and death, menstruation, and time-factored cycles relating to nature.

To indicate how the "non-sexual" aspect of the vulva worked, I present a juxtaposition of images explained by Leroi-Gourhan as a feminine-masculine combination, that is, a "male sign" with a "female sign" (Fig. 187). We see a number of red-painted bell-shaped vulvas associated with what we now recognize as a branch or plant form painted black. The panel comes from the early Magdalenian site of El Castillo in the northern, Cantabrique region of Atlantic Spain.

From the cave of Tuc d'Audoubert, which gave us evidence of seasonal ceremonies and stories associated with animals and fish, we get a plant form associated with a nearby vulva, traced in the wet clay (Fig. 188a, b).[12] The vulva in these cases is associated with a sign representing a time-factored, seasonal process in nature.

If our analysis of the abstracted, geometricized, evolved goddess and her attributes is correct, she represents one aspect of the seasonal myth, that aspect told in feminine terms.

We would expect that a mythology so complex would also have stories concerned with related masculine aspects. There is no mystical or pro-found reason for this conjecture; it is based on the nature of human relations, the nature of cognition, and the necessities of the storied equation. These male-female stories would include tales or rituals concerning the seasonal dramas of the male animals, such as the rutting, bellowing, and butting of the male stags and bulls and the fighting of the stallions. We would also expect that there would be some sort of masculine participation via story and rite in what might be considered the feminine seasonal drama, such as the periods of animal pregnancy, calving, and foaling. These male-female stories and rites would be structured, in the beginning, without a knowledge of biologic insemination and fertilization. Such stories, of course, would change as the role of the male in procreation became increasingly clear. The reasons for these conjectures have nothing to do with a philosophical world view which divides reality into male and female, as suggested tentatively by Leroi-Gourhan, but, as I have stressed, with the nature of cognition, the nature of the storied equation, and with normal relations within the human family and group.

Not all events or processes can be explained or easily conceived in terms of "male" or "female" characters acting in a characteristically male or

Fig. 188 a, b
Line renditions of a vulva and a plant marked separately upon the clay wall of the cave of Tuc d'Audoubert (Ariège) (after Leroi-Gourhan).

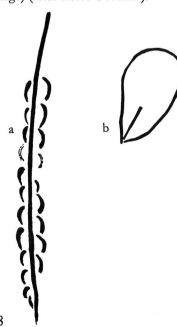

[12] After Leroi-Gourhan. TREASURES OF PREHISTORIC ART, Figs. 617 and 618, p. 454.

female way, and so we would expect that there would also be in the mythology neuter or non-sexual "spirits" or forces, phenomena, and events. Even today we conceptualize such characters or forces in our religions and fiction, our dreams and intellectual systems, whether as fate, economics, laws, disease, luck, society, history, good and evil, and so it

should not surprise us that such personalized characters would appear in earlier storytelling.

If the vulva can be used in relation to animals and plants, we would expect that other so-called "sexual" signs, male and female, could be used in comparable combinations and that these would express or symbolize other aspects of cognition, myth, or ritual. The full-belly sign of pregnancy or the phallus could be used, as the vulva was used, to symbolize a relation or process. Such symbolic combinations, though they contained "sexual signs," might, once more, be "sexual" only in a storied sense and not necessarily either in the biologic sense of a knowledge of fertilization or as an evocation of the erotic or pornographic. Since we are dealing with signs and symbols that represent attributes and processes of mytho-

Fig. 187
Painted panel in the cave of El Castillo, northwest Spain, depicting bell-shaped vulvas in red paint and a plant in black. (Photo Vertut.)

logical characters, we should also find a relation of the goddess or one of her signs to male animals such as the stag, stallion, and bull, as well as to the doe, mare, and cow or the calf, fawn, or colt. Similarly, she might be related to or conjoined with the sky, moon, sun, earth, waters, or beings like the serpent or fire.

In this storied "non-sexual" sense the phallus would be a symbol of masculine *process* before it became a symbol of impregnation; it would have been the sign of an ability that matures and declines with age, a time-factored symbol of mature virility, of power and self-creation. It would have been one aspect of the general myth with greatest relevance, perhaps, for adult, masculine members of the group. The masculine image, like the feminine image, however, would have had story and, therefore, significance for all.

Now let us look at the evidence.

One of the most puzzling and dramatic of the Upper Paleolithic compositions is a small, four inch (10 cm) bas-relief carved on a bit of reindeer bone from the Magdalenian IV level of Laugerie Basse, near Les Eyzies. The region and period have given us seasonal compositions, some with associated lunar notations, as well as images of the female with associated notations and markings. I present an enlargement of Edouard Piette's rendition (1907) (Fig. 189).[13]

Fig. 189
One face of an engraved reindeer bone from Laugerie Basse (Dordogne) depicting the hind legs and phallus of a bull apparently standing over a naked, pregnant woman lying on her back (after Piette). Other compositions that are meant to be read both horizontally and vertically suggests that the woman may be standing in prayer. Middle Magdalenian.

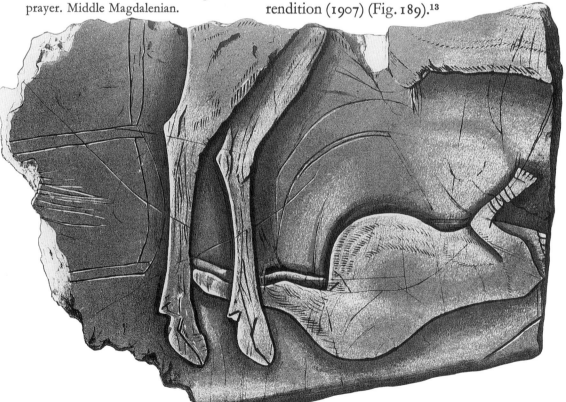

The composition shows a pregnant female seemingly lying on her back, with a male animal above her, though perhaps not directly above her. The traditional interpretation has been that the animal is a reindeer. Leroi-Gourhan, however, points out that the line of the abdomen and the place-

[13] E. Piette, L'ART PENDANT L'AGE DU RENNE (Paris: Masson et Cie, 1907).

ment of the phallus with its wick of hair resemble the bison. Reindeer or bison, the relation of the pregnant female to the male hooved and horned herd animal stands. By the nature of the drawing, the two are intended to be a single composition. The male animal was carved first and was apparently intended as the "primary" storied image. The female was carved afterwards in relation to him, her legs passing behind his. Conceptually, therefore, she is related to him, neither eliminating him nor preceding him.

This pregnant female is somewhat different from other female images we have seen. She has her hand raised as though in worship or adoration, recalling the gesture we saw earlier in relation to a huge fish above a man, from the same Magdalenian site of Laugerie Basse (Fig. 152, p. 273). In this case, clearly, since we have a pregnant female it is no hunting gesture. Is this an image, then, of a "real" woman in supplication rather than a mythological character? We saw what seemed to be a "real" woman in a pregnant state depicted in an East Gravettian sculpture and assumed it was related to a pregnancy rite, and we saw a "pregnant" bâton or wand from the Magdalenian of Petersfels and assumed the same. Is this composition, then, related to a rite of pregnancy? At the depicted late stage of the pregnancy, we do not here assume a male-female, copulative sexual relation, even mythical. Were animals related to rites of pregnancy in women, either by sacrifice or through worship, myth, or ceremony? Why is the animal male? Or does this composition depict a myth of the pregnant goddess in relation to a horned animal which may be a sky symbol? If so, does the myth have value to a woman in pregnancy? The question as to whether the female is the image of a real woman in a state of pregnancy or the goddess in myth is irrelevant since in either case we have a storied relation of pregnancy to animals. The meaning of the naked female in this composition and association is, then, storied, symbolic, and mythological. The clues as to the possible meaning are time-factored; they show a female in advanced pregnancy related by a seeming gesture of adoration to a male, horned animal. The order of drawing is animal first, woman second, then the geometric or structural forms.

From the same site and level there comes a tiny, broken, crudely carved statuette of reindeer antler, 1¾ inches high, that depicts a faceless human —much like those in the two complex Magdalenian compositions from this area which showed crudely engraved men with a bison and symbolic horse heads—bent forward as though in supplication, with arms raised as though in prayer (Fig. 190). The gesture here, too, is clearly not one of hunting or killing. The attitude, then, belongs to the culture, the area, the period.

The engraved pregnant woman on the plaque from Laugerie Basse is not decorated with signs or symbols that are aspects or attributes of the goddess or myth, as in the Mezin figurines of the East Gravettian or the geometricized image from the Abri Mège, but with jewelry, including a necklace with four beads visible and a bracelet with six bands.

The attitude of prayer, the subsidiary position of the woman in relation

Fig. 190
Figurine carved of reindeer antler from Laugerie Basse (Dordogne) depicting a human with arms raised in prayer or adoration. Middle Magdalenian.

to the animal, the stage of the pregnancy, the realistic decoration she wears, and the relation of this image to other Magdalenian images of men around animals in ceremonial attitudes or positions seem to imply that this is a "real" woman and not the goddess. If this is a representation of a pregnant woman in storied relation to a male animal, then whether it has to do with a prayer for safe delivery or is the depiction of a myth in which the goddess is also involved with the stag or bull is not really important. For the prayer by a real woman, depicted on a composition for "magical" purposes, is the telling of a mythical story in which animal and woman are related: these are acts of participation. The precise story details may be different in the myth of the goddess and the ritual of a pregnancy, yet the basic cognitive uses of story would be similar. For this reason, the storied elements in the composition may be seasonal or celestial, depicting the story of a sky god in relation to an earth goddess, and still the composition could *at the same time* represent the participation of a real pregnant woman in supplication or ceremony with a real animal. The details are not important in this early stage of interpretation. What is important is that we establish the range and potential of the uses of story and symbol, rite and art, and that we place the evidence in a frame within which analysis and comparison can begin.

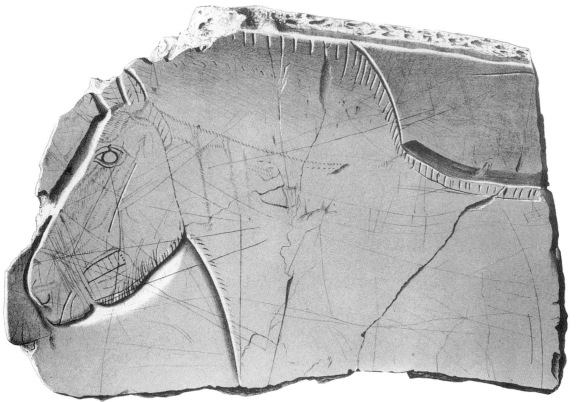

Fig. 191
Second face of the engraved reindeer bone from Laugerie Basse (Dordogne) depicting a horse with geometricized muzzle decorations, indication of a renewed mane and perhaps the marks of ceremonial killing (after Piette).

The composition, then, can have both "realistic" and "mythical" content by being the representation of an act or rite and also the telling of a tale relating pregnancy to a myth which may have included the goddess and a mythical animal. In this case the animal is the male horned herbivore, the stag or bull.

That this composition is storied and one aspect of the complex mythical relation of man to animals and of animals amongst themselves is indicated by the engraved head of a horse, symbolically marked, on the reverse face of the plaque (Fig. 191). We have already seen that the two faces of an engraved object often represent aspects of storied relation.

Horse and bison, as I have shown in terms of the engraved compositions and as Leroi-Gourhan has shown in terms of the cave compositions, are symbolic and associated with each other and with other signs and symbols. They may also have been sacrificed. The horse head is intriguing because of the subsidiary marks; one series of marks looks like an added mane, indicating a second use of the image. There are also linear marks on the muzzle which may be interpreted as a halter and muzzle (if not of a fully domesticated horse, perhaps of a horse being led to sacrifice), but which may be an example of the geometricizing of a storied, symbolic head. (See the horse heads from Mas d'Azil with notations, Fig. 57 a) Significant, too, is the fact, already mentioned, that *after* the bas-relief on the main face had been completed, two subsidiary forms or figures were added rather quickly and by a sharp engraving point, one at a side and one between the animal and the woman. The central form looks like a crescent over the swollen abdomen and the other like a frame structure with uprights and crosspiece. Intentional and precisely made, they are

Fig. 192 a, b
Two faces of an engraved bone from Isturitz (Basses-Pyrénées). On one face are two naked, decorated females, apparently in prayer when the bone is held vertically. On the other face are two bison, one of which is a bull. The bull has two engraved harpoon-like images in its thigh, an image repeated on the thigh of the woman at right on the first face. Middle Magdalenian.

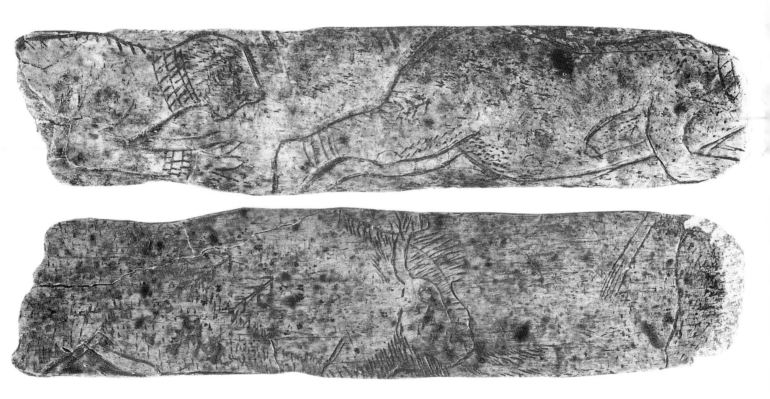

related to the symbolic composition. Were they made at different times? Unfortunately, this piece, like other important pieces in the Piette collection, is not available for microscopic analysis.

Similar to the pregnant female from Laugerie Basse, also from Magdalenian IV and in the same tradition of rendition, there comes a bone from Isturitz, in the foothills of the Pyrenees (Fig. 192 a, b). Once again we have a piece engraved on two faces; here, however, there are two human figures on one face and two animals, both bison, on the other.

On the front face is the full nude body of a squat, somewhat pregnant woman wearing necklace and ankle bracelet. Her head is broken off. Behind her is another person, wearing necklace and bracelets. The first impression is that of a man with short hair, chasing a woman, his arms reaching for her, a sort of primitive "sexual" scene. The microscope indicates that the face is hairy as though in need of a shave, but this does not necessarily mean masculinity, since the other figure has hairy breasts and thighs, as the woman of the plaque did. But, as Leroi-Gourhan has pointed out, there are the lines of a breast engraved near the arm of the second figure, so that both figures seem to be women, both comparable to the hairy nude of the Laugerie Basse composition. Both women (or the man and the woman) are in the attitude of adoration, supplication, or prayer that we saw on the previous example and that appears on other examples that have been called "hunting magic." The bent arms held up and the feet together do not give a sense of motion or chase. On the other hand, if the composition is turned lengthwise, we have the static image of two persons in an attitude of prayer. This again raises the question whether or not the woman seemingly "lying" on her back in the Laugerie Basse composition may not be *standing* in prayer. The Upper Paleolithic manner of mixing horizontal and vertical images on a single face or bone makes this feasible.

The other face shows two bison, one following the other. The enlargement indicates that the rear bison is a bull. There are two seening "harpoon" points in its flank and a similar "harpoon" is in the thigh of the first woman on the reverse face. We are, therefore, faced with the questions concerning such seeming "weapons" that we raised earlier. If the images are indicative of "hunting magic," why does the woman have it in her thigh? If these are not hunting points but storied sacrificial points why does the woman carry it? Could the composition be of a mythical sacrifice of the bison related to a sign of that sacrifice on the woman? If the scene is storied, could the "harpoons" be also storied, added at a later date as marks of renewal of the myth? Or are they not "harpoons" but rather stylized plant motifs such as we have seen associated with bison, horse, female, and notations? Or is the harpoon or plant in this case the attribute, aspect, or sign of still a third character in the story, one we do not see, either the goddess or a male in the myth?

At this point in our long analysis we find ourselves with a number of tantalizing possibilities, none of which can be proven and none of which may be correct. What we do have, however, is the certainty that all of the old interpretations of such art are too simple and were made on the basis of limited and partial theoretical concepts. It is clear that we cannot "read" or interpret an image or sign in the Upper Paleolithic as one can a sign in a structured alphabet or hieroglyphic system. For the meanings are maintained by myth and story and by their working, ritual relation to each other, as much as by definition or translation.

Two problems raised in this chapter need exploring. The first is the attitude of reverence and prayer which seems to be concurrent with expressions of ceremony and rite, and perhaps sacrifice and killing; the second is the depiction of pregnancy, which seems in some cases to be related to the reverence and to symbolic killing or sacrifice.

The attitude of the raised arms and the open hand seems to be a storied gesture when we find it in the Magdalenian. But earlier, from the first appearance of Aurignacian markings in the caves, the print of the hand, engraved or outlined as a negative in red or black paint, appears on the cave walls either alone, in groups of hands, or as an element associated with animals, notations, or symbolic forms. The meaning of these hands, often with joints missing so as to seemingly indicate sacrifice or injury, has been one of the more puzzling problems in the repertoire of Upper Paleolithic symbols. In approaching the hands, one is faced with the usual problem in analyzing art in the caves. One never knows the relation in time of hand print to nearby image, whether it was made later as a sign of renewal, as a mark of repetition of the story and a gesture of reverence or participation, or whether it stands alone. On the small engraved bones and stones, as we have seen, there is a greater surety that the elements in

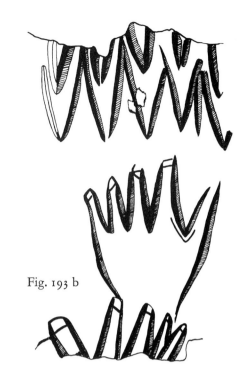

Fig. 193 b

a composition were meant to be related. It is fortunate that an extremely evolved, clarifying instance has been found on an engraved bone from the terminal phase of Magdalenian VI.

From the site of Le Morin, Gironde, France, the farmer-archaeologist Deffarges has excavated a bit of bone on which both a right and left hand are engraved, one above the other, each with fingers up and hand open as though in adoration or reverence. Above the hands is an unusual schematic image of multiple angles pointing downward that looks, again, like rain or water (Fig. 193 a, b). Both the hand and the angular series appear as symbolic elements throughout the European Upper Paleolithic. The meaning of each is often, apparently, seasonal and storied, related to horse, fish, stag, reindeer, bison, or goddess, and in one instance to lions. Since each element in this engraving from Le Morin is one symbol in a larger story, we may tentatively assume that the angles are attributes or symbols in the time-factored myth and that the hands indicate the human participation in the myth.

I have indicated that such angles can be symbolic of a phenomenon or process, or decorative, or a form of notation. They may represent the

Fig. 193 a
One face of a fragment of engraved bone from Le Morin (Gironde) depicting a right and left hand raised to a series of angles. Final Magdalenian.

Fig. 193 b
Line rendition of the unrolled composition engraved on the Le Morin bone depicting the hands and the angles which may represent rain clouds or water (after Deffarges).

Fig. 194 a
One face of a bone point engraved with schematic fish, from Petersfels, south Germany. Upper Magdalenian.

Fig. 194 b
Line rendition of the Petersfels point indicating the progressive schematization of the fish and the series of angular marks behind the first fish.

Fig. 195 a
Detail. The angular marks below and behind the first fish on the Petersfels point, indicating that the marks were made as series of intentional, rhythmic angular strokes and are neither accidental nor random.

shedding coat of summer or schematic fish scales, clouds, rain, grass, or even fire. We are dealing with a tradition of schematic and symbolic representation rather than with a limited language of set forms. Similarly, horizontal linear sequences can indicate hair in an animal or symbol outside it, hatching can indicate the scales of a fish in a drawing and be symbolic outside. The meaning of such basic forms, then, depends on the context and on the local tradition. Since the representation of an animal, plant, female image, or hand is usually recognizable, it may be advisable to show more clearly the realistic usage of a form like the angle.

From the reindeer hunter's site at Petersfels in southeast Germany, which stood by a glacial stream and gave us female figurines, there comes a long, sharpened bone that may have served as a point (Fig. 194 a, b). It is engraved on two faces with schematic fish, each fish on a face being more

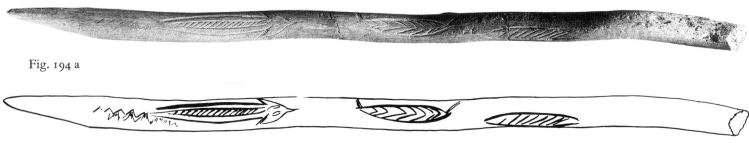

Fig. 194 a

Fig. 194 b

Fig. 195 a

Fig. 195 b

Fig. 195 b
Line rendition of all the engraved marks behind and below the fish indicating the build-up of the "water" image, as determined by microscopic analysis.

abstracted than the previous, and each fish decorated or formed by a different pattern of lines. Associated with the most realistic of these fish, below and to the rear, is a double series of angles made in a quick manner (Fig. 195 a, b). Though the form seems random, the microscope indicates that it is structured, completely unlike the random markings and over-markings in a series of work marks. We assume that this series of angles, related to but outside a fish pattern and engraved by Magdalenian hunter–fishers who had shown a gift for abstract representation, indicates water. Similarly structured, almost random angles appear in the Magdalenian associated with horse, reindeer, and deer, and in the East Gravettian with the goddess figurines. Since these animals also appear associated with fish, it may be that fish and water represent related aspects of the myth. We shall see more of these angles in a fish-and-sexual context later in this chapter.

Besides the realistic images of pregnancy we have seen, we might assume that abstracted signs or symbols of pregnancy would also be used, since this is certainly the most meaningful of the female processes. There seems to be such a sign, and it poses one of the most intriguing series of questions in the realm of supposed Upper Paleolithic "sexual" meanings.

This sign is the so-called claviform or key sign, the "P" that appears on the walls of Tuc d'Audoubert in the chamber of the ceremonial clay bear. It is one of the primary signs considered feminine by Leroi-Gourhan, and he states that it is derived from the female statuettes and engraved figures with large buttocks. In our microanalysis of the engraved stone slab from Hohlenstein, the "P"-like image, actually a reverse "Ϥ"-like image, does appear as a simplification of the fuller buttocks image. This raises a question. The engraved buttocks image of the female appears as a time-factored, recurrent image on such slabs, apparently as a *non-pregnancy* image with a flattened or hollow belly. Leroi-Gourhan has recognized the structural difference between the buttocks and the "P" images. He notes that in the "P" image the bulge is often placed high in the upper half of the upright figure, or the figure is at an angle or horizontal and the centered bulge faces upward. This is not the buttocks image or position, for in these female figures the bulge is always either in the rear or in the lower half of the female form. The schematized "P" form, therefore, seems to be a contrary or reverse image, seemingly implying pregnancy, whereas the buttocks image does not. If they are both feminine images, they would be related and be parts in a system of symbolism in which the "P" sign, too, would be time-factored. Variants of this "P" or pregnancy image appear in association with diverse animals and with notational series or groups of symbolic marks.

In the cave of Les Trois Frères, which was a sanctuary for specialized rites and stories including those of the lion, bear, bison, reindeer, and mythological animals, there is a small engraved horse, 19¼ inches long (49 cm) which has been renewed by the addition of a second back and tail and apparently by additions of a number of abdomens (Fig. 196).[14]

The horse is overengraved by a series of "P" signs, twelve seemingly in one series, plus two at the right. In addition, there is a double angle in the rump. The small-muzzled horse is not specifically masculine and may be

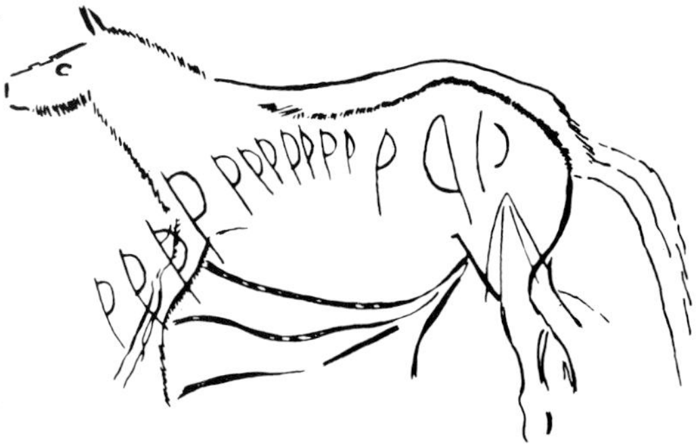

Fig. 196
Line rendition of an engraved horse with an overengraved series of "P" signs and one double angle in the cave of Les Trois Frères (Ariège). The horse also seems to have been renewed by the addition of secondary bellies, back and tail (after Begouën and Breuil).

Note
In the cave of Tuc d'Audoubert, the sister cave that adjoins Les Trois Frères, there is a tiny hidden recess with a cupola that is just large enough for the head and shoulders of one person. On the ceiling there is engraved a small crude horse that is surrounded by more than 80 "P" signs, many clearly made by different tools. Significantly, the overmarked horse in Fig. 196 is also hidden in a high recess just outside of the great chamber that is overlooked by the engraved and painted "sorcerer" (Fig. 150 a). The presence of these two secret, neighboring small accumulations or compositions confirms an Ice Age tradition involving the private ritual use of a symbolic motif made in relation to an animal image. (See Appendix, Fig. 238.)

[14] Henri Bégouën and Abbé H. Breuil, LES CAVERNES DU VOLP (Paris: Arts et Métiers Graphiques, 1958), Fig. 79, p. 76.

Note

Since publishing this book a decade of research in the French and Spanish caves has validated these early insights and findings and has documented the presence of varied symboling traditions and modes of image use. It has documented accumulations and changes to images and compositions extending over short and long periods of time.

Attempts to interpret the Ice Age cave imagery with a simple explanation or the present "structure" of the accumulations found in a cave do not adequately address this problem of the variability in such accumulations, the changes that were made to an image or a composition, or the variability found in the uses of an image or a wall.

a pregnant mare. The possibility is heightened by the "P" signs and the additions to the belly. Assuming a female animal upon which a periodic sign was made, we may conjecture that fourteen renewals or acts of participation were made by use of the sign; other renewals were made by additions to the body and still another by the addition of the multiple angle. The different forms of renewal need not necessarily have had different meanings, for each may have indicated a participation in the story and season of the pregnant mare, which may also have had a meaning for human pregnancy and general fertility. The different forms of addition may have been made by different persons, each however operating within the one tradition.

We may then have an image of twelve or fourteen rites or years in the use of the "P" image by one person as his—or her—sign of participation. Or the "P" image may be a sign, not of pregnancy, but of an *object* related to pregnancy, such as the Petersfels images, and its relation to the horse may be of the ceremonial object to a mythical or sacrificed animal. The possibilities are more important than precise answers or details, for what we are doing at this stage of the analysis is raising a number of time-factored questions, comparable to those raised with the buttocks image, questions that perhaps can be answered by research in the caves.

A cluster of seemingly evolved "P" or pregnancy signs appears in red-painted form in the cave of Altamira in northwest Spain, within the great chamber of painted bisons. They appear at a side, scattered and not in linear series, but related to the single figure of a doe. In some caves the signs stand apart, unassociated, and in one the sign has dot sequences associated with it. In other caves the sign stands in conjunction with other signs, linear uprights that lack bulges and seem to represent units of some sort, obviously not day units, but units that are additive and cumulative.

Whether animal pregnancy or animal sacrifice or renewal of the animal image was somehow related to pregnancy of women or a rite concerned with human pregnancy, or whether the stories and rites implied in the art dealt only with seasonal ceremonies related to animal pregnancy, is not important. For the "sign," being storied, was part of what I have called an open equation, a symbol that could be used in many ways. Since it represented some aspect of myth and process related to pregnancy, it could also be an attribute or sign of the "goddess" or an object in a ritual in which she was a character.

I have not yet engaged in a study of cave art with analytic techniques comparable to those I have applied to the engraved materials. A start, however, was made in working out these techniques in the cave of La Pileta, in the Malaga district of southern Spain, a few days' walk from the Costa del Sol and the Mediterranean. The cave is unusual for the range and number of its abstracted, geometric signs, symbols, and notational sequences, the most abundant perhaps in Europe. The dating is uncertain, but some of the animal art is clearly Upper Paleolithic, perhaps Solutrean, and some of the later geometricized forms are probably Neolithic or Eneolithic. The animal art is intriguing because it represents a repertoire similar to that of the Franco-Cantabrian tradition, though the ecology and culture were somewhat different. Turn back to the engraved notational limestone from Parpallo. We shall see a later example of notation from southeastern Spain in the last chapter. In La Pileta there is one huge painted fish, 4 feet, 11 inches (1.5 meters) in length, overpainted and renewed, associated with a seal, ibex, and other animals.[15] A small, narrow,

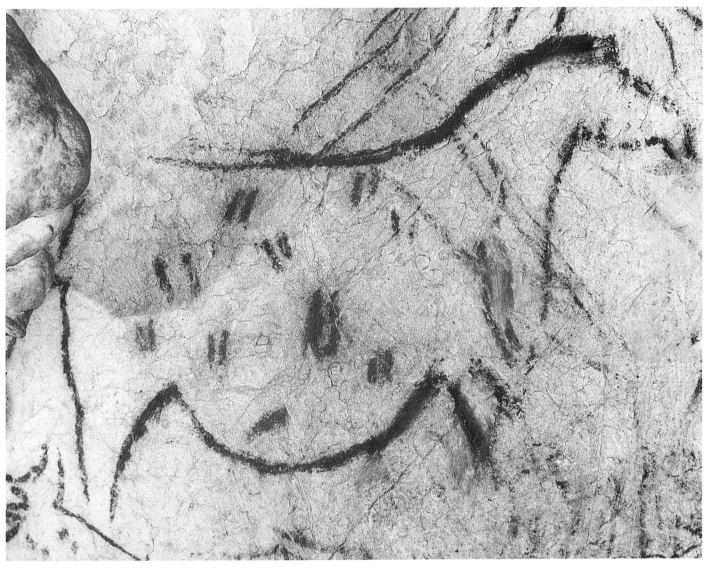

Fig. 197
Painted pregnant mare in secluded small sanctuary in cave of La Pileta (Malaga) with a sequence of double wound marks in the body, each set made at a different time.

low-ceilinged chamber, into which one climbs with difficulty and within which one has to sit crouched, had been made into a "sanctuary" large enough for one or two persons. It has many paintings on the wall, including horses, cows (though the Abbé Breuil made one of the cows look like a bull), ibex, serpentine figures, schematic stickmen, a seeming vulva sign, and oddly branched "tectiforms." The central, primary image is a painted horse, apparently a pregnant mare (Fig. 197). The black mare and cow are each marked with those double strokes we have seen before, often apparently indicating a killing or sacrifice. Significantly, the double

[15] H. Breuil, H. Obermaier, and W. Verner, LA PILETA (Monaco: Institut de Paléontologie Humaine: Peintures et Gravures Murales des Cavernes Paléolithiques, 1915), Fig. 10, p. 38.

Fig. 198
Broken bâton from Bruniquel (Tarn-et-Garonne) in the form of a phallus decorated with schematized fish and angles probably representing water (after Breuil). Upper Magdalenian.

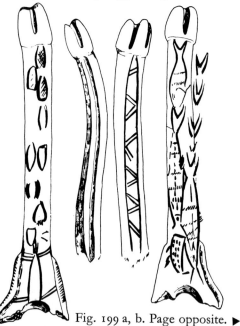

Fig. 199 a, b. Page opposite. ▶
Two faces of a broken bâton head from the Gorge d'Enfer (Dordogne) in the form of a double phallus decorated with angles. One of the projections is engraved like a fish on each side, the other like a phallus. The bâton also recalls certain forked feminine and vulvar images from the Magdalenian, a resemblance enhanced by the ovaloid bâton hole. Upper Magdalenian.

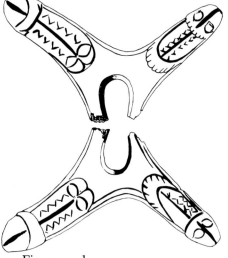

Fig. 200 a, b
Line rendition of the bâton from the Gorge d'Enfer indicating the uneven decoration of angles. As determined by microscopic analysis.

signs are made in either red or black paint, and each set seems to have been made by a different hand and at a different time. Since the sanctuary is too tight for a group ceremony, and since the change of colors and the variations in size, thickness, and deterioration of the double signs indicate a periodic marking, we assume the images and the sanctuary to have had continuity within the one culture, including the reuse of a traditional sign upon a traditional image. Use of the sign recalls the series of "P" images on the horse of Les Trois Frères, as well as the accumulations of signs in other caves in different colors or styles.

Because of the difficulty in reaching and climbing into the sanctuary, one assumes that it was not a woman in a late stage of pregnancy who entered and that the rite was probably seasonal and ceremonially and mythologically related to pregnancy, vulva, serpentine forms, ibex, and tectiforms. We assume a similar but not equivalent meaning for the painted fish in another part of the cave.

These, then, are some of the feminine images, not always or necessarily "sexual" in our meaning of the term.

Now within this tradition, as I have suggested, we should expect to find complementary masculine images, using the same equations of story and traditions of symbolism and composition.

The masked, horned, and robed images of men as shamans, sorcerers, or dancers, and of women in decorations and ornaments, seem to indicate that the participants in a ceremonial were often, except for their storied ornaments, barefoot and naked. The ceremonies may have occurred either in a covered shelter or cave or outside in a warm season or around a fire. When masculine figures are shown, they are sometimes, but not always, ithyphallic, that is, with penis erect. This would seem to indicate that one aspect of the rite had an "erotic" content, but what content is difficult to tell for the males are not related to human females but to animals. The erect phallus as a masculine process was probably storied much as were the female processes. For males it was a time-factored sign of process and power, as much as menstruation, pregnancy, and lactation were for the female. Since it was storied, it could be or become a sign, symbol, attribute, or element in a design or rite. Since the basic human processes were, of necessity, explained in storied terms in which animals were often characters, we would expect the phallic processes—erectile, copulatory, ejaculatory, and urinary—to be storied, often in terms of animal myths. Since hooved and horned male animals periodically indulge in dramatic rutting battles, the "male" story that was told in terms of these animals might be different than a "male" story concerned with the clawed carnivores. Since the phallus offers a kinesthetic and visual comparison to the serpent and fish, we might expect some storied recognition of the comparison, as was noted by the Abbé Breuil. Since the phallus was involved in the ejection of semen and urine, we might expect some storied explanation of these processes, which could compare with the vulval connection to menstrual blood. None of these stories concerning masculine processes

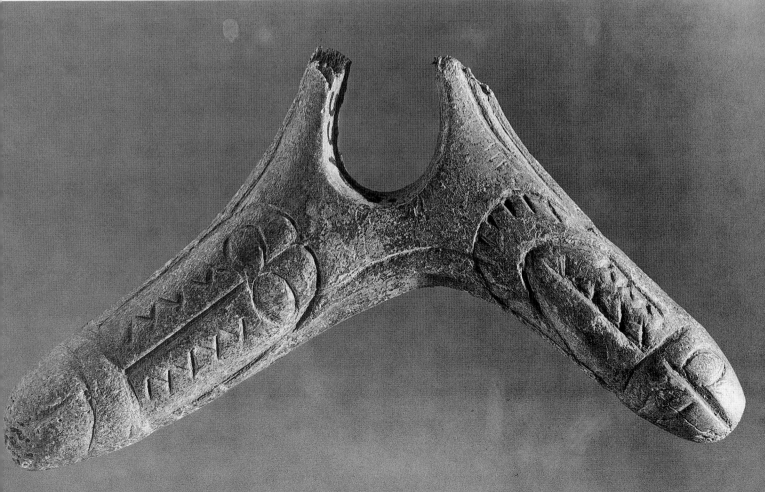

need involve the female, nor include a knowledge of insemination or fertilization. They could be part of a specialized masculine mythology, perhaps told at the initiation of boys or at a convocation of hunters or as part of the male shaman's repertory, much as there would have been another set of animals and stories for women at the time of first menstruation, pregnancy, or delivery. But within the context of the unifying story equation and the multiple uses possible for symbol, there is no reason why the masculine mythology and images should not coincide with and overlap the feminine. There is also no reason why the recognition of a division of creatures into masculine and feminine should not have had storied explanations, with the possibility that images of the phallus and vulva might be mythologically combined and then mythologically separated by a unifying concept.

All this is conjecture but possible within the context of a symbolic and storied usage that seems to have been extremely complex, varied, and sophisticated.

From an early Magdalenian level (Magdalenian II–III) at the site of Le Placard there comes a bone crudely but clearly engraved with a phallus. The ovoid head is separated by an engraved cut, and a long, linear, liquid stream issues from the engraved vent.[16] The phallus is similar to those found later, but the "liquid" in later Magdalenian phallic images is schematized in the angle fashion.

From the Late Magdalenian of Bruniquel, south of the Dordogne, there comes a broken bâton which has a phallic contour and is engraved with decorations and images (Fig. 198). On one face is a double-angle pattern which may represent schematized "water" and on another face is a series of realistic fish, with more highly schematized fish on the third face.

A Late Magdalenian level at the Gorge d'Enfer, whose early Aurignacian notations were among the first we analyzed, provides a bâton head with a double phallus image whose forked silhouette recalls the vulva image from Le Placard (Fig. 199 a, b). One phallus is marked on both sides as though it were a fish, with eyes and head at the tip and a fish tail in the rear. The other projection is phallic on both faces at the tip, but it has double "eyes" in the rear as though they also served as testes. Each of the projections is decorated with angles. The composition seems to be an example of symbolic play, of visual punning, a crossing of comparative images. In addition, the myth and tradition that allow this seem to relate the phallus to both fish and water. Fish, phallus and water seem aspects of a larger myth which apparently also includes the "goddess." These traditional visual-mythological aspects have been individualized by some person making a seemingly personal ritual object (Fig. 200 a, b).

From the Late Magdalenian of La Madeleine, near Les Eyzies, there comes a broken bone with an unusual image, the head of a bear with mouth open and a spine without body, recalling the ceremonial bison

Fig. 198. Page 330.

Figs. 199 a, b; 200 a, b. Preceding pages.

[16] Saint-Germain-en-Laye, No. 55050.

332

from Raymonden of the same period. The bear faces a phallus with testes drawn as though it were a flower or a combined vulva and phallus (Fig. 201 a). Figure 201 b is a precise rendition based on microscopic analysis and is different from earlier renditions. An emanation extends from phallus to bear, raising a number of questions that cannot be answered on the basis of this one example. But some of the questions it raises are significant and were raised before.

Is it possible that one aspect of the complex mythology related the "goddess," females, and the cultural group to the hooved and horned herbivores via seasonal and calendric rites and ceremonies, while the carnivores, the lion and bear, were related to a more specialized masculine mythology and rite? This would have practical validity if killing and sacrifice were involved, since the killing of the wild carnivore would almost certainly be an act of distant, specialized, masculine courage. Would the phallus, then, be an image in the bear mythology?

Fig. 201a
Broken bone rod from La Madeleine (Dordogne) engraved with the head of a bear facing a complex phallic form. Upper Magdalenian.

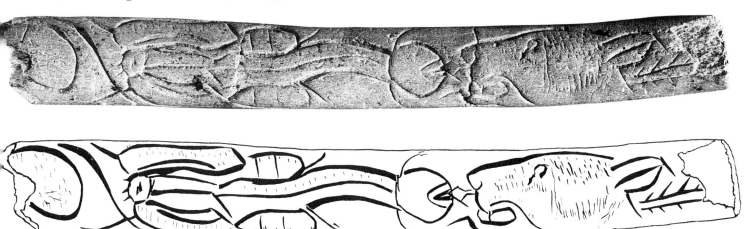

Since all animals and symbols were related by story, the lone stag, the lone ibex, and the combinations of lion-horse, horse-angles, fish-horse, fish-deer, snake-horse, snake-deer, plant-herbivore, horse-bird, or horned animal and horse may have had separate, specialized stories and meanings as part of the single mythology. Since we are also dealing with an anthropomorphized mythology, the attributes of one animal might align it in story with a god, a goddess, or a spirit, or with the sky, earth, waters, or a month, season, or year.

Since frequently these combinations appear with notations, and since notations are abstracted units that compose storied sequences and sums, I assume that the stories of these notational sequences, even when concerned with lunar observations or human activities, would be told in combined terms of these gods, goddesses, spirits, anthropomorphs, animals, plants, and processes.

I close this exploratory chapter with two examples of the female carrying a symbol or an attribute.
A famous Upper Perigordian bas-relief of a naked woman about 17 inches high (43 cm) carved on a large limestone block was found with other

Fig. 201b
Line rendition of the rod from La Madeleine indicating all the engraved marks. The phallus is almost flower-like in its complexity, making contact in one direction with a bear head via an angular emanation. In the other direction a smaller sub-phallus is placed into a vulvar form. As determined by microscopic analysis.

Fig. 202 a
Side view of bas relief from Laussel (Dordogne) indicating the relative flatness of the carving and the slight, unstressed protuberance of the stomach. The strong arc of the body is due to the camera angle. (Photo Achille Weider.)

sculpted blocks at the overhanging rock shelter of Laussel in the Dordogne region near Les Eyzies (Fig. 202 a, b). The other bas-reliefs depict female figures of the same type as well as animals, including a horse, a hind, and a carnivore. There is also one partially broken masculine figure whose posture and raised arm look as though he was about to hurl a lance. The carved man, naked except for a belt, seems to picture a ritual or mythological act. It does not seem to be a quickly made image for "hunting magic." The mythological significance of the "hunter" is enhanced when he is considered as part of the repertoire of figures which includes the naked women.

The bountiful, fat-layered female is faceless and has legs that lack feet. Her left hand rests on her abdomen, which shows a navel. Her right hand is raised holding a bison horn that is marked with thirteen lines. On her thigh there is a "Y" mark. Her faceless "moon" or "sun" head is turned to the right, looking at the horn. The figure is ochered red.

The second bas-relief from Laussel shows a woman carved in the same tradition, though crudely, holding a more arced "horn" in her raised right hand. She has the same round faceless head, pendulous breasts, and a clearly defined abdomen and navel.

What was the relation of these nude, faceless females to the crescent horns, to the male hunter, and to the animal figures found in the shelter? What was the relation of these images from a single habitation site to the sum of marked objects and representations found at other sites and in the caves of this same Dordogne region?

If, as our analysis has indicated, there was a tradition of lunar notation as early as the Aurignacian-Perigordian, and if these notations were related to a mythology that included a "goddess" in storied relation to animals, as well as a complex ceremony and ritual involving killing and sacrifice, and if the notations and myths were also related to the processes of pregnancy both in animals and women, as well as to the seasons of rutting, migration, and calving, then it is possible to conjecture that this image of the "goddess" or woman with the marked animal horn and with the red color of life is a central aspect or character in the combined myth.[17]

If this is so, then it is possible, but not yet proven, that the "goddess" with the horn is a forerunner of later Neolithic, agricultural variants. She was the goddess who was called "Mistress of the Animals," had a lunar mythology, and had associated with her signs, symbols, and attributes, including the lunar crescent, the crescent horns of the bull, the fish, the angle-signs of water, the vulva, the naked breasts, the plant, flower, bird, tree, and snake. This later goddess was associated in story with a consort or mate who was also part of the seasonal and calendric mythology, a hunter of bull and lion, stag and ibex, as well as of mythical animals

Fig. 202 b
Front view of bas relief from Laussel showing the naked, faceless female turning her head to the horn held in her raised right arm. The horn has thirteen marks. Upper Perigordian. (Photo Musée de l'Homme.)

[17] The count of thirteen is the number of crescent "horns" that may make up an observational lunar year; it is also the number of days from the birth of the first crescent to just before the days of the mature full moon. One cannot therefore conjecture on the basis of one engraved sequence any meaning to the marks, but that the usually clean bison or bovine horn was notated with storied marks is clear.

Okladnikov, an Academician of the Soviet Academy of Sciences and director of prehistoric archaeology for Siberia, had read my publications. He and I had discussed his suggestion that the motifs in the Mezin and Malta materials were "cosmological" and my related ideas that they were probably, in some measure, also abstractions derived from the perception of or the rendering of water and of time as notation or process. We had discussed the human ability to "see" concepts in terms of image, metaphor, symbol and sign. He told me that the prehistoric rock art of Siberia that he had studied and published was often oriented to the rising or setting sun. We discussed the diverse and complex role that symbol and imagery played in prehistoric cultures and in shamanism. We were not discussing art "style" but ritual and symbolic image use. When we were done he put his arm around my shoulders and said, with a self-deprecating smile, "Sasha, you and I are the last of the true shamans."

Okladnikov was familiar with the shamanistic lore and practices of Siberia and he believed that the images in the prehistoric rock art of Siberia, even when they depicted real animals such as the elk or the seasonal water bird, were depictions related to the cosmology and mythology of these cultures.

The effort of Frolov (1974, 1983), Larichev (1985, 1989 a, b), and others in the Soviet Union to suggest a sophisticated arithmetical calendar for the Ice Age cultures was based on these concepts of Okladnikov and on my evidence for an early observational astronomy. However, there is a difference between the evidence for an observational astronomy, involving an ability to count short sets, and the suggestion for a complex system of additive counting by 5's, 7's or 10's. I have not yet been able to find the evidence for such structured systems of counting in the notations.

When I went to the Soviet Union to study the plaque from Malta I discovered that almost one quarter was missing and portions had been reconstructed and replaced with wax. This wax had then

whether in the labyrinth, the depths, or in the sky. In the story he was often the "sun" to the goddess' "moon." These later cultures also depict images of men and women in attitudes of reverence, with arms raised towards either the god, goddess, sky, or animal images. They also present images of hunters engaged in mythological and ceremonial hunting, killing, or combat.

I mention these analogies not because we have the full evidence, but because the limited evidence uncovered in one hundred years of digging hints at a relation and does not exclude it, and because the possibility offers some clue as to the origins of certain basic themes of the Neolithic and early agricultural civilizations, which occur across vast distances from Europe through Asia, Africa, and the Americas, and among diverse peoples and races, speaking many languages. More important, we now have analytic and comparative techniques that may one day offer an approximate verification of these conjectures. Part of this verification will come as we track the Upper Paleolithic traditions of notation and symbolism into the Mesolithic.

This chapter on sex and the goddess has been both an inquiry into meaning and an analysis of the evidence. It has touched on old and current theories concerning the meaning of the female images. One body of theory has not been discussed.

Soviet theories were brought to my attention by an article in the English-language newspaper MOSCOW NEWS, in which the archaeologist Boris Frolov stated that Soviet archaeologists had subsidiary proofs for the lunar notations I had hypothesized in my 1964 paper in SCIENCE. An ivory buckle from the Upper Paleolithic site of Malta, Siberia, depicts three snakes on one face and a series of spiral patterns made by dots on the other. The article stated that

"Professor A. Okladnikov has come to the conclusion that the original geometric patterns on the Malta and Mezin finds [see Fig. 185: 1a-9c] were inspired by the artists' concepts of the cosmos and by their mythology, which already incorporated a conception of the Universe as an entity."[18]

My findings were more limited and did not attempt to project the philosophical world view of Upper Paleolithic man. Frolov asserted that the number "7" is a "preferred" number in this ancient decoration, a hypothesis, like Absolon's "5" and "10," that is hard to prove from the evidence.

"A number of other details also indicate the great attention that was paid to the Moon—the crescent-shaped form on the buckle, the half-moon notches on the other articles found in Malta, and especially on the figurines of women: ...The last fact is especially important because these two images—the Moon and Woman—are connected in mythology.

"Perhaps the Siberian peoples [of today] possess the key to that phenomenon; their women calculate child-birth by the phases of the Moon, according to observations made by B. Dolgikh and other Soviet ethnographists among the

---

[18] Boris Frolov, "Stone Age Astronomers," MOSCOW NEWS (Sept. 4, 1965).

Nganasans, Entses, Dolgans, Chukchi, Koryaks, and Kets.[19] Pregnancy has a duration of exactly 10 lunar months, and the woman keeps a sort of lunar calendar (it was always a woman who was the custodian of the lunar calendar among these nationalities). That calendar found original use in ornaments: thus, among the Nganasans, a mother, as distinct from a girl, sews 10 coloured stripes to her garment ...

"In any case, we can be quite sure that our ancestors peered intently at the sky and tried to use what they observed in their everyday calculations."[20]

These Siberian tribes have a complex, time-factored mythology and ceremonial, including aspects of an ancient bear ceremony and ceremonial use of the reindeer. They retain Christianized aspects of a more ancient calendric tradition, which in some instances was notational and was related not to pregnancy but to hunting seasons and periodic ceremonies. We must be careful, then, of too simple answers.

The cultures of these Siberian tribes are related to the Upper Paleolithic cultures at a distance of 15,000 to 35,000 years, and while we can consider the Paleolithic cultures central, dynamic, revolutionary, and formative, the cultures of historic hunting peoples of Siberia are peripheral, isolated, static, and in many ways degenerative and regressive. Though certain forms and traditions have been retained, they would not have the same meaning or value. I shall discuss at a later date the evidence from these northern and Siberian cultures and some from America and the Pacific, as it relates to the Upper Paleolithic.

Z. A. Abramova has published the official anthology of Upper Paleolithic engraving and sculpture in the territory of the U.S.S.R.[21] She summarizes Soviet archaeological opinion concerning the animal art and the female figurines and presents her own conclusions.

Since present-day Siberian hunting tribes offer a body of living, ethnographic comparison, Soviet archaeologists and ethnologists have leaned more heavily on such comparisons than on an exhaustive comparative analysis of the Upper Paleolithic materials. There has also been a tendency to see a confirmation of nineteenth-century Marxian theories, particularly those of Friedrich Engels concerning the origins of the family and society, in archaeological findings and ethnographic comparisons. Nevertheless, the ideas are relevant and of interest.

A. P. Okladnikov, discussing the supposedly special role of woman in the early "matriarchal societies" states that there emerged "notions about super-human beings of the female sex, sovereign mistresses operating within a definite sphere of natural phenomena, or sovereign mistresses of

been marked with an approximation of the number of marks that may originally have been present. A precise count and test could not, therefore, be undertaken. That the spirals might, however, have been related to a symbolization of time and the year, is possible and the subject will be addressed in a separate and later study.

Fig. 202 c
A schematic rendition of the spiral design on one face of the ivory belt buckle from the Ice Age site of Malta, Siberia, showing the area of the break and the modern reconstruction.

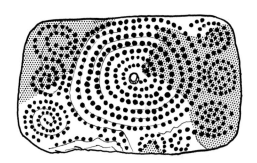

[19] Professor Arnold R. Pilling, Wayne University, wrote me on June 3 and June 10, 1968, that, according to his first tentative findings, women among the Yurok Indians had menstrual calendars and could predict births within a day, and that the Yuroks also had other tally systems. The women apparently kept a menstrual count by dropping a stick each day into a basket and kept a pregnancy count by dropping a "month" stick each lunar month into a second basket until they reached a count of ten.

[20] Frolov, op. cit.

[21] Abramova, "Palaeolithic Art in the U.S.S.R.," pp. 1-179.

definite activities."[22] He suggests that the figurines may be similar to female spirit guardians of the Arctic Eskimo, spirits related to hunting magic and exerting influence over sea and land animals:

"... a widespread ancient hunting myth about Woman—guardian of animals and owner of the forest with whom the male hunter enters into a relationship, receiving as his reward success in the chase ..."[23]

On the basis of a similarity to later female images, Okladnikov believes they were also mother-goddess images, protectresses of childbearing, and guardians of fertility.

"This point of view," writes Abramova, "is confirmed by ethnographic examples, for instance, the goddess Aiysyt of the Yakuts, and the *emegenderi* of the Altais."[24] Okladnikov also believes the female goddess may have had something to do with the cult of death, since similar images are made at the death of a female among the Yakut.

Abramova believes the female images confirm the "matriarchal" basis of man's early hunting societies.

"The image of the Woman-Mother ... was a complex one, and it included diverse ideas related to the special significance of the woman in early clan society. 'Mother—the basic idea behind the matrilineal clan society. She was neither a god, an idol, nor the mother of a god; she was the "Clan-Mother," to be understood only as something totally and concretely material' (Petrov ...). This formulation clearly shows the indissoluble relationship between the woman and the clan. The ideology of the hunting tribes in this period of the matriarchal clan was reflected in the female figurines."[25]

My analysis of the female images indicates the important role such images played in the myth, rite, and ceremony of the Upper Paleolithic, but that a "matriarchy" was involved, or the totemistic idea of a "Clan-mother," cannot be inferred from the evidence but *only* from modern theories concerning what ancient societies "must have been" or "should have been." Abramova is somewhat closer to a scientific approach, though still conjectural and political, when she states:

"By taking the ethnographic data into account, it is possible to contend that there are two different aspects of the woman's image during the Palaeolithic which do not contradict, but rather complement, one another ... mistress of the home and hearth, protectress of the domestic fire ... responsible for the well being of the household and the bearing of children ... [and] On the other hand... woman as the owner of the elements of nature, and as the sovereign mistress of animals and especially of game animals ... In either case without a doubt, there is a connection between the woman and ideas concerning fertility. Firstly, the hearth and home are linked with the image of the original mother. Secondly, we may suppose that the decisive role taken by the woman in the magical rituals preceding the chase had a special significance for its success in the eyes of primitive man.

"Thus there is essentially no contradiction between the two principal theories— the theory of fertility and the theory of magic—both of which have been accepted by Soviet scholars in the light of Marxist-Leninist ideology ... The working out of a method for the investigation of Palaeolithic habitations by Soviet scholars has made it possible to argue and substantiate the general position taken

[22] Ibid., p. 82.   [23] Loc. cit.   [24] Ibid., p. 83.   [25] Loc. cit.

by us in the above statements. The excavations of Palaeolithic settlements has established the characteristic position of the female figurines inside the dwelling hollow and most frequently of all in special storage pits dug into the floor. In a number of cases they had been carefully covered over by the bones of animals or by stone slabs as though to deliberately hide them from the eyes of strangers... the storage pits containing the figurines were located ... near the hearth ... According to the opinions of many northern Asiatic peoples, most distinctly expressed by the Tungus, the spirit of the hearth has the form of a clever old, but still strong and vigorous, woman, a portrayal of which is still stored in each tent. The idea of the female clan ancestress is still preserved among many people ... often reproduced as dolls or 'wooden *balvanchiki*' in which they believe the soul of the dead woman resides." [26]

Abramova lists ethnographic examples of the "Mother-goddess" cult. I point out that my study of the "female" images indicates a mythology and use of the image more complex and diverse than that of goddess of hearth and hunt and ancestress of the clan, though these are not excluded as aspects of the myth and ceremony. Analysis of the archaeological evidence and a beginning attempt to reconstruct certain basic cognitive and symbolic psychological processes have indicated that the images were extremely variable in meaning and use and that they played a number of specialized and generalized roles across the complex, integrated, time-factored culture. In addition, there was a separate and specialized masculine imagery and mythology, in part perhaps specialized with the male shaman but also belonging to the group, and there was a complex animal mythology associated with symbol and notation in which a female character or heroine may have played a part.

These facts do not confirm a "matriarchy," since these same general aspects of story, rite, and symbol appear in "matriarchal" and "patriarchal" societies, and since we have no proof that one evolved into the other out of the Upper Paleolithic, and since only the details of the specialized stories and uses could help clarify the problem.

Abramova also theorizes about the role of the "Woman-Mother" and animals as totemic ancestors of the clan.

"During this stage of development while man was creating his amazing art of primitive realism, the cult of animals undoubtedly carried within itself some totemic concepts, the essence of which consisted of ideas about animal ancestors. The universality of these notions and their presence among the very primitive tribes of today enables us to consider totemism as the elementary form of religion, and in general, as having been the religion of the emerging clan society ...

"The magical subjects of Palaeolithic art reflect a desire not only to kill animals, and gain mastery over them, but there is also another aspect ... the idea of fertility. This idea was inseparably linked with the cult of animals and the cult of the Woman-Mother which passes over into concepts of the zoomorphic totemic ancestor ... The cult of animals was not only concerned with their killing, but with their resurrection as well, a fact which can be found in ethnographic data dealing with rites of propitiation and expiation." [27]

These ideas are the traditional ones concerning totemism, based on early

---

[26] Ibid., pp. 83–84.   [27] Ibid., p. 86.

nineteenth- and twentieth-century anthropology and ethnology. The fact is that "totemism" is neither universal among primitive peoples nor, where present, is it specifically related to the major animals or the major gods or goddesses. It is primarily a specialized form and example of story-telling and symbol use, used between groups and sections of one culture to maintain and explain certain evolved and storied relations in the group, among the groups, and between these groups and the environment. Where "totemism" does not exist, other forms of storytelling and symbol use serve the same basic purposes.[28]

"Killing" was not always involved with hunting magic, nor necessarily with ideas of "resurrection" or "fertility," since these, too, are merely specialized examples of storytelling. Killing, more aptly, might be said to have become *storied* whether for food, in sacrifice, in ceremony, in myth or dance, as expiation or propitiation, in the dream, in the trance journey of a shaman, or in the depictions of art. The nature and uses of these storied equations have been touched on briefly in this book.

What is clear from these discussions of theories and the evidence, ranging from sexual symbolism to Marxian anthropology, is that no single or simple "explanation" will serve. What is required before any theory can be adequate is an evaluation of the human cognitive processes and the manner in which these perform in various cultures at various stages of cultural development. It may then be possible to place the specialized and specific products of a culture and a time into a more reasonable, less doctrinaire biologic and cognitive context, less and less referrable to the theories of one or another anthropological school.

Between 10,000 and 8,000 years ago the climate drastically changed. The "Ice Age" was over and the huge herds disappeared. The forest took over from tundra and steppe, the ice retreated towards the Arctic and finally disappeared. The seas rose. The reindeer and mammoth and groups of subarctic hunters went north, and eventually the mammoth became extinct. A profound change came to Europe, North Africa, and the Middle East. Not only did man's way of life in these regions change, but his images and stories also shifted and changed.

As I have indicated, certain things did not change. The periodicities of sky and season remained, and the processes of the human group remained as well. The cognitive elements involved in *Homo sapiens* culture remained; the tradition of notation and symbol-making persisted and developed, as did lunar and seasonal observation and knowledge of the periodicities and habits of plants, animals, fish, birds, and sky. Man retained the ability to function in a complex time-factored reality by use of symbol and the equations of story.

[28] Claude Lévi-Strauss, TOTEMISM, translated by Rodney Needham (Boston: Beacon Press, 1962–1963).

PART IV
THE STORY CONTINUED

CHAPTER XIV

THE STEP TOWARD HISTORY

The salmon in many rivers of the Dordogne have ceased their yearly struggles upstream to spawn, because of industrial pollution and contamination. The reindeer herds of Europe now follow their seasonal migrations only in the subarctic of Scandinavia and Siberia, primarily in a domesticated or semi-domesticated state. Fresh water birds, such as heron, crane, swan, goose, and spoonbill, still make their seasonal migrations north and south, but they are becoming increasingly rare as their flyways and nesting grounds are overbuilt and changed. Depleted seal herds still breed along rare isolated European coasts. The bison, musk ox, rhinoceros, mammoth, and lion are extinct in Europe. Ibex and chamois have been forced into the mountains as rare species hunted by gun in a limited season. Deer, bear, and wolf are now peripheral in Europe, existing only where man has not yet destroyed the forest landscape. The last

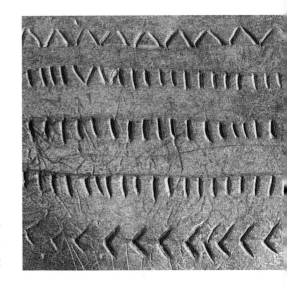

Fig. 203 a

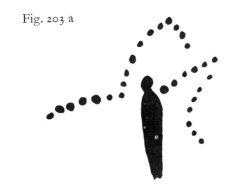

Fig. 203 b

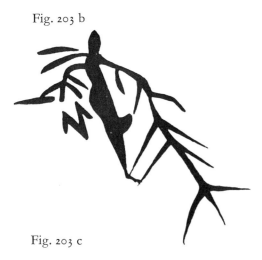

Fig. 203 c

Fig. 203 a–g
Mesolithic wall and cave paintings from Spain containing notations, anthropomorphic figures, signs and symbolic images apparently related or comparable to earlier Upper Paleolithic forms.
a) Canchal de Mahoma; b, c) Los Buitres; d) Abri de las Viñas; e, f) La Pileta.
203 g) La Pileta. Upper Paleolithic cow and associated vulva from the sanctuary with the "killed" pregnant mare (Fig. 197). The later geometric art in the cave (e, f) is related to this earlier more realistic tradition.

herd of small wild horses, once present in the millions across Eurasia, now hangs on marginally in the Siberian Gobi desert and in zoos and parks. The evidence of Ice Age man's relation to these and other creatures is still being dug out of the valley and hill sites, often as roads, factories, and homes are built, or the land farmed, and the art is still on the walls of the caves, much still undiscovered. The seasonal patterns of the animals, birds, and fish and of man's seasonal relations to them can be reconstructed. The patterns of the sky are known. The basic patterns of human life can also be reconstructed. We have the evidence of the notations, art, myth, rite, and symbol. Together this evidence has allowed us to make a beginning attempt at clarification of some cognitive aspects of culture in the Upper Paleolithic.

If our analysis of the complexity of Upper Paleolithic culture is correct, then the anatomically modern hunter-gatherers who spread across Europe, the Middle East, Africa, Asia, and eventually the Americas—carried a certain level of cognitive capacity and cultural development. They had a level of observation and story use which could, when faced with the climate and ecological changes of the postglacial period, help them in developing specialized economies and mythologies in various areas and under specific local conditions.

These post-Ice Age or Mesolithic cultures or subcultures could vary as widely as the shell-gathering and fishing cultures of the European coasts, the incipient agricultural culture of the drying hills of the Middle East Fertile Crescent, the river, lake, or forest cultures of inland Europe, the subarctic cultures of the Siberian reindeer hunter, and the coastal seal-hunting culture of the Eskimo. In some areas the adaptation included varying aspects of partial domestication or seasonal corralling of certain animals for food or for ritual. It probably included relatively stable, static groups and communities as well as seasonally roaming bands.

These possibilities for specialization were due, in part, to the skills, lore, and tradition that had been successfully brought out of the Upper Paleolithic (which included the mating, migrating, calving, sprouting, and fruiting lore we have seen), as well as to the generalized, adaptable, time-factored and time-factoring cognitive capacities of the modern *Homo sapiens*. The skills and techniques they had evolved, from notation to story-telling and symbol use, would be developed dramatically in a few thousand years into true writing, true astronomy, true husbandry, true agriculture, true arithmetic, and into highly organized comparative religion and myth. The place to look, then, as we take the first steps toward history, is in the relatively short, seemingly crude, experimental Mesolithic. It may have lasted from two to five thousand years in different areas of Europe, Asia, and Africa. The cognitive and cultural steps that were taken in those few thousands of years from the end of the Ice Age culture to the beginnings of true agriculture and the domestication of animals have only begun to be explored. The period is short, the soil layers not thick, and the amount of engraved, painted evidence less than from the earlier Paleolithic.

The evidence, however, is enough to indicate that the cognitive core of the sophisticated Upper Paleolithic cultures survived the change of animals, plants, and climate, that it developed and helped to make the transitions to agriculture possible.

Briefly, I present examples from different areas of the transitional Mesolithic, indicating the persistence and development of key elements in the tradition we have been following. More detailed analyses of the Mesolithic materials will appear later.

Turn back and look at the exquisite art and the notations of the terminal Magdalenian in the Dordogne and Pyrenean regions, particularly the material from Mas d'Azil. Over the final Magdalenian layers in these regions there appears an occupation layer with the tools and art of a "new culture," called after Mas d'Azil the "Azilian," and first discovered by Edouard Piette in the late nineteenth century. The art and compositions of this culture have the so-called nonrealistic "decadent" look. What we may have, more accurately, is a tradition in which the artist is no longer referring for his models, stories, and ceremonies to real animals and plants, as did the old hunter and gatherer, but is working rather with traditional, mythological, geometricized, and abstracted images and concepts. It is almost as though the art represents a use of image that refers to far older images and concepts, a tradition in which the basic stories and ways of thinking were retained but in which reality and relations had changed. To some extent we can sense this. The images of bison, mammoth, rhinoceros, and reindeer on the walls of caves in France and Spain would seem to these people, when they occasionally saw them, as "fantastic." They would not have been fantastic mythological animals out of their present lore but fantastic animals of a legendary or forgotten past, "known" by legendary and forgotten ancestors. The ancient images had been cut from a daily reference.

Animals were no longer rendered realistically. Creatures that the Azilian hunter did know, like the deer and fish, were schematized in simple lines. The schematization recalls the thinking involved in earlier East Gravettian abstractions, the angle images of the Magdalenian, and the abstract plant, animal, fish, vulva, female, and eye motifs. They seem to be images that refer back to older traditional images, concepts and usages and would seem, therefore, to be an *evolved* as much as, or rather than, a "decadent" imagery. The stories, ceremonies, and rites were still, apparently, related to the seasons and the sky, to water and earth, to the animals and plants, to gods and goddesses, and to symbols and notations. The art was still time-factored in origin and use. The skill in rendition, however, had deteriorated. For one thing, the 25,000 year old tradition of bone use had suffered when the herds died; for another, the social structures and ceremonial life of which the art had been a part had also deteriorated. This was a new period, archaic and revolutionary, but not entirely degenerative or regressive.

I show four Mesolithic rock-wall paintings (Fig. 203 a-f) and some from

Fig. 203 d

Fig. 203 e

Fig. 203 f

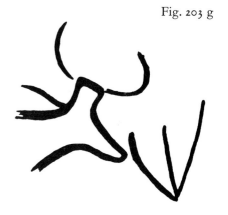

Fig. 203 g

Note

With the unraveling or "decoding" of the Taï notation, c. 10,000 B.C. and the suggestion for a indigenous European lunar/solar notation in the post Ice Age period immediately following (see Figs. 214, 215 and 217, 221), there is a strong presumption that the rock art of the later periods in Europe was often cosmological and "time-factored" and that a lore and mythology of the sky and seasons, and a diverse range of sexual metaphors of renewal were maintained, though altered, in these later cultures.

perhaps a slightly later period in the cave of La Pileta. One (a) has notation in a serpentine sequence associated with an anthropomorph or humanoid figure; another (d) has notation associated with an oval "sign"[1]; a third (c) shows a "god" and "goddess" in a solar or star wheel that may itself be notated; a fourth (b) shows a human figure with erect phallus pulling a plant form from the ground: a plant grows from his shoulders and there is an "M" or double-angle sign associated with the figure. From La Pileta there are two solar or star symbols, a typical angle-sign of the cave and a vulva image associated with a cow. All the images, with the possible exception of Fig. 203 g, come from the Mesolithic or Neolithic of Spain.

One of the crucial findings of the unfolding research was that the early notations I had discovered, and notations and accumulations generally in the Upper Paleolithic and Mesolithic, were not always calendric (see Fig. 15). In the sanctuary caves there were sets of dots, sets of finger marks, sets of hand prints, sets of signs, sets of geometric forms, which had been accumulated over time. These were often a record of periodic ritual behavior involving the use of a motif. These accumulations were not structured as notation is structured though they were periodically made. The concept of a "time-factored" ritual marking and of a periodic use of certain motifs profoundly changed the research and the nature of the inquiry. It raised questions concerning the nature of image systems and their variable use in human culture and, in particular, about their variable use in the distant past of the Upper Paleolithic. Having realized that motifs could be accumulated, either as a set of the same motif on one surface or as a motif in conjunction with other motifs, it slowly became possible to differentiate a notation, which was usually made on an easily portable and incised fragment of ivory, antler or bone, or on certain classes of long-term functional artifacts (retouchers, bâtons, flutes), from symbolic marking made on other types of objects and surfaces such as fragile, short-term tools or on hard stone and a cave wall. It was not merely the image that one had to study, but where and on what material the image was made. There was clearly practical, functional problem-solving involved in the choice of materials and surfaces for different types of marking.

The great animal art of the caves and homesites disappeared at the end of the Ice Age, but the periodic marking and accumulation of motifs and notations did not. However, to study these forms, and to distinguish between motif marking and notation, one had to understand the nature of these modes of image making and use. I therefore present examples from widely separated Mesolithic hunting-gathering cultures in Sweden, France and Austria.

When the huge ice sheets melted, hunter-gatherers moved north, inhabiting the Scandinavian coasts and the shores of inland lakes and streams. From Sweden in the north there comes a ritual axe or mattock carved of soft soapstone which was profusely incised with motifs on each of its many planes. The motifs include the water-related zigzag, and the "net" and arrayed "ladder" motif (Fig. 204 a-d).* These occur often in the

Fig. 204 a. Page opposite. ▶
Limestone slab from Parpallo near Valencia engraved in what has been traditionally called a "geometric" pattern. Magdalenian.

Fig. 204 b
Schematic rendition of all the engraved lines on the Parpallo limestone indicating the two double verticals which begin each superordinate set. On each side of these verticals subsets of marks are engraved and over-engraved at angles to each other. As determined by microscopic analysis.

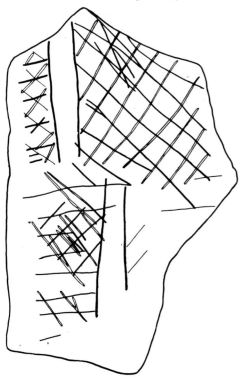

*A. Marshack. European Upper Paleolithic-Mesolithic Continuity. 1979.
[1]A. Marshack, "Lunar Notation on Upper Palaeolithic Remains," science, Vol. 146 (Nov. 6, 1964), pp. 743-745.

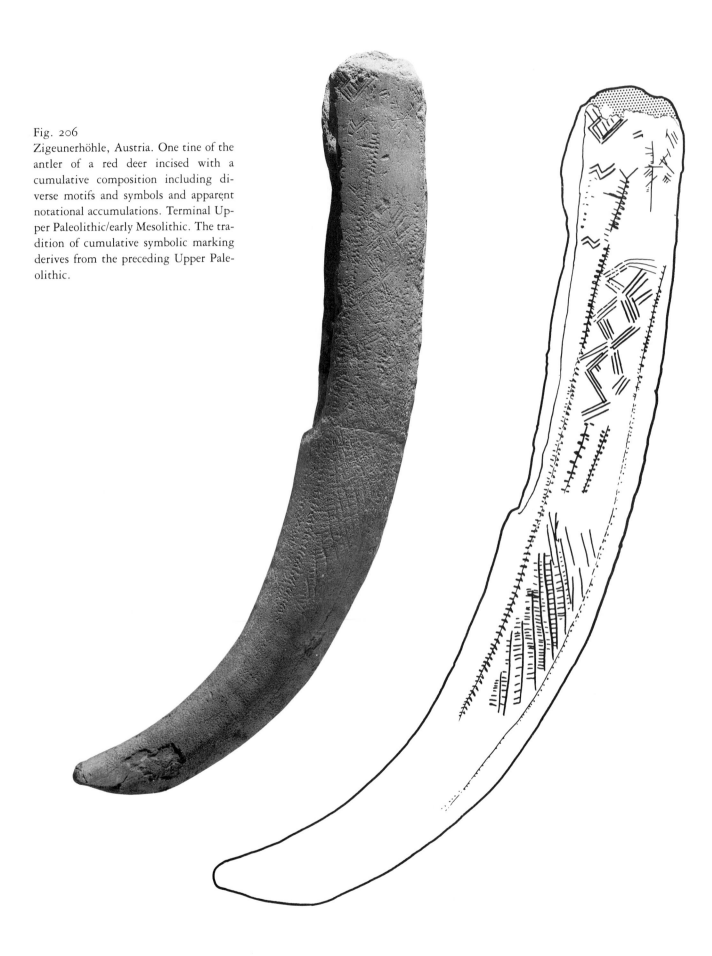

Fig. 206
Zigeunerhöhle, Austria. One tine of the antler of a red deer incised with a cumulative composition including diverse motifs and symbols and apparent notational accumulations. Terminal Upper Paleolithic/early Mesolithic. The tradition of cumulative symbolic marking derives from the preceding Upper Paleolithic.

European Mesolithic. In some areas there are linear sets of tiny marks, often on containing-lines (Fig. 205). Motifs and accumulations of this type were made in these Scandinavian Mesolithic cultures on light easily marked or carved materials such as amber or on axes and picks of antler that were used over a long period (Figs. 212-217).

The site of Zigeunerhöhle, Austria, is in central Europe on the eastern side of the Alps. It is on the Mura river, a tributary of the Drava which enters the Danube and flows eastward through the Iron Gates to the Black Sea. The site, which is terminal Upper Paleolithic-Mesolithic, c. 9,500 B.C., has provided a shaped, non-utilitarian piece of red deer antler with a complex engraved composition. Because of the surface deterioration a long and slow microscopic analysis was conducted. It revealed an accumulation of signs, symbols, motifs and sequences of marks, some of which seem related to earlier traditions from the Russian plain, and others to the motifs from the Mesolithic of Scandinavia (Fig. 206). There are double zigzags, an arrayed ladder motif (see Figs. 212, 213), notations on containing lines, and diverse small signs.** It is clear that we once again have a non-decorative accumulation of motifs apparently associated with notations. These analyses confirmed those made of the comparable Mesolithic materials in the first edition of this book.

In 1928 the team of Marthe and Saint-Just Péquart began excavating the burial grounds of a shell-gathering, fishing and hunting Mesolithic culture on small rocky islands off the coast of France, near the Quiberon peninsula of Brittany. Approximately 8500 B.C., the islands were part of the continental mainland, as was England. This was due to the slow rise of the land that came after the pressure of the vast ice on Europe had disappeared. The men of Tèviec and Hoedic were hunters of deer, wild pig, and birds, fishers of the sea and gatherers of sea mollusks and crustaceans. Their ancestors may have hunted the herds of larger animals or coastal seal of the Ice Age.

The Péquarts found graves in which skeletons were bunched together, decorated with beads, ochered red, and surrounded by tools, documenting that tradition of storied burial which went back to the Upper Paleolithic and before that to Neanderthal man of the Mousterian.

There were many indications of a complex burial ceremony and ritual. In one of the burials a crisscrossed pile of stag antlers covered the human bones, in another it seemed as if a child had been "sacrificed" to accompany the adult in the next life. But the most important evidence of symbolic usage was a surprise, a discovery I made by accident.

At the Musée Miln, le Rouzic at Carnac, there is the reconstruction of a grave excavated by the Péquarts, with the bones and accompanying objects arranged as they had lain in the earth. Among the bones of a child five to eight years old, there lay a pile of tiny, childlike ribs on a human vertebra, as though the ribs had collapsed on the spine. It seemed to me,

---

**A. Marshack. L'Évolution et la Transformation du Décor du Début del l'Aurignacien au Magdalénien Final. 1990.

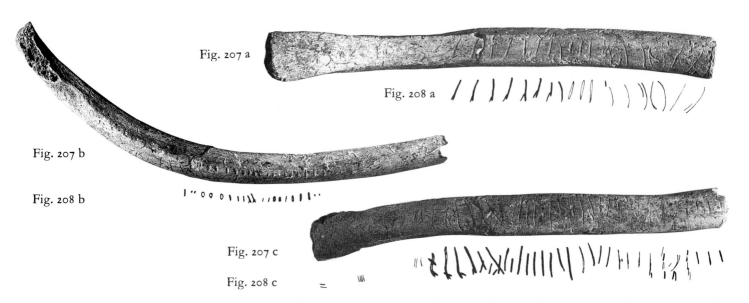

Fig. 207 a

Fig. 208 a

Fig. 207 b

Fig. 208 b

Fig. 207 c

Fig. 208 c

Fig. 207 a, b, c
The two faces and one edge of an engraved rib, probably that of a child, found in a child's grave at Tèviec (Morbihan). Mesolithic.

Fig. 208 a, b, c
Schematic rendition of all the engraved marks on the three areas of the Tèviec rib indicating the grouping by sets made by different points, angles and styles of marking, as determined by microscopic analysis.

as they lay under glass, that one rib was faintly marked. Examining the child's rib by microscope, I found that it had been intentionally "notated" on two faces and along one edge (Figs. 207 a, b, c; 208 a, b, c). These markings have never been published, and they pose one of the most intriguing problems concerned with the origins of this Mesolithic culture. Different points had been used with different pressures, angles and style of stroke, to incise 110 marks. They were clearly intentional and cumulative and, therefore, symbolic. But whether they were made for ritual purposes related to the burial or as "notation" I could not tell. Images of humans and animals were often overmarked in the Upper Paleolithic. But engraved human bones are the rarest of all archaeological finds. . . . If the rib were a human child's, the possibility of ritual,

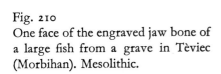

Fig. 210
One face of the engraved jaw bone of a large fish from a grave in Tèviec (Morbihan). Mesolithic.

storied marking may indicate the child's bones formed part of a secondary burial. The storied uses of death precede modern man. Human bones that were ochered red have been found in graves as far back as those of Neanderthal man. Even more significant, in a Neanderthal level at La Ferrassie in the Dordogne, a bit of stone in the grave of a child was intentionally engraved with linear sequences comparable to those in the Upper Paleolithic and to this one found in the Mesolithic (Fig. 209).[2]

Fig. 209
Line rendition of an intentionally engraved stone found at La Ferrassie (Dordogne) in a Neanderthal grave (after Peyrony).

At the museum in Carnac there was one other engraved bone found in a grave from Tèviec. It was the jawbone of a large sea fish and, as presented in the literature, it had a hatch pattern on its main face similar to those found on Upper Paleolithic bones and stones.[3] When I examined the jawbone by microscope, I found that the museum was displaying a clay copy of the original. Since the Péquarts had died, no one knew where the original was. After years of hunting through France, the original was located in a box in the reserves of the Musée des Antiquités Nationales at Saint-Germain-en-Laye (Fig. 210).

Microscopic examination revealed that it had been intentionally engraved on every available surface, on both faces and along the two edges, by groups of marks made in various angles, lengths, rhythms, and spacings. The tool or point differences were not easily determined since the relatively soft fish bone had crumbled along the edges of the engraved lines. Nevertheless, a schematic rendering reveals that the markings were intentional, sequential, and carefully structured into groups. I present only one face (Fig. 211). A full analysis of the groups on both faces must await a study being prepared of engraved Mesolithic materials. Here I

[2] Peyrony, "La Ferrassie," p. 24, fig. 25.

[3] Marthe and Saint-Just Péquart, M. Boule, H. Vallois, TÈVIEC, STATION–NÉCROPOLE MÉSOLITHIQUE DU MORBIHAN. ARCHIVES DE L'INSTITUT DE PALÉONTOLOGIE HUMAINE, Mémoire 18 (Paris: Masson et Cie., 1937).

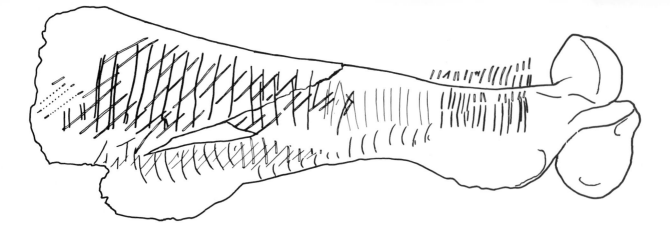

Fig. 211
Schematic rendition of all the engraved marks on the main face and upper edge of the Tèviec fish bone indicating the accumulation of sets and of groups overengraved by other sets, as determined by microscopic analysis.

need point out only that on the main face there is an accumulation and overmarking of discrete sets of marks. If they represent the results of a ritual marking they are not notational. If they are notations, perhaps representing a ritual period between death and secondary burial, we may have a record of nine lunar months of waiting. Six lunar months may be recorded on the main face:

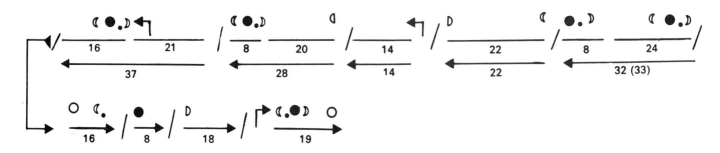

Each of these large groups is broken down further into smaller subgroups, more clearly differentiating the phases. One can see these on the schematic rendition of the main face.

Whether the markings are lunar or whether they represent engraving which, like the red ocher, is intended to say something symbolic and in sum, perhaps in a rite related to burial and death, is not crucial at this point in our analysis. The question will be decided with the use of more sophisticated microscopic techniques and by the body of Mesolithic examples.[4] Here we are concerned primarily with validation of the concept of accumulations of linear marking based on the Upper Paleolithic tradition. In Spain and France, where the Upper Paleolithic cumulative tradition evolved uninterruptedly for some 25,000 years, the tradition of meaningful marking continued past the disappearance of the ice and into the new conditions of economic and cultural change.

Earlier we saw the presence of this style and tradition among the Late Magdalenian reindeer hunters of North Germany. What happened in northern Europe still later, after the ice had retreated from north Germany and southern Scandinavia and when these areas had new coasts, bogs, and marshes, and a returning woodland?

---

[4] The instruments, using a new development in analytic microscopy, are now being readied for the purpose.

On the plains of north Germany, Denmark, south Sweden, and the Baltic region of the Soviet Union, the retreating ice around 10,000 B.C. had opened up marsh and bog lands and new coasts on huge meltwater lakes. Migrants moved in from the east and south. A post-Ice Age, Mesolithic bog or marsh culture, called "Maglemose" or "Big bog" after a large site in Denmark, evolved, stretching from England to Russia. This culture was dependent on the hunting of forest animals, instead of the vast herds of the prior steppe and tundra, and on fishing, fowling, the gathering of fruits and nuts and of shellfish in the tidal waters. Because of the rise of the land with retreat of the ice, the area of today's North Sea was not a body of water separating Britain from the mainland, and the area of the Baltic Sea was a large freshwater lake.

There were some cultural affinities between the Mesolithic coastal cultures of Tèviec and Hoedic in France and that of the Maglemose peoples of the north, but specialization and differentiation were already evident. For one thing, the new, wet north offered a somewhat richer, more varied seasonal harvest than the older coasts of France. In the new bogs and lakes vast flocks of water birds came to nest. In the enormous tidewaters one could fish for large pike. The forests held deer, elk, bear, wood, fruits, nuts. The "dying" Paleolithic culture gave way to a new scheme of life on the bog shores and in the comparatively wet woodlands.

Far to the south, around the Mediterranean and particularly in the Middle East, Mesolithic cultures took a different form, more difficult, more specialized, in comparatively dry hills and valleys. This was the area that later historians would call the "Fertile Crescent," in comparison to the deserts that now also formed in the Mediterranean regions. The practical problems faced by men in this area, particularly in extracting a minimal living in each season, were different from those to the north. The general cognitive problems, however, were the same, and the evolved time-factoring cultural skills of the Paleolithic served both areas.

The Maglemose people of the north used stone, bone, and antler tools, they had axes and adzes, they cut wood for shelter, fire, boats, tools, and weapons, and they made the first large use of the bow and arrow, though some archaeologists place the origin of the bow in the Solutrean. They also worked and decorated bone, wood, and amber and used these materials for engraving art, symbols, and sequences. Most of the wood tools and objects have decayed, but the engraved bone, antler, stone, and amber remain. The body of engraved material is surprisingly large, though it is not as large as that from the Upper Paleolithic. What has been found so far, when examined by the new analytic and microscopic techniques, reveals the continuation and development of *all* the earlier symbolic traditions of the Paleolithic. Mesolithic cultures spread across Europe, Asia, into the Americas, Middle East, and Africa carrying aspects of this tradition.

I present four representative examples from the Maglemose to document portions of the tradition.

Fig. 212 a, b. Following pages. The two sides of an amber bear from Resen Mose, Denmark, engraved in what has been traditionally called decoration in a "geometric" pattern. Mesolithic, the Maglemose culture.

Fig. 212 b

Fig. 212 a

Fig. 212 a, b. Preceding pages.

From the bog of Resen in Jutland, Denmark, there comes the palm-sized amber sculpture of a schematized bear (Fig. 212 a, b). It has been presented in the scientific literature as a carved figure with typical "geometric" patterning in the Mesolithic style.[5]

Fig. 213 b   Fig. 213 a

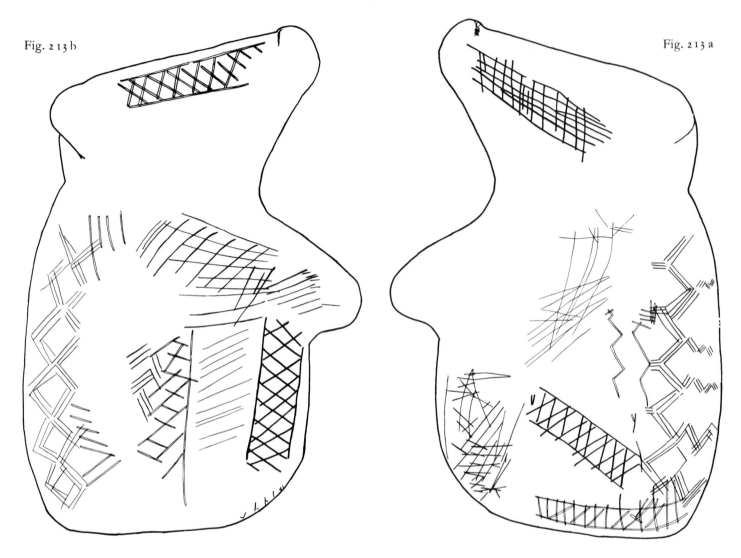

Fig. 213 a, b
Schematic rendition of all the engraved marks on the two sides of the amber bear from Resen Mose indicating the fact that the groups and patterns were made at different times and by different points. An additional pattern appears on the rear.

Under the microscope it was apparent that the sculpted ear and nose had been worn smooth by handling, that the geometric pattern along the right side of the muzzle had been made by a wide, flat point and had been polished by hand wear almost to the vanishing point, while the pattern along the left side of the muzzle was fresh and had been made by an exceedingly sharp point. Months, if not years, separated the making of the two patterns along the muzzle of the little bear.

The microscope revealed fifteen separate patterns on the two sides of the bear, made by fifteen different points, each pattern in a different stage of wear and often recognizably made by a different point (Fig. 213 a, b).

Whatever the precise meaning of the bear and its markings, it was time-factored. It was a symbolic, storied image that, like the Aurignacian horse from Vogelherd nearly 25,000 years earlier, was intended to be kept,

[5] J.G.D. Clark, THE MESOLITHIC SETTLEMENT OF NORTHERN EUROPE (Cambridge, Eng.: Camb. University Press, 1936), Fig. 7, p. 168.

handled, and used *in time*, including certain special times. It was not an object made once for "hunting magic" nor an object of decoration, since it had no hole but had to be held in the hand. Its story or use was, then, repetitive or periodic, and mythologically its meaning was continuous.

Fig. 214 a

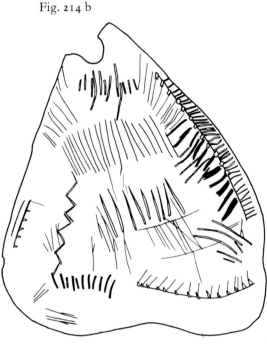

Fig. 214 b

Fig. 214 a
One face of an engraved amber pendant from Sejlflod, Denmark, engraved in what has been traditionally called a decoration in a "geometric" pattern. Maglemose culture.

Fig. 214 b
Schematic rendition of the main engraved marks on one face of the Sejlflod pendant indicating the different points engraving each set and the fact that sequences were over-engraved along certain containing lines. A comparable but different patterning occurs on the reverse face.

The geometric patterns are varied; some are hatches structured within containing lines, some are seemingly unstructured though crosshatched, some form multiple angles, some are mere linear series. It may be that the different forms have different meanings, for they were made by the one culture and probably by the same hand at different times. In one way or another, each pattern was an act of participation in the story of the bear. We can conjecture, but not know, their meanings. If the multiple angles represent sky, cloud, or water, and the structured hatches represent spirit nets or even notation, and unstructured groups represent markings made while saying a rite, we would have symbolic art and markings comparable in scope—if not in precise meaning—to those we found in the Paleolithic. These patterns, made at different times and by different points, are found on Maglemose tools, ceremonial objects, and pendants. A small pendant engraved on two faces (Fig. 214 a, b) has a complex, seemingly random patterning. Some of the sequences are notational,

Fig. 215 a,b

Sejlflod, Denmark. Details of two of the horizontal *containing-lines* on the incised amber pendant from the Maglemose culture, the Mesolithic period, c. 9,500-7,000 B.C. Each photograph documents the vertical/foot tradition of notational overmarking evidenced on the Le Placard eagle bones of the Magdalenian, c. 14,000 B.C., as well as the marking above and below a containing-line on the terminal Magdalenian notation from Taï, c. 10,000 B.C. Continuity across the Upper Paleolithic/Mesolithic transition is clear.

a) A horizontal containing-line has 16 vertical strokes attached to it; these were later overmarked by 16 small "feet." The sum of 32 makes a proper observational lunar month beginning with the last crescent of one month and ending with the first crescent of the 2nd month following. The verticals are subdivided into three or four subsets made at different angles. If this was the notation for one lunar month, the first 16 would begin with the crescent and end in the full moon period, the "feet" would then return to the crescent. Though not imaged as such, the marking might, there-

fore, have been boustrophedon. Above this main marking are two faint containing lines lightly marked with short subsidiary sets.

b) A similar but more complex notational accumulation is made at a side, in area B. A containing-line is marked with sets of verticals above the line; a set of "feet" was then added and a third group of marks, made again by different points, was appended below. These intentional accumulations are not decorative or random and are clearly made in the variable tradition of notational marking documented for the Upper Paleolithic.

These indigenous European traditions were apparently retained until the coming of neolithic farming. When the developing neolithic cultures begin building their megalithic stone alignments and mounds they document not a sophisticated arithmetical astronomy but a simple, basic mode of seasonal time-reckoning and lunar/solar observation. There is perhaps reason now to believe that these indigenous traditions began around c. 28,000 B.C. with the hunter-gatherers of the Ice Age and were not derived from the agricultural civilizations of the Middle East.

some of the forms, such as the angles, apparently symbolic. The microscope reveals that these markings were made by different tools and, showing differential wear and polish, were made at different times. An analysis of both faces will be presented later. The line drawing indicates the over-engraving and the accumulation of sets. To document the point and wear differences among the groups, I present a photographic enlargement of the central portion of face number one (Fig. 215).

◄ Fig. 215. Page opposite.
Detail. The central area of the first face of the Sejlflod pendant indicating the different tools used in the engraving and the differential wear and polish upon the varying sets. Upper sequence shows less polish than lower, the middle sequences show almost none. Evidence indicates accumulation of sets over long period.

Fig. 216 b

Fig. 216 a
One face of an amber pendant from Hjørring, Denmark, engraved in what had been traditionally called decoration in a "geometric" pattern. Maglemose culture.

Fig. 216 b
Schematic rendition of the basic pattern on one face of the Hjørring pendant indicating the complex accumulation of images and groups of marks, including a plant, a series of running angles, a vulvar image, a fallen anthropomorphic figure and a schematic hand, each apparently made by a different point at a different time.

Another amber is also engraved on both faces (Fig. 216 a, b). The microscope reveals that the groups were made by different points at different times. The symbolic forms include a plant image, angles, a schematized human form lying on its side, an apparent hand image, an enclosed, somewhat rhomboidal or vulvar structure, and two sequences of markings contained by horizontals that by their placement seem representative of sky and earth but which microscopy reveals as apparently notational.

The most important of the examples is a large axlike or mattocklike instrument made of antler horn, with a hole for what one might think was the shaft. It is heavily engraved on one face and sparsely engraved on the edges and back. The microscope reveals an unusual series of facts. There are no marks of digging or hacking on the point. Instead, it is worn smooth and discolored by what seem to be hand polish, hand oils and

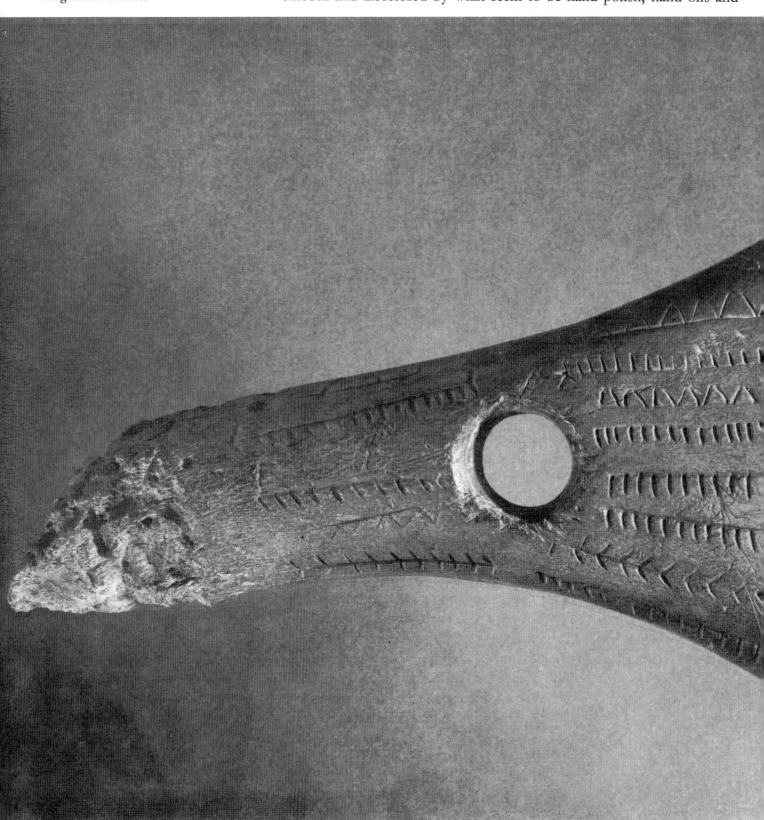

sweat, as though it had been held by the point. A similar polish appears in the later Neolithic period on axes used to dig in damp, soft soil. Whatever its original use, it was apparently also a slate or ceremonial object, even perhaps a ceremonial "ax," comparable perhaps to certain bâtons of the Upper Paleolithic (Fig. 217).

Schematic rendition of all the engraved marks on the Ugerløse "mattock" as determined by microscopic analysis. Differences in the engraving tools are schematically rendered. Intentional points of differentiation within long sequences and differences in the style of stroke among adjacent sequences are indicated. A final sequence was added at bottom center after completion of the main notations. The rendition suggests an evolved tradition of notational accumulation derived from the Upper Paleolithic.

The microscope also reveals that the marks on the point or "handle" are relatively fresh and unworn and were, therefore, made late in its use as a slate, apparently as analysis showed, among the final markings on the bone (Fig. 218). The engraving points making these marks were different from the points making the other sequences.

Even without the microscope it was clear that the central composition had a number of indications that the markings were notational (Fig. 219).

Fig. 218
Detail. The point of the Ugerløse "mattock" indicating the differences between the tools engraving these sequences and those on the central area. The marks here are not worn or polished by any use of the point.

One long series of angles began and ended with two parallel strokes (\\\\...//), as though to mark off the beginning and ending of a full sequence. The series below it ended with a figure made of four marks (←/\\\'), again indicating the close of a period represented by that long series. The series below had one lone mark as an extra in the series of

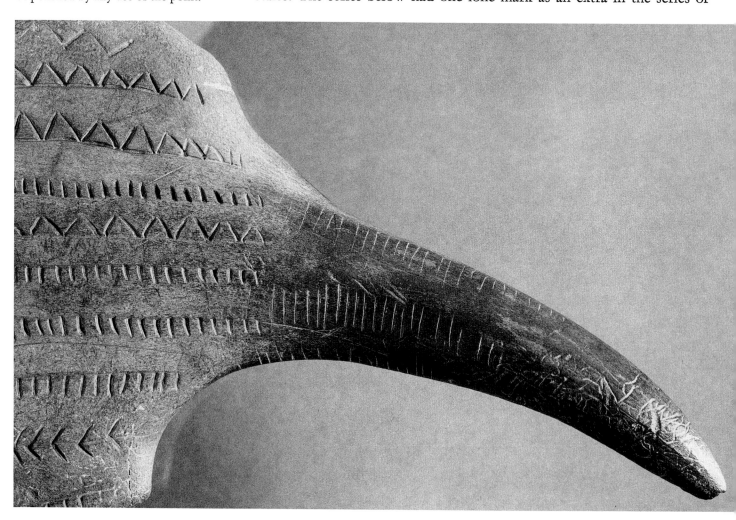

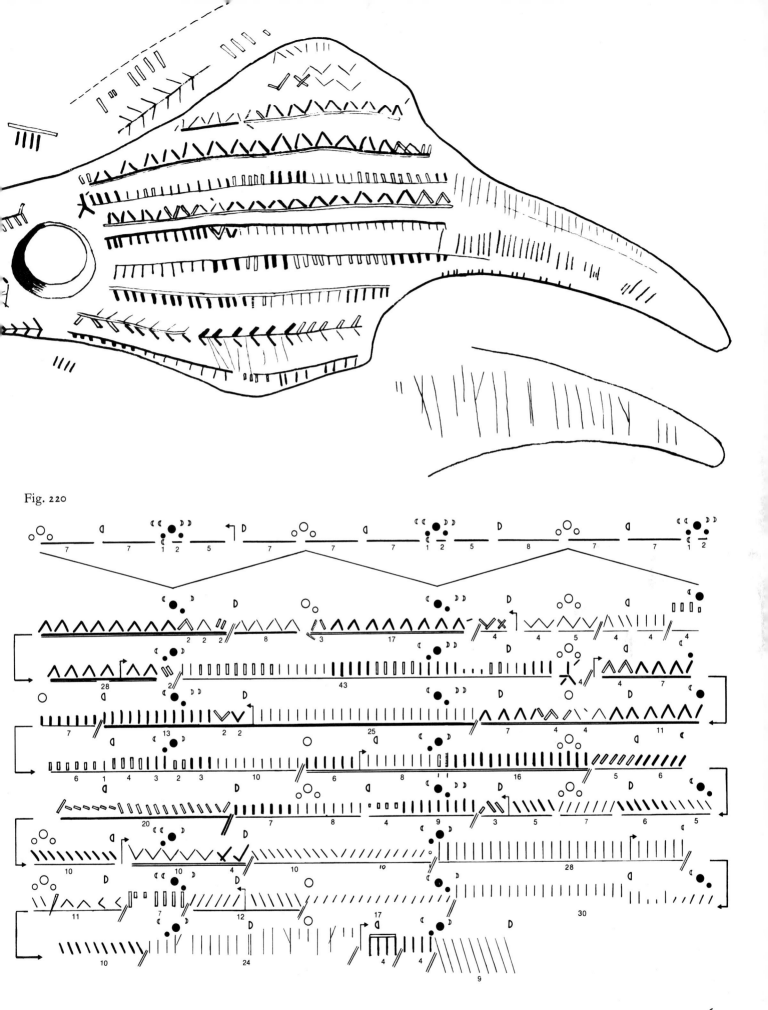

Fig. 220

Fig. 220. Preceding page.
All the engraved marks on the Ugerløse "mattock" against the lunar
model indicating a possible lunar
phrasing in the sets and subsets. The
engraved horizontal containing lines
are also used here to structure the
larger sets or groups.

Fig. 221
Detail. Enlargement of the engraved
portion at the left of the hole on the
Ugerløse "mattock" indicating that
each set was engraved by a different
point and presumably at a different
time.

angles, again indicating a point of differentiation. The series below that,
a series of verticals, was broken in the middle by two angles, again as
though to differentiate a point and sum. Even more important, each
horizontal series was divided into smaller groups made by different points.
The analysis of this slate will be published in great detail later since it
serves as the culmination of pre-literate notation.

A test of the central marks against a lunar model, beginning at the top and
working from right to left downward, revealed that the central portion
notated precisely 12 lunar months, beginning with a first crescent and ending with a last crescent. All the differentiating marks fell at phase points,
indicating either the beginning or the end of a period; all the changes
of point, as nearly as such changes could be determined by the use of a

stereoscopic zoom microscope, were indicative of lunar phase changes[6]
(Fig. 220).

The markings to the left of the hole also showed microscopic evidence of
engraving by different points (Fig. 221). The marks to the right and left

[6] These subgroupings will be refined by the new microscopic techniques now in preparation.

of the central portion gave a sum for seven months. After the central portion had been made, 9 marks had been added, very lightly, near the bottom. The total was, therefore, for a year and a half, or 17 lunar months, finishing at a half-moon. This lunar count could represent a year and a half in a lunar, solar, or stellar observational year.

If, as it seems, this is a lunar tally, it stems from the Upper Paleolithic tradition. This calendar may explain the presence of a tradition of calendric notation and observation in north and central Europe at a time when a different regional tradition was being practiced by agricultural cultures far to the south. It may point to the origins of the calendar sticks and rune calendars found in north and central Europe in the historic era. Significant in this respect is the fact that calendric notations exist across the historic Eurasian north and in other areas whose tradition can be traced to this area. These late traditions will be discussed in another publication. There is a possibility that this European tradition has relevance for the astronomic alignments of the extremely late stone circle of Stonehenge in England.[7] I urge caution and do not assert that these sparse examples and incomplete analyses have yet proved the case or indicated a direct line to Stonehenge.

I close the Maglemose with a small engraved amber in a tradition different from those shown so far. It is engraved on both faces, but I present a rendition of one face as determined by careful microscopic examination. The surface is so worn and deteriorated that the photograph may be confusing (Fig. 222 a, b). The composition shows a pattern of water birds along both sides, riding on what seems to be a series of water "angles." There are two rows of what appear to be bark or wooden floats for holding up a net, and then a long laddered figure that seems to be a net or weir for catching fish. The three triangles at the top seem indicative of land or mountains. The image, whatever its symbolic or ritual meaning, is clearly time-factored, related to the time of the large water fowl and perhaps the time of the large fish runs of late spring. Exactly this image of schematic water fowl on a band of "water" appears decoratively on a Neolithic pot from Russian Carelia, near Finland.[8]

[7] R. J. C. Atkinson, "Moonshine on Stonehenge," ANTIQUITY, XL, pp. 212–216.
Jacquetta Hawkes, "God in the Machine," ANTIQUITY, XLI, pp. 174–180.
Gerald S. Hawkins, "Astro-Archaeology," VISTAS IN ASTRONOMY, 10 (1968), 45–88.
Gerald S. Hawkins, "Stonehenge Decoded," NATURE, 200 (1963), 306–308.
Gerald S. Hawkins, "Stonehenge: A Neolithic Computer," NATURE, 202 (1964), 1258–1261.
Gerald S. Hawkins, "Sun, Moon, Men, and Stones," AMER. SCIENTIST, 53 (1965), 391–408.
Gerald S. Hawkins and J. B. White, STONEHENGE DECODED (Garden City, N.Y.: Doubleday & Co., 1965).
Fred Hoyle, "Speculations on Stonehenge," ANTIQUITY, XL (1966), pp. 262–276.
"Hoyle on Stonehenge; Some Comments," ANTIQUITY, XLI (1967), pp. 91–98.
Alexander Thom, "Megalithic Astronomy: Indications in Standing Stones," VISTAS IN ASTRONOMY, 7 (1965), 1–57.
Alexander Thom, "The Lunar Observatories of Megalithic Man," VISTAS IN ASTRONOMY, 11 (1969), 1–29.

[8] Grahame Clark, THE STONE AGE HUNTERS (New York: McGraw-Hill, 1967), p. 105.

Fig. 222 a
One face of an engraved amber from the North Sea region, Denmark, with a complex "decoration" on each face. Maglemose culture.

Fig. 222 b
Line rendition of all engraved marks on one face of the engraved amber from the North Sea region, as determined by microscopic analysis. Two bands of water birds ride on schematized water angles along each side. Fishing net floats and a fish weir seem to be lined up in the center. The mountains of the north seem to be engraved at the top. The whole is apparently a seasonal image.

Other images and symbols from the Maglemose include fish, serpents, deer, and anthropomorphic figures. There are also ceremonial axes and objects.

Far to the south in the Middle East, within this general period, agriculture began to develop out of Mesolithic roots. Dorothy Garrod and others in the 1930's excavated one of the earliest true villages in this area.
The Natufian Mesolithic culture, c. 8,500 B.C., was centered in Palestine but extended north into Syria and Lebanon and west into Egypt and Africa. Other cultures on the verge of agriculture appear as far north as Shanidar in the Zagros Mountains of northern Iraq, where Professor Ralph Solecki found a Mesolithic pebble engraved in the hatch design.
The Natufians at the village of Jericho were reaping grain with sickles and grinding it with mortar and pestle, though they were not yet full-time farmers. They had a complex religious and ceremonial life including a complex burial ritual. I present a Natufian double-breast necklace whose antecedents go back to the East Gravettian necklace we saw earlier (Fig. 223 a, b, c). With this "feminine" necklace were found "masculine" phallic forms made of stone.

Fig. 223 a

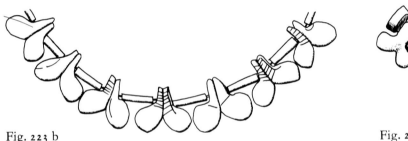

Fig. 223 b

Fig. 223 c

Fig. 223 a, b, c
Line renditions of pendant beads in the shape of the double breast image from the Upper Paleolithic and later cultures.
a) Dolní Věstonice, the East Gravettian or Pavlovian of Czechoslovakia; b) Natufian, the Mesolithic of Palestine; c) Aveyron, the Megalith builders of France.

Fig. 224 a, b, c. Page opposite.
Schematic rendition of the engraved marks on the three faces of the bone tool (Fig. 1 a, b, c) from Ishango, the Congo, as determined by microscopic analysis. Mesolithic.

Fig. 225. Page opposite.
The engraved marks on the Ishango tool against the lunar model indicating the possible observational lunar phrasing in the sets and subsets.

Thousands of years later a farming people with highly evolved burial customs and a solar mythology came out of the eastern farming areas into the ancient land of France, where once the Paleolithic hunters and the later Mesolithic hunter-gatherers had lived. They brought with them many motifs and traditions evolved from those we have seen. I present one necklace whose roots go to the Eastern Mesolithic and the earlier East Gravettian Upper Paleolithic (Fig. 223 c).

We end where we began, with the Mesolithic bone from Ishango at the headwaters of the Nile, whose markings initiated this long research. The bone was engraved at the time the northern Maglemosians were engraving and the Middle East Natufians were farming, around 6,500 B.C. When I examined this tiny petrified bone at the Musée d'Histoire Naturelle in Brussels, I found that the engraving, as nearly as microscopic examination could differentiate the deteriorated markings, was made by 39 different points and was notational. It seemed, more clearly than before, to be lunar (Figs. 224 a, b, c; 225).

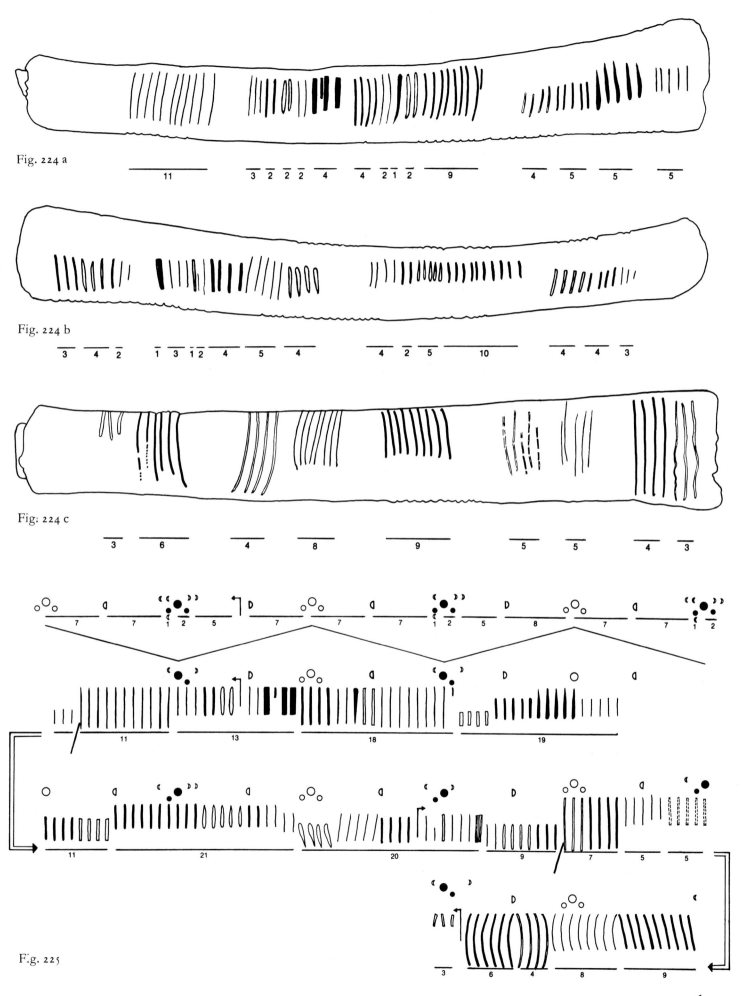

Fig. 224 a

Fig. 224 b

Fig. 224 c

F.g. 225

Engraved bone from Ishango, Congo, c. 6,500 B.C., which began the research. The three faces are placed in the order of the final analysis (Fig. 224 a, b, c) and are read from right to left.

POSTSCRIPT

In the cave of Lascaux, in the Vézère river region, in an archaeological layer containing the bones of reindeer and chipped flint tools, there was found the small carbonized fragment of a piece of cord. Its imprint was also in the clay.[1]

Because the fragment was fossilized, it was not possible to determine what variety of plant supplied the fibers. It was braided of three strands about one quarter inch wide (7 to 8 mm), all twisting to the right.

The position of the cord in the cave has led archaeologists to believe that it had been used to descend into the ritual pit or "well" containing the paintings of the wounded bison, the bird-headed "sorcerer," the rhinoceros, and the horse.

The clue is slight and is perhaps the least dramatic of those found in Lascaux with its wealth of painted and engraved animals, plants, weapons, signs, and symbols. The fragment of cord hardly compares in significance with the art or the other Upper Paleolithic images of plants we have seen depicting sprout, branch, flower, tree, and possibly cone, fruit, and nut.

[1] A. Glory, "Debris de corde paléolithique à la grotte de Lascaux," BULLETIN DE LA SOCIÉTÉ PRÉHISTORIQUE FRANÇAISE, Tome LIII (1956), pp. 263–264.

Nevertheless, by implication, the cord is of vast importance, telling us much about man, his cognition, and the nature of his early culture. There is, first, a cognitive difference between a recognition of plant forms and varieties, which to a degree can be done by all animals, and the use of a plant as an image or symbol. There is also a difference between these visual recognitions and the practical recognition required to cut the proper plant in the correct season to obtain the right fiber, a complex recognition that implies a series of skills for preparation of the fibers, twining them into string, and using the cord. It is not agriculture, but it is in a cognitive relation to it. There are different levels of cognition implied in these diverse recognitions and uses. Each extends the plant to more complex usage *in time.* How much these increasingly complex uses are due to evolved capacities of the brain and how much to the specialized culture man developed in the Paleolithic is a difficult question. Plant images and twined cord are equally parts of human "culture," contemporaneous products of the brain and society. They cannot, therefore, be functionally separated, though they can be separated for study by students of the evolution of intelligence or the evolution of culture.

Clearly, the *Homo sapiens* potential for symbol-making represents a genetic advance over the more generalized mammalian capacity for a recognition of forms. But what is the nature of that advance? Is it a factor of brain size with a greater capacity for memory storage, cross-reference and feedback? In what way is it evolved from the ancient capacity for toolmaking, which already contains these cognitive, kinesthetic, time-factored elements in simpler form?

Neanderthal man, with a larger brain than *Homo sapiens,* was an exquisite toolmaker and a user of symbols. He practiced ritual burial, used red ocher, and may have made beads (in the Chatelperronian culture of France, c. 35,000 B.C.); he made clothes of skins, tied them with thongs, and he hafted tools. He was not a maker of depictive "art," though a ritual burial and the manufacture of clothes and symbols are forms of image making. He probably could speak but there is a debate as to how well. Was there a difference in the brain or merely in the culture, or in aspects of both? What, if any, was the nature of the difference?

It would seem that the levels of cognition required for the two forms of plant usage, in one case as a sign and symbol of process and story, and in the other as a product for direct use, are different. The ape, for instance, can use a stick, branch, or leaf for specialized purposes such as probing an ant hole, chasing a leopard or sopping up water.

In Neanderthal man and even more in *Homo sapiens,* one part of the difference would seem to have been cultural, the result of an increasing "artificiality" in culture in which images, forms, and colors had themselves become products. The Neanderthal manufacture of a non-depictive image is not far from the *Homo sapiens'* manufacture of a depictive animal or human image, though a depictive image is an advance in conceptualization and in possibilities for varied use of the image.

Returning to the fossil cord of Lascaux, we can affirm that various cognitive capacities fed each other. The cord was *used* to descend into the ceremonial pit. It was a tool and not art, but it was used as part of the cultural complex involved in the "artificiality" of art, as were the stone tools, the oxides, the clays, the carbon colors, the oils and fats, the bones and the stone slates. The bit of cord was part of the same cultural complex that used plant images and symbols at special times. There are other cognitive problems. Was the cord made from fibers that had to be gathered at a particular place, say the riverside marsh, and in a particular season? Would the fibers maintain their strength through a year, into the winter or through the damp of the following spring? Or were they woven of spring rushes, vines, or branches, pliable with the new sap? The precise answers are not as important at this stage of the inquiry as the questions and the nature of the time-factored cognitions they both seek and imply.

In the painted cave of La Mouthe, in the same Dordogne region as Lascaux, there was found a shallow, ground-out stone dish that had once contained oil and presumably a wick, so that it could serve as a lamp. On the underside of the lamp is engraved the head of a male ibex, with its long crescent horns. When lit, the ibex on the underside cannot be seen. The time-factored ideas in the lamp are as vast as in the cord. Though it was not found with the cord, it belongs with it, conceptually and culturally. It was a tool used in the symbolic realm as one of the practical objects required in the making of "art." Was it a long-term object, used and reused, time after time and year after year, as opposed to a piece of cord that may have been made fresh yearly? Did the image of the ibex, which in some examples of engraved art was apparently related to the myth of spring-summer, have some meaning related to the symbolism of fire, of the lamp, of light itself, of the ceremony performed in the cave, of the season of the ceremony, or of the myth belonging to the maker and user? What animal fat was rendered to oil by heating in order to serve as liquid fuel? Was such animal fat obtained from the fatted animals of late summer and fall, or the lean animals of dead winter and early spring? Or was it obtained in any season from the marrow of animal bones? Could the oil be stored for lamp use in skins or wooden vessels? Did this oil from the animal body, which burned differently than wood and by a floating wick, and which probably savored somewhat of food or flesh, have its "story," and was it, therefore, "holy" in a way different than wood?

The questions are peripheral. They were not included in the old, traditional archaeology, nor are they part of the newer sequential analyses, deductions, and documentation presented in this book. Nevertheless, they are related to these other forms of evidence and must increasingly become part of the theorizing and research related to early man's intelligence and culture. The questions indicate the subtle range of problems involved in the search for the cognitive evolution of man.

The cord, lamp, and oil were products of the northern, Franco-Cantabrian branch of Ice Age culture. In the southeastern Spanish branch, painting was often done on the daylit rock walls of the overhangs and shelters. According to recent studies, these were often painted with red ocher dissolved in water and egg white and applied with a bird feather. If we assume that the season of egg white is limited in fowl or reptile, we can assume a spring-early summer season for these particular wall paintings, though the images themselves often give us no clue to "spring." This evidence is related to the art. A body of other archaeological evidence increases our understanding of the symbolic, artificial time-and-space realms of early man. We analyzed a bâton from the Late Magdalenian site of Montgaudier showing seals, fish,

snakes, and plants. The composition seemed to imply a spring-early summer series of images, with the possibility of seals having come up the estuary from the sea and perhaps some distance upriver, though not into the hills of the upper Vézère. In inland sites of the Upper Paleolithic one also finds sea shells and whale teeth that came from the coasts. Was there a seasonal migration or a seasonal meeting for ceremonies and "trade" at a crossing point of the great herds? In some of the Mediterranean sites there are shells both of the deeper tidewater and the shore fringes. Did the gatherers know the tides and seasons of the sea and use rafts or boats, long before the Mesolithic shellfish gatherers? In the cave of Nerja in the Malaga region of southern Spain, near the Mediterranean coast but deep in the cave and in an exceedingly difficult spot, there is a painting of three dolphins, two seemingly a male and female in face-to-face encounter. These apparently "storied" dolphins seem to imply recognition of a possible seasonal, specialized behavior known to a sea fisher.

There are other, comparable hints. In the Dordogne region Dr. Jean Gaussen has uncovered a number of outdoor Magdalenian summer campsites on hills overlooking valley and river. The tent or hut floors had "flagstone" paving to allow for drainage and to keep one off the damp ground. There was probably a fur or fiber cover over the stones. The outdoor summer site was not far from ceremonial caves and winter rock shelters. This contrasts with the North German summer campsite of the Late Magdalenian reindeer hunters excavated by Alfred Rust. That site seemed to be at the end of a long trek from the winter camp and ceremonial areas.

By analogy to modern hunting groups, and by reference to the archaeological evidence but not to the art, symbols, or notations, archaeologists have deduced some such variable seasonal life. Raymond Lantier, honorary curator of French museums, says:

"The confined life of winter was followed by a nomadic, camping existence, during which the hunters housed themselves in shallow, well-located rock shelters, facing south or east by preference in France, or in light huts built of branches and leaves. They were always on the march, in the wake of the herbivorous animals they hunted. Few traces remain today of these summer camps,[2] and it is very difficult to interpret with any exactitude the remains of the implements found on the campsites, which indicate various activities whose nature is unknown to us. But it is difficult to believe that all these journeys had hunting as their only purpose. A single group might hunt for a time, then stay put for a while to gather tubers, root plants, berries, mushrooms, eggs and wild honey. The rising of the salmon in the rivers in the spawning season was certainly the reason for fishing expeditions. And it was normal that the nature of the camps, the shape of the habitations and that of their utilitarian arrangements, should differ markedly. However, a genuine uniformity characterized the seasonal rhythm of Paleolithic life: travels and settlements were always closely related to the unending search for food.

"Scattering in summer and coming together again in winter represents a symbiosis that one finds in Eskimo societies, which are forced to live according to the habits of their game. Summer provides an almost limitless hunting field; by contrast, winter narrows it greatly. A similar alternation explains the stages of dispersal and concentration through which primitive society passed—men gathered together or scattered like their game. Society was synchronized with this wandering life, and social life was led differently at different seasons of the year. It passed through successive and regular phases of waxing or waning intensity, of activity and rest, of spending and saving.

"Thus in summer life was, so to speak, secular, while in winter men lived in a state of religious exaltation: celebrating tribal rites, initiating the adolescents into the traditions and beliefs of the tribe, the rights and duties of adults. It was also the time when one used up the savings accumulated during the summer, when one made arms and tools, prepared skins and furs, sewed clothing and made vessels of leather, basketry and bark.

"One also wonders whether a good deal of time was not spent, during this season when outdoor activity was at a minimum, in decorating the places of worship, and in such work, which could have been learned only through great patience and practiced in moments stolen from a particularly rough existence and during which the community would have to assure to the artist a life more or less free from material worries, one can recognize perhaps the beginnings of specialization.

"Isolated though these groups seem to have been, and separated from one another as were the seasonal migra-

tions, it is nevertheless possible to perceive the exchange of raw materials (flints) or of manufactured objects (stone lamps). The seashells and fossils often came from far away: the marl of Touraine and Poitou served as coin for the populations of the Dordogne, Tarn-et-Garonne, Haute-Garonne, Puy-de-Dôme and Liguria. The Paleolithic inhabitants of Laugerie-Haute (Dordogne) used shells originating in the Atlantic and the Mediterranean. At Thayngen (Switzerland) one finds Miocene fossils from the environs of Vienne.
"All these movements indicate the existence of traditional routes, rudimentary trails followed by the travelers and the hunters, passing necessarily through certain fords and passes, most often following, as is true today in primitive societies, the natural paths provided by streams and rivers."[3]

Such concepts relate to the evidence and hypotheses we have been discussing in this book. If these broad time-and-space ecologial concepts and my notational, symbolic findings are added to the new "process-oriented" archaeology discussed at the end of Chapter VI, we begin to see that a reconstruction of early man's life, which includes the dynamics of his real world, the real and symbolic relations he had to that world, as well as the cognitive processes by which that culture was created and maintained, is being made possible. At the end of almost one century of European archaeology, the mysterious maker of the chipped stone axes is beginning to seem not only human but a person we are able to study scientifically and in depth.

These new approaches to modern archeology were summarized in a paper by Professor Robert McC. Adams, Director of the Oriental Institute of the University of Chicago. The paper was published before this book and so refers only to the non-notational research being developed:
"Of the greatest importance has been the elaboration of ... an ecological approach [studying the] points of articulation between the subsistence activities of a particular human group and the wider natural and social setting within which it operated. The focus of concern ... is the shifting, complex set of adaptive responses which must characterize any community ... and which in turn can help explain the changes it undergoes through time."[4]

[2] Important exceptions are Rust's north German and Gaussen's French summer sites. A series of studies by Grahame Clark of Cambridge University, England, documents these problems at length.

[3] Raymond Lantier, MAN BEFORE HISTORY, trans. Unity Evans (New York: Walker & Company, 1965), pp. 110–112.

[4] Robert McC. Adams, "Archaeological Research Strategies: Past and Present," SCIENCE, Vol. 160 (June 14, 1968), p. 1188.

Now, "adaptive responses," as we have seen, are most effective when properly time-factored, whether these responses are realistic and practical or symbolic and storied. Describing this new archaeology, Adams writes,

"The trend has been toward reliance on greater and greater numbers of converging lines of evidence for both ancient and modern environments—soils, bones, pollen, geomorphology—in order to discover unsuspected cultural variables, to reduce ambiguities in interpretation, and to deal with the interlocking effects of the widest possible range of adaptive relationships."[5]

My analyses have begun a similar search and have opened other areas of insight and interpretation. Adams, continuing, writes:

"In some of the most important and productive undertakings of recent years, such as those concerned with the locally differentiated processes by which plants and animals were independently domesticated in the Old and New worlds soon after the end of the Pleistocene [the period of the Ice Ages], the greater part of the effort and expense has been directed at the analysis of ecological variables rather than at all of the traditional classes of archaeological findings taken together."[6]

As we saw, the evolved and complex time-factored cultures of the late Pleistocene or Upper Paleolithic provided the crucial preparations for the Mesolithic and Neolithic, within which the steps were taken towards agriculture and the domestication of animals. Various groups of these early cultures arrived in the Americas during the Upper Paleolithic and the post-Paleolithic carrying Mesolithic or Neolithic lore. Others arrived in relatively recent historic times going back to about 2,000 B.C. Under the right conditions, aspects of incipient or advanced agrculture could have developed from *any* of these groups.

After summarizing the host of new dynamic "process" approaches in archaeology, Adams states:

"... the central creative activity in archeology, like in all scholarship, lies in induction, in outstripping the narrow base of available facts to suggest new and essentially speculative unities."[7]

The leap of induction must, however, be made from a base of fact. In modern archaeology, Adams states:

"... greater emphasis is being given to the critical processes of transformation that have led from one general level of organizational complexity in human society to another."[8]

Then Adams, as a leading archaeologist, warns that:

"... most of us remain excessively timid, reluctant to tackle the grand problems of comparison, generalization, and synthesis, even though the certainty of being found in frequent error if we did so ought to be heavily outweighed by the opportunity to deepen, sharpen, and ultimately justify our inquiries."[9]

My own effort, one of these new approaches to archaeology, has consisted of the attempt to understand aspects of evolved human cognition in terms of Upper Paleolithic art, symbol, and notation, with occasional reference to other archaeological materials.

The attempt to establish a certain level of cognitive capacity and cultural complexity has perhaps given to these early Upper Paleolithic peoples an appearance of "sophistication." The modern meaning of the word "sophistication" implies a use of cross-cultural comparisons and knowledge. This modern form of sophistication was not there and it could not be.

For one thing, the general levels of the hunting and gathering cultures, though regionally specialized and variable, were not basically or profoundly different. Territories and areas were limited. The chances for a comparison of ideas and of cultures were relatively limited. Mobility always occurred within a comparative cultural uniformity. The cognitive contents that could be used in comparisons, by juxtaposition of art, symbol, myth, rite, decoration, dress, and technological skills, were not greatly different. There were variations in local skills and styles, but these were always, at least in Europe, found within the context of the broad cultural Paleolithic uniformity.

In addition, the population of mankind was sparse, a fraction of what it is today, and interrelations and cultural comparisons were, therefore, quantitatively limited. Within this limited but complex world—from our point of view—skills and knowledge were taught by word of mouth, by use of story and symbol, by ceremony and rite, and by showing and doing. Because of these factors, as I have suggested, there was a limit not so much on the amount or complexity of knowledge and lore as to the number of comparisons that were possible.

Despite these limitations, the processes of cognition were evolved and modern. The cognitive processes were not the same as the cultural data that were being

[5] Ibid., p. 1189.   [6] Loc. cit.   [7] Ibid., p. 1190.   [8] Loc. cit.   [9] Ibid., p. 1192.

offered to the *Homo sapiens* brain for cognition. The processes refer to evolved capacities and potentials. The data refer to cultural structures and the physical, ecologial reality which supply inputs to the brain.

The brain is a constant within evolutionary species limits in a period of 100,000 to 200,000 years. The data are inherently variable, though within any one area and culture the pace of that variability is itself a variable. In general, one might say that culture varied more slowly as one goes back in prehistory, though the *Homo sapiens* cultural revolution of about 35,000 B.C. seems to have been relatively rapid and widespread, compared with what had occurred before.

Because of differences in the cultural data and the way of life, a man of today would not have understood the man of the Ice Age, since languages, stories, knowledge, and skills were different. The Ice Age hunter had not the range of comparisons that even a poorly educated man has today.

Increasingly, as we understand more of what it means to be an evolved human, particularly in a formative period such as the Ice Age, we are beginning to understand some of the relevant processes though we may be perplexed by the details. Born into Upper Paleolithic society and surviving to adulthood, each of us could be either a paleolithic hunter or his wife.

There is danger in such simple generalizations. They do not present us with the enormity of the differences that did, in fact, exist between the life and thoughts of the Upper Paleolithic hunter and those of a modern man in an industrial culture.

For example, because of the relatively sparse human population, man was, and he could see that he was, a minority creature in the world of nature. Today he lives in an almost totally man-made, man-regulated world. Partly for this reason, the time-factored structures and regulations were of a different sort and order in the Upper Paleolithic.

All men were hunters and gatherers, though some hunted more on the tundra, others more by the sea, others more in the valleys and hills; some may have specialized seasonally in hunting the reindeer, the mammoth, the horse, the bison, the seal, or the mollusk. Since they were all hunters and gatherers, the practical and symbolic territories of neighboring groups and tribes must have been acknowledged generally and seasonally or, if there was overlapping or

intrusion not acknowledged, with resulting strife. It is clear that the relationships of small groups of hunters across territories, and seasonally within territories, must have included such time-factored acknowledgments. In the evolving complexity of human interrelations, the meaning of "territoriality" would have been extended from the practical, ecological range to include ranges in which the the time-factored symbol or myth was valid.

Where art and notation exist, therefore, we must recognize the play of these time-space factors and recognize a separation and differentiation among groups, though the cultures may have been generally uniform. These are deductions based on the cognitive levels implied in the symbol and art; they cannot always be made from the technology or industry of a culture or period.

Obviously something had changed and was changing by the time of the Upper Paleolithic revolution, and it continued to change as one advancd into the Mesolithic and Neolithic. The size of interrelated groups grew, at least in some crucial areas, and the relations between groups in increasingly distant territories changed. As a result the nature of the extractive, practical, and symbolic uses of a territory also changed. It may be that Neanderthal man was not so much killed and exterminated as he was "disqualified" from a symbolic realm. Within the practical and symbolic structuring of a realm, the concept of the increasing territory or inter-territory becomes meaningful. We have seen the territory of an image or symbol. But a type of stone, a seashell for decoration, a clay or pigment for a ceremony might come from outside the group's range. Specialized journeys in certain seasons might be made to get these, or practical and symbolic exchanges between groups might occur at recognized places in certain seasons. The side of a hill, which had no practical or economic use, may have had a symbolic or ceremonial use, perhaps because of a sanctuary cave or the presence of a ritual grove or because it was the place of the seasonal bear hunt or sacrifice. A river valley may have been the site at which an animal migration crossed two times a year, becoming a meeting and feasting place for related hunting groups. Time and space had begun to be divided and extended in increasingly complex human terms, and interrelations among men were involved with these time-space structures and my-thologies. It is in this sense that "sophistication" *began* to be a human cultural phenomenon.

It is within this context that the meaning of early hu-man "aggression" and "territoriality" must be dis-cussed. The symbolic and storied meanings of sacri-fice, death, and killing, and even of ritual cannibalism or aberrational murder, would change as interrela-tions among groups changed and as societies devel-oped or disintegrated. The basic cognitive and sym-bolic processes involved in these aspects of human behavior would not change, but the specific meanings of the cultural product would.

As *Homo sapiens* cultures developed, there were in-creasing opportunities and solutions possible for indi-viduals, whether of character, personality, or ideas. The growing complexity and artificiality of human culture made it possible to develop and maintain an increasing diversity of personality and character and of culturally rationalized solutions for individual problems. What role did notation, art, symbol, cere-mony, and rite play in individuality? There is a body of scientific literature that discusses the role of the shaman, sorcerer, and magician in primitive society, including his use of art, symbol, and ritual. These studies have been largely descriptive or psychologi-cal. The role of a time-factored, continuous, struc-tured culture in helping to form these specialized per-sonalities, and in maintaining them as a class through time, and the role of these personalities in maintaining the structures of the group and the culture have not yet been adequately discussed or researched. I will write about these problems too at a later time in terms of the Paleolithic and contemporary evidence.

As we saw in connection with Piaget's research, there are stages in cognitive development and in the development of the capacity for logical and symbolic thinking. The individual gradually enlarges his "ra-tional" capacity to see process within an object or symbol, to see process in the end product, to recog-nize a sequence of steps or transformations, and finally to communicate these through the use of stories and symbols. Not in the archaeological evi-dence, but important for an understanding of it, therefore, are the unconscious uses of symbol and the equations of story. These may not always be verbalized, yet they play an important role as inter-mediary between the individual, society, and the symbols and myths. The relation between the con-scious, the unconscious, society, and the body of myth and symbol is neither static nor simple. The analyses and documentation in this book serve to raise these questions for the prehistoric past.

It is clear, then, that I have barely touched on the problems suggested by the body of art, symbol, and notation of the early *Homo sapiens* cultures. I have presented only a few selected, representative examples with any degree of detail. There are thousands of rel-evant examples in the Paleolithic and Mesolithic cul-tures, not counting the stone and bone tools or indus-tries. Publication and analysis have only begun, and the scope of the cognitive, time-factored complexity implied in this vast body of evidence has just been hinted at in this volume.

What I have done is offer an introduction to a few new concepts and techniques of analysis and compari-son, presenting some of the sequential steps in the search and deduction more or less as the questions, facts and possibilities unfolded or were discovered.

THE ROOTS OF CIVILIZATION

Two Decades Later

The best of journeys, those of the mind, do not end. Each step leads to another, and each answer leads to a question. When the postscript to this book was written in 1968 it described a fragment of twined cord discovered in the cave of Lascaux. From that bit of rubbish found in a cave best known for its masterpieces of animal art I wove a fabric of implication and inference. Following the trail of that "conceptual" cord for the next two decades led the inquiry deep into little known aspects of the Ice Age cultures of Europe and backward to the earlier cultures of the Neanderthals and eventually to their antecedents, *Homo erectus*.

That bit of remnant cord, in its odd way, represents one of the major problems in archaeology. All that we normally find in the early archaeological record are the hard materials of bone and stone and, in the Ice Age, images made with mineral paints that have been preserved on the stone walls of the caves. The perishable fragment of cord was preserved only because it was in a sealed cave. Lascaux was closed for thousands of years to currents of outside air and pollution, one of the reasons that the ancient paintings retain their rich, original color. It is these animal paintings in Lascaux and in other caves, and not the bit of cord, that scholars have written about, placing them among the high points in human creativity and culture. I have, as part of the ongoing inquiry into early symbol and thought, sought to ascertain some of the "meanings," not in the images but in the contexts and uses of that "art," including the uses of the images in Lascaux. But it was that dry and blackened fragment of cord that unexpectedly led to deeper insight and to an unexpected widening of the inquiry, a widening inquiry that touched on the nature of the human symboling process and the inadequacies of the archaeological record.

In 1865, the skeletons of three anatomically modern humans (two men and a woman) from the Ice Age were discovered in a tiny Aurignacian burial cave called the "Cro-Magnon" at the base of the cliff overlooking the village of Les Eyzies. The burial cave is only a minute's walk from the overhanging cliff shelter of the Abri Pataud which looks down on Les Eyzies and the Vézère river, the shelter in which I had met and talked with Professor Movius a century after the Cro-Magnon skeletons had been found. These anatomically modern humans, the "Cro-Magnons," had incised the image of an extinct woolly mammoth on a fragment of ivory some 15,000 years ago at the nearby site of La Madeleine on the shores of the same Vézère river. It was that image, found in the 19th century a few years before the skeletons were found, that began the study of Ice Age "art." Found with the Cro-Magnon skeletons were seashell beads that had come from the distant coasts of the Atlantic to the west and the Mediterranean to the southeast. A century of interpretation was to grow up around the animal images and beads and the thousands of other Ice Age beads that soon began to be found across Europe in excavated homesites and burials. Since no beads or animal images were ever found in earlier Neanderthal homesites or burials, it was assumed that the Cro-Magnons had not only invented "art" and depiction but had also "invented" personal decoration (White 1989, 1990) and that they were, in fact, the first creatures to make symbolic images and have a sense of "self-awareness." Self-awareness was taken to be a major aspect of "being human" and, with the art, was considered to be a sign of a developing social and cultural complexity and even an indication of the beginnings of modern human language. The evidence, it was held, was present. But beads of bone, stone or seashells are preserved in the soil while other forms of personal decoration are not. Besides, there is no archaeological evidence for any widespread tradition of bead manufacture among other anatomically modern humans who lived during this period in Africa, the Middle East or Asia. Did that mean that they lacked a capacity for "self-awareness," for cultural complexity or for language? Were the "Cro-Magnons" the first humans to make and use personal decoration or did they, in creating a regional bone industry, merely begin to make adornments of materials that lasted? Do we take the beads, merely because they are in the record and in our hands, at face value?

Turn back to the black, slit-eyed female figurine of fired clay from Dolni Véstonice (Fig. 171). When I studied her I was struck not only by the eerie and ghostly "spirit" face but by the dramatically deep circle cutting into her rear and thighs. It was stated that this represented an aspect of "style" and was also an image of overhanging fat. The so-called "fat" of the

Fig. 226
Pavlov (Moravia). Fragment of a fired clay figurine with a hip belt made of twined, perishable material, probably of animal skins. Personal decorations of perishable materials are depicted on female figurines across Ice Age Europe.

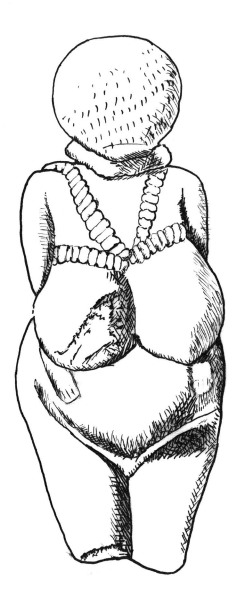
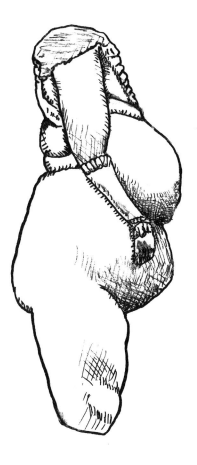

Fig. 227 a,b
Kostenki, the Ukraine. Front and side views of a fragmented female figurine wearing bracelets, arm bands, necklace, body band and collar of twined, or twisted perishable material. No beads are indicated. The head was found separately. (After photos by Praslov.)

Fig. 228
Mammoth ivory figurine from Avdeevo, the Ukraine. The Gravettian period. The figurine, found fragmented, was reconstructed. It may be "pregnant" and has the arched back and protruding stomach that is the reverse image of later, more schematized figurines from the Russian plain (see p. 312) and the Magdalenian buttocks images. The figurine is wearing bracelets, arm bands, a body band across back and chest as well as what may be a head band or cap, all apparently of twined, perishable material. Figurines from this period on the Russian plain are often depicted with schematically rendered adornments made of perishable materials, rarely with carved or manufactured beads.

Ice Age "Venus" figurines found throughout much of Europe became a subject of much study and debate. A dozen years after studying the black figurine I returned to Czechoslovakia to restudy the materials and I was shown the unpublished fragment of a recently excavated fired-clay figurine from the site of Pavlov on the same hill and from the same culture and period as the "Black Venus." The figure was that of a slim, possibly young female wearing the twined cord that, in the Ice Age, had often served as a hip belt (Fig. 226). This was, apparently, the type of tight, deeply cutting belt that the slit-eyed figurine was wearing. Such perishable adornments may, then, have served to "mark" the mature and potentially fertile female in the Ice Age, as they have marked the mature female in other later cultures. By that time I had already found that personal decorations of twisted or plaited cords—including bracelets, necklaces, anklets, collars, and arm, head and body bands—were often depicted on "naked" females throughout Ice Age Europe (Marshack 1991b). I found unexpectedly, for instance, that the famous naked "Venus" of Willendorf was wearing bracelets made of perishable, twined thongs that were abstracted and schematized as zigzags (Marshack 1991b: Pl.1a, Fig.2a). This was the same schematization of the twined thong that occurred among the "Venus" figurines on the Russian plain, to the east. Personal decorations of perishable materials may, in fact, have been far more common in the Ice Age than manufactured beads of non-perishable material (Fig. 227 a,b; 228). It was probable that humans elsewhere were using perishable materials (skins, thongs, feathers, paints, and even wood, etc.) to make personal decorations.

Could the earlier Neanderthals, then, c. 150,000-35,000 B.C., have also used perishable materials for personal decoration? Might that have been one of the reasons that "personal adornments" were never found in Neanderthal burials? When I began searching through the archaeological literature and materials for examples of earlier Neanderthal skill, problem-solving, and possible symboling, I found that they had, in fact, made awls to bore holes, apparently in skins and wooden tools. But of greater importance, a year or so after finishing the first edition of this book, my microscopic examination of the bone materials from the French Mousterian site of La Quina, in the Charente, one of the crucial Neanderthal sites in Europe, unexpectedly found that a flat shoulder-blade of a bovid, perhaps a bison, had probably been used as a platform for cutting skins (Fig. 229 a,b). Because of the delicacy of the incised lines the Neanderthals may have been cutting strips or thongs (Marshack 1991d). If the Neanderthals were cutting skins, boring holes, and making thongs, was it possible that they not only wore personal decorations but were buried with adornments of perishable skins, in addition to other perishable materials such as the seasonal flowers that seem to have been added to a Neanderthal burial at the cave of Shanidar in the Middle East? The idea that the Neanderthals, though on the "human" line, could have practiced such symbolic behavior has incited a turmoil for it goes against a contemporary desire for the "sudden" appearance of the human symboling capacity. As I write I am reading papers debating whether the Neanderthals buried their dead, had a capacity for symboling, and if they did have such capacity, ever practiced it to any degree. Evidence on each side of the debate has begun to come from many directions.

More than a decade after I found evidence that the Neanderthals were probably cutting skins to make clothes and thongs, a new generation of archaeologists, using the technique of microscopic tool-wear analysis, found that the working edges of Neanderthal stone tools showed that they were not only cutting meat but skins, wood, and grasses (Anderson-Gerfaud and P. and D. Helmer 1987; Beyries 1987; Shea 1989, 1990). In fact, their subsistence strategies and technologies were not far different from those of the anatomically modern humans with whom they came in contact towards the end of the Mousterian period in France and the Middle East. In the Middle East, where the two human groups lived as neighbors for thousands of years, it took 10,000 years for the anatomically modern humans in that region to develop a technology that was significantly and recognizably different from the Mousterian tool kit of the Neanderthals. These anatomically modern humans were, in fact, using the Mousterian tool kit. When they did develop a new tool kit, perhaps in response to ecological and climatic changes, the Neanderthals were already disappearing. Whatever the story of the now lost and perishable products of early human creativity and problem-solving by both anatomically modern humans and the Neanderthals during the period of their contemporaneity, the bit of twisted cord found in Lascaux apparently documents a concept with deep and ancient roots.

The trail from that fragment of cord continued to lead backward and forward. A bead, for instance, often requires a hole and a string so it can be worn. But a hole and string represent separate concepts and technologies in the manufacture of beads and they are made at different times and with different skills. For a century most discussions of early technology had focused on the cutting edge and the hammer. "Man the tool-maker," it was believed, was essentially a banger and a slicer. The concept of the "hole" was never addressed though "carrying bags" had been discussed by one archaeologist, Glynn Isaac, as an early means of transporting stones from a distant source back to a homesite for working. But the hole as a "concept," and as an aspect of developing hominid technology and problem-solving was never discussed. Perhaps because the creation of holes seemed to be the creation of "nothing." When I studied the early Aurignacian seashell beads of the Cro-Magnons under the microscope I found that some shells already had holes that had been bored, not by tools, but by sea-floor creatures that had preyed upon them. These shells with natural holes immediately suggested the possibility of stringing. I had found examples of fossils that had natural holes in archaeological collections, as well as fragments of waste bone that had holes bored by the larvae and worms found in soil (Marshack 1989a, 1991d). I recall as a child picking up stones and shells along the sea shore that had fascinating shapes and water-worn holes and stringing them as pendants. Could such

Fig. 229 a,b
La Quina, France, the Mousterian period of the Neanderthals, c. 40,000 B.C. Microscopic close-up of the long, absolutely straight lines incised on the flat surface of a bovid shoulder blade, suggesting a cutting of skins by the Neanderthals.

natural holes have suggested the concept of beads to early humans who were already using awls to bore holes in skins and wood and were also making thongs and cords? The "hole," I began to realize and to argue, was perhaps as important a "tool" and concept in these developing early cultures as the cutting edge (Marshack 1989a, 1990a, 1991d). The production of holes is, of course, common among many biological species. Holes, in fact, are evident in nature wherever one looks. Even the chimpanzee learns to make or enlarge a hole in a termite mound and to manufacture a simple tool with which to probe for termites. It would have been surprising if holes were not made or used by early hominids. At the Mousterian cave site of Vaufrey in France, a fossil shell, *Dentalium*, apparently collected by a Neanderthal from a fossil outcropping in the region, has been found (Rigaud 1988:408). The fractured fossil has a natural hole running through it, making it possible to have been used as a pendant or bead. Whether it was or was not so used we cannot tell, but it was clearly collected and kept. A fossil *crinoid*, a sea creature with a natural hole through its center was found in a Chatelperronian level at the rock shelter of Arcy-sur-Cure in France, c. 35,000 B.C., together with true beads that may have been manufactured by the Neanderthals. The fossil may therefore have been used as a bead. The ear bone of a cave bear, with a natural hole through the top suitable for stringing, was found in a Mousterian level at the Russian site of Prolom (Marshack 1989a).

While I was following the concept of the hole, evidence began to be published that the Neanderthals were hafting tools, that is, using a specialized type of "hole," and they were apparently also using thongs and resin to secure stone points to a wooden shaft. The concept of the hole, and the presence of cords and hafting would not, of course, have created beads, but the necessary concepts and technologies were present, and these may have made beads possible. Examples of the "hole" are so common in nature that they could not fail to be noted in the Mousterian (see Marshack 1991d Fig. 6). Do beads, therefore, as has been strongly argued by those wishing to place the "beginnings" of human culture with the appearance of anatomically modern humans in Europe, represent a sudden leap into human "self-awareness," or do they merely indicate a developing Upper Paleolithic technology for working bone which made it possible—at that time and in that place—to manufacture beads that were not only skilled but also survived?

In the odd way of science these questions concerning beads have intruded themselves into the debate over notations. R. White, an archaeologist who has argued for the importance of beads as an indication of the beginnings of human "self-awareness," wrote of the Aurignacian beads he was studying:

"If perforation technology in the early Aurignacian can be considered rudimentary, serious doubt is cast on the notion that Mousterian prototypes for Upper Paleolithic beads and pendants were manufactured in non-preservable media such as wood. If this were true, one would expect to find already well-developed techniques of perforation by the time tooth and ivory were employed as media . . . [The] sudden, intrusive, and complex character of the earliest body ornamentation remains one of the greatest explanatory challenges in all of hominid evolution" (White 1989:379).*

The great explanatory challenge, of course, does not concern "beads" but whether there was a widespread early skill for boring holes in skins, wood or bone and whether there was an early technology for making a wide range of personal decorations of perishable materials.

The search for the "origins" of personal adornment took me back to an earlier period. At the late *Homo erectus* site of Beçov in Czechoslovakia, c. 250,000 B.C.—and therefore near the time of the first appearance of the Neanderthals—a quartzite rubbing stone and a striated piece of ocher was found lying on the floor with a large spread of red ocher powder (Fridrich, 1976; Marshack 1981b). Was that ocher used for body decoration during a ritual? Was the manufacture of the red powder early evidence for symboling and, therefore, an aspect of being "human"? The evidence for an early use of ocher has also been found elsewhere and has produced its own debate. There are suggestions that such ocher may have been used, not symbolically, but to tan hides, to prevent mosquito bites or to staunch wounds. But the manufacture of ocher for any of these practical purposes would indicate processes of planning, resource acquisition and production that would have been as complex as those involved in the preparation of ocher for symbolic purposes. Would the complex production of ocher for functional purposes be any less "human" than the production of ocher for symbolic purposes? With this evidence and these questions we are faced with a problem. If one is attempting to compare the problem-solving and planning capacities of different late hominids, is it possible to determine that a "human" capacity began at one date and at one place with one set of artifacts that happen, by chance, to be found in the record? Or are we dealing with separate problems and questions, with evolving human capacities on the one hand and with regional or local stages and developments of culture and production on the other? In the first case we would be looking for the evolutionary processes that were involved in the mosaic development of the extraordinarily complex and variable human capacity; in the second case we would merely be looking for the dates and places of a particular set of cultural behaviors or products that were found archaeologically. The first inquiry is important, the second is merely interesting and, at most, indicative. Unfortunately, it is the second inquiry that is usually of interest to archaeologists. And the artifacts which are available are for that reason often also "false." There is no greater falsifier than an artifact or set of artifacts that seductively seems to prove a "beginning" or that seems to validate an interesting or novel hypothesis (Fig. 230 a,b). After finding the evidence for notation, for instance, I spent twenty years studying all the Upper Paleolithic symboling traditions, besides checking the notational hypothesis, and in doing so I found that I was led into an investigation of the different kinds of periodic symbolic behavior and forms of periodic marking found in human cultures, and into a study of the variety and range of such use in

*Many of the pre-Aurignacian beads from the Chatelperronian site of Arcy-sur-Cure, apparently made by Neanderthals, do not have holes, but instead have an incised groove around the top so that they could be tied with a string.

Fig. 230 a,b
Two faces of a non-utilitarian plaque apparently symbolic, carved from a mammoth tooth, Tata, Hungary, the Mousterian Period, c. 100,000 BP.

the Ice Age (Marshack 1977, 1989c, 1990b). As a result, I had to discard many classes of engraving that had at first seemed to be notation merely because they were accumulated over time. I found that these non-notational accumulations were often accumulated on other types of artifacts or surfaces, including stone and the cave walls, while notations were usually made on bone, that is on artifacts and materials that were easily carried and marked. An internal analysis of the accumulations and designs on stone and the cave walls indicated that though they were symbolic and often periodic, they were not "notations" (Marshack 1990b). They were neither structured internally or accumulated in the manner of notation. They represented an entirely different class of symbolic marking. That clarification was an education. But the problem is generic. The process of arguing from what one first sees and thinks, and in terms of what one first has in hand and believes, is common. It is often a definition of archeology.

At the moment I was preparing my analysis of the Taï notation for publication, for instance, R. White (1989) was publishing his studies of the early Ice Age beads arguing that they represented the beginnings of human "self-awareness" and social, cultural complexity. On finding two or three early Aurignacian beads from France that had been carved and then dotted to resemble a particular species of sea shell, he wrote: "This pattern {of dots} seems to mimic that found on Atlantic sea shells . . . Both the pattern and the probability that it was inspired by the natural punctuations on exotic seashells has seemingly been ignored by Marshack (1972) in arguing for lunar notation . . . etc." The idea that the Taï notation that I had been struggling with for two decades, and had at that moment apparently unraveled, might have been derived from the dot pattern on a particular species of seashell was amusing. There was an additional irony. I had, at the end of some two decades, just published studies indicating that such depictions of the differences in species pelage and body marking, and including even the depiction of the seasonal differences in such marking, occurred only in this Franco-Cantabrian region and nowhere else in the European Ice Age. The dotted beads came from the heart of this area. When I had studied these carved and dotted beads in the shape and pattern of a sea shell I had concluded that they documented the early beginning of this regional mode of species differentiation and marking. It was clear that the dots, which resembled the marking on a seashell, had nothing to do with notation, but had much to do with the tradition of naturalistic depiction that had begun to develop in Western Europe, particularly in France and Spain. But the irony went deeper.

R. White had done his doctoral thesis on the seasonal use of the hill, valley and riverine geography of the Dordogne region by the hunter-gatherers of the Ice Age. He had presented evidence for a network of major sites located at river crossings or fords or at river shallows that facilitated the exploitation of seasonally migrating reindeer and salmon.

These large sites located at reindeer crossings and at salmon fishing spots often had an abundance of homesite "art" since they seemed also to have served as places for seasonal human aggregation and ritual. Groups of hunter-gatherers, who dispersed seasonally to exploit regional summer resources, gathered in the spring or fall at river fords when the reindeer herds were crossing and when schools of salmon were struggling up-river through the white-water shallows. The concept of an observational "calendar" that structured economic and symbolic time-and-space, was probably more important in creating and maintaining the social fabric and the network of movement and interchange among groups than any wearing of beads. Beads may, of course, have been worn at such ritual moments of aggregation (as they could be used for a burial or for marking an individual in a changing maturational or social context), but the beads did not create or determine either the nature or the time of the ritual or the context. The hunter-gatherer's "calendar," on the other hand, whether it was merely observational or also notational, always did. The research presented in this book indicates that Ice Age observational "calendars" grew in complexity from the early Aurignacian to the terminal Magdalenian. The development of a "calendar" suggests that there was a concurrent development in the complexity of the social and cultural fabric that was being structured and maintained across time-and-space. It also suggests that beads were not so much an aspect of a newly discovered "self awareness" as they were items used to "decorate" and mark ritual periods and moments, as well as persons who had symbolically marked roles in the social interrelations of these ritual moments (Figs. 231, 232). Whether beads were imported from the coast, extracted from fossil beds in the territory, or manufactured at particular homesites perhaps during the winter, they had apparently become part of the time-and-space fabric of these cultures. Beads, therefore, argue for a "time-and-space" relevance and for the marking of persons in time-and-space more than they argue for the ' ginnings of human "self-awareness." Ice Age beads seem to do so espe__lly.

I began this book a quarter of a century ago with an analysis of the Aurignacian serpentine notation from the rock shelter or "Abri" of Blanchard (pp. 44–49), c. 28,000 B.C. That "abri" or rock shelter is one of a number that are crowded together in a small and narrow limestone valley, the Vallon de Castlemerle, through which a small stream flows into the Vézère some two hundred yards away. The stream is of the type that served as a spawning stream in the season of the salmon run. Large numbers of salmon vertebra, which are easily strung as beads, were found in a rock shelter of that little valley. After I had studied the beads excavated from these rock shelters at the neighboring little museum of Castlemerle, I went to the top and edge of the cliff that looks down into that narrow valley and across to the rolling grazing grounds behind and beyond the valley. The valley and its stream run south to north, the Vézère into which the stream flows runs east to west. Standing on the cliff

Fig. 231
Hohlenstein, Germany. Ivory carving of a lion-headed human. The Aurignacian, c. 30,000 B.C.. This is the earliest known therianthropic figure, that is, a human with animal characteristics. It comes from the same period and valley as the ivory Vogelherd horse (Fig. 129). Whether the carving represents a shaman wearing a lion mask (see the Magdalenian "sorcerer" in lion skin, horse tail and reindeer mask in Trois Frères, Fig. 150a), or a lion "spirit" and character in myth, it clearly indicates the early symbolic use of animal parts to mark a "human." If animal parts, including skins, tails, and masks (feathers?) were used in the Aurignacian and persisted through the Magdalenian, they may have had an earlier and more important beginning in the symbolic "decoration" of humans than the parochial manufacture and use of beads in Ice Age Europe. Beads themselves, like particularized skins and animal parts, may have been more important at special ritual occasions than in daily wear. Many of the early Ice Age figurines are depicted in decorations of perishable material. In only one instance is there a depiction of "beads."

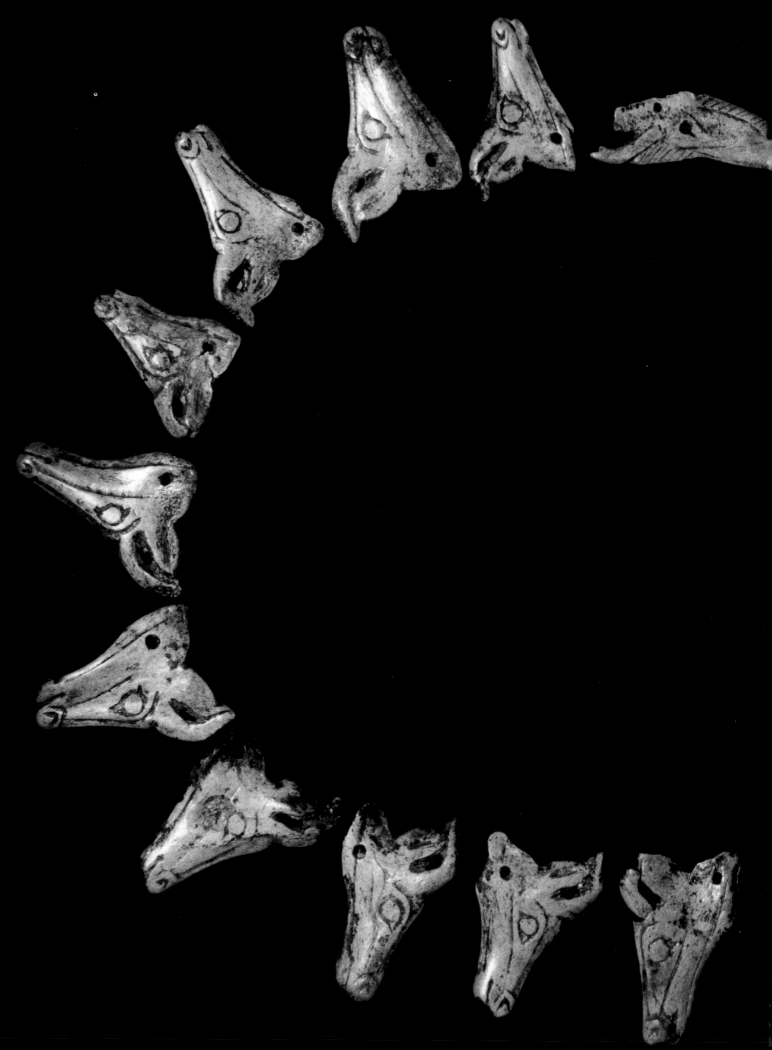

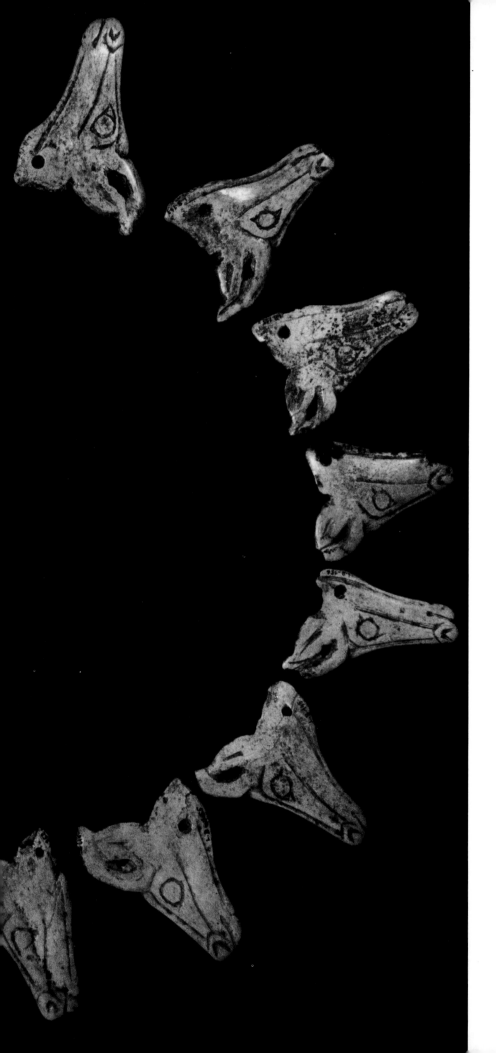

Fig. 232

Necklace of 19 carved and incised beads: 18 ibex heads and one bison. Labastide (Haute Pyrénées), France, Middle Magdalenian period (Mag. IV), c. 13,500 B.C. This is the most complex and beautiful set of beads to come from the Upper Paleolithic. Analysis indicates that the beads had once been covered with red ocher, suggesting a possible use in ritual performance. Such beads, extremely rare, may have belonged to a shaman or other person of rank. In most shamanic cultures there is a practice of wearing or using the perishable parts of symbolically relevant animals or plants during ritual in addition to manufactured items. In the limestone hill and valley regions of the Franco-Cantabrian area and in the foothills of the Alps to the east, the male ibex may have represénted a significant spiritual animal of the heights, as birds did of the air, fish of the rivers, serpents of the underground, etc. Each of these species was also strongly seasonal in behavior and occurrence. The male ibex, as an animal of these montane or limestone hill regions was, apparently, also symbolically "killed" in the spring.

The Ice Age bone industry, of which this is a unique example, has provided us with an essentially skewed evidence that suggests that early personal decoration was primarily made of bone, shell, fossils, and stone. Except for special products perhaps most common at ritual occasions, the use of perishable materials was probably more common. In France, a 5- to 7-year-old child was buried at La Ferrassie with elaborate decorations of pierced animal teeth and shells encircling the ankles, knees, wrists, elbows, neck and head. One does not assume that a child of that age was so decorated in daily life or play. At Sungir in Russia there are extremely elaborate burials; in one. there is a costume with hundreds of hand-carved ivory beads, again suggesting a unique an possibly rare ceremonial and ritual burial. The presence of manufactured beads and pendants of different types in the Ice Age is probably as much an indication of a development in the regional bone and stone working industry, and of an increased complexity in the marking of intra and intergroup relations and behaviors, as of any sudden, genetic awareness of self. When the climate changed these particular Ice Age elaborate forms of personal decoration ceased being made and other forms, often made of other materials, developed.

above the Abri Blanchard and looking into the narrow valley, one faces due west; looking around one sees the bowl of the sky in all directions. It would have taken a few seconds for an inhabitant at the shelter of Blanchard to climb to the top of the cliff (perhaps by a twined ladder or cord) in order to see the rising or setting sun and moon in the evening or dawn sky and to monitor the rolling lands upon which the huge herds grazed and the major migrations passed seasonally. Neither the sky nor animals could be monitored from the shelter in the narrow valley below. Standing on the cliff I felt that I now had some understanding as to how and why the Blanchard notation may have been made. Though the horizon and the bowl of the sky were not visible from the rock shelter, they were dramatically visible from the top of the cliff a few yards above. In his study of the beads from this tiny valley, White had written: "As Taborin (1985) has suggested, the Vallon de Castlemerle may have been an agreed-upon point of exchange (or trade) . . . this exchange would have been between groups with access to the coast, and those with access to the ranges occupied by woolly mammoth." (White 1989:377) Persons arriving from great and different distances for rituals and exchange would have timed their movements and the moment of their arrival to coincide with resource abundance (perhaps of reindeer and salmon) and they would have timed their journey and arrival to a mutually understood observational "calendar" of the sky and seasons. The notation on the main face of the Blanchard plaque is for 2 $\frac{1}{4}$ months. If after the first frost with the oncoming short and dark days of winter, one began a notation with observation of the first crescent of the month that followed a freezing of the spawning stream or the Vézère, one would probably have ended that notation within the "moon" or month of the thaw, at roughly the time of the spring arrival of reindeer and salmon and the human groups. The subsidiary marking on the back of the plaque (39 marks or a bit over a month) may have notated a period of waiting from the thaw and flood to the appearance of the migrating species or the arrival and aggregation of persons. This suggestion, of course, is conjectural, but the presence of an observational period of waiting on the reverse of the Blanchard plaque, from the beginning of the Ice Age, c. 28,000 B.C. is found also on the rear of Taï plaque, from the end of the Ice Age, c. 10–9,000 B.C.*

It is possible that some of the rock shelters in the valley of Castlemerle were workshops at which beads and other items of exchange were manufactured, perhaps in the winter, and that they were also locations at which rituals occurred, perhaps in the spring and fall. The large number of beads found there, perhaps like the notation found at the site of Blanchard, may therefore have represented aspects of a developing Upper Paleolithic time-and-space fabric, involving sequences of specialized activity at different locations, a process that began early in the Upper Paleolithic and was to be woven with increasingly complexity upon the great loom of the hill-and-valley, riverine, Franco-Cantabrian landscape. The Aurignacian Cro-Magnons buried at Les Eyzies may even have walked

*Alexander Marshack. 1991. The Taï Plaque and Calendrical Notation in the Upper Palaeolithic. Cambridge Archaeological Journal. 1(1):25–61.

along the shores of the Vézère to Blanchard for a seasonal aggregation to acquire the seashell beads that were found in the local burial. Or the inhabitants of Blanchard may, with as much likelihood, have walked to the more important and larger valley of Les Eyzies. In either case, aggregational attendance at a site was dependent on some common recognition of the processes and periods of the sky and seasons. These suggestions, so clearly and acknowledgedly conjectural, are made within a contextual, functional theoretical frame that seems increasingly, as the archaeological evidence accumulates, to have some encompassing relevance and some possibility of validation.

If beads are the primary focus of your small study, the world and the culture are necessarily seen largely through the manufacture and local presence of beads. If the seasonality of a culture and a site is your focus, one sees the culture in terms of the dispersal and use of seasonal sites with specialized seasonal activities. If cultures are conceived of as inherently variable, with varying tapestries of periodic behavior maintained in time-and-space, then even beads are seen in terms of their role and place within such a "time-factored" fabric. In such a model, not only beads, but the sanctuary caves themselves can be considered as places for periodic, regional ritual behavior. It is even possible that a specialized form of dress was worn by individuals for certain rituals in the cave.

This discussion takes us back to one of the early notations published in this book (Fig. 88) and to one of the intriguing puzzles of the Ice Age. The site of La Marche not only provides us with a notational composition that is associated with a used and reused horse (both repeatedly "killed" and repeatedly renewed) but the site also gives us the only known collection of Ice Age "self-portraits." A large number of flat, limestone blocks contain the incised images of humans and animals, sometimes together on one stone, but often separately. Because of irregularity of the stones and because of the heavy overengraving on the images, they were probably not intended to be either "communicative" or exhibited. The "portraits" not only depict generalized humans but persons of different age, sex, dress and behavior. Scattered through the often extraordinary entanglement of lines are the heads of infants, children, young adults, older adults, women at prayer, and a man depicted in what appears to be a ritual or dance performance (Fig. 231). A study of the personal decoration depicted in these images, including the indication of bracelets, anklets, arm bands, head bands, caps, skirts, etc. suggests that these were primarily made of perishable materials. No true beads are depicted, while bone and ivory bracelets and head bands are, in fact, rare in the archaeology of this period and region.

Nothing quite like this collection of human portraits exists anywhere else in Ice Age Europe (the sole other "portrait" is of late Ice Age man wearing a beard, moustache and leather cap from Italy, Fig. 234). It is not the presence of the La Marche human images that is important but also that they exist in a melange of intentional over-marking (Fig 233 a) and within

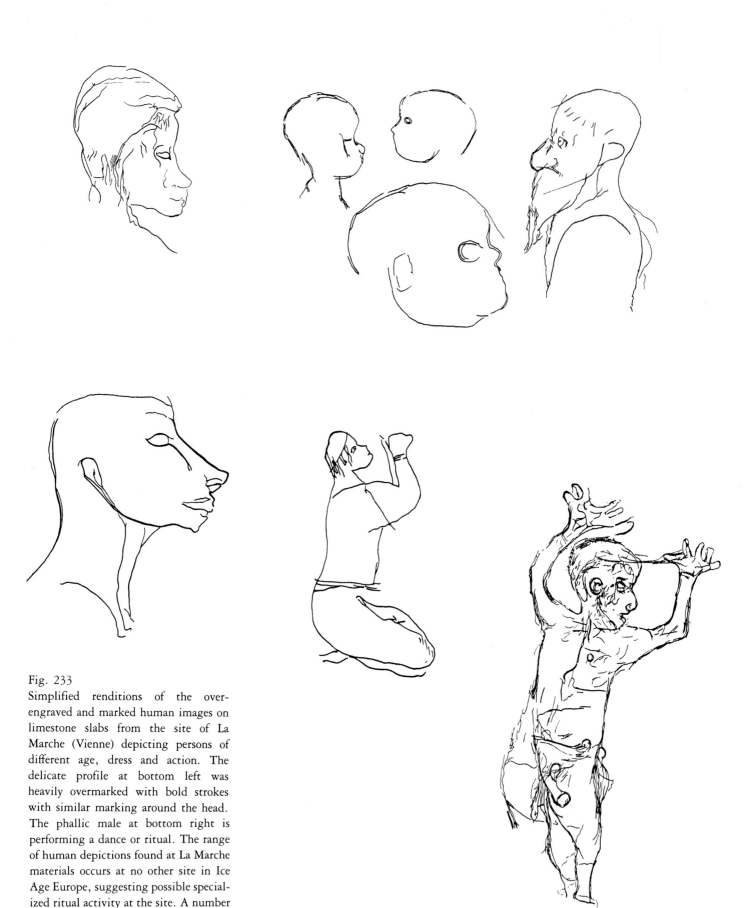

Fig. 233
Simplified renditions of the over-engraved and marked human images on limestone slabs from the site of La Marche (Vienne) depicting persons of different age, dress and action. The delicate profile at bottom left was heavily overmarked with bold strokes with similar marking around the head. The phallic male at bottom right is performing a dance or ritual. The range of human depictions found at La Marche materials occurs at no other site in Ice Age Europe, suggesting possible specialized ritual activity at the site. A number of notational artifacts were also found here. (After Pales and St. Pereuse)

a context at this site of other forms of symboling. It has been one of the crucial findings of the present research, for instance, that ritual, symbolic overmarking represents a common form of image use in the Ice Age. It occurs, for instance, on the La Marche horse in the notational composition (Fig. 88; on humans, Fig. 235 a,b) and on animals, female images and vulvas throughout Europe (See Fig. 181, 182, 185).

If, as the ongoing research suggests, the La Marche notational composition documents a tradition of observational time-keeping, and the use and reuse of the symbolic horse on the piece of antler was an aspect of that process, then it may indicate that La Marche was a ritual site at which a "shaman" engaged in a range of symbolic behaviors. This probably involved a recognition of symbolic time and a periodic use of animal and human images. These processes may have involved what is traditionally termed "magic," that is, curing and healing ceremonies, rituals for a safe pregnancy and delivery, rituals related to the end of winter and the coming of spring, rituals concerned with a late arrival of animals or herds, and even ceremonies related to a symbolic use of the carnivore lion and bear (which are depicted on these stones). This suggestion for the existence of a body of ritually produced and used animal and human images opposes many of the theories that have attempted to explain the "origins" or "meanings" of Ice Age "art." In fact, the rarity of human "portraits" in the Ice Age may have been due to the fact that they could, in such a tradition, be used ritually. Suggestions of this kind place the problem of image manufacture and use in a different light. The depicted "killing" or overmarking of an animal, for instance, may have been as symbolically effective as the actual ritual killing and sacrifice of an animal. While the ritual "killing" of a human image, which occurs, for instance, in the caves of Pech Merle and Gourdan in France, may not have referred to the "killing" of a human, but may have depicted the "killing" of an anthropomorphized evil spirit or a spirit harming a human. Depictions of "killing," therefore, need not have involved the actual killing either of an animal or human.

If these suggestions for different types of image use are valid, we may have an explanation for one image that has become part of a heated debate. One of the horse heads incised on a piece of limestone at La Marche seems to wear a halter. This unusual image was first noted by L. Pales and T. Saint-Pereuse who studied and published the La Marche engravings and then by P. Bahn who referred to their suggestion of a "halter" in his own arguments for possible domestication or semi-domestication of Ice Age horse and reindeer. There is a different way of "seeing" the image. My studies of the West European Ice Age tradition of overmarking animal images has, for instance, documented a common practice of overmarking and reuse of animal images. There is a renewal of the horse in the notational composition from La Marche by the addition of extra eyes and ears, as well as its "killing" with darts (Fig. 88). The tradition of using and overmarking animal and human images, suggests that the lines that

Fig. 234
The engraving on a stone of a moustached and bearded man in a leather cap from the Grotta di Vado all' Arancio, Italy. Late Upper Paleolithic.

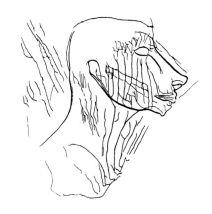

Fig. 233a
The overmarking on the head and on the stone around the head of the La Marche profile in Fig. 231. (After drawing by L. Pales)

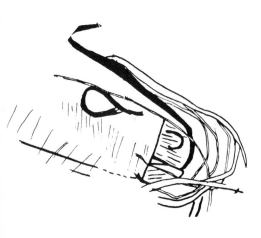

Fig. 235 a,b
a) The head of a reindeer incised on a limestone slab renewed by the addition of an extra eye and muzzle. Limeuil, France.
b) The muzzle of a stag incised on a fragment of bone renewed by the addition of 5 later muzzles. The deer was also "killed" by overengraving with engraved darts. Polesini, Italy.

seem to be a halter in the La Marche engraving may simply represent this ritual mode of overmarking an animal head. Both the stone and the horse head were heavily overmarked. As noted above, the process of overmarking an image was common among the La Marche stones. The beautiful face of the young adult (Fig. 233 a), for instance, is strongly overmarked in just this manner. Both the human head and the stone around the head are overmarked as though in acts of ritual. But a study of the tradition of representation at this time and in this region also suggests other information. My analysis of other horse heads from the Middle Magdalenian period in the Franco-Cantabrian region has suggested that many depict the morphology and appearance of the summer horse. The heavy hair of the winter horse usually masks many of the details on the muzzle that are usually so carefully depicted. This seems to hold, for instance, for the tradition of carving and engraving isolated horse heads, images that are cut out of bone to sometimes form beads in the manner of the ibex heads in Fig. 232; heads "decoupées" as they are called in France. The incised horse head on the La Marche stone is made in this style of depicting the muzzle and head of the summer horse, and the lines that seem to indicate a halter may merely represent the ritual overmarking of this image of the summer horse.

If La Marche were a ritual site, perhaps a shamanic site, such overmarking would explain much that is puzzling about the images and symbolic artifacts found there. There is, for instance, a set of horse teeth (incisors) marked with schematic "vulvas." They are not beads and seem to have been either made or used as part of a ritual (Fig. 236 a,b). La Marche also provides us with two manufactured beads in the abstracted form of the schematic female buttocks image, as well as images of an abstracted fish, the male ibex, bear and lion, a ritual bâton, as well as images of pregnant females, males in ritual costume and stance, all of which suggest a place of "shamanic" practice and of variable symbolic production and behavior. There is even a bird bone from this site marked with a notation, made somewhat earlier than the more elaborate notational composition that is published in this book. If the accumulated and overmarked images on stone, the diversity of symbolic artifacts, and the notations themselves, document aspects of repeated or periodic ritual activity, we may have one more indication for a ritual structuring of time and process at a particular site during the Ice Age. Based on the content of the images at the site, the processes that were symbolized or ritualized may have included the stages of human growth and maturation, the processes of female periodicity and the uncertainties surrounding birth, the uncertainty in the seasonal return of different animals, the curing of diseases and ailments, the ritual use or killing of the carnivore image, etc. all of which seem to have been integrated and woven into the mythic, ritual, time-factored cultural fabric.

The definition of a valid theory in science, it is often stated, is that it can either be validated or disproven by ongoing research. If my early suggestion for notation and for "time-factored" imagery in the Ice Age is eventually proven valid, it would have to be able to incorporate and accommodate the accumulating evidence. It would have to agree with our knowledge concerning the variability found in human symboling modes. It would have to encompass the symbolic variability found in the Ice Age cultures. And it must not be invalidated by any of that evidence.

With this in mind, it seems clear that the research of the last few decades has enriched and clarified the "time-factored" concepts and insights that were originally formulated in this book, has made significant corrections without altering any of those concepts, and has at the same time suggested means of expanding, enriching and coalescing the concept of time-factored culture, time-factored behavior, time-factored imagery and time-factored notation. While archaeologically rare, the Ice Age notations seem to be a reasonable and rational aspect and product of that regionally and temporally unique and complex early symbolic fabric.

The issues, however, are more complex than I have been suggesting. While I was investigating the variability and complexity of symbolic production and use in early human culture, other subdisciplines in the study of human culture, "information theory" and "artificial intelligence," were being born, primarily as a result of the theories and problems created and raised by the 20th century use of the electronic computer and the effort to understand the nature of "information." Though still in its infancy the issues raised by these subdisciplines have some relevance to the present research. A computer, for instance, encodes abstracted observational information or data (in analog or numeric form) and then presents it back in condensed and still more abstracted, visual, notational form in a manner, therefore, that is somewhat comparable to the simpler Ice Age notations. These early notations also abstracted observational information and presented them back more abstractly and visually. Yet the Ice Age notations, though early, were not as simple as they seem in such a formulation. To make an Ice Age notation observational, visual information had first to be encoded in highly abstracted form within the brain; it was then abstractly modeled in a different form in the notation that was produced and mediated by that brain. However, since such abstractions have meaning and relevance only in terms of the cultural data and the models of reference to which the original observations were keyed, the "meanings" in the notation referred to many types of cultural data which are not evidenced in the accumulating structure of simple day marks. These other forms of data and observation may have provided the reason that the notation was being kept, but they are gone and must be inferred (see the notation from Cueto de la Mina, for instance, p. 214-217). Unfortunately, most of the analyses that were conducted on the Ice Age notations addressed only certain levels of observation and problem-solving — the visual, problem-solving level involved in the abstraction, production and visualization of the periodicities of the sky. The human capacity

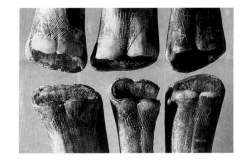

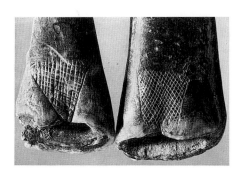

Fig. 236 a,b
Some of the horse incisors found at La Marche, engraved in the area of separation on the tooth with abstracted and schematic vulvar forms to create "female" images. The teeth were not bored through for use as beads and may have been objects made and used in ritual. The tooth form itself seems to suggest the vulvar region.

for visual abstraction and cross-referencing and association is far more complex than is evidenced in these notations and, as suggested in this research and inquiry, it is evidenced in the diverse and complex symbol systems of the Upper Paleolithic.

Turn back to the engraved bâton from Raymonden (p. 213, Fig. 101 b). It is clear that we have a composition containing different types of imagery and abstraction: a relatively realistic deer head, a few abstracted fish tails and ibex heads, a plant image, some marking that may be "notational," and a number of non-depictive signs. If this were a mnemonic composition that could be read back or used by the maker, it would have required a reading of different classes of image and abstraction, a reading whose combined meaning would have had to come not from any single image but also from the context within which the composition was made. That context, in one form or another, might have been related to, and supported by, information contained in the ritual or economic calendar. In contemporary modern graphics, the same type of multi-level, referential variability exists. A chart, graph, map or model is often composed of abstract images and symbols of many types and classes: numbers, letters, words, colors, graphs involving axes and coordinates, directions of reading, etc., each of which has to be learned separately before the system can be used or understood. Together these form an aspect of contemporary cultural, visual "literacy." Part of that literacy involves a knowledge, not only of the signs and symbols, but of the variable contexts and times within which the computer-generated notations and graphics are made and found to be relevant and useful. In surprising measure, different but cognitively comparable forms of composition involving the conceptual, visual coordination of different classes of imagery and abstraction, was common in the Upper Paleolithic. In Ice Age iconography, as in the iconography of a modern society, meanings derive not merely from single images and from their compositional association but also from the cultural, temporal context in which the images and compositions appear. Unfortunately, for almost a century, archaeologists have dealt primarily with the images themselves as discrete and separate products, and with the "style" of an image or with the structure and layout of a cave and its images.

For a number of reasons, many of which are still being explored, diverse modes and processes of abstraction and of visual, graphic equationing and modeling exploded dramatically in the Ice Age of Europe — presumably as part of the new "information" that was being woven into the cultural fabric. That explosion was therefore in some measure comparable to the even more dramatic information "explosion" that occurred in mid-twentieth century industrial cultures as the complexity and amount of information also exploded — and as the new technologies of abstraction, notation, computation and visualization increased in complexity and their speed of presentation.

I am, of course, oversimplifying the comparison as well as the complexity of the human capacity for visual symboling, problem-solving and abstraction. There were aspects of visual "information" and processes of abstraction and image use present in the Ice Age that can still not be handled by computers. It may be of interest to touch on some of these in order to note the differences between the neurological, cultural handling and use of "information" and the electronic handling of information, since these comparisons touch on the enormous differences between the potentially variable, generalized human capacity and the highly specialized capacities of the notational tools that humans devise to handle certain classes of information.

When I began research in the Ice Age caves, I was struck by the fact that some of the most complex and interesting compositions were often isolated or hidden in a difficult to find or reach recess. These images were not on those easily accessible public walls on which many of the major animal images appeared. A famous group of clay bison (a bull, a cow and a calf) carved of sheets of clay taken from the floor of the cave of Tuc d'Audoubert, was placed in what is today the most distant chamber of the cave. These carvings were made, were used, and then were apparently never visited again. They were apparently meant to be a one-time symbolic, ritual creation not intended to communicate or provide information to subsequent viewers. They therefore represented "encoded" and depicted information of a particular kind. The communication, at one level, was *ritual*, primarily between the carvers, the participants in the ritual and the images; that is, between the participants and the mythology and symbols of the culture. It was a closed temporal and spatial, physical and behavioral embodiment that involved the sharing of information among a few persons. A computer might today be able to categorically recognize the images as three bison, as a bull, cow and calf, but it could not explain their relevance, which was dependent on the mythology that informed the ritual moment. The meaning of the images was not in their form or their style, or in the fact that they were bison, but in the fact of their cultural occurrence and use at a particular, and intentionally hidden or secret, point in time and space. One can suggest, as I do, that the set of images consisting of a cow, bull and calf were a seasonal representation related to the return of life in the spring, but we cannot be certain. The ritual itself, because of the heel prints around the carvings, has been often suggested as probably involving the initiation of youths. The complex network of information, not in the imagery, but surrounding or supporting the imagery, may therefore have been more important than the imagery itself. How can these levels or types of information be handled by a computer? Or even be adequately surmised by the archaeologists who classify such imagery as Ice Age "art" or Ice Age ritual?

The cave of Tuc d'Audoubert also gives us evidence of a different kind of imagery and use. Turn to the drawing of a tiny horse overmarked with "P" signs in the adjoining cave of Trois Frères (page 327, Fig. 196). In Tuc d'Audoubert there is a tiny cubicle in which a crude, rapidly incised horse appears on the ceiling of a hidden recess that is difficult to find. To find it, one enters a long narrow passageway and after walking some distance one climbs up into a fissure that ends in a small bowl-like cupola. A crude little horse incised on the ceiling could only be made with the arms moving freely above the head. Subsequently one person at a time returned to add a "P" sign or a set of "P" signs around the small horse. The "sanctuary," big enough for only one person, was not a public wall and the return of one person at a time to make a "P" sign around the horse was clearly ritual (Fig. 237). It is, of course, reasonable to assume that the signs were added at the proper moment and for the proper purpose. The marking of similar "P" signs on the small horse in the adjoining cave of Trois Frères repeats this privacy of placement. This horse is hidden in a

Fig. 237
Schematic rendition of the small crude horse engraved on the ceiling of a hidden alcove or cubicle in the cave of Tuc d'Audoubert (Ariège) in the Pyreneean foothills with some of the 80 "P" signs engraved around it. The "P" signs, incised by many tools, are accumulated in a circle around the horse. At least one of the "P" signs is made by a finger and some of the "P" signs have been renewed or reused. An analysis of the full cave and this composition is being prepared for publication by Robert Bégouën.

high recess just outside the great hall of animal images overseen by the "sorcerer" (p. 272, Fig. 150 a). Outside the large main chamber one has to climb a steep rock to a hidden corner and lie on one's side on the rock to see the image. The horse, the place, and the overmarking of the horse with "P" signs argue again for acts of private ritual. If horse and "P" signs were, conjecturally, related either to seasonal and/or biological periodicity we may have, once again, two types of imagery, one depictive, the other abstracted, whose meanings and relevance cannot be read from their form or style but only from their association and context, and from their occurrence in a particular time and space. Given the assumption of a conceptual calendar and a knowledge of biological and seasonal periodicity, we may perhaps ask if part of the meaning was encoded in their use at a particular time within the conceptual "calendar" frame?

The use of depictive images and abstractions, and of symbols that can be conceptually associated in a particular time and space, are so crucial for a proper understanding of the Upper Paleolithic symbolic systems that I feel that I should elaborate on an example that I noted earlier and briefly in passing (p. 329) when describing the first cave panel that I studied. It was this panel that made it possible to study not only the horses and their "P" signs but the other images and compositions of the Ice Age as examples and aspects of a symboling mode, as aspects of symbol *systems*, rather than as "art" or aspects of "style." This wall panel began my research in the caves, at about the time that I was completing my manuscript for the first edition of this book. That analysis and the insights it provided would be validated repeatedly during the next two decades.

Fig. 238
La Pileta, southern Spain. The accumulation of images made in black paints of different intensity on the wall of a tiny, hidden "sanctuary." The cow and horse (see Fig. 197) at left were periodically marked by different persons with two fingers dipped in red or black paint. At right are serpentine "macaronis" made by black paints of different intensity and width. The geometric signs at the top and the stick figure in the middle may have been made in a later period.

The reused animals and the accumulated "macaronis" are typical of Upper Paleolithic or Ice Age imagery in West European caves and homesites, as is the accumulation of different classes of image and symbol on surfaces that were not intended for group viewing. These processes pose major problems for the usual interpretations of Ice Age "art" and for theories about the supposed "beginnings" of depiction and the communicative function and informational content of the images and symbols. The problem of when and why different types of image were made and used in such private, individual acts of ritual has not often been addressed.

The southern Spanish cave of La Pileta, near Malaga, is a hard two-day walk from the Mediterranean coast. Inside, before the main chamber, there is a tiny cubicle whose opening is a few feet up the wall. It is a cubicle, into which one person at a time must climb and squat. The cubicle has one wall covered with a complex accumulation of different kinds of imagery (Breuil, Obermaier and Verner 1915, Marshack 1977). Though small, the composition is as complex as any found on the great walls of some of the more northern, more famous caves (Fig. 238). There are horses and bovides in black outline which have been overmarked by double finger-marks that had been dipped in red or black paint, each set representing a hand of a different size (p. 329, Fig. 197); there are also signs and images of the ibex and, to the right there is a chaotic accumulation of serpentine "macaronis" made by different black paints. Macaroni sections made by one paint are often appended to a section made by a different paint. It was apparent that individuals had climbed into this tiny cubicle to make their images, marks and signs at different times; they had carried different skills and perhaps had different reasons for making their images and symbols. Not visible in any of the published photographs or renditions is the fact that the soft clay-like wall had itself been repeatedly touched or stroked by fingers not dipped in paint, suggesting that the cubicle and the wall may have acquired a kind of sanctity through repeated and long term use. A stylistic analysis of the animals could, of course, have determined that the animals were made in any early style and that different paints or modes of marking were used. But the far more important inference, that different persons had climbed into the cubicle at different times for different ritual or symbolic purposes and had produced different images for different purposes, could not be derived from such visual descriptions.

The walls of the cave outside the cubicle had no images of horses or bovids that I could find, but had other types of images and signs, including macaronis in red ocher that were more highly structured and carefully made than the simple meanders in the "sanctuary."

Cave compositions of this type bring us again to the difficulties surrounding those studies of "information" and symbol that began in mid-20th century. Insights from "information theory," for instance, began to be used by archaeologists in an attempt to explain the beginnings both of human "art" and Ice Age "art." This was often done without any analysis of the images or their contexts, or the manner in which they were made and used (see for example Lewis-Williams and Dowson, 1989). It was the image itself that was the object of study and interpretation. This is, in some measure, the "objective" way that a computer "sees" and then categorizes an image, by its shape and form. One of the concepts derived from "information" theory and proposed in these studies was that "style," or the form in which an image is made, is itself a kind of "information." The dispersal of a "style," for instance, it is asserted communicates information about the coherence of the group using that style and it also visualizes a separation between one group and another using a different style. The insight, of course, is valid, if not profound, and it may be of more value to the archaeologist attempting to form chronologies and maps of the dispersal of style and of style changes than it was to those who originally made and used the images — in what might be considered the "dialect" of their time and place. Such studies, while helpful, were inherently skewed and extremely limited. There was no regional or temporal "style," for instance, involved in the rendering of the little horse in Tuc d'Audoubert. It was without "style" when compared to the magnificent renderings in the larger cave. Nor was the image meant to communicate its "style" or presence to others. It was an image whose relevance was not in its "style" but in its making and its use. The "style," if there was any, was behavioral and it resided in the making and the use, not in the form or quality of the image. The "P" signs themselves, however, were apparently part of a widespread style derived from the Magdalenian tradition of abstracting the female torso in the "buttocks" style (p. 309, Fig. 181). But such a stylistic description of the shape could not tell us that the buttocks image could be used in different ways and in different contexts: as beads and pendants, as hand-held amulets, as engravings that could be accumulated on stones and repeatedly overmarked, as abstracted signs that could be accumulated around a symbolic horse but not around other animals, etc. Studies of "style" could give the archaeologist information about the chronology and geographic distribution of these forms or shapes. Other kinds of inquiry, however, were needed to tell us about their range of possible uses and meanings. These meanings and uses were patently important aspects of Magdalenian visual, cultural literacy. At this late date we see the image, but we lack that cultural literacy. We therefore attempt to create a kind of explanation or literacy of our own, using the ancient images.

Comparable to these archaeological and anthropological studies of "style" are studies of "structure," that is, of the pieces, bits and parts that make up images, symbols and motifs, studies which include an analysis of the ways in which these bits and pieces are associated. These studies, breaking images into their "design elements," are closely related to studies of "style." Such studies do not seek to determine the origin or development of the images, which are often abstractions of animals, or water, but seek instead to classify these images according to their "type," that is, ovals, chevrons, bundles of straight lines, bundles of wavy lines, single arcs, multiple arcs, etc. The Ice Age abstraction of an ibex, for instance, is often merely an image of the inturned arcs of its horns, whereas a wild ox is abstracted by its outward turning horns. A horse may be depicted by its mane and ears. The results of these studies of "design elements" were often more informative about the way in which archaeologists attempt to create categories of "information," than they were about the images or the meanings and uses of the images being studied.

When I began my research, for instance, I was faced with the "structural"

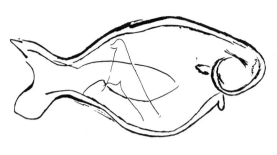

Fig. 239
La Pileta. Large fish in black paint. The fish has been renewed by the painting of another fish on the inside, following the outline, and by the addition of a smaller schematic fish in the interior. A small seal has been placed inside the fish.

and typological efforts of Leroi-Gourhan who had in mid-century classified all the "signs" in the Franco-Cantabrian caves by their shape and form, and having done so then attempted a further structural description by dividing all of these images into either "male" or "female"; that is, as images in supposed polar, sexual opposition (P. 198-199, Fig. 90). My subsequent analysis of each class of "sign" found that they were actually often abstractions of different types, and that each type had its own meaning and use. Many signs, in fact, were "time-factored," that is they referred to periodic processes or phenomena (like the water-related macaroni motif) or were used in certain contexts at certain times (like the "P" signs). Structural descriptions and categorizations, though they may seem objective and profound, are highly subjective and comparatively easy since it requires nothing but the eye and the category. It often tells us nothing except that the archaeologists have been busy and, therefore, to a certain degree, helpful. Structural studies and studies of style have continued through the period of my own research.

* * *

In the main chamber of La Pileta, outside the tiny cubicle into which one must climb and squat, is a pool of clear cool water. La Pileta, in fact, means "little pool" in Spanish. The pool was used by Ice Age hunter-gatherers and then later in the neolithic by early farmers whose pottery was found around its edge. On a wall of the main chamber is the outline of a huge oval fish in black paint (almost 5 feet in length, or 1 m 50 cm), larger than any fish that could be found in Spanish rivers (see p. 329). Breuil described the fish as a "Pleuronectes," a marine flatfish of the flounder type (Fig. 239). Because of its size it could not have been seen inland in the vicinity of the cave. Within this fish is the outline of a small seal in black paint. Since the Mediterranean coast is at least a two-day walk to the south through steep mountain valleys it is doubtful whether seals could have come this far upstream. The seal was apparently a symbol related to the fish as a symbol, neither of which could be seen among these hills, but each of which may have been related symbolically and perhaps ritually and mythologically to the pool of water in the cave. Symbolic equations can, of course, exist and function across time and space. Significantly, the large fish had been ritually reused or renewed by drawing a second fish inside the outline and then a smaller schematic third fish, drawn abstractly as an oval. On the same wall as the fish and seal are zigzag motifs that, from the Upper Paleolithic to the neolithic, were often abstractions of water. On one wall also were elaborate macaronis made with red ocher, which like the black macaronis in the sanctuary, were often made by appending one section to another, apparently periodically and over a period of time. For reasons that I could not at that time surmise, these images in La Pileta — including the pool, the animals, the abstract signs and motifs, the secret sanctuary, the modes of image use and renewal, and the aberrational large fish and seal far in these inland hills — haunted me. They seemed, even at the start of my cave research to represent more than mere "art." A few days later, along the Mediterranean coast of Spain, I found the outline paintings of both fish and dolphin far inside the Ice Age cave of Nerja. Most popular books on Ice Age art, including the volume by Leroi-Gourhan, discuss fish in passing, as minor images of the West European Franco-Cantabrian cultures. There is a widely expressed belief that fishing became important only late in the Ice Age, with the needs of an expanding population during the Magdalenian period. However, the La Pileta fish and seal are not only earlier but they do not represent species or food found in the region of the cave. They seem to have been water-related symbols like the zigzags and macaronis with which they were associated. They may even have been seasonal symbols related to the time of visiting the coast.

The questions that had begun to pervade the research in its early stages still pervade it. These questions relate not only to the images, but to the contexts within which the images are found and the manner in which they were used. The Aurignacian beads found in the burial at Cro-Magnon and at other early sites in the Dordogne of France came, for instance, from the Atlantic and the Mediterranean. The coasts of that period are today deep under the waters that rose when the ice sheets began to melt. Were there seaside camps during the Ice Age, today under water, at which groups of hunters seasonally hunted seals and shell fish? Would images of seal and fish, and rituals related to them, have been more important along these coasts then they were among the inland hills and river valleys? In the Ice Age caves of the Cantabrian hills of northern Spain, which are not far from the coast, there are many images of fish incised on the walls (for instance at Altxerri in Guipuzcoa). Some of these fish represent ocean varieties that would not have been caught in the rivers near these hills. At caves still further inland (at Altamira and Castillo) there are water motifs on the wall but not many images of fish, and the fish that are depicted tend to be schematic and abstract rather than descriptive. Were the images of fish and water at these caves seasonal? Imperceptibly, as I worked across Europe, the rivers and coasts began to form a subliminal map that structured the ongoing inquiry. In France, a ten minute walk from the burial at Cro-Magnon and the excavation at the Abri Pataud, the small cave shelter of the Gorge d'Enfer is in a small valley that like Blanchard faces a small spawning stream that flows into the Vézère a few yards below. There is a huge male salmon carved into the limestone ceiling, with the hook on the jaw that the male salmon acquires only in the spawning season. The image has been credited to the Perigordian, c. 26-24,000 B.C., thousands of years before the supposed beginning of a Magdalenian interest in fish. Was the carved salmon, then, an image of food, or was it an image of the season when salmon and reindeer returned to this area? Was the salmon a mythic "messenger" of the return of spring, arriving from an unknown deep? The salmon on the ceiling of the Gorge d'Enfer became important for my developing inquiry because one of the notations I had published in the first edition of this book was found in a rock shelter at the Gorge d'Enfer, near the salmon. Did that early notation encompass a period of waiting for the first run of salmon, at a point along the Vézère near where migratory reindeer may also have crossed in the spring and fall? If so, then these two artifacts, an incised bone with notation and a carved ceiling with a male salmon, separated by a few thousand years but coming from the same valley and set of sites, may have been analytically and conceptually related. These were questions and thoughts that could not be derived from traditional modes of archaeological inquiry.

Here I must discuss again the problem of the way in which one "sees" what one is prepared to see and does not see what one is not prepared to "see," a problem that has existed in the study of these images since they were first discovered in the 19th century.

It was only as I slowly worked my way across Europe, studying the images from the widely dispersed homesites of the Ice Age cultures, that I realized that water and fish, even if fish were not major items of diet, played a significant symbolic role within these riverine coastal cultures. The Pyrenean cave of Tuc d'Audoubert, which has a chamber containing the three carved bison and the tiny sanctuary with the horse and "P" signs, can be entered by rowboat after the spring floods have subsided. The river Volp flows through the hill. In a little known and still unpublished distant chamber of this cave, there is a wall with engraved "macaronis" that begin at a crack in the wall and then loop like interlaced meandering streams in every direction. To me, seeing this wall after years of research, the composition seemed like a model and image of the source of cave waters, streaming from the rock. In the Pyrenean cave of Gargas there is a small chamber with a clear pool whose walls are ritually covered with red ocher. At Gargas there is also one chamber where accumulated serpentine macaronis literally wrap themselves around the walls and ceiling. These seem to echo the mode and thought of the macaronis at the Tuc d'Audoubert. One of the serpentine bands at Gargas begins in a corner and crack of the wall, reminding me again of a model of the source of waters. In the Spanish Cantabrian cave of Hornos de la Peña, macaroni streams made by finger flow from a deep, round hole in the wall. Similar water-related macaroni motifs occur on bone and stone at many riverside homesites. In Germany there are images of fish at the riverside site of Petersfels (Fig. 194 b), which also gave us beads carved as the buttocks images of the female. At Gönnersdorf, on the Rhine between Cologne and Frankfurt and far into Germany, there are the engraved images of a fish, a seal, and a number of meandering water-related macaronis carefully incised on stone slates. These occur as rare, subsidiary images among the hundreds of better known female images in the buttocks style at Gönnersdorf. Far to the east on the Russian plain, along that network of rivers that drain southward to the Black Sea, among regional Ice Age cultures where animal images are always crude and relatively rare, highly abstracted images of fish and water-related zigzag motifs and designs were nevertheless common and often quite elaborate (Marshack 1979 a). Both the zigzag image of water and the spiral motif of periodicity and time are found at the riverside site of Mezin, located on the right bank of the Desna, where these motifs are associated with schematic and abstracted female figurines (p.312, Fig. 185). In Central Europe, at the Moravske Museum in Brno, Czechoslovakia, I unexpectedly found by microscopic study, the unpublished image of an abstracted and schematic fish incised on a piece of ivory tusk from the riverside site of Predmost (Marshack 1979 a: 272). This came from the Gravettian culture that also provided many of the female images published in this book. Was the image of the female, therefore, as a metaphor of periodicity and process, also related to the time-factored processes of the seasons and rivers (See Figs. 57 c, and 186 b)? The problem of what and when one "sees" when one is prepared, and that one does not see when one is not prepared, kept intruding and becoming more important as the research proceeded. Images of fish and water, for instance, are sparsely noted in most popular publications and anthologies of Ice Age "art," which are usually devoted to the images of the "Venus" figurines and the large herbivores (mammoth, horse, bison, reindeer, deer, etc.) as well as to images of the carnivores (lion, bear). Fish and water do not fit easily into most categories or theories concerning the meanings or uses of Ice Age art. But these subsidiary images persistently intruded into my research, not because fish were major items of food, but because they were apparently images and symbols of seasonal, riverine periodicity. The abstracted and schematic images of fish and water were, in fact, ubiquitous. They appear in all the later Ice Age cultures.

It is interesting that as part of an effort to use studies of "style" and "information theory" (as it related to "style"), the American archaeologist, M. Conkey, conducted a formal structural study of the Magdalenian "design elements" found on bone artifacts from homesites in the Cantabrian region of Spain. Many of these images have for almost half a century been recognized as abstractions of animals and fish and some (the zigzags, bands, and serpentines) I had also suggested were water-related motifs. Without any attempt to study the origin or derivation of these "design elements," Conkey created a catalogue of decontextualized, structural parts: arcs, ovals, bundles of lines, sets of "ticks" (strokes), etc. One of these so-called design elements, the "oval" was described structurally as "biconvergent curvilinears sometimes filled," with one variant described as "open form ovates" (Conkey 1980). These were the images that Breuil and others had earlier described as schematizations and abstractions of fish (see p. 326, Fig. 194 b). Based on her structural studies Conkey declared that multiple zigzags, banded lines, and simple "ticks" associated with a containing line, were among "the eleven design elements that are found only at Altamira." Their presence supposedly indicated "the uniqueness of the Altamira assemblage." On the basis of

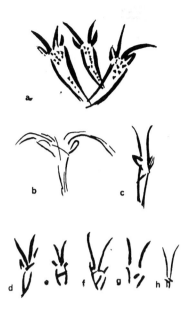

Fig. 240
Schematized and abstracted heads of the male ibex on bone artifacts from the Magdalenian period in France and Spain. Each of the heads is struck through as though in a ritual or symbolic killing. At its most abstract the male ibex in this period is represented merely by the convergent arcs of the horns. This is a regional ritual and symbolic image of the hill and mountain regions of Western Europe and does not occur elsewhere during the Ice Age.
a) La Vache (Ariège); b) Montgaudier (Charente); c) Cueto de la Mina (Llanes); d) La Paloma (Oviedo); e–g) El Pendo (Santander); h) Altamira (Santander).

Fig. 241
Incised fragment of bone from the cave of Altamira depicting four schematic fish associated with a linear representation of water. Middle Magdalenian, Santander, Spain (after Barandiaran Maestu 1973). Similar "water bands" are incised on the wall of the cave (Marshack 1977).

Fig. 242
Small bas-relief carving of a male ibex on the ceiling of the Abri Pataud rock shelter, Les Eyzies, France. Discovered after the excavation was terminated, it is an image that may be a symbol of the end of winter and coming of spring at that site. This may have been the period after the river ice broke, when the reindeer were about to return and the salmon were about to arrive (photo Delluc).

Fig. 243 ▶
Abri Pataud, France. Portion of the large limestone block incised with a serpentine accumulation and a number of vulva images. The upper vulva, top right, is lightly overengraved and the vulvar ovals within the serpentine are gouged with sets of marks. An additional vulva is apparently incised at bottom right. The stone itself had been touched with red and black paint.

these studies Conkey declared that the cave of Altamira was probably an aggregation site. Conkey may be correct. The concept of the aggregation site was being much discussed at this time in archaeology, and White, for instance, had declared the Vallon de Castlemerle in France was an aggregation site because of the presence and manufacture of large quantities of beads. Unfortunately, the images that were supposedly unique to Altamira are found throughout Western Europe during this period of the Magdalenian and are quite common, for instance, in France. The fish as a schematic or abstracted oval, for instance, appears at the Magdalenian site of Germany (Petersfels) and as far east as the Magdalenian sites of Pekarna in Czechoslovakia and Maszyska in Poland. "Convergent arcs," for instance, were recognized by Breuil and others as an abstraction of the horns of the male ibex, a species that was found among the hills and mountains of the Franco-Cantabrian area but not in northern European areas of steppe and tundra. It is, therefore, a purely regional, observational abstraction (Fig. 240). The failure of structural studies to deal with the derivation of these images or with the contexts and associations in which they appear can be illustrated by an extremely simple and schematic engraving on bone from Altamira in which four oval fish are associated with schematic band representations of water (Fig. 241). The derivation of these fish and water motifs from more realistic images can be tracked in the Franco-Cantabrian bone industry. This abstract composition of fish and water on bone at Altamira suggests an inland seasonal reference. On the walls of Altamira itself there are similar schematic, abstract representations of the water/band motif, the motif that Conkey classifies merely as incised "bundles of lines" (Marshack 1977). Incidentally, many of the famous painted bison on the ceiling of Altamira are depicted in summer molt. If Altamira was, therefore, a seasonal aggregation site and a ritual cave, a proper contextual and internal cognitive analysis of the iconography may be of relevance in determinating when it was used for ritual and aggregation. Such relevance cannot be determined or argued from a supposedly "unique" iconography derived from a decontextualized structuralism.

On the basis of these same studies, Conkey, suggested for instance, that the Spanish cave of Cueto de la Mina might also have been an important aggregation site. My analysis (p. 214, Fig. 103 a,b) of the notational composition from that site, which contains two male ibex heads with horns ("convergent arcs") in addition to plants, is probably a more significant indicator of possible periodic seasonal aggregation at this site than any reference to supposed aggregation based on the presence of "design elements." This is not intended as a criticism of the structural method, which has been extremely helpful since the early work of Breuil in creating chronologies and models of image dispersal and development, and the later work of Leroi-Gourhan in cataloguing Ice Age signs. The discussion is intended, instead, to show how one usually "sees" what one is prepared to see, either by experience or training or by current concepts

in the culture of the time. This problem of how one "sees" in a cultural context is, in fact, one that research in "artifical intelligence" has not yet been able to adequately address. There is no better instance of the problem of how one sees than the persistent and changing efforts by an army of authors to interpret the complex and variable icongraphy and imagery of the Ice Age, the images that authors have for so long presumed to be the primitive "beginnings" of human art. Since we do not have the accompanying mythology or the antecedents of these traditions we are endlessly free to create mythologies and "origins" of our own.

The South African ethnographer, Lewis-Williams, for instance, has published studies of the rock art of the technologically simple hunting-gathering San bushman who periodically practice trance ceremonies during which trance dancers "see" hallucinatory images of geometric patterns and of creatures out of the culture's mythology. South African rock art often depicts these trance ceremonies and images of real and mythologized creatures. Lewis-Williams has therefore suggested that the images of the European Upper Paleolithic, *including the notations*, are images that were originally seen in or were in other ways derived from trance (Lewis-Williams and Dowson 1989, 1990.) Assuming that the Ice Age cultures were essentially shamanistic, because there are a few images of persons in ritual costume or performance, he has suggested that the images on the walls and in the homesites were derived from shamanic visions. Like Conkey's structuralism, such interpretations have the momentary appearance of objectivity and science. Trance and shamanism do exist and have been subjects of anthropological and psychological inquiry. In the early stages of hallucination one can see geometric patterns, "entoptics," and in some stages of trance, as in some night-mares, images of animals can also undergo transformation, take on human form and even speak. But Lewis-Williams was attempting to throw a small psychological blanket over a huge and ancient city. There is nothing in San rock art, ritual or life that compares to the extraordinary complexity and variety of the symbolic materials and modes of symbolic behavior found in the European Ice Age. For instance, there is no comparable tradition of female imagery, of complex ceremonial burial, of curated objects on which different classes of symbol were accumulated. Of greater significance, the different classes of image that occur in the Ice Age occur in human cultures whether or not there is a tradition of trance or shamanism. These classes of symbol and image are usually created "consciously" as part of the culture. World mythology, in fact, offers a voluminous documentation of incessant and miraculous transformations that occur as part of the narrative equations that are integral to that form of story-telling. Folk tales are often structured with a persistent use of the concepts of change and transformation. Levi-Strauss spent a large portion of his life documenting the diverse ways in which myths and the characters in myths transform, *not* on the basis of transformations seen in trance, but on the basis of the transformations that are inherent and possible in the equationing, narrative, and mythic "story" mode. Transformations, in fact, are documented in the mythic literature of all the world's religions. These transformations are not derived from trance, but from the creative and mythic process itself. One reason, of course, is that periodicity, change, transformation, and the unexpected, are universally recognized aspects of both nature and culture, and changes even occur in individual personality. As a result they are processes that are endlessly elaborated, explained and altered in myth. These mythic modes are as variable and creative as any of the transformations or narratives that are seen or lived through in trance. It may be of interest that, as an aspect of the human, these mythic modes occur as well in the theories and models created by ethnographers and anthropologists. There is another aspect of the problem. The person in trance usually "sees" the mythic images of his own culture, not of someone else's culture, and while in trance the person will take the mythic voyage prescribed by the culture, not the mythic voyage offered by someone else's culture. The trancer will often also transcribe or translate the visions seen in trance into the words, idioms, and images that are part of the traditional imagery and mythology of that culture. San rock art, despite Lewis-Williams, is not a depiction of the universal imagery of "entoptics" or of transformation, but is also largely the stylistically and culturally transliterated and transmuted imagery of that culture. The images seen in trance, and then reported, are never merely the accultural, non-cultural products of an aberrant hallucinating neurology. They are also the product of a period and a culture.

The problem, therefore, once again concerns how one "sees" what one "sees." Lewis-Williams sees the Ice Age images, and even the rock art images of other cultures, in terms of his own acculturation, his own experience and knowledge, and what he theoretically presumes to be the universal hallucinatory mode of humanity, of shamanic cultures, and of the South African San hunter-gatherers. The fact is that shamanistic cultures create and use images of many types, at different levels of production and creation. In some shamanic cultures models of the cosmological, "astronomical" universe are made, and notations are kept. This was not done by the South African bushman. In some shamanic cultures complex geometric patterns are made and used in prognostication, healing, supplication and meditation. These are often cognized, equational structures not derived from trance. These are not made by the San. In some shamanic cultures mythological and ancestral totem animals and spirits are depicted and their images are used in ritual. These creatures are often characters derived from traditional myths. Animals with a particular pelage or color are often used or killed ritually in specialized ceremonies in certain seasons. Some animals are, in fact, mythologized because of their relation to certain seasons or realms in nature. Certain animals are regularly associated in myth because of their relations within a natural realm, a season, or a myth of origins. Some animals are symbolic because they are metaphors of a process or behavior.

To ascribe this infinitely storied and variable symbolic complexity to the imagery seen or derived from trance, because one can see geometric or "entoptic" forms in migraine or trance, or because the San bushman depict their trance images in rock art is, despite a claim to "science," anthropologically, ethnographically and psychologically naive. Even a cursory study of the Ice Age traditions, their variability and development, documents the enormous difference between these two hunting-gathering cultures and their symboling traditions.

I close with a coda, with a theme or refrain that echoes through the research.

When I stood with Professor Hallam Movius in the early summer on the cliff shelf outside the Abri Pataud, overlooking the small valley below, white pinpoint cows were grazing across the river where once the herds of wild horse and bison roamed and through which reindeer made their seasonal trek. We had been talking for two days within the shelter that had been built by farmers into the cliff overhang. The Vézère flowed iridescent in the valley below as the sun set behind the low hills on the other side of the valley. As it did so, the thin first crescent of the moon stood as a silver sliver in the sky, pointing its bow at the sinking sun. It was a few days past summer solstice and the sun was sinking near its far northern point on the horizon of those distant hills.

"You have a natural calendar in the sky," I said. Movius looked at me, apparently perplexed. We had been talking about the possibility of notations and of the new techniques that could be developed for studying the Ice Age images, as well as of the new questions that needed to be asked about culture, evolution and "man." "That sky," I said, "is a calendar." I pointed back and forth along the horizon. The sun, I said, set each evening along that horizon at a different point, from its low point to the left and the south at the winter solstice, to its midpoint at the spring equinox, just above where the cows were grazing, to that position towards the north at summer solstice, near where it was now sinking. Once each month the sliver of the first crescent would stand above the sinking sun, aiming its bow at that descending source of light, and each evening after that the moon would appear a bit higher and a bit larger, aiming at the setting sun. Movius was silent. He had clearly never thought of the changing sky as part of his excavation. He had looked down, never up, for years carefully excavating and sifting through the hardened soil. "When the sun sank midway, at the spring equinox, the river was near the time of the thaw," I said. "The salmon would soon be coming." And, as I was to realize later but did not at that time know, the reindeer would soon cross at the point where the railroad bridge now stood, the herd heading eastward to the higher lands and summer grazing behind that valley. One does not dig the sky in archaeology, but it was, of course, there for the digging.

The lesson of that scene, of that valley and sky, wove itself imperceptibly into the research, much as the walls of La Pileta did some years later. Ten minutes up river and to the north from the spot at which we stood was the male salmon carved on the ceiling at the Gorge d'Enfer.

Unfortunately, no great art was ever found at the excavation of the Abri Pataud. There were merely two engraved pebbles with animals and one crude bas-relief "Venus" figurine carved on a limestone block.

However, as Movius lay dying some two decades later of a long and slowly debilitating series of small strokes, a worker clearing out the Abri Pataud to begin a museum that was dedicated to Movius's excavation, looked up and saw a small, beautifully carved male ibex on the ceiling of the rock shelter (Fig. 242). Though Movius and his students had worked and eaten in that shelter for years, it had never been seen. During the years of my research I was to find that the male ibex was often a seasonal image of the spring, for this was the season it came down from the heights to feed on the new spring grass of the lower valleys. It descended in all-male groups days before the females and the young arrived. Did the male ibex at the Abri Pataud then mark the coming of spring, as did the setting sun over the hills to the west, the thaw, the salmon and the reindeer?

The discovery of that ibex by workers who looked up instead of down, recalled the discovery of Ice Age cave art a full century earlier. In 1879, while the landowner de Sautuola was digging in the soil of Altamira, looking for Ice Age tools and examples of bone art, his daughter looked up while playing and shouted, "Look Papa, oxen!" The painted images of bison were clearly there but archaeologists of the period would not believe them genuine until, in 1895, Ice Age images of bison were found in the cave of La Mouthe in France, a short walk from Les Eyzies and the burial at Cro-Magnon. That some of the bison in Altamira and other caves of Cantabrian Spain were depicted in summer molt, like one of the bison in Lascaux, was not perceived or recognized until, long after, I began asking my "time-factored" questions. Again, and repeatedly, one "sees" and does not "see" what one is prepared both to "see" and to not "see."

In 1988, as Movius lay dying in the United States, he did not realize that an important Ice Age symbolic composition had, in fact, been excavated at the Abri Pataud. Like other archaeologists and students of the Ice Age, he was not prepared to "see" or recognize the image or its importance. He had considered this composition to be an interesting oddity and another example of early cabalistic image making (Fig. 243). A large block of limestone, nearly 3½ feet high (105 cm) found in two pieces had a deeply incised serpentine accumulation, associated with a number of vulva images (Movius 1977:51; Marshack 1991 b). That stone block was never discussed by Movius when we would meet, I believe because he did not know what to say. It was no "masterpiece" and it was not what one might properly consider to be "art." However, I came slowly to believe that the serpentine image in the Ice Age was often, in context, a symbol and sign of time and periodicity. It was, I believed, a generalized image, apparently related both to processes in the sky, to processes in nature, and ultimately to the process of notation itself. The serpentine image at the Abri Pataud was doubly intriguing, because only a few kilometers away, at the site of Blanchard where the notation incised on a bone plaque in the serpentine mode had been found, there were also vulvas carved upon limestone blocks. The concept of periodic time, of time-factored imagery and ritual, and of cultural time, space and process had, apparently, as I came to believe, been woven like a tapestry across these hills and cultures. The large Abri Pataud serpentine, with its associated vulvas and the evidence that it had been accumulated over time and had been touched with red and black paint, seemed to close out a long and seemingly infinite odyssey through a widely dispersed labyrinth of piecemeal clues and insights. The journey had, as many do, returned to where it began, but with an increased ability now to "see" and, for that reason, to ask new questions. Did the serpentine block with its vulvas, and the male ibex on the ceiling, somehow relate to the periodic movement of the sun on the western horizon across the valley and the monthly appearance of the first crescent over those same hills?

* * *

How and why did the manufacture of image and symbol begin? It began, it now seems, like language itself began, to mark and refer to the relevant, the meaningful and the recognized—and often also to the unexplained and unexplainable—to those processes, objects and relations that were recognized in the increasingly complex phenomenological and cultural realms of human observation. This thought and insight, acquired early in the research, began a second inquiry—into the evolution and function of the human brain, and into the role of vision and imaging in the referencing capacity of language, since language, after all, is merely a mode of referring to the categories and processes or equations of the visible or envisionable world. And it began, as well, an inquiry into the different and changing worlds or "realities" that eye and brain "see" and the different and changing worlds that the brain can create and has created.

* * *

This book, first published in 1972, not only introduced the images of the Ice Age to a wide, general public, but it introduced the concept of internal cognitive analysis the study of early human image and symbol systems. This book, the cover story that I subsequently wrote for the National Geographic (1975), and the exhibition of Ice Age Art I curated for the American Museum of Natural History (New York) and the Smithsonian Institution in Washington, D.C., introduced the subject of Ice Age art to millions of persons in the United States. The European Ice Age was at that time better known in Europe. In these early efforts and in dozens of papers published since then, the "intelligence" of these early supposedly "primitive" humans and the complexity of their symboling systems was argued and has in large measure been accepted. There are dozens of practicing archaeologists who inform me that those efforts and the questions I raised had led them into the field.

It is therefore with a sense of closure and some sadness that I have found, after decades of research, that I have had to argue that the West European, Franco-Cantabrian "explosion" in creativity, in animal images, female images, personal decoration, notations, the high art of the sanctuary caves and the library of signs and motifs, constitute a skewed body of data and were, to that degree, "false." The popular and accepted belief of archaeologists and novelists of the Ice Age that these cultures represented a species difference between modern humans and earlier humans, and that the Ice Age represented the place and time of "origins" for human art and symbol rather than the historical time and place for a set of conditions that fostered a unique regional development, had, I found, now to be argued against. I found I had to address the general problem of evolving hominid and human-capacity, including the level of capacity apparently present in Homo erectus and the Neanderthals. I began to discuss the Ice Age images in terms of the cognitive and neuropsychological processes that had evolved during hominization (Marshack 1984a, 1985a, 1989a, 1991d). I found that I had to argue against the tendency to find in the European Upper Paleolithic, and in image or one set of images, proof of diverse contemporary theories about hominization and humanity, about the origins and uses of art, image, culture, social complexity, and even modern human language. Unfortunately my book, like the earlier volume about Ice Age art by Leroi-Gourhan in France, had played its part in creating a self-satisfying Eurocentric myth. I had, therefore, begun to argue about the extraordinary "potentially variable human capacity" (Marshack 1984a, 1985a, 1989a), of which the Ice Age cultures provided but an instance, and to argue about the inadequacy of the archaeological record, which could deal only with certain temporal and chronological products and processes found in the soil or on rocks, instead of with the nature of the "potentially variable capacity."

At the end of two decades, after arguing for evolution of the human capacity, I was invited to present the annual luncheon lecture to the American Association of Physical Anthropologists (Marshack 1989 a) to present these ideas and questions to the researchers who were tracking human evolution by a study of the early bones and skeletons. That paper, which represented the closing of one inquiry and the beginning of another, was a plea for an investigation, not merely of hominid or human bones (which, of course, could not "think"), but of the more important evolving "potentially variable capacity" of humans. The European Upper Paleolithic, I argued, merely documents the use of the late evolved capacity during one period and under one set of conditions. When those conditions changed, when the ice melted, when the climate warmed and the forests marched north across Europe, when the huge herbivore herds that had grazed on the steppe and tundra disappeared, the Ice Age culture collapsed. The hunter-gatherer populations, with their highly evolved potentially variable human capacity, however, remained in Europe; as did the time-factored lore and skill of the Ice Age which was by now presumably embedded in language, in myth and in the adaptive behavior and observations of the new Mesolithic hunter-gatherers.

These European traditions, developed in the Ice Age, were apparently retained by the indigenous populations until the coming of later neolithic farming technologies. When the neolithic farming cultures of Western Europe began to build their megalithic stone alignments and mounds (as at Stonehenge and New Grange) there is evidence not of a sophisticated arithmetical astronomy but of a simple basic mode of seasonal time-reckoning and lunar/solar observation. There is reason to believe that this neolithic astronomy was not derived from the agricultural civilizations of the Middle East who were developing other, arithmeticized modes of observational calendar keeping. If the present research is proven valid we have reason to believe that the indigenous European tradition of observational astronomy, which began around 28,000 B.C. with the hunter-gatherers of the Ice Age, may have been retained to play a part in the development of an indigenous European astronomy in the neolithic. Later concepts coming from the New East, including seeds and farming technology, and farming metaphors of death and rebirth in harvesting and planting, may have been absorbed into an already extant indigenous seasonal lore of the rebirth and renewal of nature and an ancient skill in astronomical observation.

The essential story, then, is not in the single and extraordinary event of the Ice Age "explosion," but in the unfolding and persistent, variable and changing human drama itself. The drama, as I have felt it, exists in the shifting uses of that "potentially variable human capacity." And it is also in the way that, periodically, we see that drama and its unfolding so differently.

ACKNOWLEDGMENTS

My deepest acknowledgment and gratitude are extended to Hallam L. Movius, Jr. His courage in supporting the needs of an untried methodology was extraordinary. He has given to the work an iron core of professional evaluation and criticism which has subtly shaped the research and publication. At the same time the author, under his aegis, has been free to walk on his own.

Lita Osmundsen and Gerald S. Hawkins have given friendship, support and advice that have helped make this work possible.

The Wenner-Gren Foundation for Anthropological Research, New York, and the National Science Foundation, Washington, D.C., have consistently funded the field work required for developing the new methodology and accumulating the data. The Bollingen Foundation and the Samuel H. Kress Foundation have supported the acquisition and preparation of materials for publication. Innumerable scientists in Europe and the United States have helped or given encouragement, often under trying circumstances and difficulties to themselves. For this I am grateful.

None of the persons or institutions above have necessarily supported the author's concepts or interpretations.

Special thanks is given to André Leroi-Gourhan. From the moment of my hesitant inquiry by letter many years ago, and in every year since, he has been both helpful and gracious, willing to meet with me in his office or home, at a dig or in the laboratory, in order to discuss the enlarging research and its ramifications and problems. His own extensive research has laid down the structure upon which I proceeded. Copies of his papers were always with me. Though it may be that we disagree in some interpretations I have found that we have consistently and mutually respected our primary search for and collection of the hard, documentary data. Interpretations, in this sense, are always secondary and tentative, in continuous process of change.

I am also grateful for the endurance and tolerance of the many museum officials and workers in collections throughout Europe, and to the owners of private collections. They have often had to put up with masses of technical equipment carted in and set up under non-standard conditions in any area and on any surface available.

The following authors, publishers, and institutions have kindly given permission to reprint quotations:

Aldine Publishing Company: A. C. Blanc, "Some Evidences for the Ideologies of Early Man," SOCIAL LIFE OF EARLY MAN, ed. Sherwood L. Washburn, 1961, pp. 120, 126, 133–134; American Anthropological Association: Lewis R. Binford and Sally R. Binford, "A Preliminary Analysis of Functional Variability in the Mousterian of Levallois Facies," AMERICAN ANTHROPOLOGIST, Vol. 68, No. 2, Part 2, 1966, pp. 242, 256, 270; American Association for the Advancement of Science: Robert McC. Adams, "Archaeological Research Strategies: Past and Present," SCIENCE, Vol. 160, June 14, 1968, pp. 1188, 1189, 1190, 1192 (Copyright © 1968 by the American Association for the Advancement of Science); Editions d'Art Lucien Mazenod: André Leroi-Gourhan, TREASURES OF PREHISTORIC ART, trans. Norbert Guterman, pub. Harry N. Abrams Inc., 1967, pp. 40, 107, 134–135; Harper & Row: Jacquetta Hawkes and Sir Leonard Woolley, HISTORY OF MANKIND: PREHISTORY AND THE BEGINNINGS OF CIVILIZATION, 1963, pp. 134–135, 106; Robert F. Heizer: MAN'S DISCOVERY OF HIS PAST: LITERARY LANDMARKS IN ARCHAEOLOGY, ed. R. F. Heizer, pub. Prentice-Hall, 1962, pp. 91, 117–121; Humanities Press and Routledge & Kegan Paul Ltd.: Jean Piaget, THE CHILD'S CONCEPTION OF PHYSICAL CAUSALITY, trans. Marjorie Gabain, 1965, pp. 60, 73, 74, 75, 77, 78, 81, 82, 85, 241; Alfred A. Knopf: Carleton Coon, THE ORIGIN OF RACES, 1962, p. 432; Macmillan & Co. Ltd.: G. Horne and G. Aiston, SAVAGE LIFE IN CENTRAL AUSTRALIA, 1924, pp. 22–24; Penguin Books Ltd.: Annette Laming, LASCAUX, PAINTINGS AND ENGRAVINGS, 1959, pp. 93–96; Press Universitaires de France and Walker and Company: Raymond Lantier, MAN BEFORE HISTORY, trans. Unity Evans, 1965, pp. 110–112; Random House, Inc.: Herbert Kühn, ON THE TRACK OF PREHISTORIC MAN, trans. Alan Houghton Brodrick, 1955, pp. 90–98; Romain Robert: His "Le Lissoir aux Saïgas de la grotte de la Vache," BULLETIN DE LA SOCIÉTÉ PRÉHISTORIQUE DE L'ARIÈGE, T. XIII, 1958, pp. 1–4; Scientific American: Jean de Heinzelin, "Ishango," SCIENTIFIC AMERICAN, June, 1962, pp. 106, 109–111, 113–114, 116 (Copyright © 1962 Scientific American, Inc. All rights reserved); Donald F. Thomson: his "The Seasonal Factor in Human Culture," PROCEEDINGS OF THE PREHISTORIC SOCIETY, Vol. V, 1939, pp. 209, 211; Trianon Press: Henri Breuil, FOUR HUNDRED CENTURIES OF CAVE ART, trans. Mary E. Boyle, 1952, pp. 118, 153, 156, 157, 167, 169, 176, 177, 230, 238, 267; Regents of the University of Wisconsin: Z. A. Abramova, "Palaeolithic Art in the USSR," trans. Catherine Page and ed. Chester S. Chard,

ARCTIC ANTHROPOLOGY, Vol. IV, No. 2, 1967, pp. 82, 83, 84, 86.

All photographs and drawings are by the author except as indicated below. Permission for the use of these illustrations has been kindly granted by the following:

Arts et Métiers Graphiques and Le Centre National de la Recherche Scientifique: Figures 121 a and b, 122, 150 a, b, c, 196 (from Henri Bégouën and Henri Breuil, LES CAVERNES DU VOLP, 1958, Figs. 55, 79, 100, Plates IX and XX); Caisse National des Monuments Historiques et des Sites, Archives Photographiques: Figures 82, 105, 106, 110, 111, 155 (photographs by Fernand Windels); Editions d'Art Lucien Mazenod: Fig. 108 (from André Leroi-Gourhan, TREASURES OF PREHISTORIC ART, 1967, Fig. 565); Field Museum: Fig. 182; Archives de l'Institut de Paléontologie Humaine: Figs. 60, 97, 198 (from Henri Breuil and René de Saint-Périer, LES POISSONS, LES BATRACIENS ET LES REPTILES DANS L'ART QUATERNAIRE, 1927, Figs. 17-1, 2, 3, 4 and 68-2, 3); Masson et Cie: Figure 183 (from François Bordes, Paul Fitte, Pierre Laurent, "Gravure féminine du Magdalénien VI de la Gare de Couze," L'ANTHROPOLOGIE, t. 67, 1963, Fig. 2), Fig. 4 a (from Henri Breuil, "Notes de voyage paléolithique en Europe centrale," L'ANTHROPOLOGIE, 1925, Fig. 11), Figure 180 (from Paul Darasse and Simone Guffroy, "Le Magdalénien supérieur de l'abri de Fontalès près Saint-Antonin," L'ANTHROPOLOGIE, t. 64, 1960, Fig. 19); Photothèque Musée de l'Homme: Figure 202b (photograph, "Venus of Laussel"); Naturhistorisches Museum, Vienna: Figure 5 a and b (from V. Scerbakiwskyj, "Eine paläolithische Station in Honci (Ukraina)," DIE EISZEIT, 1926–1927, Abb. VIII and IX); Penguin Books Ltd.: Figures 115 and 127 (from Annette Laming, LASCAUX, PAINTINGS AND ENGRAVINGS, 1959, Figs. 16 and 18); Presses Universitaires de France: Figures 159 a, b, 209 (from Denis Peyrony, "La Ferrassie," PRÉHISTOIRE, t. 3, 1934, Figs. 25 and 50); Alain Roussot: Fig. 181; Royal Anthropological Institute, London: Figure 40 (from E. H. Man, THE NICOBAR ISLANDS, 1933, illustration on p. 95); SCIENTIFIC AMERICAN: Figure 2a and b (from Jean de Heinzelin, "Ishango," SCIENTIFIC AMERICAN, June, 1962; line drawings on p. 114. Copyright © 1962 Scientific American, Inc. All rights reserved.); Société Préhistorique Française: Figure 90 a, b, c (from André Leroi-Gourhan, "La fonction des signes dans les sanctuaires paléolithiques," and "Le symbolisme des grands signes dans l'art pariétal paléolithique," BULLETIN DE LA SOCIÉTÉ PRÉHISTORIQUE, T. LV, 1958, Figs. 8 and 9 from the first article and Fig. 1 from the second article); Trianon Press: Figures 107 a, b, c, 121 a, b, 122, 150 a, b, c (from Henri Breuil, FOUR HUNDRED CENTURIES OF CAVE ART, 1952, Figs. 127, 130, 133, 139, 254, 256, 258); Karel Valoch, Moravske Museum: Figure 83 (line drawing of bison from Pekárna); Jean Vertut: Figure 187 (from André Leroi-Gourhan, TREASURES OF PREHISTORIC ART, 1967, Fig. 63); Achille Weider: Fig. 202 a. The lunar photos on pages 144–145 were supplied by CAMERA and the Lick Observatory. Georges Simonnet has given permission to use the photographs and drawings by A. Marshack of details upon two unpublished artifacts from his dig at Labastide.

I wish to acknowledge my profoundest thanks and admiration for professor Hallam L. Movius, Jr., one of the leading archaeologists of his time, who supported this inquiry from the beginning. Above all he supported the effort at first-hand analysis of the material and the development of analytical technique and new types of questions as opposed to the creation of general theories and models without adequate knowledge of the variability and complexity of the evidence. And I would like to express my special debt to professor Norman Geschwind, one of the leading neuro-scientists of the "cultural brain" who supported the research at a different level in persistently monitoring the nature of the questions and the results as they arose and as these refer to what was known of brain function and capacity.

Thanks are extended to the National Academy of Sciences in Washington, D.C. and the Soviet Academy of Sciences under whose joint auspices the material from the Ukraine, Russia, and Siberia were studied, as well as to the numerous other institutes, museums, and colleagues who made the research and inquiry possible. The added research noted in this volume was funded by the National Science Foundation, the National Endowment for the Humanities, the NATIONAL GEOGRAPHIC, the Harry F. Guggenheim Foundation, and the University of Santa Barbara Foundation.

COLLECTIONS OF UPPER PALEOLITHIC AND MESOLITHIC MATERIALS EXAMINED BY MICROSCOPE AND PHOTOGRAPHED, 1965–1970

Musée des Antiquités Nationales, Saint-Germain-en-Laye (Seine-et-Oise)

Saint-Périer Collection, Morigny (Seine-et-Oise)

Breuil Collection, Institut de Paléontologie Humaine, Paris

Muséum d'Histoire Naturelle, Paris

Laboratoire de Géologie quaternaire et Préhistoire, Université de Bordeaux, Talence (Gironde)

Musée de Saint-Antonin (Tarn-et-Garonne)

Musée National de Préhistoire, Les Eyzies-de-Tayac (Dordogne)

Faculté des Sciences, Université de Poitiers (Vienne)

Musée d'Aquitaine, Bordeaux (Gironde)

Georges Simonnet Collection, Toulouse (Haute-Garonne)

Musée de l'Ariège, Château de Foix, Foix (Ariège)

Musée d'Histoire Naturelle, Montauban (Tarn-et-Garonne)

Musée du Périgord, Périgueux (Dordogne)

J. Delsol Collection, Périgueux (Dordogne)

Louis S. Méroc Collection, Toulouse (Haute-Garonne)

Musée de l'Echevinage, Poitiers (Vienne)

Musée de Castel-Merle, Sergeac (Dordogne)

Romain Robert Collection, Tarascon-sur-Ariège (Ariège)

Louis Perricard Collection, Lussac-les-Châteaux (Vienne)

René Deffarges Collection, St.-Antoine-de-Breuilh (Dordogne)

Jean Vezian Collection, St.-Jean-de-Verges (Ariège)

Brochier Collection, St. Nazaire (Drôme)

Stephan Lwoff Collection, Paris

Musée de l'Homme, Paris

Musée d'Histoire Naturelle, Toulouse (Haute-Garonne)

Musée de l'Ain, Bourg-en-Bresse (Ain)

Faculté des Sciences, Université de Lyon, Lyon (Rhône)

Musée J. Miln, Z. le Rouzic, Carnac (Bretagne)

Musée de Guimet, Lyon (Rhône)

Abri Pataud Collection, Les Eyzies-de-Tayac (Dordogne)

Muséum Municipal, Menton (Alpes-Maritimes)

Musée d'Art et d'Histoire, Geneva, Switzerland

Museo Nacional de las Ciencias Naturales, Madrid, Spain

Museo de Prehistoria, Valencia, Spain

Museo Arqueológico y Etnográfico Vasco, Bilbao, Spain

Museo de Prehistoria y Arqueología, Santander, Spain

Museo Arqueológico (Alcazaba), Malaga, Spain

Museo Arqueológico, Granada, Spain

Museo di Preistoria e Protostoria della Lazio, EUR (Rome), Italy

Istituto di Paletnología, Università di Roma, Rome, Italy

Istituto Italiano di Paleontología Umana, Rome, Italy

Istituto di Paletnología, Università di Firenze, Florence, Italy

Istituto di Antropología e Paleontología Umana, Pisa, Italy

Museo Civico di Storia Naturale, Verona, Italy

Museo di Altamura, Bari, Italy

Museo di Archeología, Pegli (Genoa), Italy

British Museum, London, England

Miles Burkitt Collection, Grantchester, England

Institut für Ur- und Frühgeschichte der Universität Wien, Vienna, Austria

Naturhistorisches Museum, Vienna, Austria

Landesmuseum Joanneum, Graz, Austria

Museum Archeologicky, Dolní Věstonice, Czechoslovakia

Moravske Museum, Břno, Czechoslovakia

Museum Archeologiczne, Cracow, Poland

Kalectra Archeologii Polski, Cracow, Poland

Musée d'Histoire Naturelle, Brussels, Belgium

Nordiska Museet, Stockholm, Sweden

Göteborgs Arkeologiska Museum, Gothenburg, Sweden

Historiska Museet, Lund, Sweden

Historiska Museet, Malmo, Sweden

National Museet, Copenhagen, Denmark

Forhistorisk Arkaeologisk og Etnografisk Institut, Aarhus, Denmark

Kalundborg Museum, Vor- und Frühgeschichte, Kalundborg, Denmark

Schleswig-Holstein Landesmuseum für Vor- und Frühgeschichte, Schleswig, Germany

Prähistorische Staatssammlung, Munich, Germany

Rheinisches Landesmuseum, Bonn, Germany

Institut für Vor- und Frühgeschichte, Tübingen, Germany

Hegau Museum, Singen, Germany

Rosgarten Museum, Konstanz, Germany

COLLECTIONS OF UPPER PALEOLITHIC AND
MESOLITHIC MATERIALS FROM EUROPE AND
COLLECTIONS OF COMPARATIVE MATERIALS
FROM PREHISTORIC CONTEXTS IN OTHER
COUNTRIES EXAMINED BY MICROSCOPE AND
PHOTOGRAPHED, 1971–1990

MUSÉE LEMOZI, Cabrerets
LABORATOIRE DE PRÉHISTOIRE, C.N.R.S., Meudon
LABORATOIRE DE PRÉHISTOIRE, C.N.R.S., Paris
YVES MARTIN COLLECTION, Le Port Saint-Ouen
INSTITUT DE PALÉONTOLOGIE HUMAINE, Paris
MUSÉE MUNICIPAL, Angouleme
MUSÉE D' ECHIVANAGE, Poitiers
FACULTÉ DES SCIENCES, Université de Poitiers
DE LUMLEY COLLECTION, Terra Amata, Nice
MUSÉE DE CARNAC
CHATEAU DE FOIX
BEGOUEN COLLECTION, Chateâu deCujol.
SIMMONET COLLECTION,
ST. PERIER COLLECTION, Morigny
MUSÉE MUNICIPAL, ST. ANTONIN-NOBLE-VAL
MUSÉE D'AGEN
MUSÉE FERNAND DESMOULIN, Brântome
PALAIS DU RHIN, Strasbourg
MUSÉE DE MONTBELIARD
MUSÉE DE MENTON DE BARMA GRANDE, Menton
GUY CELERIER COLLECTION, Bourdeilles
FRANCIS HOURS COLLECTION
GUSTAV RIEK COLLECTION, Mauthenreuthe
ALFRED RUST COLLECTION, Ahrensburg/Holst
ULMER MUSEUM, Ulm
MUSEUM F. UR. U. FRÜHGESCHICHTE THURINGENS,
    Weimar
RÖMISCH-GERMANISCHES ZENTRALMUSEUM, Mainz.
LANDESMUSEUM FÜR VORGESCHICHTE, Halle/Saale
MUSEUM F. UR-U. FRÜGESCHICHTE, Potsdam
DIETRICH MANIA COLLECTION, Bilzungsleben
LANDESDENKMALAMT, Stuttgart
STAATLICHES AMT FÜR V. U. F., Koblentz
INSTITUTE OF ARCHAEOLOGY, Cologne
MUSEUM F. UR-U. FRÜGESCHICHTE, Schwerin
LEPENSKI VIR MUSEUM, Yugoslavia
UNIVERSITY MUSEUM, Belgrade
FILOSOFSKI INSTITUT, University of Belgrade
FRIDRICH COLLECTION, ARCHAEOLOGICAL INSTITUTE,
    Prague
ETHNOGRAPHIC MUSEUM, St. Petersburg
STATE HISTORICAL MUSEUM, Kiev

HERMITAGE, St. Petersburg
PALEONTOLOGICAL MUSEUM, Kiev
ARCHAEOLOGICAL MUSEUM, Kiev
GVOZDOVER COLLECTION, Moscow University
ANTHROPOLOGICAL MUSEUM, Moscow
HISTORISKA MUSEET, Stockholm
VILLA PALAVICINI, Pegli, Italy
ISTITUTO GEOLOGIA, Ferrara
PIGORINI MUSEUM, Rome
MUSEO CIVICO DI STORIA NATURALE, Verona
MUSEO SAN TELMO, San Sebastian
UNIVERSYTET JAGIELLENSKI, INSTITUT ARCHEOLOGII,
    Cracow
ARCHAEOLOGICAL INSTITUTE, Warsaw
KURT EHRENBURG COLLECTION, Vienna
MUSÉE D'ART ET D'HISTOIRE, Geneva
MAGYAR NEMZETI MÚZEUM, Budapest
TORTENETI MÚZEUM, Budapest
MUZEU DE ISTORIE SI ARTA AL MUNICIPOLUI,
    Bucharest
INSTITUT DE ARCHÉOLOGIE, Bucharest
MUSÉE D'HISTOIRE DE ROMANIE, Bucharest
LABORATOIRE D'ANTHROPOLOGIE ET DU PRÉHISTOIRE,
    INST. ROY. DES SCIENCES NATURELLES DE BELG.
MUSÉE D' HISTOIRE NAT. Brussels
MUSÉE ROYAUX ART ET HISTOIRE, Brussels
UNIVERSITÉ DE LIÈGE, Service Préhistoire
ARCHAEOLOGICAL MUSEUM, Cambridge University
PITT RIVERS MUSEUM, Oxford
GOUGH'S CAVE MUSEUM, Somerset
THE AUSTRALIAN MUSEUM, Sydney
PETER BEAUMONT COLLECTION, University of Witwa-
    tersrand, Paleontology
MACGREGOR MUSEUM, Kimberly, S.A.
CRANBROOK INSTITUTE OF SCIENCE, Bloomington
HEYE FOUNDATION—MUSEUM OF THE AMERICAN
    INDIAN, New York
SMITHSONIAN INSTITUTION, Washington, D.C.
PEABODY MUSEUM, Harvard University, Cambridge
FIELD MUSEUM, Chicago
LOWIE MUSEUM, Berkeley
SANTA BARBARA MUSEUM OF NATURAL HISTORY
ANDOVER FOUNDATION FOR ARCHAEOLOGICAL
    RESEARCH
DAVID H. THOMAS COLLECTION, American Museum
    of Natural History
JUNIUS BIRD COLLECTION, American Museum of
    Natural History
LOUIS DUPREÉ COLLECTION, American Museum of
    Natural History
LESLIE G. FREEMAN COLLECTION, University of
    Chicago

BIBLIOGRAPHY

In the years since the first edition of this book was published some thousands of papers have been published in different areas or disciplines that are relevant to the research. Two new subdisciplines have been established that are in some measure outside of the concerns of traditional archaeology: "cognitive archaeology" and "archaeoastronomy." A major archaeological institute, the MacDonald Institute for Archaeological Research, was formed at Cambridge University, in part to pursue aspects of "cognitive archaeology" and cultural symboling modes and a major journal, *Cambridge Archaeological Journal*, began to deal with aspects of that developing discipline.

In Europe a number of important new caves were discovered and published. They are listed below. As this edition was being prepared there was an announcement of the discovery of a possibly major new painted cave, the cave of Zubialde, in the Basque region of northern Spain. Not yet published or authenticated, it has instigated a worldwide controversy. Meanwhile, early Paleolithic rock art has begun to be found in Africa, Australia and possibly in the Americas. A new international journal on world rock art and symbolic studies, *Rock Art Research*, journal of the Australian Rock Art Association and the International Federation of Rock Art Organizations, has been publishing, in some measure to escape the traditional constraints and limitations that have become entrenched in discussions of early image and symbol as a result of traditional European and Franco-Cantabrian ethnocentrism.

A proper bibliography relevant to the research and concepts that were first presented in this book would constitute a major chapter and an argument in its own right. Since this book is the report of a single inquiry, I can do no more than selectively indicate some of the important and/or controversial publications that may have some relevance to the research. A number of the archaeological publications noted here disagree with findings of the author, and the author disagrees as often with the theories and findings found in these publications. But the following list does provide a broad sample of what seems to be new in inquiry, discovery and theory.

Specialized References

Note: In the years since this book was first published, two professional journals in the growing field of "archaeoastronomy" have appeared regularly: *Archaeoastronomy, Yearly Supplement to the Journal for the History of Astronomy*, Cambridge, and *Archaeoastronomy* Journal of the Center For Archaeoastronomy, College Park, Maryland. In addition, a large library of professional and popular books on the subject of cross-cultural archaeo- and ethnoastronomy have appeared in the English language. In one way or another these books deal with the extraordinary range and variability found in the patterns and modes of the temporal structuring and observations of the sky in societies and cultures at different levels of development and complexity. As this book goes to the printer, "time" as a factor in human behavior and culture has been further formalized with the announcement that a new international journal is to appear, *Time & Society*.

Aveni, A. F. (Ed.) 1975. *Archaeoastronomy in Pre-Columbian America*. University of Texas Press: Austin and London.

Aveni, A. F. (Ed.) 1977. *Native American Astronomy* Univeristy of Texas Press: Austin and London.

Aveni, A. F. (Ed.) 1988. *New Directions in American Archaeoastronomy*. BAR International Series 454. British Archaeological Reports, Oxford.

Aveni, A. F. 1989. *Empires of Time: Calendars, Clocks, and Cultures*. Basic Books: New York.

Aveni, A. F. (Ed.) 1989. *World Archaeoastronomy*. Cambridge University Press: Cambridge.

Aveni, A. F. and G. Urton (Eds.). 1982. *Ethnoastronomy and Archaeoastronomy in the American Tropics*. Annals of the New York Academy of Sciences, Vol. 385.

Benson, A. and T. Hoskinson. 1985. *Earth and Sky* Slo'w Press: Thousand Oaks, California.

Brecher, K. and M. Feirtag. 1979. *Astronomy of the Ancients*. MIT Press: Cambridge, MA.

Chamberlain, Von Del. 1982. *When Stars Came Down To Earth. Cosmology of the Skidi Pawnee Indians of North America*. A Ballena Press (Los Altos, Ca.)/Center for Archaeoastronomy (College Park, Md.) Cooperative Publication.

Krupp, E. C. (Ed.) 1978. *In Search of Ancient Astronomers*. Doubleday: New York.

Krupp, E. C. 1983. *Echoes of the Ancient Skies: The Astronomy of Lost Civilizations*. New York: Harper & Row.

Urton, G. 1981. *At the Crossroads of the Earth and the Sky: An Andean Cosmology*. University of Texas Press: Austin.

Williamson, R. A. 1984. *Living the Sky: The Cosmos of the American Indian*. Houghton Mifflin: Boston.

Williamson, R. A. (Ed.) 1981. *Archaeoastronomy in the Americas*. A Ballena Press (Los Altos, Ca.)/Center for Archaeoastronomy (College Park, Md.) Cooperative Publication.

Cognitive Neuropsychology

A number of subdisciplines in neuropsychology, developmental and cognitive psychology and imaging have addressed aspects of perception and cognition that have been of major concern to the present inquiry into image and symbol: visual-problem solving, visual language and visual modes of referencing. I provide a brief listing of recent publications that have some relevance to the questions raised in my own research. This neurological and psychoneurological research played as great a part in the program of research into Upper Paleolithic imagery as did archaeoastronomy and general anthropology.

Anderson, J. R. 1983. *The Architecture of Cognition*. Cambridge, MA:Harvard University Press.

Arbib, M. A. 1987. Levels of Modeling of Mechanisms of Visually Guided Behavior. *Behavioral and Brain Sciences* 10(3):407–465.

Bates, E., D. Thal and J. S. Janowski. 1991. Early language development and its neural correlates. In *Handbook of Neuropsychology, Vol. 6, Child Neurology*. Amsterdam: Elsevier. (In press)

Bellugi, U, E. S. Klima, and H. Poizner. 1988. Sign Language and the Brain. In *Language, Communication and the Brain*, F. Plum (Ed.) Raven Press, N.Y.

Bellugi, U. and M. Studdert-Kennedy (Eds.) 1980. *Signed and Spoken Language: Biological Constraints on Linguistic Form*. Report of the Dahlem Workshop on Sign Language and Spoken Language. Biological Constraints on Linguistic Form., Berlin, 3:24–28.

Bradshaw, J. L. 1989. *Hemispheric Specialization and Psychological Function* New York: John Wiley & Sons.

Damasio, A. et al., 1986. Sign language aphasia during left-hemisphere Amytal injection. *Nature* 332:363–365.

Dunlea, A. 1990. *Vision and the Emergence of Meaning*. New York: Cambridge University Press.

Eccles, J. 1989. *Evolution of the Brain: Creation of the Self*. London: Routledge. [Chapter 6, pp.117–139. Discusses Ice Age notation in terms of human "visuo-motor evolution."]

Edelman, G. 1990. *The Remembered Present: A Biological Theory of Consciousness* Basic Books: New York.

Feldman, J. A. 1985. Four Frames Suffice: A provisional model of vision and space. *Behavioral and Brain Sciences* 8(2):265–289.

Finke, R. A. 1986. Mental Imagery and the Visual System. *Scientific American* 254(3):88–95.

Finke, R. A. 1990. *Principles of Mental Imagery*. Cambridge, MA: MIT Press.

Fraiberg, S., with the collaboration of L. Fraiberg. 1977. *Insights from the Blind: Comparative Studies of Blind and Sighted Infants*. 1977. New York: Basic Books.

Gardner, H. 1983. *Frames of Mind: The Theory of Multiple Intelligences*. New York: Basic Books.

Gazzaniga, M. S. 1985. *The Social Brain: Discovering the Networks of the Mind*. Basic Books: New York.

Hamilton, C. R. and B. A. Vermeire. 1988. Complementary Hemispheric Specialization in Monkeys. *Science* 242(4885):1691–1694.

Harnad, S. (Ed.), *Categorical Perception:The Groundwork of Cognition* pp. 287–300. Cambridge: Cambridge University Press.

Jackendoff, R. 1987. On Beyond Zebra: The Relation of Linguistic and Visual Information. *Cognition* 26:89–114.

Jerison, H. J. 1991. *Brain Size and the Evolution of Mind*. Fifty-Ninth James Arthur Lecture on The Evolution of the Human Brain, 1989. American Museum of Natural History, N.Y.

Kendon, A. 1988. *Sign Languages of Aboriginal Australia: Cultural, Semiotic and Communicative Perspectives*. New York: Cambridge University Press.

Kinsbourne, M. (Ed.). 1979. *Asymmetrical Function of the Brain*. New York: Cambridge University Press.

Koedinger, K. R. and J. R. Anderson. 1990. Abstract Planning and Perceptual Chunks: Elements of Expertise in Geometry. *Cognitive Science* 14:511–550.

Kosslyn, S. M. 1981. Research on Mental Imagery: Some Goals and Directions. Cognition. *10* (1–3):173–179.

Kosslyn, S. M. 1988. Aspects of a Cognitive Neuroscience of Mental Imagery. *Science* 240:1621–1626.

Larkin, J. H. and H. A. Simon. 1987. Why a Diagram is (Sometimes) Worth Ten Thousand Words. *Cognitive Science* 11(1):65–99.

Lieblich, I. and M. A. Arbib. 1982. Multiple Representations of Space Underlying Behavior. *Behavioral and Brain Sciences* 5(4):627–659.

Massaro, D. W. 1989. Book Review of *Speech perception by ear and eye: A paradigm for psychological inquiry*. *Behavioral and Brain Science* 12:741–794.

Meltzoff, A. N. 1988. Imitation, Objects, Tools, and the Rudiments of Language in Human Ontogeny. *Human Evolution* 3(1–2):45–64.

Newell, A. 1990. *Unified Theories of Cognition*. Cambridge, MA: Harvard University Press. The William James Lectures.

Poggio, T., E. B. Gamble, J.J. Little. 1988. Parallel Integration of Vision Modules. *Science* 242(4877):436–440.

Potter, M. C., et al., 1986. Pictures in Sentences: Understanding Without Words. *Journal of Experimental Psychology: General* 115(3):281–294.

Previc, F. H. 1990. Functional Specialization in the Lower and Upper Visual Fields in Humans: Its Ecological Origins and Neurophysiological Implications. *Behavioral and Brain Sciences* 13:519–575.

Sayre, K. M. 1986. Intentionality and Information Processing: An Alternative Model for Cognitive Science. *Behavioral and Brain Sciences*. 9(1):121–166.

Schlaggar, B. L. and D. M. O'Leary. 1991. Potential of Visual Cortex to Develop an Array of Functional Units Unique to Somatosensory Cortex. *Science* 252:1556.

Tsoisos, J. K. 1990. Analyzing vision at the complexity level. *Behavioral and Brain Sciences* 13:423–469.

Author's References

Marshack, A. 1964. Lunar Notation on Upper Paleolithic Remains. *Science* 146(6):743–745.

———— 1969a. Polesini, a reexamination of the engraved Upper Paleolithic mobiliary materials of Italy by a new methodology. *Revista di Scienze Preistoriche* 24(2):219–281.

———— 1969b. New techniques in the analysis and interpretation of Mesolithic notation and symbolic art. In *Valcamonica Symposium, Actes du Symposium International d'Art Préhistorique*, 1968. pp. 479–494. Capo di Ponte.

———— 1970a. *Notation dans les Gravures du Paléolithique Supérieur*, Mèmoire 8. Edited by F. Bordes. Bordeaux: Institut de Préhistoire, Université de Bordeaux.

———— 1970b. Le baton de commandement de Montgaudier (Charente): Réexamen au microscope et interprétation nouvelle. *L'Anthropologie* 74(5–6):321–352.

———— 1970c. The baton of Montgaudier. *Natural History* 79(3): 56–63.

———— 1970d. Upper Paleolithic engraved pieces in the British Museum. *British Museum Quarterly* 35(1–4):137–145. Prehistoric and Roman Studies, British Museum Commemorative Volume.

———— 1972a. *The Roots of Civilization*. New York: McGraw Hill.

———— 1972b. Upper Paleolithic notation and symbol. *Science* 178:817–832.

———— 1972c. Aq Kupruk, Afghanistan: Art and Symbol. In *Prehistoric Research in Afghanistan* (1959–1966), L. Dupree (ed.). Transactions of the American Philosophical Society. 62(4):66–84.

———— 1972d. Cognitive aspects of Upper Paleolithic engraving. *Current Anthropology* 13(3–4):445–477. Also: 1974, On Upper Paleolithic engraving, *CA* 15(3):327–332, comments and reply; 1979, On Upper Paleolithic symbol systems, *CA* 20(3):607–608, comments and reply.

———— 1973. Analyse preliminaire d'une gravure à système de notation de la grotte du Taï (St. Nazaire-en-Royans, Drôme). *Etudes Préhistoriques* 4:13–17. La Société Préhistorique de l'Ardeche.

———— 1974a. The Chamula calendar board: an internal and comparative analysis. In *Mesoamerica Archaeology: New Approaches*. N. Hammond (ed.), pp. 255–270. Austin: University of Texas Press.

———— 1974b. Book Review of C.F. Herberger, *The Thread of Ariadne: The Labyrinth of the Calendar of Minos*, in *American Anthropologist* 76:404–405.

———— 1974c. Response to review of *The Roots of Civilization* by A.R. King, *American Anthropologist* 76:845–846.

———— 1975a. Exploring the mind of Ice Age Man. *National Geographic* 147(1):62–89.

———— 1975b. An Olmec mosaic: Internal analysis reveals prehistoric arithmetic, possibly calendric contents. In *Archaeoastronomy in Pre-Columbian America*. A. F. Aveni (ed.) pp. 341–377. Austin: University of Texas Press.

———— 1976a. Some implications of the Paleolithic symbolic evidence for the origins of language. In *Origins and Evolution of Language*. S. Harnad et al. (eds.). Annals of the N.Y. Academy of Science 280:289–311.

———— 1976b. Some Implications of the Paleolithic symbolic evidence for the origins of language. *Current Anthropology* 17(2):274–282.

———— 1976c. Complexité des traditions symboliques du Paléolithique Supérieur. In *La Préhistoire Française* H. de Lumley (ed.) pp. 749–754. Paris: Editions CNRS.

———— 1976d. Aspects of style versus usage in the analysis and interpretation of Upper Paleolithic images. In Prétirage, *Les Courants Stylistiques Dans l'Art Mobilier au Paléolithique Supérieur*, Colloque XIV, IX Congrés UISPP. Nice. pp. 118–146.

———— 1976e. The message in the markings. *Horizon* 18(4):64–73.

———— 1977. The meander as a system: The analysis and recognition of iconographic units in Upper Paleolithic compositions. In *Form in Indigenous Art: Schematization in the Art of Aboriginal Australia and Prehistoric Europe*. P. Ucko (ed.), pp. 286–317. London: Duckworth; New Jersey: Humanities Press.

———— 1978a. The art and symbol of Ice Age man. *Human Nature* 1(9):32–41.

———— 1978b. European Ice Age art and symbol. *Archaeology* 31(2):52–55.

———— 1979a. Upper Paleolithic symbol systems of the Russian Plain: cognitive and comparative analysis of complex ritual marking. *Current Anthropology* 20(2):271–311. Also discussion and reply to Boroneant and Frolov CA 20(3):604–608.

———— 1979b. ICE AGE ART. Catalogue and text, Ice Age Art exhibition. San Francisco: California Academy of Sciences.

———— 1979c. Proper data for a theory of language origins. Comment on Parker and Gibson paper, "A developmental model for the evolution of language and intelligence in early hominids." *The Behavioral and Brain Sciences* 2(3):394–396.

———— 1979d. European Upper Paleolithic-Mesolithic symbolic continuity. *International Symposium on the Intellectual Expressions of Prehistoric Man: Art and Religion* pp. 111–119. Capo di Ponte.

———— 1981a. On Paleolithic ochre and the early uses of color and symbol. *Current Anthropology* 22(2):188–191.

———— 1981b. Ice age art. *Symbols*, Winter, pp. 4–5. Peabody Museum, Harvard University.

———— 1981c. Upper Paleolithic female images of the Russian plain: A comparative, functional analysis. Paper presented at the annual meeting of the Society for American Archaeology, San Diego.

———— 1981d. Epipaleolithic, Early neolithic iconography: A cognitive, comparative analysis of the Lepenski Vir/Vlasac iconography and symbolism, its roots and its later influence. Paper presented at the symposium "The Culture of Lepenski Vir and the Problems of the formation of Neolithic Cultures in Southeastern and Central Europe," the Römisch-Germanisches Museum, Cologne, 1981.

———— 1983a. European Upper Paleolithic-Mesolithic symbolic continuity: a cognitive-comparative study of ritual marking. In *Valcamonica Symposium III: Les Expressions Intellectuelles de 1'Homme Préhistorique*. pp.111–119. Capo di Ponte.

———— 1983b. Nineteenth Century Siberian and American Indian calendar sticks. Paper presented at the First International Conference on Ethnoastronomy, Washington, D.C.

———— 1984a. The ecology and brain of two-handed bipedalism: an analytic, cognitive and evolutionary assessment. In *Animal Cognition*. H.L. Roitblat, T. G. Bever and H. S. Terrace (eds.) pp. 491–511. Hillsdale, N.J.: Erlbaum.

———— 1984b. Concepts théoriques conduisant a de nouvelles méthodes analytiques, de nouveau procédés de recherche et categories de données. *L'Anthropologie* 88(4):573–586.

———— 1984c. Book Review of "The Creative Explosion" by John Pfeiffer. *Archaeology* March/April. p. 66.

———— 1985a. *Hierarchical Evolution of the Human Capacity: The Paleolithic Evidence*. Fifty-fourth James Arthur Lecture on "The Evolution of the Human Brain," 1984. New York: American Museum of Natural History.

———— 1985b. A Lunar-Solar calendar stick from North America. *American Antiquity*. 50(1)27–51.

_____ 1985c. Theoretical concepts that lead to new analytical methods, modes of inquiry and classes of data. Article and comments. *Rock Art Research* 2(2):95–111. Journal of the Australian Rock Art Association. Also: 1986. *RAR* 3(1):62–83. Comments and reply.

_____ 1985d. On the dangers of serpents in the mind. A response to B. Mundkur. *Current Anthropology* 26(1):139–145. Also: 1985, More on serpents in the mind *CA* 26(4):537–539; 1986, More on the endless serpent *CA* 27(3):263–264.

_____ 1986a. Reading Before Writing. An essay. *New York Sunday Times, Book Review*. April 6, pp. 1, 40–41.

_____ 1986b. The eye is not as clever as it thinks it is. *Rock Art Research* 3(2):111–116. Comment on Paul Bahn article, "No sex please, we're Aurignacians."

_____ 1986c. Une Figurine de Grimaldi "Redécouverte": Analyse et Discussion. *L'Anthropologie* 90(4):807–814.

_____ 1986d. Comment on Whitney Davis article, "The Origins of Image Making." *Current Anthropology* 27(3):205–206.

_____ 1988a. L'Homme de Neandertal: La Pensée symbolique. *Dossiers Histoire et Archeologie, Special Issue: L'Homme de Neandertal* 124:80–90, 97.

_____ 1988b. The species-specific evolution and contexts of the creative mind: Thinking in time. In C.S. Findlay and C.J. Lumsden, *The Creative Mind: Towards an Evolutionary Theory of Discovery and Innovation*, E.O. Wilson (ed.) Special issue of the *Journal of Social and Biological Sciences* 11(1):116–119. Also in Findlay and Lumsden, 1988, *The Creative Mind*, New York: Academic Press.

_____ 1988c. Paleolithic Image. In I. Tattersall, E. Delson, E. and J. Van Couvering (eds.) *Encyclopedia of Human Evolution and Prehistory*, pp. 421–429. Paleolithic Calendar, pp. 419–421. New York: Garland Press.

_____ 1988d. The Neanderthals and the human capacity for symbolic thought: Cognitive and problem-solving aspects of Mousterian symbol. In Otte, M. (Ed.), *L'Homme Neandertal: Actes du Colloque International, 1986, Liège.* Vol. 5. La Pensée, pp. 57–91. Université de Liège.

_____ 1988e. Hommage to Jean Vertut [Appendix]. In P. Bahn and J. Vertut, *Images of The Ice Age*. pp. 195–202. London: Windward.

_____ 1988f. An Ice Age ancestor? *National Geographic* 174(4):478–481.

_____ 1988g. North American Indian calendar sticks: the evidence for a widely distributed tradition. In *World Archaeoastronomy*, A.F. Aveni (ed.). pp.308–324. Cambridge: Cambridge University Press.

_____ 1989a. Evolution of the Human Capacity: The Symbolic Evidence. *Yearbook of Physical Anthropology* 32:1–34. The invited luncheon lecture presented at the annual meeting of the American Association of Physical Anthropologists, Kansas City, 1988.

_____ 1989b. The origin of human language: An anthropological approach. Proceedings of the NATO Advanced Study Institute and the Language Origins Society Conference, *The Origin of Human Language,*

Cortona, 1988. In press, B. Chiarelli (Ed.), Hague: Mouton.

_____ 1989c. Theory and methodology in the study of the Upper Paleolithic signs. Paper delivered at the *First Congress of World Rock Art*, held by the Australian Rock Art Association (AURA), Darwin, 1988. *Rock Art Research* 6:17–53.

_____ 1989d. On Depiction and Language. *Current Anthropology* 30(3):332–335. [Comment on I. Davidson and B. Noble article, "The Archaeology of Perception: Traces of Depiction and Language" in *CA* 30(2):125–137].

_____ 1989e. Ice Age Art Analysis. *Science* 244(4908):1029. [Letter-to-the-editor responding to column by Roger Lewin, *Science* 244:1435]

_____ 1989f. On Wishful Thinking and Lunar Calendars. *Current Anthropology* 30(4):491–494. A response to F. d'Errico.

_____ 1989g. Response to Randall White's article "Visual Thinking in the Ice Age." *Scientific American.* 261(6):12.

_____ 1990a. Early hominid symbol and evolution of the human capacity. In Paul Mellars (Ed.) *The Human Revolution: Behavioral and Biological Perspectives on the Origins of Modern Humans*. Vol 2. Edinburgh: Edinburgh University Press.

_____ 1990b. L'evolution et la transformation du décor du debut de l'Aurignacien au Magdalénien Final. In J. Clottes (ed.) *L'Art des Objets au Paleolithique: Tome 2: Les voies de la recherche* pp.139–162. Proceedings of International Colloque in Foix-le Mas d'Azil, 1987. Ministère de la Culture, de la Communication, des Grands Travaux et du Bicentenaire. Paris: Picard.

_____ 1991a. The Methodology, Theory and Analysis of Early Notations and Calendars. Paper presented at the Third International Conference on Archaeoastronomy (Oxford 3), The Univeristy of St. Andrews, Scotland, 10–14 September 1990.

_____ 1991b. The Female Image: A "Time-Factored" Symbol: A study in style and modes of image use in the European Upper Paleolithic. The keynote address presented at the conference, *Palaeolithic Art*, organized by The Prehistoric Society and the University of Oxford, 1989, at Oxford University. Andrew Lawson and Clive Gamble (Eds.) *Proceedings of the Prehistoric Society* 57(1):17–31.

_____ 1991c. The Taï Plaque and Calendrical Notation in the Upper Palaeolithic. *Cambridge Archaeological Journal*. 1(1):25–61. Cambridge: MacDonald Institute of Archaeology, Cambridge University.

_____ 1991d. A Reply to Davidson on Mania: Symbolic Activity Before the Upper Palaeolithic. *Rock Art Research* 8(1):47–58.

_____ 1991e. The analytical problems of subjectivity in the maker and user. In *The Limitations of Archaeological Knowledge*. T. Shay and J. Clottes (Eds). Liège: Université de Liège. (In Press).

General References

Abramova, Z. A. 1967. Palaeolithic Art in the U.S.S.R.," *Arctic Anthropology*, Vol. IV, pp. 1–179, ed. by Chester S. Chard and trans. by Catherine Page

from *Arkheologiia Sssr. Svod Arkheologicheskikh Istochnikov,* Vyp. A4–3, Akademiia Nauk SSSR Moscow-Leningrad, 1962. (USSR mobiliary art. Summary of Soviet interpretations.)

Absolon, Karel. 1949. The Diluvial Anthropomorphic Statuettes and Drawings, especially the so-called Venus Statuettes, Discovered in Moravia, *Artibus Asiae,* Vol. XII, 1949, pp. 201–220.

_____ 1957. Dokumente und Beweise der Fähigkeiten des fossilen Menschen zu zählen im Mährischen Paläolithikum, *Artibus Asiae*, Vol. XX, pp. 123–150.

Absolon, K. and B. Klima. 1977. *Predmosti: Eine Mammutjägerstation in Mähren.* Prague.

Acanfora, O. 1967. Figurazioni inedite della Grotta Romanelli. *Bulletino di Paleontologia Italiana* 76:7–67. [Important late paleolithic site with geometric images. Microscopic study by Marshack [1977] revealed systems of cumulative motif marking.]

Almagro Basch, M. 1976. *Los omoplatos decorados de la cueva de 'El Castillo', Puente Viesgo (Santander).* *Trabajos de Prehistoria* 33:9–99. Museo Arqueologico Nacional. Madrid.

Altuna, J. and J. M. Appellaniz. 1976. *Las Figuras Rupestres Paleoliticas de la Cueva de Altxerri (Guipuzcoa).* *Munibe* 28(1–3). Sociedad de Ciencias Aranzadi, San Sebastian.

Altuna, J. and J. M. Appellaniz. 1978. *Ekain. Las Figuras Rupestres de la Cueva de Ekain (Deval).* *Munibe* 30(1–3). Sociedad de Ciencias Aranzadi, San Sebastian.

Anisimov, A. F. Cosmological Concepts of the Peoples of the North, *Anthropology of the North*, 4, Arctic Institute of North America, University of Toronto Press, Toronto, pp. 157–229.

L'ART DES CAVERNES: Atlas des Grottes Ornées Paléolithiques Françaises. 1984. Foreword by A. Leroi-Gourhan. Paris: Ministère de la Culture.

ARTE RUPESTRE EN ESPAÑA. 1987. *Revista de Arqueologia.* Special issue.

Aujoulat, N. 1987. *La relevé dans oeuvres pariétals paléolithiques: Enregistrement et traitment des données.* Documents d'Archéologie Française, No. 9. Paris: Editions de la Maison des Sciences de l'Homme.

Bader, O. N. 1965. *La Caverne Kapovia: Peinture Paléolithique.* Akademia Nauk: Moscow. [Ice Age paintings in the Urals]

Bader, O. N. 1978. *Sungir: Verchnepaleoliticheskaja stojjanka.* Moscow. [One of the most important of Ice Age burial complexes.]

Bahn, P. G. 1979. La Paléoéconomie Magdalénienne du Bassin de Tarascon (Ariège). *Préhistoire Ariègeoise* 34:37–46.

Bahn, P. G. 1984. *Pyrenean Prehistory.* Aris & Phillips: Warminster.

Bahn, P. G. 1986. No Sex, Please, We're Aurignacians. *Rock Art Research* 3(2):99–120. And commentary: Marshack, A. 1986. The Eye Is Not As Clever As It Thinks It Is. **RAR** 3(2):11–116.

Bahn, P. G. and J. Vertut. 1989. *Images of the Ice Age.* London: Windward. [Summarizes interpretations of Franco-Cantabrian imagery]

Bailey, G. (Ed.) 1983. *Hunter-Gatherer Economy in Prehistory: A European Perspective*. Cambridge University Press.

Bandi, H. -G. *et al* (Eds.) 1984. *La Contribution de la Zoologie et de l'Ethologie à l'interpretation de l'art des peuples chasseurs préhistoriques*. 3e colloque de la Soc. Suisse des Sciences Humaines, Sigriswil 1979. Editions Universitaires: Fribourg.

Barandiaran, I. 1973. *Arte Mueble del Paleolitico Cantábrico*. Monografias arquólogicas, 14. Zaragoza.

Barriere, C. 1976. *L'Art Pariétal de la Grotte de Gargas*. Mémoire III de l'Inst. Art Préhist. Toulouse.

Bar-Yosef, O. and A. Belfer-Cohen. 1989. The Origins of Sedentism and Farming Communities in the Levant. *Journal of World Prehistory*. 3(4):447–498.

Bar-Yosef, O. and A. Belfer-Cohen. 1991. From Sedentary Hunter-Gatherers to Territorial Farmers in the Levant. In *Between Bands and States*. S. A. Gregg (Ed.) Occasional Papers, Center for Archaeo. Investigations, Southern Illinois University. pp.181–202.

Baudouin, Marcel. 1916. La préhistoire des étoiles au Paléolithique. Les Pléiades a l'époque aurignacienne et le culte stello-solaire typique au solutréen. *Bulletin et Mémoires de la Société d'Anthropologie de Paris*, sér. VI, Tome VII, pp.274–317. (Early astronomical interpretation.)

Bégouën, R. and J. Clottes. 1986/87. Le grand féline des Trois-Frères. *Antiquités Nationales* 18/19:109–113.

Bégouën, R. et al. 1984. Compléments à la grande plaquette gravé d'Enléne. *Bull. de la Soc. Préhist. Franç.* 81(3):142–148.

Bégouën, R. et al. 1984–85. Art Mobilier sur support lithique d'Enlène (Montesquieu-Avantés, Ariège): Collection Bégouën du Musée de l'Homme. *Ars Praehistorica* 33–4:25–80.

Beltran, Antonio. 1982. *Rock art of the Spanish Levant*. Cambridge University Press.

Berenguer Alonso, M. 1979. *El Arte Parietal Prehistorico de la "Cueva de Llonin"* (Peñamellera Alta). Asturias. Oviedo:Caja de Ahorros de Asturia, Instituto de Estudios Asturianos.

Berenguer Alonso, M. (nd.) *La Cueva "Tito Bustillo"*. Tesoros de Asturias 7. Gijón: Gran Enciclopedia Asturiana.

Berenguer Alonso, M. 1986. Art Pariétal Paléolithique Occidental. Techniques d'expression et identification chronologique. *L'Anthropologie* 90(4): 665–678.

Bibikov, S. 1975. A Stone Orchestra. *UNESCO Courier*, June, 8–15

Binford, L. R. 1978. *Nunamiut Ethnoarchaeology*. New York: Academic Press.

Binford, L. R. 1983. *In Pursuit of the Past: Decoding the Archaeological Record*. London: Thames and Hudson.

Binford, Lewis R. and Sally R. Binford. 1966. A Preliminary Analysis of Functional Variability in the Mousterian of Levallois Facies. *American Anthropologist*, Vol. 68, pp. 238–295.

Binford, Sally R. 1968. A Structural Comparison of Disposal of the Dead in the Mousterian and the Upper Paleolithic. *Southwestern Journal of Anthropology*, Vol. 24, pp. 139–154.

Binford, Sally R. and Lewis R. Binford (eds.). 1968. *New Perspectives in Archaeology*, Aldine Publishing Co., Chicago.

Blanc, G. A. 1928. *Grotta Romanelli II*. Archivio per l'Antropologia e l'Etnologia. 58:365–411. [Early publication of crucial Ice Age art site with incised "geometric" motifs.]

Boas, Franz. 1884–1885. The Central Eskimo, *Sixth Annual Report of the Bureau of American Ethnology*, Smithsonian Institution, Washington, D.C., 1884–1885. (Lunar calendar.)

Boesch, C. and H. Boesch. 1984. Mental Map in Wild Chimpanzees: An Analysis of Hammer Transports for Nut Cracking. *Primates*, April 25(2): 160–170.

Bogoras, Waldemar. 1925. Ideas of Space and Time in the Conception of Primitive Religion, *American Anthropologist*, Vol. 27, pp.205–241.

Bordes, François. 1968. *The Old Stone Age*, trans. by J. E. Anderson, World University Library, Weidenfeld and Nicolson, London. (Popular summary.)

Bosinski, G. 1970. Magdalenian Anthropomorphic Figures at Gönnersdorf (Western Germany). *Bolletino del Centro Camuno di Studi Prestorici*. 5:57–97.

Bosinski, G. 1973. Le Site Magdalénien de Gönnersdorf (Commune de Neuwied) Vallée du Rhin moyen, R.F.A.) *Bull. de la Soc. Préhist. de la Ariège* 328:25–48.

Bosinski, G. 1982. *Die Kunst der Eiszeit in Deutschland und in der Schweiz*. Römisch-Germanisches Zentralmuseum. Bonn: Habelt.

Bosinski, G. 1988. Upper and Final Paleolithic Settlement Patterns in the Rhineland, West Germany. In *Upper Pleistocene Prehistory of Western Eurasia*, H. L. Dibble and A. Montet-White (Eds). University Museum Symposium Series, Vol. 1. The University Museum, University of Pennsylvania. pp.375–386.

Bosinski, G. and D. Evers. 1979. *Jagd in Eiszeitalter* Köln: Rheinland-Verlag.

Bosinski, G. and G. Fischer. 1974. *Die Menschendarstellungen von Gönnersdorf der Ausgrabungen von 1968*. Wiesbaden: Steiner.

Bosinski, G. and G. Fischer. 1980. *Mammut- und Pferdedarstellungen von Gönnersdorf*. Weisbaden: Steiner

Bosinski, Gerhard: "Magdalenian Anthropomorphic Figures at Gönnersdorf (Western Germany)," *Bolletino del Centro Camuno di Studi Preistorici*, Vol. V, 1970, pp. 57–97. (Buttocks images accumulated on single surfaces.)

Bouchud, Jean. 1954. Le renne et le problème des migrations, *L'Anthropologie*, Tome 58, pp. 79–85.

Breuil, Henri. 1909. Le bison et le taureau céleste chaldéen, *Revue Archéologique*, Tome I, pp. 250–254.

———— 1905. La dégénérescence de figures d'animaux en motifs ornementaux à l'époque du renne, *Comptes Rendus de l'Académie Inscriptions et Belles-Lettres*, pp. 105–120.

———— 1906. Exemples de figures dégénérées et stylisées à l'époque du renne, *Congrès International d'Anthropologie et d'Archéologie Préhistorique*, XIIIᵉ sess.,

Tome I, Monaco, pp. 394–403.

———— 1925. Les origines de l'art, *Journal de Psychologie*, Année XXII, pp. 289–296.

———— 1926. Les origines de l'art décoratif, *Journal de Psychologie*, Année XXIII, pp. 364–375.

———— 1912. Les subdivisions du Paléolithique supérieur et leur signification, *Compte Rendu du Congrès International d'Anthropologie et d'Archéologie Préhistorique*, 14ᵉ sess., (2ᵉ édit., 1937), pp. 165–238.

———— 1952. *Four Hundred Centuries of Cave Art*, trans. by Mary E. Boyle, Centre d'Études et de Documentation Préhistoriques, Montignac.

———— 1956. Louis-René Nougier, et Romain Robert: Les 'Lissoir aux Ours' de la grotte de la Vache, à Alliat, et l'ours dans l'art franco-cantabrique occidental, *Bulletin de la Société Préhistorique de l'Ariège*, Tome XI, pp. 1–78.

———— 1927. et René de Saint-Périer: *Les Poissons, Les Batraciens et Les Reptiles Dans l'Art Quaternaire*, Archives de l'Institut Paléontologie Humaine, Mémoire Nᵒ 2, Masson et Cie., Paris.

Brooks, A. S. and P. Robertshaw. 1990. The Glacial Maximum in Tropical Africa: 22 000–12 000 BP. *In The World at 18 000 BP. Vol. 2: Low Latitudes*. C. Gamble and O. Soffer (Eds.) Boston: Unwin. pp.. 121–169.

Brooks, A. S. and C. C. Smith. 1987. Ishango Revisited: New Age Determinations and Cultural Interpretations. *The African Archaeological Review* 5: 65–78.

Bruner, Jerome S. 1966. *Toward A Theory of Instruction*, Harvard Unversity Press, Cambridge.

———— 1956. Jacqueline J. Goodnow, and George A. Austin. *A Study of Thinking*, John Wiley and Sons, New York.

Buisson, D. and H. Delporte. 1988. Intérêt d'un raccord pour l'authentication d'une oeuvre d'art. *Bull. Soc. Préhist.Franç.* 85(1): 4–6.

Butzer, Karl W. 1964. *Environment and Archaeology: An Introduction to Pleistocene Geography*, Aldine Publishing Co., Chicago.

Câciumaru, M. 1987. *Marturii Ale Artei Rupestre Preistorice in Romania*. Bucharest.

Campbell, Jospeh. 1959. *The Masks of God; Primitive Mythology*, The Viking Press, New York.

Campbell, J. 1974. *The Mythic Image*. Bollingen Series C. Princeton: Princeton University Press

Campbell, J. 1983. *Historical Atlas of World Mythology. Vol. 1, The Way of the Animal Powers*. New York: Alfred van der Marck Editions/Harper & Row.

Capitan, Louis, Henri Breuil, et Denis Peyrony. 1910. *La Caverne de Font-de-Gaume*, Institut de Paléontologie Humaine, Monaco. (Chapters on diverse animals and forms.)

———— 1924. *Les Combarelles, Aux Eyzies (Dordogne)*, Masson et Cie., Paris. (Surveys anthropomorphic figures.)

Chollot, Marthe. 1964. *Collection Piette, Musée des Antiquités Nationales*, Éditions des Musées Nationaux, Paris. (Photographic catalogue of mobiliary art.)

Clark, J. Desmond. 1965. The Later Pleistocene Cultures of Africa, *Science*, Vol. 150, pp. 833–847.

_____ and F. Clark Howell (eds.). April 1966. Recent Studies in Paleoanthropology, *American Anthropologist*, Vol. 68, (special publication), pp. 1–394.

_____ 1932. *The Mesolithic Age in Britain*. Cambridge University Press, Cambridge, England.

_____ 1936. *The Mesolithic Settlement of Northern Europe*, Cambridge University Press, Cambridge, England.

_____ 1938. Reindeer Hunters' Summer Camps in Britain? *Proceedings of the Prehistoric Society*, Vol. IV, p. 229.

_____ 1938. The Reindeer Hunting Tribes of Northern Europe, *Antiquity*, Vol. XII, pp. 154–171.

_____ 1939. Excavations at Farnham, Surrey (1937–1938), Part IV. The Question of Mesolithic Houses, *Proceedings of the Prehistoric Society*, Vol. V., pp. 98–107.

_____ 1939. Seasonal Settlement in Upper Palaeolithic Times, *Proceedings of the Prehistoric Society*, Vol. V, p. 268.

_____ 1946. Seal-hunting in the Stone Age of Northwestern Europe: A Study in Economic Prehistory, *Proceedings of the Prehistoric Society*, Vol. XII, pp. 12–48.

_____ 1947. Sheep and Swine in the Husbandry of Prehistoric Europe, *Antiquity*, Vol. XXI, pp. 122–136.

_____ 1947. Whales as an Economic Factor in Prehistoric Europe, *Antiquity*, Vol. XXI, pp. 84–104.

_____ 1948. Fowling in Prehistoric Europe, *Antiquity*, Vol. 22, pp. 116–130.

Clark, J. G. D. 1948. The Development of Fishing in Prehistoric Europe, *Antiquaries Journal*, Vol. XXVII, pp. 45–85.

_____ 1952. *Prehistoric Europe: The Economic Basis*, Philosophical Library, New York.

_____ 1961. *World Prehistory; An Outline*, Cambridge University Press, Cambridge, England.

_____ 1965. Review of *Environment and Archaeology*, by Karl W. Butzer, *American Anthropologist*, Vol. 67, pp. 131–133.

Clottes, J. and E. Cérou. 1970. La statuette féminine de Monpazier (Dordogne). *Bull. de la Soc. préhist. franç.* Etudes et Travaux. 67(2): 435–44.

Clottes, J. 1989. The identification of human and animal figures in European Palaeolithic art. In *Animals into Art*. Morphy, H. (Ed.) One World Archaeology, 7. Unwin Hyman: London/ Boston, Ma. pp. 21–56.

Clottes, J. 1990. *L'Art des Objets au Paléolithique* T. 1 & 2. Proceedings of the Colloque international, Foix-le Mas d'Azil, 1987. Ministère de la Culture, de la Communication, des Grands Travaux et du Bicentenaire.

Clottes, J. 1990. The parietal art of the late Magdalenian. *Antiquity* 64:527–548.

Clottes, J. 1991. *The Cave of Niaux*. Boulogne: Castelet.

Clottes, J. and E. Cérou. 1970. La statuette féminine de Monpazier (Dordogne). *Bull. de la Soc. préhist. franç.* Etudes et Travaux. 67(2):435–44.

Conkey M. 1980. The identification of prehistoric hunger-gatherer sites. the case of Altamira. *Current Anthropology* 21:609–630.

Conkey, M. 1987. New approaches in the search for meaning? A review of research in "Paleolithic art." *Journal of Field Archaeology*. 14:413–430.

Conkey, M. and C. Hastorp (Eds.) 1990. *The Uses of Style in Archaeology* New York: Cambridge University Press.

Couraud, C. 1985. *L'Art Azilien. Origine - Survivance*. XXe Supplement à Gallia Préhistoire. [Study of Azilian pebbles. Theorizes numbering in the patterns].

Couts, P. J. F. and M. Lorblanchet. 1982. *Aboriginals and Rock Art in the Grampians, Victoria, Australia*. Victoria: Victoria Archaeological Survey. [p. 87. Indication of a possible precontact Australian aboriginal astronomical notation]

Dams, L. 1978. *L'Art Paléolithique de la Caverne de la Pileta*. Akademische Druck-u. Verlaganstalt: Graz.

Dams, L. 1987. *L'Art Paléolithique de la Grotte de Nerja (Málaga, Espagne)*. British. Arch. Reports, Int. Series No. 385, Oxford.

Davidson, I. 1976. Les Mallaetes and Mondúver: the economy of a human group in prehistoric Spain. In *Problems in Economic & Social Archaeology*, G. de Sieveking, I. H. Longworth & K. E. Wilson (eds.). pp.483–499. London: Duckworth.

Davidson, I. 1986. The Geographical Study of Late Palaeolithic Stages in Eastern Spain. G. N. Bailey and P. Callow (eds.) Cambridge: Cambridge University Press.

Davidson, I. 1989. Freedom of information: aspects of art and society in western Europe during the last Ice Age. In H. Morphy (Ed) *Animals into Art* pp. 440–456.

Davis, J. Barnard. 1867. Some Account of Runic Calendars and 'Staffordshire Clogg' Alamanacs, *Archaeologia*, Vol. XLI, pp. 453–478.

Davis, W. 1986. The Origins of Image Making. *Current Anthropology* 27(3): 193–215.

Delaby, Laurence. 1968. Un calendrier yakoute, *Objets et Mondes*, Tome VIII, pp. 311–320.

Delluc, B. and G. 1978. Les anneaux aurignaciens des abris Blanchard et Castanet à Sergeac. *Bull. Soc. hist. et archéo. du Périgord* 105: 248–263.

Delluc, B. and G. Delluc. 1978. Les manifestations graphiques Aurignaciennes sur support rocheux des environs des Eyzies (Dordogne). *Gallia Préhistoire* 21: 213–248.

Delluc, B. and G. Delluc. 1981. La Grotte Ornée de Comarque à Sireuil (Dordogne). *Gallia Préhistoire* 24(1): 1–97.

Delporte, H. 1979. *L'Image de la Femme dans l'art Préhistorique*. Paris: Picard.

Delporte, H. 1985. Réflexions sur la chasse à la période paléolithique. *Jagen and Sammeln: Festschrift fü Hans-Georg Bandi zum 65. Geburtstag*. Jahrbuch des Bernischen Historischen Museums, 63/64: 69–80.

Delporte, H. 1990. *L'Image de l'Animal dans l'Art Préhistorique*. Paris: Picard.

Delteil, J., Durbas, P. and L. Wahl. 1972. Présentation de la Galerie Ornée de Fontanet. *Préhistoire Ariègeois* 27: 11–20.

Dickson, D. B. 1990. *The Dawn of Belief: Religion in the Upper Paleolithic of Southwestern Europe*. Tucson: University of Arizona Press. [Popular summary of findings and theories concerning the West European Franco-Cantabrian Ice Age cultures]

Dobres, M-A. 1990. Considering Palaeolithic "Venus" Figurines: A Feminist-Inspired Reanalysis. Paper presented at the conference *Ancient Images, Ancient Thought: The Archaeology of Ideology*. Calgary.

Duhard, J-P. 1987. La Statuette de Monpazier représente-t-elle une parturiente? *Préhistoire Ariégeoise* 42: 1555–163.

Duhard, J-P. 1988. Peut-on parler d'obésité chez les femmes figurées dans les oeuvres pariétales et mobilières paléolithiques? *Préhistoire Ariégeoise* 43:85–103.

Duhard, J-P. 1989. La Realisme Physiologique des Figurations Feminines du Paléolithique Supérieur en France. Thése presentée à l'Université de Bordeaux.

Dyrenkova, N.P. 1928. Bear Worship among Turkish Tribes of Siberia, *International Congress of Americanists*, 23rd Congress, New York, pp. 411–440.

d'Errico, F. 1989. L'art gravé azilien. Doctoral Thesis presented at the Museum National d'Histoire Naturelle of the Institut de Paléontologie Humaine describing the development of an electron microscopic method for studying engraved marks on post-Upper Paleolithic Azilian pebbles. Asserts that no "notations" were found among post-Ice Age pebbles.

_____ 1990. Etude technologique à base expérimentale des coches sur matière dure animale. Implications pour l'identification des systèmes de notation. Paper presented at the Colloque International *"Les Gestes Retrouvés": Traces et fonction*.

_____ 1991. Identification of prehistoric systems of notation. *Rock Art Research* [Paper acknowledges finding a cumulative, possible "notational" bone artifact in the Upper Paleolithic]. In press.

Eisler, Robert. 1914. Der Fisch als Sexualsymbol, *Imago*, Vol. III, pp. 165–193. "Zusatz der Redaktion," Otto Rank, pp. 193–196.

Eliade, Mircea: *Birth and Rebirth*, trans. by Willard R. Trask, Harper and Bros., New York, 1958.

_____ 1954. *The Myth of the Eternal Return*, trans. by Willard R. Trask, Pantheon Books, New York.

_____ 1958. *Patterns in Comparative Religion*, trans. by Rosemary Sheed, The World Publishing Co., Cleveland.

_____ 1963. *Myth and Reality*, trans. by Willard R. Trask, Harper & Row, New York.

_____ 1964. *Shamanism: Archaic Technique of Ecstasy*, The Bollingen Series 76, Pantheon Books, New York.

_____ 1969. *Images and Symbols, Studies in Religious Symbolism*, trans. by Philip Mairet, Sheed and Ward, New York.

Fages, G. and C. Mourer-Chauviré. 1983. La flûte en

os d'oiseau de la Grotte sépulcrale de Veyreau (Aveyron) et inventaire des flûtes préhistoriques d'Europe. In *La Faune et l'Homme Préhistorique,* Mémoires de la Soc. Préhist. Franç. t. 16.

Feustel, R. 1974. *Die Kniegrotte. Eine Magdalénien-Station in Thüringen.* Hermann Böhlaus Nachfolger: Weimar.

Feustel, R. 1987. Eiszeit in Thüringen. In catalogue of *Die Anfänge de Kunst vor 30000 Jahren.* H. Müller-Beck and G. Albrecht (Eds.) Stuttgart: Theiss.

Fewkes, Jesse Walter. 1893–1894. The Group of Tusayan Ceremonials Called Katchinas, *Fifteenth Annual Report of the Bureau of Ethnology,* Smithsonian Institution, Washington, D.C., pp. 251–304. (Calendric, seasonal ceremonies of agricultural Indians.)

Fitzhugh, Wm. W. and Susan A. Kaplan. 1982. *INUA: The Spirit World of the Bering Sea Eskimo.* Washington, D.C: National Museum of Natural History, Smithsonian Institution.

Fraser, J. T. (ed.). 1966. *The Voices of Time,* George Braziller, New York. (Interdisciplinary anthology of time-factored studies in contemporary sciences. Original papers by specialists.)

———. 1987. *TIME: the Familiar Stranger.* Tempus/Microsoft: University of Massachusetts Press. [Social, biological, mathematical and physical aspects of time].

Freeman, L. G. and J. Gonzalez Echegaray. 1981. El Juyo, a 14,000-year-old sanctuary from northern Spain. *History of Religions* 21(1): 1–19.

Freeman, L. G. with J. Gonzalez Echegaray, F. Bernaldo de Quirós, and J. Ogden. 1987. *Altamira Revisited and Other Essays on Early Art.* Chicago: Institute for Prehistoric Investigations.

Frolov, B. 1974. *Numbers in Paleolithic Graphics.* USSR Academy of Sciences, Siberian Branch. Institute of History, Philology, and Philosophy. Novosibirsk: Nauka. [In Russian. Theorizes on both calendars and number systems in Upper Paleolithic]

Frolov, B. 1983. Les Bases cognitives de l'Art Paleolithique. In *The Intellectual Expressions of Prehistoric Man: Art and Religion,* A. Beltran *et al.* (eds). Acts of the Valcamonica Symposium '79. Val Camonica: Edizioni del Centro. pp. 295–298.

Gamble, C.S. 1980. Information exchange in the Palaeolithic. *Nature* 283: 522–523.

———. 1982. Interaction and Alliance in Palaeolithic Society. *Man* 17(1): 92–107.

———. 1983. Culture and society in the Upper Palaeolithic of Europe. In *Hunter-Gatherer Economy in Prehistory: A European Perspective* G. Bailey (Ed.) pp. 201–211. Cambridge: Cambridge University Press.

———. 1986. *The Palaeolithic Settlement of Europe.* Cambridge University Press.

Garrod, Dorothy. 1953. The Relations between South-West Asia and Europe in the Later Palaeolithic Age, *Journal of World History,* Vol. I, pp. 13–37.

Gaster, Theodor H.: *Thespis; Ritual, Myth, and Drama in the Ancient Near East,* Schuman, New York, 1950.

Giedion, Sigfried. 1962. *The Eternal Present; the Beginnings of Art,* Bollingen Series XXXV, Pantheon Books, New York. (Overall survey in terms of magic and symbolism.)

Gimbutas, M. 1989. *The Language of the Goddess.* Foreward by Joseph Campbell. New York: Harper & Row.

Gladwin, Thomas. 1964. Culture and Logical Process, *Explorations in Cultural Anthropology,* ed. by Ward H. Goodenough, McGraw-Hill Book Co., New York, pp. 167–177.

Glory, A. 1956. Debris de corde paléolithique à la Grotte de Lascaux, *Bulletin de La Société Préhistorique Française,* Vol. LIII, pp. 263–264.

———. 1968. L'enigme de l'art quarternaire peut-elle être résolue par la théorie du culte des Ongones? *Bulletin N° 17 de La Société d'Études et de Recherches Préhistoriques,* March, pp. 27–67. (Siberian symbolism compared.)

Graebner, F. 1920–1921. Alt- and neuweltliche Kalender, *Zeit-Schrift Für Ethnologie,* Vol. 52–53, pp. 6–37. (Comparison of Asian and New World calendars.)

Graziosi, P. 1973. *L'art preistorica in Italia.* Sansoni: Florence.

Graziosi, Paolo. 1960. *Palaeolithic Art,* trans. from the Italian, McGraw-Hill Book Co., New York. (Mobiliary and wall art.)

Guthrie, D. R. 1984. Ethological Observations from Palaeolithic art. In Bandi, H.G. et al. pp. 35–74.

Gvozdover, M.D. Spring 1989. The typology of Female Figurines of the Kostienki Paleolithic Culture. In O. Soffer-Bobyshev (Ed.). *Female Imagery in the Paleolithic. Soviet Anthropology & Archeology* 27(4). pp. 32–94.

Hadingham, E. 1979. *The Secrets of The Ice Age: A Reappraisal of Prehistoric Man.* New York: Walker & Co.

Hahn, J. 1984. L'art mobilier aurignacien en Allemagne du Sud-Ouest: Essai d'analyse zoologique et éthologique. In H.G. Bandi et al. pp. 283–293.

Hahn, J. 1986. *Kraft and Aggression. Die Botschaft der Eiszeitkunst im Aurignacien Süddeutschlands?* Archaeologia Venatoria, 7. Institut für Urgeschichte der Universität Tübingen.

Hahn, J., H. Müller-Beck and W. Taute. 1973. *Eizceithöhlen im Lonetal.* Stuttgart: Müller & Gräff.

Hallowell, A. Irving. 1926. Bear Ceremonialism in the Northern Hemisphere, *American Anthropologist,* Vol. 28, pp. 1–175.

———. 1955. Cultural Factors in Spatial Orientation, Chapter 9 in *Culture and Experience,* University of Pennsylvania Press, Philadelphia, pp. 184–202.

Haynes, R. D. 1990. The Astronomy of the Australian Aborigines. *The Astronomy Quarterly* 7: 193–217.

Hayden, B. and E. Bonifay. 1991. *The Neanderthal Nadir.* (np). [Excellent report on the symbolism of the Neanderthal burial at Regourdou.]

Heizelin, Jean de. 1962. "Ishango," *Scientific American,* Vol. 206, pp. 105–116.

Hentze, Carl. 1961. *Das Haus Als Weltort Der Seele,* Ernst Klett, Stuttgart.

———. 1928–1929. Les jades archaïques en Chine; le jade 'Pi' et les symboles solaires, *Artibus Asiae,* Vol. III, pp. 199-216; Vol. IV, 1930–1932, pp. 38–41.

———. 1932. *Mythes Et Symboles Lunaires,* Editions De Sikkel, Anvers.

———. 1936. *Objets Rituels, Croyances et Dieux De La Chine Antique et De L'Amérique,* Editions De Sikkel, Anvers.

———. 1930. Le poisson comme symbole de fécondité dans la Chine ancienne, *Bulletin Des Musées Royaux D'Art et D'Histoire,* sér. 3, Tome 2, pp. 141–152.

Howell, F. Clark. 1961. Isimila; A Paleolithic Site in Africa, *Scientific American,* Vol. 205, pp. 119-129.

Howitt, Alfred William. 1904. Messengers and Message Sticks, *The Native Tribes of Southeast Australia,* London, pp. 678–710. (Discusses forms of day-counts.)

Jaynes, J. 1976. *The Origin of Consciousness in the Breakdown of the Bicameral Mind.* Boston:Houghton-Mifflin. [Theoretical neuropsychological interpretation of consciousness and symbol in the paleolithic. The discussions are based on a cursory reading about the traditions and materials]

Jelinek, J. 1975. *The Pictorial Encyclopedia of the Evolution of Man.* London: Hamlyn. [Popular volume that deals with Central and East European archaeology and imagery]

Jochelson, Waldemar. 1933. The Yakut, *Anthropological Papers,* American Museum of Natural History, Vol. 33, pp. 100–102, 103–122.

Jochim, M. A. 1976. *Hunter-Gatherer Subsistence and Settlement. A Predictive Model.* New York: Academic Press.

———. 1981. *Strategies For Survival: Cultural Behavior in an Ecological Context.* Academic Press: New York.

———. 1983. Palaeolithic cave art in ecological perspective. In *Hunter-Gatherer Economy in Prehistory: A European Perspective.* Geoff Bailey (Ed.) pp. 212–219. Cambridge: Cambridge U.

———. 1991. Archeology as Long-Term Ethnography. *American Anthropologist* 93(2):308–321.

Jones, Rupert. 1875. On Some Bone and Other Implements from the Caves of the Périgord, France, Bearing Marks Indicative of Ownership, Tallying, and Gambling, in *Reliquiae Aquitanicae,* by Edouard Lartet and Henry Christy, London, pp. 183–201.

Jordá Cerdá F. 1983. Sur des sanctuaires monothematiques dan l'art rupestre Cantabrique. In *The Intellectual Expressions of Prehistoric Man: Art and Religion,* A. Beltran *et al.* (eds). Acts of the Valcamonica Symposium '79. Val Camonica: Edizioni del Centro. pp. 331–348.

Kelley, David H. 1960. Calendar Animals and Deities, *Southwestern Journal of Anthropology,* Vol. 16, pp. 317–335. (Asian and New World comparisons.)

Kenoyer, J. M., Clark, J. D., Pal, J. N., and G. R. Sharma. 1983. An upper paleolithic shrine in India? *Antiquity* 57:88–94, plus Plates X–XII.

Klima, B. 1984. Les representations animales du Paléolithiques Supérieur de Dolni Vestonice. In H.G. Bandi et al., pp. 323–332.

Kooijman, S. 1960. A Papuan Lunar 'Calendar'; The Reckoning of Moons and Seasons by the Marind-Anim of Netherlands New Guinea, *Man,* Vol. LX, pp. 165–168.

Kozlowski, J. 1983. Le Paléolithique Supérieur en Pologne. *Anthropologie* 87(1):49–82.

Kurtén, B. 1986. *How To Deep Freeze a Mammoth*. Columbia University Press: New York. [Chapter suggests erotic interpretation of Ice Age female images]

Landes, D. L. 1983. *Revolution in Time: Clocks and the Making of the Modern World*. Belknap Press of Harvard University Press:Cambridge, MA.

Larichev, V. E. 1985. *Drevo poznaniya* Moscow:Politizdat. [Theoretical discussion of early astronomy and calendrics. Chapter on Marshack: pp. 66–89].

Larichev, V. E. 1989. *Mudrost' Zmei*. The Academy of Science, Siberia, Novosibirsk. [Volume discusses a theory of astronomical notations and observations in Upper Paleolithic Siberia]

Lartet, Edouard and Henry Christy. 1875. *Reliquiae Aquitanicae*, ed. by Rupert Jones, London. (Mobiliary art, essays on ethnographic comparisons and zoology.)

Leason, P. A. 1939. A New View of the Western European Group of Quarternary Cave Art, *Proceedings of The Prehistoric Society*, Vol. V, pp. 51–60. (Theorizes animal images as "dead.")

Lee, Richard B. and Irven DeVore (eds.). 1968. *Man the Hunter*, Aldine Publishing Co., Chicago.

Leonardi, P. 1989. *Sacralitá Arte e Grafia Paleolitiche Splendori e Problemi*. Verona:Manfrini.

Leroi-Gourhan, André. 1964 and 1965. *Le Geste et La Parole*, Vol. I. *Technique et Langage*, Vol. II. *La Mémoire et Les Rythmes*, Editions Albin Michel, Paris. (Hypothesis on the evolution of human behavior and cognition by analogy and comparison to paleontological and ethnographic data.)

———— 1967. *Treasures of Prehistoric Art*, trans. by Norbert Guterman, Harry N. Abrams, New York. (Excellent color photos. Detailed statistical studies and summary of author's theoretical interpretation of Franco-Cantabrian art.)

Leroi-Gourhan, A. 1982. *The Dawn of European Art*. Cambridge University Press.

Leroi-Gourhan, Arl. and Leroi-Gourhan, A. 1965. Chronologie des Grottes d'Arcy-sur-Cure (Yonne). *Gallia Préhistoire* 7:1–64.

Leroi-Gourhan, Arl. and J. Allain. 1979. *Lascaux Inconnu* Paris:Editions du CNRS.

Leveque, F. and Vandermeersch, B. (1980) Les découvertes des restes humains dans un horizon castelperronien de Saint-Césaire (Charente-Maritime). Bull. de la Soc. Préhist. Franc. t. 77:35.

Levi-Strauss, Claude. 1966. *The Savage Mind*, trans. from the French, Weidenfield and Nicolson, London.

———— 1963. *Structural Anthropology*, trans. by Claire Jacobson and Brooke Grundfest Schoepf, Basic Books, New York.

———— 1963. *Totemism*, trans. by Rodney Needham, Beacon Press, Boston.

Levi-Strauss, Claude 1969, 1973, 1978, 1981. *Introduction to a Science of Mythology {Mythologiques}* 4 Vols. Harper & Row: New York. [A monumental structuralist and transformational study of North and South American myths. Of particular value for the present research because of its documentation of the astronomical, seasonal, and ecological references embedded in the mythologies of the Americas.]

Lewis-Williams, J.D. 1981. *Believing and Seeing. Symbolic meanings in southern San rock paintings* Academic Press: New York. [Excellent study of South African rock paintings with ethnographic trance interpretation. This "entoptic" interpretation was then used in an attempt to explain European Upper Paleolithic imagery]

Lewis-Williams, J.D. and T.A. Dowson. 1988. The signs of all times: entoptic phenomena in Upper Palaeolithic art. *Current Anthro.*. 29:201–245.

Lindner, Kurt. 1937. *Die Jagd Der Vorzeit*, Vol. I, Berlin. (Primitive hunting techniques and interpretation of "tectiforms" as traps, pitfalls.)

Lissner, Ivar. 1961. *Man, God and Magic*, trans. by J. Maxwell Brownjohn, G.P. Putnam's Sons, New York. (Compares Upper Paleolithic and Siberian ritual. Hypothesizes early form of monotheism. Bibliography.)

Lorblanchet, M. 1980. Les gravures de l'ouest australien. Leur rénovation au cours des âges. *Bull. de la Soc. Préhist. Franç.* 77(10–12):463–477.

———— 1981. Les dessins noirs du Pech-Merle. In *XXIe Congrés Préhist. de France,* Montauban/Cahors 1979. 1:178–207.

———— 1984. From man to animal and sign in Palaeolithic art. In *Animals into Art*. Morphy, H. (Ed.) 1989. One World Archaeology, 7. Unwin Hyman: London/ Boston, MA. pp. 109–143.

Lubine, V. P. and N. D. Praslov. 1987. *Le Paléolithique en URSS: découvertes récentes*. Académie des Sciences de l'URSS, Institut d'Archcéologie, Léningrad.

Lumley, Henry de: "A Paleolithic Camp at Nice," *Scientific American*, Vol. 220, May 1969, pp. 42–50. (Acheulian spring-summer camp, *c. 300,000 B.C.*)

de Lumley, H. (Ed.) 1976. *La Préhistoire Française*. Vol. I, Les Civilisations Paléolithiques et Mésolithiques de la France. Published on the occasion of the IXe Congrés de l'U.I.S.P.P., Nice, 1976. CNRS: Paris.

Luquet, Georges Henri. 1930. *The Art and Religion of Fossil Man*, trans. by J. Townsend Russell, Jr., Yale University Press, New Haven.

Luquet, Georges-Henri. 1938. Sur les mutilations digitales, *Journal de Psychologie Normale et Pathologique* 35ᵉ Année, pp. 548–598.

Mándoki, P. 1968. Two Asiatic Sidereal Names. *Popular Beliefs and Folklore Traditions in Siberia* V. Diószegi (Ed.) pp. 485–496. Bloomington: Indiana University Press. [Describes shamanistic use of Venus, sun, moon, stars in myth and art and importance of Venus in shamanistic practice.]

Mania, D.. and Vlcek, E. 1987. *Homo erectus* from Bilzungsleben (GDR): His culture and his environment. *Anthropologie* (Brno) 25(1):1–45.

Maringer, Johannes. 1960. *The Gods of Prehistoric Man*, Alfred A. Knopf, New York.

Martin, Y. 1973. *L'Art Paléolithique de Gouy*. Gouy: Martin. [The animal and vulva images in one of the Ice Age caves furthest north in France]

Martin, Y. 1989. Nouvelles Découvertes de Gravures a Gouy. *L'Anthropologie* 2: 513–546.

McCarthy, Frederick D. and Margaret McArthur. 1960. "The Food Quest and the Time Factor in Aboriginal Economic Life," *Records of the American-Australian Scientific Expedition to Arnhem Land*, Vol. 2, *Anthropology and Nutrition*, ed. by Charles P. Mountford, Melbourne University Press, Parkville, pp. 145–194.

Meggit, M. J.. 1958. Mae Enga Time-reckoning and Calendar, New Guinea, *Man*, Vol. LVIII, pp. 74–77.

———— 1954. Sign Language among the Walbiri of Central Australia, *Oceania*, Vol. XXV, pp. 2–16.

Mellaart, James. 1967. *Çatal Hüyük; A Neolithic Town in Anatolia*, "New Aspects of Archaeology," ed. by Sir Mortimer Wheeler, McGraw-Hill Book Co., New York.

Mellars, P. and C. Stringer (Eds.) 1989. *The Human Revolution: Behavorial and Biological Perspectives in the Origins of Modern Humans*. Vol I. Edinburgh: Edinburgh University Press.

Mellars, P. (Ed.) 1990. *The Emergence of Modern Humans*. Vol. II. Edinburgh: Edinburgh University Press.

Merrill, Robert H. Oct., 1945. The Calendar Stick of Tshi-zun-hau-kau, *Cranbrook Institute of Science Bulletin*, No. 24.

Mithen, S. J. 1988. Looking and Learning: Upper Palaeolithic Art and Information Gathering. *World Archaeology* 19(3)

———— 1990 *Thoughtful Foragers*. Cambridge University Press.

———— 1989. To Hunt or to Paint: Animals and Art in the Upper Palaeolithic. *Man* 23:671–695.

Mons, L. 1986. Les statuettes animalières en Grés de la Grotte d'Isturitz (Pyrénées-Atlantiques): observations et hypothèses de fragmentation volontaire. *L'Anthropologie* 90(4):701–712.

Mountford, Charles P. 1938. Aboriginal Message Sticks from the Nullabor Plains, *Transactions, Royal Society of South Australia*, Vol. 62, pp. 122–126.

Mountford, C. P. 1956. *Arnhem Land: Art, Myth and Symbolism*. [Chapter 6, pp.479–504. *Astronomy*. Australian aboriginal astronomical imagery and myths]

———— 1956. "Message Sticks" and "Astronomy," *Records of the American-Australian Scientific Expedition to Arnhem Land*, Vol. I, *Art, Myth and Symbolism,* Melbourne University Press, Parkville, pp. 466–475, 479–504.

———— 1976. *Nomads of the Desert*. Rigby [Chapter 8, pp. 449–483. THE MYTHS OF THE SKY. Australian aboriginal imagery and myths.]

Movius, Hallam L., Jr. 1961. Aspects of Upper Palaeolithic Art, *Three Regions of Primitive Art*, lectures given at the Museum of Primitive Art, New York. pp. 11–40.

Movius, H. L., Jr. (Ed.) 1975. *Excavation of the Abri Pataud, Les Eyzies, Dordogne)*. Stratigraphy. American School of Prehistoric Research, Bull. 30. Peabody Museum, Harvard University.

Movius, H. L., Jr. 1977. *Excavation of the Abri Pataud,*

Les Eyzies, Dordogne). Stratigraphy. American School of Prehistoric Research, Bull. 31. Peabody Museum, Harvard University.

Müller-Beck, Hansjürgen. 1966. Paleohunters in America; Origins and Diffusion, *Science*, Vol. 152, pp. 1191–1210.

Müller-Beck, H. and G. Albrecht (Eds.). 1987. *Die Anfänge der Kunst vor 30000 Jahren*. Catalogue of Exhibition in Kunsthalle, Tubingen. Theiss: Stuttgart.

Munn, Nancy D. 1966. Visual Categories; An Approach to the Study of Representational Systems, *American Anthropologist*, Vol. 68, pp. 936–949.

———— 1962. Walbiri Graphic Signs; An Analysis, *American Anthropologist*, Vol. 64, pp. 972–984.

Musill, Rudolf. 1974. Tiergesellschaft der Kneigrotte, In *Die Kniegrotte: Eine Magdalénien-Station in Thüringen* R. Fuestel (ed.) Hermann Böhlaus Nachfolger:Weimar. pp.30–95.

Napier, John. 1962. The Evolution of the Hand, *Scientific American*, Vol. 207, pp. 56–62.

Needham, Joseph. 1954–1959. *Science and Civilization in China*, Vols. 1–3, Cambridge University Press, Cambridge, England.

Nelson, Edward William. 1896–1897. The Eskimos about Bering Strait" ("Chronometry" and "Numeration"), *Eighteenth Annual Report, Bureau of Ethnology. Smithsonian Institution*, pp. 234–235, 235–241. (On lunar calendar and forms of counting.)

Neugebauer-Maresch, C. 1988. Vorbericht über die Rettungsgrabungen an der Aurignacien-Station Strazring/Krems-Rehberg in den Jahren 1985–1988: Zum Neufund einer weiblichen Statuette. *Fundberichte aus Österreich* 26:73–84. [Aurignacian stone carving of a "dancing" female].

Neumann, Erich. 1955. *The Great Mother, An Analysis of An Archetype*, trans. by Ralph Mannheim, Bollingen series 47, Pantheon Books, New York. (Jungian interpretation.)

Nilsson, Martin P. 1920. *Primitive Time Reckoning*. trans. by F. J. Fieldan, Oxford University Press, Oxford, England.

Nougier, Louis-René et Romain Robert. 1966. Les félins dans l'art quarternaire, *Bulletin de La Société Préhistorique de L'Ariège*, Tome XXI, pp. 35–46.

———— 1958. Le 'Lissoir aux Saïgas' de la grotte de la Vache, à Alliat, et l'antilope Saïga dans l'art franco-cantabrique, *Bulletin de La Société Préhistorique de L'Ariège*, Tome XIII, pp. 1–16.

Omnes, J. 1982. *La Grotte Ornée de Labastide (Hautes-Pyrénées)*. Omnès: Lourdes.

Orlova, E. P. 1966. Kalendari Narodov Severa Sibiri i Dalnego Vostoka, *Sibirskii Arkheol. Sbornik*, Izd. "Nauka," Sibirskoe otdelenie, Akad. Nauk SSSR, Novosibirsk.

Otte, M. 1974. Observations sur le débitage et le façonnage de l'ivoire dans l'Aurignacian en Belgique. In *Industrie de l'Os dans la Préhistoire*, First International colloquium, H. Camps-Fabrer (organizer). Editions de l'Université de Provence. pp. 963–96. [Describes the analysis of bead manufacture later adopted by R. White]

Otte, M. (Ed.) 1988. *L'Homme Neandertal: Actes du Colloque International, 1986, Liege* Vol. 5. *La Pensée*, ERAUL 32. O. Bar-Yosef, Coordinator. Université de Liège.

Orlova, E.P. 1966. The Calendars of the Peoples of North Siberia and the Far East. *Sibirski Arkheologies-kii Sbornik* 2:297–321. (In Russian) {Describes calendrical notations and calendars influenced and more primitive calendars not influenced by Orthodox Christian calendrics.}

Pales, L., and M. Tassin de Saint-Péreuse. 1976. *Les gravures de la Marche: Les Humaines II*. Gap:Ophrys.

Pales, L. 1989. *Les Gravures de la Marche: IV - Cervidés, Mammouths et divers*. Gap:Ophrys.

Parker, Richard A. 1950. *The Calendars of Ancient Egypt*, The Oriental Institute, University of Chicago: "Studies in Ancient Oriental Civilization," 26, University of Chicago Press, Chicago.

———— 1957. The Problem of the Month-Names: A Reply, *Revue D'Égyptologie*, Vol. II, pp. 85–107. (Lunar basis of Egyptian calendar.)

Pfeiffer, J. E. 1982. *The Creative Explosion. An Inquiry into the Origins of Art and Religion*. New York: Harper & Row.

Piaget, Jean. 1957. The Child and Modern Physics, *Scientific American*, Vol. 196, pp. 46–51.

———— 1953. How Children Form Mathmetical Concepts, *Scientific American*, Vol. 189, pp. 74–79.

———— 1960. *The Child's Conception of the World*, trans. by Joan and Andrew Tomlinson, Humanities Press, New York.

———— 1964. *The Child's Conception of Number*, Humanities Press, New York.

———— 1966. *The Child's Conception of Physical Causality*, trans. by Marjorie Gabain, Humanities Press, New York.

———— and Bärbel Inhelder. 1963. *The Child's Conception of Space*, trans. by F. J. Langdon and J. L. Lunzer, Humanities Press, New York.

———— Bärbel Inhelder, and Alina Szeminska. 1960. *The Child's Conception of Geometry*, trans. by E. A. Lunzer, Basic Books, New York.

Pidoplichko, I. G. 1969. *Late Paleolithic Dwellings of Mammoth Bones in the Ukraine* (In Russian). Kiev: КAYKOBA ДYMKA, Academy of Sciences of the Ukraine, Institute of Zoology.

Piette, Edouard. 1907. *L'Art Pendant L'age Du Renne*, Masson et Cie., Paris. (Mobiliary art.)

Pike, Tay, A. 1991. Upper Perigordian Hunting: Organizational and Technological Strategies. In *La Chasse dans la Préhistoire, Colloque International:Actes*. Treignes, Belgium, 1990. Editions du Cedarc 1991.

Pope, G. G. 1989. Bamboo and Human Evolution. *Natural History* 10/89:48–57.

Poplin, F. 1976. *Les Grandes Vertébrés de Gönnersdorf: Fouilles 1968*. Fritz Steiner Verlag GMBH: Wiesbaden.

Praslov, N. D. and A. N. Rogachev. 1982. *Paleolithic of the Kostienki-Borshechevo Area on the River Don: 1879–1979*. Academy of Sciences of the USSR, Institute of Archaeology, Commission for the Study of the Quarternary Period. Leningrad: Nauk.

Praslov, N. D. 1985. L'art du paléolithique supérieur à l'est de l'Europe. *L'Anthropologie*, **89**(2): 181–192. Paris.

Price, T. D. and J. A. Brown (Eds) 1985. *Prehistoric Hunter-Gatherers: The Emergence of Cultural Complexity*. Orlando:Academic Press.

Pritchett, W. Kendrick and Otto Neugebauer. 1947. *The Calendar of Athens*, Harvard University Press, Cambridge.

Radmilli, A. M. 1974. *Gli scavi nella Grotta Polesini a Ponte Lucano di Tivoli e la più antica arte nel Lazio* Sansoni:Florence. [Monograph on the archaeology and images of a crucial late Upper Paleolithic Italian site. Analysis of the images were published by Marshack 1969]

Raphael, Max. 1945. *Prehistoric Cave Paintings*, trans. by Norbert Guterman, Bollingen Series IV, Pantheon Books, New York.

Reinach, Salomon. 1903. "L'art et la magie. A propos des peintures et des gravures de l'âge du renne," *L'Anthropologie*, Tome 14, pp. 257–266.

———— 1913. *Répertoire de L'art Quaternaire*, Ernest Leroux, Paris.

Renfrew, C. 1982. *Towards An Archaeology Of Mind*. Cambridge University Press. Inaugural Lecture as Disney Professor of Archaeology and Fellow of St. John's College of Cambridge University.

Rice, P. C. 1981. Prehistoric Venuses: Symbols of Motherhood or Womanhood? *Journal of Anthropological Research*. 37(4):402–414.

Riddell, W. H.: "Dead or Alive?" *Antiquity*, Vol. XIV, 1940, pp. 154–162. (Answer to Leason.)

Rodseth, L., et al. 1991. The Human Community as a Primate Society. *Current Anthropology* 32(3):221–254.

Roe, Frank G. 1951. *The North American Buffalo, A critical Study of the Species in Its Wild State*, The University Press, Toronto.

Roussot, A. 1984. Peintures, gravures et sculptures de l'abri du Poisson aux Eyzies: Quelques nouvelles observations. *Bull. Soc. Préhist. Ariège* 39:11–26. [Suggests the carved fish in the Abri du Poisson at the Gorge d'Enfer may be Perigordian]

———— 1984. La rondelle "Aux Chamois" de Laugerie-Basse. *Elements de Pre et Protohistoire Europeenne*. Hommages a Jacques-Pierre Millotte. Série Archéologie No. 32. Annals Littéraires de l'Université de Besançon, Les Belles Lettres. Paris. pp. 219–231. [Author suggests the animal on the disc, Pgs. 182–183, Figs. 74 a,b, in this volume may be a chamois not a fawn, but he is not sure]

Rütimeyer, L. 1924. *Ur-Ethnographie Der Schweiz*, "Schriften der Schweizerischen Gesellschaft für Volkskunde," Vol. XVI, Basel, Ch.III "Kerbhölzer oder Tesslen," pp. 5–38. (Historic tally-sticks.)

Rybakov, B. A. 1965. Cosmogony and Mythology of the Agriculturalists of the Eneolithic, Parts I and II, *Soviet Anthropology and Archaeology*, Vol. IV, no.3: pp. 16–36 and no.4: pp. 33–52, trans. from *Sovetskaia Arkheologiia*.

Saccasyn della Santa, E. 1947. *Les Figures Humaines Du Paléolithique Supérieur Eurasiatique*, Editions De Sikkel, Anvers. (Contains bibliography.)

Sauvet, G. & S. 1979. Fonction sémiologique de l'art pariétal animalier franco-cantabrique. *Bull. Soc. Préhist. Franç.* 76:340–354.

Schmid, E. 1984. Some Anatomical Observations on Palaeolithic Depictions of Horses. In H. G. Bandi et al., pp. 155–160.

Semionov, S. A. 1964. *Prehistoric Technology*, trans. by M.W. Thompson, Barnes and Noble, New York.

Shay, T. and J. Clottes (Eds.) 1991. *The Limitations of Archaeological Knowledge*. Université de Liège: Liège.

Shea, J. J. 1989. Tool Use and Human Evolution in the Late Pleistocene of Israel. In Mellars and Stringer, pp. 611–625.

Shovkoplas, I. G. 1965. *Mezhinskaya Stoyinka*. Kiev. [Illustrates beads in the process of being made from a rod: p. 213, Pl. XLVI fIGS. 13–16.]

Sieveking, A. 1979. *The Cave Artists*. London: Thames & Hudson.

_____ 1981. Palaeolithic decorated bone discs. *British Museum Quarterly.* 35:206–229.

_____ 1987. *A Catalogue of Paleolithic Art in the British Museum*. London: British Museum Publications.

Sillen, A. and C. K. Brain. 1990. Old Flame: Burned Bones Provide Evidence of an Early Human Use of Fire. *Natural History* 4/90.

Smith, Philip E. L. 1964. The Solutrean Culture, *Scientific American*, Vol. 211, pp. 86–94.

_____ 1966. *Le Solutréen en France*, Mémoire 5, ed. by François Bordes, Institut de Préhistoire, Université de Bordeaux.

Soffer, O. 1985. *The Upper Paleolithic of the Russian Plain*. New York: Academic Press.

_____ (Ed.). 1987. The Pleistocene Old World: Regional Perspectives. N.Y.:Plenum Press.

_____ 1987. Upper Paleolithic Connubia, Refugia, and the Archaeologoical Record from Eastern Europe. In *The Pleistocene Old World*. O. Soffer (Ed.) pp. 333–348.

Sonneville-Bordes, D. de, 1986. Le Bestiaire Paléollithique en Périgord: Chronologie et Signification. *L'Anthropologie* 90(4): 613–656.

Spiess, A. E. 1979. *Reindeer and Caribou Hunters*. Academic Press: New York.

Steklis, H.D. 1985. Primate Communication, Comparative Neurology, and the Origin of Language Re-examined. *Journal of Human Evolution* 14:157–173.

Steklis, Moshe. 1966. *Civilization of the Yarmuk* (in Hebrew), Museum of Prehistory Shaar Hagalan, Nidet, Israel. (Buttocks image, circular vulvas, and hatch patterns comparable to Upper Paleolithic and Mesolithic.)

Stoliar, A. D. 1977–78. On the Sociohistorical Decoding of Upper Paleolithic Female Signs. *Sov. Anthro. and Archaeo.* 16(3–4): 36–77.

Straus, L.G. 1982. Observations on Upper Paleolithic art:old problems and new directions, *Zephyrus* 35/5:71–80.

_____ 1987. The Paleolithic Cave Art of Vasco-Cantabrian Spain. *Oxford Journal of Archaeology* 6(2):149–163.

_____ 1987. Paradigm Lost: A personal view of the current state of Upper Paleolithic research. *Helenium* 27: 157–171.

_____ 1990. The Early Upper Palaeolithic of Southwest Europe: Cro-Magnon Adaptations in the Iberian Peripheries, 40 000–20 000 BP. In *The Emergence of Modern Humans* P. Mellars (Ed.) Edinburgh U. Press.

_____ and C. W. Heller. 1988. Explorations of the Twilight Zone: The Early Upper Paleolithic of Vasco-Cantabrian Spain. In *The Early Upper Paleolithic: Evidence from Europe and the Near East* J.F. Hoffecker and C. A. Wolf (Eds.) BAR International Series 437. pp. 97–133.

_____ , et al. 1980. Ice Age subsistence in Northern Spain. *Scientific American* 242(6):142–152.

Svoboda, J. 1988. A new male burial from Dolni Vestonice. *Journal of Human Evolution* 16:827–830.

Thomson, Donald F. 1939. The Seasonal Factor in Human Culture, *Proceedings of the Prehistoric Society*, Vol. V, pp.209–221.

Toth, N. 1985. Archaeological Evidence for Preferential Right-handedness in the Lower and Middle Pleistocene, and Its Possible Implications. *Journal of Human Evolution.* 14:607–614.

Tratman, E. K. 1976. A Late Upper Palaeolithic Calculator (?), Gough's Cave, Cheddar, Somerset. *Proc. Univ. Bristol Spelaeol. Soc.* 14(2):123–129.

Turner, Lucien M. 1889–1890. Ethnology of the Ungava District, Hudson Bay Territory, *Eleventh Annual Report of the Bureau of American Ethnology*, Smithsonian Institution, Washington, D.C., pp. 202–207. (Seasonal cognitions.)

Turner, Victor W. 1962. Themes in the Symbolism of Ndembu Hunting Ritual, *Anthropological Quarterly*, Vol. 35, pp. 37–57.

Ucko, Peter J. 1962. The Interpretation of Prehistoric Anthropomorphic Figurines, *Journal of the Royal Anthropological Institute of Great Britain and Ireland*, Vol. 92, pp. 38–53.

Ucko. P. J. (Ed.) 1977. *Form in indigenous art: Schematization in the art of Aboriginal Australia and Prehistoric Europe*. London: Duckworth.

_____ 1987. Débuts illusoires dans l'étude de la tradition artistique. *Préhistoire Ariégeoise* XLII pp. 15–81.

_____ and A. Rosenfeld. 1972. Anthropomorphic Representation in Palaeolithic Art. *Santander Symposium*, Actes del Symposium Internacional de Arte Prehistórico. pp. 149–211.

_____ and Andrée Rosenfeld. 1967. *Palaeolithic Cave Art*, World University Library, London. (Critical evaluation of the major contemporary theories.)

Vandiver, P. V., O. Soffer, B. Klima and J. Svoboda. 1989. The Origins of Ceramic Technology at Dolni Vestonice, Czechoslvakia. *Science* 246: 1002–1008.

Vialou, D. 1986. *L'Art des Grottes en Ariège Magdalénienne*. XXIIe Supplément à *Gallia Préhistoire*.

Vasil'ev, S. A. 1985. Une statuette d'argile paléolithique de Sibérie du Sud. *L'Anthropologie* 89(2): 193–195.

Vayson de Pradenne, André. 1934. Les figurations d'oiseaux dans l'art quaternaire," *Ipek*, 1935, pp. 3–17.

Verbrugge, A. R. 1958. *Le Symbole de La Main Dans La Préhistoire*, Impr. Priv., Milly-la-Forêt.

Vidal (y) Lopez, Manuel. 1937. *Estudis D'Art Originari. Els Insectes En L'Art Quaternari*, "Institut d'Estudis Valencians. Seccio Histórico-Arqueológica. Servei d'Investigació Prehistórica. Serie de Treballs solts, n.3," Imp. F. Domenech, Valencia.

Vilkuna, Kustaa: "Wochenrechnung und Teilung des Jahres in zwei oder vier Teile," *Finnisch-Ugrische Forschungen*, Vol. XXXIV, pp. 43–83.

_____ 1957–1958. Zur ältesten Geschichte der Woche, *Folk-Liv,* 1957–1958, pp. 197–215.

Vrba, E. S. 1985. Ecological and Adaptive Changes Associated with Early Hominid Evolution. In *Ancestors: The Hard Evidence*, pp. 63–71. New York: Liss

Washburn, Sherwood L. (ed.). 1961. *Social Life of Early Man*, Aldine Publishing Co., Chicago.

_____ 1960. Tools and Human Evolution, *Scientific American*, Vol. 203, pp. 62–75.

Wendt, W. E. 1976. 'Art mobilier' from the Apollo 11 cave, Southwest Africa: Africa's oldest dated works of art. *South African Archaeological Bulletin* 31:5–11. [Documents painted animal images, c. 28,000 BP]

White, R. 1983. *Changing Land-Use Patterns across the Middle/Upper Paleolithic Transition: The complex case of the Perigord*. To appear in volume on M/UP Transition edited by E. Trinkaus. *British Archaeological Reports* pp. 113–121.

_____ 1985. Thoughts on Social Relationships in Hominid Evolution. *Journal of Social and Personal Relationships* 2:95–115.

_____ 1986. *Dark Caves, Bright Visions, Life in Ice Age Europe*. Exhibition Catalogue, American Museum of Natural History: New York. [Traditional academic treatment of Ice Age imagery.

_____ 1989. Husbandry and Herd Control in the Upper Paleolithic: A Critical Review of the Evidence. *Current Anthropology* 30(5):609–632.

_____ 1989. Production complexity and standardization in early Aurignacian bead and pendant manufacture: evolutionary implications. In Mellars and Stringer, pp. 360–399. [Author describes bead making technology. P. 377: Suggests that dotted beads indicate that Marshack has probably mistaken such decoration for notations.]

_____ 1989. Visual Thinking in the Ice Age. *Scientific American* 261(1):92–99. [Author suggests beads indicate early "self-awareness" and social complexity. Does not mention importance of Upper Paleolithic and even earlier personal decorations made of perishable materials]

Willetts, R. F. 1962. *Cretan Cults and Festivals*, Barnes and Noble, New York.

Wreschner, E. E. 1978. *Ochre in Archaeological Contexts and its Persistence into Recent Times: An analysis of the Structural Elements in Ochre Practices and a Study of Formative Processes of Red Ochre Symbolism.* Haifa: University of Haifa.

Wreschner, E. 1980. Red Ochre and Human Evolution: a Case for Discussion. *Current Anthropology* 21(5):631–644.

Wright, R. V. S. 1971. *Archaeology of the Gallus Site, Koonalda Cave.* Australian Institute of Aboriginal Studies, Pub. #26. Canberra. [Study of the "macaronis" and artifacts in 20,000 year old cave]

Wobst, M. 1976. Locational Relationships in Palaeolithic Society. *Journal of Human Evolution* 5:49–58.

―――― 1977. Stylistic Behavior and Information Exchange. *University of Michigan Museum of Anthropology, Anthropological Paper 61*, pp.317–342.

―――― 1983. Palaeolithic archaeology - some problems with form, space, and time. In *Hunter-gatherer Economy in Prehistory: A European Perspective.* G. Bailey (Ed.), pp. 220–225. London: Cambridge University Press.

Wynn, T. 1989. *The Evolution of Spatial Consciousness.* No. 17. Urbana: University of Illinois Press.

Yellen, J. E. 1977. *Archaeological Approaches to the Present. Models for Reconstructing the Past.* Academic Press: New York.

Zerubavel, E. 1981. *Hidden Rhythms: Schedules and Calendars in Social Life.* Berkeley: University of California Press.

Zervos, Christian. 1959. *L'Art À L'Époque Du Renne*, Cahiers d'Art, Paris. (Mobiliary and wall art.)

Zhurov, R. I. 1981/2. On the Question of the Origin of Art (an Answer to Opponents). *Soviet Anth. & Arch.* 16:43–63. And 20(3):59–82.

Zimmer, Heinrich. 1946. *Myths and Symbols in Indian Art and Civilization*, ed. by Joseph Campbell, Bollingen Series VI, Pantheon Books, New York.

SITES OF UPPER PALEOLITHIC ART IN EUROPE

425

LIST OF ILLUSTRATIONS

INDEX

Text references appear in regular type.
Illustrations appear in italics.

A

COLOPHON

The text was set in Garamond, a typeface designed by Claude Garamond (c 1480–1561). This face designed in the Paris foundry of C. Garamond was modeled after the Aldine Roman. It became one of the most used faces of its day and has engendered many typeface variations today.

Composed by Books International, Deatsville, Alabama; printed in Singapore by Palace Press, San Francisco on acid free paper.